A Psychological View of the Legal System

A Psychological View of the Legal System

Linda Anderson Foley
University of North Florida

Madison, Wisconsin • Dubuque, Iowa • Indianapolis, Indiana
Melbourne, Australia • Oxford, England

Book Team

Editor *Michael Lange*
Developmental Editor *Sheralee Connors*
Production Editor *Audrey A. Reiter*
Permissions Editor *Mavis M. Oeth*
Visuals/Design Developmental Consultant *Marilyn A. Phelps*
Visuals/Design Freelance Specialist *Mary L. Christianson*
Publishing Services Specialist *Sherry Padden*
Marketing Manager *Steven Yetter*
Advertising Manager *Jodi Rymer*

Brown & Benchmark

A Division of Wm. C. Brown Communications, Inc.

Vice President and General Manager *Thomas E. Doran*
Editor in Chief *Edgar J. Laube*
Executive Editor *Ed Bartell*
Executive Editor *Stan Stoga*
National Sales Manager *Eric Ziegler*
Director of CourseResource *Kathy Law Laube*
Director of CourseSystems *Chris Rogers*

Director of Marketing *Sue Simon*
Director of Production *Vickie Putman Caughron*
Imaging Group Manager *Chuck Carpenter*
Manager of Visuals and Design *Faye M. Schilling*
Design Manager *Jac Tilton*
Art Manager *Janice Roerig*
Permissions/Records Manager *Connie Allendorf*

Wm. C. Brown Communications, Inc.

President and Chief Executive Officer *G. Franklin Lewis*
Corporate Vice President, President of WCB Manufacturing *Roger Meyer*
Vice President and Chief Financial Officer *Robert Chesterman*

Cover design by Tara L. Bazata

Cover image © West Light

Copyedited by Siobhan Drummond

Copyright © 1993 by Wm. C. Brown Communications, Inc. All rights reserved

A Times Mirror Company

Library of Congress Catalog Card Number: 92–70087

ISBN 0–697–12982–9

No part of this publication may be reproduced, stored in a retrieval system, or transmitted, in any form or by any means, electronic, mechanical, photocopying, recording, or otherwise, without the prior written permission of the publisher.

Printed in the United States of America by Wm. C. Brown Communications, Inc., 2460 Kerper Boulevard, Dubuque, IA 52001

10 9 8 7 6 5 4 3 2 1

♦ **Dedication** ♦

*To my father,
Harry C. Anderson.*

Contents

Preface ix

1
The Disciplines of Psychology and the Law

Historical View	2
Assumptions	7
Professional Training	12
The Psychology and Law Interface	20
Summary	26

2
Crime Patterns

Sources and Accuracy of Crime Statistics	28
Reporting Crimes to the Police	35
Crime Rates and Crime Waves	41
Summary	49

3
Socialization: How People Learn to Behave

Learning to Behave	52
Modeling	54
The Effects of Punishment	57
The Development of a Conscience	62
Deviant Behavior	65
Summary	69

4
Theories of Criminal Behavior

Biological Theories of Criminal Behavior	72
Sociological Theories of Criminal Behavior	80
Social-Psychological Theories of Criminal Behavior	84
Psychological Theories of Criminal Behavior	88
Women in Crime	92
Summary	94

5
Victims of Crimes

Victimization	98
The Impact of Crimes on Victims	105
Coping with Victimization	115
Summary	123

6
Law Enforcement

Recruitment, Screening, and Training of Police Officers	126
A Psychological Profile of the Police Officer	130
Police Discretion and the Arrest Process: Police Interactions with the Public	138
Police Interrogation Methods	147
Summary	151

7
The Process from Arrest to Trial

The Jail Experience	154
Functions and Discretion of the Prosecutor	160
The Grand Jury	166
Pretrial Proceedings	169
Plea Bargaining	174
Summary	180

8
The Jury Trial

Participants in Legal Proceedings	184
The Trial Proceedings	186
The Jury Selection Process	195
Summary	207

9
Witnesses

Eyewitness Identification	210
The Expert Witness	218
The Child Witness	225
Summary	232

10
The Verdict and Sentencing

Jury Decision-Making	236
Sentencing	248
Summary	258

11
Mental Illness and Criminal Justice

The Insanity Defense	260
Incompetent to Stand Trial	276
Summary	277

12
Corrections

The Likelihood of Being Caught	280
Life in Prison	283
The Death Penalty	298
Summary	301

13
Family Law

Marriage and Dissolution	304
Children of Divorce	314
Summary	325

14
Crime Intervention and Prevention

Bystander Intervention	328
Pornography	335
Deterrence	341
Guns and Their Control	345
Summary	349

References	*351*
Indexes	*375*

Preface

♦ The most controversial issues facing society generally are argued in the courts. Thus abortion, pornography, the insanity defense, and capital punishment have been, and certainly will continue to be, addressed in the legal arena. Since these and many other issues decided by the courts are social as well as legal questions, social science can be of great assistance in their clarification.

Both lawyers and psychologists saw the benefits of collaboration early in the 20th century. However, cooperation between the disciplines started off slowly and gained momentum only in the last 20 years. Today, psychologists are researching every area of the legal system, and they are also applying their expertise to the legal system as expert witnesses in the courts, therapists in prisons, and trainers in law enforcement.

Many recent events have raised questions about the legal system which can best be answered from a psychological perspective. These events have included a videotaped beating of a California motorist by police, a well-publicized rape trial of a U.S. senator's nephew, the trial of a man accused by his daughter of killing her childhood friend 20 years before, and the arrest of a serial murderer who claims to have eaten parts of some of his victims. Each of these incidents raises questions which demonstrate the interface between psychology and the legal system. Do the police use excessive force when interacting with the public? Can an accused rapist receive a fair trial if the media publishes information not allowed at the trial? Can an adult remember events from her childhood which she had repressed for 20 years? Is someone who commits serial murder and mutilation insane and, therefore, not to be punished? These questions concerning the legal system are ones that psychology addresses.

Purpose

This book is designed to help the reader better understand how the legal system functions by applying psychological research and theory to the topic. It describes and discusses the ways in which psychology has analyzed and interfaced with the legal process. Since the legal system is composed of people, psychology—especially social psychology—can help the student understand the participants and how they affect each other. The book describes how human characteristics and psychological factors influence attitudes, decisions, and behavior throughout the legal process.

The aim of the book is to provide a comprehensive, current, and readable text for the undergraduate student in both psychology and criminology. Although an introductory text, it is challenging enough to use as a supplementary text for graduate students considering specialization in law/psychology or for law students interested in the utility of psychology in the practice of law. The book covers traditional topics in psychology and the law, plus current issues, such as: victimization, the death penalty, child custody, child witnesses, and pornography. There is discussion of victim's reactions, the psychology of police and the court system, as well as the insanity defense. The theoretical discussion is applied to real life through boxed examples of recent legal events such as the McMartin preschool case, the Hinckley trial, the rape at Big Dan's Tavern, and the abuse of Hedda Nussbaum.

Organization

Psychology and the law, although two very different disciplines, are both concerned with human behavior. They complement each other and, in cooperation, can advance the goals of each discipline. In order to understand how these two divergent fields interact, it is necessary to look at the differences and similarities between them. Chapter 1 begins this exploration with a short historical review of the two disciplines followed by an examination of their assumptions, a comparison of the training of professionals in each, and an overview of areas in which they overlap.

Chapter 2 focuses on crime patterns and the amount of crime in our society. It begins by describing the sources and accuracy of crime statistics. The chapter continues with a discussion of why victims and bystanders will or will not report crimes to the police. This chapter concludes with a discussion of crime waves and projections of future crime rates.

Insight into the reasons for criminal behavior must be based on an understanding of the acquisition of normal behaviors. Therefore, Chapter 3 outlines the theories of development used to explain how people learn to behave. This chapter includes information on conditioning, modeling, the effects of punishment, the development of a conscience, and deviant behavior. Chapter 4 progresses to theories of criminal behavior and deviance—biological, sociological, social-psychological, and psychological—and ends with a discussion of women in crime.

The 1970s saw new attention directed toward the victims of crimes and the advent of the field of victimology. Chapter 5 examines victimization and describes the problems victims face. The chapter concludes with an overview of methods victims use to cope with their situations.

Law enforcement is the main link between the public and the criminal justice system. The videotaped beating of Rodney King in the spring of 1991 focused attention on the functioning of police officers in the community. Chapter 6 describes the selection and training of police officers. It then examines the interaction of police with the public and future trends in community policing. The chapter ends with a discussion of police interrogation methods.

The logical sequel to an analysis of law enforcement is an examination of the process from arrest to trial. Chapter 7 describes the functions and discretion of the prosecutor and the grand jury. The chapter also covers pretrial proceedings and plea bargaining.

Chapter 8 continues the progression through the criminal justice system by examining the jury trial and its participants. It emphasizes the social psychology of the trial process and jury selection. The next two chapters examine the trial process more closely. Chapter 9 looks at the issues surrounding eyewitness identification. It continues with the related topics of expert testimony and the child witness. Chapter 10 deals with jury deliberation and sentencing.

Focus shifts then to the offender, first in terms of responsibility and then disposition. Ever since the institution of an insanity defense, the courts have depended on the expert testimony of mental health professionals to determine the criminal responsibility of the defendant. Issues related to the insanity plea and competence are discussed in Chapter 11. Next, Chapter 12 concentrates on the adjudicated offender. It begins with an analysis of the likelihood of a criminal ever being caught. It then discusses the disposition and rehabilitation of offenders, followed by a discussion of the death penalty.

Chapter 13 discusses a new area in psychology and law: family law. This area of noncriminal law focuses on marriage and its dissolution with special emphasis on custody and its impact on the children of divorce. Finally, Chapter 14 is a collection of topics related to intervention and prevention: bystander intervention, pornography, deterrence, and gun control.

Acknowledgments

Many colleagues reviewed drafts of individual chapters or outlines of the book prior to its publication. I would like to thank Roger Sharp, Melissa Pigott, and David Fauss, who read many revisions, for their helpful comments over many drafts of the entire manuscript. I greatly appreciate their support and encouragement. I would also like to thank Russell Jones, Iver Iverson, and Sylvia Simmons for reviewing early outlines and drafts of chapters. John Brigham, Florida State University; Robert Buckhout, Brooklyn College; Judith Chapman, St. Joseph's University; Ellen Cohn, University of New Hampshire; Francis Dane, Mercer University; Sandra Fiske, Onodaga Community College; Gary Howells, University of the Pacific; Pamela Laughon, University of North Carolina; Joseph Palladino, University of Southern Indiana; Nancy W. Perry, Creighton University; Melissa Pigott, Litigation Sciences; Camille Quinn, Tulsa Junior College; Marla Sandys, University of Louisville; Richard M. Swanson, University of South Florida; Elizabeth Swenson, John Carroll University; and Lawrence White, Beloit College, all reviewed this book in its manuscript stages.

The many recommendations made by reviewers were of particular benefit. Their suggestions did much to improve this book.

My special thanks go to the many students who assisted in different aspects of this project: Karen DeBryun Painter, Michael Clark, Carol Schickel, Gretchen Steinhilber, and Gary LeMay. Thanks also to students in my classes who brought current incidents to my attention. And last, I would be greatly remiss if I did not thank word-processing operator Ann Murphy for her help in collating the text and Matteel Jones for her assistance.

A Psychological View of the Legal System

1

The Disciplines of Psychology and the Law

Historical View
The Historical Interface of Law and Psychology
Assumptions
Assumptions about the Law
Assumptions in Psychology
Professional Training
Law School
Graduate School in Psychology
The Psychology and Law Interface
Obstacles
Legal and Psychological Methods
Differences Between the Disciplines
Similarities Between Law and Psychology
Summary

Historical View

♦ A black motorist, Rodney King, is chased and stopped by California police for a traffic violation in March 1991. The police surround King and fire a 50,000-volt Taser stun gun at him. Three police officers take turns hitting, kicking, and smashing King with truncheons while he lies helplessly on the ground. When the brutal attack is over, King has a broken ankle, a burn on his chest, a crushed cheekbone, eleven fractures of the skull, brain damage, and internal injuries. This shocking beating might have gone unnoticed if a bystander had not videotaped it and the eleven watching police officers. Later, the tape and photographs of the battered King are shown to horrified viewers of television newscasts. Is excessive police violence common practice? Can honest citizens entrust their safety to law enforcement officers? What type of training are police officers given to prevent their use of excessive force? Are police officers screened for violent behavior? Were the white police officers acting out of racism?

♦ After 13 years of marriage, Donald and Ivanna Trump announce their intention to divorce. The couple's conflict over a prenuptial agreement and the status of Donald's involvement with Marla Maples are updated daily in the tabloids. Lawyers and courts spend months coming to an agreement over the distribution of Donald Trump's vast wealth. Every aspect of the controversy is detailed in the daily newspapers. What is the impact of divorce on the couple involved? How equitable are divorce settlements? What impact does the conflict between their parents have on young children of divorcing parents?

♦ A young man in handcuffs leads police to an apartment where he was held captive and in which the police find eleven dismembered bodies. Jeffrey Dahmer, 31, confesses to killing and mutilating seventeen young men over the course of 13 years. Dahmer claims to have saved some body parts to "eat later" and painted three skulls after boiling them to remove the skin. Dahmer is alleged to have had sex with several of the victims, some after their death. Later Dahmer pleads not guilty to the charges and indicates he would plead insanity if convicted. What is the legal definition of insanity? Is Dahmer insane? How do psychologists explain his criminal behavior? How is sanity proven in court?

The incidents described above and the questions they raise are at the interface of psychology and the law. This book will attempt to describe and discuss the ways in which psychology has analyzed and interfaced with legal processes. Since the legal system is composed of people, psychology, especially social psychology, can help the reader understand the participants and how they influence each other. The book will describe how human characteristics and psychological factors influence attitudes, decisions, and behavior throughout the legal system.

Psychology and the law are disparate professions with regard to assumptions, training of professionals, and methodology, but for a number of years they have been developing a mutually beneficial pattern of interaction, as both disciplines are interested in human behavior. Research in psychology attempts to describe, explain, and predict human behavior. The law focuses on the control of human behavior in the interest of public order and provides a mechanism whereby disputes can be settled. With these similar interests, psychology and the law complement one another and, in cooperation, can advance the goals of both disciplines.

In order to comprehend the advantages of, and difficulties in, the interactions between these two fields, let us look at some of the differences between them. We begin this discussion with a historical view of the interface between law and psychology.

Law is an ancient institution that has developed and evolved over the ages. In contrast, psychology is a relatively new discipline, dating back only a little over 100 years. Although most people think of psychologists as clinicians, psychology began as a purely experimental science with laboratories modeled after those in physics. In fact, the term **clinical psychologist** was not used until 4 years after the founding of the American Psychological Association (APA) in 1892.

The Historical Interface of Law and Psychology

Professionals from both professions saw the advantages of cooperation soon after the inception of psychology. However, collaboration between the disciplines started off slowly and did not gain momentum until the 1970s. The first joint law (J.D.) and psychology (Ph.D.) degree was offered at the University of Nebraska in Lincoln in 1974. That same year, the first national convention of the American Psychology–Law Society (AP–LS) was held. This society was influential in the formation in 1981 of Division 41 (Psychology and Law) of the American Psychological Association. The two organizations merged in 1984 to form the American Psychology–Law Society/Division 41. By 1990, there were about 1,400 members (Grisso 1991).

Psychology's Research on the Legal System

Sigmund Freud in 1906 first proposed that psychology could assist the legal system in delving into the truthfulness of reported events. Two years later, an experimental psychologist at Harvard, Hugo von Munsterberg, published his book, *On the Witness Stand* (1908). This volume questioned the accuracy of witnesses and contended that psychology could assist in legal proceedings. Some psychologists criticized Munsterberg's work for not providing empirical support for his viewpoint. In fact, most psychologists either ignored or disagreed with him.

It was not until 1933 that Allport encouraged psychologists to extend their research to the real world, specifically the law. Later still, Kurt Lewin (1947, 1948) also advocated research addressed to real life concerns and suggested that social psychologists consider the effects of legal processes on society. But although a few works (e.g., Burtt's *Legal Psychology* (1931); Robinson's *Law and the Lawyers* (1935)) addressed the legal system from a psychological viewpoint, until the 1960s most work on the legal system was done by anthropologists, sociologists, or psychiatrists (Bermant, Nemeth & Vidmar 1976; Tapp 1977).

Courts Early research on the legal system focused entirely on the courts. The University of Chicago Jury Project, formed in the 1950s, was the first major research undertaking of this type. Many books and articles were derived from this project, the best known being *The American Jury* (1966) by Kalven and

A PRISON YARD. In order to maintain security and control violence, different sections of this large maximum security prison are separated by fences. Prisoners going from one area of the institution to another must pass through security check points. (Photo courtesy of David H. Fauss)

Zeisel (an attorney and sociologist, respectively). This work gave great impetus to research on jury trials and later work on jury selection.

Corrections Entry into a second area of the legal system, corrections, began slowly in the mid-century with work in the discipline of psychiatry and, to a lesser degree, psychology. At the same time professionals in the field of corrections were becoming increasingly interested in rehabilitation, many new forms of therapy were being developed. It was natural to apply these new methods to treatment of offenders. Illustrative of the acceptance of psychological methods for treatment is Menninger's book, *The Crime of Punishment* (1966), which called for a therapeutic model for corrections.

However, within ten years the tide had turned. An increase in crime, coupled with limited success in rehabilitation, provided the right atmosphere for Martinson's (1974) judgment that rehabilitation does not work. Although controversy surrounded his report, Martinson's viewpoint was widely accepted. It was not until the mid- to late-1980s that the pendulum began to swing back toward rehabilitation.

The 1970s saw mounting ethical concern about the use of prisoners as research subjects. These concerns led to large cutbacks in funding for behavioral science research in prisons, especially work on behavior modification (Bermant, Nemeth & Vidmar 1976). Meanwhile, a few psychologists were still looking at corrections. Work by Dale Smith and Dick Swanson (1979a, 1979b) on prison crowding and Rob Johnson (1987) on violence in corrections are examples of current research in corrections.

Law Enforcement In the 1970s psychological research and practice was directed at a third area of the legal system: law enforcement. Police reactions to the riots and demonstrations of the 1960s produced extremely negative public attitudes. The media reinforced those negative attitudes by criticizing law enforcement for its methods. Police departments attempted to improve their image through public service activities and community relations. While these activities were conducted with the assistance of psychologists, psychology was not theoretically advanced enough to provide insight into and solutions for the complex problems that divide citizens from law enforcement. Programs proposed by psychologists were not particularly successful. However, the failures of early programs pointed out the direction for later, more effective ones (Bermant, Nemeth & Vidmar 1976).

Other Research Areas The 1970s also saw attention directed toward the victims of crime and the advent of the new field of victimology. Today, research is being conducted on every area of the legal system. Psychologists are also applying their expertise to the legal system as expert witnesses in the courts, therapists in prisons, and trainers in law enforcement.

The Legal System's Use of Psychology

The most important and hotly contested issues facing society generally are decided in the legal arena by the U.S. Supreme Court. Thus abortion, discrimination, and capital punishment have been, and certainly will continue to be, addressed by this body. Since these and many other issues decided by the courts are social as well as legal questions, social science has much to offer in the decision-making process.

Prior to the 20th century, the Supreme Court made decisions about social issues under its consideration based on the personal experiences, opinions, or interpretations of the individual justices. A new procedure was introduced by Justice Louis Brandeis who filed what are now referred to as "Brandeis briefs." He defended social welfare legislation by referring to research and testimony given by economists, sociologists, physicians, and health workers. This technique was first used in 1908 in the *Muller v. Oregon* decision.

Not until the landmark *Brown v. Board of Education* (1954) decision did the Supreme Court again use social science findings. This decision, that "separate but equal" schools were unconstitutional, contained a brief filed by psychologist Kenneth Clark and other social scientists. In the ruling, the court cited seven studies indicating that segregation of children had a detrimental effect on

Box 1.1

Miranda

Ernest Miranda had a long history of arrests and incarcerations before moving in with Twila Hoffman and her two children. Despite Twila's legal marriage to another man, she and Ernest had a child together. Miranda avoided conflicts with the law while hopping from one menial job to another. Finally, he seemed to settle into work at United Produce in Phoenix. But this apparently conventional life-style was short-lived.

At 11:30 p.m. on March 2, 1963, a man abducted and raped an 18-year-old woman. The abductor stole $4 from the victim and fled. Less than two weeks later, Ernest Miranda was arrested for the rape and eventually confessed. Although the police denied making either threats or promises in order to obtain the confession, Miranda described the situation differently. He claimed that he was badgered, coerced, and deprived of sleep. He also alleged that the police promised to get him psychiatric help and to drop the robbery charge if he confessed to rape.

After viewing a lineup, the victim was unsure whether Miranda was the rapist and asked to hear his voice. Meanwhile, Miranda was told that he had been positively identified. Thus, when asked if she were the victim, Miranda responded, "that's the girl."

Miranda was convicted and the Arizona Supreme Court upheld his conviction. However, the U.S. Supreme Court reversed the lower court's decision, concluding that "Miranda was not in any way apprised of his right to consult with an attorney and to have one present during the interrogation, nor was his right not to be compelled to incriminate himself effectively protected in any other manner. Without these warnings the statements were inadmissable" (*Miranda v. Arizona,* 1966). In its decision the court cited social science research on police interrogation and false confessions (e.g., Frank & Frank 1957, Sterling 1965, Weisberg 1961).

As a result of this decision, police officers began to read to suspects their "Miranda" warnings:

"You have the right to remain silent. Anything you say can be used against you in a court of law. You have the right to the presence of an attorney to assist you prior to questioning and to be with you during questioning if you so desire. If you cannot afford an attorney, you have the right to have an attorney appointed for you prior to questioning. Do you understand these rights?"

The Supreme Court decision did not really help Miranda. There was enough other evidence to convict him in his new trial. He was incarcerated until 1972. Ernest Miranda was killed in a barroom brawl 4 years later.

Source: L. Baker, *Miranda: Crime, Law, and Politics* (New York: Atheneum, 1983), pp. 177–178.

blacks. While there is debate about how influential the social science data were to the *Brown v. Board of Education* decision, there is no doubt as to the importance of the precedent. Following that decision, attorneys expanded their use of social science and psychological research as documentation for their cases. As a result, the Supreme Court has increasingly turned to social science and psychology for information to support judgments. However, the justices apparently still only use social science research when more traditional legal grounds are not adequate (Kerr 1986). See MIRANDA for a current use of psychological data in a Supreme Court decision.

Expert Witnesses Ever since the institution of an insanity defense, the courts have depended on the expert testimony of mental health professionals to determine the mental responsibility of the defendant. More recently, psychologists have been asked to testify about the accuracy of eyewitness identification, the abused spouse syndrome, child custody, biases in testing, and conditions in prisons, to name only a few examples. In addition, a growing number of lawyers are turning to psychologists and other social scientists for assistance in selecting juries.

Assumptions

In order to understand the obstacles to interactions between psychology and the law, it is necessary to examine the distinguishing features of each discipline.

Assumptions about the Law

Law is based on assumptions about people's behavior and how it can be controlled. For example, criminal law assumes people are less likely to commit a crime if they know they will be punished for it (Monahan & Loftus 1982). Underlying this assumption is the belief that people are reasonable and logical—they can understand the law.

A fundamental concept in the law is that people decide what they will do by weighing the options available to them. Thus, many aspects of the legal system are based on what a "reasonable person" would do under specific circumstances. If an individual's behavior is not that of a reasonable person, that individual will be held responsible for the outcome of the behavior. This is true whether the behavior has violated criminal law or the rights of another person or body (tort).

Definitions of the Law

Over the centuries a number of definitions of the law have evolved. Bonsignore, et al. list a number of these definitions:

1. Law consists of rules and regulations of the state for the governance of society.
2. Law protects what is of value in society.
3. Law is a means to make society run more smoothly through the recognition and securing of rights.

4. Law is whatever the people want it to be.
5. Law is a means of oppression—it is designed to preserve the economic, political, and social position of the haves at the expense of the have-nots.
6. It's who you know—face it, the law is what judges, lawyers, and police say it is. (1974, p. x)

Each of these definitions contributes some insight on the legal system, but none completely defines the law. Whatever definition of law is used, it is apparent "law is a dynamic enterprise that evolves during the course of human activity. The making of decisions in legal contexts is not simply a function of the application or implementation of 'black letter' law. Claims are pressed, choices made, and disputes settled because of interactions between personal variables (e.g., legal reasoning, prior experience, personality) and legal norms—both formal and informal, written and discretionary" (Tapp & Levine 1977, p. 249).

Statutory Law and Common Law

There are two primary sources for laws: common law and statutory law. Statutory law consists of the set of laws passed by legislators. While this sounds simple and straightforward, it is really quite complicated. Legislators in every state pass laws directed at controlling the same behavior. Thus, a behavior might be legal in one state and illegal in another; for example, prostitution is legal in Nevada, but illegal in every other state. And a behavior which is universally considered illegal might have very different sanctions in different jurisdictions; for example, some states can impose the death penalty for first-degree murder while others sentence the murderer to life imprisonment.

In addition to the laws for each of the fifty states, the federal government has its own set of laws. Adding to the complexity, each set of laws is constantly in a state of flux as new laws are continually being passed. Some of these new laws contradict older laws, which are seldom repealed and are therefore still in effect. For an example of an old law that was not repealed, see THE ENFORCEMENT OF AN OLD LAW.

Common law is law made by judges. Like statutory law, it is constantly developing and evolving. Each case that comes before a judge must be decided not only on its own merit but also on the basis of past cases. In addition, the judge must take into account the constitution, statutory law, custom, and the history of cases. Common law is strongly tied to past cases. Judges must justify their decisions on the basis of precedent—what has been decided in earlier, similar cases. If a case does not follow precedence, it can be appealed and might be overruled by a higher court.

One law professor has described the legal world in this manner:

It is a world of facts, statutes, rules, and precedents, a world that demands adherence to historical and traditional roles and use of an inherited language. On the other hand, our hearts tell us that there is something more to a life in law than knowing and applying rules, or solving legal conundrums for which we make a handsome wage.

> **Box 1.2**
>
> **The Enforcement of an Old Law**
>
> A New Hampshire law forbidding extramarital sex, passed in 1791, remained on the books in 1987. In March of that year, Robert Stackelback filed a complaint against Daniel Hebenstreit for committing adultery with his estranged wife, Sharon Stackelback. Stackelback approached a number of police departments, all of which refused to investigate his complaint. Stackelback finally filed the complaint himself. Hebenstreit pled innocent.
>
> No one remembers the extramarital sex law being invoked since the early 1900s. Publicity over the law led New Hampshire Representative Michael Jones to file a bill to abolish it. However, the case was scheduled to be tried in court. The maximum punishment for the crime, a misdemeanor, is 1 year in jail and a $21,000 fine. The original law named the penalty for being convicted of extramarital sex as "standing on a gallows for one hour with a noose around the neck, taking up to 39 lashes, going to jail for up to one year, or paying a fine of 100 pounds."
>
> ♦
>
> What should legislators do to prevent the enforcement of laws which are no longer current? Do laws become outdated and no longer useful after a period of time? Should laws be reviewed at regular intervals? Should outdated laws be enforced?

Source: "200-Year-Old Adultery Law Faces Court Test," *The Florida Times-Union* (March 13, 1987), p. A–8.

The law has claimed for itself throughout modern history an association with noble purposes: justice, fairness, equality, human dignity, and social harmony. The decision to come to law school is tied—sometimes indirectly and remotely—to a set of ideals and social values that ally the student with the promise of the law. (Elkins 1988, pp. 591–592)

Assumptions in Psychology

Psychology "attempts to combine science, application of science, and professional practice into one organized endeavor" (Strickland 1988, p. 104). Psychology is not strongly tied to history like law is—it is a rapidly advancing science that is constantly changing. Advances in psychological knowledge are made through experiments and other research. New research can drastically challenge previous ideas, although major changes typically are not made rapidly or frequently.

Social psychology, the area which most frequently studies the legal system, studies the ways in which people influence and are influenced by other people. Social psychologists tend to emphasize the impact of social situations on human

♦ **FIGURE 1.1**
Scientific method (illustrated by Reen Foley)

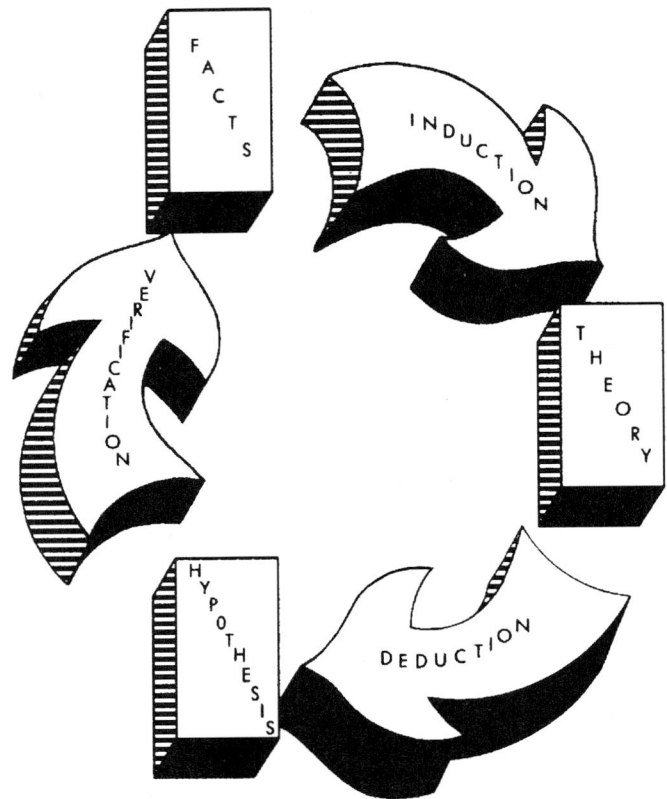

behavior. One well-researched model is the attribution theory, which will be discussed in reference to many behaviors throughout this book. This theory states that people make inferences about causes of behavior, their own and other people's, by observing the behavior.

Research Methods
Research in psychology follows the scientific method, and thus, it is cyclical in nature. The scientific method is based on facts—events which can be observed consistently and objectively by many people. From these facts researchers induce a theory to explain the facts. A theory is simply a way of organizing concepts in order to explain phenomena. Based on the theory, the researcher can then make a prediction about behavior in a specific situation or under specific circumstances. This prediction is called a hypothesis, and the process of making a prediction from a theory is called deduction. The actual research involves the verification of the hypothesis through the collection of additional facts or data. If the new data confirm the hypothesis, they support the theory. If the data contradict the hypothesis, the theory will need to be revised in order to incorporate the new information. In this manner, knowledge in psychology is constantly evolving (see Figure 1.1, The Scientific Method).

Box 1.3

Research

The following is a brief synopsis of a portion of an experiment conducted by Melissa Pigott, John C. Brigham, and Robert K. Bothwell. Forty-seven female bank tellers were approached by a confederate of the experimenters and asked to cash a United States Post Office money order that had been altered to read $110 instead of $10. When the request was refused, the confederate argued. After consistent refusals, the irate confederate took the money order and quickly left the bank. Each interaction took about one and a half minutes.

A few hours later, the female experimenter, posing as a police detective, questioned the teller. The female tellers were randomly assigned to one of three experimental groups: accurate information condition, inaccurate information condition, or neutral information condition. In the accurate information condition, the tellers were told that the experimenter believed "that a young white male was in your bank earlier today attempting to cash an altered Post Office money order. The person we're looking for is believed to be tall, slender, and having light-colored hair." The inaccurate information described the confederate as "average height, heavy-set, and having dark-colored hair." The neutral description was limited to "a white male" (p. 12).

Contrary to expectations, the information given to the tellers had little impact on their descriptions of the confederate. A post-experimental analysis discovered that tellers who had been robbed prior to this interaction were less accurate in their descriptions than those who had never been robbed.

Source: M. Pigott, J. C. Brigham, and R. W. Bothwell, "A Field Study on the Relationship Between Quality of Eyewitnesses' Descriptions and Identification Accuracy," *Journal of Police Science* 17 (2, 1990): 84–88.

Psychology, as any science, grows cumulatively with each new advance based on previous knowledge. Keith Stanovich (1986) maintains that a science such as psychology is defined by three characteristics. The first characteristic is that a science is based on **systematic empiricism.** In other words, it is based on observable events that can be measured. These observations are the objective facts collected in verification of a hypothesis. A science also must contain **publicly verifiable knowledge.** That is, research must be described in a manner which allows others to replicate it. In order to ensure findings are accurate, research is examined by others in the field. This is accomplished by submitting the research to a professional journal or organization for peer review. Finally, science looks at **solvable problems,** those that are specifiable and can be solved by an empirical technique. The definition of solvable problems is continually expanding in psychology as new techniques are developed.

In the verification stage of research there are many ways to collect data. One frequently used method is the controlled experiment. In this instance, the researcher compares the effects of two or more levels of an independent variable on a dependent variable. The primary advantage of the experimental method is that the researcher can infer cause and effect; in other words, that changes in the independent variable caused the dependent variable to change. See RESEARCH for an example of an experiment.

There are many other methods for testing hypotheses in psychology. All methods involve the collection of data in an objective manner and many will be discussed later.

Professional Training

All graduate and professional training programs have some commonalities, and graduate schools in psychology and law school are no exception. Competition for places in advanced programs is intense; thus, the best applicants are accepted. Because the students are bright, the demands placed on them are high and the work is much more difficult than undergraduate work. Students who are used to completing every assignment and being better prepared than their classmates may find that they are average performers in graduate school. The demands are such that students may find little or no time for relationships with their families and must forgo most forms of relaxation.

There are many similarities between law school and psychology graduate school. Both programs teach their participants to look at the world in a new and unique manner. Each program also requires students to learn a language specific to their new profession. Both training programs use inductive and deductive reasoning, although the emphasis in psychology is on inductive reasoning, while in law it is on deductive reasoning. There are also many differences between law school and graduate school in psychology; the major difference is the method of instruction. Law school is the beginning of legal training, whereas graduate study in psychology assumes a foundation in the discipline as an undergraduate. A description of each program will demonstrate further differences.

Law School

The majority of law school professors have graduated from the same small group of prestigious law schools. Their similar background and training are reflected in the similarity of law programs throughout the United States. The case method, combined with the Socratic technique of question and answer, was introduced by Christopher Langdell at Harvard Law school in 1870. This method is used in virtually every law school in the U.S., particularly in the first year (Stevens 1983).

The primary purpose of law school is to teach law students to "think like a lawyer." Typically law schools "emphasize the ability to analyze and advocate, placing a high value on the capacity to be precise, logical and objective" (Dvorkin, Himmelstein & Lesnick 1981, p. 1). Students are taught to examine and defend their position through objective arguments. They learn to be able to take either side of a disagreement and to argue it successfully. Law students are taught that personal values or opinions should not enter into an attorney's arguments, and certainly emotions or feelings are inappropriate.

Scott Turow, in his classic book, *One L* (the basis for the movie, *The Paper Chase*), describes thinking as a lawyer in this way: "Legal thinking is nasty. . . . Thinking like a lawyer involved being suspicious and distrustful. You reevaluated statements, inferred from silences, looked for loopholes and ambiguities. You did everything but take a statement at face value" (1977, p. 93).

First-Year Law School
The first year of law school is the most difficult; students are overwhelmed with the work and the competition. Every student is "one of the best and brightest." The vocabulary is new and unfamiliar as are the teaching methods. Uhlig (1988) reports being horrified when she did not recognize the very first word in her Contracts book—**assumpsit**.

Students in large groups of perhaps 150 are assigned seats in an immense classroom. The law professor, who has a guide to the seating arrangement, calls on a student by name and asks the student to explain the case assigned for that class period. By what is often described as hostile questioning, the professor extracts the rules or principles from the student. Using analogy, the questioning helps to determine how one case is similar to and different from other cases. Through the professor's probing with hypothetical questions, the student formulates general principles. First-year law students find the case method and the cases confusing, but they *do* learn to think like lawyers. For a description of the Socratic method in law school, see *One L*.

Grades receive a lot of emphasis in the first year. Students' grades are determined by one long (up to 8 hour) exam at the end of the course. Students panic over exams, and with good reason. The grading curve is forced, so no matter how many really good students there are in a class, only 8 percent receive an A. Fifty percent of the students receive a C or below. This is one student's reaction to the grading system and competitive atmosphere of law school:

> How do you handle the fact that you are in competition with 130 other students? Those on top are going to get better jobs. There is conspicuous competition as some students make a habit of telling others that he or she will graduate among the top thirty. It is also apparent that cliques form; it is preferable to compete in groups than alone. This does not mean that one spends every minute of the day thinking about how to outdo fellow students, but someone is going to come out on top and someone on the bottom. My goal is to come out in the middle. A close friend told me that he is at war with every other student in his class. His goal is to be number one. . . .
> The intensely competitive atmosphere into which we are forced is almost certain to engender very shallow and defensive relationships with other students. We tend to look at each other in terms of trying to gauge where we stand individually in comparison to each other with regard to comprehension of the new material, ability to express oneself in class "like a lawyer," and even in terms of whether this person or that person spends more time working, or is farther ahead on an outline. This, it seems to me, is a very unhealthy atmosphere." (Elkins 1988, p. 590)

Students find that "in the law school we seem to spend much of our time thinking like lawyers, acting like lawyers, and arguing like lawyers, even when we are not in role" (Dvorkin, Himmelstein & Lesnick 1981, p. 26).

> **Box 1.4**
>
> # One L
>
> The following is a quotation from the book, *One L*:
> "Mr. Karlin," Perini said, ambling toward my side of the room, "why don't you tell us about the case of *Hurley v. Eddingfield*?"
> Karlin already had his notebook open. His voice was quavering.
> "Plaintiff's intestate," he began. He got no further.
> "What does *that* mean?" Perini cried from across the room. He began marching fiercely up the aisle toward Karlin. "In-*tes*-tate," he said, "in-*tes*-tate. What is that? Something to do with the *stomach*? Is this an anatomy class, Mr. Karlin?" Perini's voice had become shrill with a note of open mockery and at the last word people burst out laughing, louder than at anything Perini had said before.
> He was only five or six feet from Karlin now. Karlin stared up at him and blinked and finally said, "No."
> "No, I didn't think so," Perini said. "What if the word was 'testate'? What would that be? Would we have moved from the stomach"—Perini waved a hand and there was more loud laughter when he leeringly asked his question—"*else*where?"
> "I think," Karlin said weakly, "that if the word was 'testate' it would mean he had a will."
> "And 'intestate' that he didn't have a will. I see." Perini wagged his head. "And who is this 'he,' Mr. Karlin?"
> Karlin was silent. He shifted in his seat as Perini stared at him. Hands had shot up across the room. Perini called rapidly on two or three people who gave various names—Hurley, Eddingfield, the plaintiff. Finally someone said that the case didn't say.
> "The case doesn't *say*!" Perini cried, marching down the aisle. "The case does *not* say. Read the case. *Read* the case! Care*fully*!" He bent with each word,
>
> *(continued)*

The Next Two Years of Law School

There is a law school saying that the first year they scare you to death, the second year they work you to death, and the third year they bore you to death. The second and third years of study do not have the same stresses in the classroom as does the first year. Classes are more likely to be in the lecture format than the case method; students are not as competitive; students know what to expect from exams and are not as concerned with their ranking in class (Uhlig 1988). By the second and third years of law school, students realize they do not have to memorize everything; what is important is that they learn to interpret the law.

During the third year, law students can take part in moot court or (if selected) work on law reviews. Even in the third year, students feel pressed for time.

> pointing a finger at the class. He stared fiercely into the crowd of students in the center of the room, then looked back at Karlin. "Do we really care who 'he' is, Mr. Karlin?"
> "Care?"
> "Does it make any *difference* to the outcome of the case?"
> "I don't think so."
> "Why not?"
> "Because he's dead."
> "He's *dead*!" Perini shouted. "Well, that's a load off of our minds. But there's one problem then, Mr. Karlin. If he's dead, how did he file a *law*suit?"
> Karlin's face was still tight with fear, but he seemed to be gathering himself.
> "I thought it was the administrator who brought the suit."
> "Ah!" said Perini, "the ad*min*istrator. And what's an administrator? One of those types over in the Faculty Building?"
> It went on that way for a few more minutes, Perini striding through the room, shouting and pointing as he battered Karlin with questions, Karlin doing his best to provide answers. A little after noon Perini suddenly announced that we would continue tomorrow. Then he strode from the classroom with the seating chart beneath his arm. In his wake the class exploded into chatter.
> I sat stunned. Men and women crowded around Karlin to congratulate him. He had done well, better, it seemed than even Perini had expected.
>
> ♦
>
> Does the anxiety created by the case method help students to become better lawyers? Should law professors question students in a frightening manner? Would another method of teaching enhance the learning process and thus produce better lawyers?

Source: S. Turow, *One L* (New York: G. P. Putnam's Sons, 1977), pp. 52–53.

They interview for jobs and many work part-time as well as attend classes. There still is little time for sleep and none for relaxation. This is how one third-year student describes time conflicts:

> I feel a lot of pressure. Perhaps the worst pressure is time. I find that I just don't have time to do all that I would like to do in law school or even to do the work as I want to do it. I don't have time, for example, to go off on a tangent and research an idea or point of law referred to in class. I have responsibilities other than law school with my family at home. My priorities have to shift. Law school can't always be #1 on my priority list. (Elkins 1988, p. 588)

Edwards (1988) maintains many professors are isolated in their "ivory towers," distant from, and unconcerned with, the real practice of law. Few law teachers are trying to integrate what they teach with legal practice, and few law schools have any practical courses on trial methods. Most schools have internships where students work in the public defender's office or a legal services office

LAW SCHOOL LECTURE. Law school classes are quite large, sometimes having as many as 250 students. (Photo courtesy of Robert Isaacs)

to develop the skills and practical experience necessary for litigation. Between the second and third year, students get experience through summer clerkships.

Anxiety Among Law Students

Both the Socratic method and the single exam create great anxiety in law students. Intense competition adds to the tension. Benjamin and his associates found among their student subjects a significant increase in symptoms of psychological difficulty between the time before law school and after the first few months of classes. These symptoms significantly worsened between the first and third years and remained high for two years after graduation. "The pattern of results suggests that certain aspects of legal education produce uncommonly elevated psychological distress levels among significant numbers of law students and recently graduated alumni" (Benjamin et al. 1986, p. 247). These researchers conclude it is the law school experience itself which produces the results since subjects did not demonstrate any psychological problems prior to entry. These researchers propose that the psychological problems found in law students are due to three factors: 1) the time pressures, 2) the high student–faculty ratio which creates poor relations and distance, and 3) the fact that interpersonal skills are not taught.

Students frequently complain about their law education. For example, one law student reported hearing from his colleagues "comments, all to the effect that they were being limited, harmed by the education, forced to substitute dry reason for emotion, to cultivate opinions which were 'rational' but which had no roots in the experience, the life they'd had before. They were being cut away from themselves" (Turow 1977, p. 92). However, Shaffer and Redmount found that law school did not decrease the sensitivity of students. Instead, they concluded that "moral and psychological judgments are suspended, and perhaps considered unessential, when legal solutions are so well developed and so available" (1977, p. 55).

One attorney explained that the common experience of intense stress created a group cohesiveness among lawyers. Having survived the stress also developed self-confidence. This experience produces a self-determination that is a source of strength throughout a lawyer's professional life (Uhlig 1988).

Reactions to the Case Method

There is no doubt the case method produces high levels of stress among law students. Students who are used to contemplating a question in order to formulate an answer find this habit a hindrance in law school. Students, embarrassed if they make mistakes, are reluctant to contribute to the class discussion. Law professors contend the anxiety created in the classroom is helpful, and as attorneys the students will have to answer and perform under similarly stressful situations. The questions asked in class are similar to those attorneys must address in court.

When Langdell first introduced the case method, declaring it to be the best and shortest way of teaching law, he was met with a lot of opposition. But, gradually the method became almost universally accepted. Opposition to this stressful approach, however, is making a comeback. Opponents cite the negative emotional impact the case method has upon students. In addition, critics of the case approach contend it is not a useful way for teaching analytic skills. They also maintain it has a "high cost and a low efficiency" (Teich 1986). In contrast, those in favor of this approach say:

> (1) of all potential alternatives case instruction best teaches the inductive method used by the lawyer to discern the law and so best directly teaches the most critical lawyering skill—the ability to think like a lawyer; (2) cases best provide the appropriate factual matrix for students to learn to apply the law; (3) the method demonstrates most clearly to students that the law is a growing, changing body of doctrine; (4) the method forces the student into the best possible learning mode—an "active" learning mode; and (5) the method is more pedagogically stimulating and interesting to the student than other more conventional methods. (Teich 1986, p. 170)

Advocates of any method of teaching law, whether for or against the case method, have little or no empirical data to support their positions. Teich (1986) reviewed nine empirical studies comparing contrasting methods of teaching law and found no one method superior to another. When the same author reviewed comparisons of comparable group methods in other postsecondary schools, he found similar results. Group methods of teaching are equivalent. But while all the methods employed in teaching law are group approaches, other postsecondary schools also employ "individualized" methods of instruction. These individualized methods allow each student to learn using his or her own cognitive strategies for complex material and have been shown to be superior to group methods. Teich maintains the individualized systems hold the most promise for better success at teaching law. He calls for the reexamination of law school teaching methods and assumptions about them. However, the fiscal reality is that individualized methods of instruction are more expensive than the group methods employed in law schools and thus face an uphill battle for acceptance.

Graduate School in Psychology

Students applying for psychology graduate school are accepted into a specific area or subdiscipline. The main classifications are: clinical, social, and experimental. Experimental psychology is further divided into subdisciplines of learning, memory, cognition, perception, physiological, and comparative. Some universities have additional specialties, such as: developmental, school, industrial/organizational, personality, psychometrics, and psychology and law.

While there is a lot of diversity in graduate psychology training, all training has a basic similarity to law school in that there is a great quantity of work and reading—more than can fit into the time available. However, there are also many differences between the two types of training. Very limited numbers of students are accepted for each psychology program. Some areas might only accept one or two students a year. Therefore, classes in psychology tend to be quite small after the first year. Even in the first year, when all students from every area of psychology take the same classes, the class size is seldom more than thirty students. In later years the classes are anywhere from five to fifteen.

As in law school, the first year of graduate study in psychology is difficult and stressful. Students soon realize they must work much harder than they did as undergraduates. But, unlike law school, students are not pitted against each other, and students are more likely to cooperate and help each other than compete.

Psychology is not strongly tied to history; it constantly changes and seeks social change. Psychologists are trained to be objective and qualify every statement. They seldom give a definitive answer—spending time deliberating before speaking on an issue is a sign of intelligence and abstract thinking. Psychologists are expected to report all their findings, whether the data support their position or not. They particularly must discuss any research that contradicts their conclusions. Their goal is to find the best answer, not to prove themselves accurate.

First Year of Graduate School

The first year of psychology graduate school generally consists of a series of proseminars. These are in-depth classes in every major area of psychology. Graduate students are also required to take courses in experimental methods and computer science. There is no predetermined seating arrangement, and students are not usually embarrassed by hostile questioning. Students are expected to deliberate on their answers and qualify every statement. Professors model this behavior in class.

Generally, classes consist of lectures. Class discussion is encouraged. A final exam and a written paper are usually required in each class. The final exam is usually one or two hours long and is held at the end of the semester or quarter. Exams deal with controversial issues, and students must support their positions with references to the current literature. Each professor determines his or her own grading system.

While the proseminars are difficult, and the first year is stressful, psychology students generally develop close and supportive relationships with their classmates. They develop a similar relationship with at least one faculty member who is the student's advisor. Students receive individual advice and guidance throughout their training from this professor who functions as a mentor.

Later Graduate Training

After the first year, graduate school in psychology becomes much less structured with students taking small seminars of their choice. Students proceed at their own pace, devoting most nonclass time to their individual research. The grading system for the seminars is not as stressful as in the proseminars. Frequently the grade is determined by a paper, an oral report, a research project, or a research proposal rather than an exam. Professors realize all the students are "the best and brightest" and grade accordingly. Professors who find that every student in a class has earned an A will give that grade to every student.

While graduate students are generally high achievers and want good grades, grades are not a major source of competition or determinant of jobs. Psychology students are trained to conduct research or treat patients. Evidence of expertise in these areas is the criterion for employment. Students frequently work together on research projects in order to enhance their likelihood of obtaining jobs.

In order to complete the requirements for their master's degree, graduate students are required to write a thesis based on research they conduct. Graduate students are guided in their research by a committee of faculty representatives, headed by a faculty member of their choice, their mentor. Upon completion of the thesis, each student must defend the results and conclusions to the committee of faculty. The committee will ask questions about the thesis or about prior research related to it. This defense is quite stressful to students since its outcome determines whether they receive a master's degree.

Once course requirements are completed, students must take a comprehensive exam. This exam varies by university but generally covers all the important material in the student's primary area of study, as well as statistics and research methods. Typically, the exam consists of two parts: an 8-hour written exam, followed the next day by oral questioning. This is the most stressful aspect of graduate training for the student. If the student fails the qualifying exam, he or she will be terminated from the doctoral program. Thus, students may pass all their classes and still not obtain a degree. Some universities will allow students to retake their exam one time if they fail on the first attempt.

Once qualifying exams are over, the psychology student is eligible to begin working on the doctoral dissertation. At this point, the program of study becomes even less structured. The student must conduct a second, much larger, independent research project and write a dissertation on it. The student is expected to read everything ever written on the topic selected for research. It typically takes students years to complete the dissertation. When the dissertation is completed, the student must defend the dissertation orally to a panel of faculty. Although the oral defense is stressful, the student has become an authority on the research and seldom is unable to answer the questions posed by the faculty committee.

There is a lot of freedom and autonomy in graduate school, but there is also considerable ambiguity. One reason for this ambiguity is that the standards of success are unclear. There is much emphasis placed on creativity, since the goal is to become a professional research scientist. Horowitz and Willging describe the training as "a program designed to produce an empirically oriented, analytical scientist, who searches for scientific truth by taking conceptual issues, translating them into empirical questions, and gains these truths by applying methodologies and rituals currently labeled scientific" (1984, p. 47).

Graduate students in clinical psychology receive supervision and training in treatment of clients throughout their graduate training. In addition to the requirements of a thesis, qualifying exam, and a dissertation, they must also complete an internship. Students of clinical psychology spend one year at a mental health facility working under supervision while treating clients.

The Psychology and Law Interface

Psychology and the law can work quite well together and, in the process, both disciplines benefit. Psychology can assist the legal system in the understanding and prediction of human behavior, while the legal system can provide psychology with a real-life laboratory and different perspective. However, there are a number of impediments to communications and interactions between these disciplines. As we have seen, psychology and the law are based on different assumptions, training, and methods; they use different language and value different types of information. Their different ways of finding "truth" affect the way in which they perceive and interpret events, thus interfering with communication between the disciplines.

Obstacles

Both psychologists and lawyers develop working personalities—behavioral and cognitive styles of approaching a problem. These diverse working styles, patterns of thought, and language are based on dissimilar concepts. These differences in working personalities create obstacles for members of the two disciplines who are trying to work together. The legal system sometimes looks on psychology with "suspicion and even hostility" (Kaplan 1986, p. 8).

A basic obstacle to promoting understanding between psychology and law is the type of reasoning used by each discipline. Lawyers concur with prior decisions—once a ruling has been made, it must be accepted. In contrast, psychologists are trained to be skeptics; they are constantly collecting data in an attempt to contradict or clarify earlier cases or experiments.

When psychologists testify as expert witnesses in court, their training and methodology does not mesh well with the legal system. Psychological training requires statements to be qualified. But testimony is limited by rules of evidence and can, therefore, be distorted by the adversarial process. Attorneys want to exclude any information which would be detrimental to their case and thus attempt to eliminate qualifiers and equivocal data. In order to maintain their credibility, psychologists must be perceived as objective and rational. This is a difficult role for psychologists working in the legal system where they are testifying for one adversary in a controversy. The fact that psychologists are paid for their time by the side for which they are testifying leads many observers to assume they are being paid to slant the truth in favor of that position.

Kaplan (1986) cautions psychologists to be careful not to appear as an advocate for a litigant. However, Tapp (1980) maintains that it is acceptable for a psychologist to be an advocate as long as that psychologist makes a conscious decision to do so. The psychologist must decide on a role of advocate or expert in order to lessen the probability of testimony being misused and to decrease confusion about the role held by the psychologist.

Legal and Psychological Methods

Even though both psychology and the law are empirical, "substantial differences exist between the styles and methods of reasoning, proof, and justification used in psychology and law" (Haney 1980, p. 158). Legislators and judges tend to use what Meehl (1977) calls "fireside inductions" in determining the type of laws needed and the most effective forms of punishment. These inductions are defined as "common sense, anecdotal, introspective, and culturally transmitted beliefs about human behavior" (p. 10). Attorneys, judges, and legislators have beliefs about human behavior and how behavior can be explained and controlled. There are obvious limitations to these beliefs. The common knowledge of legal professionals is based on their background and experience. Their perspective is often that of a middle- or upper-class white male. The law's acceptance of common knowledge is its major area of contrast with psychology. Psychologists distrust common knowledge—they are skeptics. Common sense and accepted beliefs are not always accurate. One common belief is that a person is safer when there are many people around than when alone. However, psychological research has shown that the more people present the less likely anyone is to help in an emergency (see "Bystander Intervention," Chapter 14).

Despite psychology's stronger dependence on scientific research, its conclusions are not always superior to those of the law. While a scientific source of information might appear better intuitively, Meehl (1977) maintains psychological research can be methodologically deficient, thus rendering the conclusions

PEANUTS reprinted by permission of UFS, Inc.

questionable. Meehl is not alone in his criticism of law research performed by psychologists. Tapp (1980) expresses concern that much more research is currently conducted on trials than on plea bargaining, while in real life 80 to 90 percent of cases are handled by plea bargaining. She is also concerned about the quality of research conducted on juries (see Chapter 10).

Differences Between the Disciplines

It is apparent that psychology and the law have very different perspectives. Haney (1980) enumerates eight ways in which the two disciplines differ:

Differences Between Law and Psychology

Law	Psychology
1. stare decisis	creative
2. hierarchical	empirical
3. adversarial	experimental
4. prescriptive	descriptive
5. idiographic	nomothetic
6. certainty	probabilistic
7. reactive	proactive
8. operational	academic

1. Academic psychology places great emphasis on **creative** views. Psychologists are rewarded from the beginning of graduate school and throughout their careers for being innovative and for using novel approaches and solutions. In contrast, the model for the legal arena is **stare decisis.** That is, attorneys depend on past cases to support their current arguments and are likely to lose arguments based on innovative reasoning. Lawyers must be conservative and look back on history for justification and methods.

2. Courts are part of a **hierarchical** system that is authoritarian. Decisions can be overruled by higher courts, so the person with the highest position has the final say. Psychology is an **empirical** science based on consistent and supporting data. Any theory can be disproved by hard data whether the data are collected by the lowliest student or the most senior research professor. Law also is empirical in that it gathers data from previous cases. However, the empiricism of the law is not scientific; the attorney arranges or rearranges the data to prove a point. In this manner, the data are used to support an opinion or convince a jury. Legal rules are stable—facts are fitted into the rules by bending and stretching. The rules can change, but they do so very slowly over time. The attorney's goal is to find the facts and the rules that best fit her position in a particular case.

3. The method used to obtain "truth" in psychology is primarily the **experimental** method. As described before, this method stresses objectivity and tries to eliminate bias and errors. The legal method for obtaining truth is **adversarial.** By presenting conflicting points of view during litigation, the truth is unfolded. Bias is an assumed and accepted part of the adversarial method. Truth is the long-term consequence of the process, not the individual goal of each attorney.

4. Law is **prescriptive;** it tells people how to behave. A trial decides what ought to be done and in what situation. In contrast, psychology is **descriptive.** Psychology describes behavior as it occurs and avoids being judgmental about the behavior. Legal proceedings assume there is some disparity between how an individual behaved and how he should have behaved. Psychology attempts to be free of values.

5. Law focuses on a single case and thus is considered **idiographic.** Each case is tried and decided on its own merits based on the facts of that particular case. In contrast, psychology attempts to be **nomothetic.** It attempts to find the general principles or paradigms that underline many different cases. Because courts are interested in the specific case, the input from psychologists about patterns is immaterial and courts are not comfortable admitting general types of evidence.

6. The law tries to give the appearance of **certainty.** During a trial, "burden of proof" and "reasonable doubt" are argued. But, once a decision is made, it is assumed to be the "truth" and is often irrevocable. The court wants the decision to be absolute and final; the defendant is either guilty or not guilty. Psychology, in contrast, is based on empirical findings and is **probabilistic.** Psychologists are

> **Box 1.5**
>
> **Is He Prejudiced?**
>
> The author was requested to testify as an expert witness at a federal hearing. The trial concerned the disproportionately small number of women and blacks who had served as forepersons of grand juries in a medium-sized southern city. Unlike petit juries, where the jurors elect a foreperson, a judge appoints the foreperson of a grand jury. The data indicated that, over the previous thirty years, one black and two women had been appointed as forepersons of grand juries in that jurisdiction. Statistical analyses showed that there was less than one chance in 100,000 that this selection could have occurred by chance. The results appeared unequivocal; therefore, I was quite comfortable in reporting on the research.
>
> Statistical information like the research I presented is typical of research in social psychology. However, statistical information is not commonplace in the legal arena. There was much questioning about both the statistical analyses and their results by lawyers from both sides of the issue. Then I was asked by the presiding judge if I thought the judge who appointed the forepersons was prejudiced. I stated that I had collected no data on the individual judge and was unable to answer. The only response I had was that the judge's behavior discriminates. The judge was very firm in demanding that I give an opinion as to whether the judge was prejudiced. This predicament is an example of the difficult interface between psychology and the legal system. I was dealing with an aggregate of data, not interviews with an individual judge. The court wanted an opinion about an individual based on data that did not address the issue.
>
> ♦
>
> Should witnesses who are experts on nomothetic data be encouraged to answer questions of an idiographic nature? Should testimony about probabilistic data be reported as certainty? How should a psychologist, bound by professional ethics to report only what is found in the data, respond to the judge's question?

ethically bound to qualify statements and mention all the conditionals that apply to a conclusion. "Their most unequivocal statement—that a relationship is 'statistically significant'—is in terms of explicit probabilities" (Haney 1980, p. 166). Clinicians who are used to dealing with categorical decisions work more easily within the legal system. Lawyers want definite conclusions, while psychologists want to give qualified results. See IS HE PREJUDICED? for an example of certainty in conflict with probabilities.

7. Psychology is **proactive.** Psychologists are free to decide what areas they want to research and how they will conduct that research. Individual interests are the primary determinants of their choices. Financial considerations have little influence on their decisions unless they are applying for funding from government or private agencies. Lawyers are **reactive.** They can only respond to the issues and cases brought to their attention by their clients. The attorney then translates the client's problem into legal terms.

8. Psychological research is generally **academic** or pure research. Most psychological research is not conducted as a way of solving problems in the real world. Even applied research in psychology is not conducted in order to change the system. Law, however, is an **operational** discipline; it is geared to solving real-world problems and is applied to real-world issues. Law is basically applied and pragmatic. While psychologists are trained to observe and use appropriate methods to define the process, lawyers are trained to intervene. Lawyers manipulate external appearances, while psychologists examine the internal workings of a situation.

Similarities Between Law and Psychology

So far we have emphasized the differences between psychology and the law. But there are ways in which the two disciplines are similar. The prediction of human behavior is a main concern of law as well as psychology. Both disciplines are interested in understanding and controlling how people behave. They are also "value-conscious and evidence-minded" (Tapp 1977, p. 8).

Ellison and Genz (1983) point out similarities between a trial and an experiment, two methods for gathering truth. The experimenter and the judge are the authority figures conducting the examination. Subjects and jurors have similar experiences. Both begin as naive and are socialized into the new experience; jurors are informed by voir dire and subjects by instructions. Both subjects and jurors are decision-makers who are debriefed following their decision. However, there are obvious differences between the two situations. The most drastic difference is in the effect of the decision.

While emphasizing the different types of data collected by the two disciplines, similarities can be overlooked. Both attorneys and psychologists are interested in evidence and the certainty of it. Lawyers present evidence and argue about "reasonable doubt." The decision concerning reasonable doubt is left to the jury. Psychologists are also interested in the certainty of decisions. They use statistical methods to calculate the level of probability of their conclusions.

Recently, there has been a definite increase in the cooperation and communication between psychology and the law. The methods and concepts used in the two disciplines are beginning to be integrated. After reviewing the interactions between psychology and the law, Tapp concludes that "the overriding themes throughout this century are: (1) the union of psychology and law can promote justice and science; (2) psychology can and has offered ways of systematically documenting a socio-legal and psychological event; and (3) the phenomena of both psychology and law require new views of science and society" (1977, p. 3). Other experts also encourage closer cooperation between psychology and the law. Concerns of both disciplines can be pursued if the methods and training of each field are directed to the same issues.

Both psychology and the law are concerned with public issues. The two disciplines are seeking empirical solutions to the same problems; their major difference is the type of data collected. Both types of information are useful and need to be shared. "Although there are still enormous gaps—substantial and theoretical, methodological and empirical—together we *can* be more systematic, *are* more committed to documenting events descriptively and *may* be more willing to ask questions from more than one perspective" (Tapp & Levine 1977, p. 368).

Summary

Psychology and the law differ with regard to assumptions, training of professionals, and methodology; they use different language and value different types of information. The two disciplines have similar interests in human behavior and, in cooperation, can advance the goals of both disciplines.

Training in psychology graduate school and law school is similar in competition for acceptance, demands placed on students, stressfulness, and socialization into a new profession. The major distinction is the method of instruction. The case method is used in law schools while graduate psychology programs use individualized instruction.

Haney (1980) enumerates eight ways in which psychology and the legal system differ: 1. Academic psychology places great emphasis on **creative** views, while the model for the legal arena is **stare decisis.** 2. Courts are part of an **hierarchical** system that is authoritarian. Psychology is an **empirical** science based on consistent and supporting data. 3. The method used to obtain "truth" in psychology is primarily the **experimental** method versus the **adversarial** method used in law. 4. Law is **prescriptive**; it tells people how to behave. In contrast, psychology is **descriptive.** 5. Law focuses on a single case and thus is considered **idiographic,** while psychology attempts to be **nomothetic.** 6. Law tries to give the appearance of **certainty.** Psychology, in contrast, is based on empirical findings and is **probabilistic.** 7. Psychology is **proactive,** while law is **reactive.** 8. Psychological research is generally **academic** or pure research. Law, however, is an **operational** discipline.

There are ways in which the two disciplines are similar. Both trials and experiments are methods of gathering truth. Both attorneys and psychologists are interested in evidence and the certainty of it.

There is a definite increase in the cooperation and communication between psychology and the law. The methods and concepts used in the two disciplines are beginning to be integrated. As we have seen, psychology can examine legal concepts from a different perspective by using methods unknown to attorneys. However, the results of this research are of little benefit to those in the legal system unless the findings are translated into language understood by lawyers.

2

Crime Patterns

Sources and Accuracy of Crime Statistics
Uniform Crime Reports
Victimization Surveys
Self-Report Studies
Reporting Crimes to the Police
The Decision to Report Crimes
Costs and Benefits of Reporting Crimes to the Police
Crime Rates and Crime Waves
Crime Rates in the United States
Crime Rates in Other Countries
Explanations for Crime Trends
Women and Crime
Race and Crime
Projections of Future Crime Rates
Summary

Sources and Accuracy of Crime Statistics

It is unusual to watch a televised news report or read a newspaper without seeing reports about criminal activity or victims of crime. At one time or another, everyone has seen a media report on the FBI "Crime Clock," indicating the frequency of various serious crimes. For example, the 1990 Crime Clock stated a violent crime occurred every 17 seconds and a property crime occurred every 2 seconds (Uniform Crime Reports, 1991). Do these statistics really tell us how many crimes are committed in the United States? No, it is actually very difficult to get accurate information on the amount of crime because the three primary sources for crime statistics (Uniform Crime Reports, victimization surveys, and self-report surveys) have many limitations and are "notorious for their inaccuracies and disagreements" (Nietzel 1979, p. 17).

Although none of the sources for statistics on crime is completely accurate, each source provides some useful information that is unique. The following discussion of the major techniques of gathering information on the incidence of crime will attempt to highlight the benefits and the deficiencies of the data from each source.

Uniform Crime Reports

The best-known source for crime statistics is the Uniform Crime Report (UCR) published by the FBI. The police report the number of crimes "known" to them, the number of arrests made, and some characteristics of the individuals arrested. The FBI then compiles the data and calculates the crime rates, which are the number of crimes committed per 100,000 people in the area.

Crimes Listed in the Uniform Crime Reports

The FBI classifies crimes as either Part I, serious crimes, or Part II, less-serious offenses. Since 1958 the Uniform Crime Reports have focused on Part I offenses: murder and nonnegligent manslaughter, forcible rape, robbery, aggravated assault, burglary, larceny-theft, motor vehicle theft, and, more recently, arson. These Part I offenses are considered an index of crime in the United States and are often referred to as Index crimes.

Data cited in the Uniform Crime Reports are accepted by most people, including the media, as an accurate representation of crime in the United States. Yet there are many problems with and limitations to the Uniform Crime Reports. For example, certain categories of crime are completely omitted from the Uniform Crime Reports, such as kidnapping, tax evasion, embezzlement, and some corporate crimes. The FBI also includes attempted crimes in the Index as if they were completed acts and only includes the most serious offense in incidents involving multiple offenses. In addition, the FBI classification of crime into different categories is somewhat vague and not clearly defined. Adding to the confusion, each state and jurisdiction can, and often does, have a different definition for a specific crime, making summary statistics somewhat questionable. For example, the Uniform Crime Reports define forcible rape as "the carnal

Chapter 2 ♦ Crime Patterns   **29**

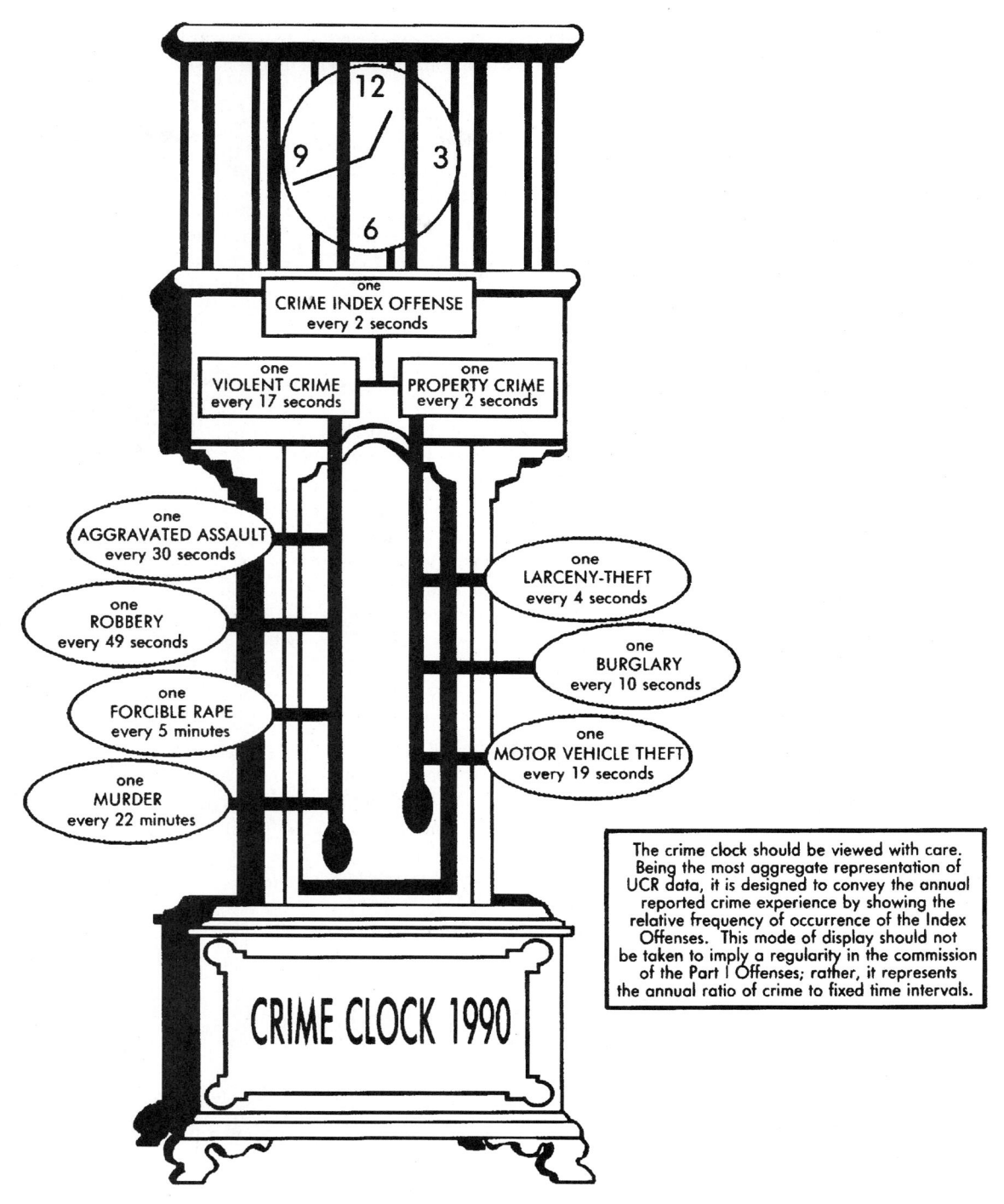

♦ **FIGURE 2.1** Crime Clock 1990 (illustrated by Reen Foley) Source: F.B.I. Uniform Crime Reports, 1991, U.S. Government Printing Office, Washington, D.C.

knowledge of a female forcibly and against her will. Assaults or attempts to commit rape by force or threat of force are also included; however, statutory rape (without force) and other sex offenses are excluded" (1985, p. 13). Many jurisdictions have sexual battery laws which allow for the inclusion of males as victims. In addition, state statutes vary in definitions of statutory rape. Statutory rape is carnal knowledge of an individual under a stipulated age. Each state has its own statute stipulating the age of the victim under which the rape is considered statutory.

Crimes Reported by the Police

Criminologists generally agree that the Uniform Crime Reports do not accurately reflect the amount of crime committed in the United States. Why are these statistics not accurate? These are data collected by the police and reported to the FBI. Who would know the number of crimes committed better than the police? To begin with, not every police agency reports to the FBI; the statistics represent approximately 95 to 98 percent of the United States population (Nietzel 1979). Also, the methods of reporting crime vary from one police department to another and fluctuate over time; the number of departments reporting to the FBI also varies. But, even if every police agency reported crime statistics to the FBI, the Uniform Crime Reports would not be complete because it only lists the crimes "known" to the police. It is generally believed that the actual number of crimes committed is a great deal larger than the number of crimes known to the police.

There are three categories of police awareness of crime: those crimes observed by the police, those crimes reported to the police, and those known to the police. The police observe very few crimes. In contrast, a great many crimes are reported to the police. But criminologists estimate fewer than half of all crimes are reported (Kalish 1974, Maltz 1975). And not all the crimes reported to the police are then reported by the police to the FBI. The police do not always believe that an offense which has been reported to them actually has taken place or that it should be classified as a crime. Thus the number of crimes "known" to the police and reported to the FBI is smaller than the number of crimes reported to the police. Therefore, the Uniform Crime Reports generally underrepresent the actual number of crimes committed in the United States.

Influences on Accuracy of Police Data

Police decisions about which crimes to report to the FBI are sometimes influenced by political factors or changes in the police agency. This creates another source of inaccuracies in the Uniform Crime Reports (Hagan 1985, Nietzel 1979). If a police department needed more money, an increase in crime rate could be a good argument for convincing the city administrators of the need. In contrast, if a police department wanted to show what a good job it was doing, a decrease in crime would document its effectiveness. "It is not at all uncommon to discover shifting criteria for the categorization of crime, depending on the manner in which a police chief or mayor or governor wishes to portray the incidence of local crime" (Nietzel 1979, p. 21).

There are many documented examples of political and agency changes affecting police record keeping. For example, the city of New York was excluded from the Uniform Crime Reports for a period of time because of questionable reporting (Hagan 1985). The reported crime rate for New York City was steadily decreasing at an unbelievable pace due to police handling of complaints. Many complaints were thrown away by the police, a practice they called "canning" or referring a complaint to "Detective Can." In 1950, a new police commissioner required accurate data keeping and reporting. As a result, reported robberies increased by 400 percent and larcenies by 700 percent (Wolfgang, Savitz & Johnston 1970). A similar improvement in record keeping in Kansas City in 1959 produced a 202 percent increase in crime (President's Commission on Law Enforcement and the Administration of Justice, 1967). In contrast, when a new Washington, D.C. chief of police declared a "war on crime," stating police officers would be fired if they did not lower the crime rate, there was a decrease in crime. Did the number of crimes really decrease? No, the police officers reclassified crimes so they were no longer Index crimes and did not have to be reported to the FBI as such (Seidman & Couzens 1974). As you can see, the manner in which the statistics are collected and the amount of crime reported can vary, depending on the honesty and capability of the police and the police departments reporting.

Presentation of Data

Some authorities believe the Uniform Crime Reports present the data in a misleading manner. By focusing on the absolute number of offenses, instead of the rate of crime, the reports tend to inflate crime statistics (Nietzel 1979). The techniques for calculating the rates of crime have also been called into question. Nietzel maintains that the Uniform Crime Reports should use the number of persons at risk for being a victim of a crime as the population base to calculate the rate of crime. For example, it makes little sense to use males as well as females when calculating the rate of rape.

The Uniform Crime Reports are the source for the Crime Clock indicating how often each serious crime is committed, and even the frequently cited Crime Clock is misleading. Wolfgang (1963) points out that the amount of time between offenses will automatically decrease every year the population increases, even if the rate of crime were to remain the same. In contrast, if the same number of crimes were committed, but the population decreased, there could be no change in the Crime Clock even though the rate of crime had increased and people were more likely to be victimized. Since the population in the United States is increasing, the frequency of crime increases and the time between offenses on the Crime Clock decreases even when there is no change in crime rate. Graham and Gurr contend Crime Clocks have "no purpose other than sheer terror" (1969, p. 382).

Despite the limitations of the Uniform Crime Report, it is considered an essential source of national crime statistics. The Uniform Crime Report is without a doubt the most extensive source for statistics. In recent years, the FBI has published a handbook which directs police agencies in the collection and classification of data, thereby decreasing some of the difficulties with variances. Advances in technology and increased use of computers are also increasing the efficiency and accuracy of reporting.

Victimization Surveys

Unreported crimes, called the "dark figure" of crime, are very difficult to document. The National Crime Survey (NCS), the major victimization survey conducted in the United States, was initiated in 1972 to determine the number of crimes actually committed, not just those reported to the police. Originally, the survey was designed to give data comparable to the Uniform Crime Report, but as we will see, that goal has not been completely successful.

Who Is Surveyed?

The National Crime Survey conducts interviews of about 100,000 people a year at about 49,000 addresses. This survey gathers information about the victims of crimes and details concerning the criminal incident. The subjects are a stratified random sample selected by address. All persons over the age of 12 living in one of the selected addresses are interviewed every 6 months for 3½ years.

The interview consists of two phases, the first part is a short questionnaire which determines if the subject was the victim of a crime during the preceding six months. If so, the respondent is given a longer, more detailed questionnaire about the incident. An adult answers the questions for 12- and 13-year-olds and one person from each address answers questions about household crimes for the same time period.

Data Collected

The NCS does not collect data on commercial offenses which constitute a large portion of the Index crimes reported in the Uniform Crime Reports. In addition, the victimization surveys do not gather information on "victimless" crimes such as prostitution, gambling, and alcohol and drug abuse. Therefore, the information from the National Crime Survey is not comparable to that of the Uniform Crime Reports. Table 2.1 indicates the differences between these two sources of information on crime statistics.

Sampling

Although the National Crime Survey statistics are probably a better approximation of the number of crimes actually committed than the Uniform Crime Reports, they are not completely without error. As indicated, the interviewers contact selected addresses. Often, transients, the homeless, or young black males are not part of the sample, and yet these are the very people who are particularly susceptible to victimization. Non-English speaking people are also less likely to be represented in the sample (Block & Block 1984).

In addition, the head of the household usually completes the initial screening for all the members of the household. This person is not always aware of the

◆ **TABLE 2.1** Comparison of the Uniform Crime Reports and the National Crime Survey. Table reprinted from the *Report to the Nation on Crime and Justice* (1988, p. 11), U.S. Department of Justice.

How Do UCR and NCS Compare?

	Uniform Crime Reports	**National Crime Survey**
Offenses measured:	Homicide Rape Robbery (personal and commercial) Assault (aggravated) Burglary (commercial and household) Larceny (commercial and household) Motor vehicle theft Arson	Rape Robbery (personal) Assault (aggravated and simple) Household burglary Larceny (personal and household) Motor vehicle theft
Scope:	Crimes reported to the police in most jurisdictions; considerable flexibility in developing small-area data	Crimes both reported and not reported to police; all data are available for a few large geographic areas
Collection method:	Police department reports to FBI or to centralized State agencies that then report to FBI	Survey interviews; periodically measures the total number of crimes committed by asking a national sample of 49,000 households encompassing 101,000 persons age 12 and over about their experiences as victims of crime during a specified period
Kinds of information:	In addition to offense counts, provides information on crime clearances, persons arrested, persons charged, law enforcement officers killed and assaulted, and characteristics of homicide victims	Provides details about victims (such as age, race, sex, education, income, and whether the victim and offender were related to each other) and about crimes (such as time and place of occurrence, whether or not reported to police, use of weapons, occurrence of injury, and economic consequences)
Sponsor:	Department of Justice Federal Bureau of Investigation	Department of Justice Bureau of Justice Statistics

victimization of everyone in the household and does not always remember every incident. For example, a young girl might not tell her father that she had been sexually assaulted on a date, and the head of the household might forget a theft of less than $10.

Telescoping and Bounding

The National Crime Survey asks respondents to report any crimes of which they have been the victim in the past 6 months. Skogan (1975) indicates a problem victims have with forward or backward "telescoping." The victim remembers the incident, but remembers it as occurring more recently or farther in the past than it actually did. More recent surveys have attempted to compensate for telescoping by "bounding." Respondents for each address are interviewed seven times at 6-month intervals and asked each time to report on crimes which occurred in the past 6 months. The first interview is not used in order to avoid backward telescoping reports. Then each subsequent interview is reviewed to be sure the incident has not been reported in prior interviews. This process is called bounding.

Inaccurate Reporting of Crimes

People who report on being victims, like others who answer surveys, are subject to problems with accuracy. People tend to forget the occurrence of incidents over time and those incidents they do remember are recollected with less accuracy the farther in the past the event occurred. Also definitions of crime vary—what is assault to one victim is merely a scuffle to another. Often people are not even aware of small amounts of money being stolen.

Both people's memory and the things they report are influenced by social desirability. Most people want others to like and respect them. In order to achieve this goal, those reporting crimes might inflate the severity of the crime or the amount of money lost in order to impress the interviewer. There is also the possibility they might not want the interviewer to know they could not defend themselves and thus were mugged. Or they might not want the interviewer to know about violence in their family: the father abuses his wife, the parents abuse the elderly grandfather, or the teenage son or daughter beats the mother. Or possibly, they do not think of these latter activities as crimes. Whatever the motivations, there is a tendency to underreport assaults by relatives and certain other types of crime. Respondents might also feel so strongly that something has to be done about the crime problem that they make up crimes as a way of doing their part in prevention (Levine 1976).

Crimes Not Reported

Although some researchers contend respondents tend to overreport crimes in victimization surveys (e.g., Levine 1976), Skogan (1977) maintains some respondents forget or just do not report crimes to the interviewers, creating a "doubly dark" figure of crime. He believes rape and assault are particularly unlikely to be reported.

Support for Levine's position is found in research showing that crimes reported to the police are not all mentioned in subsequent victimization surveys. Greenberg, Wilson, and Mills (1982) reviewed three reverse-record studies in which interviewers talked to crime victims who had reported an incident to the police. The errors in recall were different for different types of offenses, but the total error rate was about 27 percent in all three studies. The percent of victims who did not report their own crime victimization varied with the length of time since the incident. In addition, the number of errors increased when respondents were asked questions about details of the incidents.

Self-report Studies

Another source of information on the number of crimes actually committed is self-report studies, which can also be used to determine the dark figure of crime. In these studies, people are asked to respond anonymously to questions about crimes which they have committed. Most of the research in this area has been conducted with juveniles and college students (Bonn 1984, Waldo & Chiricos 1972), although at least two have been conducted with adults (Tittle & Villemez 1977). Self-report studies indicate that almost every college student and juvenile has committed at least one offense for which they could have gone to jail (Bonn 1984, Erickson & Empey 1963, Nietzel 1979). In one study of young males, 92 percent admitted to committing a theft and 32 percent to a breaking and entering, despite having no police record (Erickson & Empey 1963).

Data Collected
Most of the data are collected by anonymous questionnaire or by interviews. The questions asked of respondents determine the data collected, and many of the questions refer to minor offenses or are worded in an ambiguous manner. The data collected consist of information on many behaviors more appropriately categorized as misbehavior than criminal, for example, smoking on school grounds. In addition, most of the questions ask respondents if they have ever committed a particular infraction; they are not asked about behavior in the past 6 months or year, and as a result, data are not comparable to the National Crime Survey or Uniform Crime Reports. Most of the studies also are restricted to one geographical area, further limiting any useful comparison to national data. Evaluations of the validity of the measures used are inconsistent. They vary with the instrument ranging from very good to quite negative.

Inaccurate Reporting
The survey methods used to collect the self-report data are prone to the same problems and limitations as the National Crime Survey or any other survey. Respondents have a tendency to forget incidents and details over time. People want to appear positive in the eyes of the interviewers and will overreport in an effort to impress them or underreport incidents which might be embarrassing. Among some populations it is considered exciting or prestigious to be arrested. Hirschi (1969) found 55 percent of white and 24 percent of black boys who claimed to have been arrested actually had no police record.

Undetected Crimes
Despite their limitations, self-report surveys give us a good deal of information about the frequency of offenses committed and the likelihood of arrest. It appears that over 90 percent of the crimes committed by juveniles go undetected; however, more serious crimes are committed by adjudicated delinquents than by nondelinquent boys (Erickson & Empey 1963).

Reporting Crimes to the Police

One of the reasons often cited for inaccuracy in crime statistics is people not reporting crimes to the police. Since determination of the increase or decrease in crime rate is dependent on crimes being reported to the police or to crime survey interviewers, these statistics are also suspect if people do not report crimes. "Pervading all measures of crime is the inability to distinguish between changes in the amount of crime committed and the amount of crime reported" (Wolfgang, Savitz & Johnston 1970, p. 102). While it is generally agreed that fewer than half of the crimes committed in the United States are reported to the police

(Greenberg, Wilson & Mills 1982, Kidd & Chayet 1984), recent estimates are as low as 35 percent (Harlow 1985) or 37 percent (Bureau of Justice Statistics, *Criminal Victimization, 1986,* 1987). In addition, the proportion of crimes reported to the police varies by type of offense. For example, people are very likely to report a commercial robbery (86 percent) and unlikely to report a household theft or larceny under $50 (15 percent). In this section, we will explore the psychological and situational factors that influence people in their decision about whether or not to report a crime.

The Decision to Report Crimes

Very few personal crimes are detected by the police (3 percent). The vast majority of these crimes are reported to the police by the victim; however, a sizable number (about 40 percent) are reported to the police by someone other than the victim. Incidents of pick pocketing are almost always (87 percent) reported to the police by the victim. In like manner, only 2 percent of reported household crimes are uncovered by the police; while 88 percent are brought to the attention of the police by members of the household (Harlow 1985). Let us examine how bystanders and victims decide whether or not to report a criminal incident to the police.

Bystanders' Reporting of Crime

Kidd (1979) proposes a model of how a bystander to a criminal event decides whether or not to report it. In the first stage of the model, the bystander determines how "distant" the behavior being observed is from behavior the bystander feels is appropriate in that situation. In other words, the bystander decides whether the behavior fits his or her personal norms. If the observed behavior does not fit the bystander's definition of appropriate behavior, then the bystander decides whether to label the behavior as criminal. During this second stage, the bystander is defining the situation as a crime. If the event is labeled a crime, the bystander proceeds to the third phase of the model. At this time, the bystander considers the costs and benefits involved in reporting the incident; if the benefits outweigh the costs, the bystander is likely to report the crime. In contrast, if the costs outweigh the benefits of reporting a crime, the bystander is unlikely to report it. Before we discuss the process of defining an incident as a crime and the costs and benefits involved in reporting a crime, we will see how a victim decides whether or not to report an offense.

Victim's Decisions to Report a Crime

Ruback, Greenberg, and Westcott (1984) hypothesize a three-stage model of how a crime victim decides whether or not to report a crime to the police. The first stage of this model incorporates the first two stages of Kidd's model of bystander decision-making. In this first stage, victims label themselves as crime victims by evaluating the incident to determine if it fits into their definition of a crime. Incidents which differ greatly from the victims' definition of crime require no action. However, the closer the incident is to the victims' concept of criminal behavior, the more upset the victims become, propelling them on to the second stage of decision-making.

In the second stage, the victims determine the seriousness of the crime by considering the amount of harm caused by the incident. A victim who decides the crime was serious will proceed to the third phase, deciding what to do. Ruback, Greenberg, and Wescott identify four possible responses a victim could make: "(a) seeking a private solution, (b) cognitively reevaluating the situation, (c) reporting the crime to the police, and (d) doing nothing" (1984, p. 56). Although this process is described as a cognitive one, people are not necessarily aware of making decisions, and some may act automatically.

Defining an Incident as a Crime

Before an individual, whether victim or observer, can report a crime to the police, the person must recognize that a crime has occurred. In other words, an observed event has to be defined as a crime. As we will see, definitions of crimes are somewhat nebulous. But in addition, there are circumstances surrounding an incident which increase or decrease the likelihood that it will be defined as criminal. Events discovered after the fact are more difficult to define as criminal than are those which are witnessed while in progress or in which the observer is also a victim (Ruback, Greenberg & Westcott 1984). For example, a mother who comes home to find her door ajar would have to find something missing in order to determine whether an intruder had been there or the children left the door open. However, if she came home and found the door ajar and a stranger going through her belongings, she would know immediately that a crime was occurring.

Offenses which take place in unfamiliar places where an observer might expect a crime to occur are easier to interpret as crimes than are the same offenses in more familiar places where the observer does not expect criminal activity (Ruback, Greenberg & Westcott 1984). For example, suppose you are walking on a deserted street in a bad area of a city when you see a disheveled man approach a young woman. If the woman opens her purse and hands him her money, it is obviously a crime. However, if you were sitting at your desk at work and saw that same disheveled man approach a young woman who opens her purse and hands him her money, you might not be as sure a crime was being committed.

Other factors also influence whether a victim will perceive an event as a crime. For example, victims are not as likely to define an incident as a crime if they somehow were a participant, perhaps inciting the offender in some way. Someone who picks a fight in a bar is less likely to call the police than someone who is assaulted on the street. People are also less likely to consider an incident a crime if it is committed by a friend or relative (Block & Block 1984). If a person's brother or cousin takes some money out of a wallet, the victim is less likely to call the police than if some stranger does the same thing.

Konečni and Ebbesen (1982) point out that the legal system often evaluates the accused's motivations in deciding on whether a crime was intentional. Although it is seldom considered, the victim's cognitive state also influences whether that victim defines an event as a crime. Konečni and Ebbesen explain that when sexual intercourse takes place between two people, this act can be defined as one of love or one of violence depending on the expectations and perceptions of the participants. While it is particularly apparent in cases of sexual assault, the victims' state of mind can influence whether they define many incidents as criminal.

The nature of the incident itself also influences how easily it is defined as a crime. Some crimes are more ambiguous than others: rape occurring on a date, taking a parent's car without permission, "borrowing" money from petty cash, etc. In like manner, attempted crimes are more ambiguous than completed ones; and less serious crimes are more difficult to define than more serious crimes.

Crimes Reported to Police

Once the victim or observer of an incident has defined it as a crime, that person then makes the decision whether to report the offense to the police. The National Crime Survey estimates that in 1990 only 38 percent (13.3 million) of the crimes committed in the United States were reported to the police. The more serious a crime, the more likely it is to be reported. If someone is injured in a crime, or there was the possibility of an injury, that crime is viewed as serious and is very likely to be reported. And the more severe the injury, the greater the likelihood of reporting the crime. A crime in which a weapon, especially a lethal weapon, is used, even if there is no injury, is also defined as a serious crime (Block & Block 1984, Harlow 1985). Violent crimes, like murder, are much more likely to be brought to the attention of the police than are less serious offenses, such as household theft (Harlow 1985). And household theft is more likely to be reported than personal theft (Harlow 1985). In addition, people are more likely to report completed crimes than those that were only attempted.

Costs and Benefits of Reporting Crimes to the Police

Reasons for Reporting Crime

The most important reason respondents to the National Crime Survey give for reporting a personal theft is to regain the loss (43 percent). The same reason is often given for household crimes. However, the primary reason for reporting a violent crime is to prevent it from happening in the future (Harlow 1985).

Victims and observers often decide whether or not to report a crime on the basis of the value of the items lost or the amount of damage done. The more valuable the property, the greater probability of the crime being reported. Victims are especially likely to report a theft or burglary if they are insured, one of the reasons why a high percentage of car thefts are reported.

Reasons Not to Report a Crime to Police

When deciding whether or not to report an offense to the police, the victim or citizen compares the costs of reporting to the benefits of doing so. The individual considers the time and effort involved in reporting a crime and the likely outcome of reporting it. People who were victims of crimes which were not reported to the police are asked their reasons for not doing so on the National Crime Survey. The most frequent reason given for not reporting a crime is that it was not important enough. An experimental study of crime reporting (Greenberg, Wilson

♦ **TABLE 2.2** Reasons for reporting or not reporting crimes. Table reprinted from the *Report to the Nation on Crime and Justice* (1988, p. 35), U.S. Department of Justice.

Many Violent Crimes are Reported to Prevent the Crimes from Happening Again; Many Crimes of Theft are Reported because of a Desire to Recover Property

Percent of Victimizations Reported to the Police by Most Important Reason for Reporting the Crime

	All Responses	Economic — To Collect Insurance	To Recover Property	Obligation — Because It was a Crime	Because It was Your Duty	To Keep It from Happening Again	Stop/Prevent This Incident from Happening	To Punish Offender	Other
All crimes	100%	8%	32%	8%	7%	20%	9%	7%	10%
Crimes of violence*	100%	—	6%	7%	8%	31%	18%	14%	17%
Robbery	100	—	21	9	7	22	15	11	10
Aggravated assault	100	—	—	4	11	33	17	16	11
Simple assault	100	—	—	7	8	35	19	12	18
Crimes of theft	100%	12%	43%	8%	7%	14%	4%	4%	9%
Household crimes	100%	7%	35%	9%	7%	19%	9%	7%	7%
Burglary	100	6	26	12	7	23	12	8	7
Household larceny	100	9	37	7	7	19	8	6	8
Motor vehicle theft	100	9	63	6	4	7	4	5	—

Table reprinted from the *Report to the Nation on Crime and Justice* (1988, p. 15), U.S. Department of Justice.

Many Violent Crimes Were Unreported because They Were "Private Matters," and Many Crimes of Theft Were "Not Important Enough to Report"

Percent of Victimizations Not Reported to The Police By the Most Important Reason For Not Reporting Crime

Type of Crime	All Responses	Not Serious	Nothing Could Be Done	Police Wouldn't Do Anything	Personal Disadvantage	Personal/ Private	Reported to Someone Else	Other
All crimes	100%	35%	27%	11%	3%	9%	11%	7%
Crimes of violence*	100%	27%	9%	10%	6%	28%	11%	11%
Robbery	100	29	16	14	5	13	8	11
Aggravated assault	100	24	9	9	7	33	9	9
Simple assault	100	29	5	8	5	30	13	10
Crimes of theft	100%	34%	29%	8%	2%	4%	18%	6%
Household crimes	100%	37%	29%	13%	2%	8%	4%	7%
Burglary	100	29	31	13	3	8	7	9
Household larceny	100	41	30	12	2	7	2	6
Motor vehicle theft	100	35	27	16	—	10	—	—

Note: Figures may not add to total because of rounding.
—Too few cases to obtain statistically reliable data.
*Includes crime of rape, which is not displayed separately because of the small number in the sample.
Source: *Reporting crime to the police*, BJS Special Report, December 1985.

& Mills 1982) also found lack of importance to be the most frequently cited explanation for not calling the police.

Another reason victims gave for not reporting crimes on the National Crime Survey was a belief that nothing could be done, either because the police are inefficient or there was no evidence. Similar responses were given in the experimental study of a theft (Greenberg, Wilson & Mills 1982).

Reasons for not reporting crimes of violence tend to be different than those for not reporting property offenses. People are likely not to report a violent crime because it was a "private or personal matter" (Harlow 1985). In most assaults the two people involved either are related or know each other very well, and people tend not to report crimes in which the offender is related to the victim (Nietzel 1979).

Why Victims Do Not Report Crimes

Kidd and Chayet maintain there are psychological factors which prevent victims from reporting crimes: "(a) victim fear, (b) feelings of helplessness and perceived powerlessness of police, and (c) the threat of further victimization from authorities" (1984, p. 39). In Chapter 5, I will describe the psychological reactions of victims to crime. Let it suffice here to say there is a great deal of evidence that crime victimization produces tremendous fear in victims. Kidd and Chayet contend the fear incapacitates victims, making them unable to report the offense. The fear is so strong that victims want to avoid situations which would recreate their terror, including notifying the police.

In addition, victims feel vulnerable, helpless, and unable to control the things that happen to them. These feelings are hypothesized to be projected onto other people in the environment. Thus, the police are viewed as powerless. People who feel this way have no reason to report a crime to the police, since they believe the police can do nothing about it. "Victims reach a conclusion about police ineffectiveness that is in many respects true. Little *can* be done" (Kidd & Chayet 1984, p. 43).

Interacting with the victims' fear and feelings of helplessness is a concern with further victimization from the authorities. Some victims perceive the police as insensitive and perhaps uncaring. Many victims are concerned with the amount of time and effort they will have to put into a crime report. If the case goes to trial, they will have to attend the trial and testify at it. Attendance will require time off from work, resulting in possible financial loss, while testifying will exact psychological tolls. Victims attempt to avoid further costs by not reporting crimes. And once again the victims are right, they do experience considerable monetary and time losses from reporting crimes (Knudten, Meade, Knudten & Doerner 1976).

The three factors described above—the victim's fear, the victim's own sense of helplessness and projection of this helplessness onto the police, and the concern with further victimization by the authorities—interact to decrease the likelihood of a victim reporting a crime to the authorities.

Crime Rates and Crime Waves

While there is a great deal of skepticism concerning the accuracy of crime statistics, the statistics are helpful in determining changes in crime rate. For example, there is general agreement that the crime rate rose during the 1960s and 1970s, and this increase was particularly apparent in the amount of violent crime. Although, as Wolfgang, Savitz, and Johnston point out, it is difficult to differentiate "between changes in the amount of crime committed and the amount of crime reported" (1970, p. 102), Gurr (1979) argues that trends in crime rates should be apparent in the official statistics, even if the exact amount of "true" crime is quite different from the official rate.

Crime Rates in the United States

Crime rates appear to fluctuate over time with waves of increased activity. The Uniform Crime Reports were first published in the 1930s, but individual cities kept records of their crime rates much earlier. Gurr reviewed early studies of crime in Boston, Salem, Buffalo, New York, and New Orleans and found similar trends in each location. All of these cities reported an increase in crime in the 1850s, peaking in the 1870s, then gradually decreasing through 1940 to 1950. For example, Boston reported a 300 percent increase in arrests for serious crimes from 1849 to 1859.

The crime rate in the United States steadily increased from the early 1960s until the 1980s when it leveled off. While there were only about two robberies and assaults for every 10,000 people in the 1950s and early 1960s, that figure had risen to over fifty in 1985 (Uniform Crime Reports, 1986). In 1963 the rate of violent crime was double what it had been only 4 years earlier; by 1973 the violent crime rate doubled once again (Skogan 1979). In 1974 the "police recorded one murder, three rapes, 23 major assaults, and 22 robberies for every 10,000 Americans, which represented an increase of greater than 300 percent in little more than a decade" (Graham & Gurr 1979, p. 349). And in 1981 almost one-third of all the households in the United States were touched by crime, with some family member becoming a victim of violence or theft (Report to the Nation on Crime and Justice, 1983). By 1990 the number had declined to only 24 percent of all households (Bureau of Justice Statistics, *National Update,* 1991). The upsurge in property crimes in the 1950s and the personal crimes in the 1960s led to the concern with "law and order" demonstrated by both private citizens and politicians.

Criminologists tend to be quite skeptical of official crime rates, but agree that of the official statistics homicide rates are the most accurate and reliable (Gurr 1989, Hagan 1985). Therefore, we will look at the murder rates during the 1960s and 1970s to get some information on trends. In 1958, the homicide rate in the United States was 4.5 per 100,000 people; by 1980 it had risen to 11.0 (Report to the Nation on Crime and Justice, 1983). Media hype in the 1970s and 1980s led citizens to believe that they were in the middle of the worst crime

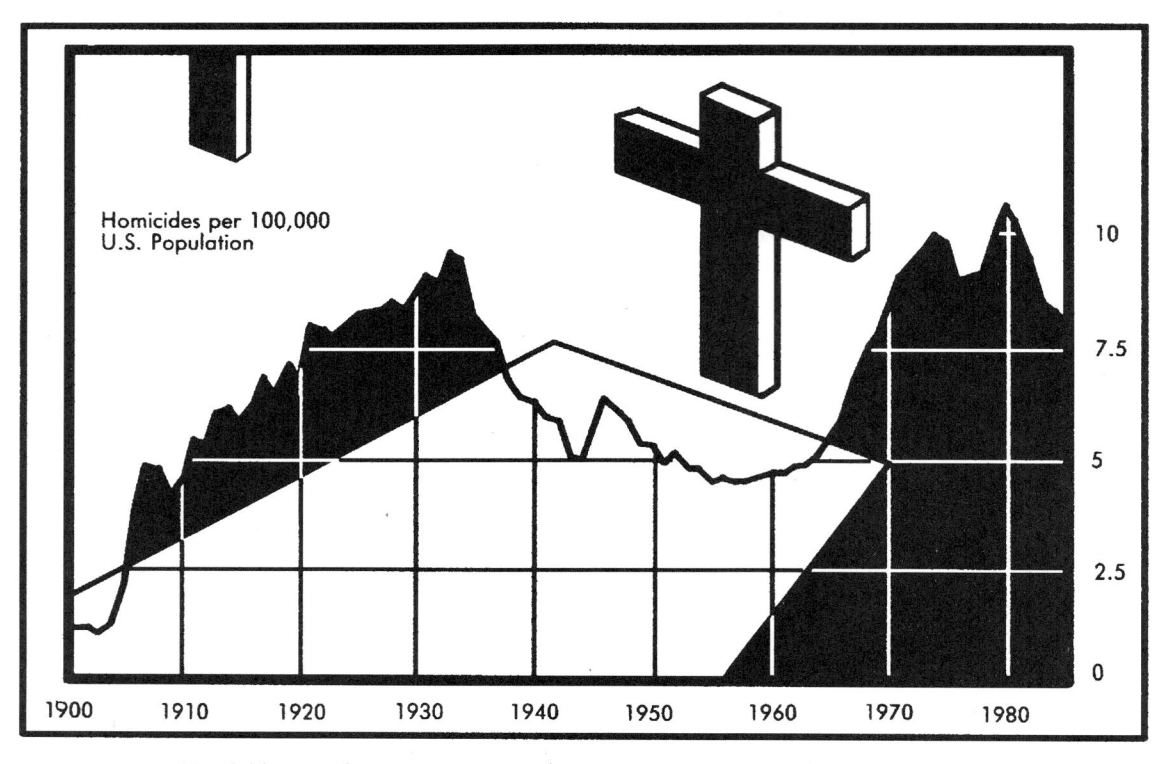

♦ **FIGURE 2.2** Homicide rates from 1900 to 1984. (illustrated by Reen Foley) Source: Federal Bureau of Investigation. *Uniform Crime Reports* (1991). *Report to the Nation on Crime and Justice* (1988) p. 15. U.S. Department of Justice.

wave in history. However, a closer look at reported crimes indicates that from 1903 until 1933 the homicide rate surged from 1.1 to 9.7 per 100,000 people in the United States.

In the late 1970s and early 1980s, criminologists contended the increasing crime rate appeared to have reached its peak; it was beginning to drop. However, after dropping in 1981, 1982, 1983, and 1984, crimes reported to the police began to rise again in 1985. The National Crime Survey reports that personal theft, household crimes, and violent crimes were lower in 1990 than in the 1970s.

Crime rates, both for violent crimes and property crimes, fluctuate over time. For example, there is an increase in all types of personal and household crimes during the summer months (Report to the Nation on Crime and Justice, 1983). This change in criminal activity probably reflects greater opportunity for offenders due to changes in the behavior of potential victims. With the warm weather, people are likely to leave their houses open for ventilation, creating easy access for potential thieves. People are also more likely to be away from home to participate in outdoor activities and go on vacations, again providing opportunities for unnoticed breaking and entering. Furthermore, spending time away from the safety of their homes makes people more vulnerable for interpersonal crimes.

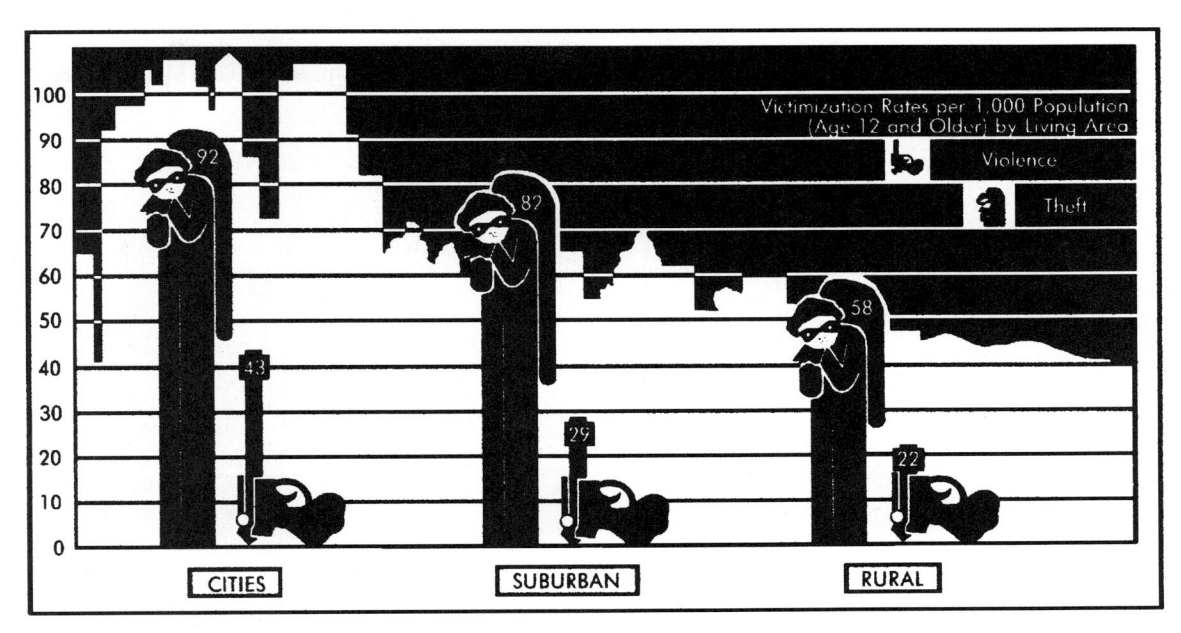

♦ **FIGURE 2.3** A large proportion of crime occurs in urban areas. (illustrated by Reen Foley) Source: Special Report: *Locating City, Suburban and Rural Crime,* December 1985. U.S. Department of Justice.

Crime rates also vary from one area of the country to another and are much higher in cities than in the suburbs or rural areas. City life contributes to criminal activity in many ways. First of all there are a variety of people from many socioeconomic classes in the city; this class differential creates both envy and opportunity. The vast number of people living in a relatively small area creates a condition that psychologists refer to as deindividuation, a lowering of inhibitions due to feelings of anonymity. Inhibitions are further decreased by city life which is less conducive to the development of social bonds (Skogan 1979). People whose inhibitions are lowered are more likely to behave in socially unacceptable ways, perhaps stealing or becoming violent.

Crime Rates in Other Countries

The U.S. crime upsurge in the 1960s was paralleled in most Western democracies. However, even with that great increase, the homicide rate in Western Europe was only 1.5 per 100,000 in 1984, compared with the U.S. rate of 7.9 in the same year. "Reported rapes were more than six times as common in the United States (35.7 vs. 5.4 per 100,000 in Europe), robberies four times as common (205 vs. 49 per 100,000)" (Gurr 1989, p. 21).

How does the crime rate in the United States compare to that of other countries? "The homicide rate of the United States is from 2 to 70 times the rate for Australia, Austria, Canada, Denmark, England and Wales, Finland, France,

◆ **TABLE 2.3** Crime rates in the United States are higher than those in most other countries. Table reprinted from *International Crime Rates*, a Bureau of Justice Statistics Special Report (May, 1988, p. 2), U.S. Department of Justice.

Homicide in Selected Countries, Rates for 1980: World Health Organization Data

Country	Number of Actual Homicides per 100,000 Population
United States	10.5
Australia	1.2
Austria	1.2
Canada	2.1
Chile	2.6
Costa Rica	5.8
Czechoslovakia	1.1*
Denmark	1.3
Ecuador	6.0*
Egypt	.9
England and Wales	.8
Finland	3.3
France	1.0
Germany (FRG)	1.2
Greece	.7
Hungary	2.6
Ireland	.7
Italy	1.9*
Japan	1.0
Luxembourg	1.9
Netherlands	.8
New Zealand	1.3
Norway	1.1
Panama	2.2
Portugal	1.3
Scotland	1.6
Spain	1.0
Sweden	1.2
Thailand	25.1
Venezuela	9.7*
Yugoslavia	1.7

*1981 data.
Source: World Health Organization, *World Health Statistics Annual*, vols. 1982–86.

Greece, Hong Kong, Hungary, Ireland, Israel, Italy, Japan, the Netherlands, New Zealand, Poland, Scotland, Spain, Sweden, Switzerland, and West Germany" (Goldstein 1986, p. 141). In 1980 there were 11,522 deaths by handguns in the United States, compared with 8 in Britain, 4 in Austria, 8 in Canada, 24 in Switzerland, and 77 in Japan. There are only a few countries with a homicide rate higher than that of the United States—Sri Lanka, Colombia, Kuwait, Taiwan, and Venezuela (Goldstein 1986).

As alarming as the statistics for violent crime in the United States are, violent crime and homicide are estimated to have been ten to twenty times higher in medieval England (Hagan 1985). Homicide rates in London during the 19th century were double the current rate, the rate in the 17th century was three times that of the 19th century, and the 13th century was three times that of the 17th century.

Explanations for Crime Trends

Why is there so much more violent crime and homicide in the United States than in most other Western democracies? There is no single or simple answer to that question. Goldstein (1986) proposes that the United States has a tradition of violence which began with the American Revolution. The violence of the revolution has become the model for behavior in many people's life-style, honest citizens as well as criminals (Brown 1979). Goldstein enumerates additional factors which are conducive to violence in American society. Most research indicates a relationship between viewing violence in the media and aggressive behavior. And there is a tremendous amount of violence depicted in films and on television in the United States. In addition, the competitiveness of the business, sports, and academic worlds generalizes to the social aspects of society. U.S. society also tends to be permissive; this is manifested both by parents with their children and in the leniency of courts with offenders. Added to these factors, lethal weapons, like handguns, are more readily available in the United States than in other countries.

But while these factors explain why the United States has a higher crime rate than other countries, they do not explain the general decrease in violence over the past seven centuries or the waves in crime rates. Gurr attributes the decrease in violence to the civilization of society. "People are socialized to restrain and displace anger" (1989, p. 45–46). The explanation for waves in crime rates is much more complex.

Two variables that are generally thought to influence short-term changes in crime rate are the number of young men in the society and war. "War is the single most obvious correlate of all the great historical waves of violent crime in England and the United States" (Gurr 1989, p. 47). The rate of crime in the United States crested during the Civil War and to a lesser extent during World War I and World War II. Wars in England also corresponded with the peaks in crime in the 18th century (1739 war with Spain, then the Seven Years' War) and the 19th century (Napoleonic Wars, 1793–1815). Why do wars influence crime rates? "Wartime social disorganization, postwar economic dislocation, the maladjustment of returned veterans, and also the legitimation of violence" all exert an influence on crime rates (Gurr 1979, p. 367).

Young men are the most likely perpetrators and victims of violence and are particularly likely to commit crimes between the ages of 15 and 25. Therefore, a society with a large proportion of young males is likely to have a higher crime rate than a society with a smaller proportion of young males. The relationship between the proportion of young males and crime rate is easily demonstrated by the changes in percentages of young men in U.S. society in comparison to crime trends. During the Depression and war years in the 1930s and early 1940s, the birth rate was extremely low. Then the postwar years brought the "baby boom."

As the increased number of young men in this age group reached their teens and early twenties in the 1960s, the crime rate in the United States soared. A similar pattern explains the English crime wave of the same time and those of other Western countries (Gurr 1979).

However, as Gurr points out, the crime rate rose by 300 percent to 500 percent during the time the population of young people only increased by 50 percent. It is, therefore, not logical to attribute the surge in crime entirely to the number of youths in American society. Other factors also influenced the rapid crime increase. Gurr sees a termination of the seven-century-long trend toward the elimination of violence; he maintains that during the 1960s the number of wars and insurrections were "glorified, vilified, and above all amplified by the media" (1979, p. 369). In addition, there was a tremendous increase in the amount and extent of violence in films and television during the 1960s. Young people were the most vulnerable to the influence of violent models and the decrease in inhibitions against violence. Along with this change in attitude toward violence there was a simultaneous change in societal values. The pursuit of happiness and material pleasure was extended to social and sexual pleasure. These outlooks were combined with a negative attitude toward authority and authority figures and a resentment toward institutions. Gurr concludes:

> that each great upsurge of violent crime in the histories of the societies under study has been caused by a distinctive combination of altered social forces. Some crime waves have followed from fundamental social dislocation, as a result of which significant segments of a population have been separated from the regulating institutions that instill and reinforce the basic Western injunctions against interpersonal violence. They may be migrants, demobilized veterans, or a growing population of resentful young people for whom there is no social or economic niche, or badly educated young black men trapped in the decaying ghettos of an affluent society. The most devastating episodes of public disorder, however, seem to occur when social dislocation coincides with shifts in values, because of war or changes in popular culture, that legitimate violence that was once thought to be illegitimate. (1989, p. 48–49)

Women and Crime

All the projections concerning increases in crime talk about youthful populations. However, it is young men who are likely to be victims and perpetrators of crimes. What about the media hype touting the rapid rise in crime among women?

Before 1950 women accounted for only 10 percent of all those arrested in the United States. The rate of offenses committed by women was slightly higher for violent crimes than for property crimes, but the amount of crime for which women accounted was consistently low. Beginning in the mid 1950s there was an increase in the amount of female involvement in crime. The percentage increases were quite high, but those increases were more a function of the low numbers from which the increases grew than an actual growth in crime. In other words, if there had been twenty counts of larceny committed by women in one year and sixty the next, that would be a 200 percent increase. But if there were 9,000 male counts of larceny one year and 10,000 the next, although there was a much greater absolute increase, the percentage increase was only 11 percent.

♦ **FIGURE 2.4**
Arrest rates by age group (illustrated by Reen Foley) Source: *Report to the Nation on Crime and Justice* (1988, p. 42), U.S. Department of Justice.

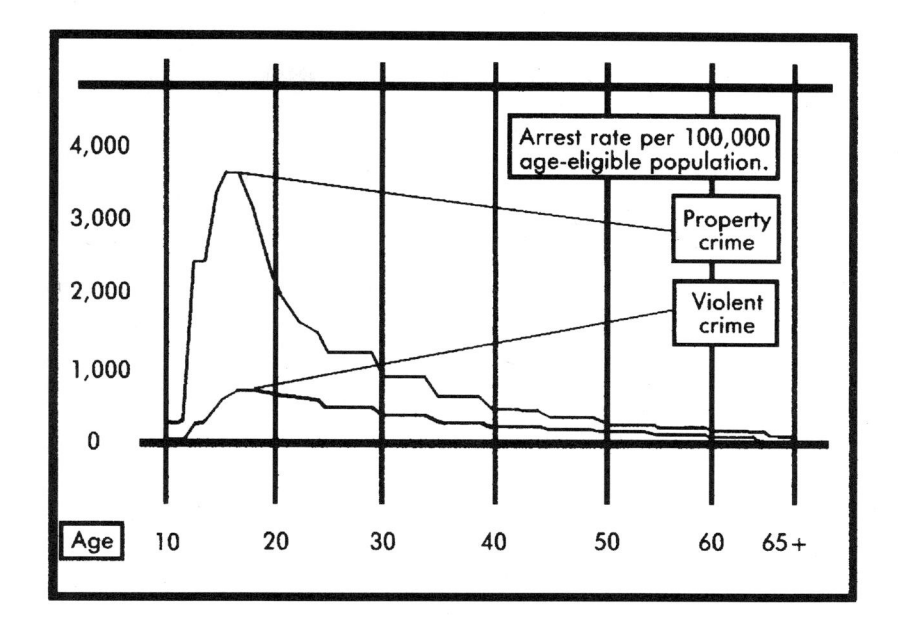

Although the percentage of homicides and aggravated assaults committed by women did increase somewhat in the 1960s and 1970s (25 percent to 35 percent), the vast majority of the increase in violent crime is attributed to violence by young males (Steffensmeier 1983). But there was a real increase in the proportion of women committing crimes of property; they currently account for almost one-third of those offenses. There are many causes hypothesized for the increase in criminal activity by females, ranging from women's liberation to a backlash by the criminal justice system against liberated women. However, economic necessity and opportunity are highly related to crimes of property (Gurr 1989). And a great deal of the increase in female criminal activity can be accounted for by changes in women's economic situations due to divorce and single parenthood, along with their entrance into the world of work, creating occasions for theft and embezzlement (Skogan 1979).

Race and Crime

A much larger percentage of blacks are arrested for crimes of violence than whites. There are some indications this could be due to the arrest practices of white police officers. However, victimization surveys indicate the percentage of black violent offenders is higher than that of white violent offenders. There are many social factors which tend to influence the commission of crime by minorities. Blacks are more likely than whites to live in cities, which have been shown to be a more probable location for crime than suburbs or rural areas. In addition, blacks have

◆ **TABLE 2.4** Characteristics of arrestees and offenders. Table reprinted from the *Report to the Nation on Crime and Justice* (1988, p. 41), U.S. Department of Justice.

What Are the Characteristics of Arrestees and Offenders in Jails and Prisons?

	U.S. Population 1980	Index Crime Arrestees Violent	Index Crime Arrestees Property	Jail Inmates Unconvicted	Jail Inmates Convicted	State Prison Inmates	Federal Prison Inmates
	226,545,805	443,686	1,707,434	88,120	132,620	405,312	31,926
Sex							
Male	49%	89%	78%	93%	93%	96%	95%
Female	51	11	23	7	7	4	5
Race							
White	86	51	66	54	61	51	65
Black	12	48	33	44	36	47	33
Other	2	1	2	2	3	3	3
Ethnic origin							
Hispanic	6	12	11	15	14	8	23
Non-Hispanic	94	88	89	85	86	57	77
Unknown	0	0	0	0	0	35	0
Age							
Under 15	23	5	14	*	*	0	0
15–19	9	23	32	14	11	7	0
20–29	18	43	32	53	54	56	34
30–39	14	19	13	23	24	25	40
40–49	10	7	5	6	7	8	17
50–59	10	3	2	3	3	3	7
60+	16	1	2	1	1	1	2

*Less than .5%.
Note: Percentages may not add to total because of rounding.
Sources: *Statistical abstract of the United States 1981.*
FBI *Crime in the United States 1983.*
Jail inmates, 1983, BJS Bulletin, November 1985.
BJS Survey of Inmates of Local Jails 1983, unpublished data.
BJS Prisoners in State and Federal Institutions yearend 1983, unpublished data.

a significantly lower mean age than other groups. Blacks also suffer disproportionately from "poverty, economic inequality, and family and neighborhood disorganization" (Skogan 1989, p. 241). All of the above are predictive of criminal and violent behavior.

Projections of Future Crime Rates

There is general agreement that the crime rate reached its peak in the early 1980s and has at least stabilized, and perhaps even begun a downward trend (Bureau of Justice Statistics, *Crime and the Nation's Household, 1989,* 1990; Hagan 1985). "Crime, like economic growth and population size, has finite limits. Call it a law of social gravitation: what goes up beyond supportable limits will eventually come down" (Gurr 1979, p. 371).

There are a number of reasons given for a hopeful outlook on crime rates. The one most often cited is the aging of the population; the baby boomers have left the crime-prone age. By 2050, the median age of people in the United States will be 10 years older than it was in the 1970s (Skogan 1979). Besides a decrease in the proportion of young people who are prone to crime, this will decrease unemployment with fewer people entering the job market. Since economic necessity and unemployment are related to high crime rates, greater employment rates also decrease crime.

But there are other factors contributing to the optimistic outlook. People are moving from high-crime areas to more prosperous and less crime-ridden sections of the country. People also are moving from the central cities and the big cities to the suburbs and more rural areas. The decrease in size of large cities since 1970 has reduced opportunity and social factors contributing to high crime rates.

Most criminologists qualify their predictions for a decrease in crime rate by saying that it is quite difficult to project changes over short time periods. Although the baby boomers have aged, they have maintained their criminality longer than anticipated. And the decrease in crime rate is only projected until the 1990s, when the children of baby boomers reach their teenage years. In addition, all the societal changes predicting a decrease in crime rate affect blacks more slowly. They are a younger, less educated population, with more unemployment and fewer opportunities to move. Blacks represent a disproportionate amount of criminal activity, particularly violent crimes. The proportion of blacks between 14 and 21 years old is projected to steadily increase until 2010, thus increasing the youthful offender rate (Skogan 1989).

The optimistic predictions for decreases in crime are conservative and most are made with a statement to the effect that some unexpected economic or societal change could reverse the trend. One change that concerns criminologists is the introduction of crack cocaine and designer drugs into society. Crack is a problem because it is so highly addictive and cheap enough for very young people to afford it. Designer drugs present different concerns; they are developed so rapidly that laws cannot keep pace with them. Unless societal reactions and antidrug campaigns are successful, the anticipated crime decline might be short-lived.

Summary

There are three primary sources for crime statistics: Uniform Crime Reports, the National Crime Survey, and self-report surveys. Each source has advantages and limitations. The Uniform Crime Reports represent national data but underreport crime. Data from the National Crime Survey better represent the actual crime rate but do not give information on commercial or victimless crimes and have problems with sampling and reporting errors.

Self-report data are perhaps the best source of information on a comparison of crimes committed to arrests, but most of the information is on juveniles. Most self-report studies are collected from a limited population and thus cannot be compared to the Uniform Crime Reports or the National Crime Survey.

One of the reasons often cited for inaccuracy in crime statistics is that people do not report crimes to the police. There are three factors which interact to decrease the likelihood of a victim reporting a crime to the authorities: the victim's fear, the victim's own sense of helplessness and projection of this helplessness onto the police, and the concern with further victimization by the authorities.

Crime rates appear to fluctuate over time with waves of increased activity. Crime rates also vary greatly by country. There is much more violent crime and homicide in the United States than in most other Western democracies.

There is no single or simple reason for the fluctuations in crime rate. Two variables which are generally thought to influence short-term changes in crime rate are the number of young men in the society and war. Although the percentage of homicides and aggravated assaults committed by women did increase somewhat in the 1960s and 1970s, the vast majority of the increase in violent crime is attributed to violence by young males, particularly blacks. There are many social factors which tend to influence the commission of crime by minorities.

There is general agreement that the crime rate reached its peak in the early 1980s and has at least stabilized, and perhaps even begun a downward trend. Unless societal reactions and antidrug campaigns are successful, however, the anticipated crime decline might be short-lived.

3

Socialization: How People Learn to Behave

Learning to Behave
Conditioning
Modeling
The Effects of Punishment
The Development of a Conscience
Child-Rearing Practices
Discipline Techniques
Conscience Development after Childhood
Deviant Behavior
Summary

Learning to Behave

In order to analyze why a person commits crimes or behaves in an antisocial manner, we need to understand how people learn appropriate behavior. Children are not born committing crimes, they learn to do so. Deviant behavior is acquired in the same way that nondeviant behavior is acquired. While it is obvious that children learn knowledge and skills, it is not so obvious that children also learn attitudes, values, beliefs, and opinions. Children must learn the behavior, language, and social norms of the society in which they live, through a process called socialization.

No infant is born with a set of values and attitudes. Likewise most parents do not have a systematic scheme for teaching their children values and attitudes. Parents do not have a lesson plan for teaching their children: 6 months—teach to love others, 12 months—teach truthfulness, 18 months—teach sympathy for others. Much of the knowledge of society is not systematically or consciously taught to children, but they learn it quite effectively anyway.

The people who teach the ways of a culture to children are called the agents of socialization. When a child is very young, these agents are primarily the child's parents. As the child grows, others such as siblings, peers, teachers, and playmates begin to influence the child. The socialization process is most apparent during childhood, but it does not stop there, it continues throughout life.

Two primary characteristics of socialization differentiate it from other changes that might occur in a person's attitude and behavior: it is an interaction process, and it results from learning. An interaction process simply means that in order to be socialized the person must interact with others. Thus the child interacts with parents in the socialization process. The socialization agent, however, does not have to be physically present in order for the person to learn from the agent. People can learn from, and be socialized by, the media—television, books, newspapers, and films. The second characteristic of socialization is that the change in the child's behavior or attitude is due to learning, not maturation. A child who knows how to walk does not need to learn to run, the child naturally begins to run as he or she matures. On the other hand, a child does need to learn to speak in the vernacular, as this does not come merely as a process of maturation. And a child will not learn a language unless there is someone with whom to speak.

The process of socialization continues throughout adulthood. People are socialized into new roles or groups, as when a person joins the military or a religious community, becomes a parent, or gets married. On each of these occasions the person must learn the attitudes and behaviors appropriate for someone in the newly acquired role or recently joined community. For example, students going to college for the first time are socialized into the role of college student. While there is no program that systematically teaches new college students how they should behave in order to be like other college students, they learn the expected behaviors very rapidly. Shortly after arriving on campus, new freshmen are wearing the same clothes, writing in the same kinds of notebooks, eating at the same places, and talking about the same topics as their classmates.

Conditioning

The process of learning that takes place during socialization follows the same form as any other type of learning. Theorists contend that people learn social behavior through three primary learning processes: classical conditioning, instrumental conditioning, and modeling. Both types of conditioning involve learning through the development of an association between a stimulus and a response. A stimulus is any event, external, as in the phone ringing, or internal, as in feeling hungry. A response is the person's behavior.

Classical Conditioning

Classical conditioning refers to the establishment of an association between an external stimulus and a response. The response in classical conditioning is a reflex action. Suppose you wanted to condition a reflex response to a specific stimulus which ordinarily does not elicit that reflex. For example, you might want to have someone blink when you ring a bell. In order to condition this response (blinking an eye), the stimulus (ringing a bell) must be paired with another stimulus which automatically elicits the response. Ordinarily a ringing bell does not elicit a blinking response; in contrast, a puff of air blown into the eye does elicit a blink. If a puff of air were to be blown into a person's eye at the same time as a bell is rung, the two stimuli (puff of air and ringing of bell) would be paired. If these two stimuli were to be paired a number of times, the person would begin to respond to the bell with a blink of the eye. In other words, when the bell was rung, the person would blink. This is an example of classical conditioning.

Operant or Instrumental Conditioning

Operant or instrumental conditioning also involves the association between a stimulus (reinforcer) and a response. However, in this case the response is not a reflex response, it is a response that is controlled by the individual. The association is not created by repeated pairing of an external stimulus and a reflex action, but by a reinforcement which occurs after the response. If a response is followed by a reinforcement, the likelihood of the response occurring again increases (Skinner 1953). This type of conditioning is called operant or instrumental conditioning because the individual operates to get the reinforcement or is instrumental in getting the reinforcement.

A reinforcement is anything which will increase the likelihood of the behavior that precedes it. The reinforcement can be either negative or positive. A positive reinforcement could be physical, psychological, or social; for example, a piece of candy, a compliment, or a gold star. A negative reinforcement is the removal of a noxious stimulus, which is something painful or unpleasant. Stopping a loud, grating noise, removal of a major concern, or the elimination of a final examination could be negative reinforcers. The following is an illustration of negative reinforcement. Jane was running in the house and broke a lamp. She is very worried about her parents' reaction when they discover the broken lamp. When her parents come home, Jane admits to breaking the lamp and says she is sorry. Her parents are upset but do not punish her because she told the truth.

Her worry about being punished is removed, thereby giving her a negative reinforcement for telling the truth. (A related phenomenon, punishment, will be discussed later in this chapter.)

Let us look at an example of operant conditioning. The ringing phone is a stimulus; your response is to answer the phone. If someone you love is on the line, that is a reinforcement. Each time you answer the telephone to find someone with whom you would like to speak, the more likely you are to answer the phone the next time it rings. Now let us suppose that the phone rings and you answer it, but this time there is no one on the line. The phone rings again and the same thing happens. If this happens a number of times, you are less likely to answer the phone in the future. You have not been reinforced for answering the phone.

In operant conditioning, the person teaching controls the rewards. Parents are not always aware that they are using behavioral techniques, but many do nonetheless. A parent who allows a child to watch an hour of television if the child clears the table or finishes his homework is reinforcing the child for a desired behavior.

There are many techniques used to teach a child the skills and attitudes necessary to live in society. One of the most common techniques, and the one parents are most aware of using, is telling the child what to do. Thus, a parent says, "You should share your toys." In this manner the parent uses words to instruct the child in the appropriate behavior. Often the parent uses reinforcement to support this form of instruction. For example, when the child shares her toys, the parent says, "Good!"

Incidental Learning Although parents think children learn primarily through verbal instruction, this is not really accurate. Children learn a lot through incidental learning. Incidental learning occurs when a child receives reinforcement for a behavior that the parent did not intend to reinforce. For example, a 6- or 8-year-old child uses an obscene word. This is the type of behavior that makes a parent wonder, "Where did my child learn THAT?" The parent does not remember when the same child was 2 or 3 years old and heard the obscene word for the first time. The child, who was then just learning to talk, repeated the word in front of a group of adults who thought it was funny. The adults laughed and asked the child to say it again. The child was not told that he was "Good!" or given a cookie for saying the word but was reinforced for saying the obscene word through attention. This reinforcement was responsible for incidentally teaching the child to use the word again. The laughter and attention reinforced the behavior and increased the likelihood that the child would use that word again. For another example of incidental learning see A PERFECT SPY.

Modeling

The other major way humans learn is by observing other people or models. Modeling requires that an actual or symbolic model be present for learning to take place. The model does not have to be physically in the same place as the learner; people can learn just as easily from models on television, in the movies, or even

> **Box 3.1**
>
> **A Perfect Spy**
>
> John le Carré's book, *A Perfect Spy,* is partially based on his own life. It describes the life story of a fictitious character, Magnus Pim, and how it prepared him to be the perfect spy. The hero was born to a sickly mother and a con artist father. The father, Ricky Pim, is a fun-loving, high-living scoundrel who periodically ends up in jail. But whenever the father is free, he reunites with his son and they have a great time. He constantly asks the son, "Do you love your old man?" Even when the law is on his heels, the father pretends all is fine. People frequently confront Ricky Pim on his con games, but he usually is able to charm his way out of trouble. He has a series of women and a group of disciples who party with him when things are good and wait for him when he is in jail.
>
> Ricky Pim sends Magnus to the best schools, paid for by his ill-gotten gains. The story describes how the young boy learns to cope with his erratic life—one minute living alone in poverty and the next having every material wish fulfilled by a loving and happy father. Surrounded by con artists, the boy learns to lie and create fantasies about his life. The boy lies to his school chums about his father's occupation and activities and develops the ability to do so without feeling guilt. Magnus also learns to lie to his father. He soon finds he can lie to anyone about anything very convincingly.
>
> When Magnus graduates from university, he is recruited as a government agent. His ability to lie and con people is a decided asset in this occupation. Magnus still loves his father and even gets him out of jail and lends him money. However, Magnus does not allow his father around his children and his wife. The son eventually becomes a double agent, using all the skills of deception learned at his father's knee. When the father dies and the government begins to close in on him, Magnus commits suicide.

Source: J. le Carré, *A Perfect Spy* (New York: Knopf, 1986).

in books or newspapers. The learner, however, does have to perceive the model's behavior. See MODELING A CHARACTER FROM A BOOK for an example of modeling.

The two basic types of observational learning, or learning from models, involve: 1) the learner observing the outcome of the model's behavior, and 2) the learner observing the actions of the model and being reinforced for imitating them.

In the first of these types of modeling, the learner profits from the experience of the model. The learner watches what the model does and observes whether the model is rewarded or punished for her behavior. The behavior is more likely to be imitated if the model's behavior is rewarded and less likely to be imitated if that behavior is punished (Bandura 1973). For example, a young child sees his

---

Box 3.2

Modeling a Character From a Book

In 1977 Stephen King wrote *Rage* under the pen name of Richard Bachman. The story describes a teenager taking a gun to school and holding his classmates hostage, in what King calls a "pathological rage fantasy about his father." In 1989 Dustin Pierce, a 17-year-old high school student from McKee, Kentucky, held eleven fellow students from his class hostage at gunpoint. In an eerie reenactment of the book, Pierce demanded to speak with the father with whom he had had no contact for years. Happily, the real hostage situation ended safely, with no one hurt, and Pierce surrendering peacefully. In the book the student killed his teacher and a classmate.

The book, *Rage,* was found in Pierce's home. The police and FBI agents who investigated the incident contend that King's book was the outline for the incident in McKee. Even though King agrees that Pierce was acting out the plot of his book, he feels strongly that books do not create this type of behavior. He says that "if they didn't do it one way, they would do it another way. . . . Crazy is crazy." Dustin Pierce denies that the book influenced his behavior. He even denies reading the book, *Rage.*

Source: "Books Not to Blame, Author Says," *The Florida Times-Union* (September 21, 1989), p. A–8.

older sister run to meet their father when he comes home from work. The older sister hugs her father. The father then takes the older sister for a ride in the car. By watching his older sister and seeing that she was rewarded for hugging their father, the younger brother learns to run and hug his father when he comes home.

Let's apply this type of learning to behavior in the inner city. A boy sees a factory worker get up early every day, go to work, and come home tired and dirty. He also sees that this worker has very few material rewards. The same boy sees a drug dealer who sleeps until noon, then hangs around on the corner until he makes a deal. The dealer drives around in a big, flashy car, spends a lot of money, and attracts a lot of pretty young women. Which behavior is the young boy likely to model? If the only influence on the boy's behavior were the comparison of the rewards of the two men in his neighborhood, he would be likely to model the drug dealer. Thankfully, human behavior is much more complex than that.

The second way in which people learn behavior from modeling is when the learner is rewarded for imitating the actions of the model. Young children are often admonished to sit still like their big sister, or comb their hair like Mommy, or brush their teeth like Daddy. When the behavior is performed, the child is rewarded with "Good!" or even a gift.

Observational learning and imitation can also instill and modify moral behavior (Bandura 1977). Research indicates that children will model self-control when demonstrated by someone they respect. One study found that children would choose a postponed reward rather than a smaller immediate one after seeing a respected model choose a delayed reward (Bandura & Mischel 1965). (Moral development will be discussed in Chapter 4.)

Bandura contends that children choose particular people as models for behavior. Children decide who merits watching, then select models on the basis of positive attributes. Children tend to model their behavior after successful and powerful adults, often their parents (Hogan & Jones 1983). If the child's imitating behavior is reinforced, the child is likely to repeat it in the future under similar circumstances. Children learn both the behavior and when to imitate it.

Early childhood modeling, particularly of parents, has a long-lasting effect on behavior. Parents can influence their offspring positively or have a predominantly negative impact. Bandura and Walters (1959) studied adolescent boys who were aggressive and delinquent. They found evidence that the boys' fathers helped develop and sustain antisocial behavior by modeling toughness and reinforcing it in their sons. Parents who physically punish their children without explaining why appear unpredictable to the children and are role models for aggressive behavior. Eron and his associates studied three generations and found that aggressiveness "as a characteristic behavior, is transmitted from parent to child" (Eron et al. 1987, p. 260). They feel that the behavior is taught rather than inherited. Children learn behavior through modeling others, particularly their parents. Once that behavior is developed, it is maintained through reinforcement by other people in new situations. Read LEARNING TO HATE for an example of modeling antisocial behavior.

Peers have an especially strong influence on young people in our society, primarily through modeling. When children observe peer models behaving in an aggressive or disapproved manner without punishment, the children are likely to imitate the inappropriate behavior. However, punishing the model does not necessarily keep the observing child from performing the inappropriate behavior. Research on this showed that the behavior of the children who saw a peer model punished is similar to children who saw no model. This led the experimenter to conclude that "the immediate impact of peer behavior may thus be more likely to weaken than to strengthen one's inhibitions, at least in our society" (Inglis 1986, p. 960).

A graphic example of peer modeling can be found in Detroit street gangs. Leaders of youth gangs encourage younger potential members to commit violent acts against innocent victims or rival gang members. Imitation of the gang members by committing an act of violence is rewarded by membership in the gang (Salpukas 1976).

The Effects of Punishment

Discipline, which is a training process, often is equated with punishment as a way of teaching children right from wrong. A lot of people, including many parents, use punishment as a way to eliminate undesirable behavior. Spanking children, imposing fines for overdue books, and sending criminals to prison are all

> **Box 3.3**
>
> ## Learning to Hate
>
> Gary Michael Heidnik and his brother Terry had an unhappy and unstable childhood. Their mother, an alcoholic, married five times. Their parents divorced when Gary was 3. The boys moved back and forth between their mother's and their father's homes, finding happiness in neither. Eventually their mother committed suicide on Mother's Day.
>
> When Gary was 8, the boys went to live with their father and stepmother on a permanent basis. Gary felt unloved by everyone and claims that his stepmother hated him.
>
> Gary and Terry report that they were beaten and forced to wear pants with a bulls-eye on the seat. Their father and children in their classes would kick them on the bulls-eye. They contend that their father hated blacks and taught them from an early age to do the same. Their father, Michael Heidnik, also hated his ex-wife (the boys' mother), who lived with black men and married two of them after their divorce. The elder Heidnik denies either beating his children or teaching them racial prejudice.
>
> The boys later moved back to live with their mother. Life was not much better at her house. She was an unstable person who alternated between living with different husbands and boyfriends. She also was arrested for theft. The boys ran away but were caught and sent to their father, who forced Gary to enlist in the Army. In a short time, Gary was discharged with a 100 percent mental disability.
>
> In 1987, Gary Michael Heidnik was arrested for kidnapping and torturing six women, two of whom he killed. All of his victims were black women.
>
> ♦
>
> Was Gary taught to hate? How much did Gary's father's attitudes toward blacks influence his son's attitudes? How much influence did his upbringing have on his mental disorder? How much of his hostility toward women was a result of his father's abuse and how much a reaction to his stepmother and alcoholic mother? Should Gary Heidnik be held less responsible for his crimes because of his childhood?

Source: "Murder-Torture Suspect's Childhood Examined," *The Florida Times-Union* (April 5, 1987), p. A–23.

examples of punishments used as attempts to change behavior. Although punishment is perhaps the most common method used to control behavior, experts conclude that it is not effective in eliminating undesirable activities (Catania 1984, Skinner 1953). While punishment may be successful in certain circumstances, there are more effective ways to change behavior with fewer negative side effects. Skinner states that, in the long run, punishment "works to the disadvantage of both the punished organism and the punishing agent" (1953, p. 183).

It is difficult, if not impossible, to study the effects of punishment on people. First, it would be unethical to impose physical punishment on subjects in an experiment. Thus, most knowledge about the effects of punishment on behavior has been garnered from research on animals. Scientists cannot say that humans would behave in the same way as animals do; there are always qualifications in the application of the research on animals to humans. However, research on animals does provide some understanding of the underlying principles regarding the effects of punishment.

Punishment is defined as the removal of a positive reinforcer or the presentation of a noxious stimulus. However, punishment is not the reverse of a reward, and it does not affect behavior in the opposite way by subtracting responses. Most research indicates that punishment only temporarily suppresses behavior; it does not permanently eliminate it. Even with the use of severe and prolonged punishment, the undesirable behavior will return when the punishment is terminated. In fact, after a period of time with no punishment, the rate of undesirable behavior returns to full strength, as if no punishment had been imposed (Skinner 1953).

Experiments conducted on rats, dogs, and cats indicate that the effectiveness of punishment depends on the level of punishment inflicted on the animal. One experiment found that shocks of very low intensity actually strengthened the undesired behavior. When the shocks were moderately low, they temporarily suppressed the behavior. When the shocks were moderately high, the suppression of behavior was more lasting. It was only when the shocks were extremely high that the behavior was completely suppressed (Solomon 1964).

What can we learn from this research on animals that can be applied to changing behavior in humans? That is not clear. There is a tendency in the criminal justice system to give those convicted of a first offense very lenient sentences or probation. Would those punishments be equivalent to low-intensity electric shocks? What level of punishment is equivalent to high-intensity electric shocks? Remember that very low-intensity electric shock in animals actually increases the likelihood of the behavior. Does that mean that if someone commits a crime and has the offense dropped or receives no sentence, the person is more likely to commit another crime? We do not know. It is impossible to translate shock intensity levels given to animals into sentencing of adults to prison.

While punishment tends merely to suppress a behavior temporarily when used alone, it becomes extremely effective when combined with a reward for alternative behavior that is incompatible with the behavior to be eliminated. Research with puppies demonstrated this phenomenon. The puppies were swatted with newspapers when they ate horsemeat, and at the same time were given the opportunity to eat food pellets. This form of punishment was so effective that the puppies learned to avoid horsemeat even when at the point of starvation (Eysenck 1984, p. 60). These same methods of pairing a punishment with a reward for alternative behavior have been very effective in decreasing self-destructive behavior in autistic children.

RAT IN A SKINNER BOX. Rats are trained in Skinner boxes to push buttons or press levers to obtain food. This training is an example of operant or instrumental conditioning. (Photo courtesy of David H. Fauss)

We have little solid scientific information about the impact of punishment on humans. Studies of the effect of punishment on children have used loud noises, reprimands, or taking candy away from the children rather than imposing physical punishment. This research demonstrates that combining punishment with an explanation of why one should not do the restricted behavior can be very effective and likely to have an enduring impact on the children (Leizer & Rogers 1974). Other research indicates that there is an interaction between the intensity of punishment and the timing of punishment which affects the outcome (Parke 1970).

There is evidence that punishment also leads to unintentional "side effects" (Skinner 1953). The person being punished learns to perform any act in order to avoid punishment. Aronfreed (1961) suggests that children become anxious if they break rules since they frequently are punished for these transgressions. Because anxiety becomes associated with a misdeed through punishment, any response which decreases the anxiety is likely to be learned, since a decrease in anxiety is a negative reinforcer. Suppose Phillip were to disobey his parents and break the VCR while playing with it. If Phillip confessed and his parents punished him, he would have learned that telling the truth leads to punishment. The next time Phillip broke something, he probably would be more anxious and might deny breaking it. If his parents did not punish him, Phillip would be reinforced for denying committing the offense (lying). Thus, he would be more likely to lie in the future to avoid being punished, which is not what his parents wanted to teach him.

Unintended teaching often occurs in the criminal justice system. Legislators who write laws believe that people will not commit crimes if the punishment is very severe. (See the discussion of deterrence in Chapter 14.) A Florida law requires that a person convicted of committing a felony with a gun will receive a minimum sentence of 3 years. Most inmates do not want to go back to prison after being released. Does this mean that they will never commit another crime after they leave prison? Or does it mean they will not use a gun while committing a crime? Most of the inmates with whom I have spoken say the next time they commit a crime, they will not leave any witnesses. They have not learned to avoid committing a felony, they have learned to avoid getting caught by killing witnesses. This is an extreme example of unintended teaching.

Research on punishment shows that in order to be effective, punishment must be "swift and sure." In other words, the punishment must immediately follow the undesired behavior and must be imposed whenever the behavior occurs. The stereotypical mother saying "Wait until your father gets home" violates this rule, as does a library fine imposed a month past the due date. Neither of these punishments is swift.

Let us look more closely at the criminal justice system, where punishment is neither swift nor sure. First, let's see how swift punishment is. A man who robs a convenience store in April might not be caught until December (if ever). If this person were to go to trial, the trial might be as long as 3 months or even up to a year or two after his capture. After the trial, or after a plea of guilty, he is finally sentenced. Thus the punishment might not be received for months, or even years, after the offense is committed. The punishment is certainly not swift.

Now let's look at how sure the punishment is in the criminal justice system. A study by Marvin Wolfgang (1978) reveals that offenders, arrested for an offense which caused injury to another, stated that they had committed an average of three "injury offenses" before being caught. Men arrested from two to four times reported committing more than seven injury offenses for each arrest. In other words, the likelihood of being arrested is quite low, making the probability of punishment unlikely rather than sure. Research with animals indicates that when a punishment is intermittent (not given for every instance of the behavior), it is very ineffective, even when quite intense. (See Chapter 12 for a discussion of the chances of being caught.)

What about the type of punishment meted out by the criminal justice system? Is that sure? No, there is a lot of disparity in sentencing. People in one state might receive a prison sentence of 5 years while someone in another state would receive probation or 60 days in jail for the same type of offense. Even within the same state, people committing the same offenses often receive disparate sentences. Thus even the type or amount of punishment is not "sure."

The Development of a Conscience

Studying inhibitions against antisocial or violent behavior is a prerequisite to understanding criminal behavior. Psychologists refer to these inhibitions as a conscience and have conducted much research and evolved many theories about how the conscience is developed. Study of the conscience dates back at least to Freud, who referred to it as the superego.

Eysenck says that a conscience makes "us behave in a moral and socially acceptable manner; that this conscience is the combination and culmination of a long process of conditioning; and that failure on the part of the person to become conditioned is likely to be a prominent cause in his running afoul of the law and of the social mores generally" (1984, p. 46). But others feel that research does not consistently support a relationship between a conscience and resistance to antisocial behavior (Strommen, McKinney & Fitzgerald 1983).

People learn social motives such as aggression, affiliation, achievement, and dependency through socialization just as they learn behaviors and skills. Socialization is also the process by which people develop a conscience. The conscience is a set of behavioral standards or norms which a child accumulates from the expectations others have of the child's behavior. Initially, these behavioral standards are external constraints, but eventually the child incorporates them into his or her motive system and they influence behavior, even in the absence of the parents (Inglis 1986). When this set of standards is accepted by the child and internalized, it becomes the conscience of the child.

In order for a child to develop a conscience, the child must have someone with whom to interact, usually the primary care-giver. This significant other has expectations concerning the behavior the child should exhibit. The child learns the expectations of the other person(s) through socialization. If the child wishes to please the care-giver, the child will use these expectations as a standard of behavior for his or her own acts or contemplated acts. Eventually, the standards of behavior are internalized and the significant other no longer has to tell the child what behaviors are expected. The child automatically compares acts or contemplated acts to the now internalized conscience and decides whether the acts are right or wrong. If the act fits into the standards, the child is more likely to perform the act and feel good about doing so. If the act does not conform to the internalized standards, the child is less likely to perform the act. If the child does complete the act, he or she will feel guilty about doing so (Bartol 1980).

Most people develop their consciences through the expectations and teaching of their parents. A good indication that you have internalized the standards of your parents is if you ever say to yourself, "If my mother ever knew that I did that. . . ." When you are making this statement to yourself, you are comparing your behavior to an internal standard, based on the expectations of your mother. These standards are internal controls which influence your behavior. These controls will not keep you from ever behaving in a manner which would violate the expectations of your mother or of your own internalized standards of behavior. However, if you were to behave in a manner inconsistent with your standards of behavior, you would feel guilty, you would feel as if the behavior were wrong.

Obviously, a child cannot be socialized or develop a conscience without interacting with other people. Reports of children who were raised in isolation indicate that they do not learn to talk or walk and do not develop social skills. Studies done in the 1940s found that children raised in institutions developed at a very slow rate, both their social and physical development were severely retarded. Without early social contact, these children became severely depressed, and many of the children died without any apparent physical cause. Researchers blame these unexplained deaths on anaclitic depression, a result of maternal deprivation. Actually, the children did not necessarily need a mother, but they needed some personal attention and affection from someone. Children who were raised entirely in institutions have also been found to be more aggressive than children raised in a more natural environment (Davis 1947, Goldfarb 1943).

Child-Rearing Practices

In order to develop a conscience, a child must have someone for whom he feels affection and also must have a set of behavioral standards. Without both of these conditions, the child's conscience is unlikely to be very strong. Unless the child wants to please his socializing agent, he has no motivation to behave according to the expectations of that person. And a child cannot internalize a set of behavioral standards that does not exist.

Much research supports the importance of parental warmth in child-rearing practices. A close and affectionate relationship between parents and child will make the child more responsive to control and guidance (Maccoby 1980). If the child feels no affection for her primary care-giver, she will feel less dependent on this person and the formation of her conscience will be weakened. The child is unlikely to internalize the standards of someone she has no desire to please. Inglis (1986) suggests that affection may make a child willing to accept discipline from her parents, model their behavior, and make her secure emotionally so she can recognize the needs of others. But a child who is raised with affection and no discipline will be unmanageable. Without a set of rules, a child can be self-centered, spoiled, and lacking in self-control.

If the parents are erratic and unpredictable in their behavioral expectations and their affection, the child will have a tendency to form an overdeveloped conscience. The child does not know what the rules are or what the parents expect. The child does not know what to do in order to have the parents love her. Thus, the child constantly monitors her behavior. In the extreme case, the child is so concerned about violating some unknown rule that she will sit still, afraid even to move.

Seldom do parents fit completely into any of the above descriptions of child-rearing practices. Those descriptions were given as if they were discrete categories; however, it is more accurate to think of child-rearing practices as dimensions. Each dimension varies on a continuum from positive to negative, from extremely affectionate to extremely unaffectionate or from an explicit set of rules and expectations to no rules and expectations. Most parents are neither perfectly good nor completely inept. The vast majority of parents are somewhere between the two ends of the continuum of showing affection and demonstrating discipline.

In addition, not every child who is raised by parents who do not love him grows up without a conscience. It is less likely that a child who is raised without affection will develop a strong conscience. However, parents are by no means the only influence on a child's development. Peers, siblings, teachers, and many others contribute to a child's formation of a conscience. These other people can show affection and have standards of behavior by which the child wants to abide.

Discipline Techniques

After reviewing eleven studies of child-rearing practices, Hoffman (1970) was able to identify three major categories of discipline techniques and their effect on the development of a conscience in the child. The first of these is the **power assertion** technique. Parents who employ this technique control their children by physical power and limiting resources; they punish their children physically and deprive them of objects or privileges. The results of the studies indicate that this technique of discipline does not aid in the development of a conscience; if anything, this technique is related to decreased conscience development.

The second type of discipline technique is **love withdrawal.** Parents who use this technique express their anger and disapproval directly but do not use physical power. They control their children's behavior by ignoring them or by verbal control. They are likely to say that they won't love the children unless they are "good," or they don't like them when they misbehave. The research finds no consistent pattern associating this technique with the development of a conscience. However, there is an impact on the child who tends to be anxious and does not express anger easily. Children raised with this type of discipline are likely to develop depression as adults.

The third type of child-rearing practice is **induction.** Parents who use this type of discipline try to explain to their children why a particular behavior is necessary. They point out how the behavior will affect others and ultimately benefit the child. Research shows that this type of discipline is associated with the development of a conscience, particularly when employed by mothers.

In summary, moral internalization or the development of a conscience is encouraged by the use of inductive discipline techniques and the presence of an affectionate relationship. It is particularly important for parents or primary care-givers to express their affection for the child frequently and in encounters other than disciplinary ones.

Conscience Development after Childhood

The major influences on the conscience of a young child are the child's primary care-givers or parents. But a conscience is not completely static. New people and their expectations continue to influence an individual's standards of behavior throughout life. A young woman who goes away to college becomes involved with a lot of new people her age who have different standards of behavior. Perhaps she meets a group of people who are active in social issues. She also takes some courses or attends some lectures dealing with such issues. She becomes very interested in social issues and at the same time becomes good friends with these new people. She wants to be liked by her new friends and wants to please them. She will probably modify her standards of behavior in order to conform to some of the expectations of her new friends.

Deviant Behavior

People in every society develop common or typical ways of doing things. For example, people in the United States answer the telephone by saying "hello," while people in England answer with their phone number, "3125," and those in Germany answer with their names, "Beck, here." These habitual ways of doing things are called folkways. Some folkways are more important to the functioning of society than others, so that violating folkways can be cute, irritating, or even dangerous. In the United States we drive on the right side of the road, while in England and Japan people drive on the left side of the road. Someone who violates folkways concerning which side of the street on which a person should drive is much more dangerous than someone who answers the phone in a different way. In civilized countries, folkways that are important for the operation of the society often are incorporated into the statutes that are set up by the society for its functioning.

Behaviors that violate the folkways of a society are deviant, and people who perform these behaviors are referred to as deviants. Deviance can be either positive or negative. People who do things faster and better than the average person are deviant, as are those who do things slower and with less proficiency than the average person. Criminal behavior is deviant but so is saintly behavior; neither one is the usual or habitual way in which people behave. Generally, the people who do things faster and better are considered superior to those who do things slower and less well.

Some folkways have strong moral connotations for the people of a society. For example, in the United States it is considered appropriate for parents to feed and care for their children. Violating the folkway of caring for one's children by abusing or neglecting them is considered immoral in our society. Folkways with strong moral connotations such as these are called mores.

Any behavior that violates the mores of a society is considered deviant and is always evaluated negatively. Societies introduce rules and regulations to ensure that people abide by the mores and folkways necessary to their functioning. These rules and regulations are incorporated into legal statutes. Behavior that violates the laws of a society is a special category of deviance, criminal behavior.

Deviance is socially defined. People in a society define what is deviant in that society and the "criteria for determining what behaviors constitute 'normality' are fluctuating, philosophical, and often self-serving for the majority or for some powerful controlling group" (Bartol 1980, p. 142). Thus what is deviant in one society or one subculture of a society may be perfectly acceptable in another society or subculture. Since the legal statutes of a society are based on that society's definition of deviance, laws are also socially defined. What is illegal or criminal in one society is not necessarily illegal or criminal in another society.

An indication of the effect of different folkways on definitions of crime can be seen by observing attitudes toward prostitution. Prostitution is legal in many European countries; prostitutes have a legal right to walk the streets in Germany and display themselves in shop windows for potential customers in Amsterdam and Brussels. Prostitution is even legal in Nevada; however, prostitution is not legal in any other state in the U.S.

The folkways and mores of a society are not static. People's attitudes change and societies change. Not everything that was considered usual behavior 25 years ago is still considered thus. Society in the United States has become much less formal. In 1960 it was unthinkable for a man to go to a restaurant without a jacket and tie or for a woman to go to dinner unless she were wearing a dress. Now many restaurants merely require that their patrons wear "shirt and shoes." The folkways have changed and the rules and regulations of society have followed suit. See UNJUST LAWS for an example of how statutes change over time.

Changes in the folkways and mores on which laws are based make the laws outmoded, and society must then change the laws in order to reflect the folkways. Alterations in the laws occur at a much slower pace than the changes in attitudes of society. Legislators are much more interested in introducing new statutes than in removing outmoded ones, and often these old laws remain on the books.

Examples of laws which have changed in response to changing attitudes in society are those related to drugs and abortion. Let's look at attitudes toward drugs first. Cocaine, opium, and heroin were legal and used by many respectable people at the end of the 19th and beginning of the 20th centuries. Products containing cocaine such as Coca-Cola, cigarettes, children's toothache drops, and face powder were sold at the neighborhood store. Opium-based solutions were recommended by doctors for use by mothers to soothe their babies. By the end of the 19th century, about one American out of 400 used opiates regularly (Thomas 1986).

As society became aware of the negative aspects of drug use, abuse, and addiction, reactions to the use of drugs changed. People were afraid of drugs and developed negative attitudes toward drug use. Reflecting the new folkways and mores of society, the government enacted laws restricting the use of cocaine and opiates in the early 1900s. Use of drugs among respectable members of society decreased until it was essentially nonexistent.

Marijuana (pot) was brought into the United States by Mexican workers in the 1920s and 1930s, but it was avoided by the mainstream of society. It was not until the 1960s that people once again changed their attitudes toward drug use. About that time LSD (lysergic acid diethylamide) came on the scene. Rebellious young people with little knowledge of the effect of drugs began to experiment with marijuana and, in smaller numbers, with LSD. Dr. David Musto, a noted expert on the history of drugs, states that "by 1960 you had a whole generation who knew nothing about drugs, and what little they did know came from people

> **Box 3.4**
>
> **Unjust Laws**
>
> In 1916 Sister Mary Thomasine Hehir and two of her colleagues were arrested. What crime had these three nuns committed? Sister Mary Thomasine was the principal of St. Benedict's School and the other two nuns were teachers there. The school had been opened to fulfill the mission that took their religious community, the Sisters of St. Joseph, to St. Augustine, Florida, 50 years before the arrests. The religious order had been asked by the first bishop of St. Augustine to educate the black children who had just been given their freedom by the Civil War. And that is the crime that the three nuns committed—they taught black children. In 1913 Florida had passed a law forbidding white teachers to teach black students.
>
> Lawyers advised the then bishop, William John Kenny, that the law was unconstitutional. Therefore, the nuns continued to teach in violation of the law. After being arraigned for teaching blacks, Sister Mary Thomasine refused to pay the $25 bond. She was then "commanded" to the county jail. However, the authorities decided to keep her under house arrest at the convent instead of in jail. About a month later the judge dismissed the case, deciding that the law deprived "teachers of privileges which were not denied any other class of citizens." ♦
>
> Should citizens violate laws that are unjust? Should they be punished for violating unjust laws? What makes a law unjust?

Source: J. Crum, "Nuns Arrested in 1916 for Teaching Blacks," *The Florida Times-Union* (February 19, 1989), p. B–3.

who didn't know anything about drugs either. When people found out that marijuana didn't drive you wild and mad, the Government lost what little credibility it had" (Thomas 1986, p. 65). The number of people using pot increased until people began to pressure the government to legalize its use. Some states did decriminalize the use of marijuana. While attitudes toward the use of marijuana have changed, pot has not been accepted by a sufficient number of people to change the folkways dealing with its use.

In the last few years, the pendulum has begun to swing back to more negative attitudes toward the use of drugs. Increased knowledge about substance abuse and publicity related to the effects of the use of crack, a potent form of cocaine, have changed the public viewpoint.

Let's turn to another example of the changing folkways of society affecting the laws, those dealing with abortion. In the 1950s and 1960s abortion was illegal; doctors who performed abortions and patients receiving abortions were subject to arrest and legal sanctions. Stories abounded of young women and girls receiving illegal abortions in slimy back rooms and becoming sick and even dying from the ordeal. Society became concerned about the consequences of illegal abortions, and some individuals became more tolerant toward abortion. As these new attitudes toward abortion spread, fewer people were prosecuted under the law. Decreasing numbers of prosecutions reduced the utility of the laws dealing with abortion, and eventually laws were passed legalizing abortion. The famous 1973 Supreme Court decision, *Roe v. Wade,* legalized abortion nationwide. The folkways and mores underlying this change in the law are still in a state of flux. There are many people throughout the country who now believe that abortion should not be legal and who are making efforts to reinstate laws against it. In its 1989 decision, *Webster v. Reproductive Health Services,* the Supreme Court gave states more freedom in restricting abortions.

Not all definitions of criminal behavior fluctuate as much as the previous examples, changing from time to time and place to place. Crimes which reflect changes in the folkways and mores of society tend to be crimes in which there is no obvious victim. But inclusion in this classification is not completely cut and dried. Even though the woman who requests an abortion does so willingly, some people say that the fetus is a victim. And while a good argument could be made that no one except the user is harmed by drugs, an equally good argument can be made for the negative effects of substance abuse on the members of the abuser's family and society. Certainly, no one will argue about the negative effects of property crime engaged in to support a drug habit. Prostitution is another crime typically classified as victimless. Prostitution usually is entered into willingly, although often out of desperation, and some people feel that women who engage in prostitution are exploited.

At the other end of the continuum from victimless crimes are violent crimes against people. Society's view of these crimes tends to be quite negative and less varying; an unjustified homicide is considered a crime by every society. Views about the legality of homicide do not tend to change over time even though evaluations of the severity of the crime have varied. Thus, there appears to be a continuum of types of crime from the ones that everyone defines as crime to those about which there is some debate or at least some fluctuation over time and across societies.

If the same behavior is considered criminal in one society and noncriminal at another time or place, it makes the definition of criminal behavior somewhat nebulous. Defining a criminal is even more so. The usual definition of a criminal is someone who breaks a law. If a criminal is someone who commits a crime, does someone who committed an act that is no longer a crime remain a criminal?

There is a tendency for people who are average citizens to think of all people who break the law as criminals. The typical image of a criminal is that of a career criminal. However, there is research indicating that a large percentage of people have committed some type of crime for which they could have gone to prison (Carroll 1982). Criminal behavior is no more one type of behavior or performed by any one type of person than is noncriminal behavior. There are many types of behavior that are criminal and many types of behavior that are considered criminal in one time or place but not in another.

Summary

Children learn behavior, values, and norms of society through socialization. The process of socialization continues throughout adulthood. Social behavior is learned through three primary learning processes: classical conditioning, instrumental conditioning, and modeling. Conditioning involves the development of an association between a stimulus and a response. Modeling involves the observation of other people or models for learning.

Punishment is not considered an effective means of learning. Punishment in the criminal justice system is neither swift nor sure—the two criteria necessary to make punishment effective. Most information about the effects of punishment has been gained from research with animals which cannot be generalized to humans. Punishment has unintentional side effects—people learn to do anything to avoid punishment.

A child develops a conscience by internalizing sets of behavioral standards from the expectations of others. In order to develop a conscience, a child needs someone for whom he or she feels affection and a set of behavioral standards. There are three major categories of discipline techniques: power assertion, love withdrawal, and induction. The development of a conscience is encouraged by the use of inductive discipline techniques and the presence of an affectionate relationship.

Behavior that violates the folkways and mores of a society is considered deviant. Since deviance and criminal behavior are socially defined, they can change over time and vary by location. Laws relating to drugs and abortion have changed over time in the U.S.

4

Theories of Criminal Behavior

Biological Theories of Criminal Behavior
Somatotypes
The XYY Chromosome
Current Biological Theories of Criminal Behavior
Genetic Evidence of Criminal Behavior
Sociological Theories of Criminal Behavior
Strain or Structural Theories
Subcultural Theories
Control Theory
Social-Psychological Theories of Criminal Behavior
Social Learning Theory
Differential Association Theory
Differential Conditionability
Psychological Theories of Criminal Behavior
Psychoanalytic Theory
Moral Development Theories
The Criminal Personality
Women in Crime
Summary

Chapter 3 described how people are socialized into society. This chapter will explore the ways people acquire criminal behavior. When speculating about the causes of criminal behavior, sociologists, psychologists, and criminologists organize their ideas into formal theories. A theory is a way of structuring knowledge or assumptions so as to explain the nature of a phenomenon, in this case criminal behavior.

There are many different motivations for people to commit crimes, many varieties of criminal behavior, and many types of criminal. Many theories of criminal behavior have been developed since no one theory has been able to account for all behavior in every situation to everyone's satisfaction. Criminology is not unique in having multiple theories to explain a single phenomenon. As Eysenck (1981) points out, there are three different theories in physics to explain gravitation, none of which is universally or even predominantly accepted by physicists.

Theories of criminal behavior can be classified into four general categories: biological, sociological, psychological, and social-psychological theories. Each theory tends to focus on one aspect of criminal behavior or one segment of the criminal population. Even though no theory completely explains the causes of criminal behavior, each theory sheds some light on the issue and increases our understanding of criminal behavior.

Biological Theories of Criminal Behavior

Biological theories center on physiological, hereditary, or genetic factors as explanations of criminal behavior. These theories postulate that there is some innate or biological condition in individuals which predisposes them to commit crimes. The first formal theory used to explain criminal behavior was based on biology. However, contradictory scientific evidence shattered this theory, and by the early 20th century there were few adherents to biological explanations of criminality. Criminal justice literature was dominated by sociological theories. In recent years there has been a resurgence in interest in biological explanations of criminal behavior, but these newly developed biosocial and sociobiological theories are quite controversial.

The first formal theory about the causes of criminal behavior was proposed by Cesare Lombroso (1836–1909). Lombroso, considered by some to be the father of modern criminology, was a physician and the leader of the Italian school of thought. According to Lombroso, some people were born to be criminals. Lombroso called these people atavistic and said they were a reversion to their more primitive ancestors. These born criminals were proposed to be a separate species described as sadistic and impulsive, insensitive to pain and without feelings of shame (Toch 1979).

People who constituted Lombroso's criminal type could be recognized by their anomalies or stigmata: a flattened nose, scanty beard, large ears, fat lips, enormous jaws, high cheekbones, a long lower jaw, and an asymmetrical cranium, to name a few. These anomalies were not postulated as causing the criminal behavior but rather were used to identify people who were criminal types. A person

Chapter 4 ♦ Theories of Criminal Behavior

BIOLOGICAL

- Lombroso's Criminal Type ♦ People are born criminals. Criminal types have anomalies.
- Sheldon's Somatotypes ♦ Body types are associated with psychological characteristics.
- XYY Chromosome ♦ The XYY chromosome associated with violent and antisocial behavior.
- Sociobiology ♦ Applies evolution to behavior.

SOCIOLOGICAL

STRAIN or STRUCTURAL
- Merton ♦ People who can't obtain rewards conventionally will resort to illegal means
- Reactance ♦ Workingclass youths reject middleclass values by developing gangs.
- Opportunity ♦ Subcultures provide opportunities to learn deviant behavior.
- Conflict ♦ Crime is result of struggle between competing groups.

SUBCULTURAL
- Focal Concerns ♦ Values and norms of lowerclass subculture lead to violation of middleclass norms.

CONTROL
- ♦ Weakening of a person's bond to society leads to crime

SOCIAL PSYCHOLOGICAL

- Social Learning ♦ Criminal behavior is developed through reinforcement.
- Differential Association ♦ Illegal behavior is learned through interactions with associates.
- Differential Conditionability ♦ Biological factors cause some people to be less conditionable.

PSYCHOLOGICAL

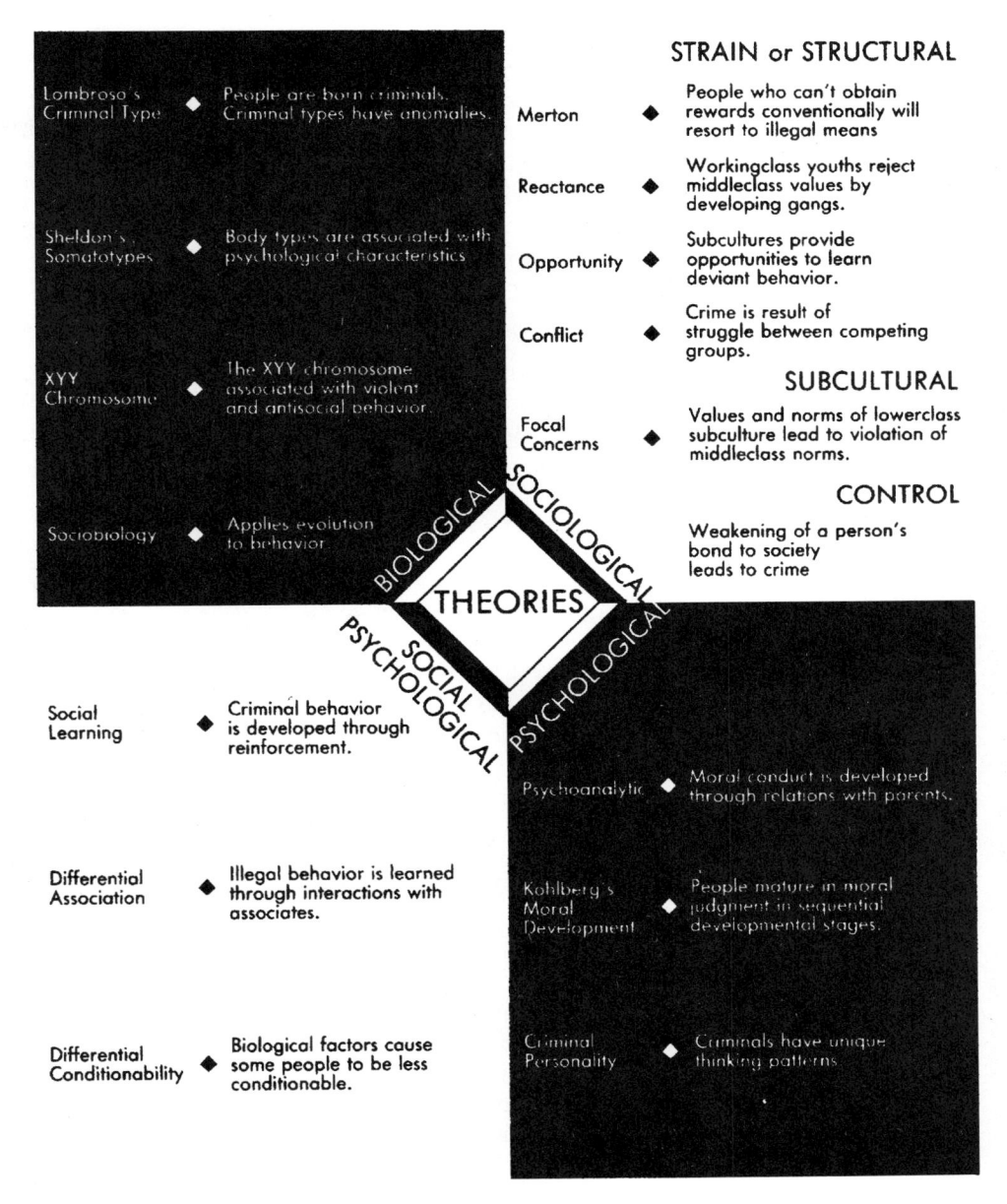

- Psychoanalytic ♦ Moral conduct is developed through relations with parents.
- Kohlberg's Moral Development ♦ People mature in moral judgment in sequential developmental stages.
- Criminal Personality ♦ Criminals have unique thinking patterns.

♦ **FIGURE 4.1** Theories (illustrated by Reen Foley)

who possessed the anomalies, and thus was a criminal type, was thought to have a strong predisposition to criminal behavior.

Lombroso's theory was challenged by another physician, Dr. Charles Goring, of England. Goring conducted a scientific investigation comparing the physiological characteristics of convicts and nonconvicts. He studied 3,000 people in each category and found no significant physical differences. His monograph reporting the results of his work, published in 1913, discredited Lombroso's theory (Bartol 1980).

Somatotypes

The next noteworthy attempt to develop a biological theory of criminal behavior grew out of the work of an American psychologist, William H. Sheldon. Sheldon's research (1949) attempted to associate physical characteristics with personality types. He identified three body builds, or somatotypes: endomorph, mesomorph, and ectomorph. The endomorph has a round, soft body and likes to relax and eat. This person is easygoing, even tempered, and likes people and affection. The mesomorph is the athletic type with a round, hard body and likes adventure, risk-taking, and vigorous physical activity. This person is aggressive, domineering, and callous. The final somatotype, the ectomorph, is thin and fragile and is reserved, restrained, and inhibited, preferring privacy and mental activity.

Sheldon postulated that mesomorphs were more likely to be delinquent than people who were predominantly one of the other somatotypes. In support of his proposal, Sheldon identified a large number of mesomorphs and some endomorphs among a large population of delinquent boys. A comparison group of college men had a lower proportion of mesomorphs than the delinquent group. Although Sheldon was a scientist, there is some evidence that he was not completely objective. The correlations between body type and personality were much higher when he measured the two variables than when someone else did. In addition, some of Sheldon's own research found a greater proportion of mesomorphs among another group of college men, children in California, army recruits, bus drivers, and truck drivers than among the delinquents (Kamin 1986).

Eleanor and Sheldon Glueck (1956) also found a relationship between physique and body type. A comparison of 500 delinquent boys to 500 nondelinquent boys showed 60 percent of the delinquents to be mesomorphs and another 39 percent to be endomorphs. The delinquent boys were also larger and stronger than the comparison group of nondelinquent boys. However, critics of the research contend that much of the difference in somatotypes between delinquent and nondelinquent groups can be attributed to ethnic group, nutrition, age, and socioeconomic status. Kamin (1986) argues that the boys in the Gluecks' study were not well matched on these variables. The delinquent boys were older and from lower socioeconomic homes than the nondelinquents, thus invalidating the results. A more recent study comparing 100 delinquent boys to 100 high school seniors, found that 57 percent of the delinquents were mesomorph versus only 19 percent of the high school boys (Cortes & Gatti 1972). But questions can be

---

Box 4.1

Richard Speck

Richard Speck was convicted of systematically murdering eight student nurses in Chicago in July, 1966. He was a 25-year-old former seaman and drifter when the attacks occurred. One of the intended victims, Corazon Amurao, lived to testify at his trial. She described the massacre, which lasted for hours, in detail.

Ms. Amurao recounted how she had been awakened by a knock. When she unlocked the bedroom door in her dormitory, Speck pushed his way into the room. He rounded up the student nurses at gunpoint and tied them up. Then he systematically dragged each woman out of the room and raped and murdered each of them. The witness heard screams and then silence. While the intruder was taking each victim out at about 20-minute intervals, Ms. Amurao managed to squirm under a bed where she was out of sight. She was hiding there when Speck raped his last victim in the bedroom about 3:30 A.M. After the assailant carried his last victim from the room, a terrified Ms. Amurao remained in her hiding place for another two hours. She finally struggled out of her bonds and found her eight dead friends.

Source: "House of Death," *Newsweek* (April 17, 1967), pp. 43–44.

---

raised about the comparability of a group of boys from a private high school and adjudicated delinquents.

Thus the research relating somatotypes to criminal behavior is still inconclusive. The evidence supporting the relationship is not strong enough to resolve the debate.

The XYY Chromosome

Another biological factor more recently associated with criminal behavior is the extra Y chromosome found in some males. It has been hypothesized that the XYY chromosome configuration is associated with violent and antisocial behavior. Research on the extra Y chromosome received a lot of notoriety when the possession of this chromosome structure was used as a defense for a few violent criminals. Defense attorneys have sometimes argued that the XYY chromosome was a mental illness or a compulsion. Infamous violent criminals, such as Richard F. Speck, Daniel Hugon in Paris, and Sean "Big Bad John" Farley were said to have an extra Y chromosome (Brown 1979, Kittrie 1984). Read RICHARD SPECK for an example of someone with the XYY chromosome.

Interest in the relationship between the XYY chromosome configuration and criminal behavior was sparked by a study of inmates in a maximum security state hospital in Scotland. Results indicated a relationship between an extra Y chromosome and a number of characteristics such as antisocial or aggressive behavior, low intelligence, and abnormal height (Ellison & Genz 1983, Kittrie 1984). A Danish study of criminal behavior furthered interest in the XYY chromosome. Since the XYY syndrome is associated with abnormal height, the researchers selected for study the tallest 15 percent of all the men born in Denmark between 1944 and 1947. Results indicated that over 40 percent of the men with XYY chromosomes had a record of one or more criminal offense, while only 9.3 percent of the men with the XY chromosome had a similar record. However, the incidence of an extra Y chromosome was very small; there were only twelve men with the XYY chromosome out of the 4,139 men studied (Wilson & Herrnstein 1985).

Despite the notoriety of the XYY chromosome, there is little evidence relating it to violent behavior. The vast majority of inmates with the XYY chromosome are in prison for property crimes (Bartol 1980), and the Danish study indicated that the XYY men were no more violent than the XY men with criminal records. Furthermore, prisoners with XYY chromosomes were found to commit fewer assaults than XY men in a comparison group (Price & Whatmore 1967). Jarvik, Klodin, and Matsuyama maintain that XYY men are "an insignificant proportion of the perpetrators of violent crimes" (1973, p. 84).

There are two obvious problems with the studies of the XYY chromosome configuration and their conclusions. First, the studies are correlational studies and not controlled experiments; therefore, it is not possible to attribute cause and effect. It has not been shown that the XYY chromosome causes antisocial or aggressive behavior. The second problem is that the men studied were in prison. Men with an extra Y chromosome are often described as having low intelligence. Their incarceration might more accurately be attributed to their low intelligence than to the fact that they are predisposed to criminal behavior. There are more men with the XYY chromosome who have never been in prison and are not aggressive than there are in prison. In any event, the number of men with the XYY chromosome abnormality is about one per 1,000. Even if every one of them were aggressive, they would account for only a small part of the aggressiveness in society.

Current Biological Theories of Criminal Behavior

By coincidence the very first theory and the most recent theories of criminal behavior are ones that explain criminal behavior through biological or physiological factors. These new biological explanations center on the controversial application of the theory of evolution to human behavior, known as the sociobiological approach.

Renewed interest in the theory of evolution was sparked by the work of E. O. Wilson on sociobiology (1975). More recently, J. Q. Wilson and R. J. Herrnstein (1985) proposed a relationship between biological factors and criminal behavior in their book, *Crime and Human Nature*. Their controversial work directed increased attention to this area of research.

The basic assumption in sociobiology is that "social behaviors evolve in much the same way as physical features" (Kenrick, Dantchik & MacFarlane 1983, p. 219). This approach advocates the use of recently developed evolutionary models, which have been helpful in understanding animal behavior, to analyze human behavior.

The sociobiological approach contends that there is an interaction between genetic constraints and ecological forces influencing the ways a person adapts to the environment. Proponents of this viewpoint state that "implicit in our argument is an assumption that at least some of the variance in tendencies toward criminal behavior is heritable" (Kenrick, Dantchik & MacFarlane 1983, p. 224). Their support for the inheritance of criminal behavior is based on evidence of the inheritance of learning dispositions, levels of motivation such as anxiety and anger, and factors such as body build or physical attractiveness which elicit various amounts of external reinforcement. All of these characteristics are assumed to interact with environmental forces.

Evolutionary theory is based on the premise that organisms will behave in a manner likely to improve their chances of producing the greatest number of offspring who are raised to mating age. Some behaviors are more functional than others, thus the differences in individuals make some more likely to reproduce than others. In order to apply this principle to human criminal behavior, we need to look at the behavior of our ancestors. Some ancestors were predisposed to use exploitative strategies. These behaviors could have increased their chances of raising offspring to mating age, causing this behavior to be passed down to their descendants. Ecological factors would then increase the criminal behavior (Kenrick, Dantchik & MacFarlane 1983).

The biosocial theory of criminal behavior contends that there are individual differences in the susceptibility to external influences which elicit criminal behavior. Theorists who support this viewpoint feel that there are physiological differences between "normal" people and people who are at a high risk of criminal behavior. They feel that variations in individual differences are due to these physiological factors.

Another area relating biological factors to potential criminal behavior is research on the impact of abnormal brain waves on aggression. Research indicates that a significant percentage of prisoners incarcerated for violent crimes have abnormal brain waves (Bartol 1980, Mark & Ervin 1970, Valenstein 1973). One estimate is that the percentage of abnormal brain waves in the general population is 2 percent, while in convicted murderers it is 8.2 percent, and in aggressive psychopaths it is 14 percent (Hare 1970). This researcher estimates that 20 to 40 percent of people who are impulsive, aggressive, or destructive have abnormal spikes in their brain wave activity.

Genetic Evidence of Criminal Behavior

Evidence to support the biological or physiological theories of criminal behavior has been sought from studies of twins and adopted children. These groups are used in order to determine the differential effect of biological factors and environmental ones. Researchers contend that based on these studies there is evidence that hereditary factors are determinants of intelligence, psychopathology, neuroses, alcoholism, schizophrenia, and criminal behavior (Cadoret 1978, Claridge 1973, Eysenck & Gudjonsson 1989, Hetherington & Parke 1975, McClearn & DeFries 1973, Rosenthal 1970, 1971, Rowe 1986, Schulsinger 1972). Most of these studies use a measure known as concordance rate as an indication of the relationship between biological factors and behavior. The concordance rate, usually expressed in the form of a percentage, is the degree to which pairs of subjects display a specific behavior or condition.

Research on Twins

Studies of twins compare monozygotic (MZ) or identical twins with dizygotic (DZ) or fraternal twins. Monozygotic twins grow from the same egg and thus are genetically identical, while the fraternal twins are formed from two eggs and are genetically different. The studies of adult twins compare the concordance rate for criminal behavior of a sample of dizygotic twins to that of monozygotic twins. The assumption is if the monozygotic twins have a higher concordance rate for criminal behavior than the dizygotic twins, then this is strong evidence for a genetic influence on behavior.

After reviewing nine twin studies, Eysenck concluded, "When averaged, they suggest that MZ twins are over four times as likely to be concordant for criminal activity as are DZ twins; this enormous difference very strongly suggests the importance of genetic factors" (1983, p. 54). Not all researchers agree with this statement. Early studies of twins have been criticized on many levels. Of primary concern is the unscientific method of determining whether the twins were monozygotic or dizygotic. In addition, the methods of sampling and the procedure for calculating concordance are questioned (Christiansen 1977). Bartol (1980) points out that early studies of twins found much higher rates of concordance than later studies which used more sophisticated methods of determining whether twins were MZ or DZ. For a description of twins, read TWINS REARED APART MEET.

There are many limitations to the study of twins. For one thing, there is no way to attribute cause and effect, so that no researcher can say that genetic factors caused the criminal behavior. As we saw in the last chapter, the definition of criminal behavior can vary over time and across settings, thus the type of behavior measured is nebulous. Also, since less than 50 percent of crimes are ever reported to police and only approximately 20 percent of those are ever solved, there is no way to measure the relationship between convicted criminal behavior and actual criminal behavior. Eysenck states that "criminal conduct is clearly a kind of human behavior, circumscribed and defined by social rules, and as such not directly inheritable" (1983, p. 58).

The most recent studies of twins have found that genetic factors account for a large percentage of the variance in characteristics generally related to antisocial behavior. However, these studies found that environmental factors also in-

> **Box 4.2**
>
> ## Twins Reared Apart Meet
>
> When Jim Lewis was in his late thirties, he first met his identical twin brother, Jim Springer. What was it like to meet a twin from whom one was separated at a few weeks of age and who one had not seen for 39 years? Springer describes it as if "we'd known each other all our lives and we'd just been gone a hell of a long time" (p. 50).
>
> The "Jim Twins," as they were dubbed by the media, found astounding parallels and similarities in their lives. They had each been married twice—once to a woman named Linda and once to a woman named Betty. They each had named one of their sons James Allan (or Alan) and had owned a dog named Toy. Both men chained-smoked Salem cigarettes, had a workshop in the basement where they made miniature furniture, drove Chevrolets, and had a tree in their yard with a white bench around it. They also had high blood pressure, chewed their fingernails, disliked baseball, liked stock car racing, and were apolitical. In addition, the Jim Twins suffered from migraine headaches that commenced at approximately the same time in their lives.
>
> The media publicity surrounding the reunion of the Jim Twins brought them to the attention of a psychologist at the University of Minnesota, Thomas Bouchard. Subsequent testing of the Jim Twins astonished the scientist. One test of personality was so similar for the two that Bouchard described it as being like the testing of one person at two different times. The similarities were also apparent in the Jim Twins' intelligence, attitudes, and interests. Even their brain waves were strikingly similar.
>
> Bouchard and his colleagues began to study other sets of identical twins who were raised apart and found as many behavioral and medical similarities as with the Jim Twins.
>
> ◆
>
> Are the similarities entirely genetic? How could heredity influence the choice of names for children and dogs? Is it possible that twins raised together try to emphasize their differences such that twins raised apart become more similar than twins raised together? How much influence do hereditary factors have on behavior and personality?

Source: D. D. Jackson, "Reunion of Identical Twins, Raised Apart, Reveals Some Astonishing Similarities," *Smithsonian* 11 (10, 1980): 48–56.

fluence these characteristics (Pedersen et al. 1988, Rose et al. 1988, Rowe 1986, Tellegen et al. 1988, Walters & White 1989).

The debate over the relative significance of genetic versus environmental factors in predicting criminal behavior continues. There is little doubt that genetic factors account for some variance in antisocial behavior. But, as Stanovich states, "whatever a person's heredity, he or she is not 'destined' to become a criminal;

everything depends on the interaction of the hereditary factors with the environment" (1986, p. 102). The same personality factors and body build found in delinquents can be found in athletes, police officers, parachute troopers, or others who are active and take risks. The personality characteristics are a predisposition to act in specific ways, not an inherent criminality. The expression of the personality characteristics is influenced by environmental factors.

Research on Adopted Children

Another method used to assess the differential impact of genetic and environmental factors is adoption studies. This method compares the rate of criminal behavior in adopted children to their biological family and their adoptive family. The assumption is that adoptive families influence behavior through environmental or external variables and biological families influence behavior genetically. One of the best known adoption studies (Crowe 1972) compared 52 children of inmate mothers who were given up for adoption to a matched control group. The results indicated that the children of inmate mothers had a greater number of arrests than the control group. Read A HAPPY? REUNION for a description of an adopted child reunited with his father.

The few studies of adopted children that have been done are fraught with methodological problems (Bartol 1980, Walters & White 1989). The adopted child is usually matched to the adoptive parents on the basis of the child's biological and socioeconomic background. This procedure confounds all studies attempting to isolate the environmental from the genetic influences on behavior. Because of this matching, the adopted child is similar to the adopted parents on some of the variables that are assumed to be randomly assigned. In addition, there is a good deal of variation in length of time spent with biological parents prior to adoption.

Sociological Theories of Criminal Behavior

Sociological explanations for criminal behavior have dominated the criminal justice literature during most of the 20th century. These theories postulate that the causes of criminal behavior can be found in the social or cultural context. Explanations emphasize the group, rather than the individual, as the motivation for criminal activity. Sociological theories generally are classified into three major categories: strain or structural theories, subcultural theories, and control theories.

Strain or Structural Theories

Strain or structural theories of criminal behavior are based on the assumption that people within a society value the same rewards and benefits, such as material possessions, but that these rewards and benefits are not equally distributed among the members of society. There are some people who receive few, if any, of the rewards available in society, putting them under the strain of deprivation. When

> **Box 4.3**
>
> **A Happy? Reunion**
>
> Shortly after his birth, Robert Magoon's parents split up and he was separated from his father. Most of Robert's formative years were spent in foster homes, until he ran away from the last one at 14. Robert's father, Michael, searched many years for his son and then happened upon him in a most unusual setting. Michael Magoon was in jail in the Santa Clara County Jail for robbery charges when his son was incarcerated for allegedly violating his parole on a burglary charge. Despite the unpleasant surroundings, the father and son were happy to be reunited, planning activities together when they were freed. They also hoped to find Robert's older brother whom neither had seen in years.

Source: "Father, Son Separated Years Ago Reunite in California Jail," *The Florida Times-Union* (June 29, 1989), p. A–19.

people cannot obtain the rewards they desire through conventional means, they seek alternative methods. If no legitimate way of obtaining society's rewards are available, these people are likely to obtain the rewards through illegal means (Warren & Hindelang 1979).

Merton
Merton (1957) theorized that people have the same goals, but social structure limits the means by which people can attain those goals. By limiting the means for obtaining goals while maintaining the ideal of monetary success, anomie or normlessness is created in society. The common goals and the social structure interact to exert pressure on some people to be deviant. This pressure is particularly evident in the lower socioeconomic classes.

Merton enumerated five types of behavior people adopt under the pressure of social structure: 1) **The Innovator** accepts the goals of society but not the socially acceptable means of achieving these goals. Merton used the robber baron as an illustration of this type of person. 2) **The Ritualist** is the reverse of the innovator. This is someone who accepts the means by which people are supposed to achieve goals, but not the goals themselves. The bureaucrat is typical of the ritualist. 3) **The Rebel** rejects and accepts both the goals and the means of attaining them at the same time. This is the person who wants to change society, the revolutionary. 4) **The Retreatist** withdraws from society, rejecting both the goals of society and the means of attaining the goals. This person drops out of society and is exemplified by the addict. 5) **The Conformist** accepts both the goals of society and the socially acceptable means of obtaining these goals.

Reactance Theory
Cohen (1955) postulated that there is a continual conflict between the values of the middle class and the working-class youth on whom these values are imposed.

Many of these values, such as ambition, rationality, manners, skills, responsibility, personal control, and nonviolence, conflict with the noncompetitive norms of the working class, who are not achievement oriented.

Cohen contends that schools are "middle-classified" and thus use middle-class standards to measure all students. Working-class youths are at a disadvantage and do poorly in school. Using the idea of reaction formation from psychoanalytic theory, Cohen explains that working-class youths reject and scorn the values of the middle class by adopting opposing values. Cohen contends these youths do not completely accept their new values. They often hide, even from themselves, the fact that they have internalized the middle-class values they publicly reject.

Working-class youths' reactions to the demands of the middle-class values lead to the development of peer-oriented delinquent subcultures, or gangs. Often gang behavior is purposeless, negativistic, and malicious with no apparent goal.

Differential Opportunity Theory

Cloward and Ohlin (1960) expanded Merton's theory to consider the influence of subcultures. These theorists centered their attention on adolescent male delinquents in lower-class neighborhoods, particularly those in large urban centers. It was hypothesized that these delinquents were suffering from the strain of deprivation. As members of the lower socioeconomic stratum of society, these adolescent boys had their aspirations blocked by barriers in society, leading them to become frustrated. The boys would then feel justified in using illegal means to achieve their material goals because they did not have enough opportunity to achieve their aspirations in a legitimate manner. Available subcultures gave them the opportunity to learn deviant behavior. In addition, there was social pressure to conform to the deviant subcultures.

Cloward and Ohlin described three delinquent subcultures: 1) the **criminal subculture,** which emphasized theft; 2) the **conflict subculture,** which centered on violence; and 3) the **retreatist subculture,** which focused on withdrawal. They describe the adolescent delinquent as an innovator in Merton's classification of behavior, which is someone who accepts the goals of society and then uses unacceptable means for attaining them. Since legitimate methods are lacking in impoverished neighborhoods, alternative means are sought through the delinquent subcultures.

Conflict Theory

Conflict theory assumes that society is constantly changing and is composed of groups which are continually interacting and struggling with each other to improve their own positions. This theory postulates that crime is a result of the interaction and struggle between competing groups. Turk (1969) focuses his attention on how those in power (authorities) maintain their authority by keeping a balance between coercion and consensus. The people in power are the ones who determine what is legal and illegal, and they enforce their beliefs on the subjects. Some members of society are constrained by those in power. The people who are constrained either become acceptors of or resistors to the laws. The theory deals with the types of conflict which are criminalized and the ones which are not criminalized. Specific groups of people, e.g., young black males, are more likely to become resistors. Those who resist the norms are categorized as criminals. Resistance to norms becomes criminal due to the social differences between those in power and those who are subject to them, and the relative power and organization of the two groups. According to Turk, however, illegal behavior is really an indication that those in authority have failed to enforce the norms that they set.

Subcultural Theories

Some theories use subcultures, defined as cultures within a culture, as a basis for explanations of criminal behavior. These theories propose some subgroups have values, standards, and norms that are in opposition to those of the larger society, which actually encourage and support criminal behavior. Most theories based on subcultures focus on low socioeconomic groups or working-class youths in urban areas. They maintain these are the youths who have difficulty coping with the frustration of deprivation and learn criminal behavior by associating with members of a criminal subculture. Subcultural theories of deviance date back to work done by Thrasher (1927) on gang behavior. This research proposed that gangs grew out of childhood play groups, the members of which became closer in reaction to the disapproval of adults. As they grew older, the gang members became more cohesive as a result of conflicts with rival gangs. The gang became the adolescents' primary group, giving support and encouragement to them when they were getting no satisfaction from school or home life. Gang membership became a status symbol and meetings were an opportunity for learning new criminal behavior.

Focal Concerns

Walter B. Miller (1958) proposed that lower-class values cluster around the "focal concerns" of toughness, excitement, trouble, autonomy, and fate. These lower-class values are in direct contrast to the middle-class values of ambition and delayed gratification. People raised in a lower-class culture will internalize the values and norms of that subculture which make them likely to violate the middle-class norms. The criminal code reflects the values and standards of the middle class, whereas delinquent behavior is said to be a direct demonstration of lower-class focal concerns.

Miller's conception of gangs is in direct contrast to that of Cohen. While Cohen contends gangs are purposeless, Miller maintains they are functional, providing a means for youth to attain status and acceptance.

Control Theory

Control theory postulates that delinquency and criminal behavior are a result of a weakening of the individual's bond to conventional society. Hirschi (1969) contends people are born without any concepts of morality or restraints against inappropriate behavior.

Hirschi proposes there are social control mechanisms which constrain an individual to behave in socially acceptable ways. These social control mechanisms are the bonds holding the individual to conventional society. If a person has a strong bond to society, that individual is likely to conform to the norms of society. However, if the bond is weakened or broken, the person will no longer conform and is more likely to violate the norms.

Hirschi describes four elements of an individual's bond to society. The first element is *attachment*. Attachment refers to the affection the individual has toward others in conventional society. If this bond is strong, the person values the opinions and expectations others have of him and is less likely to violate the norms of society. Hirschi considers this element to be the primary deterrent to criminal behavior.

Commitment to conventional behavior is the second element of the bond. Commitment refers to the amount of time and energy the individual has invested in socially approved activities, such as obtaining an education. The greater the individual's commitment to society's norms, the less the individual is likely to risk her investment by violating the standards of society.

The third element of the bond is the individual's *involvement* in conventional activities. The more active the individual is in socially approved pastimes, the less time and energy he has to devote to nonconventional activities.

The individual's *belief* that people should obey the rules of society is the fourth element of the bond. If an individual believes that society has a right to impose rules on members of society, she is more likely to obey those rules.

The four elements of the bond described by Hirschi work interdependently. If a person has one of them, she or he tends to have them all. In the same manner, if one bond is weakened, usually others are also weakened. As the bond to society decreases, the possibility of criminal behavior increases. The weakening of the bond does not mandate criminal behavior but rather makes it possible.

Social-Psychological Theories of Criminal Behavior

Social-psychological theories of delinquency and crime take into consideration both the individual and society as well as interactions between them. Control theory is really a social-psychological theory of criminal behavior. This theory emphasizes the absence or breakdown of the bonds between the individual and society, taking into account both the psychology of the individual and the social class.

Social Learning Theory

Socialization, described in detail in the last chapter, is based on social learning theory. Therefore, this section will be limited to a brief description of the different theoretical viewpoints about this theory. Social learning theory contends that all behavior is learned and maintained through reinforcement, and delinquent and criminal behaviors are developed through the same psychological processes as appropriate behavior. If a behavior is not reinforced or is followed by a negative reaction, it is less likely to be learned.

B. F. Skinner (1969) and his disciples explain behavior entirely in terms of external forces. They do not believe that internal variables play a significant role in learning. However, other social learning theorists feel this view is too simple; people are not empty boxes completely controlled by reinforcements. People are actively involved in problem solving, selectively perceiving, organizing, and coding information. In order to understand criminal behavior, one must look at the individual's cognitions, perceptions, and values. Bartol states, "criminal behaviors are acquired by daily living, in accordance with the principles of learning, and are stored and organized in a unique fashion in the individual's brain" (1980, p. 4). He further asserts that criminal behavior is not due to personality traits but to acquired responses for certain circumstances. Whether the person uses these responses depends on how he assesses the situation, what he expects to gain, and what happened to him in previous events.

Rotter (1954, 1972) focuses on the cognitions and expectations of the individual concerning the consequences of her behavior. The likelihood of a behavior occurring is determined by the expectancies of the outcomes and the individual's perceptions of the values of the outcomes. According to this viewpoint, the criminal selects the behavior which she considers the most effective one for that situation.

Bandura (1973) introduced the concept of modeling into social learning theory. Bartol (1980) illustrates the effectiveness of modeling by pointing out that every adult in the U.S. "knows" how to shoot a gun. Even though most people have never handled a gun, they know how to hold it, point it, and pull the trigger. They learned this behavior, even if they were never reinforced for acquiring it, by observing it frequently in films and television. Bandura has found a model's behavior is more likely to be copied if the model is rewarded for the behavior and less likely to be copied if the model is punished. Children learn right from wrong by modeling others, for example, their parents. By observing a number of experiences, children develop the ability to anticipate the consequences of a behavior without actually performing it. Behavior is maintained by expectancies of potential gain.

Modeling and reinforcement are major factors in the development of criminal conduct (Hogan & Jones 1983). Antisocial and delinquent behaviors are produced by contingencies in the situation. For example, delinquent behavior might be the result of intermittent reinforcement the youth receives through the attention he gets from his parents when he is delinquent. Even though his parents are very angry with him, they may pay so little attention to him at other times that even their anger is reinforcing. In addition, the youth's friends might reinforce his behavior by showing how impressed they are with his description of his exploits (Warren & Hindelang 1979).

Another possible explanation for the development of delinquent behavior is the lack of appropriate consequences following the behavior. The parents may not set contingencies for the youth, or, if contingencies are set, the parents may not impose them as threatened. In other words, inappropriate behavior does not lead to negative consequences. However, parents need to be careful about the negative consequences imposed, especially the use of physical punishment. This is because antisocial and aggressive behaviors can result from excessive or inappropriate physical punishment.

Differential Association Theory

Sutherland based differential association theory on social learning theory as an explanation of criminal behavior. This theory states that criminal behavior is learned in the same way any other type of behavior is learned (Sutherland & Cressey 1974). Both legal and illegal behaviors are learned through interactions with associates and a systematic exposure to their behavior. Thus, the type of behavior one learns is determined by how often and how long one associates with a particular type of person. Behavior is further influenced by the point in development during which these interactions occur and the significance of the contacts. Basically, the theory states if a person has greater access to models of delinquent behavior and less access to examples of nondelinquent behavior, then the person is more likely to learn the delinquent behavior. By the same token, someone who has greater access to nondelinquent models and less access to delinquent behavior is more likely to learn the nondelinquent behavior.

People learn criminal behavior by observing and modeling other people within small intimate groups. Attitudes, values, motives, and rationalizations, as well as specific techniques for committing crimes, are learned through interactions with others. By interacting with members of a criminal subculture, people learn and internalize the values of that subculture. For an example of the impact of differential association, see CHILDREN GROWING UP IN A NEIGHBORHOOD WITH DRUGS.

Differential Conditionability

British psychologist Hans J. Eysenck theorizes criminal behavior has both biological and psychological components. He maintains personality traits are inherited and these characteristics interact with environmental forces to produce criminal behavior (Eysenck 1983, Eysenck & Gudjonsson 1989). People are not born criminals but are born with a genetic predisposition toward antisocial behavior or criminal behavior.

Eysenck (1977) postulates criminal behavior is a result of an interaction between biological and social factors. He suggests people differ biologically in the characteristics of their brains or nervous systems. These differences account for the fact that some people appear to be less susceptible to conditioning than others. Behavior is a result of prior conditioning that is intensified by emotionality, a personality characteristic that is inherited. Both positive and negative behaviors are formed by prior conditioning.

Since people internalize the standards of society through conditioning (in other words, develop a conscience), those who are not easily conditioned are less able to acquire the ability to abide by the rules of society. Eysenck argues that criminals are less able to be conditioned than the average person, which accounts for criminals' deviant behavior.

> **Box 4.4**
>
> ### Children Growing Up in a Neighborhood With Drugs
>
> Kids had been playing the game for years. But the outside world was shocked when it was discovered that children from 6 to 12 were playing at drug dealing. The game was uncovered when a tackle box with "pretend" drugs and sophisticated records of "drug" transactions was found in a small town in Pennsylvania. It was an unlikely place to find children who played at drug dealing. Lebanon, in the Pennsylvania Dutch country, has only 25,000 residents. The director of the schools' curriculum maintains that the drug of choice for most high school kids is beer. But not on South 12th Street, where real drugs are in abundance. In fact, the drug transactions are so frequent and so open that one corner is referred to as a "drive-in drug store." It was in a small, dilapidated playground on South 12th Street that the tackle box was found.
>
> The tackle box contained small plastic bags of sugar labeled by size and cost: "Small half Baggie .55 (CT). Jars $3." Records of the transactions were kept in a childish handwriting on sheets of paper labeled "cocain." Bags of grass clippings simulated marijuana. The box held pennies and dimes used in the transactions.
>
> ♦
>
> How did the children learn about drug transactions? Are these children likely to use drugs when they are older? Are the children likely to stop playing the game because their parents tell them to stop? Does this behavior support the differential association theory?

Source: "Children Find New Game: Pretend Drug Dealing," *The Florida Times-Union* (August 12, 1989), p. A–15.

According to Eysenck there are three components of the personality that are related to criminal behavior: extraversion, neuroticism, and psychoticism. Each of these components is at one end of a continuum, with the opposite to that characteristic at the other end. The average person falls in the middle of each continuum.

The extravert is described as a sociable and optimistic person who is impulsive and easily loses his temper, becoming aggressive. At the other end of the continuum is the quiet and reserved introvert who does not like excitement, change, or social activities (Eysenck & Rachman 1965).

Neuroticism, or emotionality, refers to the intensity of emotional reactions. A person who is high on this variable reacts intensely and lastingly to stress, even low stress. This is an anxious and moody person who is sensitive to slights and often complains of physical ailments, a person who is very likely to develop phobias and obsessions. The stable person is at the other end of the continuum on this dimension. Eysenck considers the neurotic extravert to be the person most likely to commit crimes.

Eysenck defines his third dimension, psychoticism, differently from the clinical definition of a psychotic. The person who is high on psychoticism is cold, cruel, unemotional, and socially insensitive. In addition, the person dislikes and is hostile toward other people. The psychoticism dimension of the personality has been found to correlate with criminality in people of all ages and under varied conditions (Eysenck & Gudjonsson 1989).

Antisocial behavior is usually characteristic of someone who is extraverted, emotionally unstable, and high on psychoticism. This person finds the environment to be lacking in stimulation. Because of feelings of boredom, such a person will look for more excitement, leading to antisocial behavior. This is a person who does not have a strong conscience (Eysenck 1983, Eysenck & Gudjonsson 1989).

Bartol maintains that research has "been highly supportive of Eysenck's general theory of personality" (1980, p. 34). Neuroticism, extraversion, and psychoticism have been found to correlate with criminal and antisocial behavior in a number of studies (Allsopp 1976, Feldman 1977, Pedersen et al. 1988, Smith & Smith 1977). However after a comprehensive review of research conducted through 1971, Passingham (1972) concluded that most of the experimental designs were flawed and inappropriate control groups were used. Despite these limitations, Bartol (1980) feels the research does not disprove the theory. However, attempts to predict criminal behavior based on psychoticism, extraversion, and neuroticism have had mixed results. Some studies support the theory, while others are inconclusive or do not sustain it.

Psychological Theories of Criminal Behavior

While sociologists study social influences on group behavior, psychologists concentrate on the behavior of the individual and factors which influence this behavior, particularly personality attributes. Both lay people and criminologists are confused about the differences between psychiatric theories, psychoanalytic theory, and psychological theories. Psychiatric theories of criminal behavior generally have been based on the assumption that criminals are sick people. These theories have become outdated and fallen out of use (Bartol 1980); thus they will not be discussed here. Psychological theories address how people learn criminal behavior and how this behavior is maintained and modified. Psychoanalytic theory is a personality theory and could be classified as either a psychiatric or a psychological theory but will be discussed with the psychological theories.

Psychoanalytic Theory

Freud's psychoanalytic theory looks at the individual as both a social and a biological being. People have basic needs which they try to satisfy while dealing with the current problems in their lives. Freud postulated the personality is composed of three parts: the id, the ego, and the superego. The id is composed of the drives or urges that a person has from birth, the two basic drives being a sexual drive and an aggressive drive. The rational part of the personality is the ego, consisting of a series of functions which help the individual keep in touch with reality. The superego is composed of values and is somewhat equivalent to the conscience. These three parts of the personality are in conflict over control of the personality. Psychoanalytic theory proposes that moral conduct, which is largely unconscious, is developed through relations with parents. This theory emphasizes the importance of childhood experiences in the development of both moral character and adult personality.

Freud wrote very little about criminal behavior. However, many of his followers did. These theorists explained criminal behavior by looking for unconscious causes, usually in the criminal's childhood. Basically, most psychoanalytic theorists think delinquency and criminal behavior are due to a lack of personal control resulting from parental neglect or child-rearing practices, or the illegal behavior is a symptom of difficulties the individual is having with adjustment (Warren & Hindelang 1979).

One psychoanalytic explanation of male criminal behavior says it is a result of poor parent–child relationships. The father was either absent or not effective, depriving the child of affection, discipline, or both. Thus, the child did not internalize an appropriate standard of behavior or conscience. In addition, the child did not have a male father figure to model and did not develop a clear sex-role identification. Therefore, as an adult, the male has an inadequate conscience and is defensive concerning his masculinity. Hogan and Jones (1983) criticize this theory because it is based on the Oedipus complex, which they call a "piece of theoretical nonsense." However, even they agree that psychoanalytic theory gives us some insights into criminal behavior.

Other psychoanalytic theorists approach the explanation of criminal behavior from a different perspective (Aichhorn 1935, Friedlander 1947). These theorists maintain that a child who has difficulties in the first few years of development does not develop a strong ego and is unable to control her impulses. This child retains the pleasure orientation of an infant and does not accept reality, which leads to impulsive or antisocial behavior which can be potentially criminal.

Warren and Hindelang (1979) classify psychoanalytic interpretations of criminal behavior into five categories. The first category describes criminal behavior as a form of neurosis, a disturbance in behavior that has psychological origins. This interpretation proposes that different people manifest their neurosis in different ways—some people avoid confined places and others shoplift.

Another category of explanation says people commit crimes because they want to be punished. These criminals have feelings of guilt and think the punishment will remove their guilt feelings. The third psychoanalytic explanation proposes some people use criminal behavior to gain attention and as a way to obtain gratification of their drives and needs which are unmet in the home.

A fourth interpretation states that delinquent behavior is a manifestation of a traumatic event which was so overwhelming it interfered with the person's personality development. The person is not aware of the experience since the actual memory of this traumatic event has been repressed. A fifth psychoanalytic explanation of criminal behavior is that it is an expression of displaced aggression;

for example, a man is angry at his boss for reprimanding him. This man cannot retaliate against the boss without jeopardizing his job, but he can displace his aggression and assault a stranger in a bar. See SON OF SAM for a psychoanalytic explanation of a mass murderer.

Moral Development Theories

Moral development theories are based on the assumption that people grow and mature in their moral judgment in sequential developmental stages. People vary in how far they progress through the different stages. The amount of progression attained is theorized to be related to the moral behavior of the individual.

In the 1950s, a group of psychologists proffered the interpersonal maturity theory as a guide for understanding the personalities of offenders and determining the most effective means of treating them (Sullivan, Grant & Grant 1957). This theory identifies seven successive levels of interpersonal maturity. According to this theory, youths are not delinquent because of their immaturity; both delinquents and nondelinquents can be at any point on a continuum of interpersonal maturity. However, the interpersonal maturity stages could be used to assess the meaning of the individual's delinquency. Intervention studies in the 1950s and early 1960s attempted to match delinquents at different levels of maturity with the appropriate intervention strategies. The studies indicate this intervention method was effective in reducing delinquent behavior (Grant & Grant 1959, Warren 1976, 1983).

Kohlberg

The best known of the moral development theories is Kohlberg's (1964) moral development theory. This theory postulates that the developing child progresses in a regular sequence of stages toward moral maturity, although few attain the highest level, even in adulthood. During each progressive stage of development, the person's ways of understanding the world from a social and moral perspective becomes more complex. Successive stages of development integrate the insights gained in earlier stages. People differ markedly in their moral judgment depending on their developmental stages. These differences in moral orientation are related to moral or immoral behavior, and marked differences in the form of moral orientation may exist between serious offenders and nonoffenders (Jennings, Kilkenny & Kohlberg 1983).

Kohlberg identifies three levels of moral judgment development. In the **Preconventional Level** of development, people think of rules and social expectations as being something outside themselves. This level of development is typical of children between the ages of 9 and 11, as well as many adolescent and adult offenders. The average adolescent and adult are in the **Conventional Level** of moral development and have accepted and internalized the values and rules of society. A few adults over the age of 20 have attained the **Post Conventional Level.** People within this level define values on the basis of self-determined principles, scrutinizing societal rules and norms on the basis of universal moral rights, duties, and principles.

Box 4.5

Son of Sam

From July 29, 1976, until the following summer, the "Son of Sam" stalked the streets of Brooklyn, the Bronx, and Queens, shooting young people in parked cars at night. Six young people were killed and another seven wounded. His victims, young women and their dates, were unknown to their attacker. The "Son of Sam" wrote to the newspapers, claiming to be thirsty for more victims. Frightened young women in New York cut or changed the color of their hair so as not to fit the description of the victims—young women with long brown hair.

It was not until August of 1977 that the police had any leads. Among the cars ticketed in the vicinity of the most recent shooting was one registered to David Berkowitz. Berkowitz was described as "a pudgy man with curly black hair and a sweet smile" (p. A–19). When the police stopped him at his apartment in Yonkers, Berkowitz said, "You got me. How come it took you so long?" The gun used in the killings was found in his car and his fingerprints matched those on the letters sent to newspapers.

At the time of his arrest, Berkowitz claimed that he had killed at the direction of a 6,000-year-old demon. This demon, personified by Berkowitz's neighbor, Sam Carr, issued orders to "Son of Sam" through Carr's dog. However, court-appointed psychiatrists contended that Berkowitz was competent to stand trial, and Berkowitz pled guilty.

Dr. David Abrahamsen, a psychiatrist, examined Berkowitz after his arrest and corresponded with him in prison. He explained Berkowitz's violence as a result of reactions to his mother. Berkowitz's biological mother gave him up for adoption because he was illegitimate. The murderous drives began after Berkowitz had a reunion with his mother and she explained the circumstances of the adoption. Abrahamsen contended that Berkowitz stalked young women in cars to get even with his mother for not wanting him. Berkowitz told Abrahamsen that his mother was sitting in those cars with his biological father. Berkowitz maintained that many unwanted children are born because of "careless sexual encounters in automobiles" (p. A–19).

Abrahamsen argued that Berkowitz felt such guilt for his crimes that he purposely parked in front of a fire hydrant the night of the last murder. By doing so, Berkowitz demonstrated that he wanted to be caught and punished.

◆

Should Berkowitz have pled not guilty by reason of insanity? Would this defense have been accepted by a jury?

Source: " 'Son of Sam' Remains Mystery 10 Years after Stalking Lovers," *The Florida Times-Union* (April 19, 1987), p. A–19.

Kohlberg's theory stimulated research measuring the relationship between moral reasoning and delinquent behavior. Jennings, Kilkenny, and Kohlberg reviewed thirteen studies and found delinquents consistently demonstrate less-mature moral reasoning than matched nondelinquent controls. They conclude the "overwhelming weight of the evidence is that moral judgment is, at least, a significant correlate of some types of delinquency" (1983, p. 300). They do not propose that lower levels of moral development cause delinquency, but rather that advanced reasoning "has an insulating effect against delinquency" (p. 311).

Most of the studies finding a relationship between moral reasoning and delinquency used institutionalized delinquents as subjects and compared them to a control group of average adolescents. As Morash (1981) points out, delinquents with lower levels of reasoning might be more likely to be arrested and incarcerated, accounting for the differences found between the two groups. Other studies using self-report measures of delinquency have not found a relationship between moral judgment and delinquency (Emler, Winton & Heather 1977, Morash 1981). Thus the debate continues, and no firm conclusions can be drawn about the relationship between moral development and delinquent behavior.

The Criminal Personality

Yochelson and Samenow developed a theory of "the criminal personality" (1976) based on 15 years of clinical work and interviews with adjudicated criminals. These researchers felt criminals had a unique "thinking pattern" which differentiated them from the honest members of society. Criminals are defined by this thinking pattern rather than by conviction of a crime. The central aspect of this pattern of thinking is the person's irresponsibility. Irresponsibility is manifested by avoidance of work and obligations, including the obligation to obey the law. The criminal thinking pattern is a concrete and simplistic one seen in a person who is inconsiderate and selfish. The extreme criminal develops these cognitive patterns while very young, thus shaping his life of crime. However, he chooses his criminal behavior consciously.

This theory occasioned a great deal of debate. However, there are enough methodological limitations to the study to raise doubts about its conclusions (Nietzel 1979).

Women in Crime

Perhaps you have noticed that the majority of theories, particularly the sociological and psychological ones, have addressed only male criminality. Does that mean women never commit crimes? No, but it does reflect the fact that the vast majority of crimes are committed by males. The differential in crime rate for males and females has been about the same since the 1930s and is particularly apparent when comparing adult offenders and more serious offenses (Wilson & Herrnstein 1985).

In the last two decades, female criminals and the crimes they commit have become a highly publicized focus of attention for both the popular media and serious researchers. This increased attention can be attributed to an apparent growth in female criminal activity, particularly violent offenses, as well as a general interest in the changing role of women in society.

The new interest in women's criminal behavior has created a controversy concerning its etiology and manifestation. One of the earliest treatises on women in crime (Adler 1975) contends that women are not only committing more offenses, but these offenses are becoming more serious and aggressive. Some observers maintain that the criminal behavior of women is beginning to resemble male criminal behavior—it is becoming more violent and more masculine (Adler 1975, Noblit & Burcart 1976). Adler attributes the purported increase in aggressive offenses by women to their increasingly aggressive roles in society. This viewpoint is supported by a number of criminologists (Noblit & Burcart 1976), but is by no means universally accepted. Adler's view of women's involvement in crime is hotly contested by other researchers, who contend the absolute number of women committing aggressive offenses may be increasing, but the percentage of women committing such crimes has remained constant (Klein & Kress 1976, Norland & Shover 1977, Simon 1975, Steffensmeier 1980). One prominent authority (Simon 1975) states women are becoming involved in more serious crimes, although others (Norland & Shover 1977) contend that there is no real change in the crime patterns of women. However, the general consensus is that there is an increase in female criminal activity, but it is primarily within less-aggressive areas (e.g., fraud, embezzlement, forgery, and counterfeiting). See THE FAMILY BUSINESS: A WOMAN'S OCCUPATION for an example of female criminal activity.

Among theorists reporting a rise in the female crime rate, many attribute the increase to the women's liberation movement (Noblit & Burcart 1976, J. Q. Wilson 1975). Support for this contention is based primarily on correlational data; the purported rise in female involvement in violent crime parallels the development of the women's liberation movement. The assumption on which this contention is based is that women are committing aggressive crimes because of their more liberated sex roles. This assumption is contrary to much research on women offenders, which usually describes them as being traditional in their sex roles (Rasche & Foley 1978, Steffensmeier 1980).

However, describing female offenders as either traditional or liberated in their sex roles is too simplistic; both the motivation and the behavior involved in criminal acts are too complex to be classified so easily. Female offenders, as female nonoffenders, are a heterogeneous group. Attempting to fit all female offenders into a single classification confuses, rather than clarifies, any description. An indepth study of the sex-role orientation of violent female offenders does not support the relationship between a liberated view of women's roles and the commission of violent offenses by women (Bunch, Foley & Urbina 1983). The women who were incarcerated for violent crimes were closer to the general female population in terms of feminine characteristics than they were to women who were involved in atypical careers, such as athletes and scientists. In addition, these

> **Box 4.6**
>
> **The Family Business: A Woman's Occupation**
>
> When S. L. Kimbrough was arrested on grand theft charges, she did not have to worry about what her mother would think. Ms. Kimbrough's mother had been in prison since January, when she was sentenced to 10 years for embezzling $168,000 from the insurance company where she worked, Mobile America Corp. This was not her mother's first conviction. In 1981, Ms. Kimbrough's mother had been sentenced to 13 months in prison for stealing $42,000 worth of food stamps while working for the welfare program that distributed them.
>
> Ms. Kimbrough's sister, Alicia Hartley, received a 6-month jail sentence for receiving illegal refund checks from her mother. A family friend and the godmother of Ms. Kimbrough's daughter, Rita Macon, also was a recipient of refund checks and received a 6-month sentence in jail.
>
> So Ms. Kimbrough was only following the family pattern when she was arrested for allegedly stealing more than $5,700 in cash and money orders while working as a teller for the Barnett Bank.

Source: S. Patterson, "Bank Teller Charged in Thefts," *The Florida Times-Union* (May 13, 1989), pp. A–3, A–5.

women demonstrated a relatively large extent of sex-role conformity. They were not as egalitarian or liberated in their attitudes toward women's rights as other female populations (e.g., college students). This is not to suggest that all of the violent female offenders were traditional in their views of women's roles. They were an essentially heterogeneous sample of women who cannot be classified under one rubric.

Thus there appears to be an increase in criminal activity by women, but it tends to be in the area of nonaggressive crimes. The new attention to the criminal activity of females will undoubtedly bring forth new theories focused on the female offender.

Summary

We have discussed several theories which attempt to explain the causes of criminal behavior. The theories are classified as: biological, sociological, psychological, and social-psychological theories. Each theory tends to focus on one aspect of criminal behavior or one segment of the criminal population. Even though no theory completely explains the causes of criminal behavior, each theory sheds some light on the issue and increases our understanding of criminal behavior. There are, of course, some theories which offer alternative explanations for the same behavior or segment of the criminal population. There is no universally accepted theory of criminal behavior.

Biological theories about criminal behavior center on physiological, hereditary, or genetic factors as explanations for the causes of criminal behavior. These theories postulate that there is some innate or biological condition in individuals which predisposes them to commit crimes. The first formal theory used to explain criminal behavior was based on biology. However, contradictory scientific evidence shattered this theory. In recent years, there has been a resurgence in interest in biological explanations of criminal behavior, but these newly developed biosocial and sociobiological theories are quite controversial.

Sociological explanations for criminal behavior have dominated the criminal justice literature during most of the 20th century. These theories postulate that the causes of criminal behavior can be found in the social or cultural context. Sociological theories generally are classified into three major categories: strain or structural theories, subcultural theories, and control theories.

Social-psychological theories of delinquency and crime take into consideration both the individual and society as well as interactions between them. Psychological theories address how people learn criminal behavior and how this behavior is maintained and modified.

Most theories explaining criminal behavior focus entirely on male criminals. In the last two decades, female criminals and the crimes they commit have come under scrutiny. This increased attention can be attributed to an apparent growth in female criminal activity, most of which is in the area of nonaggressive crimes.

5

Victims of Crime

Victimization
Public Views of the Victim
Victimology
The Risk of Victimization
Groups at High Risk of Victimization
The Impact of Crimes on Victims
Psychological Reactions
Changes in Expectations
Self-Blame
Learned Helplessness
Rape Victims
Robbery
Stockholm Syndrome
Who Suffers Most?
Coping with Victimization
Psychological Methods of Adjustment
Assistance in Coping with Victimization
The Process of Readjustment
Behavioral Methods of Adjustment
Summary

Victimization

For many years, the criminal justice system seemed to forget the existence of the crime victim and concentrated entirely on punishing or rehabilitating the offender. Even today, the primary function of the criminal justice system remains the protection of the interests of society and the government; interests of the victim are secondary, at best. The victim is often a powerless participant in the legal process, usually not informed of the developments in the case, or even notified if the case is dropped. Participation by the victim is necessary for prosecution of the case, since the victim is required to go to court and be available to give evidence. The time demands of participation in court proceedings can impose great hardships on the victims of crimes. But the convenience of the victim is not a primary consideration of the court system.

The inefficiency and unpredictability of the criminal justice system often cause the victim to suffer further. The victim might be called to court many times before the case is actually tried, and can spend hours waiting in the courtroom only to be told that the case has been postponed, dropped, or settled by means of a plea bargain. It is unusual for the victim of a crime to have any influence on the sentencing of the offender; the victim is not typically consulted about or notified of the sentence imposed. And the victim of even the most violent offense seldom, if ever, is notified when the offender is released from prison. See A FAMILY VICTIMIZED BY THE SYSTEM to read about the treatment of a victim's family.

Treatment of the victims of crime by the criminal justice system has not always been so callous. Prior to the American Revolution, the victim was the central concern of the criminal justice system. To a large extent, the victim could determine the fate of the offender. Any losses to the victim were repaid by the offender at three times their value (Karmen 1984). But for the next 200 years, the status of the victim steadily declined.

Public Views of the Victim

Ignored to a great extent by the criminal justice system, the victim is viewed with ambivalence by the public. Our competitive society with its emphasis on the survival of the fittest looks down on the victim as a "loser." Victims, who tend to be depressed, are avoided by the rest of society (Coates, Wortman & Abbey 1979). After being victimized by a crime, a person is often derided and pitied rather than shown empathy by an unconcerned society (Taylor, Wood & Lichtman 1983). Private citizens are more concerned about the impact of crime on society than the effect of an offense on the victim.

Why are people so harsh in their evaluations of victims? In his "just world" theory, Lerner (1970) postulates that people try to make sense out of the world and see justice in random happenings. In order to believe the world is just, people must think victims got what they deserved. If the negative events which occur in the world are perceived as random occurrences, then they could affect anyone. By believing the world is just, people feel they are protected from victimization if they are worthy and decent. In order to maintain their belief in a just world,

> **Box 5.1**
>
> **A Family Victimized by the System**
>
> The McCulloughs were a close-knit Catholic family living in a racially mixed lower-middle-class neighborhood in South Philadelphia when tragedy struck them. Danny McCullough, one of the six children, a mild-mannered, fun-loving 15-year-old, was shot. The black youth who shot Danny mistook him for one of a group of whites who had harassed him earlier in the evening.
>
> Soon the McCulloughs realized how powerless they were in dealing with the legal system. They attempted to donate their son's eyes and kidneys in order to give meaning to his death but were prevented from doing so. Removing the organs prior to death might give the killer a defense—he could claim that Danny died from the organ transplant, not the bullet, explained the police.
>
> Two days after the shooting the McCulloughs heard through the neighborhood grapevine that the killer had been arrested. Jim McCullough asked the police officer stationed by his son's hospital room about the arrest. He was told it was none of his business. When Jim exploded, the officer reluctantly confirmed the arrest.
>
> Danny died without his family being able to donate his organs. The family became acutely aware of how little the criminal justice system considered them when they were told of the upcoming trial. Once again, the family's source of information was rumor. The family never received official notice of the trial. In fact, during the 8 months following the murder of Danny, no one from the police or district attorney's office discussed the case with the family.
>
> The family went to court for the jury selection. While there, the prosecuting attorney told Jim that he would be asked to testify. It was necessary to verify that he had identified his son's body. But, because he would be a witness, Jim would not be allowed to attend the trial. Outraged, Jim refused and after some difficulty was given the right to hear the trial.
>
> There was never any doubt that Alphonso Geiger was guilty; he had confessed to the shooting. The trial was to determine if he was guilty of first- or third-degree murder, depending on premeditation. Alphonso's lawyers argued that since Alphonso's target was "any white," there was no premeditation in the murder of Danny McCullough. The jury decided that it was third-degree murder, a decision which shocked the McCulloughs. Although the family was not intent on revenge, they did want justice. They felt they were treated like criminals, not honest citizens.
>
> ♦
>
> Should the family of the victim have more say in the sentencing of the offender? Should the family of the victim be kept apprised of the investigation into the crime? Should the family of the victim be notified of the trial? What should the criminal justice system do to assist the family of the victim?

Source: D. Magee, *What Murder Leaves Behind: The Victim's Family* (New York: Dodd, Mead, 1983).

and their own security in it, people have to derogate the victims of crime. Therefore, nonvictimized people try to find a way to blame the victims of crime for their own suffering (Ryan 1971).

It is only within the past few years that the plight of the victim has once again become a concern. With the tremendous surge in crime during the 1960s and 1970s, news reporters, the criminal justice system, and criminologists began to take notice of victims. American society started to fear victimization and became more sympathetic toward those suffering from crimes committed against them.

Victimology

As a result of the recent focus on victims, a new area of study, victimology, has emerged. The word was coined by Benjamin Mendelson in 1963. As a newly developed subdiscipline, victimology does not have a strong theoretical base, but it has gathered a great deal of information about the victim. Victimology also studies the process of and reaction to victimization (Smith & Freinkel 1988).

Crimes are generally classified into crimes with victims and those without victims (known as victimless crimes). Crime committed against persons "scares the public, preoccupies the police, and captures the notice of politicians" (Karmen 1984, p. 2). These particularly frightening offenses include homicide, assault, robbery, and rape. It is the victims of these offenses who receive the attention of victimologists.

The police have been traditionally looked upon as the "gatekeepers" of the criminal justice system. They were the ones who determined who would be arrested and processed into the criminal justice system. However, the study of victimology has led many researchers to reevaluate this assumption. The victim is the first, and sometimes only, person aware of the commission of a crime. It is the victim, therefore, who determines whether the offense will ever be brought to the attention of the authorities. Fewer than half of the crimes committed are reported to the police. The people who report the crimes, usually the victims, are the true gatekeepers of the criminal justice system (Gottfredson & Gottfredson 1988).

The Risk of Victimization

Despite the news reports to the contrary, Karmen (1984) contends that the likelihood of being a victim is not extremely high. He cites as evidence one's chances of being robbed. During 1980 only seven people out of every 1,000 over the age of 12 were robbery victims, making the probability of being robbed during the year less than 0.7 percent. Although people worry about being victims of physical violence, the chance of being injured in a crime is half that of being injured in a car accident. In fact, fewer than one percent of households suffer the death of a member due to murder, suicide, or car accident. Table 5.1 indicates the probability of suffering any of a number of unfortunate experiences.

Chapter 5 ♦ Victims of Crimes

♦ **TABLE 5.1** Comparison of crime rates with rates of other life events. Table reprinted from *Report to the Nation on Crime and Justice* (1988, p. 24), U.S. Department of Justice.

How Do Crime Rates Compare with the Rates of Other Life Events?

Event	Rate per 1,000 Adults per Year
Accidental injury, all circumstances	242
Accidental injury at home	79
Personal theft	72
Accidental injury at work	68
Violent victimization	31
Assault (aggravated and simple)	24
Injury in motor vehicle accident	17
Death, all causes	11
Victimization with injury	10
Serious (aggravated) assault	9
Robbery	6
Heart disease death	4
Cancer death	2
Rape (women only)	2
Accidental death, all circumstances	0.5
Pneumonia/influenza death	0.3
Motor vehicle accident death	0.2
Suicide	0.2
Injury from fire	0.1
Homicide/legal intervention death	0.1
Death from fire	0.03

"Based on 1982–1984 data, but there is little variation in rates from year to year" (p. 24).

While the risk of being victimized during any given year remains quite low, the likelihood of one of the negative life events occurring sometime during a lifetime are much greater. For example, Skogan and Maxfield (1981) estimate the lifetime chances of being robbed at about 50 percent, a great deal larger probability than the 0.7 percent cited by Karmen (1984). And the Report to the Nation on Crime and Justice (1988) states that "at current crime rates, almost everyone will be a victim of crime during his or her lifetime" (p. 29). Table 5.2 indicates the likelihood of being a victim over a lifetime.

Groups at High Risk of Victimization

While the debate continues over the actual probability of victimization, there is little disagreement that members of some segments of our society are at much greater risk of being victimized than other groups. The likelihood of being victimized varies by race, age, sex, and marital status.

♦ **TABLE 5.2** Percent of persons who will be victimized by crimes. Table reprinted from the *Report to the Nation on Crime and Justice* (1988, p. 29), U.S. Department of Justice.

What is the Likelihood of Victimization over an Entire Lifetime?

	Percent of Persons who will be Victimized by Crime Starting at Age 12			
	Total	Number of Victimizations		
	One or More Victimizations	One	Two	Three or More
Violent crimes, total*				
Total population	83%	30%	27%	25%
Male	89	24	27	38
Female	73	35	23	14
White	82	31	26	24
Male	88	25	27	37
Female	71	36	22	13
Black	87	26	27	34
Male	92	21	26	45
Female	81	31	26	24

Note: Except where noted, includes attempts.
—Less than .5%
*Includes rape, robbery, and assault.

♦ **TABLE 5.3** Probability of lifetime murder victimization. Table reprinted from the *Report to the Nation on Crime and Justice* (1988, p. 28), U.S. Department of Justice.

Classification		Probability of Lifetime Murder Victimization
White	Male	1 out of 179
White	Female	1 out of 495
Black	Male	1 out of 30
Black	Female	1 out of 132

Race/Ethnicity

With the exception of personal larcenies, whites have less likelihood of being victimized than blacks and Hispanics. Blacks are at the greatest risk of victimization of any racial group, particularly for crimes of violence. Young black males have the highest rate of victimization and elderly white females the lowest (Akers et al. 1987). Table 5.3 indicates the lifetime probability of being a homicide victim for racial and sexual categories.

♦ **TABLE 5.4** Average annual victimization rates by age of victim and type of crime, 1980–1985. Table reprinted from the Bureau of Justice Statistics Special Report: *Elderly Victims* (November, 1987, p. 3), U.S. Department of Justice.

	Age of Victim			
Victimization Rate	12–24	25–49	50–64	65 and Older
Crimes of violence	67.5	34.0	11.3	6.0
Rape	2.0	.8	.1[a]	.1[a]
Robbery	11.4	6.0	3.4	2.7
Assault	54.2	27.1	7.8	3.2
Aggravated	18.4	9.1	2.7	1.0
Simple	35.8	18.0	5.1	2.3
Crimes of theft	126.5	82.4	46.1	22.3
Personal larceny with contact	3.5	2.8	2.8	3.1
Personal larceny without contact	123.0	79.6	43.4	19.2
Household crimes	371.4	242.6	164.4	102.7
Burglary	144.3	86.9	59.4	44.0
Household larceny	196.8	136.5	92.3	53.7
Motor vehicle theft	30.3	19.3	12.7	5.1

Note: The victimization rate is the annual average of the number of victimizations for 1980–85 per 1,000 persons or households in that age group. Detail may not add to total because of rounding.
[a]Average annual estimate is based on 10 or fewer sample cases; see Methodology.

Sex and Age

Females and the elderly feel more vulnerable to crime but in fact are much less likely to be victims than males and younger people (Akers et al. 1987, Gordon et al. 1980, Stinchcomb et al. 1980). The only crimes in which elderly people are more likely victims than younger people are having their pockets picked or their purses snatched. However, elderly women are in great fear of crime and their fear is not completely unfounded. Although the likelihood of victimization is smaller than other groups, elderly women are more vulnerable physically, and some young male offenders consider them such easy targets that they concentrate on them (Karmen 1984). Table 5.4 indicates the annual victimization rates by age and type of crime.

It is the least fearful and vulnerable members of our society who have the highest victimization rates. Young men are the most frequent victims of crime and have the greatest probability of being injured while being victimized. With the exception of rape and purse snatching, men in general are more likely than women to be victims of theft and violent crimes (Report to the Nation on Crime and Justice, 1991).

Marital Status

Those individuals who have never married or who are divorced are more likely to be victimized than are the married or widowed. These differences in victimization are probably due to life-style variables. Single and divorced people are more likely to go out alone, thus presenting a more vulnerable target to a potential offender. Married and widowed people are less likely to frequent places where singles congregate and where offenders may search for potential victims.

Offenders Known to the Victim

With the exception of murder and assault, most violent crimes are committed by strangers to the victim. For many years, about two-thirds of the homicides were committed by relatives, friends, or acquaintances of the victim (Hepburn & Voss 1970, Wong & Singer 1973). However, there is some evidence that this high proportion of homicides committed by persons known to the victim is decreasing (e.g., see Block 1977; Bureau of Justice Statistics, *Violent Crime in the United States,* 1991). Bartol (1980) explains the change in proportion of murderers knowing the victims by the increased use of firearms in the course of robberies leading to more deaths of strangers.

Almost half of all assaults are committed by people known to the victim. Women are more likely to be assaulted by acquaintances and relatives than men. And victims of both sexes are more likely to be seriously injured by an assailant who is a relative than one who is an acquaintance or stranger (Report to the Nation on Crime and Justice, 1988).

Income Level and Employment Status

The deprived members of society are at a higher risk of victimization than are the employed, the affluent, and the educated. With the exception of theft, which also plagues the high-income members of society, the poor, those with lower incomes, lower educational levels, the unemployed, and students are those most likely to be the victims of crime and violence. In addition, the economic impact is greater on the poor who are twice as likely as the wealthy to suffer property loss (Wright & Rossi 1981).

General Factors

There appears to be a pattern of victimization related to living area. People living in cities, in rental homes, and in the North and East have a greater probability of being victims of crime than do those living in rural areas and other parts of the country (Report to the Nation on Crime and Justice, 1991; Skogan 1979). There also appears to be specific locations within a city where a large proportion of crimes occur (Sherman, Gartin & Buerger 1989).

According to Karmen (1984), the most likely location for a theft or violence by strangers to occur is in a public place after dark. Frequenting these locations is closely tied to life-style and probably explains the increased vulnerability of the young male and decreased vulnerability of the elderly and married. Those who feel most vulnerable take the most precautions against crimes. Since the elderly are more frail and women tend to be weaker than men, they are more likely to avoid situations which are frightening or likely to result in violence. In contrast, the young male feels invulnerable and is not likely to curtail his activities out of concern for his own physical safety. Thus, he is more likely to travel alone, particularly at night, and to frequent locations which are more likely to be the stage for violent activity (Karmen 1984).

The Impact of Crimes on Victims

Most people think of the consequences of victimization as being the monetary loss of property or physical injury. While losses in these areas can be extensive, psychological damage far exceeds the loss of property and, in many cases, the physical hurt caused by a crime. Victims of violent and/or personal crimes experience deep psychological pain which creates changes in their belief systems and behavior.

Psychological Reactions

Victims of a disaster have similar reactions whether the trauma is a violent crime, natural catastrophe, terminal illness, or automobile accident. Bard and Sangrey (1979) identify a pattern exhibited by victims in reaction to crises. First the victim feels helpless and numb, is disorganized, and unable to function. The initial shock is replaced with emotional ups and downs, sleeplessness, loss of appetite, and concentration problems. Finally, the intense emotions of fear, anger, and guilt decrease. The victim can emerge from the crisis stronger than before by overcoming the reactions. However, some victims are never able to recover completely from the incident and continue to have negative reactions.

Victims of a trauma typically experience tremendous emotional turmoil, reacting with feelings of anxiety, low self-esteem, fear, depression, and helplessness (Friedman et al. 1982, Taylor et al. 1983). This group of symptoms, or syndrome, which occurs in reaction to traumatization is called the posttraumatic stress disorder. Posttraumatic stress syndrome is described as "1) reexperiencing the trauma via memories, intrusive thoughts, or dreams; 2) numbing of responsiveness demonstrable by feeling of detachment from others, constricted affect, or diminished interest in significant activities; 3) other symptoms, including exaggerated startle response, sleep disorders, guilt, memory impairment, or trouble concentrating, and phobias about the activities triggering recollection of the event" (Janoff-Bulman & Frieze 1983, p. 2).

Criminal victimization is a traumatic experience. The person who has been the victim of a crime no longer considers the world as safe as he did beforehand. Feelings of excessive stress and anxiety are coupled with helplessness, making victims think they cannot control events in their lives (Krupnick 1980, Notman & Nadelson 1976, Scheppele & Bart 1983). Victims of violent crimes feel so helpless and dazed that sometimes they have difficulty reporting the crime (Skogan 1976).

The psychological reaction to criminal victimization occurs even if the person has not been physically threatened. Those who find that their homes have been

Reprinted with special permission of King Features Syndicate, Inc.

burglarized also feel vulnerable, insecure, helpless, and unable to control events in their lives. People consider their homes as extensions of themselves and as such feel violated when an intruder breaks into it. They feel unable to protect themselves and their property.

Changes in Expectations

People develop perceptions about themselves and expectations concerning what is likely to occur in their world. Being a victim of a crime makes people question the accuracy of their assumptions. Taylor, Wood and Lichtman (1983) enumerate three types of assumptions which victims are particularly apt to question: "1) the belief in personal invulnerability; 2) the perception of the world as meaningful and comprehensible; 3) the view of ourselves in a positive light" (p. 3). Criminal victimization tends to destroy these assumptions. The victim feels apprehensive and helpless, now viewing the world as unpredictable, threatening, and dangerous. Let us now examine the three assumptions and see how each is affected by criminal victimization.

Invulnerability

Most individuals have a natural tendency to expect that more positive events and fewer negative ones will occur in their lives than chance would predict. They feel invulnerable and believe that extremely negative events like crimes and accidents cannot or will not happen to them. Feelings of being less vulnerable to victimization are particularly apparent in individuals who have never been victims of crime (Weinstein & Lachendro 1982).

People who believe that they are invulnerable feel in control of their lives. They have an "illusion of control." Perloff (1983) explains that this feeling of invulnerability alleviates the feelings of stress and anxiety that would be apparent if people always expected the worst. A belief in invulnerability could be a defense mechanism that allows individuals to conduct their lives without constant concern for their own safety. However, feelings of invulnerability have both positive and negative repercussions. While people who feel invulnerable are able to function well since they are less anxious and concerned, they are not as likely to take precautions as those who feel more vulnerable. The lack of caution in these individuals increases their real vulnerability. And if someone who feels invulnerable is victimized, that person finds it much more difficult to cope with the victimization.

Criminal victimization destroys feelings of invulnerability; victims feel vulnerable, which is defined as "a belief that one is susceptible to future negative outcomes and unprotected from danger or misfortune. Accompanying this cognition is an affective component, consisting of feelings of anxiety, fear, and apprehension" (Perloff 1983, p. 43). Victims are constantly concerned and fearful that they will be victimized again. The world is no longer viewed as safe and other people can no longer be trusted. Depressed, anxious, wary, and cautious, victims are unable to function due to fear. This reaction is especially strong in victims of rape (Burgess & Holmstrom 1974a).

Victims feel life is no longer predictable. Even familiar places are threatening to the extent that they must be constantly alert for future victimization. Those who have been victimized feel more vulnerable to future crimes and less secure. They no longer feel in control of their lives (Kidd & Chayet 1984, LeJeune & Alex 1973).

Positive Self-Perceptions
Ordinarily, people tend to view themselves in a positive light, believing themselves to be generally good and perceiving their lives as worthwhile. However, victimization causes people to reevaluate their self-perceptions. They now see themselves as weak, afraid, powerless, and unable to protect themselves. They wonder why they have been selected for victimization and why they are not worthy of a peaceful life. They feel unworthy and unable to control their lives (Janoff-Bulman & Frieze 1983, Krupnick 1980).

Perception of the World as Meaningful
Most people tend to think of the world and life in it as meaningful and logical. Events are supposed to be understandable, and individuals should have control over what happens to them. Lerner's just-world theory (1970, 1980) proposes that people believe the events that occur are fair, or just. People have good things happen to them if they are good, and bad things only happen to the people who deserve them. If a person is good, kind, and honest, that person will be protected from negative events because the world is just. People have control over events in the world, and someone who avoids dangerous situations should not be victimized. See A JUST WORLD for an example of the phenomenon.

However, victimization does not make sense. People who have been kind and gentle are sometimes harshly treated. People who have been cautious and avoided questionable situations are victimized. Women who have been raped despite being cautious tend to remain fearful for longer periods; their world is no longer predictable or just, and they feel particularly insecure (Scheppele & Bart 1983). The world is no longer comprehensible and predictable to victims who have been

Box 5.2

A Just World

Betty Jane Spencer lived with her husband of 10 months, her 22-year-old son, and her three teenage stepsons in a peaceful rural area in Indiana. Her serene existence was shattered in February, 1977, when four armed gunmen entered their unlocked house and shot Betty Jane and killed her sons. Although seriously injured, Betty Jane managed to get to a neighbor's house and call the police.

There had not been a real murder in Parke County in 50 years. People could not believe that the murderers had just chosen a house at random to go into to kill people. If violence occurred that way, no one was safe. Rumors began to circulate. Most of them focused on Betty Jane, who was an "outsider." One rumor ran that Betty Jane had killed the boys to share the insurance money with her husband, Keith, who shot her to cover it up. Even Keith seemed to blame her silently for not doing something to prevent the murders.

Doctors were unable to take the 109 pellets out of Betty Jane's back and shoulder without doing more damage. Betty Jane's arm was paralyzed. But her injuries were not the only source of suffering. The memory of the horrible event was overwhelming. In addition, she had no one with whom to share her trauma. Her husband wanted to be left alone with his grief and her relatives and friends avoided her.

Finally, 2 months after the murders, the murderers were arrested. The community continued to blame Betty Jane. The arrested men were involved in drugs and rumors flew tying Betty Jane and Keith to drug activity.

When the first defendant went to trial, Betty Jane had to describe the whole incident. The murderer was convicted and received four life sentences, one for each murder. With Betty Jane's permission, the local newspaper described the trial in detail. Her courageous testimony converted the people in the county to her supporters. They realized Betty Jane was not to blame for the incident and felt very guilty about the rumors. People now treated her like the hero she was. After the second defendant received a guilty verdict on four counts of first-degree murder, the other two defendants pled guilty.

By the end of the trials, Betty Jane weighed only 93 pounds, down from her normal 115. It was not only weight that Betty Jane lost, she lost all will to live. She alternated between anger at the whole world and guilt over being alive. Friends and family avoided her and everyone seemed to stare. She hated to be alone during the day and was terrified at night if her husband was not with her. She was even afraid of driving. It was not death that she feared, it was the terror preceding death. Betty Jane had been through a horrible experience, and the reactions of the community exacerbated it.

Source: D. Magee, *What Murder Leaves Behind: The Victim's Family* (New York: Dodd, Mead, 1983).

good and cautious. Victims try to figure out what they did to deserve this treatment and cannot find meaning in the world.

Self-Blame

Researchers have observed that victims of severe illness and violent crimes often assume more blame for the unfortunate event than would seem logical or even possible (Burgess & Holmstrom 1974b, Janoff-Bulman 1979). Wortman (1976) suggests that self-attributions of blame might reflect a desire on the part of victims to regain some control over the victimizing experience. Attributing blame to themselves might be preferable to feelings of lack of control. Not knowing what precipitated the event would lead victims to believe that they are living in a meaningless, unjust world. However, if the victim blames herself, she now has some understanding of why the unfortunate event occurred. Furthermore, she also knows what she needs to do in the future to avoid a repetition of the unfortunate experience.

Miller and Porter (1983) postulate that self-blame fills three psychological needs for victims. First, victims feel in control over their lives again; second, they can reestablish their belief that the world is just and orderly; and third, they can find meaning in what appeared to be random events.

Even though victims often blame themselves, this does not mean that they take responsibility for the incident. Guilt still remains with the offender. Miller and Porter maintain that a rape victim who blames herself is "not necessarily exonerating her assailant. He still is responsible for his actions. She sees herself as to blame for being the victim of his actions" (1983, p. 144). In other words, the victim is taking the blame for being the one chosen to be a victim but is not the one morally responsible for the crime. Wortman (1976) differentiates between attributions of causality and those of moral responsibility, with victims attributing causality to themselves and moral responsibility to the offender.

Learned Helplessness

Peterson and Seligman propose "learned helplessness" as a model for the "emotional numbing and maladaptive passivity" that sometimes follows victimization (1983, p. 104). The learned helplessness model was developed by Seligman (1975) in his work with animals. Animals who received uncontrollable aversive stimuli, for example, electric shock, were less likely to avoid future controllable aversive stimuli. Dogs learned from the original shock situation that their responses would not control the aversive stimulus. Response and outcome were not related; therefore, they were helpless. This helplessness was generalized to new situations and 24 hours later the dogs made few attempts to evade what were now avoidable shocks. The dogs' reaction of not avoiding the shocks was called learned helplessness.

> **Box 5.3**
>
> **The Destruction of Hedda Nussbaum**
>
> Joel and Hedda appeared to be an ideal couple. He was a successful attorney, good-looking, charismatic, and intelligent. She was a lovely, bright, and vibrant young career woman, an editor of children's books for Random House. They met at a party in 1975, and she moved in with him in 1976. They were deeply in love and life seemed wonderful. And it was wonderful for the first 3 years—then Joel hit her. Hedda does not remember what precipitated that first attack but does remember that both of them were shocked and, although he did not express any regret, Joel was very affectionate following the attack. It was easy for Hedda to believe that it would never happen again.
>
> Hedda continued to believe that each incident of abuse was the last—even when she required surgery to repair a ruptured spleen after a beating in 1981. After each episode, Joel was affectionate and Hedda believed that it was an isolated incident, one that would never happen again. She loved Joel and believed that he loved her. Then, in 1981, a client retained Joel to find a home for her illegitimate daughter. Joel decided to keep the child and brought "Lisa" home to live with him and Hedda. Hedda was thrilled to be a mother, and life was wonderful for all of them for about 6 months. Then the abuse of Hedda began again.
>
> When her injuries were apparent, black eyes or facial injuries, Hedda was embarrassed to go to work. As the beatings became more frequent and severe, she missed more and more work until Random House fired her in 1982. Her job was not only her sole source of income, it had provided her with outside relationships. With her termination these relationships ceased, leaving her even more dependent on Joel. Although he was quite wealthy, Joel took Hedda's savings. When he persuaded Hedda that her friends and family were not good for her
>
> *(continued)*

Research on learned helplessness in animals may have considerable relevance to the study of victimization. Victims of crime are also exposed to an uncontrollable aversive situation and may learn during the incident that responding is useless and response and outcome are unrelated. They are learning helplessness. Once they have learned that responses are independent of outcomes, victims generalize this learning to other behaviors. This overgeneralization explains their apathy and passivity (Peterson & Seligman 1983). Seligman contends that learned helplessness is at the core of reactive depression. For a description of an actual case of learned helplessness, see THE DESTRUCTION OF HEDDA NUSSBAUM.

Rape Victims

Rape and its impact on the victim have been studied extensively because of their severity. Rape is a crime of violence, not one of sexual desire. However, because

> and eliminated her contact with them, Hedda was completely isolated and entirely dependent on Joel. Joel and Hedda began to use drugs. Joel's use became heavy, and he coerced Hedda into using more and more.
>
> The abuse increased and the cruelty escalated. Joel devised new and more horrible ways of tormenting Hedda: he hung her from a bar with handcuffs, burned her with a blowtorch, broke her nose a number of times, and choked her. Hedda ran away six times, going to friends or to shelters. But each time she went back to Joel, swayed by his tenderness and apparent love, or wanting to be with Lisa. In 1986, Joel brought home another child, an infant, Mitchell. As with Lisa, Mitchell was never legally adopted. Despite Joel's cruelty to her, Hedda did not think that he would abuse the children.
>
> In November, 1987, Hedda was no longer the attractive, independent, happy, capable young woman who fell in love with Joel and went to live with him. She had lost 25 pounds, was permanently disfigured, defenseless, and psychologically traumatized. She was the typical battered woman, completely isolated from the outside world. That was her condition the night Joel brutally beat Lisa. Not only was Hedda incapable of defending herself from her lover, she could not prevent him from attacking Lisa. Joel prevented Hedda from summoning help for the child who lay unconscious for 12 hours. By the time Lisa was taken to the hospital, it was too late to help her and she died. After a year of hospitalization for physical and mental problems, Hedda was able to testify against her former lover who was convicted of first-degree manslaughter in the death of 6-year-old Lisa.
>
> ◆
>
> Could Hedda have done anything to prevent her exploitation by Joel? How much influence did drugs have on the behavior of Joel and Hedda? What could society do to prevent the abuse of people like Hedda and Lisa? How can people avoid destructive relationships?

Source: N. Weiss and B. Johnson, "A Love Betrayed, A Brief Life Lost," *People Weekly* (February 13, 1989), pp. 82–95.

the crime involves unwanted subjection to sex, victims feel particularly violated and their psychological reaction is more severe than the reaction to other violent crimes (Greene, Schooler & Loftus 1985). Rape victims often manifest a "rape crisis syndrome"—a collection of psychological, behavioral, and physical reactions to the crime. These reactions are similar to reactions manifested by victims of other violent crimes, but tend to be stronger (Burgess 1984, Hilberman 1976, Symonds 1976).

Immediately after the rape, the victim demonstrates physical distress characterized by an inability to sleep, intestinal problems, muscle tension, nausea, and physical pain. She manifests emotional reactions, primarily fear, but also experiences anger, embarrassment, and self-blame. This acute phase of the rape crisis syndrome lasts for 2 or 3 weeks. The longer second phase consists of the

> **Box 5.4**
>
> **A Tragic Event at Big Dan's Tavern**
>
> This is the story of a tragic incident in the life of a 21-year-old divorced mother who lived in New Bedford, Massachusetts, with her two children. Although the victim's name has been published by a number of newspapers, the author will not use it in this report. March 6, 1983, was a happy day for the young mother, who spent it celebrating her older daughter's third birthday. About 9 P.M. the young woman went out to get some cigarettes. Unsuccessful at finding any at a couple of stores, she went into Big Dan's Tavern, a local bar. She saw another young woman she knew and decided to stay for a drink. After her friend left, the young woman was grabbed from behind by a patron of the tavern. He stripped off her pants and raped her on the floor. Several of the other patrons lifted her to a pool table where she was repeatedly raped for an hour and a half. Her screams for help were met with cheers and laughter from the other patrons.
>
> Although one of the customers said "Knock it off—this is getting out of hand" (Starr 1983, p. 25), the attack continued. And when the bartender, Carlos Machado, and a customer tried to leave the bar to call the police, they were stopped by the other patrons. At the trial, Machado testified that the onlookers shouted "That's how it's done. That's how you do it" (Starr 1984). Finally, the half-naked young woman was able to run from the tavern and flag down a passing van. When the police, called by the people in the van, arrived at the tavern hours later, two of the attackers were still there. It was business as usual at Big Dan's Tavern.
>
> Police quickly arrested the four men who actually committed the rape. Later the state prosecutor filed charges against two other men who cheered the rapists,
>
> *(continued)*

victim's personality reorganization. During this stage, the victim is plagued with nightmares, phobias, and psychological problems. She is likely to have difficulties in her sex life and to encounter conflicts in her interpersonal life, particularly with men (Burgess & Holmstrom 1974a).

Rape victims are very likely to demonstrate symptoms of depression and fear, be unable to feel pleasure, and to develop phobias and physical illnesses. They may also develop eating and sleeping problems. Victims may manifest any number or combination of reactions from anxiety, shock, disbelief, and guilt to anger and outrage. And emotions may rapidly change from one reaction to another. The reactions are so intense and negative that many victims attempt suicide (Feldman-Summers 1976, Katz & Mazur 1979, McCahill, Meyer & Fischman 1979). See A TRAGIC EVENT AT BIG DAN'S TAVERN.

The rape victim attempts to recover control over her life. However, fear lingers and she often makes drastic changes in her life-style to avoid possible danger. Scheppele and Bart (1983) found that about a third of the rape victims limited their definitions of dangerousness to situations very similar to that of the rape

> contending that they were accomplices. When the national media disseminated news of the horrible gang rape with cheering bystanders, the country was horrified and outraged. The owner of Big Dan's Tavern closed the bar permanently 2 days after the rape. And a week after the incident 2,500 people held a candlelight procession to offer sympathy for the victim and express their concern.
>
> This incident ignited the anger and concern of society, not only because of the vicious nature of the assault, but also because of the insensitivity of the bystanders. One witness is reported to have asked, "Why should I care?" (*America* 1983, p. 252).
>
> There is growing concern with the callousness of witnesses to crimes in the United States. Some citizens propose that the United States should institute "duty to rescue" laws. These laws would require that bystanders to an incident such as the rape at Big Dan's Tavern report the incident to the police. Bystanders who did not attempt to terminate the incident by calling the police would be held criminally responsible and could be arrested. Many European countries have "duty to rescue" laws and impose criminal sanctions, including jail sentences, on those who violate them. In reaction to the incident at Big Dan's and other similar incidents, three states have instituted "duty to rescue" laws with fines instead of jail sentences.
>
> ◆
>
> Should "duty to rescue" laws be instituted? Should they include stricter penalties than a small fine? Would a "duty to rescue" law have prevented the rape at Big Dan's?
>
> For information on the outcome of the trial and the response of the New Bedford community, see COMMUNITY REACTION TO THE RAPISTS IN BIG DAN'S, Chapter 14.

Sources: "The Crime That Tarnished a Town," *Time* (March 5, 1984), p. 19; M. Starr, "The Tavern Rape: Cheers and No Help," *Newsweek* (March 21, 1983), p. 25; M. Starr, "Gang Rape: The Legal Attack," *Newsweek* (March 12, 1984), p. 38; "Violence and the Social Fabric," *America* (April 2, 1983), pp. 251–252.

and only changed behavior in reference to those situations. However, almost a third of the women generalized their perceptions of dangerousness to other places, and about one fourth of the victims thought the whole world was dangerous. These women might avoid social interactions, stay at home, or miss work in order to avoid dangerous situations.

The emotional reaction to rape can last a long time, much longer than either the victim or her friends and relatives realize. Burgess and Holmstrom (1978) found that a quarter of rape victims were still experiencing repercussions of their victimization 4 to 6 years after the incident. And victims of incest report emotional problems as long as 20 years after the experience (Silver & Wortman 1980). The extended period of recuperation is very difficult on people who are helping the victim to cope. Both the victim and the people in her support group become impatient and willingness to bolster the victim decreases with time.

Robbery

Robbers seldom injure their victims and those injuries that do occur tend to be minor. However, there are some victims who are more likely to be hurt than others: the elderly, those with lower incomes, and those who know the robber.

There are a number of reasons why a robber will injure a victim. Perhaps he might want to intimidate the victim so she will cooperate with him. Or possibly he is sadistic or wants to show off to his companions. A robber might panic and injure a victim who resists or is uncooperative. Another possibility is that the robber wants to keep the victim from getting assistance or identifying him later.

Karmen found most victims reported resisting to some extent, and about two out of five did so successfully, thereby foiling the robbery attempt. However, if the robber had a gun, the robbery was completed 80 percent of the time. Younger people, whites, and women tended to resist more than older people, blacks, and men. And people who knew their assailants were more likely to resist the robbery attempt than those accosted by strangers. Most people who resisted did so by trying to escape; very few victims used a weapon. Men tended to resist by fighting back, whereas women were more likely to scream to frighten the robber. Some people who resisted were injured.

Stockholm Syndrome

A very unusual reaction to victimization, the Stockholm Syndrome, is sometimes displayed by victims who are held hostage. This syndrome was first noticed in, and named for, a 1973 incident which occurred in Stockholm, Sweden. After being held hostage for some time by a bank robber, a young woman fell in love with her assailant and married him.

Terrorists, skyjackers, robbers, gunmen, or kidnappers take innocent persons hostage in order to use them in their negotiations with the police, family, or government. The hostages and the terrorists often spend a considerable amount of time together. During this time, the hostages may develop a feeling of warmth and closeness to the lawbreakers. By the time the authorities are able to gain the release of the hostages, the victims are actually angry and resentful toward the authorities. They are unaware of the efforts made on their behalf and only know of delays in negotiations. The hostages feel more grateful to the terrorists for not hurting them than they do to the authorities who risk injury of the hostages during their rescue.

Who Suffers Most?

Interviews with victims show the already-disadvantaged suffer the most from crime victimization: the poor, undereducated, inner-city residents, and minorities. These deprived people, who are already having difficulty coping with the day-to-day problems of living, have greater emotional distress due to victimization than the average person. All the problems of victimization already discussed are magnified for this population. This magnification occurs because the disadvantaged have more practical problems and fewer sources of support than the more-affluent members of society. Their problems remain for longer periods of time, and they have greater difficulty getting assistance. Their friends and relatives, who suffer secondary victimization, are already stretched to the limits of their emotional and financial resources and find it difficult to assist the primary victim. Joanna Shapland (1986) cites the incident of a victim whose eyeglasses were broken in an offense. The victim was unable to return to work because he could not afford to replace the glasses.

Coping with Victimization

While all victims of crime are traumatized to some extent, some people appear to cope with the experience rather well, while others seem never to recover from the traumatic event. In this section, I will discuss some of the psychological and behavioral strategies for adjusting to the experience of being victimized and the effectiveness of these different coping mechanisms.

Before evaluating the effectiveness of different methods of coping, we need a definition of effective coping. Wortman (1983) maintains that most definitions of coping include a number of common factors. For example, a person who is coping well does not display any active psychiatric or emotional problems and holds both the world and herself in a positive light. This person should be able to handle both occupational and social activities well, while remaining healthy physically. It is important that the individual herself thinks that she is coping well.

However, some of the factors often cited as signs of poor coping can actually be helpful in the long run. These signs of intense reactions to victimization may motivate victims to find other means of coping. For example, the people who are most distressed emotionally and suffer the greatest decrease in self-esteem may be the ones most actively motivated to try coping behaviors (Wortman 1983).

Psychological Methods of Adjustment

The psychological methods of adjustment described are processes the victim goes through naturally or spontaneously while coping with the victimization. Although the methods are not psychotherapies, some of the processes are similar to those a therapist would use to assist a client in coping with the traumatic event. Even if the victim progresses through the coping strategies described, a mental health professional usually is necessary to help a victim overcome the psychological trauma.

De-victimizing Self

One of the cognitive or psychological reactions victims sometimes have to victimization is a process of "de-victimizing" themselves. By doing so, victims are able to decrease the chances that their basic assumptions about the world will be destroyed. In addition to financial losses, victims suffer a decrease in status and value. Victims lose their sense of control over their lives while becoming vulnerable, fearful, and depressed. Other people react negatively to victims by avoiding them and looking down upon them. Therefore, viewing themselves as victims, or having others view them that way, is a negative experience for most people. Because the evaluation of victims is so negative, victims are motivated to de-victimize themselves. They do this by cognitively minimizing their victimization.

Taylor, Wood and Lichtman (1983) describe five coping mechanisms used by victims to make themselves feel less victimized. These mechanisms enhance the victims' view of themselves and decrease their perceptions of themselves as victims. The first method entails the victims' *comparing themselves with other victims who are less fortunate.* Comparisons with victims who have received greater injuries make the victims feel less sorry for themselves. In this way, the victims can feel that they are doing better than others. This helps to raise their self-esteem. For example, rape victims often contrast their victimization with that of other women who have been severely injured or suffered tremendous humiliation during the episode. No matter how frightening their experience was, they consider themselves lucky in comparison.

The second method victims use to minimize their own victimization is *selectively to choose an attribute on which they compare themselves* with others. By selecting an attribute which is favorable to them, they can perceive their victimization more positively than the other person's. For example, a victim who has terminal injuries might compare herself to someone who is going to live, but not compare herself on that attribute. Instead, the victim might think, "At least I was not raped." On that attribute, she has a more favorable view of herself than other victims, so she can feel less victimized.

Another group of researchers (Brickman et al. 1982) further distinguish between responsibility for the problem and responsibility for a solution. These authors maintain the victim can assume responsibility for resolving the problems associated with the victimization without taking the blame for causing it. In other words, the victim can take control of future events, while not feeling he controlled the past incident.

Victims also decrease their perceptions of victimization by *considering worse worlds.* Victims think of the worst thing that could have happened during the incident. By comparison, the actual event was not so bad, and the victim feels fortunate. For example, a victim might think that the offender could have killed or maimed him.

A fourth strategy used by victims to de-victimize themselves is *manufacturing benefits derived from the victimization.* Victims might decide that the experience made them stronger, more understanding of themselves and others, or improved their lives in some other way. Taylor, Wood and Lichtman (1983) describe an event reported in the *Los Angeles Times* which demonstrates this cognitive process. A woman who barely lived through a horrible beating and shooting felt she benefited from the experience because her mother and she were brought back together. The woman was able to see herself as less of a victim because of the happy event resulting from the victimization.

If victims cannot find a comparison person to whom they feel superior in rate of recovery, they may *manufacture a standard of comparison.* Female cancer patients who have had radical mastectomies often compare themselves to the wives of hypothetical husbands who divorce their wives because of the disfigurement of a mastectomy. These women patients can say at least their husbands supported them during their time of crisis. Despite the persistence of rumors about husbands who do, there is little evidence of husbands divorcing their wives because of a radical mastectomy (Taylor, Wood & Lichtman 1983).

Psychological Evaluation of Victimization

Another coping mechanism apparent in victims of crimes is to appraise the victimizing experience cognitively. Janoff-Bulman and Frieze (1983) maintain the victim's psychological perception of the victimization influences how psychologically damaging the event is to the victim. For example, Scheppele and Bart (1983) found women were better able to cope with being sexually attacked if they perceived that they had avoided being raped. Their self-definitions of avoiding rape were unrelated to the amount of violence experienced. These women believed they had avoided being raped as long as they only endured sex acts that did not involve intercourse. Regardless of the amount of violence involved in the incident, women coped better and had less severe reactions if they thought they had avoided rape.

Attributions of Causation

Victimization is an uncontrollable event. When people are victimized, they look for explanations and causes of the event. Peterson and Seligman (1983) propose three possible dimensions to the attributions of causation of an event. In the first place, victims decide whether there is something about themselves or the situation which has precipitated the event. They attribute the event to an **internal or external** cause. A second domain involves whether the factor which precipitated the victimization will persist for a long or a short time, whether that factor is **stable or unstable.** And third, the victim decides whether the factor will affect a variety of outcomes or be limited to the event, a **global or specific** attribution. People have a typical way of explaining events in their lives, no matter what the event. If they tend to explain events as being due to internal, stable, and global causes, they are likely to explain their victimization in the same way. A person who explains his victimization in that way is likely to adjust poorly. Self-blame that is explained by a mistake made by the victim is unstable and specific. Self-blame explained by a personality characteristic (e.g., I am so naive) is stable and global. Someone who explains his victimization in this latter manner will tend to develop lower self-esteem and have greater difficulty overcoming his trauma (Peterson & Seligman 1983).

Self-blame assists in readjustment only if the victim attributes the blame to his behavior. If the victim blames the incident on a personality characteristic, the attribution is likely to lead to feelings of depression and helplessness (Janoff-Bulman 1979, Peterson & Seligman 1983). Someone who blames his behavior for causing his victimization can avoid that behavior in the future. By doing so, that person believes he decreases the likelihood of future victimization. However, if the cause of victimization is perceived to be a personality characteristic that is enduring, the person is unable to control that attribute and foresees the future likelihood of victimization.

Assistance in Coping With Victimization

Coping with and adjusting to victimization are determined to a large extent by interpretations of the event and cognitive appraisals of it. While some victims are able to readjust and cope on their own, many victims need the assistance of a trained professional. Since the primary function of cognitive therapy is to help clients reinterpret the events in their life, Peterson and Seligman (1983) contend that this therapy is particularly geared to using the psychological methods described previously to prevent future or solve current problems in coping with victimization.

Support from Friends and Family

Not every victim of a crime has access to a mental health professional for counseling. Counseling is expensive and time consuming, and for some people seeking or obtaining professional help would be an added indignity. But these victims still need emotional support. Victims of crime often turn to family and friends for many types of support and assistance. Family, friends, and loved ones can help victims with practical solutions to problems and with emotional adjustment. The emotional and social support of others is extremely important in the adjustment of victims and the maintenance of their self-esteem. Ruback, Greenberg, and Westcott (1984) found that victims who received support from family and friends displayed less emotional and physical damage and generally appeared better adjusted than those without social support.

Victims have a great need to talk about the crime and release their intense negative emotions. It is difficult for those who care for the victims to relive the experience with them. However, it is extremely helpful to victims if others are willing to listen and be accepting of their reactions. It is particularly important that victims know support is available without any conditions or limitations (Janoff-Bulman & Frieze 1983).

Friends and family who help victims expect the adjustment time to be much shorter than it usually is. Oftentimes, both the victims and those close to them think they are taking an abnormally long time to adjust. It is a typical response for helpers to feel victims need to get on with their lives and stop dwelling on this one incident. Family and friends may get tired of hearing about the victims' trauma, become intolerant of their depression, and begin to avoid them. Often people react by saying, "Don't be upset." Statements such as this make victims think they are overreacting to the attack. Victims may then feel even more isolated and concerned about being emotionally disturbed. This is where professionals and peer groups can be of assistance. They can assure the victims that their reactions are normal and their feelings are typical (Coates & Winston 1983).

Peer Support Groups

Sometimes family and friends are not available, are unable to assist, or are unwilling to devote the time or energy to provide the support a victim needs. Even with the support of loved ones, victims often feel their reactions are abnormal and unhealthy. In these cases, the victim is well advised to join a peer support group.

Peer support groups are composed of people who have experienced similar incidents. Victims help each other feel normal. By participating in such a group, victims are able to discuss their feelings and reactions with people who have similar emotions. Victims tend to feel alone and different from others. Many victims also think they are "inordinately and inappropriately" distressed (Coates & Winston 1983). Support groups help victims see that they are not the only ones in that situation and their reactions and emotions are typical. The support group can aid victims in realizing their feelings and reactions are appropriate and normal, thus restoring the victims' self-esteem.

Peer support groups usually have a counselor or psychologist to guide the group interactions. The professional member of the group is primarily a facilitator; the peer group members are the ones who give the assistance and support to each other. Membership in the group gives victims a sense of belonging and decreases their feelings of isolation. By helping others, they also develop a feeling of purpose in life.

Self-Help Groups

Recently, different categories of victims have gotten together to assist others like themselves. Their support is not limited to therapy groups, but rather includes other types of assistance for victims. "Notable achievements have been made by rape victims who set up crisis centers, battered women who established shelters, targets of racist violence who organized self-defense groups, and bereaved parents of murdered, missing, or molested children" (Karmen 1984, p. 23). Well known among the self-help groups are organizations such as MADD (Mothers Against Drunk Driving) or SADD (Students Against Drunk Driving) or the Adam Walsh Society. Less well known self-help groups include Parents of Murdered Children, Child Find, and Society's League Against Molestation. See MADD—ONE MOTHER'S CAMPAIGN for a description of the formation of a self-help group.

Each of the self-help groups consists of members who have suffered a particular type of victimization. These people organize groups to help prevent future incidents of the same offense and to support and assist victims of similar traumas.

The Process of Readjustment

In a previous section of this chapter, we saw that victims of crime have their assumptions about themselves and the world destroyed. They no longer view themselves as invulnerable, no longer have positive self-perceptions, nor do they find meaning in the world. In the process of readjustment, victims have to face these destroyed assumptions and rebuild their concepts of the world in order to

Box 5.5

MADD—One Mother's Campaign

Candy Lightner, a single parent, was raising her three children when her life was changed forever. Her 13-year-old daughter, Cari, was walking to a church carnival when a drunk driver swerved and killed her. The driver, Clarence Busch, kept going. His attempts to hide his car raised his (then) wife's, Sharlene's, suspicions. She was so distressed when she found out about Cari's death that she implicated her husband.

Clarence Busch had had three convictions for drunken driving within the previous 4 years and had been released on bail for a drinking-related hit-and-run offense only 2 days before killing Cari. Despite his long record of arrests for drinking and driving, Clarence Busch had spent only 48 hours in jail.

Candy Lightner was enraged that a person could kill an innocent child and avoid punishment with the excuse that he was drunk. Even before Cari's funeral, Candy had resolved to change the system. She organized Mothers Against Drunk Drivers (MADD) both as a support group for families who suffered as the result of drunk drivers and as a lobbying group to change the laws. Beginning in her home state of California, Candy Lightner went to see Governor Jerry Brown. She pestered him until he agreed to form a task force on drunk driving and appointed her to it. California led the way for stricter laws against drunk driving. Candy Lightner criss-crossed the country, speaking to citizen groups and lobbying legislators until all fifty states followed California's lead.

MADD soon had expanded throughout the United States, boasting over 300 chapters and 600,000 donors and volunteers. Candy Lightner then expanded her goal to prevent teenage alcohol-related accidents. She became determined to raise the drinking age. With the same dedication and perseverance with which she prompted the changes in drunk driving laws, Candy Lightner pressured Congress to raise the drinking age. In 1984, she succeeded. Congress passed an amendment that penalized states, by restricting federal highway funds, if they did not raise the drinking age to 21.

But Candy Lightner is not through. She has many more goals, among which are an automatic prison sentence for drunk drivers who are repeat offenders and a bill of rights for victims. And what happened to Clarence Busch? Despite Cari's death and the hit-and-run offense 2 days before, he was allowed to plead *nolo contendere* for one count of vehicular manslaughter. Of his 2-year prison sentence, he served 3 months in a work camp and 18 months in a halfway house. Upon release, he was told he could get his driver's license contingent on obtaining liability insurance.

◆

Are the stricter laws against drunk driving having an effect? Do you know any people who drive while drunk? Will automatic prison sentences deter people from driving after drinking?

Sources: "You Can Make a Difference," *Time* (January 7, 1985), p. 41; M. B. Sellinger, "Already the Conscience of a Nation, Candy Lightner Prods Congress into Action Against Drunk Drivers," *People Weekly* (July 9, 1984), pp. 102–103; M. Wilhelm, "A Grieving, Angry Mother Charges That Drunken Drivers Are Getting Away With Murder," *People Weekly* (June 29, 1981), pp. 24–26.

function. To reconstruct their conceptual system, victims must integrate the event that shattered their assumptions with their new concepts. Although victims can no longer view themselves as completely invulnerable, they can begin again to see some meaning in the world. Victims can begin to regain their self-esteem, think of themselves as worthy and strong, and see that the world is not completely unpredictable and threatening.

Victims often complain that negative memories of the victimization intrude into their thoughts at unexpected and inconvenient times and places. Intrusive thoughts about the victimization are symptoms of the experience, but they also provide a way for the mind to incorporate the negative experience into the new conceptual system. These thoughts make victims review their assumptions about the world and themselves. In the process, the assumptions are changed and reviewed again until the traumatic experience is incorporated into the victim's conceptual system. Sometimes victims will redefine the experience itself so that it will fit into their revised conceptual system (Janoff-Bulman & Frieze 1983).

Vulnerability

One of the most intense reactions to victimization is a feeling of fear and vulnerability. This feeling is particularly extreme in victims who were being cautious and avoiding dangerous situations when attacked. Scheppele and Bart (1983) report rape victims who were being cautious when raped were most likely to sustain feelings of intense fear for an extended period of time. Because these victims know their behavioral attempts at safety did not work, they no longer feel secure. Those who felt most invulnerable and were still victimized are the ones who suffer the greatest psychological damage and have most difficulty coping (Perloff 1983).

Behavioral Methods of Adjustment

The psychological reactions to victimization which are described before, assist victims in coping with the negative experience. These psychological reactions are spontaneous. Usually victims are not aware that they are adjusting to the event with these cognitive responses. In contrast, behavioral changes by the victims are consciously decided upon in order to adjust to the victimization.

Environmental Control

Some victims make a conscious effort to control their environment in order to avoid future victimization. These behaviors help decrease the victim's feelings of vulnerability and lack of control over the world. People who have been robbed will put great effort into protecting their homes: replacing locks, installing burglar bars and alarm systems. However, prevention of future victimization can become an obsession, with victims constantly worrying about the possibility of crime. Victims sometimes make changes in their life-styles that make their lives less enjoyable: they change jobs, stay locked in their homes at night, or move to avoid future victimization (Burgess & Holmstrom 1974b, Cohen 1974, Wortman 1983). See TAKING THE LAW INTO YOUR OWN HANDS for a description of how one man reacted to repeated crime victimization.

> **Box 5.6**
>
> **Taking the Law into Your Own Hands**
>
> Prentice Rasheed owned a variety store in the Liberty City area of Miami. Like many of his neighbors, he was frequently burglarized. In fact, his store was robbed nine times in a 2-year period from 1984 to 1986. Mr. Rasheed decided that enough was enough. He rigged a crude booby trap for the robbers by attaching two metal grates to an extension cord. He said later that he knew nothing about electricity and only intended to shock any potential robber. However, his trap electrocuted a 27-year-old man attempting to enter his store. Apparently, the grand jurors believed Rasheed—they refused to indict him for manslaughter, saying he did not intend to kill anyone.
>
> Rasheed's homemade trap and the resulting death of a potential thief sparked national controversy over the use of deadly force in protecting one's property. Some of the debate against Rasheed's behavior focused on the fact that people do not have the right to take the law into their own hands. Another point made was that a criminal does not receive the death penalty for theft. Further, the law condemns the use of deadly force to protect property. Even the grand jury which decided Rasheed's fate reinforced that law, stating that the use of deadly force to protect property "should never be tolerated" (Lacayo 1986, p. 85). However, despite their comment, the grand jury refused to press charges against Rasheed, and some feel that the grand jury's actions speak louder than words.
>
> The public tends to sympathize with honest citizens who fight against criminals, even if their behavior is not legal. There is much public concern that the police are not protecting these citizens from crime. However, as James Mullin, chairman of the local ACLU points out, there is no way that a booby trap can distinguish between a potential thief and a police officer or firefighter who is legally entering the store.
>
> ◆
>
> As citizens become more concerned with the amount of property crime, do you think people will be more inclined to use deadly force to protect their property? Should people be held accountable for the injury of someone who is attempting to break into their homes or businesses? What if the potential thief is killed?

Sources: R. Lacayo, "Trouble with Fighting Back," *Time* (November 10, 1986), p. 85; "Deadly Force: A Target Again," *Newsweek* (December 15, 1986), p. 10.

Rape victims are particularly susceptible to feelings of vulnerability. In reaction to these feelings, the women are likely to change their behavior in order to avoid future victimization. It is obvious that some situations are more dangerous than others, and it is within the ability of women to avoid them. On this basis, many women develop a set of "rules of rape avoidance" (Scheppele & Bart 1983). For example, most rapes occur at night and when the victim is alone. Therefore, women often travel at night with other people, particularly men.

However, there are some situations the victim could not avoid. Anywhere from 18 to 56 percent of rapes occur in the home (Amir 1971). In these cases, rape victims often move or have their phones unlisted. These behavioral reactions have a positive effect; victims who take these precautions adjust and cope faster than those who don't (Burgess & Holmstrom 1974b).

Training in Self-Defense
Another behavioral method of coping with criminal victimization involves training in self-defense. Victims of rape and mugging are particularly apt to use this approach to decrease their feelings of vulnerability (Janoff-Bulman & Frieze 1983).

Training in self-defense and also in assertiveness does have an impact on the people taking the course. A victim who is afraid and timid is more likely to have an assault completed than a victim who responds with anger or suspicion. Kidder, Boell, and Moyer found that training in self-defense and assertiveness decreased women's feelings of helplessness and fear. They state that "women felt significantly stronger, braver, more in control, and able to defend themselves after" the self-defense training (1983, p. 156).

Summary

The primary function of the criminal justice system is the protection of the interests of society and the government; interests of the victim are secondary, at best. The inefficiency and unpredictability of the criminal justice system often cause the victim to suffer further. Society's reaction to victims is not much better. In order to believe the world is just, people tend to assume that victims got what they deserved.

As a result of the recent focus on victims, a new area of study, victimology, has emerged. Victimology studies victims and the process of and reaction to victimization. The likelihood of being victimized varies by age, sex, race, and marital status.

Victims of violent and/or personal crimes experience deep psychological pain which creates changes in their belief systems and behavior. Feelings of excessive stress and anxiety are coupled with helplessness, making victims think they cannot control events in their lives. Many victims blame themselves. Self-blame fills three psychological needs for victims. First, victims will feel in control over their lives again; second, they can reestablish their belief that the world is just and orderly; and third, they can find meaning in what appeared to be random events.

While all victims of crime are traumatized to some extent, some people appear to cope with the experience rather well, while others seem never to recover from the traumatic event. Psychological methods of adjustment are processes the victim goes through naturally or spontaneously while coping with the victimization. One of the cognitive or psychological reactions victims sometimes have is a process of "de-victimizing" themselves. Other coping mechanisms apparent in victims of crimes are appraising the victimizing experience cognitively and attributing blame to themselves.

While some victims are able to readjust and cope on their own, many victims need the assistance of a trained professional. However, not every victim of a crime has access to a mental health professional for counseling. Victims of crime often turn to family and friends or join a support group for support and assistance.

Some victims make a conscious effort to control their environment in order to avoid future victimization. These behaviors help to decrease the victim's feelings of vulnerability and lack of control over the world.

6

Law Enforcement

Recruitment, Screening, and Training of Police Officers
Recruitment
Screening
Suggested Methods for Selecting Police Officers
Police Training
A Psychological Profile of the Police Officer
Studies of Police Personality
Diversity in Police Behavior
Stress and the Police Officer
Police Discretion and the Arrest Process: Police Interactions with the Public
Police Discretion
Reactive Activities and Decisions
Proactive Activities and Decisions
Effectiveness of Reactive vs. Proactive Approaches
Styles of Policing
Current Trends in Policing Styles
Police Interrogation Methods
Coerced Confessions
Summary

Recruitment, Screening, and Training of Police Officers

The lengthy, involved process of hiring new police officers can take as long as a year and a half. The screening process, particularly in large urban settings, is quite stringent and only a small percentage of applicants are hired. The selection process varies greatly by department, city, and state, but despite their differences, the procedures in most jurisdictions have some basic similarities. Territo, Swanson, and Chamelin (1977) identify the following steps in the screening process: initial application form, written test, file review, agility test, medical examination, psychological screening, polygraph and psychological stress indicator, character investigation, and oral interview. Although not all departments employ every one of these steps, they are the ones that are commonly used.

Recruitment

Candidates applying for positions on the police force generally come from the lower middle class or upper working class, but vary in terms of other demographic and background variables (Yarmey 1990). Recruits have similar motivations for wanting to become police officers. The most common motivations for applying for the job are a desire for security (Cohn & Udolf 1979, Yarmey 1990) and an interest in enforcing the law and helping others (Hunt 1971).

Many police departments make a special effort to recruit minority and female applicants in response to community concerns and affirmative action requirements. Minority groups are particularly difficult to recruit due to negative attitudes toward the police and beliefs that police are prejudiced and antagonistic toward minorities (Stotland & Berberich 1979). For a description of a minority police officer, see UNLIKELY COP.

Screening

Considerable concern is expressed among professionals about the efficacy of the procedures used to screen police candidates. The usual screening process, which has remained the same for decades, involves written tests (e.g., for intelligence, reading and writing ability), physical tests, oral interviews, and an investigation of the applicants' background and character (Trautman 1988).

Psychological Testing

Applicants who successfully complete the written and physical screening are usually interviewed and tested by a psychologist or psychiatrist. These mental health professionals attempt to eliminate candidates who might be inappropriate for work as police officers, for example, those who are overly aggressive or have psychological disorders. Written and projective tests (e.g., Rorschach) are also used to determine whether the candidate is emotionally mature, has adequate interpersonal skills, coping ability, and appropriate motivations. While Yarmey (1990) questions whether these scales are capable of predicting how well individuals will perform as police officers, Hiatt and Hargrave (1988) have found some evidence of their predictive validity.

> **Box 6.1**
>
> **Unlikely Cop**
>
> When Police Officer Robert Chung dresses in civilian clothes, he is really undercover. As a 5'5" oriental, this unimposing man does not look anything like a police officer. However, his size and race can be an asset when dealing with street people. Officer Chung describes going to a housing project in Bedford-Stuyvesant to look for a robbery suspect, the "Choker." Seeing a woman leaning out a window, he yelled up and asked for the Choker. The woman called the suspect who came down to see Chung after evaluating him from a window. The Choker could not believe it when this unimposing oriental said he was a cop and arrested him on the spot.
>
> ♦
>
> Many police departments restrict their recruits to specific heights. Should police officers be required to be large and muscular? Should extra efforts be made to recruit minorities?

Source: M. Daly, "New Wave Cops," *New York* (November 14, 1983), pp. 24–30.

The Oral Interview

Almost all screening procedures include some type of oral interview, the purported primary purpose of which is to evaluate the applicant on communication skills, poise, and appearance. An unpublicized, but important, aim of the oral interview is to ensure that the applicant agrees with conventional morality and is willing to enforce unpopular laws or laws directed at behavior that is not universally considered deviant, such as personal drug use, viewing or selling pornography, or aberrant sexual behavior. The interview board would like recruits to be "comfortably religious, defiantly heterosexual, and appropriately punitive toward moral deviants" (Kinnane 1979, p. 6).

Many times the interviewers themselves are not sure exactly what they are trying to determine through the interview (O'Leary 1979). The evaluations made by different board members tend to be quite dissimilar and not good predictors of police performance (Burbeck 1988), leading most researchers to conclude that structured interviews are a poor method for evaluation and selection (Landy 1976). Despite doubts expressed by experts concerning its usefulness, the oral interview is employed by over 90 percent of police departments looking for recruits (Territo, Swanson & Chamelin 1977).

The Background Investigation

Every conceivable attempt is made to verify the information provided by candidates through a background investigation. Most departments thoroughly investigate the applicants' educational, family, military, and financial background, as well as their criminal records (including juvenile) and personal references.

> **Box 6.2**
>
> ## The Hard Way to Become a Chief of Police
>
> A high school visit to a police department in her hometown of Lansing, Michigan, determined Penny Harrington's career choice—she wanted to be a police officer. She still had that goal when she graduated from Michigan State University and headed to Portland, Oregon, to join the police force. But there was a large obstacle to her goal; it was 1964 and Penny was a woman. Despite the difficulties, she did not give up her plan to become a police officer. Finally, she was hired in the Women's Protection Division to work with juveniles in Portland.
>
> Now Penny found other difficulties. The police department was segregated by sex and the notices for advancement tests asked for "policemen." Penny filed a suit to require the tests to be open to "police officers," not just policemen. Not only did she win the suit, she became the first woman detective on the Portland police force. She advanced through the system and became the first woman to earn the ranks of sergeant, lieutenant, and captain. The advances were not due merely to her good work; they came as a result of her filing a whopping forty-two complaints and winning almost all of them.
>
> Penny's latest advance is not a result of a suit—it is entirely due to her outstanding work, particularly her work with the community. For two and a half years prior to her new promotion, Penny Harrington was commander of a precinct in Portland. She developed an excellent reputation with both the officers in her command and with the community. It was Penny Harrington's precinct's community relations that led to her latest promotion. The Mayor of Portland, Oregon, appointed Penny Harrington as the first woman police chief in a major city in the United States.

Source: P. Allen, "Penny Harrington," *MS* (January, 1986), pp. 68–76.

Intensive probes into the personal lives of the applicants also are conducted by many departments.

The intensive screening of candidates for the police force produces a cadre of recruits who tend to accept the values of conventional conservative society. These recruits are about average in intelligence and have not been involved with drugs, crime, or any type of extremist group (Kinnane 1979). For a description of a police candidate who overcame many obstacles, see THE HARD WAY TO BECOME A CHIEF OF POLICE.

Suggested Methods for Selecting Police Officers

Most personnel selection specialists contend that the current hiring process for police officers is inadequate and does not identify which applicants will perform best on the job. These experts suggest applying current personnel selection procedures to the screening and hiring of police candidates.

The first step in the hiring process should be a job analysis to specify the skills, abilities, attributes, and qualities necessary to perform in the job (Yarmey 1990). Stotland and Berberich reviewed a number of studies on screening procedures, all of which agree that "most police selection methods have not been adequately tested because there are no agreed-on criteria or measures of good police performance" (1979, p. 51). These researchers suggest that some of the characteristics appropriate for good police work would be: decision-making ability, human relations skills, emotional maturity, communication skills, and physical qualifications.

Once the job analysis has determined the skills and abilities appropriate for police work, methods must be selected or developed to measure these qualities. There are many adequate scales and instruments already available to evaluate some of the qualifications; however, the quality of these measures varies widely.

Situational Testing

Neal Trautman (1988) suggests the use of assessment centers to improve personnel selection. Assessment centers place police candidates in an environment which elicits the behaviors to be evaluated, such as competitive discussion groups or role-playing situations. Multiple observers can assess the candidates' performance in a variety of realistic situations and provide a standardized evaluation of their behavior. This type of situational testing is one way of measuring performance for comparison with written instruments. It is also recommended for assessing some of the characteristics necessary for police work which cannot be measured through paper-and-pencil tests.

Police Training

Police training consists of an extended two-phase process of classroom instruction at an academy and street experience supervised by an experienced officer. While police training has been expanded, American recruits still have one of the shortest training programs in the world (Das 1988).

The Police Academy

Police officers spend about 15 percent of their time in law enforcement-related activities (Trautman 1988). The preponderance of their time is devoted to alleviating conflicts, giving directions, answering questions, assisting injured people getting to hospitals, locating lost children, and quieting drunks. However, training in the typical police academy allocates time in the reverse proportion, focusing primarily on crime control, with almost no training in how to deal with juveniles, the mentally disordered, or alcoholics (Bennis & Cleveland 1980, McEvoy 1975a, Schwartz, Liebman & Phelps 1975).

Even within the area of crime control, there is concern with the way police officers are taught. Patrol officers on duty have a tremendous amount of discretion. However, recruits are not taught about making decisions; they are taught to follow laws, rules, and procedures (Kelling, Wasserman & Williams 1988).

Classroom instruction is not the only source of training for recruits; they also learn from modeling. While in the academy, recruits go through a process of "anticipatory socialization," which involves observing the experienced officers in order to learn appropriate behavior (Yarmey 1990). Recruits listen to the "war" stories of the experienced police officers, picking up their attitudes, values, language, and philosophy.

Field Training

After graduation from the academy, the recruit usually goes on field training, a type of apprenticeship, and works on patrol with a more experienced police officer. Experienced officers usually begin the field training by telling rookie police officers to forget everything they learned in the academy (McEvoy 1975a, Stotland & Berberich 1979).

While on field training the rookie is further socialized into the life of a police officer. During this initiation period rookies are not trusted until they demonstrate that they have internalized the norms of their new occupation. The recruits are never explicitly told what the norms are; they must find out for themselves by observing experienced officers. To be accepted, the rookie must appear competent, confident, and decisive while at the same time displaying deference to the more experienced officers in acknowledgment of their superior experience and know-how.

Police Locker Room Culture

Each police department or precinct develops informal rules and sets of behaviors that their officers need to follow and new recruits must learn in order to be accepted by their peers (Goldsmith 1988). This macho set of norms, called the "locker room culture," decrees that a police officer must be self-confident, capable, in control, and powerful (Stotland 1982, Stotland & Berberich 1979).

Long-time members of the department watch new recruits to determine whether they should be accepted into the culture. Police officers are a close-knit group; their work is dangerous and they need to feel that they can depend on their fellow officers. New rookies who cannot be relied upon in time of trouble are ostracized and never accepted. Socialization into the locker room culture grants new police officers admission to the "brotherhood," a close-knit society in which police officers protect and defend each other from the outside world.

A Psychological Profile of the Police Officer

Obviously not all police officers have the same personality attributes, anymore than all students, lawyers, or psychologists have the same characteristics. However, members of the same occupational group tend to be more similar to each other than they are to members of another occupational group.

There are two primary explanations for this similarity. One reason is that people with similar interests tend to go into the same field. The other reason is that people working together under similar conditions begin to develop norms for behaviors, attitudes, and values. Eventually these standards are internalized and become characteristic of the people working in the situation. These factors appear to be magnified in police officers. People selected for hiring are generally similar in attitudes, values, and behavior to members of the police force (Gray 1975). Then candidates are trained to behave in the same way other police officers behave.

In his social-psychological theory of self-perception, Bem (1972) proposes that people often infer their attitudes from observations of their own behavior. Research indicates that behaving in a particular manner will influence an actor's attitudes; even imitating the overt behavior associated with a particular mood can produce the mood. Thus people who walk in a depressed manner, with heads down and shuffling their feet, begin to feel more depressed and tired than people who walk with a long stride, looking ahead and swinging their arms (Snodgrass, Higgins & Todisco 1986).

The research on how style of walking influences mood had subjects taking a mere 3-minute walk. Imagine the impact of having someone behave in a particular manner 8 hours a day, 5 days a week for years. This is exactly what happens when someone has a job requiring a particular type of behavior, such as being a police officer.

Studies of Police Personality

While no researcher maintains that all police officers have the same personality, many do contend that working as a police officer socializes people into viewing the world and behaving in similar ways (e.g., Kroes 1988, Skolnick 1975, Yarmey 1990). Westley (1970) proposes that the social-psychological aspects of the job shape police officers into a "working personality." The danger and pressures inherent in the work elicit specific perceptions of the world and behavioral reactions in the police. Most researchers agree that the behavior exhibited by police is not a reflection of underlying psychological characteristics, but rather is a result of occupational socialization (Horowitz & Willging 1984, Skolnick 1975, Yarmey 1990).

Much has been written about the "police" personality, particularly the police "working personality." The following are some of the characteristics most often attributed to police officers in performing their duties.

Authoritarianism

Many researchers contend that being a police officer shapes the person who holds the job into someone who is extremely authoritarian. Police departments are paramilitary organizations which place a lot of emphasis on chain of command, obeying orders, and internal discipline. Police believe many problems in society are due to negative attitudes toward legitimate authority. In addition, police officers see themselves as authority figures who must maintain their authority and control in order to be effective during their interactions with the public. Thus they demand that the public treat them with respect. Research in Great Britain has found that police officers who work in high-crime areas become authoritarian but not those who work in low-crime areas (Colman & Gorman 1982).

Suspiciousness

Police work is dull and at the same time dangerous, creating police officers who are both bored and afraid while on the job. The vast majority of duty time is spent on dull, routine tasks, but police officers must always be alert for the unexpected, violent incident. Police officers often deal with the outcasts of society and even seemingly respectable people are sometimes violent and dangerous. Thus police officers know they are in constant danger and must be on the lookout for potential threats. Beginning with their training in the academy, police are taught to be suspicious (Yarmey 1990).

Isolation

Because police officers are suspicious of the population as a whole, they tend to distance themselves from the rest of the community. By the same token, nonpolice members of society, knowing that the police have the authority to arrest even when not on duty, tend to be uncomfortable with, or afraid of, police officers and feel intimidated if police are at a social function. Other citizens use the opportunity of social gatherings to complain to the police about traffic tickets, arrest policies, and other police officers. All of these circumstances increase the likelihood that police officers will tend to avoid social functions with citizens and socialize entirely with other police officers (Kroes 1988). Even the families of police officers tend to isolate themselves from nonpolice families.

Police officers are not just isolated from the average citizen, they are also alienated from other members of the criminal justice system. Police think that they are the main source of justice in society. Other members of the criminal justice system frustrate the police by showing leniency toward criminals. In addition, judges, juries, and attorneys are so concerned with protecting the rights of criminals that they are perceived by the police as interfering with crime control. Police tend to think they are doing their jobs but that the rest of the criminal justice system is working against them (Blumberg 1979, Trautman 1988).

Cynicism

Constantly being alert to the possibility of danger trains the police officer to be cynical as well as suspicious. Police officers have to expect the worst from people, and eventually they define some types of people as "symbolic assailants," meaning these people are likely to assault them (Skolnick 1975). These views interact with their feelings of isolation until they view the public as hostile and unappreciative, the "enemy." They develop very negative attitudes toward a large portion of society and do not trust anyone who is not a member of the police force (Baker 1985, Kroes 1988).

Secrecy

Closely related to, and growing from, the loyalty police officers feel for each other is a secrecy, the "silence that must be maintained among the police 'brotherhood' in the face of official inquiry or review to shield one's colleagues" (Blumberg 1979, p. 82). Not only will police officers not report their colleagues, they will protect fellow officers from disclosure of misuse of police authority, brutality, stealing, and corruption (Lester & Brink 1985). There are only a few bad police officers, but the others will protect them by looking the other way. See THE DEATH OF ARTHUR McDUFFIE for a description of an incident demonstrating police secrecy and aggressiveness.

Aggressiveness

Police officers deal with a great deal of stress and frustration. Considerable social-psychological literature indicates that aggression is one of the possible responses to frustration (Baron 1977, Berkowitz 1982). Berkowitz (1969) postulates that frustration is the basis of the aggressiveness seen in the police. Fear and anger are often the causes of police brutality.

Lack of Emotion

In the course of their work, police officers come across many sad, frustrating, depressing, and traumatic incidents: they see children abused or neglected, innocent people injured in accidents or victimized by crimes, malicious criminals released without sentences, and mentally disabled individuals unable to care for themselves. In order to deal with the series of problems they encounter, police officers become somewhat detached; they separate themselves psychologically from their emotions. They become toughened and suppress their emotions in order to be able to perform their jobs (Territo & Vetter 1981).

Diversity in Police Behavior

Blumberg (1979) contends that the "working personality" of a police officer is a myth and that there are many different ways of behaving while being an accepted member of the police department. Evidence of the diversity in police officers, as well as support for some of the characteristics described as typical of police, can be found in the work of Mark Baker (1985). Baker made no attempt at conducting a scientific study but rather collected a number of vignettes from the lives of more than 100 police officers. Each of the vignettes provides some insight into the pressures and stresses in the lives of police officers, as well as an understanding of their viewpoint toward the public.

Police officers vary in their temperament, their humanitarianism, attitudes, and effectiveness on the job as do any other group of people. The vignettes provided by Baker give the reader an idea of the diversity in behavior and attitudes of police officers. One vignette describes a police officer who found a 6-year-old child in the middle of a street after an accident. The child had a broken leg and was lying in the street surrounded by people. The police officer could see the child was frightened, so he laid down on the street with the child and cradled him in his arms, telling the child to ignore the other people and just talk to him. They stayed on the ground talking until the ambulance arrived.

Another vignette describes a traffic violation in which the person who was stopped gave the officer a hard time. The police officer took the citizen's license and ate it; then he gave the person a ticket for driving without a license. This police officer maintained that there are officers throughout the country who do

> **Box 6.3**
>
> ## The Death of Arthur McDuffie
>
> The police report of an incident occurring in the wee hours of the morning on December 17, 1979, was not out of the ordinary. A black male on a motorcycle ran a red light. Traveling at speeds up to 100 mph, he attempted to elude police, running a number of red lights. The report stated that his motorcycle crashed, the suspect banged his head on the curb but still struggled with police, who had to subdue him with nightsticks. Paramedics arrived 7 minutes later to find the suspect's face covered with blood, and it was not long before he went into a coma. As it turned out, this was not an ordinary incident. By the time Arthur McDuffie died 4 days later, the authorities had begun to question inconsistencies in the police report.
>
> Arthur McDuffie, 33, was a hardworking, honest citizen, with no police record, although he had had his driver's license suspended for a series of traffic violations. A former Marine, McDuffie was an associate manager with the Coastal States Life Insurance Co., a volunteer worker with unemployed ghetto youths, and the father of two children.
>
> The authorities investigated the conflicting stories surrounding McDuffie's death and notified the Dade County State's Attorney. Nine days after the incident, Charles Veverka, one of the police officers involved in the incident, went to state prosecutors to tell the truth. He told the shocking story of how he and nine other police officers beat Arthur McDuffie senseless. McDuffie had gone through a red light the night of the incident and tried to outrun and evade the police. However, after a period of time, McDuffie stopped and surrendered. Veverka admitted that he pulled the 138-pound McDuffie off his cycle and punched him. Other police officers arrived at the scene and joined in the beating, using
>
> *(continued)*

the same thing when someone calls them names or hassles them. If the person goes to court and tells the judge what happened, the police officer will say the citizen is insane and no one would believe that the officer ate the citizen's license.

Some of the police officers who were interviewed think they are above the law. They can speed or break the laws governing traffic, even when off duty. Officers "become reflections of the people they police," taking the law into their own hands (Baker 1985, p. 300). Baker describes police officers riding through a neighborhood shooting dogs. They rationalized their behavior by saying that the ASPCA (American Society for the Prevention of Cruelty to Animals) is not going to do anything about wild dogs.

nightsticks and heavy metal flashlights. One witness was quoted as saying, "They looked like animals fighting for meat" (*Newsweek* 1980, p. 39). Even after McDuffie was lying handcuffed and still, Officer Merrero continued to hit him on the head. When it was apparent that the beating had gotten out of hand and McDuffie was obviously injured seriously, one police officer drove a squad car over the motorcycle so it would appear to have crashed. The police on the scene agreed to cover up the real story.

The police officers indicted for involvement in the beating of Arthur McDuffie had a history of brutality charges and citizens' complaints. Ira Diggs, Alex Marrero, Michael Watts, and William Hanlon were indicted for the beating. Herbert Evans was also involved in the cover-up.

The response in the black community was one of outrage; they picketed the courthouse and marched through the streets. McDuffie's family filed a $5 million suit against the county and the police. The Dade County Commission reacted by instituting better screening procedures for police officers. Among the changes were the institution of a psychological testing procedure for police officers with a view to eliminating those who are prone to violence and a new procedure for handling complaints of brutality.

Eventually eight police officers were dismissed from the force and five were tried for charges related to the incident. For the story of what happened to the police involved in the McDuffie incident, see THE MCDUFFIE VERDICT in Chapter 10.

♦

Should harsher disciplinary actions be taken against police officers found guilty of brutality? Did racial attitudes of the police influence their behavior? Should police officers be screened on racial attitude?

Sources: D. A. Williams, "Three Days of Black Rage in Miami," *Newsweek* (June 2, 1980), pp. 34–39; "Crazy Cops," *Time* (January 21, 1980), p. 32; "What Happened to 'Duff'?" *Time* (June 2, 1980), p. 14; "How Safe Is Immunity?" *Time* (August 11, 1980), p. 58.

Women Police Officers

Women are not easily accepted as police officers because of the macho orientation of the "locker room" culture. Most male officers do not think females have the physical strength or disposition to handle police work (Hindman 1975, Vega & Silverman 1982) and exclude women from the "brotherhood." Male police officers are evaluated on their working personality, which is composed of stereotypically male characteristics. However, physical ability tends to be the primary standard used to evaluate female officers. Vega and Silverman (1982) found that male officers perceived female officers as less effective in dealing with riot and violent situations because of their lack of physical strength and assertiveness.

> **Box 6.4**
>
> **Life as a Woman Cop**
>
> A petite, black woman cop was such a novelty that people thought Vertel Martin was "cute" in her Transit Police uniform. Some men even pursued her romantically while she was on duty. That was when she decided to change her demeanor. She stopped smiling on duty and started walking "bad" and holding her nightstick in a more masculine manner.
>
> Her new image commanded respect. A group of men drinking in the subway began to disperse when she approached them in her uniform. Then one of the men realized that the police officer was a very little woman and he was a very big man. He decided to challenge her, stating, "I ain't afraid of no police." Using her new tough demeanor and holding her nightstick, Martin responded with authority, "If you raise your hands to me, I will lay you out." The large man decided that he really had a great deal of "respect for the law" and quietly left at her order (p. 24).
>
> Officer Martin cannot handle every situation as easily as dispersing the group of men. In another incident, Officer Martin attempted to arrest a man who had punched out a window in the subway. Not only did he attack her but his family joined in the fight. In the fray, the officer felt someone trying to get her gun and rolled over on it. Officer Martin was trying to hold her own when backup arrived. She looks on the fight as the "best time" she's had. It taught her that she could really make it.

Source: M. Daly, "New Wave Cops," *New York* (November 14, 1983), pp. 24–30.

Research by Love and Singer (1988) discovered female officers have similar perceptions of themselves. However, there was no difference between the male and female officers' perceptions of their general effectiveness or specific effectiveness in other aspects of the job. Male and female officers also were found to be similar in psychological well-being, job satisfaction, and job involvement. For an idea of what it is like to be a woman police officer, see LIFE AS A WOMAN COP.

Women have been accepted very slowly into the ranks of the police and still account for a very small percentage of sworn officers. Female officers were housed in separate divisions where their professional activities were limited primarily to service or social work activities (e.g., searching female prisoners or handling children) until the 1970s (Bell 1982, Janus et al. 1988). Policewomen were prevented from advancing by restricting the promotional examinations to "policemen." Then, in 1961, a female officer in New York City won a suit to take the promotional exam. Four years later she became the first female sergeant (Bell 1982).

In the late 1970s, women police officers were considered "tokens." When the 1973 Crime Control Act banned sex discrimination in police departments, the number of female officers gradually began to increase. In 1974, fewer than 2 percent of sworn officers (2,857) were women (Janus et al. 1988). By 1987, that percentage had grown to 7.6 percent (17,000) sworn officers (Bureau of Justice Statistics, *Profile of State and Local Law Enforcement Agencies, 1987,* 1989).

Despite numerous studies with findings that indicate women police officers perform their jobs as effectively as males (Balkin 1988, Sherman 1975), attitudes of male officers toward female officers remain quite negative. In a comparison of male and female police officers in Washington, D.C., few differences were found in their competence or skill. However, women experienced hostility from male officers (Kinnane 1979). According to Golden, "male officer attitudes, and not female officer performance, appear to be the main problem in introducing women into law enforcement agencies" (1981, p. 29).

Janus and his colleagues interviewed 135 women police officers in New York City and vicinity. They found most of these officers enjoyed their work and felt the public responded to them in ways equivalent to male officers. Many officers believed being female actually helped them to be more successful in their interactions with the public. However, over half of the women reported being "assigned a demeaning detail solely because they were women" (Janus et al. 1988, p. 125). A large proportion of the female officers (68 percent) reported being sexually harassed while on the job and a good number (30 percent) suffered some difficulty in being accepted by their male colleagues.

Police Families

Most of the research on police families has dealt with the families of male police officers. Niederhoffer and Neiderhoffer contend that all police families are similar, "patterned by the lathe of the police occupation" (1978, p. 1). These researchers maintain that the police officer is so tied to his job that it becomes a "jealous mistress." Territo and Vetter agree, asserting that police work becomes a "way of life for the officer, his spouse, and his family" (1981, p. 202).

Wives do not like their husbands to be police officers, not just because of fear for their safety, but more importantly because of the impact the job has on their husbands' emotions. As described earlier, in order to deal with the traumatic and horrible incidents seen every day, police officers distance themselves psychologically from their emotions. It is difficult to abandon this cold and aloof behavior after work, and most men bring this aspect of their "working personality" home with them (Kroes 1988). Therefore, wives believe their husbands become tough and cold and are "less loving and lovable" (Kinnane 1979, p. 65).

Officers also bring their suspicious and cynical attitudes home with them. They worry that something might happen to a member of their family and therefore want to know where they are at all times. Often this concern is interpreted as suspicion and distrustfulness by the family (Kroes 1988, Territo & Vetter 1981).

Stress and the Police Officer

Police work is considered one of the most stressful occupations (Band & Manuele 1987). Police officers have to cope with danger, fear, anger, boredom, bureaucracy, responsibility for the lives of others, and feelings of isolation. They are frustrated by their dealings with the rest of the criminal justice system and feel no support from the administration or the community (Ellison & Genz 1983, Kroes 1988). In addition, the irregular hours and weekend work decrease the time officers can spend with their families, putting stress on their domestic lives. It is no wonder that, with this emotionally hazardous occupation, officers often experience marital and family problems, as well as emotional problems such as depression, alcoholism, and even suicide.

There is evidence that emotional problems are the primary cause of police officers leaving the police force. Many who do not quit are dissatisfied with their jobs and do not perform at high levels. They often exhibit "burnout syndrome" due to extensive amounts of stress. Burnout consists of "emotional and physical depletion, negative self-esteem and negative attitudes toward people, life, and work" (Band & Manuele 1987, p. 122).

Police departments have begun to institute programs to alleviate the stress faced by police officers in an attempt to retain the people they have spent an average of $30,000 to train. There are many methods that have been employed to decrease problems with stress. Some departments offer confidential treatment for both the officer and his or her family, and stress management courses are offered by other departments.

Police Discretion and the Arrest Process: Police Interactions with the Public

Wilson (1968) identifies three general types of responsibilities or functions which police officers have: legal, order maintenance, and service. Police officers accomplish their legal responsibilities through arrests and law enforcement. The maintaining of order involves controlling public disturbances, family altercations, and traffic, while service functions include taking people to the hospital, giving information, and helping people in distress. Different police departments place different amounts of emphasis on each of these functions, but in general, 70 to 80 percent of the incidents to which police respond are service requests (Bennis & Cleveland 1980, Webster 1973) and from 80 to 90 percent of police staff and resources are used for peacekeeping or helping duties (Bayley 1979).

On-duty police officers devote most of their time to routine activities, such as driving around, writing accident reports, helping people open locked cars, rushing women in labor to the hospital, or making reports on minor incidents. But even the police themselves believe the common stereotype that their primary function is law enforcement. They regard service as an annoying burden and often complain that these demands on their time prevent them from performing their *real* job—law enforcement. Most criminologists (e.g., Kelling 1988, Skolnick & Bayley 1986, Sparrow 1988) maintain that service duties are an important aspect of the police function, if not the primary purpose, while a few believe service is peripheral to the job (Cohn & Udolf 1979, Cumming, Cumming & Edell 1965).

Police Discretion

The image of the police as law enforcer conceals the tremendous amount of discretion inherent in police behavior. The police have more discretion than other members of the criminal justice system because much of their day-to-day behavior cannot be observed. The police officer on the street can decide not to arrest someone and no one else in the criminal justice system will be aware of that decision.

Although police manuals generally instruct the police to enforce every law against all people, very few police contacts lead to arrests or even citations. Laws which the police are supposed to enforce are ambiguous and do not encompass all aspects of socially disapproved behavior. To the police officer, the law is a constraint, indicating what the officer is not allowed to do, but not specifying what behavior is appropriate in a particular situation (Kelling, Wasserman & Williams 1988). Law enforcement policies and procedures are also somewhat vague and do not designate exactly what the police officer should do in specific instances. In addition, there is not enough time for the police to investigate every incident or arrest every law violator. These ambiguities and time constraints give the police a lot of leeway as to which laws to enforce. Every police officer at the scene of an incident is an arbiter of the law who decides what behavior constitutes an infraction of the law, who should be arrested, and what charges should be filed (Gottfredson & Gottfredson 1988, Moore, Trojanowicz & Kelling 1988).

Police officers evaluate a situation and then do what they feel is necessary to control it (Fisk 1974). As Bayley states, the police are authorized "to utilize force within the community to handle whatever needs doing" (1979, p. 113). If they need to use force, then they invoke the law as a justification (Rumbaut & Bittner 1979). The police have the authority to make an arrest, but they do not *have* to make an arrest. When a police officer arrests someone, it is not because the person broke the law; the formal charge is used to *justify* the arrest. The real reason the officer arrests someone is that the officer thinks it is necessary to do so in order to handle the incident (Bittner 1974). See JOGGING CAN BE DANGEROUS TO YOUR FREEDOM.

Reactive Activities and Decisions

Reiss (1971) distinguishes between "reactive" and "proactive" activities of the police. Reactive activities are those in which the police officer is responding to a report of criminal activity, while proactive activities are those which the officer initiates, e.g., traffic violations. Police spend the vast majority of their time in reactive activities.

Police officers want to demonstrate that they are in control of all interactions with the public. They also want to ensure that they are respected by society. These two motivations underlie many of the decisions police officers make.

Pepinsky outlines four ways in which the police demonstrate their control: "(1) meeting what they perceive to be expected of them; (2) anticipating what kinds of situations will warrant offense reports and then fulfilling their own

Box 6.5

Jogging Can be Dangerous to Your Freedom

Benjamin L. Wall, a health-conscious 69-year-old retired Navy chief warrant officer, used to jog until he was arrested for it. He lives in a nice neighborhood near the river in Jacksonville, Florida. Ever since he moved into his apartment, he had taken the same jogging route along the river and through the neighborhood. He regularly ran about 2 miles by going six times around the route.

Then something happened that stopped his jogging. One night he just could not sleep; at 2:45 A.M. he finally gave up trying and went out to jog. Dressed in his all-white jogging outfit (including a cap with "America" on it), he began to run his usual route. He ran down the middle of the street and had completed five laps when a police car stopped him. The officer asked for identification, which Wall was not carrying. When asked what he was doing, Wall responded sarcastically, "I'm exercising my constitutional rights." Annoyed, the police officer said he had been getting calls about Wall for prowling.

Wall could not believe that anyone thought a 69-year-old man running in white shorts down the middle of the street could be prowling. Both men were now agitated and began to argue. Wall felt victimized and the police officer did not feel he was getting the respect he deserved. Then Wall made an obscene gesture. But the police officer had the last word: "You're under arrest." The officer charged Wall with breach of peace and took him to jail. Wall spent 37 hours in jail before he could find a neighbor to lend him the $252 bail money.

But Wall's troubles were not over. He hired a lawyer to defend him in court. Almost immediately the attorney had a plea bargain for him. Charges would be dropped if Wall agreed not to sue. Wall would have none of that; he wanted his day in court to prove his innocence, and he wanted to sue. Although people almost never have jury trials for misdemeanors, Wall's attorney was able to win the right to one for Wall. But the jury decided that Wall was guilty of breach of the peace because he was screaming and hollering. His sentence? A fine of $100 plus court costs of $225. Wall also paid his attorney $750 to defend him for jogging. Jogging was no longer the enjoyable pastime it had been, and Wall bought himself a ten-speed bicycle.

♦

Was Benjamin Wall committing a crime when he was stopped by the police officer? Do you think the police officer handled the situation in an appropriate manner? Should Benjamin Wall have been arrested? Should the prosecutor have taken the case to court? Was the jury decision an appropriate one?

Source: R. Blade, "Jogger Runs into Trouble with the Law," *The Florida Times-Union* (August 22, 1985), p. B–1.

> **Box 6.6**
>
> **Robin and the Police**
>
> Robin is an attractive and vivacious young black woman with a quick smile and enthusiastic nature. One night Robin was driving a car belonging to a friend. She was going very fast and hit a car pulling out of a driveway. She immediately knew it was her fault, apologized, and offered to pay for the damages. The driver of the car would not be pacified. He ranted and raved, continuing to do so even after the police arrived. Robin explained the circumstances and took complete responsibility for the accident. Again, she said she would pay for the damages. The other driver continued to scream at both the police officer and Robin. Finally, the police officer gave the other driver a ticket for causing the accident and told Robin she was free to go (personal communication 1988).
>
> ♦
>
> Should the other driver have received a ticket for an accident that Robin admitted causing? Should Robin have been alleviated from all responsibility because of her demeanor?

prophesies; (3) asserting their control by making decisions opposite to those they believe any parties who challenge their control would want them to make; and (4) making decisions as to whether to report offenses in such a way as to show that they identify with respectable people of apparently attractive social status and to show they identify against the unrespectable" (1975, p. 32).

The latter two ways of demonstrating control are characteristic of rookie officers who tend to react on the basis of the citizen's demeanor and status. After being socialized into the police department, officers demonstrate control by doing what they think is expected of them and by anticipating which situations will call for offense reports. Let us first look at how rookie police officers decide whether to invoke the law during incidents.

The Influence of Demeanor on Police Decisions
New police officers are particularly concerned with demonstrating their authority and control in law enforcement situations. They are very sensitive to their perceived status and the demeanor of those with whom they interact. In most situations, police officers can lecture suspects, issue them a citation, or arrest them and take them to jail without much reference to the severity of the offense. Since they have limited time in which to gather information, the police will, in many instances, decide what to do on the basis of the activities or demeanor of the people involved (Adams 1972, Horowitz & Willging 1984).

If the alleged offender is disrespectful or hostile, the officer is very likely to invoke the law; however, if the offender is cooperative and respectful, the officer is less likely to file a report (Horowitz & Willging 1984, Smith & Visher 1981). ROBIN AND THE POLICE demonstrates how demeanor influences police decisions.

Behavior of the person making the complaint also influences decisions of police officers. For example, if the complainant is very respectful to the police and really wants to have a report filed, the officer is likely to go along with those wishes (Black 1971).

In order to understand the motivation behind these decisions, one must realize that police officers identify with the law. They believe someone's behavior toward a police officer is indicative of that person's attitude toward the law in general. Thus, when a police officer decides in favor of someone who is respectful toward her, she is rewarding the citizen who has respect for the law. Likewise, when a police officer arrests someone who is hostile, he is punishing a person who does not respect the law (Pepinsky 1975).

The Influence of Status and Race on Police Decisions

New police officers try to identify with people who have high status and dissociate themselves from those with low status. They do this by following the requests of people with high status and acting in such a way as to oppose the desires of those with low status. Thus, if a complaint is made against a suspect who is poor and black, the police officer is more likely to file a report and/or make an arrest than if the same complaint were made against a middle-class white person (Lundman, Sykes & Clark 1978, Piliavin & Briar 1964, Smith & Visher 1981).

Sometimes police officers cover cases in which the race and socioeconomic status of the offender are unknown. For example, someone reporting a burglary of his home probably has no idea who perpetrated the crime. The officer investigating this type of crime cannot make a decision on the basis of the characteristics of the offender and, therefore, decides on the basis of the status of the victim. In these cases, the officers are more likely to file charges if the complainant has high socioeconomic status.

The Influence of Socially Expected Responses on Police Decisions

After years of reacting to people on the basis of their demeanor and status, these reactions become internalized into the behavior of the police officer. Police maintain that it takes anywhere from 1 to 5 years for a new police officer to become "streetwise"—to be able to decide whether someone is a criminal by observing that person's behavior.

Streetwise senior police officers react to incidents in the manner they perceive is expected of them and make the socially expected response. For example, if they have been sent to the crime scene by the dispatcher, their behavior often depends on whether the dispatcher has identified an offense. Once an offense has been identified, the police officer is likely to file a report for that offense. If the dispatcher has not mentioned an offense, the decision to file a report and the offense recorded depend on the request of the complainant (Pepinsky 1975, Davis 1975).

Senior officers tend to invoke the law when the offense is serious and to handle less-serious offenses informally. By taking formal actions against serious offenses, senior officers indicate to their superiors that they are concerned with law enforcement activities and are performing up to expectations. Police officers tend to handle more situations informally the greater their length of service (Bozza 1973).

The Influence of Self-Fulfilling Prophecy on Police Decisions

After a number of years of treating suspects differently based on their demeanor and socioeconomic status, streetwise senior officers have learned the stereotypes; they know who is likely to commit an offense because they have arrested that type of person many times before (Pepinsky 1975). And since they know this person is a criminal type and likely to commit an offense, they are more likely to arrest him now. This process demonstrates the self-fulfilling prophecy. If person A expects person B to behave in a particular manner, then person A is likely to elicit that behavior from person B without being aware of it. For example, when deciding whether an activity is an offense, the police officer uses his experience and the concepts he has internalized. If this officer has arrested many minorities and poor people, then he will believe that these people are criminals. When the officer observes someone who conforms to the stereotype, that is, a poor person or a minority group member, he will be more likely to perceive that person as a criminal and make an arrest. Once arrested, the person is a criminal and it reinforces the police officer's stereotype.

Commonly held police stereotypes have a systematic impact on police behavior. Police officers are more likely to arrest minorities and low socioeconomic status individuals because these people fit the police stereotype of an offender (McEvoy 1975b, Lundman, Sykes & Clark 1978, Smith & Visher 1981, Stotland 1982).

Treatment of Females by the Police

Historically, females have received more lenient treatment by police than men (Anderson 1976, Crites 1976, Moulds 1980, Nagel & Weitzman 1971). Pollak (1950) contends women are not as likely as men to commit *visible* crimes; so police are unlikely to stereotype females as criminals and less likely to treat them as offenders. However, other researchers attribute the differential treatment of females to chivalry on the part of the male-dominated police force. Visher says chivalry "represents the phenomenon whereby women receive preferential treatment during the criminal justice process" (1983, p. 6). However, chivalry is not equally accorded to all women, and it is not given without qualifications. Chivalry appears to be given only to white females who display what police consider appropriate sex-role behaviors of submissiveness and deference. Blacks and hostile or aggressive white females, particularly young ones, are likely to receive harsh treatment (DeFleur 1975, Visher 1983).

Proactive Activities and Decisions

When police officers intervene in the behavior of a citizen, they are involved in proactive activities. People do not like police to interfere with their behavior and can become very hostile; therefore, the police are careful about their proactive activities and justify them before intruding in the citizen's affairs (Grant, Grant

& Toch 1982). Officers have the same basic goal or motivation for maintaining control and respect as they do when reacting to a complaint. However, when making proactive decisions, officers are not as likely to rely on status as they are in reactive decisions, and they use the demeanor of the individual only after deciding that they should intervene in the activity (Pepinsky 1975). In other words, the police adjust their responses to reflect the demeanor of the citizen. For example, the officer might give a very polite and courteous person a warning instead of a ticket for speeding.

Traffic violations are one of the most common proactive activities of the police. They are likely to stop anyone committing a violation, but once stopped, the citizen's demeanor influences the likelihood of getting a ticket. After a thorough study of the police in Minneapolis, Pepinsky (1975) enumerated responses by the citizen which increase the likelihood of receiving a ticket. Any response that indicated the citizen did not have respect for the officer resulted in a ticket. Drivers admitting that the officer was right, that they had committed the violation, and calling the officer "sir" were likely to receive a warning. Behaving in the latter manner shows respect for the police officer and for the law and demonstrates that the officer is in control. However, arguing displays disrespect for the police officer and the law, so the officer feels compelled to teach that driver to respect the law.

Effectiveness of Reactive vs. Proactive Approaches

Inability to control rising crime rates has led to critical evaluation of policing strategies. Moore, Trojanowicz, and Kelling feel that during the 1970s and 1980s, "confidence in the reactive approach has been eroded by the accumulation of empirical evidence suggesting that these tactics are of only limited effectiveness" (1988, p. 6). For example, the Kansas City Preventive Patrol Study found that doubling the number of patrol cars had no significant impact on crime. In response to criticism, the police have developed proactive strategies to deal with specific problems that reactive tactics do not resolve, for example: child abuse, drug dealing, and vice. These proactive strategies involving the use of informants, decoys, sting operations, and undercover agents have been shown to increase arrests.

Wilson and Boland (1978, 1982) found that crime rates decrease with an increase in proactive and aggressive police strategies. (These strategies are apparent in departments with legalistic styles of policing, described in the next section on styles of policing.) These authors speculate that the decrease in crime is due to the greater likelihood of arrest of people breaking the law and the deterrence of potential offenders who perceive the likelihood of arrest as greater.

Sampson and Cohen support Wilson's and Boland's theory, proposing that aggressive or proactive policing reduces social disorder, which in turn decreases criminal activity. They define a proactive police strategy as the "extent to which officers invoke a formal law enforcement response even for minor infractions" (1988, p. 169). They hypothesize that social disorder (e.g., public intoxication, disorderly conduct) leads to an increase in crime because criminals believe no one will intervene. Therefore, a decrease in social disorder produces a decrease in crime. These researchers collected data from every U.S. city with a population over 100,000 in 1980 to test their theory. The data support the theory; more arrests for DUI and disorderly conduct per police officer were correlated with lower robbery rates. However, the data is correlational and cannot show cause and effect.

Styles of Policing

Wilson (1968) identifies three primary styles of policing: the watchman style, the legalistic style, and the service style. These styles are related to the makeup of the community, local politics, and the administrative policies of the department.

The **watchman style** places most of its focus on order maintenance rather than enforcing laws. Members of police forces dominated by this style tend to have very little training and receive low pay. Acceptance into the department and promotions within the department are dominated by the local controlling political party. These factors result in a high turnover rate within the department.

Departments with a **legalistic style** concentrate on strict enforcement of the law; officers make many arrests and give many citations. Police officers are instructed to view every incident from a law enforcement perspective. These strictly controlled departments are devoted to professionalism and protected from community influence.

A department emphasizing a **service style** is sensitive to the interests and concerns of the community, devoting much energy to public relations. Its police officers are not likely to arrest or give citations in most situations.

Current Trends in Policing Styles

Kelling and Moore (1988) trace the history of police strategy through three phases: the *Political Era* dating from the 1840s through the early 1900s, the *Reform Era* from the 1930s through the late 1970s, and the *Community Problem-Solving Era* beginning in the 1980s. They do not maintain that all police departments used the same strategy during these periods but that these were the predominant ones.

During the Political Era, police were an appendage of the local political machines running the cities. Police provided diverse services to members of the community: helping immigrants find work or shelter, running food lines, as well as crime fighting. Their close association with the people provided police with easy access to bribes and graft, giving rise to police corruption.

In response to the corruption of the Political Era, the Reform Era initiated the separation of police from both politics and the people. The main function of the police became law enforcement. However, this style of policing was not a panacea. In the 1960s and 1970s there was a tremendous increase in crime rates. Citizens became afraid of victimization, minorities felt they were not treated equitably, and civil rights groups challenged the police. Meanwhile, research disputed the effectiveness of police strategies, cutbacks were made in funding, and police officers were discontented.

According to Kelling, Wasserman, and Williams (1988), the primary focus of most police departments today is counterproductive for fighting crime. The problems with current police methods are summarized by Skolnick and Bayley: "increasing the number of police officers, for example, does not reduce crime; random motorized patrolling does not enhance public safety; rapid emergency response neither produces more arrests of criminals nor reassures the public; and crimes are rarely solved by policemen acting on the basis of physical evidence but require victims and witnesses to identify perpetrators and give persuasive testimony" (1986, p. 212).

Innovative police departments are addressing these problems by using community problem-solving strategies for policing. This approach is described as "a police department striving for an absence of crime and disorder and concerned with, and sensitive to, the quality of life in the community" (Sparrow 1988, p. 1). This type of policing is less militaristic and more participatory in its management style than the Reform Era departments. It deemphasizes the old police manuals and increases problem solving or reasonableness of actions; it involves a shift from dependence on rules and regulations to values and principles.

One of the features of community policing is a return to foot patrol which has "reduced fear, increased citizen satisfaction with police, improved police attitudes toward citizens, and increased the morale and job satisfaction of police" (Kelling, Wasserman & Williams 1988, p. 10). However, foot patrol alone does not identify a department's style as being community policing. Community policing is not a single concept or program. Skolnick and Bayley (1986) enumerate four elements necessary to identify a department's strategy as community policing: 1) **police–community reciprocity,** which means the police and residents really interact and communicate and the police truly believe community involvement is necessary for policing; 2) **a real decentralization of command,** involving the location of substations within the neighborhoods and the long-term assignment of officers to the same substation; 3) **reorientation of patrol,** meaning the institution of foot patrols or the combination of motor and foot patrols where the officer leaves the patrol car periodically to walk; and 4) **civilianization,** which involves having civilians perform many of the non-law enforcement tasks: clerical, traffic, dispute mediation, research, and training.

Individual Styles of Policing

While the above styles of policing are determined by the police departments, Kinnane (1979) has identified a different set of policing styles, based on the behavior of the individual officer: safe, producing, crime fighting, avoiding, and street policing.

The police officer who demonstrates the **safe** style of policing does not put much effort into his job. Concerned primarily with security and safety, this kind, peaceful officer tends to try to diffuse tense situations and avoid making arrests. This style of policing is usually found in older officers who are close to retirement.

The **producing** officers legalistically enforce the law and measure their own worth in terms of the great number of tickets they give and the car stops they make. They consider themselves enforcers and do not want to be bothered with service activities. These officers tend to be immature and even dangerous, causing other officers to avoid them.

The **crime fighting** police officers view themselves as heroes and act the part of the movie version of a dedicated police officer. These officers really want to control crime and put a great deal of effort into their jobs. Believing that they can be promoted to detective if they make the "big arrest," they are always looking for serious offenders.

At the other end of the continuum from the crime fighting officer is the **avoiding** police officer who does anything possible to avoid work. Happily there are only a few of these unproductive officers. They pursue easy assignments and hide while on the job so as to keep from doing too much work. They refrain from making arrests which would require them to attend court on their days off and are particularly careful not to get involved in an incident which might require them to work beyond the end of their shift.

Street policing is a common style, especially for the young police officer. These police officers are enthusiastic about the crime fighting aspect of their jobs but do not care to perform service duties. They enjoy the risk-taking of high-speed chases and physical confrontation. Tending to be aggressive and courageous, they have a big influence on the police subculture. Almost all police officers have some degree of this style in their attitudes.

While the styles were described as if they were discrete, most police officers have some of the characteristics of more than one of these styles. In fact, it is quite likely that an individual officer will manifest attitudes or behaviors of several different styles during the course of a career.

Police Interrogation Methods

During the investigation of a serious crime, the police are concerned primarily with determining who committed the offense. Thus, if they have a suspect or a possible accomplice, they want to find out everything that person knows about the crime. By the time the police arrest a suspect, they are usually thoroughly convinced the suspect committed the crime. Then all they have to do is convince the suspect to confess to the crime and tell them everything that he knows about the crime.

In their pursuit of information or a confession, the police can become coercive in their interrogation methods. The psychological procedures used by police departments to elicit statements may even extract a confession from someone who is innocent (Horowitz & Willging 1984, Kassin & McNall 1991). After studying police manual instructions on how to conduct interrogations, Zimbardo (described in Horowitz & Willging 1984) identified five psychological methods recommended to police for eliciting information and confessions.

1) **Demand characteristics of the situation.** The police are advised to set up an environment for interrogating suspects that would help elicit information. This area should not look like a police station and the officers doing the interrogating should not wear uniforms. Inbau and

Reid, authors of a popular police manual, suggest the use of a special room without windows and with very little furniture. This same manual urges keeping the suspect from communicating with family or friends. These psychological characteristics of the situation make it more likely the suspect will eventually tell the police what they want to know.

2) **Techniques of distortion.** Police are encouraged to change the suspect's perception of the incident. For example, if the police either greatly increase or decrease the seriousness of the crime, propose mitigating circumstances, or suggest the crime was committed in self-defense, the suspect is more likely to confess.

3) **Distortion of the social-psychological situation.** These methods include establishing rapport with the suspect by displaying empathy and understanding. One suggested technique is the "good cop/bad cop" method, where one officer plays the nice guy, pretending to protect the suspect from the mean cop, played by a second officer. The suspect is likely to cooperate with the nice police officer and give him a confession.

4) **Use of personality and clinical techniques.** Some police manuals suggest evaluating the psychological state of the suspect and gearing the questioning methods to these evaluations. Both verbal and nonverbal behavior should be observed to form an assessment of the suspect.

5) **Semantic and verbal distortion.** Interrogation manuals suggest that police play on the guilt of a first-time juvenile by saying how devastating the crime will be to the juvenile's mother. The manuals also give instructions on how to word a question to extract the information, for example, by asking where something is rather than whether it exists.

Although there is no way of knowing how many people have confessed to a crime they did not commit, there is anecdotal evidence of a number of cases (Frank & Frank 1957, Rattner 1988). Kassin and Wrightsman (1985) identify three types of false confessions: voluntary false confessions, coerced-compliant confessions, and coerced-internalized confessions. See CONFESSIONS OF A MURDERER.

There are many motivations for making a **voluntary false confession,** ranging from protecting someone else to mental illness. After the Lindbergh baby was kidnapped, more than 200 people confessed to the crime, which Kassin and Wrightsman attribute to a "morbid desire for notoriety" (1985, p. 76).

The second type of false confession, the **coerced-compliant confession,** is elicited from a suspect who is in an altered state of consciousness, similar to being under hypnosis. The suspect, through fatigue and stress, becomes extremely suggestive and complies to the request for a confession. In the **coerced-internalized** type of false confession, the person being interrogated is also in a trancelike state. Because of the coercive methods used to elicit the confession, the suspect begins to believe that she or he actually committed the crime.

Box 6.7

Confessions of a Murderer

Henry Lee Lucas was an unknown drifter in 1983 when he confessed to killing his 15-year-old niece and traveling companion as well as an 80-year-old widow in Texas. It was not the first time Lucas had been convicted of murder. He had spent 10 years in a Michigan prison for the stabbing death of his mother, a prostitute. Less than a year after his release, he was convicted of an attempted abduction. He spent another 5 years in prison for that offense until his 1975 release.

With his conviction on the Texas murders, Lucas faced an unpleasant life on death row in the Huntsville, Texas, prison. But Lucas found a way to postpone, if not avoid, death row. He confessed to other murders. Not one or two, but hundreds of unsolved murders. At one time, police estimated that he might be responsible for up to 600 murders in 27 states. He claimed to have committed some of these murders alone, some with casual acquaintances, and many with his friend and lover, Otis Elwood Toole. Lucas and Toole met in 1976 and claimed to have wandered around the country killing victims at random. After his confessions, Lucas was taken by jet plane to the scenes of the incidents where he impassively described brutally killing and mutilating random victims of every age, race, and sex.

Then, in 1985, Lucas recanted all his confessions, saying he had confessed as a perverse way of ridiculing the police. He said it was an attempt at legal suicide. Lucas claimed he made the confessions because of the attention, to receive gifts and favors from the police, and to avoid death row. There were even claims that he received a milk shake for each unsolved death for which he confessed.

Closer scrutiny found that Lucas had confessed to crimes committed in distant sections of the country at about the same time. One series of six crimes occurring within a month would have required 11,000 miles of driving in his 13-year-old station wagon. By the time he recanted his confessions, Lucas had been convicted of ten murders. In one of the murders for which he was convicted, there was a great deal of evidence that Lucas could not have committed it: witnesses said he was 600 miles away at the time of the crime, and blood and semen samples from the scene did not match Lucas's. In addition, someone else had confessed to the crime. An indictment for a murder of a 72-year-old Texas woman was dropped by a judge who felt that Lucas's confession was involuntary. Citing the favors and treatment given by the police, the judge stated, "You can catch as many flies with honey as with a fly swatter" (Lacayo 1987).

♦

Should the police give special treatment to suspected criminals in order to encourage them to confess to crimes? Should convicted felons be given attention and favors if they confess to crimes? Should all confessions be treated with skepticism? What danger does a false confession pose for society with the actual criminal still on the loose?

Sources: R. Lacayo, "Master of Cant and Recant," *Time* (January 12, 1987), p. 66; A. Stanley, "Catching a New Breed of Killer," *Time* (November 14, 1983), p. 47; "A Mass Murder Reconsidered," *Time* (April 29, 1985), p. 50.

In order to avoid acquiring false information from witnesses and suspects, Freedman (1988) suggests guidelines for investigative interviewing and interrogation. He recommends that a special police unit be created to conduct interrogations and experts in behavioral science be trained or hired for the unit. He also advises audio- or videotaping of all statements.

Coerced Confessions

A confession by a suspect is one of the strongest pieces of evidence a prosecutor can present in a trial. Armed with a confession, a prosecutor can win a conviction with little or no additional evidence. Because a confession is such a strong weapon against a defendant, and because a false confession can be coerced, the admission of a confession has been hotly contested in numerous cases. The defense argument to exclude a confession as evidence has generally centered on the manner in which the confession was elicited.

In 1897 the United States Supreme Court ruled that confessions are not admissible if they were elicited by threats or promises whether direct or implied (*Bram v. United States*). In actual practice, confessions tend to be excluded if they were obtained through the use of direct threats or promises but allowed if the promises and/or threats were implied (Kassin & McNall 1991).

The United States Supreme Court stated in the *Miranda* (1966) decision that the then-current police methods of interrogation were psychologically coercive. As a result of the Supreme Court decision, police modified their interrogation techniques to "noncoercive" methods. These noncoercive techniques, which include implied promises and threats, are the current methods used to obtain confessions.

Saul Kassin and Karlyn McNall (1991) identify two methods using implied threats or promises which could "coax" suspects into confessing to a crime that they did not commit. The first method, **maximization,** is defined as "a 'hard-sell' technique in which the interrogator tries to scare and intimidate the suspect into confessing by making false claims about evidence (e.g., staging an eyewitness identification or a fraudulent lie-detector test) and exaggerating the seriousness of the offense and the magnitude of the charges" (pp. 234–235). The second technique is **minimization,** "a 'soft-sell' technique in which the police interrogator tries to lull the suspect into a false sense of security by offering sympathy, tolerance, face-saving excuses, and even moral justification, by blaming a victim or accomplice, by citing extenuating circumstances, or by playing down the seriousness of the charges" (p. 235).

In a series of experiments, Kassin and McNall (1991) found that the implied threats and promises of maximization and minimization were communicated to subjects and influenced their sentencing expectations. Confessions elicited by these methods most likely would be admissible in court. Prior research shows that mock jurors consider confessions elicited by threats as involuntary and thus discount them when deciding on a verdict. However, confessions acquired through promises of leniency are not entirely discounted (Kassin & Wrightsman 1985). Similarly, mock jurors were much more likely to convict a defendant on the basis of confessions elicited by promises or minimization than involuntary confessions or those elicited by threats (Kassin & McNall 1991).

At the same time that social scientists are documenting the effect of implied threats and promises in eliciting confessions, the Supreme Court has reversed the precedent of almost a century by approving the admission of some coerced confessions into evidence. In *Arizona v. Fulminante* (1991) the court ruled that some cases of coerced confession could be "harmless error" if other evidence indicating guilt was present.

Summary

The lengthy, involved process of hiring new police officers can take as long as a year and a half. The selection process varies greatly by department, city, and state, but despite their differences, the procedures in most jurisdictions have basic similarities. Considerable concern is expressed among professionals about the efficacy of the procedures used to screen for police officers. These experts suggest applying current personnel selection procedures to the screening and hiring of candidates for police officer positions.

Police training entails an extended two-phase process of classroom instruction at an academy and street experience supervised by an experienced officer. While in the academy, the recruits go through a process of "anticipatory socialization." Then, while on field training, the rookie is socialized into the life of a police officer and has to earn acceptance. Women have a great deal of difficulty in being accepted as police officers because of the macho orientation of the "locker room" culture.

Westley (1970) proposes that the social-psychological aspects of the job of police officer shape the people in that occupation into a "working personality." Blumberg (1979) maintains the "working personality" of a police officer is a myth, contending there are many different ways of behaving while being an accepted member of the police department.

Police officers have three general types of responsibility or function: legal, order maintenance, and service. Police officers want to demonstrate that they are in control of any interaction with the public and ensure that they are respected by society. Police officers are likely to be influenced by the demeanor and status of the complainant and accused when deciding on a reaction.

Three primary styles of policing determined by police departments are: the watchman style, the legalistic style, and the service style. A different set of policing styles based on the behavior of the individual officer consists of: safe, producing, crime fighting, avoiding, and street policing.

The history of police strategy is traced through three phases: the Political Era dating from the 1840s through the early 1900s, the Reform Era from the 1930s through the late 1970s, and the Community Problem-Solving Era beginning in the 1980s. The primary focus of most police departments today is counterproductive for fighting crime. Therefore, innovative police departments are using community problem-solving strategies for policing.

Research indicates confessions are sometimes made by innocent people. Suspects have many motivations for giving false confessions, not the least of which are the coercive methods used by the police to extract confessions. False confessions provide law enforcement officials with an arrest and enable them to clear the case. However, the actual offender is still free to commit future offenses while the victim of the crime and the public have been given a false sense of security.

7

The Process from Arrest to Trial

The Jail Experience
Booking
Bail and Bond
Consequences of Not Making Bail
Functions and Discretion of the Prosecutor
Functions of the Prosecutor
Roles of the Prosecutor
The Decision to Press Charges
Overcharging
Pretrial Diversion Programs
The Grand Jury
History of the Grand Jury
Minority Representation on the Grand Jury
Advantages of the Grand Jury
Pretrial Proceedings
First Appearance
The Public Defender
Preliminary Hearing
The Arraignment
Pretrial Motions
Plea Bargaining
The Bargain for the Defendant
The Bargain for the Prosecutor
Plea Bargaining for the Defense Attorney
The Judge and the Plea Bargain
Evaluation of the Plea Bargaining System
Elimination of Plea Bargaining
Summary

The Jail Experience

What happens after a suspect is arrested? The suspect goes to trial and, if adjudicated guilty, is sent to jail, otherwise he is released. Right? Well, yes, but not as quickly as most people think. The legal system is complex and involved; it also moves slowly. See Figure 7.1 for an overview of the criminal justice system. People do not go to trial the day after their arrest or, in most cases, even the week or month after their arrest. In this chapter, we will see what happens to the accused from the time of arrest until the beginning of a trial.

Booking

Someone arrested for a criminal act is "booked" at the jail. Booking is "the procedure by which an administrative record is made of the arrest" (Cole 1986, p. 125) and is tantamount to being admitted to jail. The entire process of booking a suspect might take as long as 2 or 3 hours and is traumatic for the accused, particularly if this is the person's first experience with jail.

The suspect is searched immediately upon reaching the jail and relieved of all personal belongings. Then the accused is taken to the identification room for fingerprinting and photographing. In a large facility, medical staff evaluate the accused upon admission to determine if there is any immediate need for medical attention, drug or alcohol counseling, or if the person has any chronic condition requiring daily medication. The accused is then taken to a holding cell.

The typical holding cell is about 10' × 10' and can hold up to twenty people. It is a windowless room with concrete seats around the wall. There is a toilet in one corner without any form of privacy. Sometimes phones are located in the holding cells so people can contact their lawyers, families, or bail bondsmen. During busy times, such as weekend nights, the holding cell is brimming with people, many of whom are very intoxicated.

Jails are used as temporary holding facilities for people accused of crimes until they are released on bond or go to trial. Jails are also used to incarcerate people adjudicated guilty of less serious offenses, while people convicted of serious offenses and sentenced to long terms are sent to prisons. Many of the people incarcerated in jails are awaiting trial. According to our constitution, these people are innocent until proven guilty by a court of law. However, the U.S. Supreme Court has ruled in *Bell v. Wolfish* (1979) that persons awaiting trial may be treated as convicted offenders in the interests of security.

Whenever people are admitted to large institutions, even universities, these people are socialized into their new group. The effectiveness of socialization is increased by the elimination of prior roles, a process called desocialization. There are a number of ways in which desocialization can be encouraged. One example is removal of a person's clothing and jewelry, which people wear as a means of self-expression, demonstrating individuality. Another way of eliminating prior roles is to sever people's connections with members of their previous social groups. These people then are identified solely as members of their new group, in this case, inmates in jail. The goal of jail administrators is not to desocialize people

Chapter 7 ♦ The Process from Arrest to Trial

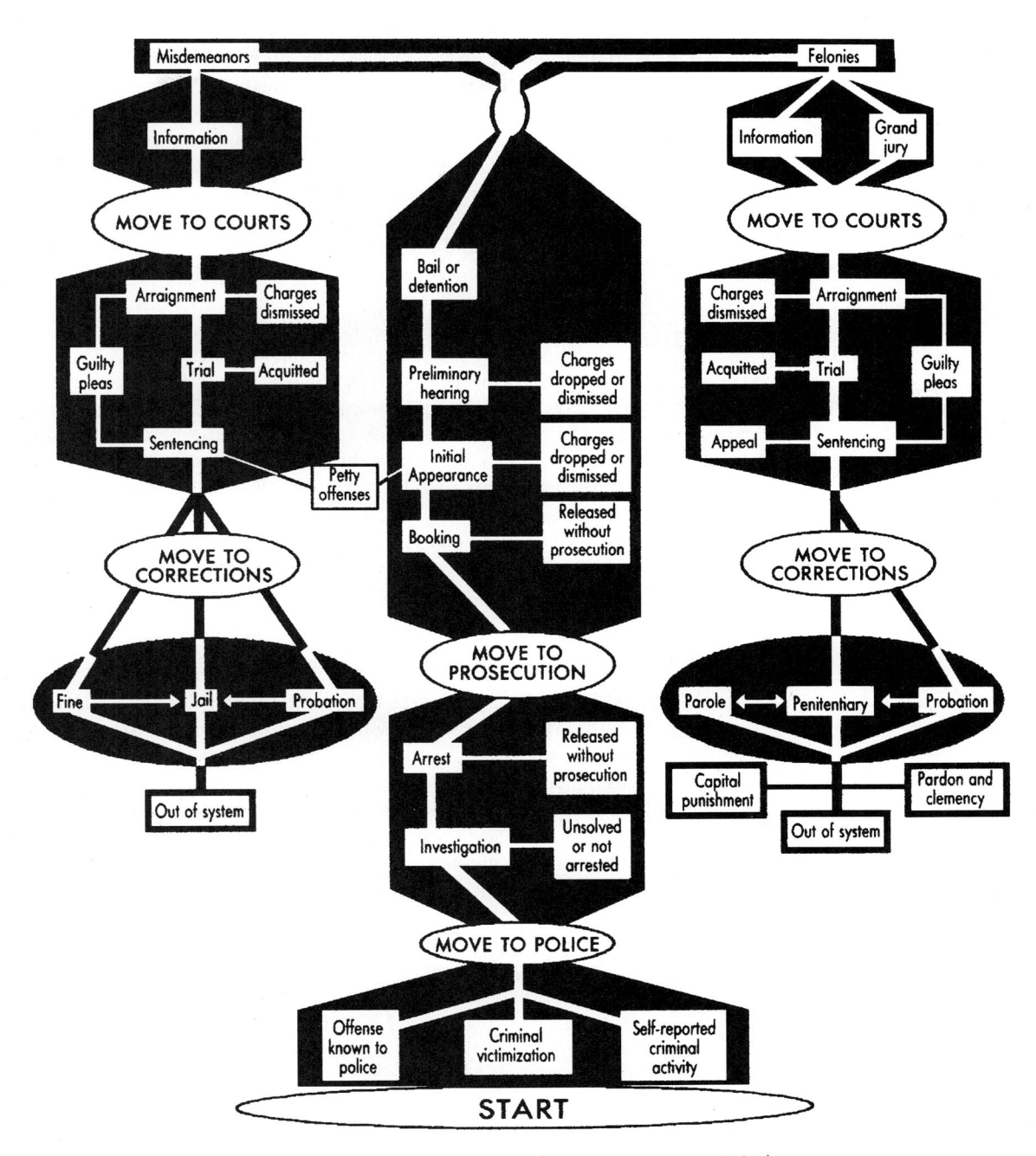

♦ **FIGURE 7.1** Overview of the criminal justice system (illustrated by Reen Foley)

Source: *Report to the Nation on Crime and Justice,* 1988, inside front cover. U.S. Department of Justice.

sent to jail. The administrators merely are attempting to hold suspects safely in custody. In order to accomplish this objective, administrators remove personal valuables from inmates to prevent fights among those in custody and to protect the personal belongings of the inmates. The administration is also responsible for protecting the public from possible victimization by people thought to have committed crimes. In order to do so, the accused must be removed from society. It is only a by-product of incarceration that the accused's normal contact with family and friends is eliminated and they are desocialized. We will discuss desocialization more in the chapter on corrections.

Bail and Bond

The time from arrest to trial can be quite lengthy; it is not unusual for a trial to be held 3 or even 4 years after the offense was committed. Therefore, the legal system has provided the bail system whereby the accused can be released until the time of trial. Conventional bail requires the accused to provide a set amount of money to the court and to promise to appear at all court proceedings. The accused is then released until the first required court attendance. If the accused fails to appear, she will forfeit the money. Bail is an amount of money defendants must pay to the court in order to be released until they go to trial, while bond is a written agreement to pay a specified amount if the defendant does not attend the court proceedings related to the case.

There are many differences of opinion about what bail is supposed to accomplish and even less agreement about how successful it is in accomplishing these goals. Bail is supposed to guarantee that the accused will appear in court. However, agents of the criminal justice system are also concerned with protecting the public from further victimization, as well as safeguarding witnesses and jurors. If someone who has not committed a crime is incarcerated until trial, that person is being punished for something he or she did not do. However, if someone has committed a crime and is released until trial, that person might not return for court or might commit more offenses. Both possibilities are taken into account when setting bail (Reaves 1991).

Bail Bondsmen

An arrestee can either pay bail or contact a bail bondsman to assist with bail. The accused pays the bail bondsman a percentage of the bail, typically 10 percent. For example, if the bail is set at $2,500, the accused pays the bondsman $250 and the bondsman will put up a bond for the full $2,500. If the accused pays the full $2,500 herself, she will get the money back when she goes to trial. However, if the accused pays the bondsman a percentage of the bail, the bondsman keeps that money as his fee when the accused goes to trial. See COLLATERAL FOR BAIL BONDSMAN.

The person who uses a bail bondsman and is adjudicated not guilty has in essence paid a fine despite not being legally guilty of a crime. Since the low income and indigent are more likely to use a bail bondsman, they are more likely to pay this fee. However, courts are aware of these inequities and have introduced other

> **Box 7.1**
>
> **Collateral for Bail Bondsman**
>
> The woman arrested for kiting checks appeared to be in her early 30s. She opened a number of checking accounts at different banks for nonexistent companies. Then she proceeded to write checks back and forth among the accounts so that it appeared that there was a flow of cash through the accounts. There were insufficient funds to cover the checks. First Union Bank figured out her scheme and notified the police, who arrested her when she tried to make a cash withdrawal.
>
> The woman, arrested under the name of Jane Doe, refused to allow the police to photograph her. She had two Florida driver's licenses in different names. Judge Dorothy Pate set her bond at $25,000. But that was no problem for Jane Doe. Freddie's Bail Bonds advertises that "We'll put your feet on the street" and that's exactly what it did. A colleague of the defendant gave Freddie's a bogus check for $19,000 as collateral for the bail. The check appeared to be a cashier's check, but the bail bondsman was unable to check with a bank for 2 days. When the bank was finally contacted, it reported that the check was drawn on one of the bogus accounts that Jane Doe had been manipulating. It seems that Jane's first appearance in court may also be her last.

Source: G. Thomas, "String of Bad Checks Lands Woman In, Then Out of Jail," *The Florida Times-Union* (June 20, 1989), pp. B–1, B–5.

methods of release. In a small number of jurisdictions, the court will allow the accused to pay a percentage of the bail to the court and sign an affidavit promising to pay the full amount if she does not appear in court. Greenberg and Ruback (1982) describe two other types of release sometimes used: 1) an unsecured appearance bond, in which the accused promises to pay a specific amount of money if he does not appear at court but does not have to provide any money to be released; and 2) a release on one's own recognizance, which is based on a review of the accused's background. If the court feels that the person is very likely to show up for the trial, she can sign a promise to appear which has no financial requirements. Long-time residents with permanent jobs and families in the area who have been arrested for misdemeanors or lesser offenses are usually released on their own recognizance.

Factors Used to Set Bail

State or administrative guidelines are usually provided for setting bail. A study of the nation's seventy-five largest counties found that bail decisions are primarily influenced by the likelihood that the defendant will appear in court and the possible danger he or she poses for the community. In addition, many jurisdictions use criteria such as "personal character and mental condition, employment and financial resources, family and community ties, prior criminal record, prior court appearance record, the weight of the evidence against the defendant, offense seriousness, and the sentence which may be imposed upon conviction" (Reaves 1991, p. 3).

Most studies find that the severity of the crime and the accused's prior record are the only two factors that affect bail. Ebbesen and Konečni (1982a, 1982b) conducted two studies to determine the factors which influence judges' bail decisions. In the first, a simulated study, it was found that judges who reviewed robbery case records used community ties, the prosecutor's bail recommendation, and the accused's prior record to determine bail. The bail recommendation by the defense attorney had no impact on the judges' decisions. However, the second study of actual cases found that the prosecutor's bail recommendation was the primary predictor of bail. These researchers propose that the prosecutor takes the severity of the crime and prior record into account when making the bail recommendation; thus these factors do not influence the judge's decision independently of the prosecutor's recommendations. See SETTING BAIL for a description of a case.

Greenberg and Ruback (1982) found that in addition to the severity of the crime and the prosecutor's recommendation, "local ties" and community sentiment influenced bail decisions. Local ties are factors binding the accused to the area, such as living in the local area, steady employment, and character references by responsible people. Community sentiment is particularly likely to affect bail decisions in notorious cases. Greenberg and Ruback give the example of the "Son of Sam" case (described in Chapter 4) in New York. In this well-known murder case, Berkowitz (the Son of Sam) was accused of a series of apparently motiveless murders. Most jurisdictions do not allow bail in capital offenses. However, a pretrial services agency recommended Berkowitz be released without bail. Due to the reaction of the public, and particularly the mayor, the defendant was not released. The public reaction was so intense that the services agency later stopped making recommendations in murder cases.

Factors Which Predict Appearance

The factors used to determine bail do not seem to be strongly related to whether or not the accused will actually appear for court proceedings. Different studies have isolated different predictors of court appearance but have found no consistently valid predictors. Particularly apparent by its absence is the relationship between ties to the community and the likelihood of appearing (Clark, Freeman & Koch 1976, Landes 1974).

Arrests While Out on Bail

Appearance at trial is not the only consideration when setting bail. Protection of the public and prevention of further victimization are also important. Using these latter considerations, at least some of the criteria used to determine bail appear to be valid. It appears that the severity of the crime and the prior record of the accused are related to the likelihood of an accused being rearrested for a serious offense while awaiting trial. There appears to be no relationship between other demographic variables and pretrial arrests (Ebbesen & Konečni 1982a).

> **Box 7.2**
>
> **Setting Bail**
>
> When Chris Cole appeared in court in June, 1989, for possession of cocaine, his bail was set at $5,000. Bail probably would have been at least $25,000 if authorities knew that he was really Terry Bing. Bing was on probation for kicking a pregnant woman so many times that the assault possibly caused her miscarriage. However, the police did not match the fingerprints of Cole to those of Bing, so the subterfuge was not discovered. The lower bail made it easier for Bing to get out of jail. A month later, Bing was accused of beating a stranger to death on a city bus. The latter offense was witnessed by a dozen bystanders and is discussed further in Chapter 14.

Source: D. Hosansky, "Suspect Got Lower Bond Using Alias," *The Florida Times-Union* (July 18, 1989), pp. A–1, A–2.

Consequences of Not Making Bail

If the accused is not released on his own recognizance and does not have the money for bail or to pay a bail bondsman, that person must remain in jail. The bail system obviously discriminates against the poor. Bail is costly, particularly for the poor. It is also costly to remain in jail. The effects of not making bail are well documented. People kept in jail are likely to lose their jobs and have trouble raising money to pay an attorney. These people are isolated from their families and friends, deprived of the comfort of their own homes, and do not have the freedom of movement to seek evidence in their own behalf.

In addition, there are physical and psychological consequences of the jail stay. There is little or nothing for inmates to do while in jail. Most spend their time lying on their bunks or watching television. Many inmates describe the conditions in jail and the time spent there as worse than in prison (Casper 1972). Why would conditions in prison, an institution for convicted criminals, be better than conditions in a jail for people who are still considered innocent? There are many reasons, but primarily, prisons are facilities for long-term incarceration, and as such provide activities for the inmates. There are work, social, vocational, and educational programs in prison. Since jail is a temporary holding facility and the accused is not yet convicted, programs and activities available in prison to "rehabilitate" inmates are not offered. Some larger facilities have drug and alcohol programs, but unadjudicated inmates cannot be required to take part in the programs. Therefore, inmates have little to do to take their minds off their personal problems.

In addition to the social and psychological problems described above, the person who remains in jail until trial is more likely to have legal difficulties. Pretrial release affects the treatment defendants receive from others in the criminal justice system. Probation officers, public defenders, and private attorneys tend to

Reprinted with special permission of King Features Syndicate, Inc.

treat released defendants more sympathetically than those who are kept in jail (Ebbesen & Konečni 1982a). But, more importantly, people detained until trial are more apt to be found guilty and to receive longer sentences than those who are released prior to trial (Reaves 1991). The psychological impact of seeing a person brought to trial in prison garb by jail personnel is strong. Members of the jury often assume the person is guilty of something or that person would have been released prior to trial. By the same token, someone who appears in court dressed in a nice suit and accompanied by a private attorney has the advantage of appearing to be a law-abiding citizen.

People released prior to trial receive more lenient treatment than those detained in jail. A study of felony defendants in the nation's seventy-five largest counties found that 79 percent of those detained in jail prior to trial were convicted, while only 66 percent of the people released prior to trial were convicted. Similarly, "detained defendants who had been convicted were about twice as likely as released defendants to receive a state prison sentence" (Reaves 1991, p. 8). The primary factor in their treatment was whether or not they were released prior to trial.

Functions and Discretion of the Prosecutor

After arrest and booking, the prosecutor, called the District Attorney or State Attorney, has almost total control over what happens to the accused. The prosecutor has a tremendous amount of discretion, with little supervision; even the courts have refused to review prosecutorial decisions (Albonetti 1987, Gelman 1982). In this section we will discuss the duties and roles of the prosecutor, as well as how the prosecutor makes decisions.

Functions of the Prosecutor

The prosecutor generally receives cases from the police, at which point the prosecutor can press charges, dismiss them, increase or reduce the charges. Once charges have been filed, the prosecutor is influential in determining the amount of bail. She also interviews witnesses and reviews the evidence before arguing a case. Once the defendant pleads or is adjudicated guilty, the prosecutor usually recommends a sentence to the judge. See THE MCMARTIN PRESCHOOL CASE for a description of the discretion and power of the prosecutor.

Roles of the Prosecutor

Alschuler (1968) enumerates four roles that the prosecutor fulfills in the course of duties. The first role is that of an **administrator.** In this role the prosecutor is concerned with the efficient disposition of cases and the avoidance of backlogs. When prosecutors play the role of **advocate,** their primary interest is convicting offenders and making sure they receive the longest possible sentence for their offenses. The role of **judge** calls for the prosecutor to evaluate the case against the accused and decide whether or not it is fair and appropriate. Finally, in the role of **legislator,** the prosecutor evaluates existing statutes and decides on their fairness. For example, a prosecutor might decide to reduce charges against all defendants accused of a particular offense, because the sanction is too severe. Obviously, there can be a great deal of conflict among the different roles held by a prosecutor at any given time.

The Decision to Press Charges

Prosecutors are required to seek justice and are morally bound to dismiss charges brought against someone they believe to be innocent. Therefore, the most important consideration in filing a charge is the prosecutor's belief as to whether the accused really committed the offense. Prosecutors not only decide whether or not to press charges, they also decide what type and how many charges to file. These decisions influence later plea bargaining, so the prosecutors use them to their advantage.

Likelihood of Conviction

Once the prosecutor has decided to her own satisfaction that the defendant is guilty, other factors come into play to influence her decisions. Prosecutors are generally required by law to be attorneys and most often are elected officials. As an elected official, the prosecutor is subject to pressure from the community, particularly from political and business leaders who can influence the outcome of elections. The public wants the prosecutor to convict criminals, therefore, he tries to attain a high conviction rate.

Although assistant prosecutors are not elected, they realize that their jobs and their careers are dependent on conviction rates. Therefore, they also pursue convictions. Aside from the political and job-related incentives to obtain a high conviction rate, having a record of many convictions frightens defendants into pleading guilty, thus making the prosecutor's job easier.

Prosecutors are most likely to pursue cases in which they are likely to gain a conviction. Therefore, the prosecutor will evaluate a case based on the amount

> **Box 7.3**
>
> ## The McMartin Preschool Case
>
> The McMartin Preschool was a nice school located in an upper-middle-class neighborhood in a suburb of Los Angeles. The clientele were children from respectable homes. Thus, the whole community was shocked when the owner and several faculty at the school were arrested in March, 1984, on 300 counts of child molesting. The district attorney, Robert Philibosian, believed the accused were so dangerous to society that they should be held without bail to await trial. The owner of the school, Virginia McMartin, was eventually released on $50,000 bail. But her grandson, Raymond Buckey was held without bail until he went to trial in 1987. Raymond's mother, Peggy McMartin Buckey, was also held in jail for 2 years without bail. The other teachers were finally released after spending time in jail and/or paying high bail. Babette Spitler and Betty Raidor spent a couple of months in jail before being released on bails of $400,000 and $750,000 respectively. A third teacher, Marianne Jackson, was released on $100,000 bail. Ms. McMartin's granddaughter, Peggy Ann Buckey, was released on $100,000 bail after 2½ months in jail.
>
> Then in 1987 a new district attorney, Ira Reiner, reviewed the evidence in the McMartin case. He decided the evidence against five of the women was so weak that he dropped the charges against them. Both Raymond Buckey and his mother, Peggy McMartin Buckey, were still scheduled to go to trial.
>
> Meanwhile the lives of the five women had been destroyed. Their careers had been ruined and they had lost all their material possessions—$400,000 or $750,000 is a lot of money on a teacher's salary, even $100,000 represents several years' salary. (Even if they used a bail bondsman they still would have to produce
>
> *(continued)*

of evidence, how the evidence was obtained, and the willingness of witnesses and victims to testify (Albonetti 1987). All of these factors will influence the outcome of a case brought to trial. Read UNJUST JUSTICE? for a description of a case in which the prosecutor appears to have been overzealous.

Prosecutors evaluate the credibility of witnesses and victims when deciding whether to press charges. There is some evidence that the sex and race of witnesses influence the prosecutors' evaluation of their credibility. Males and whites tend to be evaluated as more credible witnesses than females and blacks (Albonetti 1987, Myers & Hagan 1979).

The prosecutor also considers the credibility of the victim. Even if the victim would make a credible witness, a victim unwilling to testify could hurt the case. Often the victim of an offense will decide to drop charges. This is particularly apt to occur if the victim and offender are involved in a long-term relationship, for example, if the offender assaulted his mother-in-law. If the victim no longer

> 10 percent of the bail or $40,000 to $75,000. And if a bondsman is used, the money is not returned.) In addition, one of the teachers, Babette Spitler, lost the custody of her children while she was in jail. Peggy Ann Buckey spent only 5 weeks teaching at the school and was not there at the time some children accused her of molesting them. But her career is finished. The state of California has revoked her teaching credentials—the special education degree she spent 6 years in college to get is now useless.
>
> Ira Reiner did not deny that some children were molested at the McMartin school. There appeared to be evidence of some molestation. However, instead of 350 victims molested, it seemed to him that there were only a few (*60 Minutes*). And, in fact, Peggy McMartin Buckey and her son, Raymond Buckey, were acquitted in fifty-two of the charges. The jury was unable to reach a decision on twelve counts of sex abuse against Raymond Buckey and one count of conspiracy against him and his mother. The judge dismissed the conspiracy charge against Peggy McMartin Buckey.
>
> The prosecution retried Raymond Buckey on eight of the charges. After two juries were unable to reach a unanimous decision, charges were dismissed. After 7 years, Raymond Buckey was a free man (Weber 1990).
>
> ♦
>
> Should the prosecuting attorney have so much power over the indictment of defendants? Should people who have spent time in jail and paid large amounts for bail be reimbursed if found not guilty? Has society gone overboard looking for cases of child molestation?

Sources: *CBS News, 60 Minutes*, "The McMartin Preschool" (July 5, 1987); "Pair Acquitted of Fifty-Two Counts Child Sex Case," *The Florida Times-Union* (January 19, 1990), pp. A–1, A–6; D. Webber, "After a $15 Million Case and Seven Years, Raymond Buckey Is Cleared of All Child Molestation Charges," *LA Daily News* (August 2, 1990), p. 7.

wishes to pursue the case, it will be very difficult for the prosecutor to convict the accused.

Other Considerations

As an elected official, the prosecutor is particularly susceptible to public opinion. He is likely to prosecute the most serious crimes and ones the public finds most abhorrent. Other factors which influence the prosecutor's decisions include the case load of the office, community sentiment regarding particular crimes, and administrative policies.

The prosecutor also will evaluate whether the punishment which the court may impose fits the crime. The prosecutor can dismiss the case if he feels the likely punishment is too severe for the offense. This is particularly likely to happen in cases such as euthanasia, especially if the victim had asked for assistance in committing suicide.

Box 7.4

Unjust Justice?

Officer Robert Wood was killed in the line of duty on November 28, 1976. When he stopped a car just outside Dallas in the wee hours of the morning, the driver took out a gun and shot the police officer. Police later questioned 16-year-old David Harris who had been boasting about killing a policeman. Harris denied killing Wood but admitted seeing Randall Adams commit the murder. Harris said that Wood stopped the car which Adams was driving, and Adams shot the officer five times.

Adams admitted that he was with Harris during the day but said Harris dropped him off at his motel about 10:00 P.M. The car the two men were driving was one that Harris had previously stolen, as was the gun used in the murder. But Adams was arrested, tried, convicted of murder, and sentenced to death. Subsequently, his sentence was commuted to life. Still claiming innocence, Randall Dale Adams was facing life in prison.

Then filmmaker Errol Morris became interested in Adams's story. While probing into the case, he found so much evidence that the wrong man had been convicted that he produced a documentary, *The Thin Blue Line.* The film portrays the bogus evidence used to convict Adams. For example, the partner of the slain officer identified Adams during the trial even though she originally stated that she could not see into the car. Further, a witness who could not pick Adams out of a lineup was not allowed to testify. Harris, who is now under a death sentence for a 1985 murder, virtually confessed to the murder of Wood in the movie.

After 12½ years in prison for a murder he insisted he did not commit, the Texas Court of Criminal Appeals set aside Adams's conviction. The court ruled unanimously that the prosecutors in the case were "guilty of suppressing evidence favorable to the accused, deceiving the trial court . . . and knowingly using perjured testimony." The district attorney decided not to retry Adams, who was finally set free in mid-March, 1989. Despite the time spent in prison and the evidence of misconduct on the part of the prosecutor, Randall Adams cannot sue the prosecutor for compensation.

♦

Should the police have dropped their case against Harris when he identified Adams as the murderer? Should charges be brought against the prosecutors who allowed perjury in the trial? Why did the prosecutor take Adams to trial with all the evidence against Harris? Should states allow persons who have unjustly spent time in prison to sue for compensation?

Source: "Court Sets Aside Conviction in Officer's Slaying," *The Florida Times-Union* (March 3, 1989), p. A–2.

Immunity

Finally, the prosecutor considers whether the accused could be helpful to other members of the criminal justice system. If the accused could testify against others who have committed more serious offenses, the prosecutor might offer immunity in return for testimony. This option is most likely to be given to someone who has had minor involvement but can testify against one of the primary perpetrators in a large crime. For example, the prosecutor might offer immunity to the lookout in a drug-smuggling ring if the accused can give evidence against the people running the operation.

Another situation that might warrant immunity is one in which the evidence against the defendant and his accomplices is not strong. In that case, the prosecutor might offer immunity or a reduced charge or sentence to one of the defendants, usually the one least involved, in exchange for testifying against a codefendant.

Overcharging

Prosecutors are often accused by defense attorneys of overcharging defendants. Overcharging occurs when the prosecutor initially charges the defendant with more severe offenses or a larger number of offenses than the case would warrant in order to be in a good position for plea bargaining.

Alschuler (1968) describes two types of overcharging: horizontal and vertical overcharging. The former occurs when the prosecutor charges the defendant with every possible offense which might have occurred. Someone who is arrested for sexual battery might be charged with sexual battery, assault, battery, kidnapping, and commission of a felony with a firearm. In contrast, vertical overcharging occurs when the prosecutor makes a single charge, but it is much more serious than the offense would justify. For example, if the prosecutor charges the accused with first-degree murder when second- or third-degree murder was clearly appropriate under the circumstances, it would be a case of vertical overcharging.

While plea bargaining (which will be described later in this chapter) is the most obvious motivation for overcharging, there are other explanations for its use. The prosecutor might overcharge in case future investigations turn up evidence of additional or more serious offenses. In addition, the defendant who is overcharged is likely to be reluctant to go to trial and therefore more apt to plead guilty (Cole 1986). If the case does go to trial, the jury tends to be influenced by a long list of charges. They tend to think the accused must have committed *some* crime and are more likely to turn in a guilty verdict (Greenberg & Ruback 1982).

One motivation for vertical overcharging is to make the offense a felony. Most jurisdictions have laws or rules limiting the time from arrest until the person goes to trial. The length of time is longer for felonies than for misdemeanors. Thus, a felony charge allows the prosecutor more time to prepare the case than a charge of misdemeanor.

Finally, vertical overcharging could raise the offense to a capital one (allowing the death penalty) in one of the thirty-six states with the death penalty. Prosecutors trying a death penalty case are allowed to ask potential jurors about their attitudes toward the death penalty. The Supreme Court has ruled it is constitutional to have "death qualified" juries, those in which the members are willing to invoke the death penalty. This type of jury is advantageous to the prosecution—it is more likely to rule in favor of the prosecution than the defense (Cowan, Thompson, & Ellsworth 1984, Luginbuhl & Middendorf 1988, Moran & Comfort 1986).

Pretrial Diversion Programs

The prosecutor has enumerable options besides criminal prosecution to use with people accused of crimes. In some instances, the defendant is in greater need of therapy than incarceration, and both the public and the defendant are better served if the behavior can be permanently changed. Few prisons claim to be able to rehabilitate offenders.

The prosecutor can require the defendant to attend driver education classes for charges of driving under the influence of alcohol, go to a drug or alcohol treatment program for offenses related to substance abuse, attend sex therapy sessions for incest or child abuse charges, etc. The pretrial diversion programs usually require the defendant to finish the program in order to have charges dismissed.

Dispute Settlement Programs

In cases involving an ongoing relationship between the victim and the offender, both parties are better served if the dispute is settled through some type of arbitration. Frequently, prosecutors will refer these cases to a dispute settlement program. In these programs, a mediator will listen to the victim's complaint and the explanation of the behavior by the accused. Then the mediator will suggest a resolution. If both parties agree to the resolution, the case does not go to court. If the defendant later violates the agreement, he will be sent to court and prosecuted. This type of resolution is particularly effective for people in long-term relationships who have a dispute. For example, mediation could resolve a dispute between a divorced couple arguing over visitation rights with the children. After many months of conflict, emotions rise and suddenly there is violence or destruction of property. The disputants are still involved with child visitation and are not able to avoid each other in the future. Therefore, a mutually agreed upon resolution formulated with the help of a mediator can avoid future problems.

The Grand Jury

The previous section described the many ways the prosecutor can control the pretrial process. In addition, the prosecutor influences the legal system through indictments and investigations made by the grand jury. In a felony case, a precise statement or written accusation of the charges made against a defendant must be filed with the court. This statement may be made by the prosecutor in what is called an information or by the grand jury in an indictment. Defendants are guaranteed the right to a grand jury indictment in felony offenses by the federal Bill of Rights and by the constitutions of many states (Clark 1975).

History of the Grand Jury

The legal right to a grand jury indictment is a reflection of the historic view of the grand jury as a protection for citizens against the power of the government (Felkenes 1973). A serious charge against a citizen should be one made by a group representing the community. The view of the grand jury as protecting the innocent has persisted despite its historical use as a political vehicle reflecting the biases and prejudices of the community and the times. Different segments of society have also been excluded from serving on grand juries. "For example, in the colonial period, women, slaves, and indentured servants were ineligible to be grand jurors" (Frankel & Naftalis 1977).

Members of the grand jury are laypeople without an extensive knowledge of the law. Sessions are private and the only lawyer allowed to address the jurors is the prosecuting attorney. Since the grand jury lacks the means to complete an in-depth investigation of the large number of serious charges presented to it, it must depend on the guidance of the prosecutor. The defendant cannot cross-examine witnesses, present his side of the story, nor can he have a defense attorney present during the hearings. Only a few states require the prosecutor to give favorable evidence as well as incriminating evidence during grand jury deliberations. If the grand jury decides that the evidence is sufficient to bring the accused to trial, it files an indictment.

The grand jury was abolished in England in 1933. It still exists in the United States, but its practices vary from state to state and in the federal government. In about 80 percent of the cases, the defendant waives the right to a grand jury hearing (Cole 1986). Read COMATOSE SON for a description of a grand jury decision.

Minority Representation on the Grand Jury

Although Congress passed a law in 1875 prohibiting the exclusion of blacks from jury duty and the Supreme Court forbade their exclusion in 1880, it was not until well into the 20th century that the law was enforced. Until the Federal Jury Selection and Service Act was passed in 1968, members of a grand jury were selected by a "key-man" method. The clerk of the court would contact well-known men in the community. These men, in turn, would recommend other men to serve as grand jurors. "The poor, the racially disfavored, the young, women, and others thought inferior were at best minimally represented" (Frankel & Naftalis 1977, p. 34).

The Federal Jury Selection and Service Act requires all grand juries to be "selected at random from a fair cross section of the community in the district or

> **Box 7.5**
>
> **Comatose Son**
>
> Sammy Linares swallowed a balloon at a birthday party in August, 1988. He remained in a coma and "partially brain dead" at Rush-Presbyterian-St. Luke's Medical Center until April of the next year. When Sammy's parents were refused the right to have their son's respirator turned off, his 23-year-old father, Rudy, decided to act. On April 26th, Rudy Linares went to his son's hospital bed and, while holding the hospital personnel at bay with a .357 hand gun, he disconnected the life-support system. He tearfully held his 16-month-old son in his arms until little Sammy died.
>
> The state attorney charged Rudy Linares with first-degree murder. However, the Cook County grand jury refused to indict Rudy Linares and the prosecutor did not pursue the case. Rudy Linares did plead guilty to a charge of "unlawful use of a weapon," which is a misdemeanor. The judge sentenced him to 1 year conditional discharge. He served no time in jail.
>
> ♦
>
> Should parents be allowed to decide when to have life-support systems disconnected for their children? Should Rudy Linares have been charged with a crime?

Sources: "Pulling Tot's Life Support Draws Ethicists' Sympathy," *The Florida Times-Union* (April 28, 1989), p. A–16; "Grand Jury Refuses to Indict Man Who Let Comatose Son Die," *The Florida Times-Union* (May 19, 1989), p. A–4.

division wherein the court convenes." The law forbids the exclusion of members on the basis of "race, color, religion, sex, national origin or economic status" (Frankel & Naftalis 1977, pp. 41–42). The foreperson of the grand jury is appointed by the judge in some jurisdictions. A study of the appointment of grand jury forepersons in one Florida county found that in a 15-year period (1966 through 1980) only one female and two blacks were selected as forepersons of a grand jury (Foley 1981).

Advantages of the Grand Jury

The grand jury is useful in protecting the prosecutor from public and political pressure. If a member or members of city government are suspected of corruption, the prosecutor can take the evidence to a grand jury and protect herself from the political coercion that might interfere with her filing charges on her own. In like manner, if the case is one which arouses great public sentiment in both directions, the prosecutor can shield himself from public outcry by bringing the case to the grand jury. For example, in the case of Bernhard Goetz (who has been called the subway vigilante), the public had very strong opinions; some people thought he was a hero and others considered him a racist. By bringing the case to the grand jury, the prosecutor was able to deflect some of the public reaction. See the box, THE SUBWAY VIGILANTE, in Chapter 14 for a description of this case.

The grand jury is also useful as an investigative tool. The grand jury can subpoena witnesses and documents in order to decide whether a case should proceed. The grand jury is not limited to information which would be allowed in a criminal trial or to probable cause; it can use information gathered in illegal searches, wiretaps, etc. (Wrightsman 1986). These advantages are particularly important in cases involving organized crime and political corruption.

Pretrial Proceedings

From the viewpoint of the accused, the time before trial is tedious and uneventful, as well as tense, uncertain, and frustrating, particularly if this time is spent in jail. From the perspective of the legal participants, the court system is really quite busy with the case. There are a number of events that take place in the legal system prior to a criminal trial. Procedures, systems, and administration of cases vary in each state and jurisdiction as well as in the federal system. However, there are many similarities and the U.S. Constitution guarantees certain events will occur in each case. The typical sequence of events is as follows: first appearance, preliminary hearing, indictment, and arraignment. In this section, we will discuss the legal pretrial proceedings, those activities that take place in the courtroom. (Refer to Figure 7.1, p. 155, for an outline of the pretrial proceedings.)

First Appearance

Within a short time after arrest, the accused attends a first appearance, or initial appearance, in court. Technically, the presiding judge can rule on whether the case should be dismissed or should proceed. In actuality, the court docket is so overloaded in most jurisdictions that the judge has little time to do more than agree with the recommendation of the prosecutor. The judge also rules whether the complaint really constitutes a crime and whether the court has jurisdiction over the case. Again the judge almost always follows the recommendation of the prosecutor. In some states, the judge may try minor cases (e.g., public drunkenness, traffic violations) during the first appearance.

At first appearance charges are read and the accused are advised of their rights. These rights include a right to an attorney, so the judge will ask if the accused has one. (Actually, if the accused can afford an attorney, he most likely has been released from jail before first appearance and the attorney is present at the hearing.) If the accused does not have an attorney and cannot afford to hire one, a public defender or court-appointed attorney will be assigned to the case. Read WHO'S THE CRIMINAL? for a description of the judge's discretion at these hearings.

A major function the judge performs during first appearance is setting bail for the accused. The accused must be allowed to post bail within 24 to 48 hours after being arrested. In many jurisdictions, the amount of bail is predetermined

> **Box 7.6**
>
> ## Who's The Criminal?
>
> Broward Circuit Judge Mark Speiser has twice jailed women who filed sexual assault charges for refusing to testify against the alleged assailants. Judge Speiser defends his actions, saying that one instance was a mistake by the correctional staff and in the other case the woman lied in court. In June, 1989, a 22-year-old woman spent 6 days in jail because she did not want to testify in court against the stranger who allegedly kidnapped and raped her. When she did not show up for court hearings, Speiser issued a warrant for her detention. Jailers, following orders, kept her in custody when she was brought to the Broward County Jail. The judge contends that he intended her to be brought to his courtroom, but there was a mix-up.
>
> A 27-year-old woman had a similar experience. She filed charges against a former boyfriend and another man for rape and kidnapping but later said it was a domestic dispute. Despite her signing a "waiver of prosecution," police felt the assault had occurred and pursued the case. The assistant state attorney agreed. At the bail hearing, the victim testified on behalf of the accused. Judge Speiser ordered her jailed. Prosecutor Tim Donnelly opposed sending her to jail. However, Judge Speiser later explained that he "wanted her to think about this right then and there, to reflect upon the trauma of that incident and tell the truth. The problem from the state's vantage point was that after she came in and lied under oath, their case was shot. If, in fact, the rape didn't occur, and she lied, I wanted her to remember this experience in court."
>
> The terrified victim was taken away in handcuffs to spend the night in jail. The next day she again appeared before the judge. She admitted lying because she was afraid of the assailants' families who were in the courtroom. The men in the second case eventually received 1-year suspended sentences for attempted rape. A description of the outcome of the first case can be found in Chapter 10, THE JURY DECIDES ON A RAPE CASE.
>
> ◆
>
> Should judges have the authority to jail victims who do not want to testify? Should victims be required to press charges in rape cases? Should victims be required to press charges against people with whom they have an ongoing relationship?

Source: "Judge Defends Jailing Alleged Rape Victims," *The Florida Times-Union* (August 1, 1989), p. B–2.

and the accused has already had an opportunity to post bail. However, in some jurisdictions, no bail is set prior to first appearance. Then the judge decides on the amount of bail. Cases move quickly so the judge does not have very much time to review the offense or the accused's intentions very thoroughly. After a short time on the bench, judges usually develop their own personal bail schedule. In some jurisdictions, the judges as a group have set up standard amounts for specific offenses and use these to determine bail. Even in courts where the bail is set according to a schedule, the first appearance provides an opportunity for the defense counsel to argue for a reduction in the bail. If the accused cannot make bail, he must go back to jail until the next court appearance.

After studying cases in a New England court, Swigert and Farrell (1976) concluded certain categories of people were treated more harshly throughout the legal process. Persons who were black, of a low socioeconomic status, and those of lower occupational status were stereotyped as "normal primitive." These categories of people were less likely to be released on bail, more likely to be assigned a public defender, and more likely to waive a jury trial. The authors interpret this treatment as indicating that these people were presumed guilty until proven innocent.

The Public Defender

Almost two-thirds of the defendants are indigent and in some cities the percentage increases to 90 percent (Cole 1986). These defendants are represented by an attorney appointed by the judge. Usually this will be a public defender, an attorney who is in the employ of the city or town. Although the public defender is not formally assigned to a case until first appearance, she actually begins her work prior to the initial appearance by visiting all the people in jail scheduled for first appearance. In a medium-sized city, the public defender might have thirty to forty new cases to handle in one day.

Typically there are extenuating circumstances surrounding every offense or some personal reasons why each of the accused should have his or her bail reduced, or be released, or have the case dismissed. Unfortunately, in the short time the public defender has to interview all the accused, he cannot determine what these extenuating circumstances are for every case before court is in session.

The public defender, like the prosecutor, has discretion in handling cases. Each case cannot be given the same amount of time and energy. Therefore the public defender must decide how much attention to devote to each case. Since time is at a premium, the decision must be made on limited knowledge of the case and on the characteristics of the client. Sudnow (1965) proposes that public defenders develop their own intuitive psychological evaluation of clients. They develop stereotypes about the kind of person who is likely to commit a specific type of crime. They also have preconceived notions about the manner in which crimes are committed. These untested ideas often influence important decisions made by the public defender.

Court-Appointed Attorneys

Some jurisdictions are too small to warrant the services of a full-time public defender. In these jurisdictions, the judge will appoint a private attorney to defend accused people who are indigent. Some large cities utilize court-appointed attorneys, maintaining it is more cost-effective than having a public defender's office. In some areas, the fee for the court-appointed attorney is so low these attorneys may pressure the client into plea bargaining (Cole 1986).

Jurisdictions with a public defender's office occasionally use court-appointed attorneys if the case load of the public defender is too large to handle all the cases. Court-appointed attorneys also are likely to be assigned cases in which a number of people are accused of taking part in the same offense and each one accuses the other of being the perpetrator. In such a case, the defendants cannot be represented by the same public defender's office because of a possible conflict of interest.

Preliminary Hearing

The Fourth Amendment to the Constitution guarantees people accused of crimes the right to have a judge review the case and decide whether there is probable cause to proceed with it. Therefore, the defense attorney may demand a preliminary hearing. A grand jury indictment prior to the preliminary hearing renders the preliminary hearing unnecessary because it satisfies probable cause. The preliminary hearing is used instead of the grand jury in about half of the states in the United States. Generally, an indictment by the grand jury prevails in the eastern half of the country, while the prosecutor writes the formal charge or information in the West (Cole 1986).

At this hearing, the prosecutor presents evidence to convince the judge that there is "probable cause" to believe a crime was committed by the suspect. The prosecutor also presents the state's evidence and the defense attorney presents the case for the defendant. This allows the two attorneys to evaluate the case. The prosecutor may decide the case for the defense is too strong to justify going to court and be willing to offer a plea bargain. In like manner, the defense attorney may decide the evidence is so overwhelming it would be better to negotiate than to have a jury review the case. Thus, the hearing could make it more likely that a plea bargain will be negotiated.

After reviewing the evidence, the judge can reduce or dismiss the charges. However, the judge seldom rules that probable cause does not exist.

The Arraignment

A few weeks after first appearance, an arraignment—the formal decision to continue with the prosecution—is held. The judge reads the indictment to the accused, who is asked to enter a plea. In some states, the defendant has an attorney appointed at this hearing. The defendant can enter a plea of guilty, not guilty, or, in some states, may stand mute or in others is allowed to enter a plea of **nolo contendere** (no contest). With a plea of nolo contendere, the defendant accepts the punishment but does not admit guilt. A nolo contendere plea may not be used against the defendant in later civil suits. For example, if someone arrested for driving under the influence pleads nolo contendere, that plea cannot be used when the victim of the auto accident sues the defendant for damages.

If the accused pleads guilty or nolo contendere, he is scheduled for sentencing. If the plea is not guilty, the defendant is scheduled for trial. Once a plea has been made, the accused is called a defendant.

Reprinted with special permission of King Features Syndicate, Inc.

Pretrial Motions

Prior to the actual trial, the defense attorney has the option of filing any number of pretrial motions which can affect the case. A motion is a legal method of requesting the judge to review an issue. The following are examples of the type of motions that can be made but is by no means a exhaustive list. Most motions are attempts to gather further information or attempts to get the court to rule on the defense's claims.

Discovery

In almost every trial, the defense counsel makes a motion for discovery. This motion asks the prosecutor to share with the defense the evidence to be used against the defendant. In civil cases, either side can request information from the other. In criminal cases, the U.S. Supreme Court has ruled that the defense is entitled to any material that is favorable to the defendant.

Pretrial Publicity

Pretrial publicity has been shown to bias jury decisions (Kramer, Kerr & Carroll 1990). If the case to be tried has been highly publicized, the defense might make a motion to alleviate the impact of the publicity. One way of doing this is to make a motion for a "change of venue." In other words, the defense counsel will ask the court to move the trial to another location where there has not been so much publicity detrimental to the defendant. Another possible way of alleviating the impact of pretrial publicity is to make a motion for a "continuance." This motion is one that will delay the onset of the trial for a period of time until the publicity has abated.

Suppression

The motion to suppress evidence is a request by the defense attorney that information gathered in an illegal manner not be used in the trial. A request for the exclusion of evidence would be made in cases where the police made an illegal search, the lineup was suggestive, or the defendant made a confession without benefit of counsel or without being told of her rights. Sometimes a pretrial hearing is held to decide the issue of suppression. If this motion is successful, the charges might be dropped or reduced.

Other Motions

Other pretrial motions might include: a motion concerning competence to stand trial, a motion to dismiss the charges, or a motion to disqualify a judge or attorney due to conflict of interest. In addition to these typical motions, defense attorneys may file any additional motions that are relevant to the case.

Plea Bargaining

If the attention television programs and newspaper accounts give to jury trials were an accurate reflection of the legal system, it would appear that every person accused of a crime has his or her case heard in court. Despite the fascination of the press and the public with jury trials, in actuality very few cases ever go to trial. As indicated in the section on the likelihood of being caught (Chapter 12), 80 to 90 percent of cases do not go to trial; the vast majority of accused people plead guilty. Why would people plead guilty when they have the right to a jury trial? Why not take the chance and perhaps be adjudicated not guilty even if they are guilty? They have nothing to lose—or do they?

People who go to trial and are adjudicated guilty are likely to receive a much longer sentence than those who plead guilty to the offense. In fact, the sentence received from a jury trial is often twice as long (Wrightsman 1987). The person who has gone through a jury trial using the extremely limited resources and time of the courts, knowing full well he is guilty, is one who has tried to beat the system and is not repentant for his crime. If he were repentant, he would have pled guilty and said he was sorry. Therefore, this unrepentant criminal deserves a stiff sentence; at least this is the view held by many judges.

The Bargain for the Defendant

There are other incentives for defendants to encourage them to plead guilty. Usually the prosecutor will offer the defendant a "deal." The concessions made by the prosecutor fall into three categories: count bargaining, charge bargaining, and sentence bargaining. In count bargaining, the prosecutor will drop a number of the charges against the defendant if she will plead guilty to one or a few of them. For example, if the defendant has been charged with thirty-five burglaries, the prosecutor might offer to drop thirty charges if the defendant will plead guilty to the other five. Or perhaps the defendant has been arrested for selling narcotics. The prosecutor might have charged him with selling cocaine, possession of cocaine, selling heroin, possession of heroin, possession of drug paraphernalia, resisting arrest, etc. The prosecutor could offer to drop the other charges if the person will plead guilty to selling cocaine.

Charge bargaining refers to the situation where the prosecutor offers to reduce the charge if the defendant will plead guilty to a less-severe offense. For example, the so-called "preppie killer," Robert Chambers, admitted killing Jennifer Levin, age 18, with whom he had had a brief affair. After an 11-week trial for second-degree murder in which the lurid details of the sex killing were revealed, the defense agreed to a plea bargain. Chambers pled guilty to first-degree manslaughter. The penalty for this offense is 5 to 15 years in prison instead of the 25 years to life 19-year-old Chambers faced for the second-degree murder (Linden 1988).

In the third type of plea bargaining, sentence bargaining, the prosecutor will promise a lighter sentence for the defendant if she will plead guilty to the charge. For example, the penalty for armed robbery might be 5 to 15 years. The prosecutor might promise the defendant a sentence of 5 years if she pleads guilty, so there is no risk of getting the full 15 years. A common sentence bargain is one for first-degree murder, where the prosecutor promises not to request the death penalty if the defendant will plead guilty.

In the previous section, we saw that many defense attorneys feel prosecutors "overcharge" defendants in order to give them more negotiating power in plea bargaining. Given the workings of the plea bargaining system, it is easy to see the advantages of overcharging from the prosecutor's point of view.

The U.S. Supreme Court has ruled that the defendant must voluntarily plead guilty without any coercion. It has further stated that the defendant must understand all his rights, particularly those he waives. However, there is some doubt as to whether every defendant—particularly those naive to the court system, those with little formal education, and those with limited intelligence—really understand either the plea bargain or the rights which have been waived. Judge Ralph Adam Fine (1986) describes a case he heard in juvenile court. A 16-year-old boy's attorney said that "they" wanted to plead guilty to carrying a concealed weapon since the prosecution was offering probation. Upon questioning the boy, the judge found that the knife had been used for peeling an apple. When he got into a fight with some friends, the boy had put the knife in his boot to avoid hurting anyone. Despite the defense attorney's protests that he was wasting time, Judge Fine rejected the guilty plea and insisted the case go to trial. The boy was acquitted.

The Bargain for the Prosecutor

There are a lot of incentives for the defendant to enter into a plea negotiation, but why would the prosecutor want to plea bargain? The primary motivation for the prosecutor is the heavy load of cases going through the court system. The courts cannot try every case. Therefore, the prosecutor is anxious to have some, if not most, of the defendants plead guilty without going to trial. Cases in which the defendant pleads guilty count the same as court cases in which the defendant is found guilty in terms of the prosecutor's conviction rate. In addition, if the defendant pleads guilty, the prosecutor is assured the defendant will receive *some* punishment, even if it is not as much as the offense warrants.

The primary motivating factor in the decision to plea bargain is the amount of evidence the prosecutor has (Alschuler 1979). If there is little evidence, or if it is questionable, the prosecutor will not want to go to court. He is therefore likely to offer a good bargain. If he has a lot of concrete evidence, he will not make many concessions to the defendant.

The plea bargain situation favors the prosecutor as he has most of the power in the situation (Maynard 1988). The prosecutor is considered to have more "esteem" than the defense attorney since he represents the state. He has greater monetary and time resources, and generally the plea bargain is more favorable toward the state than the defendant.

Plea Bargaining for the Defense Attorney

Defense attorneys also benefit from plea bargaining. These negotiations enable them to handle more cases and devote more time to the cases that actually go to trial. Many defense attorneys begin their careers as prosecuting attorneys and therefore are sympathetic to the prosecutor's viewpoint and have good relationships with the staff in the prosecutor's office. In addition, defense attorneys, particularly public defenders, deal with the prosecutors on a daily basis and like to remain on good terms with them. They will have many more cases to handle with the prosecutor than they will for their client, therefore they must be careful not to go overboard in their negotiations. Greenberg and Ruback (1982) maintain that defense attorneys are more concerned with maintaining their relationship with the prosecutor than with the outcome for their clients.

Court-appointed attorneys also benefit from plea bargaining. These attorneys usually receive the same fee for defending a case whether it is plea bargained or goes through a trial (Greenberg & Ruback 1982). Therefore, since plea bargaining is less time consuming than a trial, it allows the court-appointed attorney to handle more cases and earn more fees.

Maynard (1988), having recorded the negotiations in fifty-two cases, made the following observations. Most of the negotiations are made by the defense attorney, who must convince the prosecutor that the case under consideration is atypical. The prosecutor is rather passive in the bargaining. Maynard found four patterns of negotiations: 1) **Routine processing** where both attorneys agree that the case is routine and proceed directly with negotiations. 2) **Assessing character** occurs in cases where the defense attorney does not dispute the facts of the case. He does, however, ask for leniency for his client based on the good character of the client and/or the presence of difficult circumstances. 3) **Disputing facts** arises in cases in which the defense attorney does not accept the description of the facts at face value. The attorney denies some component of the case, and there is an attempt to reconcile the alternative versions of the facts. 4) **Arguing subjectivity** is the final pattern of negotiation. In this situation, the defense attorney proposes excuses for her client's behavior. She might maintain there was no intention to commit the crime, which tends to be a weak defense. Or she might contend that the defendant's psychological state interfered with the defendant's subjectivity and ability to form intent. This last circumstance is likely to occur when the defendant was using drugs. Read PLEA BARGAINING for a description of a negotiation.

Alschuler (1979) points out that while the prosecutor definitely has an advantageous position when negotiating with one defense attorney or one defendant, that power dissipates if the defense attorneys act in unison. As a unified group, the defense attorneys can wield a great deal of power. For example, if the attorneys thought a particular judge was treating them and their clients unfairly, those defense attorneys could agree to take every case in that judge's court to trial. Since ordinarily only 10 to 20 percent of the cases reach a trial, the judge would have five or ten times as many cases on the docket. The judge would be overwhelmed with cases, which would slow down everything handled in that court. In like manner, if the defense attorneys felt a particular type of offense was not receiving fair treatment, they could take all of those cases to trial, thereby completely bottlenecking the court. The attorneys who are most capable of accomplishing this type of unified protest are the public defenders. These lawyers handle the greatest percentage of cases and work for the same office, so they are more likely to cooperate and create a large impact.

The Judge and the Plea Bargain

Different states and jurisdictions have varying regulations about the amount of involvement the judge can and should have in plea bargaining negotiations. In some states and the federal courts, the judge is not allowed to participate in the negotiations. Other jurisdictions require the judge to be present and/or to participate. The remaining jurisdictions leave it up to the discretion of the judges as to how much participation they have in negotiations (Horowitz & Willging 1984).

Judges who do not participate in the negotiations do not have to agree to the plea bargain. Although there is some chance the judge will refuse the recommended sentence, in almost all cases the negotiated settlement is accepted. Judges have pressures to encourage plea bargains, too. Their case load is constantly growing and creating large backlogs. If a judge refuses a plea bargain in court, it weakens the prosecutor's position and future defendants will not believe the offers made by that prosecutor. In the future, fewer defendants will plea bargain in that court and the case load of the court will increase dramatically.

Evaluation of the Plea Bargaining System

In our system of justice, very few criminals receive severe punishments while most get away with their criminal activities. Rosett and Cressey (1976) maintain that the system is designed to pressure people to plead guilty. Even honest citizens who receive an unjust traffic ticket are more likely merely to gripe and pay it rather than going through the inconvenience of attending a court session.

Box 7.7

Plea Bargaining

The following is a transcript of the negotiating sessions of a case which Maynard (1988) reports. The negotiators are the public defender and the district attorney. The judge, who is present, asks some questions.

PD1: Um, the only other one I have is Maria Zamora-Avila.

DA3: Sure, Zamora-hyphen-Avila, we've got a probation report on this.

PD1: They're recommending straight probation, but she's not gonna plead 'cause we have a good good defense.

DA3: Oh yeah?

PD1: Yeah. It should be dismissed. [Referring to the contents of a file that DA3 is reading:] Those are letters that other people've written about her character. *Lemme briefly tell ya 'bout the case.*

DA3: Mm hmm.

PD1: She goes inta Davidson's. . . .

PD1: Situation is this. She's a 65-year-old lady. Mexic—speaks Castillian Spanish, she's from Spain. Uh, she goes into Davidson's. Oh, incidently, by way of background, for 20 years she's worked in the Catholic church at San Ramon as the housekeeper for the nuns an' the fathers an' all this stuff, and, uh, very religious, well known. I've interviewed half of San Ramon concerning her background. Wonderful lady, no problems, 65 years old.

PD1: But on this particular occasion, she goes into Davidson's, goes into a fitting room, takes two hundred dollars worth o' clothes, pins them up underneath her dress, and leaves.

[1.2 seconds of silence]

PD1: And they pick her up outside, she's with a companion, they pick her up outside, and they, uh, cite 'er for petty theft, later discover how much was involved and hit 'er with four eighty seven point one [grand theft].

(continued)

PD1: She had no explanation except to say that she was sorry, her companion with whom she lives is here in court today, says that night, *she,* the companion, was crying, saying—look what've you done, why are you doing this, an' all the lady could say what've I done? Y'know what've I done? It wasn't til the next day that she realized when she found the ticket in her purse that the police had given her what she had done. And then in subsequent investigation, uh, it was discovered that she had taken two different drugs, one for her arthritic condition, she'd taken more than what she should've, and another drug, combined them which was improper, and was obviously under the influence of drugs.

J1: What're the drugs, ya got any idea?

PD1: Darvoset.

J1: Yeah.

PD1: And Seconal. Now I've checked with the county pathologist and he's researched the thing out. He says that if those drugs are mixed, it will cause a state of confusion, delirium, and put the person in a situation where they're just in a dream world, don't know what in the world they're doing. I've also talked with a pharmacist at Middleton Medical who says the exact same thing.

DA1: I just can't believe that the drug is—if the drug affects you that badly you're gonna do something bizarre, in other words, you're gonna walk out swingin' around your arm or carryin' out bananas in your ear or something crazy. Here she was extremely sophisticated, go into the dressing room, pin it up underneath her coat, uh, her dress like that. Uh, I just can't buy it.

Stated differently, the DA does not directly dispute who the woman is or what she did but rather argues against the defense attorney's depictions of her subjective state and capacity to form intent. Of course, this can indirectly call into question the character of the defendant and can provide for a different, retrospective interpretation of the "facts" as told during the story proper. Nevertheless, the PD, telling his story several times as the case was continued over a period of weeks, stuck to his portrayal and interpretation of events and eventually won a dismissal.

Source: D. W. Maynard, "Narratives and Narrative Structure in Plea Bargaining," *Law and Society Review* 22, pp. 454, 457–458, 463, 473.

Trade-Out Agreements

A trade-out agreement occurs when a defense attorney and prosecutor are involved in negotiations over separate cases with different defendants. These lawyers might come to an agreement that involves more than one defendant. For example, the prosecutor might agree to drop or reduce the charges against a defendant accused of petty theft if another defendant in a sexual battery case will plead guilty. Obviously, the defense attorney never tells the client in the sexual battery case that his guilty plea was negotiated so that another one of the attorney's clients would receive lenient treatment (Alschuler 1979). There is no way of knowing exactly how often trade-out agreements are made. These agreements are considered unethical, therefore they are negotiated in strict confidence.

Elimination of Plea Bargaining

Concern about the ethics and wisdom of plea bargaining and criticism of its use have led to attempts to eliminate it. In 1975, both El Paso, Texas, and the state of Alaska abolished the use of plea bargaining with very different results. Alaska, in the only statewide attempt to eliminate plea bargaining, was very successful in its effort. The legal system ran smoothly, even efficiently, while convictions and guilty pleas did not change. However, results in El Paso were quite negative. This city employed a point system to determine the sentence for each defendant. Apparently, when defendants evaluated their possible sentences, they decided they were better off going to trial. So many defendants chose the option of going to trial that the system slowed down to a crawl. The resulting trial delays worked to the advantage of the defendants, decreasing the likelihood of a conviction and increasing the likelihood that other defendants would go to trial. Since then, New Orleans and Oakland County, Michigan, have also eliminated plea bargaining (Fine 1986).

Summary

Jails are used as temporary holding facilities for people accused of crimes until they are released on bond or go to trial. The factors used to determine bail do not seem to be strongly related to whether or not the accused will actually appear for court proceedings. The person kept in jail prior to trial suffers financially, socially, psychologically, and legally.

After the arrest and booking, the prosecutor has almost total control over what happens to the accused. Prosecutors have a tremendous amount of discretion and are often accused of overcharging defendants. The prosecutor is an elected official and tries to please the public by attaining a high conviction rate and prosecuting crimes that the public finds most abhorrent. The credibility of witnesses and victims also influences decisions made by the prosecutor.

The prosecutor influences the legal system prior to an actual trial through indictments and investigations made by the grand jury. The view of the grand jury as protecting the innocent has persisted despite its historical use as a political vehicle reflecting the biases and prejudices of the community and the times.

There are a number of events that take place in the legal system before the actual trial. The typical sequence of events is as follows: first appearance, preliminary hearing, indictment, and arraignment. If the accused does not have an attorney and cannot afford to hire one, the court will appoint a public defender or another court-appointed attorney will be assigned to the case.

At the preliminary hearing the prosecutor presents evidence to convince the judge that there is "probable cause" to believe a crime was committed by the suspect. The arraignment hearing is the formal decision to continue with the prosecution.

The prosecutor often will offer the defendant a "deal" if he will plead guilty to a charge. The plea bargain situation favors the prosecutor as she has most of the power in the situation, but defense attorneys also benefit from plea bargaining. Concern about the ethics and wisdom of plea bargaining and criticism of its use have led to attempts to eliminate it.

8

The Jury Trial

Participants in Legal Proceedings
The Judge
The Prosecutor's Role in the Trial
The Defense Attorney's Role in the Trial
The Trial Proceedings
The Importance of Jury Trials
The Trial
The Levels of Courts
Views of the Court System
The Jury Selection Process
The Jury Pool
Voir Dire
Methods of Voir Dire
Research on Jurors
Characteristics of Jurors
Summary

Participants in Legal Proceedings

Courtrooms are not used exclusively for major trials, they are the site of many other important legal functions as well. As the last chapter indicated, a person can go to court a number of times and never have a trial. The following is a description of a typical courtroom and the participants who assist in the functioning of sessions held in it. The described courtroom could be a criminal or a civil courtroom in a county or the federal system.

The courtroom is designed to emphasize the power and authority of the judge presiding over it. Thus, the focus of the courtroom is the bench at which the judge sits. This bench is quite high, requiring all those who come before the judge to look up in order to see her. In front of the bench and to one side is the witness stand.

Directly in front of the bench and perpendicular to it, are two parallel, oblong tables, one for the defense and one for the prosecution. Attorneys, assistants, and the defendant sit at these tables during the court sessions. To one side of the room and set off by railings are the seats reserved for members of the jury. At the far end of the room from the bench and separated from the rest of the courtroom by another railing are the seats for the observers.

We have already discussed the activities of the prosecutor, judge, public defender, and defendant prior to the trial. Now we will be introduced to their roles as participants in the trial. These roles are more formal and regulated more closely by the law than their previous activities. We will also meet some new actors in the trial: the victim, witnesses, and jurors.

The Judge

Prior to the trial the prosecutor has almost total control over what happens to the defendant. However, once the trial begins the judge is in charge. The judge presides over the trial, functioning somewhat like a conductor or a referee, maintaining order and deciding all questions pertaining to the law. The judge decides who can testify at the trial, what evidence can be admitted, what evidence the jury can hear, and what the attorneys and witnesses are allowed to say during the trial.

The judge has tremendous power over the trial proceedings and outcome. The judge even has the authority to direct a verdict, which means to instruct the jury on what verdict they should reach. The judge can also decide to set aside a verdict although that would be unusual (Guinther 1988). For a description of a judge's activities, read MAXIMUM MORPHONIOS.

The judge is supposed to maintain neutrality and be unbiased during the trial, not unduly influencing the jury. Unfortunately, however, judges tend to have a predisposition toward either the prosecution or the defense, in most cases the prosecution (Winick 1979). The judge's predisposition is important because the favored opponent is frequently the successful one. This predisposition manifests itself in the manner in which the judge treats the two adversaries in the courtroom. The judge responds in a more positive and respectful manner to the attorney

> **Box 8.1**
>
> **Maximum Morphonios**
>
> Dade County Circuit Court Judge Ellen Morphonios is somewhat of a legend in Miami. Her reputation is well earned. She is outspoken and harsh in her sentencing. She is also fair. A 59-year-old grandmother who has been married and divorced three times, Judge Morphonios has an unusual background for a judge. She is a former beauty queen and a former talk show host. She was working as a legal secretary when she entered the University of Miami Law School at the age of 23 without ever attending college.
>
> As interesting and unusual as her background is, it is not the source of Judge Morphonios's reputation. She is a colorful judge who speaks her mind in and out of the courtroom. She is tough on criminals, particularly violent ones. She maintains that, "You do the crime, you do the time." At one point, she sentenced a multiple felon to 1,698 years in prison while reassuring him that he probably would not serve even half that time. Probably the most circulated story is about her lifting her robes to show a rapist sentenced to life the last set of gams he would see for a long while. She denies having ever lifted her robes, although she thinks it's a great story. She assures people she would tell them if she did it, and it is easy to believe her. She is extremely straightforward.
>
> She readily describes a case in which a woman shot an attempted rapist in the groin and Judge Morphonios congratulated her on a nice shot. She also describes a "crazy" armed robber who took his pants off in court. He was not wearing underwear. When the judge ordered him removed from the courtroom, the nude defendant asked to put on his pants. The judge replied, "Boy, you walk bare-assed inside my courtroom, you'll walk bare-assed out." The defendant is now serving 900 years in prison.

Source: E. Morphonios and L. Marx, "Crime and Punishment: A View from a Broad," *People* (July 3, 1989), pp. 79–82.

toward whom she is predisposed, and this differential treatment is apparent to members of the jury. The judge communicates his beliefs and attitudes to the jurors through nonverbal behavior (Blanck, Rosenthal & Cordell 1985). Kerr (1982) postulates that the judge becomes an "emotional model" for the jurors. The judge's behavior toward, and treatment of, the attorneys representing the two opposing sides becomes the model for the jurors' attitudes toward the two attorneys.

Judges spend a great deal of time in monotonous and routine tasks. Even the courtroom proceedings themselves can be quite monotonous. Cole maintains that "bored judges paying little attention to the arguments of the lawyers before them can often be observed in the courtroom" (1986, p. 399).

The Prosecutor's Role in the Trial

The prosecutor presents the case for the state. The prosecutor's job is to prove to the jury that the defendant committed the offense for which he has been indicted. Prior to the trial, the prosecutor interviews all potential witnesses; that is, everyone who might know anything about the case. Based on this information, this attorney puts together the case for the prosecution.

The Defense Attorney's Role in the Trial

The defense attorney represents the defendant and attempts to disprove the case of the prosecutor. The defense attorney can be a private attorney paid by the defendant, a public defender paid by the state, or a court-appointed attorney. The defense attorney prepares for the trial in a manner similar to that of the prosecutor by interviewing all the potential witnesses prior to the trial. This attorney also interviews people who know the defendant and might be willing to testify about his good character. In addition, the defense attorney files a number of pretrial motions.

The Trial Proceedings

The trial system is an adversarial one, with each attorney only presenting one side of the case. In this way, the facts are revealed to the members of the jury who then must determine the truth: whether or not the defendant committed the crime. And, as we will see, the jury evaluates the attorneys, as well as the evidence in a trial, in coming to a decision.

Greenberg and Ruback (1982) compare the jury trial to a stage performance, with the attorneys performing as actors and also functioning as producers and directors. During the trial the attorneys are always on stage. The prosecutor "acts" aggressively toward the defendant to demonstrate her confidence in the accused's guilt. Meanwhile, the defense attorney attempts to show how likeable the defendant is. At the same time, the victim or complainant is denigrated by the defense in order to create uncertainty as to the guilt of the defendant. Both attorneys use "tricks of communication and presentation of self" in an attempt to sway the jury to their viewpoint (Winick 1979, p. 73).

The prosecution must prove beyond any reasonable doubt that the defendant committed the offense and had "criminal responsibility"; that is to say, the defendant committed the crime while in a criminal state of mind or *mens rea*. The defense attempts to show one or the other of these two factors was not present: either there was no voluntary act (e.g., the defendant did not commit the act or did so involuntarily) or that there was no *mens rea* or criminal intent. The former factor includes insanity, which we will discuss in detail in Chapter 11, Mental Illness and Criminal Justice. During the trial, the prosecution attempts to make the case appear as clear and simple as possible, while the defense tries to point out how complex it is. The motivation for the defense in increasing the perceived

> **Box 8.2**
>
> **Reasonable Doubt**
>
> The following is a definition of reasonable doubt that is read to jurors by the judge in a trial:
>
> "To overcome the presumption of innocence of the defendant, the law places the burden upon the state to prove the defendant is guilty to the exclusion of and beyond a reasonable doubt. The law does not require the defendant to prove his innocence. Accordingly, you must assume that the defendant is innocent unless you are convinced from all the evidence in the case that he is guilty beyond a reasonable doubt.
>
> You should evaluate the evidence admitted in the case and determine the innocence or guilt of the defendant entirely in accordance with these instructions. It is from the evidence introduced upon this trial, and it alone, that you are to determine the guilt or innocence of the defendant. A reasonable doubt as to the guilt of the defendant may arise from the evidence or the lack of evidence. The test you must use is this: If you have reasonable doubt as to the truth of any charge made by the State, you should find the defendant not guilty as to that charge. If you have no reasonable doubt as to the truth of any charge, you should find the defendant guilty as to that charge."

Source: The Supreme Court Committee on Standard Jury Instructions in Criminal Cases, in *Florida Standard Jury Instructions in Criminal Cases,* 2nd ed. (Tallahassee: The Florida Bar, 1975), p. 31.

complexity of the case is to show that the facts are uncertain, providing reasonable doubt. Read REASONABLE DOUBT for a legal definition of this complex concept.

The Importance of Jury Trials

As we have already seen, the vast majority of criminal cases are settled through the process of plea bargaining. In cases that are not plea bargained, the defendant may waive the right to a jury trial and have the case heard by a judge in a "bench trial." Defense attorneys prefer to have jury trials, since many judges are former prosecutors who tend to favor the prosecution (Dershowitz 1982, Winick 1979). However, some defendants do choose to have their cases heard by a judge. The number of defendants who make this choice varies by location. For instance, Los Angeles and New Orleans have a high proportion of bench trials while Washington, D.C., has very few (Report to the Nation on Crime and Justice, 1983).

Despite the small number of cases determined by a trial, the importance of jury trials should not be underestimated. Cases with strong evidence against the defendant tend to be plea bargained, while those with insufficient evidence usually are dismissed. The remaining cases, those going to trial, are the contentious

JUDGE DOROTHY H. PATE presides over a courtroom in the Fourth Judicial Circuit, Duval County, Florida. (Photo courtesy of Roger Sharp)

ones and tend to be more serious. In most cases which go to court, the defendants are found guilty and are likely to appeal the decision. The appeal process is very important because appellate court decisions influence future cases by precedence. In a very few cases, decisions are appealed all the way through the legal system to the U.S. Supreme Court. Decisions by this body influence interpretations of the law throughout the United States and all future cases.

The Trial

Before any evidence is presented, the attorneys select a jury. This can be a long and intricate process. We will discuss the process and the psychological factors influencing the selection of the jury in the next section. The jury can consist of as many as twelve members or, in some jurisdictions, as few as six people.

Criminal cases handled through jury trials require considerably longer to resolve than do cases that are plea bargained. The disposition of most criminal cases takes 6 months or less in the majority of jurisdictions. However, those cases going to trial usually require well over 6 months (Report to the Nation on Crime and Justice, 1983).

In 1974 the Federal Speedy Trial Act was passed. This act specified the amount of time allowed to elapse between each of the parts of the legal process from arrest to sentencing. For example, it was stated that no more than 70 days could pass between the time of an indictment to the beginning of the trial. Since the act was passed, many states have followed the lead of the federal government and instituted speedy trial laws. Of course, if the defense requests a continuance or delay in the trial, the speedy trial requirement is no longer in effect and that time is not counted.

The Opening Statements

The order of presentation in a trial is prescribed by law. The prosecutor begins the trial with an opening statement, giving the jury an overview of the case and what the prosecution intends to prove. Then the defense attorney gives an opening statement. The defense indicates the flaws in the state's case and talks about how he intends to show his client is innocent. The opening arguments can be very persuasive and have a lasting influence on opinions formed by jurors. These statements are helpful in establishing rapport with the jurors. The opening statement can influence what jurors remember by providing a well-organized overview for jurors to use as a framework for information presented later in the trial. Ambiguous cases or those relying on the conflicting testimony of witnesses can be particularly susceptible to influence by opening statements (Linz, Penrod & McDonald 1986, Pyszczynski & Wrightsman 1981).

There are legal constraints on both the opening and closing statements. Attorneys are restricted in their opening statements to discussing the evidence they will present. They are not allowed to make legal arguments, discuss inadmissible evidence, argue about the facts or merits of the case, or give their own speculations. The prosecutor has more restrictions than the defense attorney. The prosecutor's inflammatory remarks or personal opinions given during the course of the trial may be grounds for a mistrial (Horowitz & Willging 1984, Lind & Ke 1985, Loh 1985).

Alan Dershowitz contends that "the courtroom oath—'to tell the truth, the whole truth and nothing but the truth'—is applicable only to witnesses. Defense attorneys, prosecutors, and judges don't take this oath—they couldn't! Indeed, it is fair to say the American justice system is built on a foundation of *not* telling the whole truth" (1982, p. xix).

The defense attorney may waive his opening statement until just prior to the presentation of the case for the defense. There is some debate about the advantages for the time of presentation. Some legal experts contend that the defense attorney should immediately contradict the opening statement made by the prosecutor so that jurors will not make up their minds before the defense presents its case. Others argue that the jurors will forget the defense opening statement unless it is given immediately prior to the actual presentation. The latter contend that the opening statement is necessary at that time so the jurors will understand the case. There is little empirical evidence for either argument, although most attorneys choose not to waive their right to present immediately. However, there is little doubt that the prosecution has the advantage by being allowed to present its case first.

The judge instructs the jury not to make a decision based on the opening statements; however, it is unlikely all jurors are able to refrain from doing so. Psychologists who have studied the decision-making process have found that some people make quick and permanent decisions. For example, people who are described as highly authoritarian or dogmatic tend to have "speed of closure." This personality trait entails making quick decisions on the basis of little information. People with this characteristic will make decisions very rapidly and are probably unable to hold their decision in abeyance until the end of the trial.

The Case for the Prosecution
Following the opening statements, the prosecutor presents her case. The prosecution is required to prove "beyond a reasonable doubt" that the defendant committed the crime. Most of the evidence is presented through witnesses: people who saw the crime or who saw the defendant in the area of the crime, the police officer who arrested the defendant, the evidence technician who gathered the physical evidence, such as fingerprints, the doctor who examined the victim, and anyone else who knows anything about the case. After each witness testifies under direct questioning by the prosecutor, the defense attorney is allowed to cross-examine that witness. During cross-examination, unlike direct examination, the attorneys may ask leading questions (questions which imply what answer the witness should give). Usually the attorneys spend some time with the witnesses prior to the trial, rehearsing them in how to behave while testifying at the trial.

The Case for the Defense
When the prosecutor has completed presenting her evidence and rests the case for the state, the defense attorney presents his case. According to our constitution, people are presumed innocent until proven guilty. In other words, the prosecution has to prove the defendant is guilty, but the defense does not have to prove innocence. If the defense attorney believes the prosecutor has not proven the defendant guilty, he can make a motion for a directed verdict. This motion is a request for the judge to decide that there is not enough evidence to prove the defendant committed the offense. The judge will review the merits of the motion and decide whether there is enough indication of guilt to have the jury review the evidence, but judges seldom dismiss cases at this point in time.

The defendant does not have to prove he is innocent. Practically speaking, though, it is foolish of the defense not to present some evidence. Usually the defense attorney has a number of witnesses: people to provide an alibi for the defendant or witnesses to the crime who say it was not the defendant who committed the offense. The defense attorney attempts to provide the jury with a reasonable doubt as to the guilt of the defendant (Kassin & Wrightsman 1988). After each witness, the prosecutor has the opportunity to cross-examine that witness. Defense attorneys show their confidence in their case and create credibility by introducing damaging evidence themselves. The jury will think they are so sure of the defendant's innocence that they don't have to be concerned with the opposing case.

HERMAN copyright 1990 Jim Unger. Reprinted with permission of UNIVERSAL PRESS SYNDICATE. All rights reserved.

"Your honor, he's leading the witness."

The Defendant's Testimony

The defendant does not have to testify in criminal cases, since citizens of the United States have a constitutional right not to incriminate themselves. In civil cases, the plaintiff can be required to testify as an "adverse witness," but not in criminal cases. If the defendant testifies and is a credible witness, he is likely to be viewed favorably (Efran 1974, Kaplan & Kemmerick 1974, Widgery 1974). But jurors tend to distrust defendants who do not testify, feeling these defendants are hiding something from them. The judge and prosecutor are restricted from making comments to the jury about defendants not testifying, but the jurors usually question it without attention being drawn to the fact.

If nontestifying defendants are viewed more negatively by the jury, then why do some defendants not testify? There are at least two major reasons. The defense attorney might advise the defendant not to testify if the attorney feels the defendant will not make a good presentation or if the defendant has an extensive past record. Information about the defendant's past criminal record cannot be entered into the record at the trial. However, if the defendant testifies, he can be asked questions about his past convictions in order to call his character into question. The Fifth Amendment protects the rights of defendants not to incriminate themselves. Thus, a defendant who testifies in his own behalf can refuse to answer incriminating questions. However, refusal to respond has a boomerang effect on jurors, who tend to believe that the defendant who invokes this right is attempting to hide his guilt (Hendrick & Shaffer 1975, Shaffer & Case 1982).

A case described by Alan Dershowitz demonstrates how putting the defendant on the witness stand can backfire. "Eager to show the jury that he was not trying to hide anything, the lawyer asked his own client whether he had ever been convicted of a crime. 'Yes,' the client answered. The lawyer asked whether he had ever been convicted of a felony. The client again answered, 'Yes.' The lawyer then asked the client to tell the jury the exact number of felonies he had been convicted of. The client paused and started to count on his fingers. Finally he looked his lawyer in the eye and said, 'This one will make four' " (1982, p. 403).

The Victim's Testimony
The victim is required to testify because the U.S. Constitution guarantees the defendant the right to face his accuser. It appears somewhat inequitable that the victim has to go through the trauma of testifying at the trial while the defendant does not. It is particularly difficult and traumatic for the victim in cases of sexual battery, especially when the victim is a child (see "The Child Witness" in Chapter 9 for an extensive discussion of this issue).

Rebuttals
After the presentation of its evidence, the defense rests its case. At that point, the prosecution is allowed to present witnesses who will refute the case made by the defense. Following this rebuttal by the prosecution, the defense is also allowed to bring new witnesses forward in order to rebut the case for the prosecution. Rebuttals are restricted to information or evidence that will contradict the evidence presented by the opposing side.

Inadmissible Evidence
There are legal restrictions concerning the evidence presented at a trial. First of all, the evidence must be relevant to the case. Second, persons who testify can give evidence only about factual occurrences; they cannot give personal opinions (with the exception of expert witnesses) or hearsay evidence. Hearsay refers to something the witness heard another person say about the incident or the defendant; it is secondhand information. Since defendants have the right to confront their accusers, any secondhand information or hearsay evidence is inadmissible (there are some exceptions to the hearsay rule, such as deathbed utterances and excited utterances). A third important category of inadmissible evidence is evidence that was collected in a manner violating the rights of the defendant, such as illegal searches. The judge decides what evidence is admissible and can be admitted to the record and will exclude things prejudicial to one side. See DNA for an example of evidence.

Closing Statements
Once the witnesses have completed their testimony, the prosecutor makes her closing statement. She uses this statement to summarize and clarify the case and to reiterate what she has shown to be evidence of the guilt of the defendant. Following the closing argument of the prosecutor, the defense attorney makes a closing statement. This is the last chance to convince the jury that the defendant

did not commit the offense. The prosecution is then allowed to rebut the defense. Both attorneys use the closing arguments to point out the weaknesses in the other's case and to persuade the jury to their point of view. The lawyers may not give legal instructions to the jurors, but they may present their opinions and discuss the credibility of witnesses. Attorneys are also allowed to point out factors which may cause the jury to be sympathetic to their cause. Both attorneys are obviously trying to persuade jurors with their opening and closing statements. Realizing this, jurors tend to be skeptical of these arguments (Lind & Ke 1985, Loh 1985).

Research in social psychology has shown a strong primacy effect for information. A primacy effect means that people tend to form impressions on the basis of the first information they receive. This effect is particularly apparent in research on first impressions. There is also some evidence for a recency effect, indicating that the most recent information received also has an impact on decisions (Thibaut & Walker 1975, Walker, Thibaut & Andreoli 1972). In either case, the prosecution has the advantage, since it makes both the first and the last presentation. In civil cases, the order is such that the plaintiff has the first and last word (Loh 1985).

Prosecuting attorneys are usually careful to appear unbiased throughout the trial. If they are too aggressive toward witnesses, they can appear to be primarily concerned with winning the case rather than seeking the truth. This aggressive behavior is very apt to be drawn to the attention of the jury by the defense attorney. Greenberg and Ruback (1982) postulate that concern with appearing unbiased accounts for the prosecution saving its most negative and emotional condemnation of the defendant until the final arguments. By doing so, the prosecutor appears to have been objective throughout the trial and finally is herself convinced of the defendant's guilt and cannot control her repulsion for the horrible criminal.

The Verdict

The jury retires to the jury room for its deliberations following instructions. The process of the jury deliberations will be described in Chapter 10. Once the jury has decided on the verdict, the bailiff notifies the judge and attorneys, and the courtroom is reconvened. Then the judge asks the jury foreperson to state the verdict: guilty or not guilty. Once the jury announces its decision, it is dismissed.

The Levels of Courts

Both the state and the federal court systems in the United States consist of three levels. The first or lowest level is the trial court, where cases are heard initially. Once a decision is reached in a trial court, the losing side has the option of appealing the decision to an appellate court. The appeals court reviews the trial decision and rules whether to uphold or reverse it. The highest level in the court system consists of the supreme courts. There are supreme courts in each state system and in the federal system. When requested, the supreme court in each system can review the rulings of appellate courts. Each supreme court decides

> **Box 8.3**
>
> # DNA
>
> Deoxyribonucleic acid, commonly called DNA, determines characteristics such as hair color, susceptibility to certain illnesses, and height, as well as every other inherited physical trait of an individual. Found in the nucleus of every cell, DNA is unique for each individual—a genetic fingerprint. DNA from any tissue, sperm, skin, blood, or any other cell can identify the individual from which it came. Recently scientists have found that DNA is extremely useful in criminal investigations. The genetic code of a sample of blood, sperm, or tissue found on the scene of a crime can be matched to that of a suspect and is extremely accurate in identifying the person who left the sample. The identification is so conclusive that there is only one in two billion chances of its being wrong. It has proved to be particularly useful in identifying rapists and the parents of children.
>
> One of the first cases in which DNA proved useful in the United States was that of the Congress Avenue rapist. The Boynton Beach, Florida, rapes began in December 1986 with an attack on a young mother pushing her baby in a stroller through a park on Congress Avenue. Subsequent victims in the vicinity were joggers. The rapist always wore a black knitted ski mask and surgical gloves so there was no way for the victims to identify him. The assaults lasted for 10 months while the police were unable to find any suspects.
>
> But then a police officer spotted a pickup truck in the vicinity of a rape. Tracking the license to a golf course in the area, police searched the locker of the truck's owner, George Forrest, a groundskeeper and found a black knitted mask and surgical gloves. Confronted with the evidence, George Forrest confessed. Later he recanted his confession, accusing the police of coercion. However, one victim who had been raped in her home became pregnant. Using the
>
> *(continued)*

which cases it will review and limits those cases to ones with wide ramifications or those in which the law is ambiguous. The decisions made by appellate and supreme courts are published and referred to by lawyers when they argue cases. Trial court decisions are sometimes published and can be referred to in the absence of relevant higher court decisions.

Views of the Court System

There are different ways of interpreting and evaluating the functions of the court system. Bonn (1984) describes three of the most typical views of the court system in the United States. The first view maintains that the court is a **due process** system. This viewpoint focuses on the constitutional rights of the defendant and sees the system as a method of delineating and extending those rights. From this

> DNA from the fetus, scientists were able to identify the suspect as the father. Confession or not, there was no doubt that George Forrest was the Congress Avenue rapist.
>
> Another demonstration of the detection power of DNA comes from a case in Great Britain. In 1983, a young woman was raped and murdered in Narborough, a small village in England. No clues were found and no suspect was apparent. Three years later, another young woman was raped and murdered in the same small town. This time a tip led to the arrest of a kitchen porter who confessed to the crime. However, the suspect's father, aware of the discovery of DNA as a genetic fingerprint and convinced of his son's innocence, insisted that his son's blood be compared to semen taken from the body. The samples did not match. The police demanded that every male in the vicinity born between 1953 and 1970 be tested. An employee at a local bakery, Colin Pitchfork, paid a co-worker to take the test for him. When the police were informed of the payment, they tested Pitchfork. Sure enough, he was identified as the rapist.
>
> ♦
>
> The use of DNA as evidence is being contested in court. There is some question as to the procedure used in analyzing it in some laboratories. Is the use of DNA an invasion of a person's privacy? Should a defendant be allowed to refuse testing? Should the police keep a bank of DNA samples as they do fingerprints? Should people who are arrested automatically give DNA samples? Should everyone in an area be required to be tested, as in the case in Narborough? Would it be right for the police to take a hair from a suspect surreptitiously and have this tested?

Sources: H. Italie, "Controversy of 'Blooding' Keeps Wambaugh Up Nights," *The Florida Times-Union* (March 19, 1989), p. D–3; "DNA Joins Crime War As New Way to Pinpoint Identity of Rapists," *The Florida Times-Union* (April 6, 1988), p. B–6; J. Wambaugh, *The Blooding* (New York: Morrow, 1989).

point of view, the courts are seen to have created a "trend toward fairness and equity in criminal court procedure" (Bonn 1984, p. 425). Others view the courts as **bureaucracies.** They contend that the increase in the use of negotiations and plea bargaining has led to the demise of the adversarial system and replaced it with a "bargain" justice. The third view sees the courts as **perpetrators of injustice.** This viewpoint emphasizes the inequities in sentences and maintains that the courts are a system by which the ruling class maintains state control over the lower classes.

The Jury Selection Process

A trial by a jury of one's peers is supposed to protect the individual rights of the defendant and guarantee justice. However, the jury selection process often eliminates "peers" and, in the process, does not necessarily protect rights or mete out justice. The Fourteenth Amendment guarantees defendants the right to a trial by a jury that is representative of the community. In a clarification of this right, the U.S. Supreme Court has ruled that juries must represent all groups with reference to sex and race (Winick 1979). However, the jury is seldom selected from a cross-section of the community and is not representative of the people likely to be tried. For example, although most defendants are from the lower socioeconomic groups, the jurors tend to be middle-class with the poor, young, and minorities underrepresented (Kassin & Wrightsman 1988). Eliminated from jury duty are the extremes of education and wealth. It is estimated that only about 15 percent of Americans have been selected for jury duty (Report to the Nation on Crime and Justice, 1983).

The Jury Pool

People are selected for the jury pool randomly, usually from the voter registration lists. However, voter registration lists are not representative of the community, since blacks tend to register less frequently than other groups and females tend to register more frequently than males. In attempts to compensate for these discrepancies, many jurisdictions have started using other sources for their jury pools, such as vehicle registration lists and property and tax roles (Guinther 1988).

Prior to formation of the jury pool, people selected from the voter registration list (or one of the other sources) are sent a questionnaire to determine if they are eligible for service. This screening is to ensure all members of the jury pool are over 18, can read and write English, and have no felony convictions or any handicap that would prevent them from serving on the jury.

Most jurisdictions exempt specific categories of people from having to serve on a jury. While each jurisdiction has its own exemptions, there are many similarities and the results tend to be the same: the elimination of the highly educated and wealthy from the jury pool. For example, some of the groups which are frequently excused from jury duty are professionals (doctors, lawyers, teachers), members of the criminal justice system, clergy, elected officials, and firefighters. People are often excused if service will create an economic hardship; for example, proprietors of small businesses might be excused.

Contrary to popular opinion, trials do not necessarily have juries with twelve members. The U.S. Supreme Court has ruled that juries can be as small as six members; nevertheless, most trials are heard by twelve-member juries (Report to the Nation on Crime and Justice, 1983). Therefore, most courts select twelve jurors and two alternates for most trials. The alternates will take part in deliberations if one of the original jurors is unable to continue.

Voir Dire

The judge inquires whether any potential juror has a reason why he or she should not serve on this particular jury. First, people are excused for hardship: parents who stay at home with small children, people with handicaps, etc. Next, people are asked if they know any of the participants in the trial: the attorneys for the

Reprinted with special permission of King Features Syndicate, Inc.

prosecution or defense, the defendant, the victim, or the judge. These people are excused since it is assumed that they could be biased due to their acquaintance with one of the participants.

Challenges

The people who remain after this screening are questioned further in the *voir dire* process. Voir dire is loosely translated as "truth talk." It is the process whereby the opinions of the jurors are evaluated to determine whether they may be biased toward either side in the case.

A person can be eliminated from the jury by one of two types of challenge: a **challenge for cause** or a **peremptory challenge.** If the potential juror is obviously biased, one of the attorneys can request that the judge eliminate that person for cause. Usually the attorneys disagree over whether the person should be eliminated because the person who is biased against the defense is usually one the prosecution wants on the jury, and vice versa. The judge decides whether there is enough evidence of bias to necessitate a challenge for cause. There is no limit to the number of challenges allowed for cause. Read AN UNINFORMED JURY for a description of the people selected for the Oliver North trial.

If a potential juror appears to one of the attorneys to be someone who will not be fair (or more accurately, not favor his side), but the bias is not such that the judge would exclude the juror for cause, the potential juror can be eliminated by a peremptory challenge. No justification is necessary for a peremptory challenge. The number of peremptory challenges allowed varies by jurisdiction and by type of case. In a few states (e.g., Florida and New Jersey) and the federal courts, the defense is allocated more peremptory challenges than the prosecution (Winick 1979).

The method for voir dire varies by jurisdiction. In some courts, the judge asks the jurors questions, while in others the attorneys do the questioning. In still others, the lawyers submit their questions to the judge who screens them and only asks questions that the judge considers appropriate (Bermant 1985).

The purpose of voir dire is to determine if a potential juror is biased and, therefore, unlikely to be fair in evaluating a trial. In truth, attorneys prefer jurors

---

Box 8.4

An Uninformed Jury

In the spring of 1989, Oliver North was brought to trial in the Iran-Contra affair. North was accused of twelve felonies, including: lying to Congress, shredding evidence, and using tax-exempt funds to finance the Contras. Oliver North received immunity for testifying to the United States Congress. Because his 6 days of testimony was nationally televised and his photograph was on the front page of most newspapers, it seemed unlikely that there would be anyone in the United States who was not familiar with the case. However, the courts determined that the only jurors who would be unbiased would be those who did not know anything about the case. After much screening, a pool of forty-five people was found who said they knew just about nothing about Oliver North.

Some of the jurors are quoted as saying, "Whatever I heard I didn't understand," "The front page is the last thing I look at," "I don't like the news." Others said that they paid no attention to North's nationally televised testimony or just were not interested. Finally a jury of twelve people who were totally uninformed about national events was formulated to hear the case.

♦

Can people who are completely uninformed about national events make an intelligent decision about the Iran-Contra affair? Is it possible that these people really knew nothing about Oliver North? Can people be informed about political events and remain unbiased? Can people who say they do not understand or do not care about national events make valid decisions in cases of this sort?

Source: "Juror: 'I Don't Like the News,'" *The Florida Times-Union* (February 10, 1989), p. A–7.

to be biased, but only in favor of their position. Alan Dershowitz (1982) recounts the old tale of an attorney who cables his client to announce that he won the client's big case. The cable stated, "Justice has prevailed." In response the client cables, "Appeal immediately." Dershowitz's point is that attorneys do not want justice, they want to win (1982, p. xvi).

It is highly questionable whether jurors' biases can be determined through the voir dire practice. Often attorneys merely ask jurors to state their prejudices. This is unlikely to elicit a truthful response. But if jurors state they are not biased, they usually are accepted for the jury. Social psychologists have found that people have a strong need to answer questions in a socially acceptable manner, a phenomenon called social desirability. People do not like others to know of their biases and are particularly reluctant to disclose them in a public situation, such as a trial (Suggs & Sales 1979). At least one study has found that many jurors respond differently to questions asked privately after the trial than they did during voir dire (Murray & Eckman 1974). While potential jurors usually are questioned in groups, there are jurisdictions that allow them to be questioned in private. This latter method has been found to be more effective in determining biases of jurors (Nietzel & Dillehay 1979).

Evaluating biases is not a simple task. Psychologists who specialize in the study of prejudice find it difficult to determine whether someone is prejudiced and to develop a valid measure of prejudice. If someone wishes to conceal a bias, it would be very difficult to uncover it. Many people are not aware that their attitudes are biased or that they hold prejudices. Few, if any, people are completely free of all biases.

Wrightsman defines bias as "a human predisposition to make interpretations based on past experience, to try to fit all new stimuli and information into one's already developed system for looking at the world" (1987, p. 241). Using this definition, he maintains that juries are biased, with individual jurors being selected by attorneys on the basis of favoring one or the other position. In addition, attorneys may attempt to create biases in the jurors during voir dire.

Methods of Voir Dire

Although much advice given to attorneys on jury selection is based on stereotypes, most attorneys realize that following this procedure is not effective and use other tactics. Attorneys tend to use one of two primary approaches to voir dire: the "grand stand play" or "in-depth questioning" (Blunk & Sales 1977, Nietzel & Dillehay 1979).

Grand Stand Play

Attorneys who use the grand stand play accept the first twelve jurors selected but do so with a good deal of theatrics. These attorneys generally make an elaborate speech telling the jurors how much they trust them and the faith they have in the jury system. These lawyers point out that they have not questioned the jurors because they have such faith in their fairness. The implication is that their case is so strong, any fair-minded person will rule in their favor. The flaw in this approach is that it is rather transparent. Jurors who feel they are being manipulated or patronized might resent this approach and react against the case presented by that attorney.

In-Depth Questioning

Most lawyers use the voir dire process to select jurors who they think will be favorable to their viewpoint. These attorneys generally ask potential jurors about their background, family, experience with crime, and similar questions. They also might attempt to determine the person's attitudes toward race, the police, criminals, or other issues related to the trial.

Greenberg and Ruback (1982) propose that attorneys use extensive questioning in the hope selected jurors will feel as if they "passed" a difficult test, thus creating positive attitudes toward the attorney. However, others have found it is just as likely these jurors will feel resentment at being put through the ordeal instead of pride in having succeeded (Broeder 1965).

Indoctrination

Indoctrination is an attempt to influence and educate jurors about the case during voir dire. The attorney tries to persuade jurors to accept her view of the case.

Reprinted with special permission of King Features Syndicate, Inc.

The voir dire process is also used to build rapport with jurors. One strategy used is to ask each juror if he or she believes some point critical to the case. Each juror who agrees is accepted. During the summary statement, the jurors are reminded of their beliefs. An example would be a case of assault. Suppose the defendant is accused of hitting a worker on a construction site. During voir dire, the defense attorney asks jurors if they believe individuals have the right to defend themselves if threatened. During the case, the attorney provides evidence that the assaulted construction worker shouted in a threatening manner and appeared about to strike the defendant. During closing arguments the defense attorney will remind the jurors of their belief in an individual's right to defend themselves when threatened and indicate that the defendant was in such a situation.

Scientific Jury Selection

Actual jurors cannot be interviewed prior to the voir dire process. Therefore, attorneys attempt to gather as much information as possible about potential jurors prior to selection. In recent years, scientific methods for jury selection have been developed and used, particularly by the defense. These methods generally include some combination of the following procedures: 1) a community survey, 2) an informal community network, and 3) observation and evaluation of the jurors' behavior in the courtroom.

Most scientific jury selections include the administration of a survey. This method allows the lawyers to gather information on the average person in the community. A questionnaire reflecting the issues of the case is developed and distributed to a random sample of people living in the community. The questionnaire generally collects demographic information and asks questions dealing with general attitudes as well as attitudes toward the specific case. Analysis of the data from the questionnaire provides a profile of the person most likely to convict and that of the person most likely to acquit the specific defendant. The profiles obtained by regressing questionnaire responses on demographic data are compared to demographic profiles of potential jurors. It is presumed that those demographically similar will have similar attitudes toward the defendant and the case. For example, in the Mitchell-Stans case (see THE MITCHELL-STANS TRIAL later in this section), the person most likely to convict was described as liberal, Jewish, Democrat, someone who read the *Post* or *New York Times,* and watched Walter Cronkite. A person who was quite knowledgeable about the Watergate incident was described as someone who would be prejudiced against the defendants and likely to convict them (Zeisel & Diamond 1976).

The second scientific method, an informal community network, is used sometimes in conjunction with the survey and sometimes alone. The community network is formed by friends and relatives of the accused and the attorneys involved in the case. These people contact others whom they know in the community in an effort to find people who know the jurors. The contacts are interviewed in order to find out as much as possible about the potential jurors and their predispositions before the voir dire (Saks & Hastie 1978, Schulman 1973). Some states even have organizations which produce "jury books" describing potential jurors in terms of their characteristics, criminal records, and prior jury service, including the verdict from these previous juries (Winick 1979).

The third scientific method involves observation of the jurors during voir dire to determine their predisposition toward the case. Typically, a psychologist is employed to evaluate the verbal and nonverbal behavior of the jurors. Sometimes this assessment is used alone; at other times, data such as survey results or network information are combined to predict the decision each juror is likely to make. A number of highly publicized trials have used some type of scientific method, for example, the Angela Davis, the John Mitchell and Maurice Stans, the Harrisburg Seven, and the Gainesville Eight trials.

Nietzel and Dillehay (1979) present a theoretical model for jury selection. They divide the trial into two phases and propose that jurors need to be selected on the basis of different qualities for each of the phases. The first of these, the **opinion formation phase,** encompasses the time from when the juror is called to voir dire until the deliberation. The second phase, the **social influence phase,** overlaps with the first phase and continues until it becomes prominent during the deliberation. In the first phase, factors such as the juror's experience, sentiment, and intelligence tend to influence decisions. Experience refers primarily to experience as a juror, but also includes other courtroom activities, for example, testifying in trials or involvement in civil cases. The attorneys particularly will want to know the verdict from any other case in which the potential juror served on the jury. Sentiment is a combination of personality, attitudes, values, and authoritarianism. These characteristics are used to predict whether the juror will tend to be harsh or lenient. Sentiment is evaluated by factors tending to correlate with it (e.g., education, occupation, residence, membership in organizations, etc.). Intelligence is the easiest to assess but the least emphasized, unless the trial will entail the use of very technical testimony. A trial in which scientific jury selection was used is described in THE MITCHELL-STANS TRIAL.

The second phase, the social influence phase, is concerned with how the jurors interact and influence each other. Social influence is determined by such characteristics of the juror as conformity and reactions to group pressure. These characteristics are inferred from the person's education, occupation, and leadership

Box 8.5

The Mitchell-Stans Trial

John Mitchell and Maurice Stans were accused of conspiracy. They were alleged to have hindered the Security and Exchange Commission's investigation of Robert Vesco in exchange for a $200,000 contribution to President Nixon's reelection campaign. The defense team included social scientists who conducted a survey of the community to obtain a profile of people who were likely to find the defendants guilty. People most likely to convict these defendants were liberals, Jewish, Democrats, those who read the *Post* or *New York Times* and watched Walter Cronkite. The person described was someone quite knowledgeable about the Watergate incident and, therefore, likely to be prejudiced against the defendants and likely to convict them.

During voir dire, 138 jurors were excused for reasons ranging from hardship and impartiality to illness. In addition, there were twenty-six peremptory challenges, six by the prosecution (who did not use their other two) and twenty by the defense. The results of the jury selection process was a jury that was similar to the jury pool in race and sex distribution, somewhat different in age distribution, and drastically different in education level. While almost half of the jury pool had some college education, only one member of the final jury did. None of the other members of the jury had any education beyond the high school level.

Outsiders are not allowed to observe jury deliberations. However, after the trial, jurors in the Mitchell-Stans case were interviewed to reconstruct their deliberations. The fact that only one member of the jury, Mr. Choa, had any college education made that member different from the others. Mr. Choa was not only well-educated, but as the vice president of the First National City Bank of New York, he also was much higher in status than the other members of the jury.

Mr. Choa was described as persuasive and confident of his opinions. Due to these characteristics, as well as to his education and status, he had a great deal of influence on the other jury members and the final verdict. The original vote was eight for conviction and four for acquittal. The final vote was unanimous for acquittal, the position that Mr. Choa originally espoused.

One of the most incriminating pieces of evidence in the trial was a memo from Vesco to President Nixon's brother. In the memo, Vesco threatened to reveal his $200,000 contribution to the reelection campaign if the case against him by the Security and Exchange Commission was not terminated. Mr. Choa, as the only member of the jury having any experience with memos, convinced the other members of the jury that this memo was "trash."

It is interesting to note that Mr. Choa was an alternate for the jury and would not have participated in the deliberations except for the illness of one of the original jurors. It is also important that the prosecution did not use its three challenges for the alternates despite the fact that Mr. Choa was very conservative politically and sympathetic to Mitchell and Stans. Challenging Mr. Choa might have changed the verdict in this case.

Source: H. Zeisel and S. S. Diamond, "The Jury Selection in the Mitchell-Stans Conspiracy Trial," *American Bar Foundation Research Journal,* vol. 87, pp. 151–174.

experience and are particularly important during jury deliberations. A juror who is predisposed to an attorney's point of view and decides in that direction will not impact the final verdict if this juror is also easily influenced by others and changes his opinion during deliberations.

There is much debate over both the ethics and the effectiveness of scientific jury selection. The question of ethics centers on the fact that scientific jury selection may have an unfair impact on the verdict. This method is used primarily by the defense, which tends to equalize the advantages of the two sides since the prosecution has more resources available to it.

Obviously, the time and expense necessary for scientific jury selection is available to only a few: the wealthy or those involved in a popular cause which elicits professional volunteers. The poor and those involved in unpopular activities are unlikely to have the advantage of scientific jury selection. Of course, the ethics are no longer relevant if the method is not effective, but there is no universal agreement on the effectiveness of the scientific jury selection method. Most trials in which scientific jury selection is used have outcomes supporting its effectiveness. However, these trials tend to be ambiguous ones, such as conspiracy, in which the outcomes would be difficult to predict and in which people might be reluctant to convict. Simulated jury trials designed to evaluate the effectiveness have not been able to resolve the question to everyone's satisfaction (Horowitz 1980, Penrod 1980).

Research on Jurors

Both psychologists and lawyers are interested in predicting decisions an individual juror is likely to make. Psychologists are interested because they wish to understand people and the decision-making, while attorneys would find this information useful during voir dire. In pursuit of this knowledge, psychologists have studied the jury trial and jury decision-making in great depth. Since people are prohibited from observing or recording actual jury deliberations, much of the research has been conducted with mock or simulated juries. These juries often are composed of college students, although some researchers have used actual jury pools for subjects (for example, Horowitz 1988).

Criticisms of Mock Jury Research

There is some controversy over whether the results obtained by research conducted on simulated juries can be generalized to real juries. Kerr contends there is "good reason to hesitate in generalizing" these results (1982, p. 264). One criticism of this type of research is that the trial reviewed by mock jurors usually is quite short, only giving the highlights. Therefore, the variable being studied (e.g., attractiveness of the defendant) becomes very obvious to the subject and its impact is inflated. Thus, the results from the laboratory studies may be much stronger than they would be in real trials (Bray & Kerr 1982).

After analyzing seventy-eight simulated jury trials, Linz and Penrod (1982) expressed reservations concerning the results. They found the effects of the manipulated variable were stronger when the realism of the settings decreased.

However, recent research by Kramer and Kerr (1989) contradicts these criticisms of simulated trials. These researchers found variations of the length and complexity of simulated trials had no impact on the decisions of mock jurors. While allowing that results of simulations should not be accepted unquestioningly, they maintain "even highly artificial simulations are not **inherently** distorting and may actually inform us on relationships of real significance for law and human behavior" (1989, p. 99).

Another criticism of simulated trials centers on the verdict. Many simulated jury studies have each mock juror decide on a verdict independently, rather than deliberating in a group. Often the choices are whether the person is "certainly guilty," "possibly guilty," "undecided," "possibly not guilty," or "certainly not guilty." In contrast, real jurors reach a group decision and only have a choice between guilty or not guilty. In addition, mock jurors realize nothing will happen to the defendant as a result of their decisions, whereas real jurors sometimes have control over whether the defendant lives or dies. Therefore, mock jurors are less likely to take the decision as seriously as real jurors do. However, there is no consistent finding that real and mock juries reach different verdicts. While some research indicates mock jurors are less likely to convict than real jurors (Diamond & Zeisel 1974), other studies found the verdicts to be the same (Miller 1975, Kerr, Nerenz & Herrick 1979).

Comparisons between mock jurors, usually college students, and real jurors have found many differences, the most obvious being in age and education (Nemeth & Sosis 1973, Sealy & Cornish 1973, Simon & Mahan 1971). However, despite concerns with simulated studies, there is no universal agreement that the results are invalid and should be discounted. More recent studies have sought to overcome the limitations of simulated jury studies by using subjects from actual jury roles, having juries deliberate as a group, and increasing the realism and complexity of the simulated trial. Still, results from simulated jury studies cannot be automatically generalized to real juries. Bearing in mind the limitations of simulated jury studies, we will now look at the results of the research.

It appears that jurors, at least in simulated trials, have a predisposition toward one or the other side before the trial begins. Research with mock jurors found that they were either pro-defense or pro-prosecution prior to hearing any evidence in the simulated trials (Kassin & Wrightsman 1983). These predispositions were found to influence the verdicts to a very large extent. Although all the subjects reviewed identical evidence, decisions were predicted by the predisposition of the mock jurors in three out of the four cases. The exception was a rape case, which we will see is likely to be influenced by the sex of the juror.

Characteristics of Jurors

Most attempts at predicting decisions have focused on the characteristics of jurors. Greenberg and Ruback (1982) maintain that a "folklore" has developed among attorneys about what type of person makes the best juror for each side of a case.

This folklore has evolved from "personal experience, hunches, intuition, and common sense" (p. 139). These predictions are passed on in the writings of attorneys as advice to other lawyers (for example, Darrow 1936). The older pieces of advice tend to be based on stereotypes without much evidence of veracity.

The psychological approach has been more scientific without much more success. In an attempt to determine underlying factors that influence individual decisions by jurors, psychologists have studied the relationship between jurors' personality characteristics and their decisions. Despite the collection of a considerable amount of data on the topic, researchers have not found any conclusive evidence of specific demographic characteristics that consistently predict the direction of verdicts. However, some personality traits have been found to correlate with decisions, the most consistent ones being dogmatism and/or authoritarianism (Alexander & Licker 1975, Mitchell & Byrne 1973). Although these characteristics are measured by different instruments, they both suggest a simple cognitive structure. The syndrome related to a simple cognitive structure has been similarly described by theorists under many rubrics: authoritarianism (Adorno et al. 1950), dogmatism (Rokeach 1960), low cognitive structure (Bieri 1955, Scott 1962), and concrete cognitive structure (Harvey, Hunt & Schroder 1961).

The description of the cognitively simple individual is of someone who tends to make extreme evaluations, is punitive, rigid in beliefs, has speed of closure (defined as making quick decisions on little information), and has a low tolerance for ambiguity. These individuals have also been found to seek less conflicting and novel information (Feather 1967) and to have low recall of inconsistent information (Kleck & Wheaton 1967). All of these characteristics would tend to influence the decision-making processes of the jurors. In fact, researchers have found that persons high in dogmatism give more guilty verdicts, and both dogmatic and authoritarian persons have been shown to give longer sentences (Alexander & Licker 1975, Berg & Vidmar 1975, Jurow 1971) than persons who are low in these characteristics. In addition to the attributes described, simple cognitive structure is strongly correlated with prejudice (Adorno et al. 1950, Foley 1976, Pettigrew 1958).

Race of Juror

Given that simple cognitive structure correlates with both prejudice and the imposition of harsh sentences, it would seem logical that jurors with these characteristics would be particularly harsh toward defendants of another race. However, research on juries has been conducted almost exclusively with white subjects, and some evidence indicates that the relationship between cognitive structure and prejudice is reversed for blacks (Foley 1976, 1977). Whites who score high on dogmatism tend to be prejudiced toward blacks, while blacks who score high on dogmatism tend to be low in prejudice toward whites. In a simulated jury study, Foley and Chamblin (1982) found dogmatic white jurors were more likely to find the defendant guilty than those low in dogmatism, and the reverse was found for black jurors. The differences in verdicts for the highly dogmatic subjects are probably a reflection of the norms for the respective subcultures. The white subculture has negative attitudes toward crime and dogmatic whites attribute more likelihood of guilt to defendants. In contrast, the black community tends to be less punitive than the white community (Gallup 1976). Therefore, dogmatic blacks would tend to attribute less likelihood of guilt to the defendant. The authors hypothesize that these results are an indication of a relationship between dogmatism and conformity found previously by Thomas Pettigrew (1959) and O. J. Harvey (1966). However, since the number of black subjects in the study were limited, the results need to be viewed with caution.

Sex of Juror
Although attorneys are often given advice about the different ways in which males and females make decisions on juries, there appears to be little consistent evidence of a difference. The exception is in rape cases, where females are more likely to find the defendant guilty and males to find him not guilty (Davis et al. 1977, Selby, Calhoun & Brock 1977, Ugwuegbu 1979). Greenberg and Ruback (1982) attribute this difference to males and females viewing the evidence from the perspective of different participants: the male from the perspective of the rapist and the female from the perspective of an observer or victim. A psychological principle, known as the "actor-observer bias," maintains that people tend to attribute their own behavior to external factors and the behavior of others to internal factors. In other words, people think that they themselves behave differently based on the situation, but others have consistent ways of behaving due to motivations or personality characteristics. In the case of jurors hearing a rape case, male jurors are apt to identify with the male defendant, thus perceiving his behavior as being elicited by external factors. In contrast, female jurors are likely to evaluate his behavior as observers, making them more likely to attribute it to internal causes.

Ambiguity of Evidence
Characteristics of the juror only influence decisions in ambiguous cases. When the evidence is very clear and consistent, jurors' characteristics have little impact. Indications of the relationship between juror characteristics and clarity of evidence were discovered in a study of mock jurors by Kaplan and Miller (1978). These researchers found a difference between people with harsh and lenient attitudes when the evidence was considered unreliable but no difference between these groups when there was reliable evidence. Those jurors with harsh attitudes were more likely to attribute guilt than those with lenient attitudes, but only when the evidence was ambiguous. However, the reader is reminded that only cases which are ambiguous are likely to go to trial.

    A more recent study by Christy A. Visher (1987) found that decisions made by actual jurors were largely dependent on evidential issues, particularly the use of force and physical evidence. She based her opinion on interviews of 331 jurors who served on thirty-eight forcible sexual assault juries. Most research has found that the characteristics of the jurors have an insignificant impact on their decisions.

Summary

The courtroom is designed to emphasize the power and authority of the judge. The judge presides over the trial, functioning somewhat like a conductor or a referee, maintaining order and deciding all questions pertaining to the law. The prosecutor's job is to prove that the defendant committed the offense for which he has been indicted. The defense attorney represents the defendant and attempts to disprove the prosecution's case. The trial system is an adversarial one, with each attorney only presenting one side of the case.

Despite the small number of cases determined by a trial, the importance of jury trials should not be underestimated. Cases that go to trial are contentious and serious ones. They are also the cases that reach appeals courts, determining precedence for future trials.

The order of presentation in a trial is prescribed by law. The trial begins with opening statements by the prosecutor and defense attorney. Then the prosecutor presents the case for the state and the defense attorney presents his client's case. The defendant does not have to testify in criminal cases, but the victim is required to testify. Both sides are allowed to present witnesses to rebut the opponent's case. The trial ends with closing statements by the prosecution and the defense.

There are different ways of interpreting and evaluating the functions of the court system. Bonn (1984) describes three of the most typical views of the court system in the United States: courts as **due process** systems, as **bureaucracies,** and as **perpetrators of injustice.**

Juries are selected through the voir dire process. Attorneys from each side use challenges to select jurors who are sympathetic to their point of view. Two primary methods of voir dire are the grand stand play and in-depth questioning. Attorneys also use voir dire to indoctrinate jurors to their position. In recent years, scientific methods of jury selection have been developed. Debate over the ethics and effectiveness of this latter process continues.

Most attempts at predicting juror decisions have focused on the characteristics of the jurors. Some support for the relationship between cognitive structure and decision-making has been found. In addition, the sex of the juror seems to be related to decisions in rape cases. However, characteristics of jurors only influence decisions in ambiguous cases.

9

Witnesses

Eyewitness Identification
Acquisition
Retention
Retrieval
Eyewitness Identification and the Courts
The Expert Witness
Ethics
Roles of Expert Witnesses
The Effect of Expert Testimony
The Courts and Expert Testimony
The Child Witness
The Courts and Child Witnesses
Accuracy of Children's Testimony
Children's Emotional Reaction
Children's Credibility
Summary

Eyewitness Identification

Eyewitness accounts of incidents and identification of perpetrators are given tremendous credibility by laypersons, the media, and members of the criminal justice system. The legal system depends on accounts of victims and witnesses to decide whether an incident was a crime and, if so, to determine who was responsible for it. Police will arrest, prosecutors will indict, and jurors will find someone guilty on the word of an eyewitness. The testimony of the eyewitness is often given greater weight than the alibi of the offender, testimony contradicting the eyewitness, and even physical evidence.

The many limitations of eyewitness accounts and identification seem to be a well-kept secret. The average person thinks memory functions like a videocassette recorder; if someone wants to remember a past experience, all that person has to do is pull out the appropriate cassette and replay it. The vividness of recollected events leads people to assume that they are accurate. Actually, as vivid as memories appear to be, they are not necessarily accurate.

Memory is not a static filing system but rather an ongoing process which continues after the event is perceived. Memory consists of three separate phases: acquisition, retention, and retrieval (Goodman & Hahn 1987). The acquisition step refers to the process by which we see or perceive an event or an object. Retention encompasses the time during which we keep the memory in our minds. The last phase, retrieval, occurs when we try to recall the event or the object from our memory. A host of internal and external factors can interfere with any of the phases.

Acquisition

Memory can only be as accurate as the original perception, so acquisition is an important aspect of memory. Most people assume they see and hear things as they really are. However, this is not necessarily so; there are many incidents of misperceptions. Everyone has had the experience of misunderstanding something someone told them or being misunderstood. Certainly most people have seen someone they recognized and after approaching him or her, realized it was not who they thought.

The Influence of Race

Experience with members of another racial group influences perceptions. People have more difficulty identifying someone of another racial group than people from their own group (Bothwell, Brigham & Malpass 1989, Barkowitz & Brigham 1982, Elliott, Wills & Goldstein 1973). Whites tend to use eye color, hair color, and hair texture as identifying characteristics, and these cues are not helpful in identifying blacks and orientals (Ellis 1975). Cross-race identification may also be affected by the perceiver's attitudes toward the other race (Luce 1974). A classic study by Allport and Postman (1947) illustrates the effect of prior attitudes on perceptions of members of another racial group. In this study subjects were shown a picture of a black man and a white man interacting on a subway.

Chapter 9 ♦ Witnesses   **211**

♦ **FIGURE 9.1** Subway scene used in rumor experiments (illustrated by Reen Foley)

The white man was carrying a razor. After viewing the picture, the first subject described it to a second subject. The second subject told a third subject, and so on, through six links in the rumor chain. When asked to describe the scene, more than half of the chains reported that the black man was carrying the razor and some even thought he was holding it in a threatening manner.

Cognitive Influences on Perception

Past experience is not the only factor influencing perception; both attention span and span of immediate memory are highly restricted. A person can only perceive and encode a limited amount of information at any one time. In order to make sense out of information and remember it, people organize what they perceive. Perceptions are organized by cognitive processes through leveling, sharpening, and assimilating (Allport & Postman 1947). In other words, people eliminate some of the details, highlight other factors, and organize their cognitions according to their experiences, values, and needs. People attend to and perceive things better if those items are important (Walker, Thibaut & Andreoli 1972) or salient. People do not purposely distort what they see; they are simply unaware of the cognitive influences on their perceptions.

People also tend to see what they expect to perceive. Brian Inglis (1986) describes how six independent witnesses were asked to observe a man use the power of his mind to make a vase of flowers levitate. Only one of the observers reported seeing the vase rise. The other witnesses did not see it rise, even though it rose 6 inches into the air through mechanical devices. Controlled experiments have also shown the impact of expectations on perceptions. Subjects asked to judge the colors of familiar items said that orange-colored tomatoes were redder than orange-colored lemons (Bruner, Postman & Rodrigues 1951) and that a black ace of diamonds was red (Bruner & Postman 1949).

Situational Influences on Perception
The situation in which the perception occurs, the circumstances surrounding the perception, and the physical limitations of the person doing the perceiving also determine the accuracy of perceptions. Perception is limited or distorted by the length of time the person observes the event, the distance between the person perceiving and the object being perceived, and lighting in the area. Obviously someone who observes an event taking place in a few seconds at the other end of a parking lot in the dark will not perceive the event very accurately. However, if the same event took place over a period of hours in a small, well-lit room, the eyewitness's perceptions would be more accurate. The physical condition of the perceiver also influences the accuracy of what is perceived. For example, if the person has poor eyesight or is not wearing necessary glasses, is under the influence of drugs or alcohol, is ill or in pain, that person's perceptions will not be extremely accurate.

Psychological Influences on Perception
There are many psychological factors which influence perception, such as the primacy and recency effects. The reader will remember from the section on trial proceedings (Chapter 8) that the primacy effect refers to the tendency of people to be greatly influenced by the first information they perceive. For example, people form first impressions of others and these first impressions continue to influence perceptions of later behavior which might be quite different. Another frequent influence on perception is the recency effect, the opposite of the primacy effect. The recency effect occurs when someone's perceptions are influenced more by the most recent information than by previous perceptions.

Conformity
Much social-psychological research centers on how people influence other people's perceptions and attitudes, particularly through conformity. In a well-known study, Solomon Asch showed subjects three lines and asked them to select the line that was the closest in length to a stimulus line. The correct answer was obvious and most subjects were correct close to 100 percent of the time when they were alone. However, when other subjects (actually, confederates of the experimenter) chose obviously inaccurate lines, the subjects also chose the incorrect line in about one-third of the trials. Afterwards, many subjects reported that they

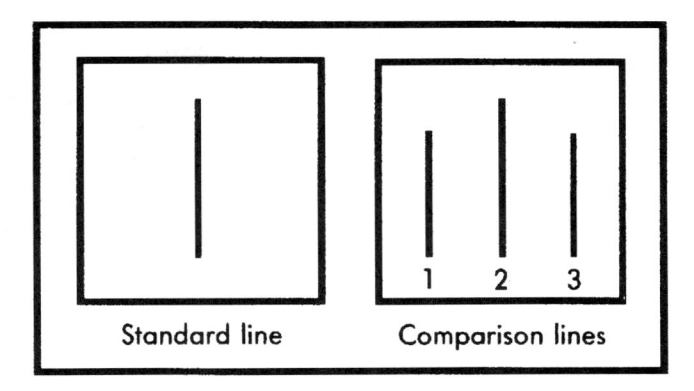

♦ **FIGURE 9.2** Sample comparison from Solomon Asch's conformity procedure. The participants were asked to judge which of three comparison lines was equal to the standard. (illustrated by Reen Foley)
Source: D. G. Myers, *Social Psychology,* 2d ed. Copyright © 1987 McGraw-Hill, Inc. Reprinted by permission of McGraw-Hill, Inc.

knew the correct answer but went along with the crowd. But some subjects said they actually saw the line in the way the confederates did (Asch 1956).

Perceptions of Crimes

Crimes happen quickly and are not usually anticipated, so the attention of the observers is reduced. Crimes often go unnoticed by passersby because they do not appear to be significant. Thus, witnesses to a crime might not have very accurate perceptions of the event.

When people observe a crime in progress, it is an unusual, ambiguous, and oftentimes threatening event. Under these circumstances, people lack confidence in their perceptions and interpretation of the event. They are less sure of themselves and rely more on information from other people to interpret the event and to integrate contradictory perceptions. Thus witnesses to a crime are very susceptible to the influence of others' interpretations of the event (Levine & Tapp 1982).

Observing a crime, particularly as a victim, is stressful. People under stress tend to narrow their attention, and the chances of misperceiving an event increase. Anxiety produces a loss in abstract abilities, and people tend to be less accurate in their perceptions of aversive events. Inaccuracies in perceiving the perpetrator are even more likely. Observers might be paying such close attention to the event that they do not accurately perceive the offender. Other thoughts, such as how to stay alive, are so engrossing that witnesses are not concentrating on the offender.

Another factor found to interfere with perception is "weapon focus." This refers to the phenomenon in which a witness's attention is directed toward a gun or knife during the commission of a crime and, therefore, he is less attentive to other items in the environment reducing his ability to remember other details.

Loftus, Loftus, and Messo (1987) showed subjects a series of slides depicting an incident in a fast-food restaurant. The slides were identical for two groups of subjects with the exception of what the stimulus person showed the clerk. Half the subjects saw a gun and the other half saw a check. Eye movements of subjects watching the slides were recorded; more and longer eye fixation was demonstrated by those seeing the gun than by those seeing the check. Subjects viewing the person with the gun displayed poorer memories than those seeing the check and were less able to recognize the stimulus person.

Retention

Let us assume the original perception was accurate and see what happens during the second phase in the memory process, retention. Most people assume events are stored in a permanent file in their memory. Unfortunately, this is not the case. At the very least, memory diminishes the longer items are held in retention. Incidents occurring after the original incident, both internal and external, can modify the memory while it is in storage (Wells 1986). New information about the original event, impressions created by other witnesses, and questions about the event all influence the memory in storage.

Research Studies
Of particular interest in the area of eyewitness identification is research demonstrating that events during storage can affect memories for faces (Loftus 1979). For example, photographs of suspected offenders shown to witnesses can modify their memories of the offender. Brown, Deffenbacher, and Sturgill (1979) had actors interact in an incident observed by subjects. The subjects subsequently searched through many "mug shots" for the actors. Several days after the staged event, subjects were asked to pick the actors out of a lineup. Included in the lineup were actors involved in the incident, people whose photographs were in the mug shots, and some totally unfamiliar people. Faces seen in the mug shots were as likely to be chosen as the actual participants; but subjects seldom chose unfamiliar faces. Apparently subjects' memories of the participants were altered during the retention stage by viewing a large number of photos of other faces.

Unconscious Transference
Research indicates that people will engage in unconscious transference of aspects of the situation. A study conducted using a videotape of a staged purse snatching demonstrated the occurrence of transference. In the videotape, there was a group of young men standing around talking. One of the men snatched a purse from a passerby. A significant percentage of subjects viewing a photo spread of the young men thought the innocent young man facing the camera was the culprit. In another study, a large percentage of witnesses to a feigned incident identified an innocent bystander, who was a stranger, as the culprit (Loftus 1979).

Questioning

Any statements or questions asked about an event can influence memory of it (Loftus 1979). In one study, experimenters showed subjects slides of an automobile accident. One half of the subjects saw slides in which the accident occurred after a red Datsun pulled up to a yield sign. The other half of the subjects saw the same accident after the car pulled up to a stop sign. Following presentation of the slides, half the subjects in each group were asked, "Did another car pass the red Datsun while it was stopped at the stop sign?" The other half of the subjects in each group were asked the same question except the sign mentioned was a yield sign. At a later time, subjects were asked to choose the slide they originally saw from two choices, one with a stop sign and one with a yield sign. Subjects tended to choose the slide which had the sign that matched the question they were asked, no matter what they actually saw (Loftus, Miller & Burns 1978).

Retrieval

It is difficult to know whether storage has been affected until the last phase of memory, retrieval. And it is often this step which tampers with the memory in retention. This is the stage in which an eyewitness is asked to describe the incident and/or the assailant. Questions asked can influence the responses of the witness. For example, Loftus and Palmer (1974) reported on two studies they conducted involving a simulated car accident. Subjects were asked how fast a car was going when it "smashed," "collided," "bumped," "contacted," or "hit" another car. People's perceptions of the speed of the car were influenced by the verb used to describe the impact.

A number of studies by Loftus and her colleagues indicate that new information about an incident is incorporated into the person's original memory during the retrieval stage. In a study which illustrates this effect, subjects were shown a videotape of a classroom incident (Loftus, Altman & Geballe 1975). After viewing the videotape, subjects were asked either aggressive questions (Did the professor shout something to the activists?) or nonaggressive questions (Did the professor say anything to the demonstrators?). One week later, those subjects who were asked the aggressive questions described the demonstrators as noisier, more violent, belligerent, and antagonistic than did the subjects who were asked the nonaggressive questions.

Eyewitnesses

Levine and Tapp (1982) conclude, after a thorough review of the literature, that the procedures used to investigate a crime might well influence the witness in unintentional ways, unknown to any of the participants. Expectations of other people influence retrieval even if conveying the expectation is unintentional. Interviews of witnesses by the police are particularly susceptible to influence since the police have legitimate power and authority. Eyewitnesses try to impress the police and behave in the appropriate manner. They want to answer questions the way the police indicate they should. The police are not purposely trying to get the witness to identify the wrong person. The police are convinced the suspect is the criminal. Levine and Tapp suggest that the biasing influence of the police should be counterbalanced by giving specific instructions to witnesses in order to alleviate their apprehension.

Research indicates that the form of questioning will influence the accuracy of the information given by witnesses. Geiselman and Fisher (1985) have developed a cognitive interview procedure based on scientific knowledge of memory. When used by trained police professionals, this process was shown to enhance greatly the recollections of victims and witnesses to crimes (Fisher, Geiselman & Amador 1989). Read COGNITIVE INTERVIEW PROCEDURE for a description of the instructions given to witnesses by Geiselman and his associates (1986).

Questioning under Hypnosis

Once a person has made a statement about an incident, if said statement is somewhat inaccurate, the person is likely to remember the incident in the way stated rather than the accurate way. In other words, the witness is likely to believe his or her erroneous statement. Concerns have been expressed that people questioned under hypnosis are particularly susceptible to the creation of pseudomemories and have more confidence in their inaccurate recollections than do nonhypnotized subjects (e.g., Diamond 1980, Sheehan & Tilden 1983).

Research directly addressing the above concerns found no support for the conviction that pseudomemories are facilitated by questioning under hypnosis (Spanos et al. 1989). Hypnotic procedures did not increase the number of misattributions of characteristics to the offender nor the number of misidentifications above those of leading questions. There was also no difference in the amount of confidence in inaccurate memories displayed by the hypnotized and nonhypnotized subjects. Some researchers feel hypnotic procedures can immunize subjects against changing their opinion during cross-examination (Diamond 1980). However, other research determined that pseudomemories generated by hypnotic interrogation are not especially resistant to cross-examination (Spanos et al. 1989).

Advantages to questioning under hypnosis are questionable. Some researchers contend that questioning under hypnosis does not increase the accuracy of eyewitness recall (Wagstaff 1984, Yuille & McEwan 1985). The majority of studies have found no evidence that hypnosis is more effective than other procedures for memory retrieval (Yarmey 1990).

The Lineup

In an attempt to demonstrate the limitations of a lineup, Buckhout (1975) showed a film of a mugging during a televised news program. Afterwards, a lineup of six people was televised and viewers were invited to call in to identify the offender. A total of 2,145 viewers called. Only 14.1 percent were accurate, a rate expected by chance.

Recently, attempts have been made to evaluate empirically the fairness of lineups. Doob and Kirshenbaum describe a biased lineup as one in which "a person who was not a witness to the crime (a mock witness) is more likely to pick the

> **Box 9.1**
>
> **Cognitive Interview Procedure**
>
> Geiselman and his associates propose giving witnesses the following instructions:
>
> "1. *Reinstate the context.* Try to reinstate in your mind the context surrounding the incident. Think about what the surrounding environment looked like at the scene, such as rooms, the weather, any nearby people or objects. Also think about how you were feeling at the time and think about your reactions to the incident.
> 2. *Report everything.* Some people hold back information because they are not quite sure that the information is important. Please do not edit anything out of your report, even things you think may not be important.
> 3. *Recall the events in different order.* It is natural to go through the incident from beginning to end. However, you also should try to go through the events in reversed order. Or, try starting with the things that impressed you the most in the incident and then go from there, going both forward in time and backward.
> 4. *Change perspectives.* Try to recall the incident from the different perspectives that you may have had or adopt the perspectives of others that were present during the incident. For example, try to place yourself in the role of a prominent character in the incident and think about what he or she must have seen."

Source: R. E. Geiselman, et al., "Enhancement of eyewitness memory with the cognitive interview," *American Journal of Psychology* 99 (1986), pp. 390–391.

suspect out of the lineup than we would expect by chance" (1973, p. 290). They found almost half of the mock witnesses selected the identified suspect out of a photo spread when he was described as "good-looking." Similar results were found in a study in which the suspect was described as a "husky 175-pound man with dark hair" (Buckhout et al. 1988). The fairness of a lineup or photo spread can be assessed by using mock witnesses.

Eyewitness Identification and the Courts

The U.S. Supreme Court has addressed the limitations of eyewitness identification in two cases: *Neil v. Biggers* (1972) and *Manson v. Braithwaite* (1977). In the first of these cases, the court specified guidelines for the evaluation of eyewitness evidence, and in the second case it reaffirmed these guidelines. The court specified the following be considered in the evaluation:

1) the opportunity of the witness to view the criminal at the time of the crime;

2) the length of time between the crime and the identification;
3) the level of certainty demonstrated by the witness at the identification;
4) the witness's degree of attention during the crime; and
5) the accuracy of the witness's prior description of the criminal.

Guidelines 1 and 4 refer to events which occur in the acquisition stage of memory. Research cited above supports the utility of the first guideline, and there is some support for the fourth one. Guideline 2 refers to retention and is supported by research. Guidelines 3 and 5 focus on the retrieval of information. There is little or no empirical evidence to support or dispute the fifth guideline. The third guideline is the most controversial. Wells and Murray (1984) reviewed thirty-one studies and found the correlation between confidence and accuracy divided. Thirteen of the studies found a significant correlation and eighteen found none. Bothwell, Deffenbacher, and Brigham (1987) were somewhat more optimistic. They estimate the correlation to be about .25. However, the controversy is far from resolved.

The Supreme Court and many state courts have encouraged judges to caution juries about the limitations of eyewitness identification. However, some judges are not convinced of the necessity of a cautionary instruction and decline to give it. See LENELL GETER—A TRAVESTY OF JUSTICE for a description of a case in which a man was convicted by mistaken eyewitnesses.

Rattner (1988) reviewed actual cases of wrongful conviction and found that 52 percent were due to eyewitness misidentification. Because the sample used in this study was nonrepresentative, the percentages must be accepted with caution. However, Rattner suggests "that in cases where the eyewitness identification is the sole evidence, a jury or a judge should hear, in a special session, all information related to the issue and should decide the adequacy, validity, and reliability of the eyewitness identification. In cases where eyewitness identification is involved, the court should permit the use of an expert witness and/or should issue precise, cautionary instructions to juries" (1988, p. 292).

The Expert Witness

There are times when the evidence in a case is so complex or technical that the average juror would have difficulty evaluating it. In these cases, the defense attorney or the prosecuting attorney may ask an expert witness to testify. An expert witness is someone with special expertise in a relevant area who evaluates complex evidence and explains it to the jury in order to help them understand the case. For example, a psychiatrist or psychologist might testify as to the mental state of the defendant or a pathologist might testify about the cause of death of a victim.

Psychologists were first allowed to testify about mental disorders and crime in 1940. These experts, forensic psychologists, testify about the sanity, competency, and dangerousness of individuals. More recently psychologists with specialties in experimental, social, and cognitive psychology have begun to testify

Box 9.2

Lenell Geter—A Travesty of Justice

Lenell Geter was a quiet, soft-spoken, young black engineer working for E-Systems near Dallas, Texas, when he was arrested. What had Geter done? He had a habit of driving to a park to feed the ducks and read during his lunch break. An elderly woman noted his license number and reported this "suspicious" behavior to the police. There had been a number of holdups in the Dallas area by a young black man. So the police showed Geter's photo to the robbery victims at a nearby fast-food restaurant. The victims said Geter was not the robber. In fact, one victim recognized Geter as a customer and said it definitely was not he who committed the robbery. However, the police sent Geter's photo to nearby towns where robberies had occurred. A witness to one of those robberies said Geter might have been the man, so the police circulated his photo further. Finally some witnesses at another fast-food restaurant identified Geter's photo from a photo spread, and he was arrested.

Geter's private attorney dropped the case when Geter's money ran out. The court-appointed attorney was paid $200 to defend Geter. Most of the attorney's energy went into trying to convince Geter to plead guilty. At his trial, nine of Geter's colleagues testified that Geter had been at work at the time of the robbery. There was no physical evidence connecting Geter to the scene of the crime, no gun or fingerprints were found. But five eyewitnesses identified Geter as the robber. The arresting officer, James Fortenberry, testified at the sentencing hearing that the sheriff from Geter's hometown in South Carolina had described Geter as "a bad character." The all-white jury found Geter guilty and sentenced him to life in prison.

Geter's friends, relatives, and colleagues did not give up. They contacted the NAACP who sent an attorney, George Hairston. Geter's colleagues from E-Systems raised $11,000 for his defense fund. The South Carolina sheriff testified at a hearing for a new trial that Fortenberry had been inaccurate in his statements. Geter had no police record anywhere. However, the judge refused to grant a new trial. Then, George Hairston brought the case to national attention through the media. The public was outraged. Even the governor contacted the prosecutor. With all the public pressure, District Attorney Henry Wade agreed to a new trial for Geter. After 16 months in prison, Geter was released in December, 1983. The following March, charges against Geter were suddenly dropped and an ex-convict was arrested for the crime.

♦

Should retribution be made to Geter? Should rules of evidence be made tougher so that it is harder to convict someone based on circumstantial evidence?

Sources: J. Adler and J. Schwartz, *Newsweek* (December 19, 1983), p. 51; "Similarities in Robberies, Suspects Raise New Questions in Texas Case," *The Florida Times-Union* (December 18, 1983), p. A–10; J. Hammer, "An Innocent Man Set Free," *People Weekly* (July 16, 1984), pp. 61–62; A. Toufexis, "Some Doubt Has Been Raised," *Time* (December 26, 1983), p. 14.

about other phenomena, such as: the impact of memory and perception on eyewitness identification; "whether the average person would notice the warning label on a can of lighter fluid; about the comprehensibility of product information provided with birth control pills; about whether an allegedly libelous statement represents fact or opinion; or about whether two trademarks are sufficiently similar that they are likely to be confused by consumers" (McCloskey, Egeth & McKenna 1986, p. 2).

An expert witness must be accepted by the judge prior to testifying. There are two aspects of acceptability on which the judge rules: 1) the witness is an expert in the area under question, and 2) the jury needs the assistance of someone with this particular expertise. The major obstacle to expert testimony is the judge's evaluation of the necessity of the testimony for the jury. For example, psychologists with expertise in eyewitness identification or the battered woman syndrome frequently are asked to testify at trials. Generally, they are ruled to be experts. However, many judges will decide that the jurors do not need the information these expert witnesses can provide.

The standard for experts testifying on scientific evidence was set in *Frye v. United States* (1923). Although this case referred to lie detectors, it is used to define what constitutes expert testimony in other areas. This ruling states that expert testimony is that which is "deduced from a well-recognized scientific principle or discovery, the thing from which the deduction is made must be sufficiently established to have gained general scientific acceptance in the particular field in which it belongs" (p. 1014). Read DOCTOR DEATH for the description of one expert witness.

There is much conflict over whether juries need the assistance of expert witnesses in order to evaluate the accuracy of eyewitness testimony or the existence of the battered woman syndrome. There is no general agreement in the judicial system. More progressive judges who are aware of the fallacies of eyewitness identification and the impact of abuse are more likely to allow experts to testify.

Ethics

The ethics involved in a psychologist testifying in court as an expert witness have been hotly debated in the psychological literature. Some people question whether psychologists should testify at all, especially in an adversarial way. Much of this debate has centered on eyewitness identification testimony. McCloskey and Egeth (1983) are not convinced that the research on eyewitness identification has advanced to the point where there is general agreement among the scientific community on its theoretical base. Therefore, these researchers believe psychologists do not have enough solid scientific basis for testifying in court. Other researchers agree that the methodologies used in research on eyewitness identification are inadequate for drawing firm conclusions, therefore making it inappropriate to testify in court (Konečni & Ebbesen 1986, Pachella 1986). Pachella maintains that "psychologists who routinely offer expert testimony to the courts about the problems of eyewitness testimony demonstrate an unwarranted degree of faith in experimental psychology" (1986, p. 145).

> **Box 9.3**
>
> **Doctor Death**
>
> Psychiatrist James Grigson has earned the nickname "Dr. Death" by testifying at the sentencing hearing in death penalty trials in Texas. Each time, he has been hired by the prosecution and, invariably, he decides that the defendant is dangerous and likely to commit a violent crime in the future. Dr. Grigson has testified that the defendant is a dangerous "sociopath" in seventy cases. In every case except one, the jury has agreed with him and imposed the death penalty.
>
> Testimony such as that given by Dr. Grigson is questioned by the psychiatric community. In the case of Ernest Smith, the American Psychiatric Association filed a brief stating that such testimony "gives the appearance of being based on expert medical judgment, when in fact no such expertise exists."
>
> In a few cases, Grigson has testified about the dangerousness of a defendant without ever interviewing him. Grigson defends his position by claiming that examination of the defendant's record provides enough information to determine his potential for violent crime. One defense attorney, Richard Anderson, was able to get his client a life sentence instead of the death penalty despite Dr. Grigson's testimony. Anderson accomplished this by asking the psychiatrist to evaluate a hypothetical deprived black who was arrested several times and finally imprisoned for a violent offense. After Grigson predicted a life of violent crime for the hypothetical black man, Anderson revealed that the man described was Ron LeFlore, a star for the Chicago White Sox.
>
> ♦
>
> Should a psychiatrist be allowed to testify against a defendant if the psychiatrist has not personally examined the person?

Source: "They Call Him Dr. Death," *Time* (June 1, 1981), p. 64.

Loftus (1986) strongly disagrees. She argues that psychologists have an obligation to share their expertise with the legal system. Many researchers agree with Loftus that findings in the psychological research are consistent enough to draw conclusions and that it is appropriate to testify in court cases based on such research (Buckhout 1986, Goldman 1986, Woocher 1986).

Among those who agree that testimony can be given in eyewitness identification cases, discussion centers on the ethics of the testimony itself. It is generally agreed that a psychologist should never testify outside his or her area of expertise and that the psychologist has the responsibility to present the research accurately, including strengths and weaknesses. "Expert witnesses have obligations to both the court and to the science and profession of psychology" (Yarmey 1986, p. 111). Kargon (1986) maintains that only scientifically well established research with clear conclusions should be offered in court. But, Wagenaar argues that there is "no absolute certainty in science" (1988, p. 507). For this last reason, some experts (e.g., Yarmey) believe testimony should provide the best science can offer, the currently available information.

Goldman (1986) encourages psychologists to testify since the psychological information available to them on eyewitness identification is more accurate than that known by the typical attorney or juror. But, he and Lempert (1986) caution psychologists to consider the moral consequences of testifying. They believe that experts should be helping the courts reach an accurate decision. Unlike attorneys, psychologists have no obligation to assist the guilty. Therefore, a psychologist should not testify if convinced of the defendant's guilt, particularly if the testimony is likely to free the defendant. Buckhout (1986) disagrees with their viewpoint, maintaining that the psychologist is not in a position to determine the guilt of the defendant. He believes every defendant deserves to have expert testimony presented at the trial.

Most experts on eyewitness identification are hired by defense attorneys. These attorneys obviously want the expert to limit testimony to evidence that supports the defense position and may try to coerce the expert into making a biased presentation, thus presenting an ethical dilemma for the psychologist.

Loftus (1986) indicates that the impartiality of an expert witness is questionable if that expert:

1) does not discuss the **generalizability of results** found in the lab to the real world;
2) neglects to mention factors which would **support the opposition's case**;
3) conducts **special purpose experiments** for the case that are biased; and
4) **leaves out relevant studies** or does not review all the relevant work in the area.

Wagenaar states that "witnesses who cannot present a balanced account of the literature are not really experts" (1988, p. 508).

Wagenaar maintains that the controversy over the appropriateness of expert testimony is due to a lack of clear understanding of the differences between the roles and responsibilities of the expert and of the court. The expert witness merely provides the information necessary for the court to decide the specific issue under consideration. Wagenaar argues that the expert should not give a final opinion on a specific case. The court has to form the opinion.

Roles of Expert Witnesses

Loftus (1986) describes two roles psychologists assume when testifying as expert witnesses. In the role of an **adversary** the psychologist presents only the evidence supporting one side of the case. In defense of this role, Loftus reports that the law does not require "full disclosure" by the expert. Many psychologists are opposed to the role of adversary. A major objection is that the opposing side is likely to bring in its own expert to refute the testimony of the first expert, leading to a "battle of the experts." While many psychologists are opposed to a courtroom battle between experts, it is a common occurrence for other areas of expertise. For example, it is not unusual for the defense to have an expert on ballistics and the prosecution to produce another ballistics expert with differing opinions.

The second role described by Loftus is that of **impartial educator.** This role is somewhat difficult to maintain under questioning. McCloskey, Egeth, and McKenna (1986) differentiate the two roles on the bases of the testimony given. If an expert gives the same testimony whether testifying for the defense or the prosecution, that person is an impartial educator. If, however, the expert gives different testimony depending on who hires him, he is an advocate. The current tendency is for experts in eyewitness identification to be advocates rather than impartial educators.

A conference was held at Johns Hopkins University in 1983 to discuss the ethics of expert testimony (papers presented at this conference were published in the June 1986 issue of *Law and Human Behavior*). Most of the participants at the conference maintained that the impartial educator was a more desirable role to play (e.g., Goldman 1986, Lampert 1986). However, this role is difficult to maintain in an adversary system. If the expert is truly impartial, the attorney may decide not to have her testify. And, it is very difficult for the psychologist not to identify with the side that hired her. Therefore, some authorities contend that it is acceptable to present one side of the research, provided the evidence is presented in an objective manner without distorting or misrepresenting the research.

Hastie (1986) advocates a different role, that of **watchdog.** He contends that a psychologist should be neither a lapdog, who does not confront misleading experts or testify about unreliable eyewitnesses, nor a rabid attack dog, who assaults every eyewitness. He strongly advocates an impartial stance, evaluating each case on its own merits.

The Effect of Expert Testimony

Most research has found that lay people, as well as police, lawyers, and judges are not completely aware of the factors that influence eyewitness identification (Brigham & Bothwell 1983, Brigham & WolfSkeil 1983, Noon & Hollin 1987). These data support the use of expert testimony on the topic. But does expert testimony improve the decisions made by jurors? Research consistently finds that when an expert testifies, there is an increase in the amount of time jurors spend discussing the eyewitness testimony, a decrease in belief of the eyewitness, and a decrease in convictions (Fox & Walters 1986, Maass, Brigham & West 1985). However, Wells (1986) points out that it is difficult to determine if all these changes are an improvement in decision-making by jurors. Certainly, the increased discussion is beneficial. But, the decrease in belief of the eyewitness and in convictions could be either positive or negative depending on whether the defendant is innocent or guilty. Wells concludes that "at this point . . . there has not been a persuasive demonstration in the published literature that expert testimony on eyewitness matters improves the judgments of jurors" (1986, p. 86).

In a well-controlled experiment, Cutler, Penrod, and Dexter (1989) attempted to document the effect of expert testimony on juror decisions. They classify the effect of expert testimony on jurors into three categories. The first category is **juror confusion.** Rule 403 of the Federal Rules of Evidence indicates that expert testimony should not be admitted if it is likely to prejudice, mislead, or confuse the jury. It is possible that expert testimony will be misinterpreted by jurors, who then draw unwarranted conclusions. These authors give credit to this assumption because of the difficulty jurors have with legal concepts and their application.

The second category of effect is **juror sensitivity: knowledge and integration.** Knowledge refers to an "awareness of how units of information should be combined to form a judgment," while integration is the "ability to form judgments that reflect the unit combinatorial scheme about which the judge is knowledgeable" (Cutler, Penrod & Dexter 1989, p. 313).

Category three is **juror skepticism.** When an expert's credentials are extremely impressive, the jury may rely heavily on the expert's opinion rather than the evidence in reaching a verdict.

Cutler, Penrod, and Dexter (1989) found that expert testimony increased jurors' sensitivity to eyewitness evidence. Typically the confidence shown by an eyewitness influences jurors' evaluations of that witness's credibility. However, those jurors hearing expert testimony gave less weight to confidence than those who did not hear the expert. After hearing expert testimony on eyewitness identification, jurors considered the conditions under which the incident was witnessed and the person was identified. Apparently, the expert testimony improved jurors' knowledge without changing their skepticism toward the eyewitness evidence.

The Courts and Expert Testimony

While psychologists continue their debate over the appropriateness and usefulness of expert testimony in eyewitness identification, the debate will ultimately be decided by the courts. In the past, the courts have often excluded expert testimony by psychologists because it was deemed unnecessary. Woocher (1986) summarizes the general view of evidence as follows: "*Only* relevant evidence is admissible, and all relevant evidence is admissible in the absence of some countervailing policy" (p. 48). Evidence is excluded if it is unfair or prejudiced, or if the judge thinks it confuses the issues or could mislead the jury.

In *United States v. Amaral* (1973) the appellate court ruled that expert testimony would be allowed under the following criteria: "(1) the witness must be a qualified expert; (2) the testimony must concern a proper subject matter; (3) the testimony must be in accordance with a generally accepted explanatory theory; and (4) the probative value of the testimony must outweigh its prejudicial effect" (p. 50). Although recent decisions have expanded or modified these criteria, they are still principally the current standards.

The second criterion above has been the one most frequently employed to exclude the testimony of experts in eyewitness identification. The reasons given for exclusion of experts in this area were either that the jury already had enough information on the subject to evaluate the witness or the expert would usurp the jury's role. These arguments are no longer used, having been rejected in most jurisdictions. Most rulings now acknowledge that there is sufficient research evidence of which the average person is unaware to justify the testimony of experts (*United States v. Downing,* 1985; *United States v. Smith,* 1984).

Other arguments against the use of expert testimony focus on the third criterion—a generally accepted explanatory theory. Two early cases excluded expert testimony on this basis (*United States v. Jackson,* 1975; *United States v. Watson,* 1978). However, more recent cases have ruled that enough scientific data exists to support a generally accepted theory in eyewitness identification (*United States v. Downing* and *United States v. Smith*).

Both Arizona (*State v. Chappele,* 1983) and California (*People v. McDonald,* 1984) have overturned lower court murder convictions in eyewitness cases. The decisions were attributed to some extent to the fact that the lower courts did not allow experts on eyewitness identification to testify. Since these decisions, there has been an increase in the number of experts testifying on eyewitness identification in these two states. Woocher (1986) believes there has been a significant shift and predicts courts will be more open to the admission of testimony by experts in eyewitness identification in the future.

The Child Witness

Many cases are dropped by prosecuting attorneys who are reluctant to pursue a case that depends entirely on a child witness. There are many reasons for this decision. Frequently, state laws make it difficult for a child to testify. For example, most state statutes specify children above a certain age (some say 10, others 12 or even 14) are competent to testify. The assumption is that a child under that age is incompetent. Some states have additional obstacles for a child testifying in a sexual assault case. For example, a sexual assault case cannot be pursued in some jurisdictions unless there is some evidence corroborating the child's word (Goodman 1984).

Increased concern with child abuse and victimization has led states to revise laws in order to make it easier for children to testify. These new laws are leading to the prosecution of increased numbers of cases involving child victims and/or witnesses. But these changes are not universally applauded.

The Courts and Child Witnesses

Children who are below the age specified in state statutes must be interviewed by the judge to determine if they should be allowed to testify. The criteria for determining if a child is qualified to testify are that the child: "(a) can receive and relate information accurately, (b) can understand the difference between telling the truth and telling a lie, and (c) can appreciate the necessity of telling the truth in court" (Berliner & Barbieri 1984, p. 131). Berliner and Barbieri maintain that attorneys can demonstrate a child's competence rather easily. By asking children to describe details of their everyday activities, the first criterion will be satisfied. The second criterion can be satisfied by asking the child a question such as, "If I said your dress is red, would I be lying or telling the truth?" Asking the child what the consequences of lying are and having her promise to tell the truth in court satisfies the final criterion. Children as young as three can demonstrate their ability to testify. Very young children may not be able to meet the legal criterion for testifying. Even older children may be too traumatized to testify or may have problems with memory.

Historically, the court has a duty to protect children, known as *parens patriae*. Therefore, laws allow some special considerations for children. For example, in Colorado, a medical expert can testify about what he or she was told by the child victim in a sexual assault case. Thus, a psychiatrist could testify as to what a child told her and protect the child from the trauma of testifying. Another example of special consideration for children relates to hearsay evidence. Although hearsay is not allowed in evidence, some states make an exception for children in the case of an excited utterance (*rea gestae*). In other words, if the child says something immediately after the incident while still upset and excited, an adult can testify as to what the child said. The assumption is that, while in this state of excitement, the child will not lie. The problem with this exception is that it is limited to what the child says immediately after the incident, and many children do not discuss the event for a long time. Other attempts to protect children include restricting the audience at the trial during the child's testimony or removing the defendant during the child's testimony.

As society has become more aware of child victimization, laws have begun to reflect more sympathetic views toward the child witness. At least thirteen states and the federal courts have eliminated the examination for competency for children, allowing juries to decide on the child's credibility. Although some states still require corroboration for a child's claims of victimization, there is much controversy surrounding this requirement. Corroboration is usually required for cases of sexual assault. Since there is little evidence that children falsely report sexual assault (Berliner & Barbieri 1984), even this requirement is being removed in some jurisdictions. While leading questions are allowed only in cross-examination of adults, there is a trend to allow them for direct examination of children. There is also a movement to allow children to give videotaped depositions. This allows the child to testify once and not repeatedly experience the trauma of describing the crime. There is also a move to make children immune from perjury (Goodman 1984, Goodman & Reed 1986).

The Sixth Amendment gives citizens the right to a public trial in which they can confront their accuser. The First Amendment gives the public access to trials through the press. These rights have been limited by giving special consideration to children, and attempts have been made to regain these rights through the courts. In one such instance, the Globe Publishing Company challenged the right of the state of Massachusetts to bar those not "having a direct interest in the case" from being in court during the testimony of a minor sex victim. The U.S. Supreme Court in *Globe v. Superior Court* (Globe III, 1982) overturned the Massachusetts law. Melton contends, based on the Globe decision, that "procedural reforms to protect child witnesses are unlikely to pass constitutional scrutiny" (1984, p. 119).

Accuracy of Children's Testimony

Questions concerning the reliability of a child witness frequently center on whether a child can differentiate fantasy from reality. In addition, it is assumed that a child is likely to change his or her story when leading questions are asked. A third concern is whether the child is a reliable eyewitness. Each of these issues has been addressed in the research described as follows.

The assumptions that children notice fewer events, omit more details, and forget faster than adults are not supported by research. While it is well-documented that children recall less than adults, there is little evidence for the other assumptions.

In a series of experiments comparing 6-year-olds, 9-year-olds, and 17-year-olds, Johnson and Foley (1984) found the number of items recalled increased with age. They assumed that this result was "associated with the developmental trend in the acquisition both of enriched knowledge structures (e.g., an apple is a fruit) and of memory strategies (e.g., organizing or generating images)" (1984, p. 45). Children frequently do not have the prior experience to help organize elements or relate events to one another. When children have experience related to a specific event, their memories are at least as good as memories of adults. For example, Chi (1978) found that children who were experienced with chess had a better recollection of a chess board than adults who were not experienced with the game.

Comparing the children on reality monitoring, Johnson and Foley (1984) concluded that children have no "generalized confusion" between fact and fantasy. The 6- and 8-year-olds were as good as the older students in differentiating memories from imagined and perceived pictures and words. The researchers conclude that children have difficulty with some, not all, reality monitoring situations and "even young children may be able to recognize who did what" (p. 45). In fact, in some situations children are more reliable than adults. One example is the Allport and Postman (1947) study discussed above ("Eyewitness Identification"), where adults frequently saw the black man with the razor. Those children who noticed the razor were not confused about who held it.

Goodman and Reed (1986) compared 3-year-olds, 6-year-olds, and adults in a study on identification. The subjects interacted with a man for 5 minutes. When they were asked to identify him later, adults and 6-year-olds performed equally well. The 3-year-olds made fewer identifications. In the same study, these experimenters tested another stereotype of children: that they are susceptible to suggestions. In other words, children can be influenced to remember incidents that did not occur or inaccurate details. The 6-year-olds were more suggestible and had less recall of the event than adults. The 3-year-olds were most suggestible and had little recall of the event. However, other research has found little evidence that children are more susceptible to suggestion (Duncan, Whitney & Kunen 1982, Marin et al. 1979).

The reliability of child witnesses is a new area of research; as such, it is difficult to draw many firm conclusions. Some studies (Brigham, van Verst & Bothwell 1986, Chance & Goldstein 1984, Saywitz 1987) find that children under 10 have poorer memory skills than adults. Some studies (Ceci, Ross & Toglia 1987, Cohen & Harnick 1980) find that children have a greater susceptibility to leading questions than adults. But then other studies (Goodman & Reed 1986, List 1986) find little difference by age in staged, crimelike events. Melton and Thompson (1987) maintain that the inconsistent results indicate adults and children differ on memory performance depending on variables like task and context.

While older studies have found a correlation between age and accuracy of facial recognition, research conducted during the 1980s found little or no relationship in photo identification (Davies, Stevenson-Robb & Flin 1988, Parker, Haverfield & Baker-Thomas 1986). There is some evidence that preschoolers are somewhat inferior in identification (Goodman & Reed 1986, Peters 1987, King & Yuille 1987). "On balance, research so far seems to indicate that if the memory task is structured appropriately, children are more adept (and closer to adults) at accurate recognition and recall than Western jurisprudence traditionally has assumed" (Parker & Carranza 1989, p. 104).

Children's Emotional Reaction

Often a child is the sole witness to a crime or provides the main evidence in a case. If the child does not testify, the offender cannot be prosecuted. However, most legal professionals believe the experience of participating in the investigation and testifying at the trial will be traumatic for the child. The child is typically frightened by having to face the defendant. The child might also have to interact with untrained or insensitive officials.

Children who have been sexually abused face further trauma and embarrassment. Adults are frequently skeptical of children's reports of sexual abuse, despite there being "little or no evidence indicating that children's reports are unreliable, and none at all to support the fear that children often make false accusations of sexual assault or misunderstand innocent behavior by adults" (Berliner & Barbieri 1984, p. 127). If the accused is a family member, the child may feel guilty accusing the person. These confused children have mixed feelings; they want the assaults to stop, but they do not want to hurt the accused or disrupt the family. Often the nonoffending parent and the victim are financially and emotionally dependent on the accused. In addition, the child's family might side with the accused and become hostile toward the child. Adding to the trauma are attempts by the defense attorney to suggest that the child was a willing participant.

Cases typically get to trial in about 6 months. But Goodman reports that some child witness cases take as long as 8 years. During that time, the child is questioned repeatedly. Not only is it emotionally upsetting for children to keep reliving the incident, but by the time they actually testify, their description of the crime sounds rehearsed and unreal. "The number of children who actually testify is much smaller than would happen if investigators knew more about interviewing children, if attorneys thought they could win their cases when a child is a key witness, and if the legal process could be geared more toward children's needs" (Goodman 1984, p. 6).

Berliner and Barbieri have dealt with hundreds of victims of sexual assault. They believe the trauma to the child and the difficulties inherent in the legal system can be avoided or overcome. These authors argue that even very young children can testify if they are assisted through the process. They suggest that "professional personnel appropriately trained, a criminal-justice system that accommodates its procedures to the needs and capabilities of the child victim/witness, and a set of procedures designed to give support and comfort to the child—seem to be highly facilitative (if not necessary and sufficient) conditions for effective use of child witnesses in sexual assault cases" (1984, p. 130).

The primary necessity is for some adult to establish rapport with the child and provide emotional support throughout the legal process. In some cases, a very young child can be allowed to sit on the lap of a familiar adult, provided the adult does not prompt the child. Berliner and Barbieri (1984) maintain that a child should testify if the testimony increases the chances of convicting the perpetrator, but not if testifying will cause serious harm to the child. Testimony can be therapeutic for the child by instilling a sense of empowerment. But acquittal of the defendant can be devastating for the child. In any event, posttrial follow-up is necessary to assist the child through the emotional trauma.

Pynoos and Eth (1984) studied children who have witnessed the murder of their parents. A minor child was a witness in 10 percent of the 1982 homicides in Los Angeles. While only 10 percent of homicide cases go to trial, children who witness the crime are almost always interviewed and required to assist in the criminal proceedings. These authors recommend a specialist in psychic trauma be assigned to each child. By helping the child in interactions with criminal justice officials, the specialist can ease the trauma and at the same time improve the child's ability to testify.

Children who have witnessed a parent's murder suffer psychic trauma and perhaps posttraumatic stress disorder (PTSD). In addition to the symptoms typical of adults, children with PTSD have changes in personality and become pessimistic. They do not suffer the amnesia of adults, but they sometimes reenact unconsciously some acts similar to the homicide. "Parental homicide leaves indelible, highly accurate, and detailed visual images" (Pynoos & Eth 1984, p. 95). The children are preoccupied by their own and the parent's vulnerability, the injuries to the parent, and the murderer's loss of control. One young boy is quoted as saying, "It was awful, my heart hurt; it was beating so loud" (p. 91).

Relatives and guardians of child witnesses frequently attempt to keep the child from discussing the event. In an attempt to protect the child, they make it harder for the child to adjust. Open discussion would assist the child in coming to terms with the trauma. For this reason, involvement in the legal proceedings actually can help the child to cope.

Sometimes the legal proceedings can be quite terrifying for the child. Postponement of the trial may prolong the child's anxiety. Pynoos and Eth (1984) describe a 5-year-old who had seen his mother beaten to death by her estranged boyfriend. Eighteen months passed before the case went to trial. The longer the wait, the less the boy wanted to testify; he did not want to think about the horrible event. The defense attorney confused the child with his questions and tried to trick him. He was on the stand for hours. The judge finally realized the child was frightened and allowed him to testify in chambers.

Because they are often unaware that the child is afraid of the defendant, judges seldom use their discretion to assist the child witness. Pynoos and Eth (1984) describe a judge's insensitive treatment of a 4-year-old girl who saw her father kill her mother. The child was kept waiting for hours before being put on the witness stand. No familiar adult was allowed in the courtroom, except the child's father, whom she had not seen in months. Without introducing himself, the judge immediately intimidated the child with a few questions, then summarily decided she could not testify. The child, who had recounted the crime a number of times, regressed after being denied the opportunity to testify and became almost mute. She was returned to her father's care. Older children who are not allowed to testify report feeling that they failed their dead parent.

Pynoos and Eth (1984) have a number of suggestions for assisting the child witness through the legal process. First of all, they advise the police to allow a familiar person to stay with the child during questioning. The child who witnesses a parental homicide should receive psychological care from an expert in childhood trauma as soon after the event as possible. The traumatized child needs the opportunity to examine and discuss the ordeal. This process will prepare the child for testifying and make her a better witness. In addition, judges need to be sensitized to the special needs of children. And finally, the child needs to be kept informed, particularly of the trial outcome.

Children's Credibility

It is always difficult to determine whether someone is telling the truth. But adults tend to be unusually doubtful when they are evaluating the truthfulness of children. This judgment becomes particularly serious if the adults are jurors and the child is a witness. Sixty-nine percent of those asked to judge the reliability of an 8-year-old's testimony thought the hypothetical child would answer in the way the questioner wished or with "I don't know" (Yarmey & Jones 1983). Adult witnesses are believed if they are perceived to be consistent, confident, trustworthy, certain, and objective. Children are at a disadvantage because they tend to be less confident. They are also inclined to answer questions literally, which appears inconsistent and undermines their credibility. See CHILD ON THE WITNESS STAND for an example of a child's literal interpretation of questions.

Jurors' biases about the credibility of a child witness can be overcome. Goodman, Golding, and Haith (1984) conducted an experiment in which they varied the age of a witness whose testimony was crucial to the trial. The adult was considered the most credible, then the 10-year-old, and finally the 6-year-old. But the evaluations of guilt did not vary with the age of the witness. These

> **Box 9.4**
>
> ## Child on the Witness Stand
>
> A child's approach to answering questions can have serious consequences for the unwary attorney. In the following case example, a 5-year-old child, on direct examination, told the jury about her father putting his penis in her mouth. On cross-examination by the father's defense attorney, the following exchange took place:
>
> *Defense Attorney*: And then you said you put your mouth on his penis?
> *Child*: No.
> *Defense Attorney*: You didn't say that?
> *Child*: No.
> *Defense Attorney*: Did you ever put your mouth on his penis?
> *Child*: No.
> *Defense Attorney*: Well, why did you tell your mother that your dad put his penis in your mouth?
> *Child*: My brother told me to.
>
> At this point, it looked as if the child had completely recanted her earlier testimony about the sexual abuse and had only fabricated the story because her brother told her to. However, the experienced prosecuting attorney recognized the problem and clarified the situation:
>
> *Prosecuting Attorney*: Jennie, you said that you didn't put your mouth on daddy's penis. Is that right?
> *Child*: Yes.
> *Prosecuting Attorney*: Did daddy put his penis in your mouth?
> *Child*: Yes.
> *Prosecuting Attorney*: Did you tell your mom?
> *Child*: Yes.
> *Prosecuting Attorney*: What made you decide to tell?
> *Child*: My brother and I talked about it, and he said I better tell or dad would just keep doing it.

Source: L. Berliner and M. K. Barbieri, "The Testimony of the Child Victim of Sexual Assault," *Journal of Social Issues,* vol. 40, no. 2 (1984), p. 132.

same results were obtained in a number of studies with students and potential jurors as subjects and with video or written mock trials.

Leippe and Romanczyk (1989) conducted five studies in which jurors evaluated eyewitnesses who varied by age. The reactions varied across studies. The authors conclude that "it seems that adults' negative preconceptions about children's memory will not dispose them to reject a child's memory message if the message's quality is sufficiently 'mature' to belie the stereotype" (p. 127). While stereotypes of children greatly influence reactions to testimony, child eyewitnesses are not perceived as negatively as past research and stereotypes would lead us to believe.

Three experiments examining views of different aged witnesses (6, 10, and 30) obtained similar results (Goodman et al. 1987). The studies conducted by the same researchers utilized different subjects, different trials, and different methods. There were only slight, nonsignificant tendencies for the subjects to give lower guilt ratings if the witness was a child. At the same time, the child, especially the 6-year-old, was rated as less credible. During deliberations, some people expressed concerns with the reliability of children as witnesses but still came to the same conclusions. The authors assume jurors may rely more heavily on other incriminating evidence when they doubt a child. Ross, Miller, and Moran (1987) support the findings of Goodman and her associates. Their study found no perceived credibility or verdict differences in child and adult witnesses.

Summary

The many limitations of eyewitness accounts and identification seem to be a well-kept secret. Eyewitness identification is based on memory, which is not static but rather an ongoing process. Memory consists of three separate phases: acquisition, retention, and retrieval.

There are many physical and psychological factors which influence and distort our perceptions in the acquisition phase. Incidents that occur after the original incident can modify the memory while it is in storage, during the retention phase. It is difficult to know whether storage in memory has been affected until the retrieval phase occurs. The retrieval phase in memory is particularly susceptible to the expectations of other people.

Crimes are unexpected and happen quickly, so witnesses might not have very accurate perceptions of the event. The U.S. Supreme Court has addressed the concerns about eyewitness identification by specifying guidelines for the evaluation of eyewitness evidence.

When evidence in a case is complex or technical to the extent that the average juror would have difficulty evaluating it, an expert witness may be asked to testify. The ethics involved in psychologists testifying in court as expert witnesses have been hotly debated in the psychological literature. Much of this debate has centered on eyewitness identification testimony and whether the research has advanced to the point where there is general agreement among the scientific community on its theoretical base.

Loftus (1986) describes two roles psychologists assume when testifying as expert witnesses: **adversary** and **impartial educator.** The majority opinion is that the impartial educator is a more desirable role to play. However, the current tendency is for experts in eyewitness identification to be advocates.

Cutler, Penrod, and Dexter (1989) classify the effect of expert testimony on jurors into three categories: **juror confusion, juror sensitivity: knowledge and integration,** and **juror skepticism.** Psychologists continue their debate over the appropriateness and usefulness of expert testimony in eyewitness identification, but the debate will ultimately be decided by the courts.

Criminal justice professionals are reluctant to prosecute a case that depends entirely on the identification and testimony of a child witness. This reluctance is due to the many stereotypes concerning the reliability of children's identification and testimony. It is generally assumed that children notice fewer events, omit more details, and forget faster than adults. However, these assumptions are not supported by research. Historically, the court has a duty to protect children. Therefore, laws allow some special considerations for children, although special treatment of children has been successfully challenged in the courts.

Often a child is the sole witness to a crime or provides the main evidence in a case. By helping the child in interactions with criminal justice officials, the child's trauma can be overcome and, at the same time, the child's ability to testify will improve. Although jurors doubt the credibility of a child witness prior to the trial, these biases can be overcome.

10

The Verdict and Sentencing

Jury Decision-Making
Predeliberation Activities
Jury Deliberations
Extralegal Factors
Death-Qualified Juries
Sentencing
Judges' Discretion
Sentencing Options
Sentencing Hearings
How Judges Make Decisions
Discrimination
Sentencing Reforms
Summary

Jury Decision-Making

If we extend the analogy of the trial as a play, with the attorneys as the actors and directors, the members of the jury become the audience and critics. It is the jury that the attorneys are trying to influence with their presentations.

Predeliberation Activities

So much attention is given to the decision-making function of the jury that often the jury's activities prior to deliberations are overlooked. Some authorities think members of the jury make their decisions before deliberations despite the judge's instructions to hold the decision in abeyance.

Jury Instructions

Early in the trial, the jury is given preliminary instructions by the judge. Included in these instructions are a description of the contrasting roles of the judge and the jury: the judge is the interpreter of the law while the jury decides the facts. The judge also instructs the jurors about restrictions and prohibitions concerning their behavior during the trial. For example, jurors are not allowed to discuss the case they are hearing with anyone, including other jurors, before deliberations begin. With the commencement of deliberations, jurors may discuss the case only with other members of the jury and only during official sessions. They are not allowed to receive opinions or information concerning the trial from any other source. Therefore, jurors are prohibited from reading newspapers, listening to the radio, or watching television commentary pertaining to the trial. In addition, jurors are not allowed to visit the site of the crime.

Although instructions to the jury can be given throughout the trial, in the vast majority of cases, instructions are presented following the closing arguments when the judge charges the jury. At that time, the judge tells the jury how the law defines the offense, points out the rights of the defendant, and explains the possible verdicts. Since instructions are given at the end of the trial, jurors who make decisions while the case is in progress do not have the benefit of legal instructions.

The judge's instructions to the jury are long, boring, complicated, and couched in legal jargon. As a result, jurors often cannot understand the instructions and thus do not follow them (Elwork & Sales 1985, Pennington 1982, Saks & Hastie 1978, Severance & Loftus 1982).

The Foreperson

The jury's first order of business is to select the foreperson. Although some jurisdictions specify that the first person chosen is designated to be the foreperson, most juries elect the foreperson. Mock jurors generally select a male, the person sitting at the head of the table, or the one who initiates discussion; all of these characteristics can be interpreted as indicators of high status (Bronson 1970). The foreperson of the jury usually does not advocate any position but rather acts as a facilitator in the deliberation process.

Juror Notetaking and Questions

Jurors must listen to long, monotonous testimony without taking notes. Yet they are required to make a decision based on details of the evidence which greatly impacts the defendant, sometimes even determining whether he lives or dies. The legal system assumes jurors can recall all the testimony they have heard (Marshall 1969). In order to compensate for the difficulty the jurors might have in remembering details of the trial, they may request portions of the transcript or they may ask to have the judge's instructions reread during deliberations.

There is much debate in legal circles about the advantages and disadvantages of allowing jurors to take notes during a trial. Proponents of notetaking maintain it would assist the jurors in remembering trial testimony and judges' instructions. Notetaking would also lead the jurors to be more interested in and attentive to the trial. In addition, jurors would think their application of the judge's instructions was appropriate and have more confidence in their decisions. Opponents of notetaking contend that jurors, inexperienced in notetaking, would take inaccurate notes and might miss some important information while writing something of less importance. Jurors who take notes also might have undue influence over non-notetaking jurors during deliberations. Support for both positions can be found in the literature (Flango 1980, Sand & Reiss 1985).

Some legal authorities maintain that jurors should be allowed to ask questions of the witnesses. But there is considerable opposition to this position. Only a few jurisdictions allow jurors to submit questions for the judge to ask the witness. Proponents of juror questioning argue that jurors would have fewer doubts about their decisions and perhaps their questioning would uncover important issues. Opponents worry that the questions would be a nuisance and would interfere with the attorneys' trial tactics, prolong the trial, and decrease its decorum. The jurors might also ask improper questions to which the attorneys would be reluctant to object for fear of offending the juror.

In order to resolve the debate over juror notetaking and questioning, Heuer and Penrod studied thirty-four civil and thirty-three criminal trials in Wisconsin. The judges conducting these trials agreed to allow the trials to be randomly assigned to conditions. Jurors were either allowed to take notes or not and to question the witnesses or not. The researchers found none of the disadvantages to notetaking or questioning by jurors listed above. They did find support for many of the advantages for both procedures. They conclude that "both of these procedures deserve serious consideration by the judicial system" (Heuer & Penrod 1988, p. 257).

Leakage

Sometimes during the course of a trial a witness will say something which should not be admitted as evidence in the trial. Usually, one or the other of the attorneys will object to the statement. If the judge agrees that the evidence should not be admitted, she will instruct the jury to disregard it. However, put yourself in the position of a juror. Suppose you had sat through the presentation of a great deal of monotonous technical and repetitious testimony. Suddenly, the attorneys get all excited and argue in front of the judge about whether a particular statement should be admitted. What is the likelihood that you will be able to disregard the most exciting thing that happened all day? It is unlikely. Research supports this logical conclusion by showing that jurors remember evidence better after being told it is inadmissible than if no objection had been made to it. However, there is a limitation to the impact of inadmissible evidence; this type of evidence only affects decisions when the case is weak (Sue, Smith & Caldwell 1973, Wolf & Montgomery 1977).

Innocent Until Proven Guilty?

Although people in the United States are considered innocent until proven guilty, jurors do not act as if that were the case. Winick (1979) reports research finding that a quarter of jurors surveyed believed the defendant was guilty or he would not have been brought to trial. Fahringer (1977) found an even higher proportion of subjects (36 percent) who believed that the defendant must prove his innocence, not that the state must prove the defendant's guilt. Foley and Chamblin (1982) discovered a high relationship between these beliefs and a guilty verdict in a study of mock juries.

Jury Deliberations

The most important function of the jury is to decide on a verdict. The jury is instructed not to make a decision until all the evidence has been presented. Then the jurors are to discuss the case and come to a decision (usually it must be unanimous). Kalven and Zeisel (1966) conducted a scientific survey to determine how important deliberations were in influencing individual jurors. In close to 90 percent of the trials studied, the ballots of the jurors taken prior to deliberations were identical to the verdict. The authors concluded that the "real decision" was made prior to deliberations. In other words, the jurors decided individually on the verdict prior to deliberating and did not change their minds after hearing other viewpoints. In a similar study, Kalven (1957) found an even higher agreement between the first ballot and the verdict. This does not mean the decisions were unanimous on the first ballot; this happened in fewer than a third of the cases. It does indicate that when a majority of jurors hold the same view, they are likely to convince the remaining members to change their opinions or at least their votes. If the first ballot revealed almost equally divided opinions, the jury was unlikely to reach an unanimous agreement.

Compliance

Juries spend a good deal of time in intense negotiations, becoming a cohesive group. Those who hold a minority viewpoint are pressured to conform and become uncomfortable unless they do so. These jurors want to do what is right; but they also want other members of the jury to like them. Sometimes they will comply with the majority because their desire to be liked overrides their desire to be right. Social psychologists have been studying conformity and compliance since Solomon Asch initiated the research in 1952 (see Chapter 9, p. 212). Basically, conformity is a change in behavior or attitude due to group pressure. Compliance is one aspect of conformity, referring to people changing their behavior or public attitude but not their internal attitude in response to some pressure. Studies of mock jurors have found that some jurors comply with the majority decision but privately maintain their prior beliefs (Bray & Noble 1978, Simon 1967). This phenomenon has also been found in actual trials. For an example, see the box THE JURY DECIDES ON THE JUAN CORONA CASE in Box 10.1.

What about members of the group who agree with the majority opinion? Do their opinions change? Yes, group discussions tend to create a shift to the extreme, a phenomenon psychologists refer to as a group polarization effect. In other words, more members of the jury will agree with the majority decision after deliberation than prior to it and, in addition, many individuals will hold their opinions more strongly after discussing them (Bray & Noble 1978, Kaplan & Miller 1978, Myers & Kaplan 1976, Myers & Lamm 1976).

Interviews with Jurors

Although no one is allowed to observe jurors during deliberations, a few authors have reconstructed deliberations by interviewing jurors. *Jury: The People vs. Juan Corona* by Villasenor (1977) describes the pressures members of the jury impose on those whose opinions do not coincide with the majority. See THE JURY DECIDES ON THE JUAN CORONA CASE.

Attribution/Exchange Model of Deliberations

Greenberg and Ruback (1982) use an attribution/exchange model to explain decisions by jurors. In the first phase of the decision-making process, individual jurors attribute dispositions to the defendant. These attributions are influenced by the evidence but also by characteristics of the defendant such as physical appearance and demeanor. The dispositions assigned to the defendant also are influenced by attorneys and other jurors. See MERCY KILLING—COMPASSION OR MURDER? for a jury decision that was influenced by demeanor.

After the jurors have attributed dispositions to the defendant, they decide on a verdict. Greenberg and Ruback (1982) use the social exchange model to explain how juries look for equity in the decision. An example of how equity influences jury decisions is found in cases where the defendant is seen to have suffered enough and, therefore, the jury decides not to inflict further punishment (Shaffer, Plummer & Hammock 1986). For example, suppose the defendant has been kept in jail for a long time awaiting trial for a relatively minor offense, or the defendant was seriously injured during the offense or even in an unrelated act after the offense. In these situations, the jury might acquit the defendant. The acquittal is given because the defendant is perceived to have suffered enough, not because he is thought to be innocent.

Equity also can work against the defendant. For example, the jury might find someone guilty who did not do anything really illegal but whose behavior was an affront to human decency. The evidence in the case may not be strong enough to prove beyond a reasonable doubt that the defendant committed the offense. However, the evidence may seem to indicate the defendant did do something, and the victim really suffered, so the jury issues a verdict of guilty.

Box 10.1

The Jury Decides on the Juan Corona Case

After sitting through 4 months of the Juan Vallejo Corona trial, the jury of ten men and two women returned its verdict—Juan Corona was found guilty of twenty-five counts of first-degree murder. Ordinarily, that is all the public would learn about a jury's decision. However, in this instance, author Victor Villasenor spent 7 months interviewing the jurors to reconstruct their 8 days of deliberations.

In the jury's first straw vote, seven voted innocent and five guilty. How did they come to a unanimous decision that Juan Corona was guilty of every count? A number of jurors voted not guilty on the first ballot in order to ensure thorough discussion of the case so that a decision would not be reached lightly. The jurors meticulously went through the evidence, discussing each of the twenty-five deaths and all the evidence for and against Corona's conviction.

Villasenor's description of the deliberations was both enlightening and disappointing. While it was heartening to see citizens so dedicated to making a fair decision, it was upsetting to see some jurors blatantly disobey the instructions of the judge. The jurors were instructed not to discuss the case with anyone or to read the newspapers. Yet some of the jurors read the papers every day, and some discussed the case with the bailiffs.

One juror apparently lost touch with reality. The lone holdout for innocence, she confused the case presented in trial with one she had read about in the papers and with detective stories. She felt that if Corona were really guilty, the evidence against him would have been airtight, without any holes—the way detective stories are. She had difficulty making a decision on circumstantial evidence. Other jurors were also uncomfortable with circumstantial evidence, but this juror refused to consider it in terms of its overall effect on the great deal of evidence.

As the trial progressed, this juror became more and more agitated. Other members of the jury became impatient with her, and she refused to listen to their views. After holding out for some time, she suddenly changed her vote. Now some jurors were concerned that she had changed her vote so they would not be angry with her or in order to go home and feed her cats. However, she insisted that she really believed Corona to be guilty. But after the verdict was given, this juror told the press that she still felt Corona was innocent and that she had been pressured to change her vote.

The jurors were quite frustrated with the system. Whenever a difficult point was discussed, the judge and attorneys for both sides would retire to the judges chambers, out of hearing of the jury, to come to a decision. The jury wanted to know why the defense did not present any case after outlining what it would prove in the opening statement. There were many questions that the jury felt were unanswered. They would have liked to be able to ask questions of the witnesses that the attorneys neglected.

◆

Should jurors be allowed to submit questions to the judge for witnesses? Why should jurors not be allowed to read newspapers and watch television? Should jurors who are having emotional problems be dismissed from juries?

Source: V. Villasenor, *Jury: The People vs. Juan Corona* (Boston: Little, Brown, 1977).

Box 10.2

Mercy Killing—Compassion or Murder?

Roswell Gilbert, a retired engineer, was happily married to Emily for 51 years. The Gilberts were a loving couple with one daughter and three grandchildren. Then Emily Gilbert developed Alzheimer's disease, emphysema, and osteoporosis, a painful and degenerative bone disease.

Emily Gilbert was in constant pain, and her mental and physical condition was quickly deteriorating. By the time of her death, she had lost 30 pounds and 2 inches in height. She had broken three ribs and almost every bone in her lower spine due to the osteoporosis. Roswell Gilbert took care of his wife. He took her to lunch and pacified the waitresses when she forgot what she ordered. But she often did not recognize him or her daughter; she did not even remember that she had grandchildren. Sometimes she wandered off. She begged for help. Roswell suffered seeing his lovely and bright wife lose her mental capacity and her physical health. The day after an incident at the hospital where she refused to be examined and tore a needle out of her arm, Roswell shot and killed her.

Gilbert says that he did it because he loved her and could not bear to see her suffer. The jury did not see it that way. They convicted him of first-degree murder and sentenced the 75-year-old man to life in prison without possibility of parole for 25 years. Gilbert's conviction set off a national debate on euthanasia, or mercy killing.

The Gilberts' daughter testified that he had killed her mother out of love and compassion. Emily's sister agrees. Why did the jury convict him? Apparently a number of factors influenced this decision: 1) When Roswell shot his wife, she did not die immediately. He went to his workshop to get another bullet and shot her a second time. The jury interpreted this second shot as proof that the murder was premeditated. 2) The jury interpreted Gilbert's maintenance of his composure on the witness stand as an indication that he was uncaring and cold. 3) The jury were sympathetic toward Gilbert but felt that the law did not give them any other option.

Once the jury returned the verdict of "guilty of first-degree murder," the judge had no option but to sentence Gilbert to life in prison. Roswell Gilbert was granted clemency and released on August 2, 1990, after serving 5 years in prison.

Most euthanasia cases never get to trial. The police have the discretion not to arrest, the prosecutor has the option to drop the case, and the grand jury has the option not to indict. One of those options generally is used. But when a euthanasia case does get to trial, the jury usually turns in a verdict of "not guilty."

♦

Should Roswell Gilbert have been kept in prison? Did his detention protect society? Should our society allow euthanasia as does the Netherlands? Should people be allowed to commit suicide or to help others to commit suicide? Should we have laws that differentiate euthanasia from murder?

Sources: "'Mercy Killing' Verdict May Spark New Support for Euthanasia Laws," *The Florida Times-Union* (May 12, 1985), p. B–6; B. Bearak, "Gilbert's Second Shot Decisive," *The Florida Times-Union* (October 20, 1985), pp. H–1, H–4.

Jury Nullification

Equity is also the motivation behind the phenomenon of jury nullification. Juries have the prerogative to evaluate a case on the basis of the jury's own collective conscience. The jury can decide that although a person obviously committed a particular offense, it would not be fair to convict that individual. The jury might come to this conclusion because it thinks the punishment was too severe for the crime, the law was not fair, or the crime did not warrant punishment. Whatever their reasoning, the jury can decide to ignore the instructions given to them by the judge. Jurors are not required to justify their decisions and the decisions cannot be overturned by the trial judge (Horowitz & Willging 1991).

Jury nullification was frequent during Prohibition, is still common in cases of euthanasia, and has occurred in other cases as well. Jury nullification was used occasionally during the 1960s and 1970s in trials involving antiwar protestors (Horowitz 1985, Loh 1985). For an example of a recent case of jury nullification, read THE McDUFFIE VERDICT.

Much evidence supports the existence of jury nullification and equity in jury decisions (Kerr 1978, Simon 1967). For example, Vidmar (1972) studied a simulated murder trial. Subjects were most likely to acquit the defendant when their only choice was between very long imprisonment and not guilty. However, when other choices of intermediary sentences were available to them, jurors would more often choose these lesser sentences over a not guilty verdict. It would appear that if the sentence is perceived as too severe, juries are likely to acquit the defendant.

Although juries have the option of ignoring the law and the evidence, juries are seldom told of this option. Judges are allowed to instruct juries about their option of nullification in only two states (Indiana and Maryland) (Scheflin & Van Dyke 1980). Horowitz (1988) studied the effect of jury nullification instructions on 144 six-person juries composed of people from the jury roll. These juries heard an audiotape of a mock trial. Those juries that heard instructions concerning nullification from the judge or defense attorney were "more likely to acquit a sympathetic defendant and judge a dangerous defendant more harshly" (p. 439) than the juries that did not hear this information. When juries heard challenges to the nullification information, they were less likely to act on their sentiments.

Size of Jury

Although most trials have twelve-member juries and require unanimous verdicts, the U.S. Supreme Court (*Williams v. Florida,* 1970) has ruled that juries can be as small as six members and do not have to come to a unanimous decision (Report to the Nation on Crime and Justice, 1983). Social scientists have researched both aspects of juries, size and unanimity. First, we will discuss the size of the jury.

Research with real juries has found that twelve-person juries are superior to six-person ones. Juries composed of six persons tend to be more limited on a number of variables: age range, educational range, representation of females, and representation of blacks (Winich 1979). The decisions reached also seem to be affected by the size of the juries. Valenti and Downing (1975) compared decisions

Box 10.3

The McDuffie Verdict

After a short investigation of Arthur McDuffie's death at the hands of the police, the Dade County state's attorney filed charges against six police officers. (For a complete description of the McDuffie incident, see THE DEATH OF ARTHUR McDUFFIE in Chapter 6.) The charges ranged from second-degree murder to participation in the cover-up. Charges were eventually dropped against one officer and dismissed in court against another. The four officers whose cases went to the jury were Ira Diggs, Alex Marrero, Michael Watts, and Herbert Evans, Jr. Three officers were given immunity to testify against their coconspirators: Charles Veverka, Mark Meier, and William Hanlon.

The defense was successful in challenging all blacks selected for the jury. Therefore, the case was heard by a jury of six white men.

Meier testified that McDuffie had said "I give up." Despite his surrender, the police beat him with their nightsticks and flashlights even when he lay motionless on the ground. Hanlon testified that he had driven over McDuffie's motorcycle to make it appear as if it had crashed. The defense argued that the incident was like a "barroom brawl"—claiming there was no way of determining who had done what.

It seemed like an open-and-shut case—the defendants admitted taking part in the beating. But, after 2 hours and 45 minutes of deliberation, the jury proclaimed that the defendants were not guilty on all counts. The jury seemed to feel that the witnesses for the prosecution were as guilty as the defendants and, therefore, no one should be punished. "It wasn't fair to send one person to prison while others just as guilty were going free," said jury foreperson David Fisher, an air-traffic control specialist at the Tampa airport. Fisher insisted that there was no racial favoritism in the verdict.

The jury's verdict touched off 3 days of rioting in the black neighborhoods of Miami. The United States Justice Department reviewed the case. A federal grand jury with five black members indicted Charles Veverka on four counts of violating McDuffie's civil rights. A jury in San Antonio, Texas, acquitted Veverka, touching off rock-throwing episodes in Miami's black community. The McDuffie case was over—with no one punished for his murder.

♦

Juries often react negatively to witnesses being given immunity to testify. Does the fact that the witness for the prosecution is also guilty mean that the defendant should not be convicted? Was justice served by adjudicating these police officers not guilty?

Sources: D. A. Williams, "Three Days of Black Rage in Miami," *Newsweek* (June 2, 1980), pp. 34–39; "What Happened to 'Duff'?" *Time* (June 2, 1980), p. 14; "A Whistle Blower Is Acquitted," *Newsweek* (December 29, 1980), p. 17; "How Safe is Immunity?" *Time* (August 11, 1980), p. 58.

by mock juries of six and twelve members. When the evidence was weak, the two different-sized juries came to the same decision. However, the decisions were quite different when the evidence was strong. In the latter case, a conviction was much more likely in the six-person juries than in the twelve-member ones. These researchers also found twelve-member juries were more likely to end deliberations in a stalemate (a hung jury) than a six-member jury. This result occurred no matter how weak or strong the evidence was. Most social scientists believe juries should consist of twelve members.

Unanimity of Decision

Unanimous decisions are required for capital offenses in every state and for criminal cases in almost every state (forty-five). Very few states (five) have no requirements for unanimous jury verdicts. The situation is somewhat different in civil cases: twenty-six states do not require a unanimous verdict in these cases. In the states allowing nonunanimous decisions, the percentage of jurors who must reach agreement varies from two-thirds in Montana to five-sixths in Oregon (Report to the Nation on Crime and Justice, 1983). Once again, most social science research supports the superiority of unanimous verdicts (Guinther 1988).

The Supreme Court decision in *Williams v. Florida,* which upheld the use of smaller juries and nonunanimous decisions, cited "research" to support its ruling. Unfortunately, the cited research consisted of uncontrolled studies and personal opinions published in legal journals. The sole research study taken from the psychological literature (Asch 1956) was misinterpreted. Although later research on jury size and unanimity of decision have not produced huge impacts on decisions, there have been detrimental effects on the deliberation process (Saks 1977). A subsequent decision by the Supreme Court (*Ballew v. Georgia,* 1978) considered social science research but did not reverse its earlier decision. In this ruling, the Supreme Court decided juries could not be smaller than six persons.

Extralegal Factors

The public assumes juries make decisions on the basis of the legal evidence presented to them. While evidence is an important determinant of the verdict, it is not the only influence (Visher 1987). Jurors have been found to make decisions on the basis of extralegal attributes of the defendant or victim such as sex, attractiveness, race, or demeanor (Kerr 1982).

Juries are comprised of individuals, each of whom brings individual biases and prejudices to bear on the case which is to be decided. Defendants are judged more harshly by mock jurors when the defendants are black, poor, and uneducated (McGlynn, Megas & Benson 1976, Rokeach & Vidmar 1973, Ugwuegbu 1979). The race of the victim also affects judgments, with mock jurors tending to be harsher on defendants when the race of the victim is the same as the juror's (Ugwuegbu 1979). Negative attributes of the defendant bias judgments against that individual even when the mock juror has been instructed not to consider personal attributes of the defendant (Kaplan 1977). However, these extralegal factors influence decisions primarily when the evidence is ambiguous. The decision is determined by the evidence when it is quite clear and strong (Kaplan & Miller 1978, Ugwuegbu 1979).

The results of these laboratory studies are consistent with the outcomes of actual trials. Characteristics of actual defendants also influence jury decisions. The poor are treated more severely than others by the courts (Clarke 1975, Gordon 1976, Stephens 1975) and blacks are convicted on less evidence and receive harsher sentences than whites (Chambliss & Seidman 1971, Dodge 1990, Johnson 1974, Perry 1977, Quinney 1970). The race of the victim also affects the decisions in the legal system. Offenders receive very harsh sentences when the victim is white, but much more lenient sentences when the victim is black (Foley & Rasche 1979, Johnson 1970, Wolfgang & Reidel 1973).

The Attorneys

Balzac is quoted as defining a jury as "twelve men chosen to decide who has the better lawyer" (cited in Kerr 1982, p. 273). Support for this position is found in research by Kaplan and Miller (1978). These researchers set up a simulated trial with four different scenarios: either the prosecutor, the defense attorney, both the judge and the experimenter, or no one acted obnoxiously. The results confirmed the influence of the attorney on the verdict.

Kerr (1982) collected data on the personal characteristics and behavior of judges and attorneys in more than 100 trials. Although the study did not involve the evaluation of the evidence in the trial, it did show that "moods, styles, and skills" of attorneys influence the verdict of the juries (p. 281).

Greenberg and Ruback (1982) use attribution theory to explain how attorneys influence the jury's decision. Jurors attribute characteristics to the attorneys such as credibility and confidence in the case. The attorney's demeanor, particularly in reference to the defendant, influences the attributions of the jurors. The defense attorney tries to convince the jurors that he believes the defendant, while the prosecutor treats the defendant with disdain, indicating that she knows the defendant is guilty. Jurors use attorneys to help them decide whether the defendant is guilty.

The Defendant and Victim

Clarence Darrow (1936) maintained that the primary function of a defense attorney was to make the jury like or feel sympathetic toward the defendant. Research with juries supports this theory; attributes of the defendant do influence jury decisions. Attractive defendants or those with positive traits are assumed to be less guilty (Efran 1974, Izzett & Leginski 1974, Kaplan & Kemmerick 1974). However, the attractiveness of the defendant can work against her if she is shown to have used her attractiveness in the commission of crimes (Sigall & Ostrove 1975).

Jurors evaluate the nonverbal behavior of witnesses in order to determine whether or not they are telling the truth. The way the defendant speaks and his demeanor influence verdicts (Savitsky & Sim 1974). If a witness appears nervous by hesitating or squirming, the juror is likely to assume the witness is hiding something (Miller & Burgoon 1982). Unfortunately for the defendant, many of the speech patterns and nonverbal behaviors attributed to someone who is lying are actually the behavior typical of someone who is truthful but tense and nervous (Miller & Burgoon 1982, Lind & O'Barr 1978).

If the defendant is believable and provides a good alibi or rationale for the behavior, the verdict will be favorable. But a mere denial of the crime holds no weight. And anything the defendant says will be outweighed by evidence that he committed a similar offense in the past or that he is lying (Shaffer 1985). Probably the behavior of the defendant most likely to influence a verdict is a confession (Kassin & Wrightsman 1985, Wigmore 1970). A confession will override other evidence (McCormick 1972, Miller & Boster 1977).

Jurors are likely to attribute dangerous behavior to those who are not granted bail prior to trial. A mock jury trial comparing jurors' reactions to a defendant in prison garb and a defendant in regular clothes found the former defendant was evaluated more harshly than the latter (Fontaine & Kiger 1978). The evidence that juries treat defendants in prison garb differently is so strong that in 1976 the Supreme Court prohibited states from having defendants appear at trial in prison uniforms.

Verdicts also have been shown to reflect attitudes toward victims (Myers 1980). One study found a defendant who stole a car from an attractive victim had a greater likelihood of conviction than one who stole a car from an unattractive victim. However, if the victim's carelessness contributed to the crime, attractiveness no longer affected the outcome (Jones & Aronson 1973). Jurors who believe the victim contributed to the victimization attribute less guilt to the defendant. This is especially true in rape cases where divorce, the past sexual history of the victim, prior rapes, and evidence of promiscuousness have been found to influence decisions (Calhoun, Selby & Warring 1976, Feldman-Summers & Lindner 1976, L'Armand & Pepitone 1977). Current laws forbid the introduction of evidence about the victim's sexual history. Read THE JURY DECIDES ON A RAPE CASE for a description of how attitudes toward the victim influenced a verdict.

Comparison of Decisions by Judges and Juries

Kalven and Zeisel (1966) conducted a comprehensive review of jury decisions in 3,576 trials. They asked 555 judges to compare their own hypothetical decisions to the actual decisions made by juries in their courtrooms. The judge and jury agreed in 78 percent of the civil trials and 75 percent of the criminal trials. In the cases in which there was disagreement, the judge tended to be more likely to convict than the jury. The judges believed the jurors were deciding on emotion rather than evidence. For example, the jury might think that the punishment was too severe for the crime, the law was not fair, or the crime did not warrant punishment. These responses generally occurred in cases involving unpopular laws. The authors maintain that the differences in opinion were due to jury sentiment and conflict over evidence. Of course, this interpretation is based on the information furnished by the judges and, therefore, can be somewhat biased. In addition, judges receive more information than do juries.

> **Box 10.4**
>
> **The Jury Decides on a Rape Case**
>
> A 22-year-old woman was jailed for 6 days because she did not want to face the stranger she accused of rape and kidnapping in court (see WHO'S THE CRIMINAL in Chapter 7 for further details). Testifying at the trial in Florida was a Georgia woman who said the same man, Steven Lamar Lord, had raped and kidnapped her. She reported that the accused said, "It's your fault. You're wearing a skirt." The Florida victim was forced to testify against her wishes. And what was the outcome of the trial? The alleged rapist, Steven Lamar Lord, was acquitted. The foreperson of the jury, Roy Diamond, said the jury felt that the victim "asked for it" because she was dressed provocatively and was wearing no underwear. The acquittal set off a national outcry. Later, Diamond explained that he meant she was asking for sex, not to be raped.
>
> But the rape victim was vindicated. Steven Lord pleaded guilty to rape and kidnapping in the Georgia case. He was sentenced to life plus 20 years. He had been charged in another county in Georgia of false imprisonment and attempted rape.
>
> ◆
>
> Should a description of what a rape victim was wearing be admitted in a trial? Should rape victims be forced to testify against their wishes?

Sources: "Man Acquitted of Rape Pleads Guilty to Attack," *The Florida Times-Union* (December 6, 1989), p. B–7; "Florida Rape Victim Sees Vindication in Georgia Case," *The Florida Times-Union* (December 7, 1989), p. B–9.

Death-Qualified Juries

Thirty-six states allowed the death penalty to be imposed as of 1989 (Greenfield 1990). Potential jurors in those states are asked their opinions about capital punishment. In order to serve on a capital case each juror must be "death-qualified"; that is, the juror must indicate willingness to vote for the death penalty, if appropriate. In *Witherspoon v. Illinois* (1968), the United States Supreme Court ruled that jurors who would never invoke the death penalty, no matter what the facts or aggravating circumstances of the case, could be excluded from a jury. Jurors must also indicate that they will be fair and impartial in their decisions. It should be noted that those persons who would automatically vote for the death penalty are also excluded from death penalty trials (Luginbuhl & Middendorf 1988, Neises & Dillehay 1987). A more recent decision (*Wainwright v. Witt,* 1985) reduces the standard for excluding jurors. This ruling states that a person can be excluded if that person's opposition to the death penalty would "prevent or substantially impair the performance of his duties as a juror in accordance with his instructions and his oath" (p. 849).

Research with death-qualified jurors has found them to be more authoritarian, more punitive, and have a stronger belief in a just world than other jurors.

All of these characteristics have been shown to be related to a likelihood to convict. It is not surprising, then, that death-qualified jurors have also been found to be more likely to convict than others (Cowan, Thompson & Ellsworth 1984, Fitzgerald & Ellsworth 1984, Jurow 1971, Moran & Comfort 1986, Rubin & Peplau 1975). This result has been so consistent that the American Psychological Association filed an *amicus curiae* brief stating that there were no contrary research results (Bersoff & Ogden 1987). Since that time, two researchers have found results in a series of studies which have led them to question the relationship between death penalty attitudes and juror decisions (Elliott & Robinson 1991).

Most states have a bifurcated trial in capital cases. Bifurcated trials, in essence, involve two trials: one to establish guilt and a second one to determine the penalty, life imprisonment or death. Typically, the vote for death must be unanimous or the sentence automatically becomes life imprisonment. However, some states, such as Florida, allow a nonunanimous decision. There are other jurisdictions which allow the prosecutor to retry the penalty phase.

When juries deliberate in the penalty phase of a capital trial, they are asked to evaluate the aggravating and mitigating circumstances of the offense. The aggravating circumstances are those which make the offense more severe than the average first-degree murder, for example, a particularly heinous offense. In contrast, the mitigating circumstances are those which decrease the blameworthiness of the offender. Death-scrupled jurors (those who will not vote for the death penalty) cannot serve on either phase of the trial.

Luginbuhl and Middendorf (1988) found that jurors who were strongly opposed to the death penalty were more responsive to the mitigating circumstances and less responsive to the aggravating circumstances than were other jurors. These researchers state "that the present system of death qualification in capital cases results in biases against the interest of the defendant at all stages of the trial process—jury selection, determination of guilt, and sentencing" (p. 263). They maintain that death-qualified juries "substantially depart from the ideal of neutrality" (p. 265).

Sentencing

The drama of the criminal trial is not over with the announcement of a guilty verdict; the defendant must be sentenced. The sentence imposed on the offender is usually determined by the judge. However, in some states the jury decides the punishment, and in others the defendant can choose whether the judge or jury decides.

Sentencing decisions reverberate throughout the whole criminal justice system. A series of long-term sentences can create overcrowding in prisons, while a large number of probations increases the case load of probation officers. Defendants who receive suspended sentences, probation, or short terms are back in the community very rapidly. If they commit more crimes, they become problems to law enforcement authorities and the courts. Both police and prosecutors find the "revolving door" of the legal system very disheartening.

> **Box 10.5**
>
> **An Unusual Santa**
>
> Alachua County Judge Aymer "Buck" Curtin decided to share the blessings of those convicted in his courts with the needy during the Christmas holidays. Judge Curtin gave some minor offenders the option of donating food instead of paying a fine. People convicted of traffic offenses or misdemeanors could donate food or a supermarket gift certificate to families for holiday meals. The offender even gets a bargain. The typical fine is about $100, but Judge Curtin will allow a $35 food donation plus $25 court costs, for a total of $60.

Source: L. Schnell, "Gainesville Judge Hands Out Food-for-Needy Sentences," *The Florida Times-Union* (December 6, 1989), pp. A–1, A–2.

Judges' Discretion

Judges have wide discretion and their decisions are seldom reviewed. Judges are prohibited by the Eighth Amendment from imposing cruel and unusual punishment. But the only real limitations to judges' discretion are the charges made by the prosecutor and the sentencing guidelines designated by the legislature. Nevertheless, even these restrictions can be circumvented through a number of techniques. For example, the judge can impose an alternative to incarceration, such as a fine, probation, or probation and restitution. In addition, the judge can rule whether a number of sentences will run concurrently or consecutively, or the judge may even suspend the sentence.

Sentencing Options

Judges have a number of sentencing options available to them. Both the statutes governing sentencing options and the amount of discretion judges have vary by jurisdiction. Despite these variations, most jurisdictions have most of the following options (Report to the Nation on Crime and Justice, 1988):

1) A **suspended sentence** gives the convicted offender freedom without court supervision. However, the court is able to reinstate the sentence if the offender commits another offense during a specified time period.

2) **Fines** are used primarily in minor offenses. There is some concern that offenders without resources have to steal in order to pay the fine (Cole 1986). Read AN UNUSUAL SANTA for a description of a judge's use of fines.

3) **Probation** releases the offender into the community with some restrictions. The offender is supervised by a probation officer and must abide by specific conditions. Probation is the most widely used disposition in the United States (Report to the Nation on Crime and Justice, 1988).

4) **Restitution** requires the offender to pay the victim compensation for financial losses. Many states have restitution centers which are somewhat like halfway houses. Offenders live in the centers while working to pay restitution.

5) **Incarceration** is the imposition of a term in a prison, jail, or other detention facility. Incarceration can be for a specified period of time, a range of time, or an indeterminate amount of time. When judges impose **indeterminate sentences,** the power to determine sentencing is relinquished to the parole board. The indeterminate sentence allows for the individual treatment of each defendant.

Legislatures that enact **determinate sentences** limit the disparity between sentences. Usually, these sentences involve a minimum to a maximum amount of time and can be reduced by a parole board or by gain time. The judge may increase or decrease the sentence because of mitigating or aggravating circumstances (Report to the Nation on Crime and Justice, 1988). Legislatures that enact **mandatory sentences** require a defendant serve a minimum amount of time. In this case, the judge does not have the discretion to reduce the sentence, suspend it, or give parole (Report to the Nation on Crime and Justice, 1988). However, the prosecutor can reduce the charge, thereby eliminating the mandatory sentence.

6) The **death penalty** could be imposed for homicide in thirty-six states as of the end of 1989 (Greenfield 1990). In most jurisdictions, the jury determines the sentence. But in some states the judge makes the final decision or can reduce the sentence recommended by the jury.

7) **Other types of sanctions** can be quite creative. For example, judges can require community service, the financial support of children whose parents have been killed in traffic accidents, public apologies printed in the newspapers, or special license plates for those convicted of driving under the influence of alcohol or drugs. Sometimes judges feel the loss of reputation and the costs of defense are punishment enough for minor offenses. Judges also have the option of giving split sentences which provide that the offender be incarcerated for a certain amount of time and then be placed on probation (Report to the Nation on Crime and Justice, 1988).

Sentencing Hearings

Sentencing hearings are usually held several weeks after conviction. Because of the frequent use of plea bargaining, judges often sentence offenders with whom they are unfamiliar. The attorneys present aggravating and mitigating circumstances in hopes of influencing the judge. And the defense attorney asks for leniency. As with other decisions in the criminal justice system, the judge does not have enough time to consider all aspects of the case and characteristics of the defendant before imposing a sentence. The hearings are quite short (about 5 minutes), since the decision about the sentence was probably made prior to the hearing.

Some experts think the prosecutor, not the judge, decides the sentence (Cole 1986). Others believe the prosecutor has a minor role in sentencing or that both the judge and the prosecutor decide the sentence (Horowitz & Willging 1984). The prosecutor certainly influences the sentence by determining the offense for which the defendant will be tried. However, most researchers contend that the judge follows the recommendation of the probation officer in the majority of cases (Carter & Wilkins 1967, Konečni and Ebbesen 1982, Report to the Nation on Crime and Justice, 1983). In fact, Konečni and Ebbesen describe the sentencing hearing as a ritual, stating that the judge is not the main decision-maker but rather the "main broadcaster of sentencing decisions reached by the probation officer" (1982, p. 302).

Prior to the sentencing hearing, the judge generally requests that a probation officer prepare a presentence investigation or PSI. The lengthy PSI is primarily based on hearsay. This report covers the circumstances of the offense, the characteristics of the offender, and interviews with the offender, family members, employer (if there is one), social workers who have dealt with the offender, and anyone who might have insight into the prognosis for this defendant's rehabilitation. It also includes an evaluation of the offender and makes a recommendation for sentencing. The severity of the offense and the defendant's prior record are the most important considerations in the sentence recommendation (Cole 1986).

Sentencing Disparities

Legislatures determine behavior considered criminal and indicate the punishment for these offenses. Statutes are not very explicit in terms of punishments, giving added discretion to judges. In addition, more flexible sentencing statutes create a wider range of possible sentences. Both ambiguity and flexible sentencing statutes increase disparity in sentences given by different judges for the same offense to similar offenders (Report to the Nation on Crime and Justice, 1988). These differences vary across geographical location, jurisdiction, and federal and state courts. For example, there is some evidence that judges in the South impose harsher sentences than those in the North (Harries & Lura 1974).

Bonn (1984) attributes disparities in sentencing to a number of factors related to information and supervision. First, judges' decisions generally are not reviewed. Another reason for sentencing disparity is that judges lack experience or training in making sentencing decisions. In addition, judges tend to work alone; they do not review the decisions made by other judges and seldom discuss sentencing with their colleagues.

Hogarth (1971) attributes disparities in sentencing to differences in the judges' attitudes, personalities, and value systems. In a similar vein, M. A. Levine (1976) found a relationship between judges' socioeconomic background and the sentences they imposed. Judges from lower-class backgrounds in Pittsburgh imposed shorter sentences than Minneapolis judges from higher socioeconomic backgrounds. However, Myers (1988) found that the social background of judges was not very predictive of their decisions.

Another explanation for disparities in sentencing centers on the conflicting goals of the criminal justice system. Cole (1986) explains that both the individual values of the judge and community values influence sentencing, accounting for some disparity. In addition, various judges have different views of the law. They also react differently to diverse types of offenses and disparate types of offenders. Cole maintains that judges' decisions reflect "tradition, precedent and lack of information."

How Judges Make Decisions

Judges cannot review all the information they obtain on every defendant. Greenberg and Ruback (1982) propose that judges depend on past experiences to create "causal schemas." Judges infer the disposition of the offender based on the type of crime committed and their evaluations of people who have committed that crime in the past. If the defendant has a prior record, that defendant is assumed to have a stable criminal disposition. Sentences are, then, a result of the judge's evaluation of the defendant's disposition.

Characteristics of Judges

We have already seen that authoritarian mock jurors are inclined to impose longer sentences. There is the same tendency in authoritarian mock judges (Berg & Vidmar 1975, Boehm 1968, Bray & Noble 1978, Mitchell & Byrne 1973). Authoritarian people espouse the conventional values of society. Their commitment to these values is so strong and rigid that they are very punitive toward those who violate them by involvement in criminal activities. Therefore, highly authoritarian subjects impose more severe sentences on defendants committing serious crimes (murder, manslaughter, and rape) than do nonauthoritarian subjects. However, in the case of less serious offenses (e.g., car theft, shoplifting, and forgery), there is no difference in the sentences imposed by low- and high-authoritarian subjects (Ryckman, Burns & Robbins 1986).

Another personality characteristic that relates to sentencing by judges is internal-external locus of control. People who have an internal locus of control believe that they control what happens in their lives. In contrast, people with an external locus of control believe that outside events are the controlling force in their lives. Apparently, those with an internal locus of control believe that people are responsible for their own behavior and should be punished accordingly. Thus, people with an internal locus of control are likely to impose more severe punishments than those with an external locus of control (Phares & Wilson 1972).

A review of studies evaluating sentencing practices and characteristics of judges found a relationship among length of sentence and religion, socioeconomic status, and membership in organizations. "Generally, these studies show that Republicans give longer sentences than Democrats, that Protestants give longer sentences than Catholics and Jews, that members of the American Bar Association

Reprinted with special permission of King Features Syndicate, Inc.

give longer sentences than nonmembers, and that former district attorneys give longer sentences than former defense attorneys" (Greenberg & Ruback 1982, p. 199). These authors conclude that members of the "political right" tend to give more severe punishments than others.

Other studies have had conflicting conclusions. For example, while Gibson (1978) concluded that fundamentalist judges discriminated against blacks, Myers (1988) found that these judges and Baptist judges were simply more punitive than other judges. Although these judges were more likely to incarcerate blacks, they would impose lighter sentences. Myers also found older judges and former prosecutors to be selectively more punitive.

Philosophies of Sentencing

Researchers categorize the underlying philosophies on which judges make sentencing decisions as follows: retribution, rehabilitation, deterrence, incapacitation, and moral outrage.

The philosophy of **retribution** maintains that the offender should receive a sentence that fits the crime. There is no concern with how the sentence will affect the offender in the future. Judges take the offender's prior record into account and try to give fair sentences. If the victim was injured or defenseless, judges with this philosophy tend to impose a more severe sentence on the offender. In addition, the more positive the judge's attitude toward the victim, the more severe the sentence imposed. Read A SENTENCE THAT FITS THE CRIME for a description of one judge's innovative sentencing.

Rehabilitation is the view that the sentence should resocialize the defendant in order to produce a functioning and contributing member of society. The indeterminate sentence was supposed to accomplish this by releasing the offender when he was capable of functioning as a contributing member of society. Judges who use this orientation tend to provide assistance in an attempt to change the person's behavior (Hogarth 1971).

Individual deterrence proposes that the purpose of sentencing is to see that the offender's sentence is severe enough to convince him not to commit another offense. In contrast, **general deterrence** maintains that the offender's sentence

> **Box 10.6**
>
> **A Sentence That Fits The Crime**
>
> Neurosurgeon Dr. Milton Avol acquired the nickname "Ratlord" because of the deplorable condition of the four apartment buildings he owned in Los Angeles. Despite hundreds of citations for health, fire, and building code violations, the neurosurgeon refused to repair and improve the apartments. The apartments were described as filthy and unhealthy, littered with rodent droppings and infested with roaches. In addition, there were many safety problems related to faulty wiring and plumbing. Finally Municipal Court Judge Veronica Simmons-McBeth sentenced the slumlord to a 30-day sentence. In what jail was he to serve this sentence? In one of the worst places in the area—one of his own apartments. The 63-year-old physician was fitted with an electronic monitor to guarantee that he actually stayed in the roach-infested building, complete with falling plaster and broken windows for the entire sentence.
>
> ♦
>
> Is this an appropriate sentence for this defendant? Should judges make better attempts to have the sentence fit the crime? Will the defendant be more likely to comply with the law in the future? How can slumlords be made to improve their buildings? Are professionals treated the same as nonprofessionals who commit the same crimes?

Source: "L. A. Slumlord Sentenced to 30 Days in Tenement," *The Florida Times-Union* (July 14, 1989), p. A-4.

should be severe enough to dissuade other members of society from committing similar offenses. Judges who function from this point of view want to make people aware of the certainty and severity of punishment. Disparity in the length or severity of sentences makes sanctions unsure. Since the concept of deterrence is based on certainty of sanctions, disparity of sentencing eliminates the deterrent effect (Report to the Nation on Crime and Justice, 1983).

Incapacitation refers to detaining the offender in jail or prison in order to prevent him from committing crimes while under sentence. Cole (1986) gives another example of this philosophy: the castration of some rapists in order to incapacitate them.

Moral outrage is the philosophy that the sentence should express the community's disapproval of the offense. In sensational cases, judges are particularly likely to consider the community response. Since they are elected officials, judges are eager to please the community.

Each judge uses his or her own philosophy, emphasizing one or more of these orientations when deciding on sentences. There is no universally accepted philosophy of punishment. Both the public and professionals debate which orientation is the most appropriate. Shifts in sentencing patterns have paralleled changes in views about rehabilitation. Rehabilitation went out of favor in the

1970s but now appears to be regaining popularity. Cole (1986) reports a trend in which judges give more psychological and social sanctions, moving away from a physical orientation.

Research with male undergraduates attempted to differentiate the sentencing strategies used by high- and low-authoritarian subjects. The strategies described previously (except for moral outrage) were included. When asked to sentence for serious crimes, high-authoritarian subjects used deterrence (general and specific) more and retribution less than low-authoritarian subjects. The low-authoritarian subjects were not more likely to use rehabilitation for less serious crimes (Ryckman, Burns & Robbins 1986).

Theoretical Explanations
One theoretical explanation for judges' decision-making is based on equity theory (Greenberg & Ruback 1982). This theory maintains that judges are concerned with restoring equity between the offender and the victim. Equity can be restored by having the offender pay restitution or by having the offender suffer. At times, it is impossible to restore physical equity, particularly if the victim has been permanently disabled. In these latter cases, the judge might attempt to restore equity by lessening the disparity through psychological means, such as derogating the victim, minimizing the extent of the victim's suffering, or denying the responsibility of the defendant. "Restoration of equity through psychological means almost always implies that the judge will show greater leniency in sentencing the defendant" (Greenberg & Ruback 1982, p. 208). This has been particularly true in rape cases.

Judges also consider the defendant's family in trying to obtain an equitable sentence. If the defendant is the sole supporter of small children, the judge would be punishing the children as well as the offender by incarcerating her or him.

Support for the theory of equity in sentencing decisions is found in a study by Austin (1979). College students were asked to sentence hypothetical persons convicted of various crimes. The crimes varied in severity and the defendant also suffered various amounts of physical or emotion pain. The more the defendant suffered, the less punishment was imposed in minor crimes. However, this reduction in sentence did not occur in the case of serious crimes unless the offender's suffering was much more extreme than that of the victim. The effect of suffering on the sentence was obtained even if the suffering was not a consequence of the crime. In addition, suffering of the criminal did not lead the subjects to think that the criminal should be adjudicated not guilty.

Lerner's (1970, 1980) just-world hypothesis is another theory that might help explain sentencing decisions. For example, in a study by Jones and Aronson (1973), it was found that men convicted of raping married women or virgins received a longer sentence than those who raped divorced women.

Other Factors Influencing Judges' Decisions
The court system is vastly overloaded. Therefore, judges are evaluated more positively if they process a large number of cases through the system and get their opinions out on time (Edwards 1988). Judges who hand out very severe sentences

are less likely to have cases plea bargained in their court. Without plea bargaining, the process of handling cases is much slower; therefore, these judges are seen as less competent (Greenberg & Ruback 1982).

Judges work with the other members of the criminal justice system to advance the cause of justice. Sometimes this cooperation requires the judge to impose a lenient sentence on a defendant who has assisted the prosecution in another case or is an informant for the police. These defendants have valid concerns that they not go to prison, because their safety might be at risk there. Judges are aware of these concerns and tend to cooperate.

Konečni and Ebbesen (1982) conducted a series of studies in order to determine the factors influencing the decisions made by judges. They used four different methodologies: 1) interviews with judges; 2) questionnaires filled out by judges; 3) rating scales completed by judges, defense attorneys, and students; and 4) experimental simulations with judges, probation officers, and students. Results differed for each of the four methods, reducing confidence in all the methods. However, two factors were found consistently in all four studies: severity of crime and prior record. Therefore, credence can be placed in the finding that judges are influenced by these two factors.

Discrimination

Although most criminologists agree that in the past the offender's race influenced the sentence received, more recent studies have challenged the continued assumption of the existence of differential treatment of offenders because of race (Bernstein, Kelly & Doyle 1977, Chiricos & Waldo 1975, Hindelang 1978).

The contradictory results of studies relating race to sentencing can be explained to some extent by taking into account the race of the victim. Blacks who commit crimes with black victims receive the most lenient sentences, while blacks who commit the same offenses against white victims receive the most severe sentences and have very high conviction rates (Johnson 1970, Wolfgang & Reidel 1973). The influence of the victim's race is particularly apparent in rape cases (LaFree 1980). As Green (1964) points out, imposition of lenient sentences on blacks for crimes against blacks is discrimination as much as the imposition of heavier sentences on blacks for crimes against whites.

Differential treatment of offenders has been particularly apparent in capital cases. The data show that blacks and males are much more likely to receive the death penalty than whites and females even when other factors, such as circumstances of the offense, additional offenses, and presence of weapon are controlled (Dodge 1990, Foley 1987, Foley & Powell 1982, Kleck 1981). Race of the victim also influences sentencing in capital cases. In a study of murder indictments in three southern states, Johnson (1970) found that blacks were much more likely to receive the death penalty for interracial murder than for murder of another black.

The influence of race on sentencing decisions is a complex question to evaluate. The many studies in this area have utilized diverse methodologies, subject pools, and, not surprisingly, have obtained different results. Debate over the existence of racial discrimination in sentencing continues. Hindelang (1978) used the Uniform Crime Reports and victimization surveys to evaluate the impact of race on sentences. He concluded that blacks were not disproportionately represented in prison because of discrimination. He contends, rather, that blacks are disproportionately involved in crime, which accounts for their greater incarceration rate. Kleck (1981) reviewed sixty studies that had conflicting results; some studies found evidence for discrimination and others did not. The only consistent evidence of discrimination was found in capital cases. The defendant's prior record was more predictive of the sentence than the race in noncapital cases.

Another category of offender who has received differential treatment in the criminal justice system is the indigent. Research indicates that the poor are treated more severely than the wealthy by the courts (Clarke 1976, Gordon 1976, Silverstein 1965, Stephens 1975). Defendants of low socioeconomic status are more likely than wealthy defendants to receive prison sentences (Clarke 1976, Stephens 1975). In addition, the defendant who is indigent and, therefore, represented by a public defender or a court-appointed attorney, tends to receive a harsher sentence than someone represented by a private attorney (Nagel 1969).

A study by Foley and Powell (1982) found that both judges and juries in capital cases in Florida were influenced by the sex of the offender. Judges were influenced also by the race of the victims despite the recommendation of juries, which were not influenced by this factor. These results were obtained even when a variety of legal and extralegal factors were controlled statistically.

Sentencing Reforms

In the 1970s, sentencing and the effectiveness of corrections came under scrutiny. Led by Martinson (1974), many legal professionals began to question the effectiveness of the programs used to rehabilitate inmates. Concern with disparity of sentences and the impact of lack of certainty on deterrence created a push toward sentencing reform and a decrease in discretion of judges. Professionals began to look for clarification of the goals for sentencing. The move was toward a more "predictable" system which imposed sanctions in accordance with the "just deserts concept" (Report to the Nation on Crime and Justice, 1983, p. 71).

The current tendency is to increase the role of the legislature in sentencing and to decrease the influence of judges and parole boards. There are many ways in which this is being accomplished. For example, between 1975 and 1982, parole boards were eliminated in ten states (Report to the Nation on Crime and Justice, 1983). Another approach is to have the legislature specify the sentence for each type of offense (Hirsch 1976). This can be accomplished through a **presumptive sentence** in which the judge can increase or decrease the sentence specified by the legislature on the basis of aggravating or mitigating circumstances. Or, the legislature can specify a **mandatory minimum sentence,** in which case the judge could increase the sentence but not decrease it. There are, of course, proponents and opponents of each approach (e.g., Hirsch 1976, Alschuler 1979, Brewer, Beckett & Holt 1981). Reforms have also been instituted by enacting administrative guidelines for judges and parole boards for the purpose of determining the punishment or parole release.

Sentencing Guidelines

Sentencing guidelines are being introduced in many states but are still controversial. The purpose of the guidelines is to limit the discretion of judges. These guidelines assign weights or scores to attributes of the offender and to circumstances of the crime. For example, the prior record and employment history of the offender would be used along with other characteristics to obtain a score. When these weights are compared to a chart, they specify the kind and length of sentence. Although the judge does not have to follow the guidelines in every case, if the judge chooses to go outside the guidelines, a justification must be given in writing (Cole 1986; Report to the Nation on Crime and Justice, 1988).

Summary

Instructions to the jury are long, boring, and complicated. Therefore, jurors often cannot understand the instructions and do not follow them. The most important function of the jury is to decide on a verdict. Jurors are influenced by extralegal factors as well as the evidence. The social exchange theory is used to explain how juries look for equity in their decisions. Although juries have the option of ignoring the law and the evidence, juries are seldom told of jury nullification. In order to serve on a capital case, each juror must be "death-qualified." Death-qualified jurors are more likely to convict than others.

Judges have a great deal of discretion in sentencing convicted offenders. Two factors found consistently to impact sentencing decisions are severity of crime and prior record. Disparities in sentencing have been attributed to a number of factors: information and supervision; judges' attitudes, personalities, and value systems; judges' socioeconomic background; and different judges receiving different types of cases. Researchers categorize the underlying philosophies on which judges make sentencing decisions as follows: retribution, rehabilitation, deterrence, incapacitation, and moral outrage.

Despite variations in sentencing options, most jurisdictions employ: 1) a **suspended sentence,** 2) **fines,** 3) **probation,** 4) **restitution,** 5) **incarceration,** and 6) the **death penalty,** as well as other innovative sanctions. One theoretical explanation for judges' decision-making is based on equity theory. Most researchers believe the judge follows the recommendation of the probation officer in most cases.

The influence of race on sentencing decisions is a complex question to evaluate and continues to be debated. Differential treatment of offenders has been particularly apparent in capital cases. Concern with disparity of sentences and the impact of lack of certainty on deterrence created a push toward sentencing reform and a decrease in discretion of judges in the 1970s. The current tendency is to increase the role of the legislature in sentencing and to decrease the influence of judges and parole boards.

11

Mental Illness and Criminal Justice

The Insanity Defense
History of the Insanity Defense
Public Attitudes Toward the Insanity Defense
Recent Attempts to Abolish the Insanity Defense
Incompetent to Stand Trial
Summary

The Insanity Defense

Despite tremendous advances in knowledge in recent years, no one claims to have the definitive answer to what causes or even constitutes mental illness. Needless to say, the answer is even less clear as to how it can be controlled. Mental health professionals continue to debate the nuances of the diagnoses and treatment of those needing help. In 1987, the American Psychiatric Association published the revised third edition of its *Diagnostic and Statistical Manual* (DSM III-R) for mental illness. This manual is considered the standard for evaluating and diagnosing patients. Yet even within the discipline of psychiatry, there is a great deal of debate as to the accuracy of the descriptions in the DSM III-R. Definitions of mental disorders are constantly being refined and changed as new information and research increase knowledge within this discipline. Debate continues between and among professionals in every discipline dealing with mental health as to what constitutes mental illness and the appropriate treatment for it.

At the same time that definitions of mental illness are evolving in the mental health disciplines, the legal profession is reviewing its definition of "insanity" for use in the court system. Insanity is a legal defense, not a psychological term. Legal definitions of insanity are not comparable to those used by the psychological or psychiatric professions. And while psychology and psychiatry were making great strides, the laws governing insanity did not change for almost 100 years. Controversy rages within the legal arena over the definition of insanity as well as whether insanity should be used as a defense for those accused of criminal activity.

The public became aware of the controversy concerning the use of the insanity defense when John W. Hinckley, Jr., was acquitted despite most of the nation observing him on television shooting and wounding four people, including the President of the United States. The jurors at his trial decided that he "lacked substantial capacity to appreciate the wrongfulness of his conduct" or "lacked substantial capacity to conform his conduct to the requirements of the law" (Maeder 1985, p. xiii). See THE HINCKLEY TRIAL for a complete account of the trial.

History of the Insanity Defense

During the Middle Ages, people who were insane were considered to be possessed by the devil. Insanity was used not as a defense for a crime but rather as a reason for the king to grant a pardon after a person was convicted. The pardon allowed the convicted person to be confined instead of being put to death, which was the typical punishment for an offense.

Until the M'Naghten rule of 1843, there was no consensus on a definition of insanity or any uniform criteria for determining whether a person was insane. Often the person was compared to a wild beast or evaluated on whether he knew good from evil (Gerber 1984; Low, Jeffries & Bonnie 1986).

Finally, a series of trials in England led to a defined test of insanity. The first of these trials in 1724 was for Edward Arnold, who was accused of shooting and wounding Lord Thomas Onslow. Local people, who had long been aware of Arnold's odd ways, testified to his strange behavior. For example, Arnold complained that Onslow was in his belly and that Onslow was the source of his having bugs and plagues. However, as the prosecutor argued, Arnold appeared rational and demonstrated foresight in borrowing a gun, buying the ammunition, testing the gun, running away, and saying he was sorry. The presiding judge, Justice Tracy, found Arnold guilty, stating the criteria for insanity were that such a person was "no more than an infant, than a brute, or a wild beast" (quoted in Maeder 1985, p. 11). Arnold was thus sentenced to death. However, Onslow interceded for mercy for his attacker, which was granted. Instead of execution, Arnold was jailed for the rest of his life (Maeder 1985, Low, Jeffries & Bonnie 1986).

The second trial that affected the outcome of insanity trials was that of James Hadfield, who claimed insanity in 1800 after shooting at King George III. The prosecutor argued that Hadfield used reason and purpose in the commission of the crime. The defense advanced the argument that insanity is not an inability to think, but rather a delusion. Hadfield, who had received serious head wounds in the French Revolutionary War, had experienced delusions ever since, believing himself at various times to be King George, God, or Christ. Prior to shooting at the king, Hadfield felt that he was doomed and that the only hope for his salvation was his martyrdom. Since he believed suicide to be a sin, Hadfield reasoned that he could accomplish his goal by being put to death for an attempt on the king's life. The jury decided that he was insane and, therefore, not guilty.

Prior to Hadfield's case, the disposition of someone found not guilty due to insanity was determined by the judge. It was not unusual for the judge to give custody of the defendant to his or her family. However, the Hadfield case involved an attempt on the life of the king and received a great deal of publicity. As a result, a new law was passed requiring that people adjudicated not guilty by reason of insanity were to be held where the crown decided. Therefore, Hadfield was sent to the Bethlehem Hospital (later called Bedlam).

Another case affecting the insanity defense occurred in 1840. Edward Oxford nodded to Queen Victoria and Prince Albert, then proceeded to shoot, missing them both. He immediately identified himself as the perpetrator. Oxford, whose father and grandfather were considered insane, was also well-known for his strange behavior. For example, he would suddenly laugh for no reason or sit and cry. Further evidence of his mental state was found in letters he wrote to himself from a nonexistent revolutionary group. After hearing the evidence, the chief justice instructed the jury to decide "whether the evidence given proves a disease in the mind as of a person quite incapable of distinguishing right from wrong" (Maeder 1985, p. 21). The jury decided Oxford was not guilty because of insanity, and he was committed to Bethlehem.

The M'Naghten Rule

The most important advance in the definition of insanity came out of the 1843 M'Naghten case. (The name in this case is spelled differently by different sources. The London *Times* researched the accurate spelling and determined that it should be spelled McNaughton. However, most U.S. sources use the spelling in the sen-

> **Box 11.1**
>
> **The Hinckley Trial**
>
> There was no doubt that John W. Hinckley, Jr., had shot President Reagan and three others; Hinckley's trial revolved around his sanity. The law in effect in the District of Columbia at that time was the Brawner Rule. Judge Parker read the jury many pages of instructions including the following: "The burden is on the Government to prove beyond a reasonable doubt either that the defendant was not suffering from a mental disease or defect on March 30, 1981, or else that he nevertheless had substantial capacity on that date both to conform his conduct to the requirements of the law and to appreciate the wrongfulness of his conduct. If the Government has not established this to your satisfaction beyond a reasonable doubt, then you shall bring a verdict of not guilty by reason of insanity" (Caplan 1984, p. 98).
>
> Psychological experts for both the defense and the prosecution agreed that John Hinckley had some sort of psychological disturbance. However, they differed on the nature and extent of the disorder. The defense had four experts who testified that John was psychotic, although they differed in the precise diagnosis for him. They did agree that John Hinckley was not responsible for his actions.
>
> The prosecution's psychiatric team diagnosed Hinckley as having dysthymnic disorder or depressive neurosis as well as three types of personality disorder—schizoid, narcissistic, and mixed with borderline and passive-aggressive features. These psychiatrists testified that Hinckley was not too impaired to distinguish right from wrong or to be able to conform his conduct to law.
>
> John Hinckley's life was described in bits and pieces by his family and people who observed his behavior. John had no friends and few acquaintances. After he left home in 1973 to attend college at Texas Tech in Lubbock, Texas, he became
>
> *(continued)*

tence above.) On January 20th of that year, M'Naghten shot and killed the private secretary to Robert Peel, the prime minister of Great Britain. M'Naghten thought he was assassinating the prime minister, but instead killed the secretary who was in the prime minister's carriage. The prosecutor cited the forethought and planning apparent in the crime as evidence that M'Naghten was sane. But the defense was able to provide evidence of strange and paranoid behavior and delusions. M'Naghten alleged that Catholic priests, Jesuits, or various political parties were responsible for his difficulties. In addition, he had been evicted from his rental home for generating loud moans. Without hearing further evidence, the judge stopped the trial, stating that M'Naghten was insane and had him committed.

The public was outraged. Queen Victoria was upset and asked Peel to arrange for a definitive rule on insanity. At Peel's request, fifteen judges wrote what was later called the M'Naghten rule. In part this rule stated that "to establish a defense on the ground of insanity, it must be clearly proved that, at the time

> even more isolated. He had strong negative reactions to having a black roommate and moved off campus. He claimed but later denied joining the Nazi party. He formed the "American Front," a fictitious and racist organization with no members for which he published a newsletter. John periodically stopped attending classes. Then, in April, 1976, John quit college and went to Hollywood in hopes of having his music published. He wrote his parents that he was involved with an imaginary girlfriend.
>
> While in California, Hinckley saw the movie *Taxi Driver* fifteen times. He became obsessed with the movie and an actress in it, Jodie Foster. Unsuccessful in Hollywood, dissatisfied with his life and lacking direction, Hinckley embarked on an odyssey. He spent the next several years criss-crossing the country and living in at least seventeen places. During this time, he frequently visited Yale, where Jodie Foster was a student. During these visits, he left her notes and phoned her, taping the conversations. During his travels, Hinckley accumulated guns, practiced shooting them, and was arrested for possession of guns.
>
> His parents were concerned with John's strange behavior and lack of direction in life. At different times, they sent him to a psychologist and a psychiatrist. But John did not confide in his psychiatrist, Dr. Hopper (despite their twenty-two sessions together) much more than he did in his parents. Dr. Hopper set John the goal of having a job by the beginning of March and leaving home by the end of that month. When the end of March arrived, John had no job. His parents followed the psychiatrist's advice to make John leave home.
>
> John took one last trip to Hollywood, then rode a bus to Washington, D.C., where he arrived March 29th. The next day, he attempted to assassinate the President of the United States. The jury decided that John Hinckley was not guilty by reason of insanity.

Source: L. Caplan, *The Insanity Defense and the Trial of John W. Hinckley, Jr.* (Boston: David R. Godine, 1982).

of the committing of the act, the party accused was laboring under such a defect of reason, from disease of the mind, as not to know the nature and quality of the act he was doing, or if he did know it, that he did not know that he was doing what was wrong" (Maeder 1985, p. 33). By 1900, the M'Naghten rule had become law in Great Britain and most U.S. states.

The M'Naghten rule is referred to as a cognitive measure of insanity since the person is required to know two things: the nature and quality of the act and that the act was wrong. There was much conflict over this cognitive test for insanity. In its strictest sense, the M'Naghten rule referred to cognitive knowledge, but sometimes people can know something intellectually without really appreciating or internalizing this knowledge. Low, Jeffries, and Bonnie (1986) cite an example from the 1939 *American Journal of Orthopsychiatry* of a young child who said that he hit his sister, she bled, and fell. He was able to say he killed her but did not really "know" what he did. This case illustrates the difference between verbal and affective knowledge.

Many judges felt that the M'Naghten rule was too restrictive and thus would instruct the juries that they did not have to limit their decisions to the cognitive issues delineated in it. Frequently, judges would add a test of "irresistible impulse" to the M'Naghten rule. This test required that the defendant was unable to prevent himself from committing the crime even though he knew that it was wrong. In a similar vein, other judges used the test of the "policeman at the elbow." This was a test that attempted to determine whether the person would have committed the crime even if a policeman was standing at her elbow.

Opponents to the use of irresistible impulse as a test of insanity argued that everyone has impulses. Even psychiatrists had difficulty differentiating "could not control behavior" from "did not control behavior." When do these impulses become irresistible? Resisting impulses is what makes people law-abiding. Thus, the irresistible impulse measure is too similar to normal behavior. Despite these reservations, by 1900 about half of the states had laws which supplemented the M'Naghten rule with an irresistible impulse test. Later irresistible impulse was used as a separate insanity defense. England was opposed to the use of the irresistible impulse test, as were some states. Other states were unclear on the matter (Maeder 1985, Low, Jeffries & Bonnie 1986).

Early Attempts to Abolish the Insanity Defense

A further change in the laws dealing with insanity occurred in 1883 with the passage of the Trial of Lunatics Act by the British Parliament. This act was an outcome of another attempt on the life of Queen Victoria, this one made by Roderick Maclean, a former inmate of a lunatic asylum who was delusional. When Maclean was acquitted by reason of insanity, Queen Victoria was furious and demanded a change in the law. The new law replaced the not guilty by reason of insanity (NGRI) plea with "guilty but insane." The consequences were the same for the defendant—commitment for life. Because there was no change in the consequences, many people felt the change in the law was unnecessary (Maeder 1985). It is interesting to note that the most recent changes in the insanity defense in the United States are to a guilty but mentally ill (GBMI) plea.

Attempts to abolish the insanity defense have occurred periodically in the United States. These attempts generally follow notorious cases in which the defendant was acquitted on the basis of insanity. When Harry K. Thaw was acquitted on grounds of insanity for the murder of a well-known architect in Madison Square Garden in 1906, the public tended to agree with the decision. During the trial, the victim, Stanford White, was described as a villain who had had an affair with Thaw's wife. The public believed that the victim deserved what he got. However, Thaw's behavior after his acquittal gave the public second thoughts about his acquittal. A wealthy man, Thaw seemed to make light of his commitment by throwing an elaborate party to celebrate his trip to the institution. He then used his wealth to manipulate the institution in which he was confined, thereby enabling him to come and go at will. Those doctors who attempted to restrict him were fired.

Soon after his admission, Thaw began to work on his release. He filed numerous petitions for reevaluation of his sanity which were carried all the way to the Supreme Court with no success. Thaw eventually decided to leave the hospital permanently and went to Canada. Two years later he returned and was declared sane. Subsequently, he was arrested for kidnapping, and his family committed him to a private hospital. In response to this case, the New York State Bar decided that the insanity defense should be eliminated and that persons previously committed on this defense should have strict limitations on their right to file petitions (Maeder 1985).

The states of Washington and Mississippi attempted to abolish the insanity defense in the early 1900s. Subsequently, both states' laws were found unconstitutional and repealed. California attempted a different solution; it instituted a bifurcated trial for the insanity defense in 1925. In the first part of the trial, the defendant attempted to prove his innocence. If he was found guilty, he would proceed to a second trial to address his sanity. During the first trial, the defendant was assumed sane and was not allowed to present evidence concerning mental health. However, it was quite difficult to distinguish between motivation and mental state. Eventually, appeals gradually reduced the subtle differentiation that existed between the two trials.

Testimony in an Insanity Defense

Until the mid-1800s, medical experts rarely testified at insanity trials. When they did testify, they frequently did so without examining the defendant. For example, two doctors testified in M'Naghten's trial on the sole basis of having watched the trial. The judge decided M'Naghten's insanity primarily on what he called these doctors' "unbiased" testimony. Most medical doctors in the 1800s had no experience with mental illness. It was considered hereditary and incurable prior to this time. Since nothing could be done for patients, doctors were not interested in dealing with these kinds of disorders. The best doctors could do was suggest bloodletting as a solution to mental problems, which they thought to be caused by black bile and blood congesting the brain. Early in the 19th century, medical people began to take more interest in mental illness. They gradually took over the running of asylums and initiated more humane treatment of people confined in them. They also began to accumulate more understanding and knowledge of mental disorders.

The M'Naghten rule remained the legal standard of insanity well into the 20th century despite tremendous advances made in psychiatry and psychology. As medical personnel acquired more knowledge of mental disorders, they realized that the M'Naghten rule was not an appropriate test of mental illness. The legal question of whether the defendant knew right from wrong does not fit into psychiatric definitions. Even the term *insanity* is used only by the legal profession and not by the mental health professions. Furthermore, the adversarial nature of the legal system is not conducive to lengthy descriptions of the nuances of diagnoses necessary to convey the psychiatrist's findings. The medical profession's focus on evaluating health does not concern the legal community, whose only interest is legal responsibility. Both legal and psychiatric experts were aware of this problem.

Psychiatrists, placed in a moral dilemma, were reluctant to testify. They knew the defendant was not responsible for the act but that he had "knowledge of right or wrong." Some handled the dilemma by merely testifying that the defendant did not know right from wrong. Others refused to testify or answered truthfully that he did know right from wrong. Maeder highlighted a common view of legal experts in the 1950s. "Both in England and in America it was believed that if a man was truly insane, the procedures would contrive to have him acquitted, and it little mattered what the rule happened to be. Why then should one change it and swap errors one had learned to live with for new and untried mistakes?" (Maeder 1985, p. 79).

Psychiatry is not an exact science. No X-rays and blood tests yield specific diagnoses. Psychiatrists must take into account many factors regarding the patient's behavior and personality. Psychiatrists often differ in their diagnoses of and prognoses for patients. If the patient has a severe mental disorder, psychiatrists tend to agree with one another. It is in cases where there is less evidence of psychological disorders that there is disagreement. When these ambiguous cases go to court, each side can find psychiatrists to testify in its behalf. One psychiatrist will state that the patient is ill and the other will swear he is sane. When psychiatrists give contradictory evidence, the jury is caught in the dilemma of trying to decide which psychiatrist to believe, rapidly losing faith in psychiatry.

Many critics accuse psychiatrists of being bought, contending that their testimony is unreliable. Low, Jeffries, and Bonnie quote George Will's column in the Washington *Post* (June 23, 1982) to this effect: "Psychiatry as practiced by some of today's itinerant experts-for-hire is this century's alchemy. No, that is unfair to alchemists who were confused but honest. Some of today's rent-a-psychiatry is charlatanism laced with cynicism" (Low, Jeffries & Bonnie 1986, pp. 132–133). The American Psychiatric Association acknowledges the criticism but points out that the problem is a function of the adversarial system. Only ambiguous cases go to trial and experts can have contradictory views on individual cases. Medical experts, engineers, ballistics experts, etc., also have conflicting expert opinions that are voiced in court.

Comparisons of decisions by practicing forensic experts found relatively high agreement on relevant symptomatology in a mock case of the insanity defense. The psychiatrists and psychologists relied on different types of information to reach their conclusions, but there was no difference in decision from one discipline to the next. Approximately 30 percent of the respondents thought the defendant was guilty and 64 percent thought she was not guilty by reason of insanity. There was no difference in opinion based on whether the request came from a judge, prosecutor, or defense attorney. However, since the experts were not employed by a particular side, they did not interact with the participants. Due to this lack of interaction, the incentive to internalize a particular position might not have been very strong (Beckham, Annis & Gustafson 1989).

The Durham Experiment
New Hampshire developed its own rule for the test of insanity, which evolved out of cases in that state in the late 1800s. The rule that New Hampshire still uses

is that the crime "was the offspring or product of mental disease in the defendant" (Low, Jeffries & Bonnie 1986, p. 16). No other state followed New Hampshire's changes until the *Durham* decision made by Judge David Bazelon in 1954 in Washington, D.C. Low, Jeffries, and Bonnie (1986) point out that the *Durham* rule assumes that behavior is a product of an illness in the same way that a seizure is the product of epilepsy. However, mental disorders are not the same as physical ailments.

Judge David L. Bazelon was already unhappy with the test for the insanity defense when he heard the case of Monte Durham in the U.S. Court of Appeals for Washington, D.C. Durham's long history of psychiatric problems began when he was 17. He had been institutionalized and incarcerated a number of times. At his most recent arrest, Durham was found huddled in a corner with a shirt over his head. After Durham spent some time in St. Elizabeth's Hospital, he was found competent to stand trial and was convicted. The experts who testified on his sanity said he had an "unsound mind," but did not discuss his ability to distinguish right from wrong. Judge Bazelon ruled that "an accused is not criminally responsible if his unlawful act was the product of mental disease or defect" (*Durham v. U.S.*, 1954). He based his decision on the New Hampshire rule and indicated that no rule could be written that adequately addressed every case. In later discussions of the ruling, Judge Bazelon stated that there needed to be enough flexibility in the law to accommodate the growing knowledge of psychology.

Opponents of the Durham experiment argued that it gave too much protection to the defendant. The prosecution was in the difficult position of having to prove the sanity of the defendant beyond a reasonable doubt. And while the Durham rule was in effect, the number of NGRI decisions did increase. However, the actual number of these decisions was still quite low. Opponents of the Durham rule also argued that the rule removed the decision concerning insanity from the jury. If a psychiatrist testified that the defendant's act was a result of mental disease or defect, the judge and jury would have to accept that diagnosis as fact. The jury could hardly disallow the testimony of a psychiatrist and make an independent decision. Congress responded to that concern with a law in 1984 limiting testimony of psychiatrists to mental disorder and specifically disallowing opinions or inferences about defendant's "mental state constituting an element of the crime."

The American Law Institute's Model Penal Code Test

In 1962 the American Law Institute developed a Model Penal Code Test (called the ALI rule) for insanity. This rule stated that "a person is not responsible for criminal conduct if at the time of such conduct and as a result of mental disease or defect he lacks substantial capacity either to appreciate the criminality of his conduct or to conform his conduct to the requirements of law" (Report to the Nation on Crime and Justice, 1988, p. 87). As of 1985, this ALI test was used in many states and in every federal circuit court except one. It was accepted in Judge Bazelon's court in 1972.

Box 11.2

The Use of the Insanity Defense in State Courts

According to the American Bar Association—

- ♦ Twenty-four states use the definition adopted by the American Law Institute (ALI) in 1962 as part of the ALI Model Penal Code. It states that "A person is not responsible for criminal conduct if at the time of such conduct and as a result of mental disease or defect he lacks substantial capacity either to appreciate the criminality of his conduct or to conform his conduct to the requirements of the law."
- ♦ Sixteen jurisdictions use the McNaughton rule, formulated by the British House of Lords in 1843. It states that, to establish a defense on the ground of insanity, it is necessary to prove clearly that at the time of committing an act the accused party was laboring under such a defect of reason from disease of mind as not to know the nature and quality of the act, or if he did understand the act, he did not know that it was wrong. Lawyers call this the cognitive test because the language hinges on "knowing."
- ♦ Some jurisdictions modify the McNaughton rule by reference to "irresistible impulse."
- ♦ New Hampshire uses a rule devised by its Supreme Court in 1871 that a person is absolved of responsibility if the act committed is the offspring or product of mental disease.

Source: Report to the Nation on Crime and Justice (Washington, D.C.: Department of Justice, Bureau of Justice Statistics, 1988), p. 87.

The Appreciation Test

In 1984 the Comprehensive Crime Control Act made the Appreciation Test the law in all federal courts. This test relies on a cognitive test, making it similar to the M'Naghten rule. There is no requirement for a defendant to prove a lack of control as in the ALI test. This "new federal law changes previous standards in the federal courts by shifting the burden of proof to the defense, limiting the scope of expert testimony, eliminating the defense of diminished capacity, creating a verdict of 'not guilty only by reason of insanity,' which requires a civil commitment proceeding, and by providing for federal commitment of persons found insane after conviction or incarceration" (Report to the Nation on Crime and Justice, 1988, p. 87). See THE USE OF THE INSANITY DEFENSE IN STATE COURTS.

Despite all the controversy over legal tests and the refinements in definitions of insanity, research indicates that mock jurors come to the same conclusions no matter what test of insanity is given to them (Finkel 1982, Finkel & Handel 1989, Finkel et al. 1985). Critics of decisions in insanity cases contend that the jurors either misunderstand or disregard the judges' instructions. Others maintain that the jurors construe insanity in a simplistic and irrelevant way and do not discriminate between different types of cases. Finkel and Handel (1989) found just the opposite result. Mock jurors used complex constructs of insanity and applied these constructs differentially according to their relevance to the particular case. In fact, Finkel and Handel conclude that the jurors used "a more complex picture of insanity than past, current, and most proposed new legal tests of insanity propose" (1989, p. 55). See JOSEPH KALLINGER for a description of a man found sane by the jury but diagnosed as a paranoid schizophrenic by psychiatrists.

Public Attitudes Toward the Insanity Defense

Prior to the 20th century, the NGRI defense was used primarily for murder. Persons acquitted on this basis would be committed to an institution for the rest of their lives instead of being executed. Hospitals for the criminally insane were at least as bad as penitentiaries and often were worse, so that defendants had no incentive to fake insanity. Most of the defendants who used this defense were genuinely mentally ill. Someone electing this defense could not plea bargain or present evidence of innocence. Since the defendant would be institutionalized for life, prosecutors had no reason to contest the defense.

The mid-1900s brought drastic changes in the treatment of those found not guilty by reason of insanity. In the 1950s, the advent of psychoactive medications allowed severely ill mental patients to be released. Then, in the 1960s and 1970s, the exposure of horrible conditions in institutions led to public demand for changes. Involuntary commitment was greatly limited by court action. No one could be involuntarily committed without a hearing and legal representation. Only those who were a danger to themselves or others were involuntarily committed. They were then entitled to treatment and had a right to a review of their progress.

The changes in commitment requirements eventually were expanded to include people adjudicated not guilty by reason of insanity. The new commitment requirements meant that, if these people were not guilty, they could not be held involuntarily. Once defendants were adjudicated not guilty, they had to be committed in a civil commitment proceeding. They then received all the rights and entitlements of any other person who was involuntarily committed. Thus, they were entitled to treatment and to regular review of their progress. If patients were considered to have made sufficient progress toward recovery, they were released. The tendency now is for people adjudicated not guilty by reason of insanity to spend less time in the hospital than those convicted of a similar offense spend in prison (Pasewark, Pantle & Steadman 1982, Phillips & Pasewark 1980). Heilbrun, Heilbrun, and Griffin (1988) drew similar conclusions in a study of women. Women involuntarily committed to a mental hospital without committing a crime, but with similar disorders to those found not guilty by reason of insanity, spent the least amount of time institutionalized.

Prior to the introduction of new medication and widespread concern for the rights of patients, people who were found not guilty by reason of insanity were permanently institutionalized. With the changes in laws, these people could leave the hospital, often a short time after commitment. Maeder states that "in a very

> **Box 11.3**
>
> **Joseph Kallinger**
>
> Joseph Kallinger was 22 months of age when he was adopted by Stephen and Anna Kallinger. His adoptive parents were emigrants from the Austro-Hungarian Empire in their 40s. The Kallingers wanted a child to inherit their successful shoe repair shop. Their motivations were not altruistic, what they really wanted was someone to take care of them in their old age.
>
> The Kallingers were good to Joseph materially, but they were psychologically and physically abusive. The Kallingers burned Joseph's fingers on a gas burner, beat him with a cat-o'-nine-tails, and hit him with a hammer on the head. The latter punishment was imposed for requesting permission to go to the zoo with his class. In addition, Joseph had to work in the shoe repair shop and could not play with other children.
>
> When Joseph was 6, he required surgery to repair a hernia, an experience made traumatic by his adoptive parents. Anna Kallinger frightened the boy by saying that a knife would be used on him in the hospital. The Kallingers frequently threatened to send Joseph back to the orphanage. Left alone in the hospital, Joseph felt abandoned, believing he had been returned to the orphanage. The Kallingers further frightened Joseph by telling him the doctor had made his "bird" (their term for penis) small and removed the demon which used to live in it. Now his penis would never grow or get hard so he would not get into trouble. After this traumatic incident, Joseph began to fantasize about knives.
>
> The psychiatrist who examined Joseph as an adult felt that knives became "instruments of power and authority through which those giants called grownups enforced their will by cutting leather or a little boy's flesh" (Arieti & Schreiber 1980, p. 506). When he was 8, Joseph was sexually assaulted by three older boys at knife point, increasing his fantasies involving knives and their association with sexual activities. Joseph thought of knives as magical weapons and began to imagine castrating boys. As a 12-year-old, he would stab photographs of nude women's breasts while he masturbated. Later he was able to have intercourse only while handling a knife kept near his bed.
>
> At 15, Joseph began to display physiological abnormalities. Writhing and jerking his head, Joseph would laugh uncontrollably. Frightened by Joseph's behavior, the Kallingers installed a lock on their bedroom door. Joseph left his adoptive parents' home and married when he was 16, but continued to work in
>
> *(continued)*

real sense, those who satisfy the criteria for legal insanity—who do not know the difference between right and wrong, who lack the capacity to keep their behavior under control, are precisely the people society should fear most and whom some judicious agency ought most closely to supervise. It would be very odd for us to feel ourselves entitled to less control over those who *could* not control themselves than we have over those who simply *did* not" (1985, p. xviii).

> the shoe repair shop. Joseph quickly fathered two children to whom he was a conscientious parent. Joseph was happy for the first time in his life, and his symptoms abated. But then his wife ran off with another man. Joseph soon remarried and had five more children. He wanted a large family to make up for the lonely life he had as a child.
>
> Joseph was an attentive father, caring for the children when they were ill and keeping in touch with their teachers. But Joseph had periodic bouts with madness. He hallucinated and developed a private language. Afraid that his wife would leave him if she became aware of his illness, Joseph hid his illness and the rituals associated with his madness.
>
> Joseph was not only protective of his children, he was extremely possessive and tried to keep them away from friends. Punishments for violating his arbitrary rules were so severe that Joseph spent 8 months in prison for child abuse. A psychiatric examination by the court revealed major mental disorders and two psychiatrists recommended hospitalization. However, on the advice of a third psychiatrist, the judge released Joseph because he believed that he was needed at home.
>
> Joseph became even more delusional, believing that he was God and that he had to destroy all the people on earth. Joseph had the hallucination that he would mutilate and torture the people before killing them. Joseph enlisted one of his sons in his mission to kill everyone. They broke into a number of homes with the intention of killing the occupants. Together they mutilated and killed two children, one of whom was Joseph's own son. Joseph heard voices and had an imaginary companion, Charlie, who goaded him to accomplish his violent goals (Schreiber 1983).
>
> Joseph was arrested in January, 1975, after committing his third murder. Juries in three separate trials found him guilty and sane. During his imprisonment, psychiatrist Silvano Arieti examined Joseph Kallinger and found him to have hallucinations and to be delusional. Dr. Arieti diagnosed Joseph as a paranoid schizophrenic, stating that he "must be considered not only psychotic, but also legally insane, according to the M'Naghten law and the Durham law because, although he knew the nature and quality of the crimes that he committed, he did not know that they were wrong; in fact they were commands from God, and presumably good" (Arieti & Schreiber 1981, p. 517). However, Dr. Arieti's opinion has not occasioned a change in the sentence of Joseph Kallinger.

Sources: S. Arieti and F. R. Schreiber, "Multiple Murders of a Schizophrenic Patient: A Psychodynamic Interpretation," *Journal of the American Academy of Psychoanalysis,* vol. 9, no. 4 (1981), pp. 501–524; F. R. Schreiber, *The Shoemaker* (New York: Simon and Schuster, 1983).

One of the cases that gave impetus to the changes in NGRI decisions was that of Johnnie Baxtrom. Convicted in New York in 1959 on second-degree murder, Baxtrom was sentenced to 2½ to 3 years in prison. While incarcerated, he was sent to Dannemora State Hospital. At the end of his sentence, he was kept in Dannemora because the civil hospitals refused to take him. When his petitions for release or transfer reached the U.S. Supreme Court, it ruled in his favor. Based on this decision, almost 1,000 patients were transferred to civil hospitals. The transfers generated great fears and protests, but there were few problems. Four years later, only 3 percent of the 1,000 transfers remained in corrections or hospitals for the criminally insane (Maeder 1985).

Recent Attempts to Abolish the Insanity Defense

Laypersons do not understand psychiatry, but they think they know about people who use the insanity defense. The public mistakenly assumes that the insanity defense is used frequently, especially by savvy criminals as a method of manipulating the system. Laypersons feel that psychiatrists are fooled by lying criminals. Actually, the insanity defense is seldom employed and rarely does it succeed. When the insanity defense is used, it tends to be a valid defense. For example, a child who has been abused for years and eventually grows large enough to retaliate against his abusive parent might plead not guilty by reason of insanity. The vast majority of NGRI cases are settled informally, with the prosecutor agreeing with the insanity verdict. Fewer than 20 percent of cases are disputed. The cases that are disputed tend to involve serious offenses and those in which the experts disagree about the diagnosis (Rogers, Bloom & Manson 1984). See THE BURNING BED for a description of a recent case using the insanity defense.

Boehnert (1989) compared thirty men who successfully attempted an NGRI defense to thirty men who were unsuccessful in the same attempt. A large proportion (80 percent) of the successful acquittees had been found to be incompetent to stand trial earlier in their case. In contrast, only 30 percent of those found guilty had been declared incompetent to stand trial. Almost all the men (96 percent) who were successful in their attempt to plead not guilty by reason of insanity had their cases tried before a judge without a jury. Only 24 percent of those found guilty had a bench trial. It is possible that juries are harder to convince than judges, but it is more likely that the more controversial cases are heard by juries. Often, laypersons assume that the insanity defense is used by the wealthy. However, that view does not appear to be supported by this study. Both groups of men were "skilled or unskilled laborers, white, had been defended by a public defender, possessed a 10th-grade education, and had a previous arrest record" (Boehnert 1989, p. 36). The men who were unsuccessful in their NGRI attempt had higher intelligence scores and the potential for "intact reality testing."

Society's reaction to the insanity defense has fluctuated over the years. When society is concerned with law and order, people tend to view the insanity defense as a form of coddling criminals and try to restrict its use. When crime is not of such great societal concern, professionals in the field try to make the insanity defense more applicable. An example of the latter time was after World War II when experts from Europe came to live in the United States. The public became more aware of psychological problems, and the government established the National Institute of Mental Health and the Veterans Administration, which opened many psychiatric hospitals. These innovations paralleled the advent of new psychoactive drugs for mental disorders.

Public outrage over John Hinckley's 1982 acquittal elicited new interest in changing the insanity defense. One attempt was the Insanity Defense Reform Act of 1984, which gave the burden of proof to the defense to prove insanity. Prior to this law, the prosecution was required to prove sanity as in the case of Hinckley.

New laws changing the insanity defense tend to address the *mens rea* or intention component of criminal behavior. The rationale behind this change is to restrict psychiatrists' testimony to the intentions of the accused, so that they may not discuss psychiatric evaluations and diagnoses. However, the *mens rea* test of insanity is quite stringent, and the psychiatric community feels that it will eliminate the insanity defense in cases where it should be used. Some experts argue that the test is so restrictive that it could only be used in murder cases in which, for example, the accused did not know it was a gun that he was holding or thought that he had shot a tree. The frequently cited example is that of a man strangling his wife, thinking she was a lemon. However, switching the law to evaluation of *mens rea* will not necessarily solve the problem. *Mens rea* is a vague concept. There has not been much debate over intention in the past because if the defendant's mental capacity was so deficient that he did not understand the law, he was usually considered incompetent to stand trial.

The effect of the new laws requiring those adjudicated not guilty by reason of insanity to be treated as innocent persons was that these people often were released. After their adjudication, these people went through civil commitment proceedings. For those who did not satisfy the requirements of civil commitment, there was no alternative but to release them. This is because the courts had determined they were not guilty (by reason of insanity). If these people did meet the requirements of civil commitment, they had the same rights as anyone else who was committed. In other words, they had the right to have their status reviewed at specified times and, if they were determined to have been cured, they were released. Because of the new medications available, many of these people were released quite soon after commitment. Alternatives to the NGRI defense, therefore have been sought. Federal law, and many state statutes, now require NGRI acquittees to be committed automatically. They are subject to periodic review, but the acquittee must meet a more-stringent burden of proof than those seeking release under civil procedures.

Guilty but Mentally Ill

Guilty but mentally ill is an alternative to not guilty by reason of insanity but not a replacement for it. However, Montana, Idaho, and Utah abolished not guilty by reason of insanity as a separate defense for conviction and criminal sentence. Nine other states also have a guilty but mentally ill (GBMI) verdict; in these states, the insanity plea also exists (Report to the Nation on Crime and Justice, 1988). The definition of guilty but mentally ill varies by state. Most states require the jury to decide if the person is mentally ill (but not insane) when convicted. Usually, the definition for mentally ill used in conviction is the same as that used for commitment. A few states use criteria for guilty but mentally ill that are similar to NGRI criteria in other states (e.g., ALI).

> **Box 11.4**
>
> **The Burning Bed**
>
> Francine Hughes lived with Mickey Hughes and her fear of him for 12 years. Mickey had a violent temper and frequently beat his wife. Insanely jealous and possessive of his wife, Mickey was known to rip off her clothes and tear them up if they looked "too good" on her. He was so domineering that Francine was not allowed to leave their home, even to visit her mother. It was not unusual for Mickey to quit his job impulsively, often after only a few weeks of work, and he was frequently unemployed. When he did work, Mickey spent his money as fast as he earned it, drinking and running around with other women. Mickey and Francine moved constantly, on Mickey's whim or because they were evicted for lack of rent payment.
>
> The police often intervened when Mickey was beating his wife, but they arrested Mickey only if he fought with them. Francine frequently ran to Mickey's parents' house to hide while they called the police. Once he chased her there with a knife. He threatened to kill Francine if she left him and even hit his parents and threatened them.
>
> The Hughes had four children in 6 years. The children often went hungry, but Mickey refused to apply for welfare and would not let Francine work. He was satisfied as long as he had enough money for his food, beer, and cigarettes. Mickey frequently abandoned his family. Francine tried to stay with Mickey because she was afraid she could not support the children and believed they needed a father. But eventually she left Mickey. In fact, she left him a few times. Each time he found her and convinced her to return to him either by persuasion, force, or threats. At one point, when the children were starving and she had no other recourse, Francine divorced Mickey in order to qualify for welfare.
>
> At the time of the divorce, Francine was 23, pregnant, and already had three young children. She found her own place and got a job. But Mickey barged into her home and refused to leave. They lived together for 6 years after the divorce. No public agency would or could help Francine keep Mickey away.
>
> Then Mickey was in a car accident which left him near death. He begged for Francine to come to the hospital and she went. As an invalid Mickey was even more demanding of Francine. After he left the hospital, he stayed with his parents next door, but he wanted Francine's constant attention and would not allow anyone else to care for him. When she finally refused to jump at every request by Mickey, he hobbled on crutches to her house and refused to leave.
>
> *(continued)*

States also vary in the process of determining guilty but mentally ill. Generally, the department of corrections evaluates the person after he or she has been sentenced as a criminal. If treatment is appropriate and available, it is given. When the treatment is completed, the person completes his or her sentence in prison. Typically, the judge has no input concerning the treatment. Critics of this

> Soon after he recovered from his injuries, Mickey asked Francine to remarry him. When she repeatedly refused, he beat her. "You're my wife. Go get ten divorces. It won't do you any f——ing good" (McNulty 1979, p. 109).
>
> Francine worked hard, bought a car, and obtained a grant to attend Lansing Business College. Mickey constantly berated her and denigrated her abilities. But she persevered and did well in school. Then on March 9, 1977, Mickey Hughes beat Francine for the last time. Francine described the incident at her trial. "He began hitting me. The kids were outside. He told them to stay out. I remember he was pulling my hair and he was hitting me with his fist and he had hit me on the mouth and my lip was bleeding. . . . Then I got away from him and ran around the dining-room table" (p. 5). Francine's daughter summoned the police. Mickey continued to beat Francine and then ripped up her books and notes from the business college. Next he made Francine pick up the books and burn them in the trash. He insisted that Francine say she would stop going to school, but she refused. He threatened to pulverize the car so she could not attend classes.
>
> When the police arrived, Mickey sat down and appeared calm. After the police left, Francine let the children in to feed them. Mickey began screaming at Francine, pounding the table, spilling milk and making the children cry. He sent the children to bed and spilled the food on the floor. He then made Francine clean it up. When she had finished, he dumped the garbage on the floor and said, "Now, bitch, clean it up again" (p. 6). While she crawled around cleaning up the mess, Mickey smeared food into her clothes and hair. He kept hitting her. Then he took a beer into his bedroom and told her to fix him something to eat. After eating, he demanded sex. When Mickey finally fell asleep, Francine poured gasoline around his bed and set it afire. Hysterical, she drove the children to the police station.
>
> Dr. Arnold Berkman, a clinical psychologist, testified at Francine's trial that she "experienced a breakdown of her psychological processes so that she was no longer able to utilize judgment . . . no longer able to control her impulses . . . unable to prevent herself from acting in the way she did" (p. 255). He said she was behaving under an "irresistible impulse." A psychiatrist, Dr. Anne Seiden, testified that Francine's "fragile personality made her vulnerable to becoming temporarily insane under certain types of stress" (p. 257). Even the psychiatrist for the prosecution maintained that Francine's act was impulsive and was not premeditated. The jury found Francine Hughes not guilty by reason of temporary insanity.

Source: F. McNulty, *The Burning Bed* (New York: Harcourt Brace Jovanovich, 1980).

alternative say that the law has no impact on the Department of Corrections, there being no guarantee that the convicted person will receive treatment. In addition, the Department of Corrections has procedures for the treatment of mentally ill inmates without a GBMI decision (Low, Jeffries & Bonnie 1986).

Incompetent to Stand Trial

There are some people who are so impaired intellectually or psychologically that they are unable to assist an attorney in the preparation of their own defense. People who are greatly impaired cannot even comprehend the charges against them and the process through which they are going. As such, they are considered incompetent to stand trial (IST). Up until the 1960s, people who fell into this category were sent to institutions, often permanently. It made no difference whether the offense was minor, the disposition was the same. Maeder (1985) describes a 19-year-old boy who was arrested for burglary in Brooklyn in 1901. He was never convicted of an offense but was still in Matteawan Hospital at the age of 83. Prosecutors sometimes used IST as a way in which to have someone suspected of a serious crime, but for which there was little or no evidence, receive justice. Often the charges were dropped as soon as the accused was committed. Maeder describes this procedure as an "odd form of psychiatric vigilantism" (1985, p. 116).

In the 1960s, studies of hospitals in New York and Massachusetts found that most of the IST patients had been there more than 10 years, some for more than 60 years. In the Massachusetts hospital, the most common means of release was death (cited in Maeder 1985). Steadman and Cocozza (1974) found that 40 percent of those confined in New York hospitals for the criminally insane had not been convicted of crimes. Many were confined for longer than they would have been in prison if convicted of an offense. In addition to the inappropriate length of confinement, these patients received no treatment to enable them to become competent.

There was little or no differentiation between NGRI and IST in old English law. The outcome of either decision was the same, permanent institutionalization. As the differences between the two categories became clearer, most legal experts focused on NGRI. Laws dealing with IST in the United States varied by state, but all were vague. There were ten times as many people determined to be incompetent to stand trial as those declared not guilty by reason of insanity. Psychiatrists were as confused with the criteria for IST as anyone else. Often they used the M'Naghten rule to determine IST. There was a great deal of pressure to conduct an initial evaluation of the accused, but little attention was given to treatment or reevaluation once that person was declared incompetent. For this reason, people found incompetent to stand trial were seldom released.

Beginning in the 1960s and 1970s, laws addressing the injustice of IST dispositions were initiated. In 1960, the U.S. Supreme Court in *Dusky v. United States* ruled that specific factors had to be considered in order to declare someone incompetent to stand trial. The person had to be unable to assist in his own defense and unable to understand the charges. With this ruling, the number of IST cases dropped drastically.

A 1972 U.S. Supreme Court decision (*Jackson v. Indiana*) addressed the release of someone found incompetent to stand trial. This case involved a 27-year-old mentally defective deaf-mute who was accused of stealing about $9 worth of goods in 1968. He was declared incompetent and committed. Experts said there was no hope of improvement. Since people could only be released if they improved, he had no hope of ever leaving the institution. The Supreme Court ruled that someone cannot be deprived of rights to due process on the filing of criminal charges without a trial. The case was sent back to court and dismissed. This decision meant that someone declared incompetent to stand trial had the right to treatment and that progress should be made. If someone cannot improve, that person is entitled to a commitment hearing or must be released. Other laws provided guidelines for involuntary commitment for IST cases. These guidelines were generally the same as for a civil commitment. People committed because they were incompetent to stand trial had the right to treatment and the limits of legal confinement were specified. The length of evaluation for incompetence was also limited (Report to the Nation on Crime and Justice, 1988).

All states and the federal government have provisions for an individual to be declared incompetent to stand trial. Usually a court-ordered mental evaluation is used to determine if the individual is incompetent to stand trial. A determination of IST is the most common reason for a defendant to be sent for psychological evaluation. Forensic evaluators use traditional diagnostic tools and instruments designed specifically for this type of screening. These instruments measure "legally relevant functional abilities" (Nicholson et al. 1988). Most defendants referred for evaluation are declared incompetent (Roesch & Golding 1980). Although some states require release after a specified amount of time, all states provide that these persons can be committed under civil hearings (Report to the Nation on Crime and Justice, 1983).

Summary

Until the M'Naghten rule of 1843, there was no consensus on a definition of insanity or any uniform criterion for determining whether a person was insane. Finally, a series of trials in England led to a defined test of insanity: the trials of Edward Arnold, James Hadfield, and Edward Oxford.

The most important advance in the definition of insanity came out of the 1843 M'Naghten case. When M'Naghten was adjudicated not guilty by reason of insanity, Queen Victoria asked for a definitive rule on insanity. In part, this rule stated that "to establish a defense on the ground of insanity, it must be clearly proved that, at the time of the committing of the act, the party accused was laboring under such a defect of reason, from disease of the mind, as not to know the nature and quality of the act he was doing, or if he did know it, that he did not know that he was doing what was wrong." The M'Naghten rule is referred to as a cognitive measure of insanity. Frequently, judges would add a test of "irresistible impulse" to the M'Naghten rule.

A further change in the laws dealing with insanity occurred with the passage of the Trial of Lunatics Act by the British Parliament. The new law replaced the not guilty by reason of insanity plea with "guilty but insane." Attempts to abolish the insanity defense have also occurred periodically in the United States. These attempts generally follow notorious cases in which the defendant was acquitted on the basis of insanity.

When these ambiguous cases go to court, each side can find psychiatrists to testify. One psychiatrist will state that the patient is ill and the other will swear he is sane. When psychiatrists give contradictory evidence, the jury, in the middle, tries to decide which psychiatrist to believe and rapidly loses faith in psychiatry.

A new rule for insanity was instituted in 1954 by Judge Bazelon. This rule, known as the Durham rule, stated that "an accused is not criminally responsible if his unlawful act was the product of mental disease or defect." Opponents of the Durham experiment argued that it gave too much protection to the defendant; the prosecution had to prove the sanity of the defendant beyond a reasonable doubt.

In 1962, the American Law Institute developed a Model Penal Code Test for insanity. As of 1985, this ALI test was used in many states and in every federal circuit court except one. Then, in 1984, the Comprehensive Crime Control Act made the Appreciation Test law in all federal courts.

The mid-1900s brought drastic changes in the treatment of those found not guilty by reason of insanity. Prior to this time, people who were found not guilty by reason of insanity were permanently institutionalized. With the introduction of new medication and increased concern for the rights of patients, these people could leave the hospital, often a short time after commitment.

Laypersons mistakenly assume that the insanity defense is used frequently, especially by savvy criminals as a method of manipulating the system. Actually, the insanity defense is seldom employed and rarely does it succeed. Society's reaction to the insanity defense has fluctuated over the years. New laws changing the insanity defense tend to address the *mens rea* or intention component of criminal behavior. Alternatives to the NGRI defense have also been sought, such as guilty but mentally ill.

There are some people who are so impaired intellectually or psychologically that they are unable to assist an attorney in the preparation of their own defense. Such people cannot comprehend the charges against them and the process through which they are going. These people are considered incompetent to stand trial (IST). Up until the 1960s, people who fell into this category were sent to institutions, often permanently. Beginning in the 1960s and 1970s, laws addressing the injustice of IST dispositions were initiated. In 1960, the U.S. Supreme Court in *Dusky v. United States* ruled that specific factors had to be considered in order to declare someone IST. With this ruling, the number of IST cases dropped drastically.

Other laws provided guidelines for involuntary commitment for IST. These guidelines were generally the same as for a civil commitment. People so committed had the right to treatment and the limits of legal confinement were specified. The length of evaluation for incompetence was also limited.

12

Corrections

The Likelihood of Being Caught
Life in Prison
Functions of Prisons
Psychological History of Prisons
Prisoners
Coping with Life in Prison
The Death Penalty
Summary

The Likelihood of Being Caught

Arguments in favor of punishment as a deterrent are based on the assumption that people will not commit crimes if the punishment is very severe. Origins of this argument can be traced back to the theories of Bentham and Baccaria in the mid-1700s. These authors speculated that if the punishment was so unpleasant that the rewards from the offense were not worth the suffering, fewer people would commit crimes. Advocates of deterrence would maintain that if a criminal robbed someone and got $300 worth of valuables and only spent an hour in jail, it would be worth it to the thief. However, if the thief had to spend 5 years in jail, it probably would not be worth $300 to him and he would not commit the robbery. The flaw in this argument is that the thief might not know what the punishment for his crime is. Furthermore, most criminals do not believe they will be caught, so they do not worry about being punished. And, for the most part, criminals are right; the likelihood of any offender being caught and punished is very slim.

In order to discuss the probability of an offender being punished for an offense, I will combine statistics from a number of sources. Statistics on the amount of crime committed have many limitations and deficiencies (see Chapter 2, "Crime Patterns"). None of the sources used in this discussion claim to be completely accurate, particularly in the beginning stages of the criminal justice process. However, an estimate of the likelihood of someone being punished for a specific crime can be obtained by using these statistics.

Let us begin with 1,000 crimes of all sorts, even though different types of crimes have different reporting, arrest, and punishment rates. For example, it is estimated that only one household larceny in four is reported, whereas most car thefts are brought to the attention of the police. In order to get a general idea of the likelihood of being punished for a crime, these divergent offenses will be combined. The discussion centers on crimes committed, rather than the criminals who commit them, because that is the way the statistics are gathered. It is possible, and highly likely, one person has committed a number of crimes. But, it is not possible to trace criminals with our current methods of gathering data, so crimes will be used.

Nothing will happen after a crime is committed unless it is detected. It is estimated that only about half of the crimes committed are detected (Nietzel 1979). Obviously, no one is going to be punished unless the authorities know about the crime. However, only 30 to 50 percent of the crimes detected are ever reported to the police (Ebbesen & Konečni 1982a, Johnson & DeBerry 1990). Therefore, someone who commits an offense has a 50 to 70 percent chance the crime will not even be detected. Of those crimes which are detected, there is a 30 to 50 percent chance the police will never learn about the crime. Therefore, of the 1,000 crimes that were committed, about 500 were detected and only 150 to 250 were brought to the attention of the police.

Assuming the crime *is* reported to the police, what happens then? The police arrest a suspect in approximately 20 to 25 percent of the Index or Part I crimes they investigate (see Chapter 2 for a description of Index crimes) (Bonn 1984, Wolfgang, Savitz & Johnston 1970). Therefore, of the 150 to 250 reported crimes, suspects are arrested for only 30 to 63 offenses. Please note: in order to ensure

Chapter 12 ♦ Corrections

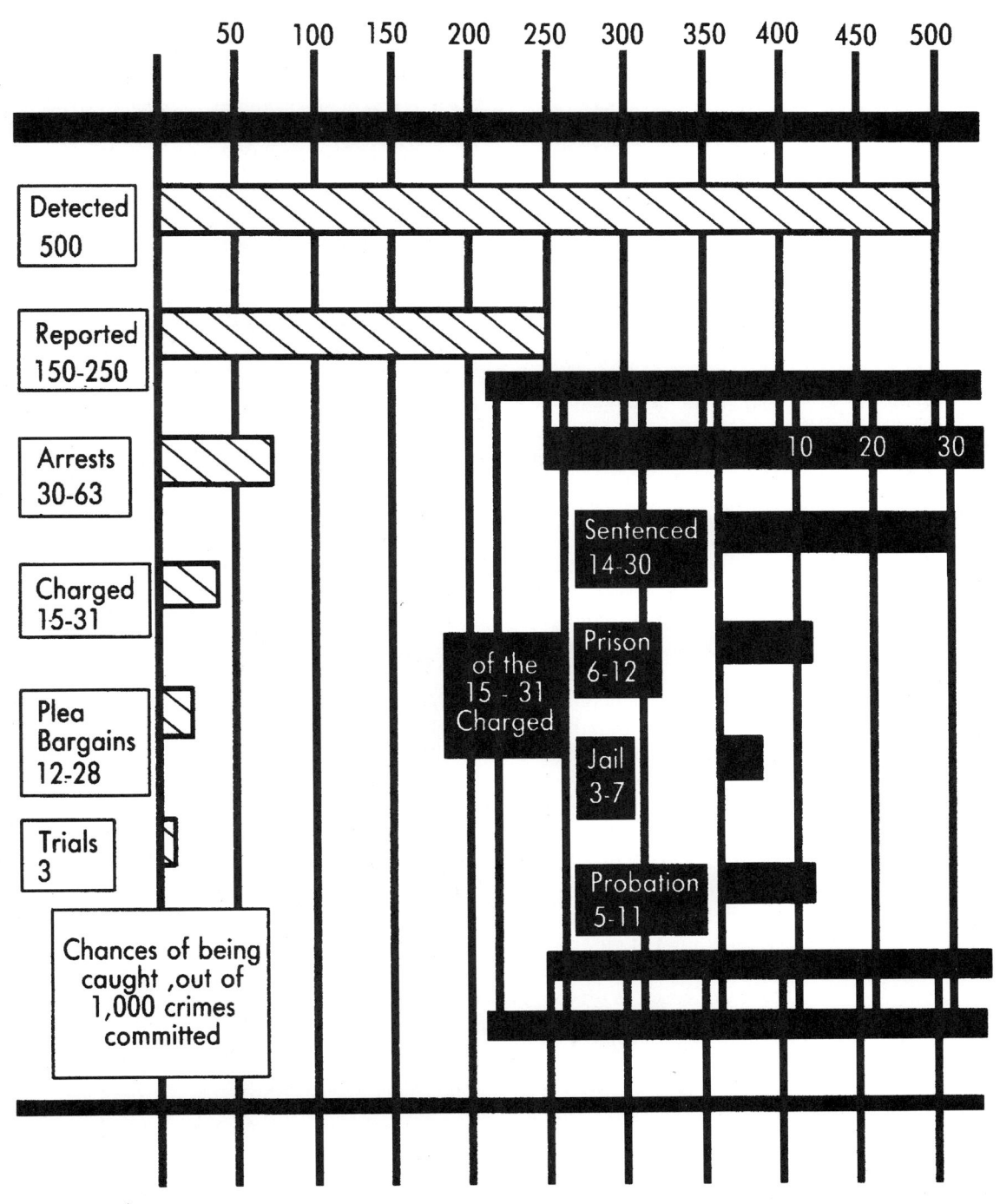

FIGURE 12.1 Chances of being caught (illustrated by Reen Foley)

Data from various sources.

that the widest range of possible incidents are included in the estimates, the calculations for these and later estimates were made in the same manner. That is, the lower percentage was taken of the lower number and the higher percentage of the larger number. For example, in this case 20 percent was taken of 150 crimes (30 offenses) and 30 percent of 250 crimes (63 offenses).

Wolfgang, Savitz, and Johnston (1970) estimate that about 10 to 20 percent of those arrested are sentenced to jail or prison. What happens to the other arrestees? Once the suspect has been arrested, the statistics are easier to keep and thus tend to be more accurate. However, these statistics are not kept nationally, so data collected at a number of different geographic locations will be used. A study conducted by the Law Enforcement Assistance Administration (LEAA) in thirteen jurisdictions found approximately half the cases were dismissed or never formally charged because of insufficient evidence or lack of witnesses to testify (LEAA Newsletter, 1979). This figure varied from 40 percent in Milwaukee to 76 percent in Los Angeles, but the average of 50 percent will be used. To continue with our original example, then, the police have arrested suspects for 30 to 63 of the original 1,000 offenses. If 50 percent of the cases are dropped, only 15 to 31 charges remain.

At this point, the vast majority of charges are plea bargained. The estimates for the number of cases in which the defendant pleads guilty or are plea bargained vary from 50 to 90 percent, with most estimates in the range of 80 to 90 percent (Cole 1986, LEAA Newsletter 1979). The remaining cases go to trial. Using the most frequently cited figures of 80 to 90 percent pleading guilty, in 12 to 28 of the cases the defendant pleads guilty. That leaves 3 people who go to trial (15 − 12 = 3 and 31 − 28 = 3). Of those going to trial, most (70 to 93 percent) are found guilty (LEAA Newsletter, 1979). If the 12 to 28 people who plead guilty are combined with the 2 people found guilty in the trial, that means between 14 and 30 people are sentenced for the 1,000 crimes with which we started. But does that mean they go to prison? No. Ebbesen and Konečni (1982a) estimate that of those sentenced, 39.38 percent go to prison, 21.88 percent go to jail, and 35 percent receive probation. Thus, of those 1,000 original offenses, between 6 and 12 people go to prison, about 3 to 7 go to jail, and 5 to 11 receive probation.

Bear in mind there are a lot of limitations to the estimations made in this section. First of all, this whole discussion has been in terms of crimes committed, not criminals who commit crimes. One person could be responsible for any number of the offenses. With that person's arrest, a number of crimes could be accounted for without the police knowing it. In addition, the likelihood of being caught and prosecuted varies by offense, and we have lumped all offenses together. But despite these limitations, the fact remains that the likelihood of being caught and punished for any given offense is very low.

Professional criminals realize that their chances of getting away with crime are quite high. Most people commit crimes under the assumption that they will not be caught, and statistics support their assumption. The likelihood of any offender being caught and punished is very slight. For this reason, it is surprising that one of the primary reasons legislators give for imposing severe punishments for criminal offenses is to deter people from committing crimes. The evidence is that punishment by the criminal justice system is given in a very small percentage of the offenses committed. Punishment for criminal offenses is neither swift nor sure, making it extremely ineffective in changing behavior. All of this is to say legislation of stiff sentences for particular crimes is futile unless the punishment is likely to be imposed.

The likelihood of going to jail or prison for an offense is very low, one out of one hundred or less. This small percentage of offenders who are incarcerated is the object of the vast correctional apparatus.

Life in Prison

Although society has been imprisoning people during most of known history, it usually has been for the purpose of detention. The use of incarceration as punishment is a relatively recent phenomenon dating back only to about the 1770s. Prior to that time, prisons were used as holding places to keep prisoners until they went to trial or after a trial until they received some other form of punishment (e.g., execution or banishment).

For more than 200 years, incarceration has been used as punishment for crime. During that time, corrections has been the subject of considerable research and reform leading to the development of many new treatment strategies and other innovations. But how successful have these advancements been? Are our prisons now humane and safe institutions that effectively reform all who are sent there? No! Robert Johnson (1987) considers current prisons to be merely "custodial warehouses," little better than banishment. Present-day prisons are dangerous, violent, and overcrowded. There is no doubt that incarceration is punishment; it is a painful experience. However, not only is incarceration generally considered ineffective in rehabilitating those confined to correctional institutions, but many experts contend it actually corrupts those confined. Inmates are of more danger to society upon release than when first imprisoned. Recidivism seems to be the major result of incarceration; the likelihood that people sent to prison will change their behavior for the better is slim.

The goals and objectives of corrections and the functions of incarceration are hotly debated issues among professionals. The only agreement appears to be that corrections do not correct. In the 1970s, rehabilitation was considered a lost cause, but now many proponents say it was never adequately attempted. Meanwhile, the number of prisoners incarcerated has increased at an alarming rate. At the end of 1990, there were 771,243 prisoners (43,845 women) being "corrected" by federal and state authorities, an increase of about 133 percent since 1980 (Cohen 1991). Of every 100,000 people in the United States, 293 were sentenced prisoners in 1990. While most institutions have some sort of rehabilitative treatment programs for the inmates, the severe overcrowding limits access to these programs so that the majority of inmates do not receive treatment.

Functions of Prisons

The primary goal of a prison is security—to ensure that the inmates housed there remain in prison. But prisons also have a number of other functions, some of which are mutually supportive and others which conflict. The order of priority of conflicting functions is the source of considerable debate among professionals. Different functions are considered to be more important by individual professionals and by the majority of experts at various points in time. The functions of incarceration correspond to the philosophies of sentencing discussed in Chapter 10.

One function of prisons is to deter future crime; incarceration should provide both **specific deterrence** and **general deterrence.** Specific deterrence assumes that an individual who receives a prison sentence will not commit criminal acts in the future. Unfortunately, instead of vowing to avoid future crime as a result of imprisonment, many inmates use their time in prison to learn from more experienced criminals and to plan future crimes. General deterrence, "the prevention of crime in the general population by the imposition of penalties on those committing criminal acts" (Gottfredson and Gottfredson 1988, p. 16), is similarly ineffective. As we have seen, very few criminals are actually caught. With the likelihood of being caught so slim, the knowledge of someone being punished for a crime is not a deterrent to others.

Prisons also perform the function of *incapacitation.* While incarcerated, an individual is prevented from committing any further crimes. Obviously, this function is performed quite well for the person in prison. However, the function of incapacitation is limited by the number of criminals who are incarcerated. Fewer than 1 percent of felons are actually sent to prison (Humphrey & Milakovich 1981). Thus, society is not protected from 99 percent of felons. (For a detailed examination of the percentage of offenders sent to prison, see the first section in this chapter.) In addition, the vast majority of felons who are sent to prison will eventually be released. Many of these convicted felons will be more hostile after release than they were prior to incarceration due to the conditions in the prisons. See A REFORMED MURDERER? for a discussion of the impact of incarceration on one man.

The third function of prisons is *retribution.* The punishment of going to prison should pay back the victim for the harm that was done by the offender. This function of prisons satisfies the moral outrage society feels for the crimes.

The final function of prisons is *rehabilitation.* This function has come in and out of favor with the correctional establishment over the course of history as indicated in the discussion in Chapter 10. Rehabilitation was considered an unobtainable goal in the 1970s, but it is currently regaining favor.

Psychological History of Prisons

The history of social control in the United States paralleled that of England and Europe, emphasizing revenge and brutal physical punishment during colonial times. The major punishment for serious offenses was banishment or execution.

> **Box 12.1**
>
> **A Reformed Murderer?**
>
> On the night of December 22, 1980, Clay Boyer and his wife Rebecca were celebrating their purchase of a house by cooking steaks. Both had been drinking and taking drugs when a fight broke out between them. This was not an unusual occurrence; they had fought often and Clay had beaten Rebecca many times in the past. Both went to bed nursing their injuries. Rebecca did not wake up. Clay called the police and paramedics, but Rebecca never recovered. Clay had killed his wife.
>
> The attorney who prosecuted Boyer called the murder premeditation based on Clay's history of battering his wife. Clay pled not guilty by reason of insanity, but the jury decided he was sane and convicted him of first-degree murder. The state asked for and got a life sentence without possibility of parole for 25 years. So Clay went to prison.
>
> While in prison, Clay Boyer became active in the Worldwide Church of God. Nine years after his wife's death, Clay Boyer said he had reformed, and many members of his denomination agreed. More than fifty letters were sent to the governor of Florida asking that Clay Boyer be set free because he had been rehabilitated. What is particularly interesting about these letters is that some are from correctional officers, people who are not easily "conned" by inmates.
>
> Not everyone believes that Clay Boyer should be released. Rebecca's parents feel strongly that Boyer should be kept in prison. Her mother is even afraid for her life if Boyer is set free. The state attorney agreed with Rebecca's parents. (Ritchie, 1989, Feb. 19). It was now up to the governor of Florida to decide.
>
> ♦
>
> Can someone who has committed murder be reformed? If someone is rehabilitated, should they still be punished for the crime they committed? Should premeditation be based on prior violence against the same person? Should someone be convicted of first-degree murder if they did not intend to kill the victim? Should the victim's family have a say in a reduction of sentence for an offender?

Source: B. Ritchie, "Murderer Says He's Reformed," *The Florida Times-Union* (February 19, 1989), p. B–5.

Offenders were publicly humiliated and physically punished with branding, flogging, stocks, pillory, or worse. Offenders were often made to stand by their own coffins on the morning of their execution while a preacher gave a sermon on their sins. The family was responsible for the prevention of offenses by its members, and children who were disrespectful to their parents or particularly incorrigible could be put to death (Clare & Kramer 1976).

In 1773, a former copper mine located 40 miles north of New Haven, Connecticut, was converted to New-Gate Prison, thus becoming the first prison in the United States. Several other states followed the lead of Connecticut and built prisons, some even imitating New-Gate's underground living areas. The newer

NEW-GATE PRISON. The first prison in the United States was constructed underground from a former copper mine 40 miles north of New Haven, Connecticut in 1773. (Photo courtesy of Roger Sharp)

THE OLD BAILEY, the Central Criminal Court in London, England, is built on the site of the original New-Gate prison. (Photo courtesy of Roger Sharp)

facilities duplicated the conditions at New-Gate, which in turn had adopted the deplorable conditions and inhumane policies in English prisons. The administration provided very little food or heat and no clothing. The conditions were unsanitary, and there was no attempt to protect the weaker inmates from the more aggressive ones or to separate the inmates according to sex (with the exception of New-Gate) or seriousness of offense.

Penitentiaries were developed as a means of changing criminal behavior and alleviating some of the psychological and physical abuses of prisons. People sent to prison prior to the advent of penitentiaries were often the victims of brutality from both the guards and the other inmates. The penitentiary isolated the men from one another in order to prevent their abuse at the hands of other inmates. Inmates were also isolated from family and friends and restricted from speaking to one another in the mess hall, at work, or while marching lockstep from one place to another. The isolation and limited activity of the inmates produced severe psychological disorders. In addition, the men were often physically punished and were required to perform hard physical labor. The strict discipline of the penitentiary limited the amount of violence between inmates, but produced psychological trauma (American Correctional Association, 1983).

Big Houses
Penitentiaries evolved into less physically and psychologically abusive places at the turn of the century, but nevertheless maintained their oppressiveness. These "big houses" were still relatively safe for inmates who obeyed the rules of the authorities as well as the inmate culture. Inmates gradually were allowed some activities, visitors, and interactions with other inmates. However, rigid discipline and control by the staff were maintained and often imposed brutally. The inmates suffered severe emotional and psychological reactions to institutionalization and often appeared to be in a stupor (Irwin 1980).

Violence was rare in big houses. This is because these institutions were stable and orderly, with many rules and regulations and a rigid routine. But the health care and physical facilities were adequate. The high-status inmates worked with the guards to operate the institution and keep things running smoothly. These inmates coerced other inmates into obeying the institutional and inmate rules. For their efforts, these high-status inmates were rewarded with sought-after jobs and were given influence over life in the institution (cell assignment, etc.). Irwin describes the inmate code as "do not inform, do not openly interact or cooperate with the guards or administration, and do your own time" (1980, pp. 11–12). By doing your own time, inmates meant not being concerned with the problems of others. If an inmate observes someone being attacked, he should not help the victim or report the incident to authorities. Even victims of violence should not report the incident to guards. Those men, called "rats," who reported attacks to the authorities were low in status and likely to receive further abuse.

The inmate culture had its own hierarchy with the "right guy" at the pinnacle. The right guy was a "real man" who showed no emotions, was detached, dispassionate, and imperturbable. He and his "main men" stuck together to pro-

PRISON WALLS. The walls of this maximum security prison consist of parallel fences with coils of razor wire between them. Armed guards survey the walls from strategically placed guard towers. (Photo courtesy of David H. Fauss)

tect one another. Violence and exploitation were sanctioned by the inmate code and "right men" did not notice unless they were directed at their "main men." There were swindles, tricks, cheating, sexual assaults, and many weapons within the institution, but the violence was controlled. Every once in a while there would be a riot.

Correctional Institutions
In the 1940s, correctional institutions emerged, and many institutions were renamed, leading to the decline of big houses in the 1950s and 1960s. However, the biggest change was in the name, as little correction actually took place. New administrators were concerned with rehabilitation, humane treatment, and social relations. They increased recreation, mail, visitation, and programs of all sorts. Inmates could learn a new trade, get an education, or even receive counseling. But there were limited resources and the institutions were understaffed. Much time was spent in meaningless and menial work or in cells. Unfortunately, the reforms eliminated the rigid control in the institutions but did not replace it with another method of controlling the violence. See INSIDE THE WALLS for a description of life in prison.

Box 12.2

Inside the Walls

The following is an inmate's description of a prison in 1970:

"Waking up in a cell is an old story now. It was a different penitentiary last time, but cells always look the same. They rarely send you back to the same place in this system. And they've got so many in this state that it's no problem. Besides, they have a built-in graduating system. A guy normally starts in the 'country club' in the southern part of the state. Next time he goes a little farther north for medium security. From there it's on to the 'Big Top,' what they call their close security prison. And the final stop on the list is really the end of the road, the 'Fortress,' and just the name alone is enough to make most guys want to stay out of it.

But they all look pretty much the same. Most of them have the same furniture; the supplies all come out of the same pot. The bed is a steel frame bolted to the wall. The springs are heavy wire that give little comfort. The mattress label says it's stuffed with cotton fiber, but it feels like straw. Where the state gets them is anybody's guess, but they'd better not lose their connection, because it can't be accidental and must also be part of the treatment. The sheets feel like burlap and are manufactured in one of the other joints in the system. I was in that one last time. The clothing manufacturing is part of what they call their 'vocational training' program. But what they teach you is how to get along in the penitentiary. They teach you a lifetime penitentiary trade so you'll always be useful to them when you come back the next time, and the next time. They won't ever have to retrain you. They only manufacture maintenance materials and supplies for themselves and the other state institutions. On paper it looks good. They are able to say they're teaching trades to convicts: trades like the textile mill, clothing manufacturing, and furniture manufacturing. A textile mill trade would be fine if we were in the South, or at least in the East, because that's where most of them are. But we're in an "enlightened state," where they don't have textile mills, and most other kinds of slave labor, so they're actually teaching us a nonexistent trade. And clothing manufacturing, that's a real laugh! What they do is teach you how to make prison clothes, and you can get quite good at making them. The only problem is after you've learned the trade here you can't get a job doing it outside. State specifications, by which they manufacture things, aren't exactly competitive in the open market! And what you've been taught isn't good enough for the higher standards on the outside. All you can learn is to make prison clothes—so the only place you can get a job at the trade they teach you is in the penitentiary. And the same goes for their other trades."

Source: A. J. Manocchio and J. Dunn, *The Time Game: Two Views of a Prison* (Beverly Hills, Calif.: Sage, 1970), pp. 30–31.

PRISON LIFE. Inmates in a maximum security institution sit in a commons area watching television. Two-man cells line the upper and lower corridors. (Photo courtesy of David H. Fauss)

The 1960s and 1970s saw the emergence of new rights for inmates won in the courts. The courts restricted the discipline and authoritarian discipline of the big houses. The correctional profession did not replace the structured discipline with new methods of control, and violence became commonplace and epidemic.

Prisons Today

Overcrowding has overloaded the correctional system; there are too many inmates to provide work, adequate medical attention, and programs for everyone. In addition, physical conditions in our prisons have deteriorated. Guards are demoralized because they cannot control the prisoners given the situational constraints. Today's prisons provide more freedoms for the inmates through furloughs and work and study release programs. In reality, these programs are more an attempt to control the overcrowding than to serve a rehabilitative function. The prisons, therefore, function primarily as storage facilities for convicted criminals. There are so few activities for so many men that the available activities provide little assistance in the inmate's rehabilitation and no benefit to society.

Present-day prisons are much more unstable and violent than were the penitentiaries and big houses. With the disintegration of the order and discipline in correctional institutions, conditions have deteriorated; violence, assault, and open

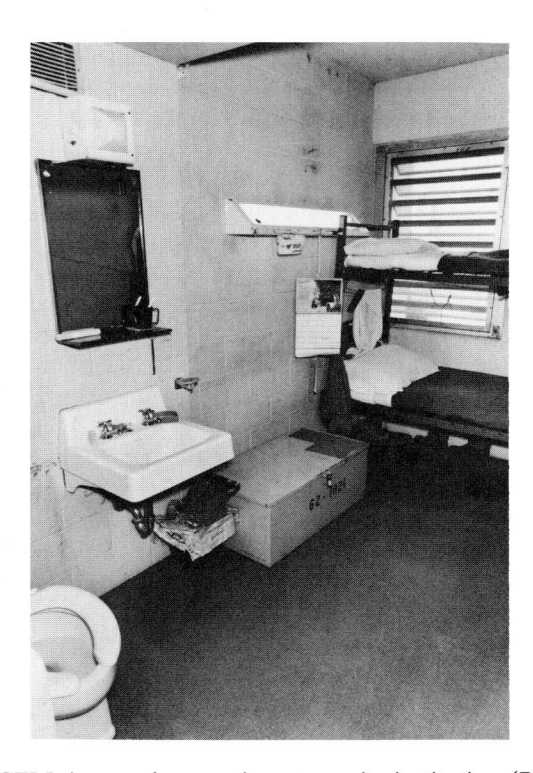

TWO-MAN CELL in a modern maximum security institution. (Photo courtesy of David H. Fauss)

predators have become rampant. Power is divided between the staff and the inmates with the institutions running on fear. The amount of power wielded by each of the two sources varies by prison and among areas of the same prison. The administration controls the perimeters of the institutions and the formal activities, but the inmates run the cells and public areas of the prisons. Gangs have replaced the "right guys"; they run freely in the open areas of the prisons and rule the yard. Prisons are dangerous places for inmates and guards alike.

The new prisons are ruled by the "cruel." "Convicts" are the most violent inmates who use power to obtain rewards and goods. Their power is derived from violence and toughness, and they consider all others potential victims. "Naturally, the extent prisoners are permitted (by officials) and encouraged (by their peers) to treat others in need with indifference and even contempt, the greater will be their willingness to victimize others when it suits their interests" (Johnson 1987, p. 63).

The most violent and dangerous inmates are those who were state-raised, "men reared on rejection and abuse in orphanages, detention centers, training schools and youth prisons" (Johnson 1987, p. 85). These men have become institutionalized. They have been in all-male institutions for such a large part of their lives that women have been replaced by "punks" and "queens" as sexual objects; sexual gratification is obtained by sexually assaulting men. Traumatized by the system, these men are brimming with hostility and anger and filled with impotent rage. These men particularly resent the guards, calling them "pigs" and looking for excuses to attack them. Johnson describes these violent men as "perpetual, impulsive adolescents." Like adolescents, they do not have control of their lives and cannot mature without control. Violence is their only method of proving their manhood and gaining respect—the ultimate respect is obtained by killing another inmate. These men are proud of their lack of feelings and emotion. They must kill to protect themselves and cannot depend on anyone. For this reason, the "main man" concept is now nonexistent. The number of men seeking protective custody has greatly increased as more inmates find shelter only in their cells. Even the "convicts" avoid the open areas.

An increase in the number of black inmates has added a racial tone to the violence. Many black inmates resent the white administrators and the predominantly white guards. With the destruction of the inmate code, men need to belong to racially segregated gangs in order to survive. The gang provides the only support and stability they have; Latin gangs are even referred to as "the Family." It is important to remember that most inmates are not members of gangs and that they try to avoid violence. However, the violent prisoners, those "who are least equipped for life in the civil world, set the tone of adjustment on the prison yard" (Johnson 1987, p. 89).

Prisoners

Life in prison is meant to be painful. "Virtually everyone agrees that incarceration is punishment. The inhumanity, arbitrariness, unjustness, and degradation that often accompany it can even go beyond punishment to subtle cruelty" (Humphrey & Milakovich 1981, p. 128). Prisons are not supposed to be comfortable, but they have become terrifying and intimidating places of violence. It is difficult for anyone to maintain a dignified life-style while in prison. JACK HENRY ABBOTT is a description of an inmate's life.

Separation from people in the community increases the loneliness and depression felt in prison. People in prison are isolated from their family and friends, which puts great strain on their relationships and limits their ties to the rest of the world. Often, people in prison are divorced by their spouses while incarcerated, leading to a severance of their ties to their children.

Most men avoid violence and do not get involved in the inmate culture. They just want to serve their sentences without being victimized. Many want to learn a trade or obtain an education and be law-abiding citizens when they get out. However, it is difficult for ex-offenders to get jobs and the recidivism rate remains about 33 percent. Despite the gloomy statistics, there is some hope. Age appears to be related to crime and to recidivism. As men age, they are less likely to commit crimes and go back to prison (Hoffman & Beck 1984). Research documents that rehabilitation does occur for a great many men in prison, and most inmates say they want to change. Robert Johnson (1987) reminds us that few inmates are

> **Box 12.3**
>
> **Jack Henry Abbott**
>
> Jack Henry Abbott spent most of his life in prison. He began his life behind bars at age 12 and, with the exception of 9 months of freedom, remained there. One 5-year sentence for cashing a check with insufficient funds was extended for up to 19 years when he murdered another inmate. During his incarceration, he was placed in solitary confinement for 5½ years. He used this time to educate himself until he became a "self-made intellectual."
>
> While in prison, Abbott read that Norman Mailer was writing a book about condemned murderer Gary Gilmore. Abbott contacted Mailer offering to explain life in prison. Mailer was so impressed with Abbott's letter that he engaged in a continued correspondence with him. The letters sent to Mailer were later used as the basis of the book, *In the Belly of the Beast.* Mailer, convinced of Abbott's writing talent, assisted in gaining him parole. Mailer states, in the foreword of Abbott's book, that "we may yet have a new writer of the largest stature among us" (p. xvi).
>
> Abbott was paroled in the summer of 1981. He was out of prison for less than 1 month when he was arrested and convicted in the fatal stabbing of a New York restaurant owner on July 20, 1981.

Source: J. H. Abbott, *In the Belly of the Beast* (New York: Random House, 1981).

first offenders; they were recidivists before incarceration. Thus, if only one in three goes back to prison, two-thirds are doing better than before they went to prison.

Types of Prisoners
The present-day prison is described as a "contained but turbulent ghetto" (Johnson 1987, p. 45). Prisoners act tough and manipulative, especially in the public areas of the prison. Their behavior is the same in prison as it is on the street, making the transition back to the outside world easy. Tough prisoners believe rules do not apply to them and that they are above the law. But these beliefs lead to behavior that soon returns them to prison. These tough inmates desperately want approval from their peer group, so they act in ways to impress them. They accomplish this by becoming hardened criminals and committing more crimes.

Institutionalized inmates adjust well to prison. They serve so much time that prison becomes a natural place for them to be. They do well materialistically in prison but do not adjust to the outside world. They feel secure in prison and often go back very quickly after their release. They appear to be model prisoners, but actually they are simply manipulating the system. Read A FORGED RELEASE to see how one man attempted to manipulate the system.

> **Box 12.4**
>
> **A Forged Release**
>
> The official-looking document entitled "Revocation of Sentence and Termination of Incarceration" which was sent to the Department of Corrections bore the return address of the sentencing judge. It also displayed both the stamp placed on legal documents in the Duval County Court Clerk's Office and the signature of Judge Hudson Olliff of Jacksonville. The document "Ordered and Adjudged . . . That the sentence imposed on the above cited cases has hereby been revoked, and . . . That the incarceration of the Defendant, MICHAEL V. HERNDON, is hereby terminated." But Herndon, serving a 15-year sentence for forgery, was not released. Although the document appeared authentic, an employee with the Department of Corrections became suspicious. She noticed that the form came from the "Fourt Judicial Circuit" and was a "defence" motion. Even Judge Olliff said the signature was his, but the name below the signature was misspelled.

Source: K. Stott, "Prison Release Form Forged," *The Florida Times-Union* (November 3, 1989), pp. A–1, A–6.

Most inmates do not fall into either of the categories: tough or institutionalized. They try to survive a dangerous and painful experience and leave others alone. The men who suffer the most are the ones who are chronic victims. They are psychologically destroyed by their prison experience.

Coping with Life in Prison

Toch (1977) identifies seven ecological dimensions of prisons that correspond to the needs of incarcerated men:

1. **Activity**: a concern about understimulation; a need for maximizing the opportunity to be occupied and to fill time; a need for distraction.
2. **Privacy**: a concern about social and physical overstimulation; a preference for isolation, peace and quiet, absence of environmental irritants such as noise and crowding.
3. **Safety**: a concern about one's physical safety; a preference for social and physical settings that provide protection and that minimize the chances of being attacked.
4. **Emotional feedback**: a concern about being loved, appreciated, and cared for; a desire for intimate relationships that provide emotional sustenance and empathy.
5. **Support**: a concern about reliable, tangible assistance from persons and settings, and about services that facilitate self-advancement and self-improvement.

6. **Structure**: a concern about environmental stability and predictability; a preference for consistency, clear-cut rules, orderly and scheduled events and impingements.
7. **Freedom**: a concern about circumscription of one's autonomy; a need for minimal restriction and for maximum opportunity to govern one's own conduct (Toch 1977, pp. 16–17).

Men vary in terms of these listed needs. For example, younger men tend to have more need for activity, freedom, and safety, while older men have more need for privacy. The ways in which these needs are satisfied vary by prison and within the same institution. Robert Johnson (1987) finds that men adjust to prison life by finding niches within the institution which fulfill their individual needs. These niches could be in a work setting, school, or living area. For example, a man might find that a job in the nursery will provide both privacy and safety. Or a man might satisfy his need for activity through athletics.

Finding a niche that corresponds to a man's needs helps him survive physically and psychologically while existing in a painful situation. If a man can find a niche, he can often avoid the convict culture. Men can adjust by pretending to live by the prison code in public while developing a very different private life within their niche. Different men need different types of niches and life-styles within the institution. Some inmates find it easier than others to find an appropriate niche or sanctuary, and some are unable ever to find a niche.

The highest priority, in terms of survival within an institution, is to find some type of protective relationship with one or two other men. In the violent institutions, individuals cannot survive alone. It also helps to join organizations. There are many groups within the prison: Jaycees, religious groups, AA, self-help groups, cultural groups, etc.

Experienced inmates advise newer ones to avoid crowds. They counsel them not to think about their sentences in terms of months or years, as those kinds of thoughts can be overwhelming. Instead, they advise a new prisoner to live as structured a life as possible, and to make every day as similar as possible to every other day. By living each day one at a time, the days fade together and seem to go faster. Experienced prisoners recommend going through each day like a robot without thinking about time. THE REVOLVING DOOR describes one inmate's methods for coping with prison life.

The most vulnerable men in prison are the young and inexperienced. This is particularly true if they are the least bit effeminate. These are the men who become the sexual targets of the hardened convicts. It is very difficult for these men to find a niche. It is almost impossible for them to find safety unless they elect to be put in protective segregation. Many institutions have whole areas of isolation cells for the protection of threatened or frightened men. Unfortunately, these men have to give up their other coping methods while in segregation, and they will probably have to stay in segregation for their whole sentence. While in segregation, they must forfeit their freedom and any participation in programs or sports. Segregation can lead to severe psychological trauma. But many men elect to have safety and privacy in exchange for freedom.

> **Box 12.5**
>
> **The Revolving Door**
>
> "I know what I am. I'm a convict and nothing the state can do can make me change, because I know I got the better go. I've got something that most guys, especially the Joe Squares, don't have. I've got hope! I've got the streets, and I'm going out there again. I've got something to look forward to. Joe Square has the rut, the routine, and there's no hope for him. When I get out there again, I can make up for everything that's happening to me now. I'll be free, free to live the way I want and to do what I want. I know Joe Square can't make that statement. I can shoot dope, steal, rob, pimp whores. I can live as fast and as good as I want. And when they nail me again, I can come back "home" for a vacation and wait it out until the next time. But I'll always have the knowledge that I'll get out again, and again, and again. So I can do the time they give me, this time and the next time. The judge who gave me this jolt thought he was hurting me, but he doesn't know that I'll live to piss on his grave.
>
> So I'll get up this morning, like every other morning, and I'll go through the routine, because the routine is what saves me. The days are all the same. Each one exactly like the one preceding it and like the one following it. They're all the same—just a blur—and looking back a year ago when I got this jolt, it seems like only yesterday because yesterday was just like it was a year ago."

Source: A. J. Manocchio and J. Dunn, *The Time Game: Two Views of a Prison* (Beverly Hills, Calif.: Sage, 1970), p. 33.

Mature Coping Methods

Most prisoners find prison life painful and difficult. Not only are they not rehabilitated, most are worse off after serving time. Robert Johnson (1987) maintains that inmates do poorly because their coping is immature and destructive. But he contends men do not need to be worse off when released than when first incarcerated. People can adjust in mature ways and be rehabilitated if prisons provide constructively painful living conditions. Correctional staff and programs can assist prisoners in their efforts at coping and rehabilitation. Johnson defines mature coping in prison as "(1) Dealing directly with one's problems using the resources legitimately at one's disposal; (2) refusing to employ deceit or violence (other than in self-defense); and (3) building mutual and supportive relationships with others" (1987, pp. 4–5).

Problems found in prison are often quite similar to those faced in the outside world, particularly the world of the ghetto. The harshness and deprivations of life in the ghetto are intensified and amplified in prisons. Both slum streets and prison yards are places for manipulation. Everyone is a potential victim of exploitation, even friends are not immune. Both victim and manipulator are less able to function in the real world after prison. One is less sensitive and more aggressive; the other is weaker and more vulnerable. "Virtually all chronic felons

SEGREGATION. Men held in isolation or segregation communicate through small openings in the cell doors. These openings allow for food trays to be passed to the inmates. (Photo courtesy of David H. Fauss)

experience degenerating relations with friends and family (who may too often double as victims), failed work careers and downward social mobility (which add to pressures to prey on others), and a haunting sense that theirs is a pointless, dead-end existence" (Johnson 1987, p. 58).

In order to cope with prison life, inmates need to develop assertiveness, a sense of personal efficacy, and internal locus of control. Life in prison is conducive to introspection. Mature coping is found in prison, but it is quite difficult because there are constraints on methods of adjustment. However, these constraints also work against self-destructive behaviors such as alcoholism or spouse or child abuse. Saying there are constraints on alcoholism does not imply drugs and alcohol are not available in prison—they are. However, men are not free to sit in their cells all day and drink or take drugs.

Johnson contends that mature coping is the basis for rehabilitation. "Prison citizenship can serve as a rehearsal for citizenship in other harsh environments, most notably the low-income, high-crime (and distinctly prisonlike) milieus from which most prisoners are drawn and to which the vast majority of them will return" (1987, p. 6). The need for reforms in prison rehabilitation becomes apparent when the statistics are considered. *One in every twenty males will spend some time in prison.*

The Death Penalty

During the Middle Ages, people in western Europe were very religious, and they tended to impose supernatural causes on any unusual event or behavior. A behavior that was either unusually good or unusually bad was thought to have been caused by a supernatural power—God or the devil. Thus, people who committed sins or crimes were thought to have been motivated by the devil. In order to eliminate the devil's influence in the community, people who committed these offenses had to be removed from the area, either through banishment or execution.

Society was very harsh on criminals. Offenders received some form of harsh physical punishment: exile, torture, mutilation, branding, flogging, execution, or slavery. Physical punishment, torture, or banishment was the typical result of any violation of the mores of society.

Execution was a common form of punishment for what were considered serious offenses. At the end of the 17th century, there were fifty crimes for which death was the penalty. More and more offenses were considered worthy of the death penalty. The seriousness of the offense for which death was imposed varied from treason and heresy to adultery, witchcraft, and swearing (Fox 1972). In England, the number of crimes for which execution was the punishment reached a peak of 350 in the late 1700s. After that time, the number of death penalty crimes in England decreased steadily until by the 1860s there were only four (Carter, Glaser & Wilkins 1972). The death penalty is no longer used in Great Britain.

Society was also harsh in the imposition of the death penalty. Execution was not administered in the rather antiseptic manner in which it is administered today. It was not imposed in an isolated area of an isolated prison. People were executed in public, and there was no attempt to make the execution a humane event for the offender or for the witnesses. Death was imposed in innumerable grotesque ways: drawing and quartering, boiling in oil, burning at the stake, and guillotining, to name a few. Even though harsh torture and inhumane forms of execution are not a part of modern corrections, punishment still is a major motivation in the treatment of offenders.

Since the 19th century, there has been a continual decline in the use of the death penalty in Western democracies. "Nearly every European nation has either formally abolished the death penalty for civil crimes or has abandoned it in practice" (Zimring & Hawkins 1986, p. 1).

The death penalty was abolished for a short time in the United States. In 1972, the U.S. Supreme Court ruled (*Furman v. Georgia*) that capital punishment, under the then-existing statutes, was imposed in an arbitrary and standardless manner. The death penalty thereby violated the Eighth Amendment, which prohibits cruel and unusual punishment. All nine of the Supreme Court justices issued independent opinions in the *Furman* decision. These separate decisions took into account studies that related the imposition of the death penalty to the race of the offender (Riedel 1976).

Racial discrimination has been particularly evident in the imposition of the death penalty. Between 1930 and 1975, 3,859 persons were executed in the United States. Of those, 2,066 (53.5 percent) were black (Criminal Justice Research Center, 1978). Of the 455 men executed for rape, 89 percent were black. During that same time period, about 10 to 11 percent of the population of the United States was black (U.S. Bureau of Census, 1979).

The Supreme Court's ruling in *Furman v. Georgia* was influenced primarily by consideration of racial discrimination. However, the sex of the offender has also influenced the imposition of the death penalty. Of the 3,859 persons executed in the United States between 1930 and 1975, only 32 (.8 percent) were women (Criminal Justice Research Center, 1978). In contrast, during that period, women committed approximately 15 percent of the homicides (FBI Uniform Crime Report, 1976).

The *Furman* decision stated that a state law that provides a choice between death and imprisonment must have guidelines for making the determination. This decision, in effect, overturned the death penalty for cases tried on the basis of statutes existing prior to 1972. Florida, Georgia, and Texas responded to the *Furman* decision by enacting new legislation that conformed to the Supreme Court ruling. The Supreme Court reviewed these statutes in 1976. In a series of decisions (*Profitt v. Florida, Gregg v. Georgia,* and *Jurek v. Texas*), the Supreme Court ruled that states having guided discretion statutes could enact the death penalty (Paternoster 1984). In the 1976 decisions, the Supreme Court "did not even examine whether the new death sentences would constitute cruel and unusual punishment if applied discriminatorily, thus bypassing the ground of the 1972 decision" (National Council of Crime and Delinquency, 1978, p. 29).

Since the 1972 *Furman* decision, thirty-six states have reinstituted the death penalty. Between 1976 and the end of 1989, 3,746 people were sentenced to death and 120 people were executed. During the same time period, 1,376 people were removed from death row for a variety of reasons: retrial, death by means other than execution (e.g., from natural causes or suicide), resentencing, or commuted sentence. Of the persons under the death penalty at the end of 1989, 1,310 (58.2 percent) were white, 903 (40.1 percent) were black, 23 (1 percent) were American Indian, 14 (.6 percent) were Asian, and 25 (1.1 percent) were female (Bureau of Justice Statistics, 1990).

The Bureau of Justice Statistics reports that "a total of thirteen states have carried out executions since 1977. During the period, 70 white males, 41 black males, and 1 white female have been executed. The largest number of executions occurred in Texas (33), Florida (21), Louisiana (18), and Georgia (14)" (1990, p. 8).

The effectiveness of the *Furman* decision in eliminating discrimination in the imposition of the death penalty has been the focus of continued debate in legal circles. Research conducted in the South since the *Furman* decision still finds people accused of killing whites much more likely to be indicted for a capital homicide than those accused of killing blacks (Paternoster 1984). Foley and Powell (1982) examined the effects of the race and sex of the defendant and the victim

By permission of Johnny Hart and Creators Syndicate, Inc.

on the processing of capital offense charges in Florida between 1972 and 1978. The judicial treatment of the offenders was traced from their indictment for first-degree murder through the trial to their final sentencing. The study looked at the effect of legal and extralegal variables on the trial outcome, conviction offense, and sentence. The data indicate extralegal factors impinge on all three of the legal events examined. The age and sex of the defendant, the race of the victim, and the county where the trial was held all impacted the results. These variables affect the outcome even when other legal and extralegal variables are statistically controlled. The results indicate that Florida's post-*Furman* statute has been unsuccessful in eliminating differential treatment of offenders from the imposition of the death penalty. In each step of the judicial process, there is evidence that offenders are treated differentially based on extralegal factors.

On April 22, 1987, the United States Supreme Court ruled in *McCleskey v. Kemp* that state death penalty statutes are constitutional even if statistics indicate that the laws are carried out in a racially disproportionate manner. However, the Supreme Court has not overturned its 1972 decision contending that the imposition of the death penalty must be sufficiently controlled in order to avoid arbitrariness and discrimination (Davis 1978).

On September 6, 1991, a white person was executed for killing a black person. David Gaskins was put to death in South Carolina for the killing of Rudolph Tyner. Gaskins was serving time for nine murders and was suspected of others when he killed a fellow inmate, also in prison for murder. The son of one of Tyner's victims had hired Gaskins to commit the murder. Gaskins's execution was the first since 1944 in which the death penalty was imposed on a white for killing a black (Margolick 1991).

Summary

Arguments in favor of punishment as a deterrent are based on the assumption that people will not commit crimes if the punishment is very severe. However, most criminals do not believe they will be caught, so they do not worry about being punished. And they are right; the likelihood of any offender being caught and punished is very slim.

Present-day prisons are dangerous, violent, and overcrowded. Incarceration is generally considered ineffective, and many experts believe it actually corrupts those confined. The primary goal of a prison is security. But prisons also have a number of functions: specific deterrence, general deterrence, incapacitation, retribution, and rehabilitation.

Penitentiaries, developed as a means of changing criminal behavior, evolved into less physically and psychologically abusive places, big houses, but maintained their oppressiveness. Present-day prisons, renamed correctional institutions, are much more unstable and violent than the penitentiaries and big houses were. Power is divided between the staff and the inmates, leading the institutions to run on fear.

Toch (1977) identifies seven ecological dimensions of prisons that correspond to the needs of incarcerated men: activity, privacy, safety, emotional feedback, support, structure, and freedom. Men adjust to prison life by finding niches within the institution which fulfill their individual needs.

During the Middle Ages, people in western Europe were very harsh on criminals. Execution, slavery, physical punishment, torture, or banishment were the typical result of any violation of the mores of society. Since the 19th century, there has been a continual decline in the use of the death penalty in Western democracies.

In *Furman v. Georgia* (1972), the U.S. Supreme Court abolished the death penalty imposed under then-existing statutes. A series of Supreme Court decisions in 1976 (*Profitt v. Florida, Gregg v. Georgia,* and *Jurek v. Texas*) allowed states with guided discretion statutes to enact the death penalty in cases tried under new statutes (Paternoster 1984). Since the *Furman* decision in 1972, thirty-six states have reinstituted the death penalty.

There has been a continual debate in legal circles as to the effectiveness of the *Furman* decision in eliminating discrimination in the imposition of the death penalty. Research conducted in the South since the *Furman* decision still finds people who are accused of killing whites much more likely to be indicted for a capital homicide than those accused of killing blacks. On April 22, 1987, the United States Supreme Court ruled in *McCleskey v. Kemp* that state death penalty statutes are constitutional even if statistics indicate the laws are carried out in a racially disproportionate manner. In September, 1991, a white man was executed for killing a black man for the first time since 1944.

13

Family Law

Marriage and Dissolution
Marriage
Cohabitation and the Law
Dissolution of Marriage
Spousal and Child Support
Children of Divorce
Child Custody
Visitation
Relitigation
Impact of Divorce on Children
Summary

Marriage and Dissolution

Marriage

Until the middle of the 18th century, marriage was the only career opportunity open to a middle-class woman. It was virtually impossible for her to obtain an education or learn marketable skills, which eliminated the possibility of getting a job. She needed a husband to support her. The woman's part of the bargain was to provide sexual favors and keep the house. If the wife had to work, the law required her to get her husband's permission and give all her earnings to him. Without skills or education, her job possibilities were limited to those which paid a pittance.

Traditional Marriages

Lenore Weitzman (1985) enumerates five central principles of the traditional marriage. First, **roles and responsibilities** were divided on the basis of gender. The family had a **patriarchal structure;** in other words, the husband was in charge of the family. The wife became a "legal nonperson"; she assumed the name and identity of her husband. There was a **moral underpinning** to marriage, which was considered to be a **lifelong commitment.** Marriage was a **partnership,** a joint enterprise, whereby the partners performed their gender-appropriate roles and shared in the benefits of each other's endeavors.

As the previous paragraphs illustrate, women had no rights in a marriage. Women were considered the property of their husbands, who had the legal right to beat their wives. Although these marital restrictions on women sound like ancient history, many continued until quite recently. Until 1951, a wife's separate earnings were under the exclusive control of her husband in California. Even after that year, they were under the husband's exclusive control if she "commingled" the funds. In other words, if a husband and wife had a joint bank account, the husband had exclusive control of it, even if the wife earned most of the money.

As recently as 1971, a man living in California could sell, mortgage, or transfer community property without telling his wife, let alone getting her permission. The husband had the legal right to decide where the couple lived, and the wife had no right to disagree. This right of a husband was not unique to California. More than one-third of the states still considered the husband's place of residence as the legal domicile of the couple. Women, until quite recently, were required to take their husband's name in marriage. Riane Eisler (1977) gives a number of examples of women who were deprived of their rights because they did not take their husbands' names. In the mid-1940s, one woman in Illinois was not allowed to vote because she registered in her own name and not her husband's name. A 1926 case in Massachusetts prohibited a woman from collecting damages for injuries received in a car accident because the car was not registered in her married name. In 1934, a woman was deprived of citizenship papers because she used her maiden name. This woman was a professional musician who continued to use her professional name after her marriage. Up until the 1970s, most states would not allow women to take back their birth names after a divorce if they had minor children.

Modern Marriage Laws

The mid-1970s saw the advent of some changes in the legal implications of marriage which alleviated some of the inequality of males and females. California gave both partners equal control over community property, and both members now have to agree to the sale, lease, or mortgage of community property. The majority of women still take their husband's name in marriage, but now most states allow the woman (and the man) to use a hyphenated name combining both of their names or to keep their original names. This is referred to as a "common-law" name change (Sack 1987). Women have seen great gains also in the financial arena with the enactment of the Equal Credit Opportunity Act. Prior to that law, women could have no separate credit after marriage, only their husband's. This restriction made life very difficult financially for women after a divorce.

Laws Related to Marriage

Marriages are regulated by state laws which designate, among other things, the minimum age of the couple and a waiting period. Prior to marriage, the couple must obtain a marriage license and, in some states, take a blood test to determine if they have syphilis. Two states (Louisiana and Illinois) enacted laws requiring potential newlyweds to be screened for AIDS, but these statutes were repealed within 6 months in both states (Landers 1989). See LOVE DOES NOT CONQUER ALL for a description of the problems facing some modern couples.

State laws also address very personal areas of marriage. For example, married women are expected to have sexual relations with their husbands, but many states have recently made it illegal for a husband to rape his wife. Other intimate areas of marital life that have been legislated include family planning. Women have the right to use birth control methods, but their right to have an abortion is still a hotly contested area. The U.S. Supreme Court recently gave power to the states to regulate abortions in *Webster v. Reproductive Health Services* (1988). The woman does not have a right to an abortion after 6 months of pregnancy (Sack 1987). Courts are still battling over the rights of a father to prevent an abortion. In addition to these laws, adultery is illegal in many states. It is against the law for a married person in these states to have sexual relations with a person other than the marital partner.

Cohabitation and the Law

Cohabitation by two opposite sex, unmarried people who are unrelated used to be a crime in every state. Laws concerning cohabitation have relaxed somewhat, and now these laws vary by state. The major legal concern with cohabitation occurs if the couple separates or one member dies. What happens to the joint property? In some states, if a person dies intestate (without a will), all of his or her property goes to the next of kin, not the person with whom that person was

> **Box 13.1**
>
> **Love Does Not Conquer All**
>
> Reece Sloan found Cindy McClellan's name in a publication by Date-Connection. Seeing that they had many common interests, he called her and they began dating. The couple quickly became very close. Both were adopted. Reece knew who his father was and Cindy had hired a private investigator to locate her biological parents. After they had been dating for about 5 months, the private investigator called to give Cindy the identity of her father. The name was somewhat familiar, but it was awhile before she put it together. She and Reece had more in common than they thought—they had the same biological father, Cecil Deardorf. The couple were stunned and saddened to discover that each had fallen in love with a half sibling. They found it difficult to shift from a romantic relationship to a platonic one.
>
> ◆
>
> As surrogate parenting and artificial insemination become more common, the problem faced by Reece and Cindy will become more frequent also. There are many biological reasons why persons who are closely related should not have children. What happens in the case of people who do not realize that they are related?

Source: "Couple Learns Their Love Runs in the Family," *The Florida Times-Union* (May 13, 1988), p. A–5.

living. Most states do not have laws pertaining to unmarried couples living together. Therefore, there are no bases for dividing property unless there is a written contract. Some states will honor only written agreements between cohabitants, while others will honor oral agreements as well. Still other states will not acknowledge any agreement between unmarried persons who cohabit. Read STAR-CROSSED LOVERS for a description of the legal problems of two people who cohabited.

Dissolution of Marriage

Marriage is "an agreement between a man and a woman who love one another to spend the rest of their lives together as husband and wife" (Sack 1987, p. 56). While that definition reflects the traditional view of marriage, the well-publicized increase in divorce rates has altered the public perception of the projected longevity of marriages. But not every new bride and groom are cynical about marriage. While newlyweds no longer naively believe every marriage will last forever, many still believe their marriage will. And most marriages at least begin with the man and woman loving each other.

Divorce laws vary by state in terms of grounds but have followed a trend in which the focus in dissolution cases has shifted from contention over the divorce itself to conflict over how to divide economic resources. Many states now have "no fault" divorces. Some states currently allow marriages to be dissolved on the basis of "incompatibility," "irreconcilable conflict," "breakdown of the marriage," or "irretrievable marital breakdown." One state allows an uncontested divorce by registration; no one even has to go to court. Other states still have stringent criteria for divorce, maintaining that the individual filing for divorce must prove adultery or, in other states, the parties must live apart for a specified length of time (some require as much as 3 years) (Sack 1987).

Separation
A separation is an agreement by two married people to remain married but live apart. The agreement is prepared by attorneys for the two parties and a decree is issued through the court. This settlement usually specifies support, custody of the children, and property procedures. Some states only require a couple to live apart for a specified length of time in order to get a legal separation. Other states require the couple to have grounds for a separation (Sack 1987).

A separation allows the parties to adjust to a divorce. But there are disadvantages to a legal separation: if the couple eventually divorce, they have twice the legal expenses, a nonworking spouse does not receive property distribution, and both parties still have the legal obligations of marriage.

Annulment
If persons get married when they are not free and able to do so, the marriage can be annulled. An annulment declares a marriage void, that it never took place in proper form. If one or both of the partners is too young to marry legally, already married, or concealed some important information from the partner (for example, an illness or an inability to have sex or children), the marriage can be annulled. Some people prefer an annulment to a divorce because of religious beliefs or the social stigma attached to divorce.

History of Divorce
The legal origins of divorce in the United States are found in Great Britain, where laws were closely bound to Christianity and its view of marriage. Marriage was considered a sacrament in which a man and woman were wed for life. A divorce had to be obtained from the ecclesiastical courts. The only acceptable grounds for divorce were adultery, cruelty, or unnatural practices, and the person receiving the divorce could not remarry (Eisler 1977). Beginning in the 17th century, after Henry VIII's argument and break with the Pope over divorce, a divorce could be granted by an act of Parliament, which of course had to have royal assent. This requirement led to some unusual and rather amusing acts of Parliament. For example, Parliament might pass a law to incorporate a city and tack on someone's divorce.

In England and Wales, the Matrimonial Causes Act of 1857 changed jurisdiction for divorce from the religious to the legal system. Laws governing divorce originally were designed to punish people who broke their vows while rewarding those who would abide by them. The only grounds for divorce was adultery. Divorce was rare and still available only for the wealthy, which meant it was really primarily available for men.

Box 13.2

Star-Crossed Lovers

Karen Thompson grew up in the family-oriented area of northern Minnesota. Like her friends, she expected to marry young and raise a family and could not understand why she never seemed to find the right man. She immersed herself in the job she held as a physical education professor at the state university in St. Cloud. One of Karen's former students, Sharon Kowalski, assisted with teaching track. Sharon also grew up in conservative and religious northern Minnesota. She was an athletic and willful young woman who worked as a teacher.

The two women became good friends. Then the friendship evolved into a much deeper relationship, and Karen was shocked to find that she had fallen in love with a woman. The love was mutual and after 2 years Karen Thompson and Sharon Kowalski "married" each other in a personal ceremony in which they exchanged rings. They moved in together but meticulously hid their relationship, even from their families. Because they lived in a conservative area where homosexuality was looked upon as sinful, even criminal, they were concerned about losing their jobs.

After four happy years together, everything suddenly changed. In 1983, Sharon was hit by a drunk driver who swerved into her lane (for more information on drunk drivers, see MADD in Chapter 5). Sharon was in a coma for 5 months and suffered severe brain damage. When she came out of the coma, Sharon was a quadriplegic, unable to speak, and only able to move her right hand. However, Karen worked untiringly with her lover, teaching her to communicate with a letter board and typewriter.

But while Karen worked with Sharon to help her recover and communicate, Sharon's parents viewed her as an incapable infant in diapers. Donald Kowalski, Sharon's father, was described by Sharon's neurologist as visiting as if he were visiting a funeral home to show respect for a corpse. Eventually, conflict developed between Karen and the Kowalski family. Donald Kowalski told Karen that if she did not let the family have some time alone with Sharon, he would not allow her to visit.

Horrified that she would not be allowed to visit Sharon, Karen wrote to the Kowalskis, telling them that she and Sharon were lovers. The Kowalskis refused

(continued)

to believe that their daughter was involved in a lesbian relationship. They insisted that since she did not tell them about the relationship, it did not exist.

The year after the accident, Donald Kowalski began procedures to move Sharon 200 miles away from Karen. Karen asked the court to name her custodian of Sharon. She lost her case but was allowed visitation rights. Donald Kowalski did not want Karen to visit his daughter and returned to court. The case was taken to court twenty times in 5 years. Kowalski maintained that there was no lesbian relationship between Karen and Sharon and that Karen might sexually molest his daughter. Sharon's father described his daughter as incapable of making decisions such that she was not allowed to testify, even though Jan Goldman of the Minnesota Civil Liberties Union interviewed her and found her completely lucid. Communication was slow with Sharon using the typewriter; however, Sharon told Goldman that she and Karen loved each other and had a gay relationship.

Despite the attempts by the MCLU and Karen, Donald Kowalski was given total custody of his daughter on July 25, 1985. It took him less than 24 hours to bar Karen from visiting his daughter. He moved Sharon to a nursing home in northern Minnesota where he restricted visitors and censored her mail.

Karen decided to take her story to the public in an attempt to raise funds to continue the court battle over her lover. Karen contended that Sharon was not receiving rehabilitation which would help restore some of her functioning. Early in 1989, the courts finally gave Sharon the right to choose her own visitors, and Karen was allowed to visit again. However, the case was far from closed. Doctors planned to reevaluate Sharon's competence and report back to the judge. Once again, the court would decide what it thinks is best for Sharon Kowalski.

In 1991, the courts finally gave custody of Sharon to Karen.

♦

There are many issues highlighted by this case. The rights of unmarried lovers, parents, and the handicapped come in conflict in this sad situation. Should lesbian and homosexual couples be allowed to marry? Should they inform their parents in order to avoid this type of controversy? Should handicapped people be allowed to testify as to whom they would like as guardian? Do handicapped people have the right to decide on their visitors? Do handicapped people have the right to rehabilitation?

Sources: N. Brozan, "Gay Groups Are Rallied to Aid Two Women's Fight," *New York Times* (August 7, 1988), p. 26; N. R. Gibbs, "Tragic Tug-of-War," *Time* (August 22, 1988), p. 71; J. Linsley, "Courts Separate Lesbian Couple," *The Progressive* (July 19, 1986), pp. 15–16.

U.S. laws governing marriage and its dissolution usually were secular. Many states had no provisions for divorce. Although states that did allow divorce varied in legal requirements, all had very restrictive grounds. Lenore Weitzman isolates "four major elements of traditional divorce laws: fault-based grounds, one party's guilt, the continuation of gender-based marital responsibilities after divorce, and the linkage of financial awards to findings of fault" (1985, p. 7). These characteristics were in effect throughout the United States by the beginning of the 20th century. Grounds for divorce varied by state but were generally limited to adultery, cruelty, or desertion. Alimony was awarded only to an "innocent" wife as punishment of a guilty husband. Many states would not grant a divorce if the person filing the divorce was also found to be at fault. Therefore, if a wife filed for a divorce because her husband beat her and he said she did not iron his clothes, the judge could not grant a divorce.

Typically what happened was that the couple agreed on a divorce and then made up the most innocuous fault acceptable; for example, the wife was a poor cook or the husband would not repair the house. Usually the wife filed the case and, as a form of chivalry, the man admitted guilt. Even if the spouse agreed he was at fault, the parties had to have witnesses to corroborate the case. This led to a farce of the courts with all parties, including lawyers and judges, playing into it.

No Fault Divorce

In 1970, California passed the first "no fault" law for divorce. With this new law, no grounds were necessary for divorce and fault no longer had to be proven. Therefore, fault was not tied to the financial outcome. The sexes were treated equally, and one spouse could get a divorce without the consent of the other. The purpose of this system was to eliminate the adversarial aspects of the divorce. By 1985, all states except South Dakota had no fault divorce laws, with most of them following many of the provisions of the California law. The same trend is apparent throughout the rest of the Western world (Weitzman 1985).

Dissolution Litigation

Litigation for a divorce is not composed of a single trial with a judge and jury deciding the outcome. There are many months of negotiation and litigation, requests for temporary orders, negotiations between attorneys, filed motions, and *ex parte* hearings. There are also investigations and a proliferation of documents. Typically, there is a preliminary hearing to resolve pressing problems such as child custody and support. The actual trial is usually quite short. For example, the average uncontested divorce trial in Connecticut was found to take about 4 minutes (Wheeler 1980).

One would assume that a friendly, uncontested divorce could be handled by a single lawyer acting for both parties, but the bar associations in many states have ethical codes prohibiting the same attorney from representing both sides. Read A SIMPLE NO FAULT DIVORCE? for an account of one complicated divorce.

> **Box 13.3**
>
> **A Simple No-Fault Divorce?**
>
> After 9 years of marriage, Junior Davis, 30, expected a simple no fault divorce from his wife, Mary Sue, 28. Instead, the childless couple are involved in a heated custody battle—over seven fertilized eggs held in cold storage at the Fort Sanders Regional Medical Center in Knoxville, Tennessee. The eggs were taken from Mary Sue and fertilized with semen from Junior at the fertility clinic 6 years previously, when the couple found they were unable to have children. Several other eggs, fertilized at the same time, were implanted in Mary Sue's uterus. However, these attempts at impregnation were unsuccessful.
>
> Then the Davises began the process of a divorce. Mary Sue could not have children unless fertilized eggs were implanted in her uterus. She wanted custody of the eggs to ensure the opportunity of bearing children in the future. Junior did not want to be forced into fatherhood after a divorce. Despite Mary Sue's willingness to forego child support from Junior, he would be legally liable to support a child born from those eggs.

Source: "Future Shock," *Time* (March 27, 1989), p. 42.

Although it is not required by law, most people use attorneys to handle their divorces. There are law manuals available from libraries to assist parties in the preparation of a divorce. There are also "do-it-yourself" kits available in some locations. Often, the local bar opposes self-help kits and has had them banned in some states. Although the court procedures are confusing, if the divorce is uncontested and friendly, most people can probably handle their own divorce (Wheeler 1980).

People criticize attorneys for adding to the conflict in divorce and often maintain that the attorney could help resolve the conflict and perhaps save the marriage. But a lawyer is in a touchy situation. If he or she advises reconciliation, it could be interpreted as meddling. The client is, after all, an adult who is seeking legal services. It can be assumed that the decision was not made lightly or without first exploring other options. In any event, lawyers are not trained in counseling and are not capable of deciding which marriages can and cannot be saved. In addition, ethical codes in some states prohibit attorneys from working in the same practice as a marriage counselor.

Spousal and Child Support

Financial support of a spouse now works for both sexes. Since the advent of no fault divorce, there has been a trend toward lower and shorter maintenance (formerly called alimony), with a higher cash settlement. There is also a trend to encourage a nonworking spouse to be retrained and go to work, a policy called "rehabilitative maintenance." Some states do not give maintenance to a nonworking spouse who caused the divorce, and many states will discontinue maintenance if the supported spouse cohabits with someone else. Spousal support is paid in very few cases (6 to 7 percent) (Wheeler 1980).

If so few women receive alimony, why do so many men complain about paying it? This confusion is due to a misuse of terms. Child support is paid to the custodial parent, usually the mother, and the noncustodial parent, usually the father, often views it as supporting his ex-spouse; that is, paying alimony.

Economic Impact of Divorce

There is general consensus that many women and children become impoverished after a divorce. Within 1 year of a divorce, men average a 42 percent increase in their standard of living, while women and children average a 73 percent decline in their standard of living (Weitzman 1985). Why does this happen? Assume a family has two children and the mother stays home to care for them. During a divorce, the settlement calls for the father to support the children. Typically, he is ordered to pay about 13 to 25 percent of his salary toward the support. Now, you have one member of the family living on 75 to 87 percent of the former family income and three members living on the remaining 13 to 25 percent.

The Office of Child Support Enforcement (1984) estimates that 15,000,000 children live in homes without fathers. Almost one-third of these children live in poverty. About 35 percent of these households receive some amount of child support.

The vast majority of divorced women work. However, women still earn only about 60 to 70 percent of what men earn, and often a divorced woman is entering the work force for the first time or reentering it after some time away from her career. Thus, her salary tends to be even lower than the average career woman's salary. Divorced women's earnings are so low that most cannot afford the necessities of life. The difference in income tends to be much more drastic for older women and women who were married longer, and they are unlikely to catch up through jobs and retraining because they are older, have no marketable skills, and no recent work experience (Weitzman 1985).

Women who have been married to men in the highest income brackets tend to have the biggest discrepancy in standard of living after a divorce. These women have less potential for earning the incomes their ex-husbands have achieved over years of business or professional experience. Mothers with small children also suffer tremendous financial hardships. They are unable to devote the time to education or career that would enable them to earn large salaries. Some women are able to move out of poverty through extreme effort, increased education, better jobs, or by remarrying. But the short period of time spent in poverty does not decrease its impact.

If the family has small children, they place restrictions on the woman's job opportunities. After a divorce, small children are an added liability to a woman's career. She has to consider the children when asked to work overtime or relocate, travel, etc. At a time when she has less time to devote to the care of the family and home, she also has fewer resources to hire help. She has added expenses of babysitters or childcare to be taken from her smaller income (Weitzman 1985).

Division of Property
No fault divorce laws typically require the equal division of property. If the only asset the couple has is their house, it must be divided. Since few divorcing people can afford to buy their partner's share in the house, it must be sold to be divided. However, this forced sale of homes is unfair to the children and the custodial parent. Prior to the no fault divorce laws, the home typically went to the wife, the "innocent party." Then the children were able to stay in the family home and be kept in a stable atmosphere. Since the advent of no fault divorce, a large percentage of homes must be sold. The existence of minor children appears to have no effect on the decision to force the sale of the home (Weitzman 1985).

Community Property, Equitable Distribution, and Common-Law States
Community property is a concept that grew out of the French and Spanish colonies. States with community property laws (nine states) view marriage as a community and maintain that everything acquired during the marriage belongs equally to both partners, no matter whose name is on the property. Property, therefore, is divided equally upon divorce. Most states are "equitable distribution" states. In these states, the judge divides the property equitably between the partners while considering things such as: the length of marriage, age and health of the partners, standard of living, contribution to acquisition and maintenance of property, earning potential, contribution of homemaking, marketable skills, and the custodial parent's need to work or stay with children. Common-law states (there are three) maintain that anything one earned during the marriage belongs to that person. The example Steven Sack (1987) gives is of a man who bought a house in his wife's name. Upon divorce, the house was entirely hers. There is a trend to change these common laws.

Intangible Assets
Weitzman found that "over 60 percent of divorcing couples have less than $20,000 in total assets" (1985, p. 68). Fewer than half of these couples owned their own home or were in the process of purchasing one. This author maintains that most divorcing couples have invested in other types of assets—careers and earning capacity. Most couples can earn the equivalent of their assets in 6 months. The intangible assets should be divided when considering maintenance and child support. Marriage, even today when a number of married women work, is a disadvantage to a woman's career. Women tend to subordinate their careers to their husband's career and put their families first. Therefore, at the time of divorce, the man is further along in his career and has a larger salary and greater earning capacity. Robert Weiss (1984) and Thomas Espenshade (1979) document the discrepancy in income for divorced men and women.

The definition of assets is rapidly changing. Women are requesting a division of their ex-husbands' pensions, medical insurance, professional degrees, professional practices, businesses, and other income-producing assets. Judges are beginning to recognize these intangible assets and differential earning power.

Court-Ordered Child Support

Most judges view equality as each parent having equal responsibility for the support of the children without reference to an unequal ability to earn. Judges are reluctant to require the supporting spouse (usually the father) to pay a very large percentage of his salary toward child support. Their rationale is that if they order the father to pay too much in child support, the father will lose his incentive and not pay anything. Weitzman (1985) contends that judges are more concerned with the father's life-style and his right to start life anew than with the proper support of the children. The children get what is left after the father is first considered.

Payment of Child Support

Despite the inadequacy of child support awards, compliance with support orders is incredibly low. Studies indicate that fewer than half the mothers receive the amount of child support ordered by the courts (Freed & Foster 1984). A Wisconsin study found that only 38 percent of the fathers paid the amount of child support ordered by the courts. Another 20 percent paid some of the award, while 42 percent of the fathers paid none. In addition, noncompliance appears to get worse with time. Seven years after the divorce, only 17 percent of the fathers paid all the child support, while 71 percent ignored the court order. Wheeler (1980) maintains that these compliance rates are comparable to those throughout the United States.

Children of Divorce

Divorce is a very unpleasant experience for the couple involved, but they are adults and usually at least one of them has decided divorce is the only viable solution to an unhappy marriage. The ones who suffer without having had any "fault" in the conflict or control over it are the children. Over 2,000,000 children suffer through the divorces of their parents every year in the United States (U.S. Bureau of the Census, 1983). This number tripled between 1960 and 1980 even though the number of children decreased in those years. Experts estimate that from one-half to two-thirds of the children in the United States will undergo the traumatic experience of having their parents separate or divorce before they reach the age of 18 (Morgan 1989).

Childless couples can divorce and never have any further interactions, but divorced parents find themselves still tied to each other through their children. People who have decided to terminate their marriages because of "irreconcilable differences" must spend a good part of their lives trying to negotiate in the raising of their children, which may have been a contributing cause of the divorce in the first place. The conflict and animosity often associated with these negotiations are felt most keenly by the children of divorced parents.

Child Custody

The laws related to custody of children are evolving and changing to reflect the changing norms of society. Generally the preference for naming the mother of a "child of tender years" as the custodial parent is referred to as a traditional viewpoint, but actually it was not until 1839 that the British Parliament first declared that the mother should have custody of children under age 7. Prior to that time, fathers had the absolute right to custody, being considered the owners of their children. The trend has since progressed to a "gender free" decision concerning which parent should have custody of the children, followed by a preference for joint custody. These latter changes are a reflection of a shift in the emphasis of the courts from the preferences of the parents to the interests of the children.

Custody can be divided into two domains: physical custody and legal custody. Physical custody determines the parent with whom the child lives, while legal custody concerns the parent who has responsibility for the education and welfare of the child. Usually physical and legal custody are given to the same parent, most frequently the mother. The noncustodial parent then has the right of visitation. With the trend toward joint custody, more judges are deciding that parents should share the legal custody of the children while one parent retains physical custody. There is also a tendency to have the couple come to an agreement instead of the court imposing a decision on custody. Read BABY M—AN UNUSUAL CUSTODY BATTLE for a description of an unusual child custody case.

Custody Disputes

Despite great variation in wording, custody laws are similar throughout the U.S., with most legislation recommending awarding custody on the basis of the "best interests of the child"—a nebulous phrase. Any decision can be rationalized as best for the child. If there are no obvious reasons for granting one parent custody, the courts have to search for some grounds, often relying on insignificant ones.

The Uniform Marriage and Divorce Act, drafted to alleviate some of the problems with divorce and custody, is used as a model in some states. It states, "the courts shall not consider conduct of a proposed custodian that does not affect his relationship to the child" (Wheeler 1980, p. 37). Therefore, the adultery of a mother should not prevent her from obtaining custody of her child. This act further suggests that judges consider a number of factors while deciding what is in the best interests of the child, for example, the child's relationship with the parents and others, and the child's place in the family, school, and community. Judges are advised to consider the wishes of all those involved and the mental and physical health of each.

The new laws are more flexible than the old ones, but they are also less predictable. No fault divorce has affected custody decisions because it is the only area of the settlement that can still be affected by fault. Adultery or spouse abuse, while not relevant to a divorce, can be important for custody. Although technically parents' behavior which does not affect the child is not supposed to enter into the decision, it is sometimes the only means of differentiating between the ability of the two parents to provide a good home for the child. Custody is often awarded to the innocent or injured party, replacing the designation of "guilt" formerly found in divorce cases.

At times, custody disputes are merely used to publicize grievances, get public vindication, or even as a means of getting revenge. Some attorneys maintain that

Box 13.4

Baby M—An Unusual Custody Battle

In 1985, Mary Beth Whitehead contracted with William and Elizabeth Stern to bear them a child—she agreed to be artificially inseminated by William Stern. For a fee of $10,000 plus medical expenses, she agreed to be their surrogate mother. All went well until the baby girl was born in March of 1986. When she saw the child, Mary Beth Whitehead decided that she could not give her up. She allowed the Sterns to take the child for a short time, then begged to have her back. After a heated discussion, the Sterns agreed to Mary Beth's plea because they were concerned that Ms. Whitehead was suicidal. When the Sterns went to retrieve the baby, Richard Whitehead, Mary Beth's husband, sneaked out a back window with the baby and the Whiteheads fled. The authorities found the Whiteheads 3 months later, and a hotly contested custody battle ensued over "Baby M," whom Mary Beth Whitehead named Sara and the Sterns called Melissa.

In 1987, Judge Harvey Sorkow declared that the contract giving the baby to the Sterns was valid. He felt that the contract was protected under the Constitution but was not automatically enforceable. Based on "the best interests of the child," he awarded custody of Baby M to the Sterns. In addition, the judge decided that Mary Beth Whitehead had no parental rights and thus could not even visit her child. The judge, in a move that surprised everyone, immediately allowed Elizabeth Stern to adopt the child legally, now called Melissa Elizabeth Stern.

However, in February, 1988, the New Jersey Supreme Court overruled all but the custody decision of Judge Sorkow. The court maintained that the contract between Mary Beth Whitehead (now Whitehead-Gould, since remarrying) and the Sterns violated the adoption laws in New Jersey because of the payment involved. The court said voluntary surrogacy was acceptable, provided the mothers were allowed to change their minds. The court ruled that Mrs. Whitehead-Gould would be allowed visitation with her child and voided the adoption by Mrs. Stern. The court did agree with the lower court that it would be in the child's best interest to be raised by the Sterns.

◆

Advances in medicine have led the way for infertile parents to have children. Some of these advances have created ethical and legal problems for the children and the parents. Should society legitimize surrogacy? What recourse do infertile couples have if surrogacy is prohibited? What rights should a surrogate mother have? Are surrogate mothers being exploited? Will wealthy women opt for surrogacy as a way of avoiding the inconvenience of pregnancy?

Sources: R. Lacayo, "Whose Child Is This?" *Time* (January 19, 1987), pp. 56–58; R. Lacayo, "In the Best Interests of a Child," *Time* (April 13, 1987), p. 71; R. Lacayo, "Is the Womb a Rentable Space?" *Time* (September 22, 1986), p. 36; "Surrogate Mother Denied Baby," *The Florida Times-Union* (September 11, 1986), p. A–10; "Jersey Court Condemns Surrogacy," *The Florida Times-Union* (February 4, 1988), p. A–21.

custody battles are really conflicts over money. A father who gains custody of the children usually retains the house and pays no child support. Mothers, afraid of losing custody of their children, are more likely to bargain away financial support. Custody is usually quite important to the mothers, putting them at a disadvantage in the bargaining situation (Polikoff 1983).

Sometimes judges make creative decisions concerning child custody. For example, when Jane Borloff filed for divorce from her husband, Rich, and both parents requested custody of their two young daughters, the presiding judge made what appeared to be a Solomon-like decision. The ruling required that the children stay in the family home while the parents alternated staying with them 3 days one week and 4 days the next. Unfortunately, the parents' animosity escalated, making the situation untenable for everyone. Since both parents had to find other living arrangements for the days they were not in the family home, expenses increased as well. Apparently, much of the conflict centered around differing housekeeping standards. Eventually, the mother was awarded permanent custody of the children. Mrs. Borloff believes that the animosity, fueled by conflict over shared custody, caused her ex-husband's lack of regularity in child support and visitation (Wheeler 1980).

Fathers and Custody
In the early 1970s, California began to change laws to acknowledge the rights of fathers to have custody of their children. The legal trend has been toward a gender-neutral evaluation of child custody, with every state now giving both fathers and mothers equal rights. The change in laws was the result of pressure by fathers. But mothers were also becoming sympathetic to fathers having the opportunity to raise their children and less anxious to shoulder all the responsibility of child rearing. Women's groups supported mothers' decisions not to seek custody, maintaining that there was no necessity for guilt feelings associated with that decision. Despite the publicity, there has been little change in the number of single-parent families headed by fathers. The slight increase in the number of fathers gaining custody has been due primarily to agreements with the mothers rather than court decisions. But in contested cases there has been an increase in the number of fathers who obtain custody (Blades 1985, Morgan 1989).

Mothers still tend to receive custody for a number of reasons. Social norms lean toward mothers having custody, and people are reluctant to go against social pressure. Most divorcing couples believe young children should be kept with their mothers. In addition, divorcing fathers complain that attorneys often try to dissuade them from attempting to gain custody.

Forward-thinking fathers who wanted to maintain custody of their children applied pressure to change the laws before the majority of society accepted their position. However, the norm is slowly changing; society's viewpoint appears to be following the changes in the law. Fathers are more interested in receiving custody, women are more willing to allow it, society is more open to men having custody, and laws are making it easier. A bias still exists toward giving the mother custody of preschool children, especially if there is no clear-cut reason why one or the other of the parents should have custody (Freed & Foster 1984). Usually the decision is made on the basis of who the more nurturing parent is. Generally, but not exclusively, it is the mother, since she is more likely to stay at home with infants. Mothers are still awarded custody in 85 percent of the cases, while fathers get custody 10 percent of the time, and custody is shared in the remaining cases (Weitzman 1985).

Some states are following West Virginia's lead with laws giving custody to the primary caretaker (Weitzman 1985). But "primary caretaker" can also be ambiguous. Mothers are often assumed to be more nurturing, but there is no biological basis for that assumption. Courts attempt to review the parent–child relationship and the quality of the care each parent can give in making the determination, but the decision is never simple.

Judges are likely to attribute better quality of care to the parent who has the greater financial resources, equating financial success with stability. Women who are homemakers cannot compete in the financial arena. Laurie Woods, Vicki Been, and Joanne Schulman (1983) found that even working women were at a disadvantage, since they tend to earn less money than men. Nancy Polikoff (1983) maintains that judges punish women who work for their independence and use work as an excuse to keep from giving mothers custody. Fathers are *supposed* to work, so it is not held against them. These authors contend that using financial criteria for custody undermines the importance of nurturing.

Children's Testimony

The discussion so far has focused on the wishes and needs of the parents, but the justice system is shifting its attention to the interests of the children. Although only half the states instruct judges to listen to the children, judges who want to take the child's desires into account often speak directly to the child. However, testifying on the witness stand is difficult for most people and can be overwhelming for children, particularly if asked to choose publicly between the two people whom they love most. Many judges, sympathetic to the concerns of the child, will do the questioning *in camera* (in chambers).

The children of divorcing parents have been through a lot of emotional trauma and often have a preference for a particular parent. Children need to be reassured that they are loved by both parents and that the love will continue despite any preference. Children can be coerced or bribed to state a preference. The judge must decide what is truly in the best interests of the child, and the child's preference is only one piece of information used in the decision.

Some legal experts contend that children should have their own attorney and a voice in the decisions. Judges can appoint an attorney for the children in most states; however, they seldom do. Some courts and/or attorneys enlist the expertise of psychologists or psychiatrists. However, professionals can be as biased as anyone else, and if they are hired by one or the other side of the litigation, they tend to reflect that viewpoint. It is usually better if the mental health professional is retained by the court to report on the needs and wishes of the child, rather than having an affiliation with one of the contesting parties.

Mediation

The use of mediation to assist in resolving divorce and custody disputes is encouraged by experts to defuse the adversarial atmosphere of a contested divorce, particularly when dealing with children (Pearson & Thoennes 1984). Mediation helps parents compromise while assuming the responsibility for the future of their children. Some researchers, however, believe that there are people who are not capable of resolving disputes through mediation. For example, couples who are particularly antagonistic, couples who are not sure they want a divorce, and those who cannot or will not communicate are not likely to find mediation helpful (Kressel et al. 1980).

Joint Custody

Joint custody (also called shared custody, dual custody, or coparenting) was initiated by parents. Fathers wanted more involvement in their children's lives. Mothers were in agreement, as they wanted assistance in the responsibility of child rearing. Prior to the legalization of joint custody, parents sometimes found themselves in the frustrating situation of having negotiated an agreement to share custody of a child which the judge then refused to accept. Judges and attorneys tended to oppose joint custody, maintaining that parents who were unable to get along well enough to stay married would never be able to cooperate in the joint responsibility of raising children after a divorce. Parents who were refused joint custody by a judge often went ahead with their agreement without the court's approval.

In 1980, California became the first state to institute laws allowing parents joint custody of their children following divorce. By 1989, thirty-four states had laws allowing joint custody. These laws were an attempt to maintain the child's contact and relationship with both parents. They were also considered a means of having both parents take the responsibility in raising their children and a way to encourage the noncustodial parent to continue child support (Morgan 1989).

Schulman and Pitt (1982) differentiate four types of joint custody legislation. **Joint custody as an option** allows the court to award joint custody even if the parents do not request it. **Joint custody when the parents agree** can be awarded only when the parents request it. Although widely approved, this type of custody is ripe for coercion. If a parent does not agree to joint custody, the other parent can use this as evidence that the first parent will make visitation difficult. Therefore, the cooperative parent could possibly be awarded sole custody. **Joint custody at the request of one parent** can be even more coercive than when parents agree. One parent can force joint custody on the other. The child is often in the middle and the courts have to mediate. If a parent is opposed to joint custody, that parent can be viewed as "unfriendly" and lose all custody. **Joint custody as a preference or presumption** is the most coercive form of the law. Six states require the judge to give preference to joint custody.

The most coercive laws are those which presume joint custody is best for the child and only allow sole custody as an exception which must be justified. A battered wife is one example of a person who can be coerced into joint custody when sole custody might be better for the child. This mother realizes her ex-husband has abused her and has the potential for violence. She is worried about the safety of the children. However, this mother might lose custody if she opposes joint custody and can be considered "unfriendly."

Problems with Joint Custody

Joint custody is not a panacea. Some people believe that this arrangement is more beneficial to the parents than to the children. After studying twenty-four couples in California who had joint custody of their children, Steinman (1981) concluded that the children were anxious and confused. The lives of these children were very complicated, making the children feel disorganized and lacking in control. For example, a child might live part of the week with one parent and the rest with the other, or a child might spend one month with one parent and the next with the other. In any case, the child has to remember differing rules and regulations, different locations for belongings, and different routes home. These children were under a great deal of stress—they worried about getting lost, taking the wrong bus, or going to the wrong home when no one would be there.

Parents with joint custody of their children must maintain a cooperative relationship. The relationship tends to disintegrate if either parent remarries or moves. Joint custody is ironic in requiring that the divorcing parents cooperate at the very time when they are in the process of dissolving their marriage. Their relationship is particularly acrimonious at this point in time, such that it seems foolish to try to force the idea of shared parenting. Judith Wallerstein and Joan Kelly (1980) found that children who have the most difficult time adjusting to a divorce are those who are caught in the middle of their parents' continuous fighting.

Joint Custody in Practice

The new laws for joint custody were hailed as a way for fathers to maintain parenting bonds with their children. It was assumed that the fathers would be more likely to continue payment of child support and there would be less conflict between the parties if they shared custody. In actuality, most of the change has been in the labels applied to this agreement rather than the resulting behavior. The pattern of actual living arrangements for joint custody is not much different from the old single custody with liberal visitation. Most of the children in joint custody arrangements live with their mother, and the father has a say in decisions about schooling and other concerns. Alternatively, the children live with their mothers on weekdays and with their fathers on weekends.

Visitation

Divorce decrees generally indicate that the noncustodial parent will have "reasonable" visitation with the children. However, very few decrees (5 percent) define exactly what is meant by reasonable; most parents have to work out an agreement. It can be quite difficult to arrange visitation that satisfies both parties, especially if they do not want to cooperate. The visitation agreement thus becomes an ongoing source of conflict and aggravation. Sometimes one or both parties use visitation as a means of getting revenge on the former partner. The mother makes sure the children are out when the father comes to pick them up, or the father does not bring the children back when expected.

Visitation, particularly immediately after the divorce, can be the source of conflict and antagonism. Frequently, the mother complains that the father is having a negative influence on the child because he lives with a lover. Taken to court, this complaint has sometimes led to rulings forbidding the father from having a lover spend the night. Sometimes requests for extensive visitation are used as a bargaining chip to be negotiated against less support. For example, the noncustodial parent might ask to have the children spend their summer vacation with him/her and then ask to eliminate child support during these periods. While it is quite equitable to decrease payments, since there is no expense for food, the custodial parent still has to maintain a living area for the children. Mothers, who are generally the custodial parent, sometimes deny fathers visitation in order to collect back child support. And sometimes the reverse is used. The father stops paying child support in order to force his ex-wife to allow him to visit the children. The loser in these situations is always the child (Wheeler 1980). Read A MOTHER IN CUSTODY for an extreme example of contested visitation.

Visitation usually is a highly emotional event. Some divorced parents find it impossible to interact with their recent antagonist over the care of their mutual children without renewing the conflict or the pain. Any contact is avoided if possible. A specified visitation schedule, agreed to before a divorce, avoids future conflict and decreases the emotional trauma. Having a predictable schedule increases stability for the children and allows the parents to plan ahead.

But, despite many attempts on the part of parents to withhold visitation through the courts (for example, making allegations concerning abuse or improper conduct in front of the children), visitation rights are usually upheld. Visitation is considered a right of the child as well as a right of the noncustodial parent. Some professionals go even further, contending that noncustodial parents have an obligation to visit their children (Wheeler 1980).

Child's Relationship with Noncustodial Parent
Most children of divorced parents still live with their mothers and visit with their fathers. Noncustodial fathers appear to separate emotionally from their children after a divorce. A national sample of 11- to 16-year-old children of divorce found a very low frequency of visitation by the father (Furstenberg et al. 1983). This survey discovered that most children (52 percent) had had no contact with their fathers within the year surveyed. Only 16 percent of the children saw their fathers once a week, another 16 percent saw their fathers once a month, and 15 percent saw their fathers once a year. The researchers conclude that divorce puts a wedge between noncustodial fathers and their children which serves to break the bond between them. This severing of the relationship begins shortly after the divorce and escalates over time. By 10 years after the divorce, 64 percent of the

> **Box 13.5**
>
> **A Mother in Custody**
>
> Dr. Elizabeth Morgan, a Washington, D.C., plastic surgeon, and her husband, Dr. Eric Foretich, were divorced. Eric Foretich was allowed visitation rights with their daughter, Hilary. But, Elizabeth Morgan believed that her ex-husband had raped his daughter and, therefore, Dr. Morgan refused to allow the visits. Foretich denied the accusations and demanded unsupervised visitation with his daughter. When the court ordered Elizabeth Morgan to produce Hilary for the visits, she refused. Judge Herbert Dixon ordered Dr. Morgan jailed for contempt of court, where she remained from August, 1987, until her release in 1989. During her time in jail, Dr. Morgan refused to reveal the whereabouts of her daughter, vowing to remain jailed until the child was 18 rather than allow Hilary to visit her father unsupervised.
>
> Judge Dixon would not permit testimony about an older daughter of Dr. Foretich's by a previous wife. This child also claims to have been sexually abused by her father, a claim supported by a child abuse expert. During her tenure in jail, Judge Dixon told Dr. Morgan that her release was in her own hands; she merely had to reveal Hilary's location. Dr. Morgan was released in 1989, but not due to a decision by the judge. The U.S. Congress passed a bill requiring the release or filing of criminal contempt charges against anyone held more than 12 months for civil contempt of court.
>
> Meanwhile, Dr. Foretich, Hilary's father, continued to search for his daughter and offered a $50,000 reward for information about her. In early 1990, Dr. Foretich traced his daughter to New Zealand. The New Zealand courts would not enforce U.S. court decisions in a child custody case. Therefore, Hilary's parents had the custody issue decided by another court. The New Zealand court granted Dr. Morgan custody of Hilary with the proviso that she remain in Christchurch, New Zealand, and refrain from further publicity in the case. Hilary's father indicated that he would not pursue the case farther.

Sources: "House Votes to Bar Terms Given for Court Contempt to Twelve Months," *The Florida Times-Union* (June 29, 1989), p. A–12; M. McGrory, "Mother Determined to Shield Child from Father," *The Florida Times-Union* (June 14, 1989), p. A–9; "Woman Jailed in Custody Fight Wins Ruling," *The New York Times* (December 1, 1990), p. 16(N).

children reported no contact with their fathers. Noncustodial mothers maintained more contact with their children.

Characteristics of the parents predicted who were likely to maintain contact with their children. In general, blacks, less educated, and remarried men were less likely to maintain contact with their children. Men also were less likely to maintain contact with their children if the mother remarried. If both parents remained unmarried, slightly fewer than half the fathers maintained weekly contact. However, if both remarried, only 11 percent had weekly contact with the children (Furstenberg et al. 1983).

Relitigation

Child support and custody tie parents to each other for many years after a divorce. People who could not live together because of conflict must interact and negotiate over the highly emotional aspects of support, custody, child rearing, and visitation. Because these people have been unable to agree in the past and many have been through a contentious divorce, the animosity and hostility are likely to continue. If there are changes in the lives of the parties affecting support or custody which they cannot work out between them, they are likely to go back to court. A study of cases in Wisconsin found that more than 50 percent of divorced couples returned to court within 2 years of the divorce. Most of these couples went to court more than once, some as often as ten or twenty times in that period. One couple in New Jersey went to court seventy-six times in the two years following their divorce. Most of the conflict is over visitation. As Wheeler states, "custody cases are never closed" (1980, p. 176).

Feeding into the frequency of relitigation are ambiguous decrees and the fact that lawyers do not inform parents of future problems. Most divorce decrees give the noncustodial parent "reasonable visitation rights." What is reasonable to the noncustodial parent can seem quite unreasonable to the custodial parent (or vice versa). The attorneys who negotiate the agreement often neglect to anticipate future problems. By omitting items that will eventually lead to conflict, the likelihood of relitigation is quite high. Often, the animosity and conflict are so consuming that the divorced parties cannot communicate well enough to settle the smallest problem without the assistance of the courts. See DIVORCE RELITIGATION.

When a divorce and custody case are first settled, the participants cannot predict every life change likely to occur. An ex-husband who was a poor graduate student prior to the divorce, who subsequently graduates and becomes a high-income earning professional, can be taken back to court to increase the child support payments. But the system works to the advantage of both parties. The well-paid executive who loses his job can also have the court decrease his payments.

Remarriage and Relitigation

Remarriage is one of the primary life changes precipitating relitigation. For example, a father who did not want custody of the children because of concerns about his effectiveness in raising them or the amount of traveling he does in his work remarries. Now he has a wife who will stay at home and care for the children. He believes it would be less expensive to raise the children than pay child support. Thus, he goes back to court to get custody of the children.

If a man remarries and has children by his second wife, that is no excuse for stopping child support payments to the children of his first wife. However, some men decide to stop payments at this time on their own. The remarriage of the ex-wife is also not a reason for the ex-husband to discontinue child support payments. Alimony stops upon the wife's remarriage, but child support does not, unless the stepfather adopts the children.

> **Box 13.6**
>
> **Divorce Relitigation**
>
> In the fall of 1988, Michele Smith went to court to demand that her ex-husband, Lorenzo Lamas, spend more time with their two children, Alvaro Joshua, 4, and Shayne Dahl, 3. Their mother claimed that the children only saw their actor father while viewing *Falcon Crest*. Since their divorce in early 1985, the former Mrs. Lamas claimed that the children's father had seen them only a few times. She contended that this was psychologically unhealthy for the children. Lamas countered that he loved his children and had seen them regularly.
>
> As with many couples who divorce, Michele Smith and Lorenzo Lamas had spent a lot of time in court with relitigation. Lamas brought Smith to court in an attempt to keep her from taking their son out of Los Angeles while she was pregnant with their second child. Even Michele's mother brought her to court, asking for custody of the child, citing Michele's emotional instability as interfering with her daughter's care of the child.
>
> ♦
>
> Should fathers be required to spend time with their children after a divorce? Does frequent relitigation have a negative effect on children? Does the publicity which frequently accompanies celebrity divorces have a negative impact on the children?

Source: J. Kaufman, "Lorenzo Lamas' Ex-Wife Goes to Court to Deliver an Unusual Message: Spend Time with the Kids," *People Weekly* (November 14, 1988), pp. 81–82.

Impact of Divorce on Children

Psychologists maintain that change of any type, even positive change, is stressful. While moving to a new house or getting a new job are happy events, even these create stress. Holmes and Rahe (1967) have developed a scale to measure the amount of stress in a person's life. The most stressful event identified by these researchers is the death of a spouse, followed by divorce and separation.

After a divorce, there are many changes in the lives of the mother (generally the custodial parent) and children. The mother frequently must find a job or pursue retraining for job skills. Both of these activities involve time and produce pressure and stress on the mother. Even if she was working prior to the divorce, she often has to upgrade her job skills by going to evening school. In addition, the mother is in the midst of her own psychological trauma from the divorce, and she is attempting to build a new social life. Therefore, at the very time the child is traumatized by losing one parent, the other parent may be so physically stressed that she is often psychologically unavailable to assist the child in coping. The mother has so many additional time demands in her hectic schedule that she is often physically exhausted and unavailable to help the child adjust (Wallerstein & Kelly 1980). Often the mother and children have to move for economic reasons (two-thirds move within 3 years, many move three times or more). The child then faces adjustment to new surroundings, the pressure of finding new friends, coping with a new school and new neighborhood. All semblance of stability and continuity is gone. The effects of the move are exaggerated by the psychological trauma of losing one parent and having the other less available (Wallerstein & Kelly 1980).

The emotional impact of divorce is so common that mental health professionals describe a "divorced child syndrome." Children whose parents have divorced manifest a variety of symptoms. Often the children are depressed and, in extreme cases, even suicidal. Sometimes the depression is displayed in less dramatic ways, with children being accident prone, constantly fatigued, or bored. These children cry a lot, do not eat well, and complain of stomach pain. Children's behavior sometimes changes drastically, and they begin to do poorly in school or become delinquent. Usually the worst aspects of the divorced child syndrome are manifested during the year following the divorce and then tend to dissipate (Wheeler 1980).

Although children are quite resilient, it is difficult for them to adjust to the changes involved. Young children frequently are unable to maintain their bonds with their former neighborhood and school friends. During one of the most stressful experiences of their lives, children have few familiar comforts in their lives. The turmoil in a child's life due to divorce is often more severe than that of their parents, who maintain the same friends and jobs and frequently have developed a social support system.

Judith Wallerstein and Joan Kelly (1980) followed children for 5 years following a divorce to evaluate the emotional trauma they suffered. Children actually adjusted quite well to the divorce if the parents could cooperate and if both parents retained their relationship with the children. In contrast, parents who were in constant conflict and displayed their animosity interfered with the coping mechanisms of their children. Later studies following children for up to 15 years after a divorce found that the divorce was the most stressful event in the children's lives. Some of the children adjusted well, others had difficulty with long-term relationships. These problems were particularly apparent in females (Wallerstein 1985, Wallerstein & Blakeslee 1989).

Summary

The five central principles of the traditional marriage were: 1) division of **roles and responsibilities**; 2) a **patriarchal structure**; 3) a **moral underpinning**; 4) a **lifelong commitment**; and 5) **partnership**. The middle of the 1970s saw the advent of some changes in the legal implications of marriage which alleviated some of the previous inequality of males and females.

Divorce laws vary by state in terms of grounds for divorce but have followed a trend in which the focus in divorce cases has shifted from contention over the divorce itself to conflict over how to divide economic resources. In 1970, California passed the first "no fault" law for divorce. The purpose of this system was to eliminate the adversarial aspects of the divorce. By 1985, all states except South Dakota had no fault divorce laws.

Despite the inadequacy of the child support awards, compliance with support orders is incredibly low and gets worse over time. Many women and children enter poverty after a divorce. However, both laws and divorce decisions are changing. Judges are beginning to recognize intangible assets and the differential earning power of males and females.

Divorce, always difficult, becomes traumatic when children are involved. The legal system shifted first to a more gender-neutral viewpoint and from there to a system that encourages joint custody of children. These changes are a reflection of the changing emphasis from the parents' rights to consideration of the best interests of the children. Current legislation tends to favor the joint custody of children. While the underlying assumptions of this viewpoint are quite positive, joint custody is not a panacea. There are many financial and life-style problems associated with joint custody.

Children of divorce must withstand the conflict between the two people with whom they are closest. The psychological stress on children is so strong that mental health workers recognize a "divorced child syndrome." These children display many manifestations of depression.

Many parents continue their adversarial relationships and use visitation as a method to continue the conflict. After a divorce, the noncustodial father tends to separate himself emotionally from his children. While there are no perfect solutions to custody questions, it appears that children cope best when there is little conflict between the parents and the children maintain their ties to both parents. When custody and divorce are hostile, the children are the innocent victims.

14

Crime Intervention and Prevention

Bystander Intervention
Witnesses to Crime
Intervention
Cost-Reward Model
Pornography
Presidential Commissions on Pornography
Research on Violent Pornography
Violent Pornography and Rape
Nonviolent Pornography
Violence
Alleviating the Effects of Sexual Violence
Deterrence
Limitations of Early Research on Deterrence
Survey Research
Guns and Their Control
Collective Security Model
Firearm Accidents
Guns and Deterrence Theory
Summary

Bystander Intervention

It was 3:00 A.M. and Kitty Genovese, 23, was returning to her home on Long Island, New York. Kitty worked as a waitress and was accustomed to late hours. However, this night was different; someone was waiting for her. A man attacked Kitty with a knife and killed her outside her Kew Gardens apartment complex. This 1964 incident has gained international notoriety. The infamy of the event is not due to an unarmed woman being killed, because as horrible as that is, unfortunately, meaningless murder is not an unusual event in major cities in the United States. This particular murder has gained widespread notoriety because it was later discovered that there were thirty-eight witnesses to the crime. Again, this is not an unusual situation in large urban areas. What is so appalling about this event is that none of the eyewitnesses to the crime called the police until the victim was dead. Had the police been summoned earlier, Kitty Genovese might have survived the attack. The murderer took more than 30 minutes to kill the victim and left the scene three times during the attack. When the police were finally summoned, they arrived within a few minutes. But, it was too late for Kitty Genovese; she was dead.

The death of Kitty Genovese induced social psychologists to study the phenomenon of bystander intervention. They have explored the reasons why, and the conditions under which, one person will assist another during an emergency. Previous chapters have discussed crime and the criminal justice system's reaction to it. This chapter will explore intervention and prevention of crime. The following discussion will center on the findings related to bystander intervention during the commission of a crime.

Witnesses to Crime

Apparently it is not unusual for crimes to go unreported by witnesses. One survey found that only one in four witnesses to a crime called the police or intervened (van Dijk 1986). An experiment conducted in The Hague, Netherlands, found that even fewer witnesses responded when they saw someone cutting locks off bicycles. The author concludes that offenders have no need to worry about bystanders. Without social reactions by witnesses, technical means of crime prevention such as bike locks will not be very effective. See COMMUNITY REACTION TO THE RAPISTS IN BIG DAN'S for people's evaluation of a crime, p. 330.

Adolescents tend to be the most frequent offenders, victims, and witnesses to crime. Jan van Dijk (1986) hypothesizes that this occurs because adolescents have considerable free time which they spend away from home. Male adolescents are the least likely to intervene, although they are the most frequent bystanders to crime in big cities. They appear to be disinclined toward prevention or intervention. Because adolescents are unlikely to intervene in crime, offenders are not worried about intervention in areas populated by adolescents. As a consequence, crimes are more likely to occur in areas where adolescents congregate.

Adolescents are more likely to commit crimes than are people of other ages and are unlikely to be caught. Van Dijk (1986) found a high correlation between being a victim and an offender in boys who spend a lot of time away from home.

This relationship was particularly strong in boys from more affluent social backgrounds. Those boys who witnessed, or were victims to, theft were more likely to be future offenders. He explains this relationship as being due to a learning process. Victimization creates a need for compensation for the loss by the victim, thus providing a motivation. Likewise the witnesses have observed an easy way of obtaining goods. The victims and witnesses can model the method used by the offender to obtain goods and often become offenders themselves. Therefore, an increase in crime and victimization has a snowball effect. Crime is self-perpetuating.

A related issue is that bystanders cannot be effective unless they are present. Fear of crime means that people, especially women, are less willing to go out at night. With fewer people on the streets, social control of the area decreases. It logically follows that if an area of a town becomes known as unsafe, it quickly becomes very unsafe. People avoid the area, thereby decreasing the amount of social control. When people fear an area, they do not go into it and, therefore, they are not there to intervene in a crime.

Intervention

Intrigued by the Kitty Genovese murder, Bibb Latané and John Darley studied the phenomenon of bystander intervention. From their extensive research, these social psychologists developed a five-stage model to explain helping in an emergency. This model is described below.

Before an individual intervenes in an emergency, that individual must **notice the incident.** Crimes, as do other emergencies, typically happen quickly and unexpectedly. Witnesses are not anticipating criminal activity and, therefore, do not attend to the incident. Even next-door neighbors might not notice that a delivery truck is removing goods instead of delivering them. The likelihood of noticing an incident is decreased if the observer is far from the event, if it is dark, or if loud noise drowns out the sounds associated with the event. Apparently, people are more likely to notice an incident if they observe it transpire (Piliavin, Piliavin & Broll 1976). It is much easier to decide that your neighbor's house is being broken into if you observe two men using a crow bar to open the front door, than if you merely notice that the door is ajar.

Once the incident is noticed, the witness must **define the situation as an emergency.** Many emergencies are ambiguous, particularly criminal activity. Are those delivery men taking a stereo in to be repaired or stealing it? People tend to define situations by using the behavior of other observers. Thus, if other people are acting in a casual, unconcerned manner, the witness is likely to assume there is no emergency. This behavior is explained by the concept of informational influence. The observer gathers information and makes decisions about the situation by observing the reactions of others.

Having decided the situation is an emergency, the witness must determine whether he or she should **assume responsibility for acting.** Someone might notice an event and decide it is a crime but not feel he or she should do anything about it. This is what occurred in the Kitty Genovese murder. Thirty-eight people witnessed the crime and did not call the authorities.

> **Box 14.1**
>
> ## Community Reaction to the Rapists in Big Dan's
>
> National attention was directed to New Bedford, Massachusetts, when the details of the horrifying gang rape in Big Dan's Tavern became public (for details of the incident see Chapter 5, A TRAGIC EVENT AT BIG DAN'S TAVERN). Six men were brought to trial for the gang rape of a young woman. Three defendants received 9- to 12-year prison sentences, one received a 6- to 8-year sentence, and the other two defendants were found not guilty. Was the community satisfied that justice had been accomplished and that women were now safer? A resounding "No!" is the answer.
>
> The victim was blamed for the offense and further victimized by the trial, the media, and the community. People in the community felt that the rape was the victim's fault—she should have been at home with her children "where she belonged." She should not have gone into a tavern alone and should not have been drinking. The women in the community were harder on the victim than the men. One woman was quoted as saying, "She should have been hanged" (*National Review,* p. 21). Thousands of people joined a march (led by the two men acquitted in the trial) to protest the verdicts and sentences in the trial.
>
> The defense attorneys fed into already existing community prejudices against rape victims and divorced mothers. They brought the victim's sex life, her social life, and even her alleged receipt of welfare payments under fraudulent premises into the trial. They accused her of embellishing the story in order to get a book contract and even brought up that she had been raped 2 years prior to this incident.
>
> *(continued)*

At each of the first three stages, there is an inverse relationship between the number of observers and the likelihood that any one of them will intervene. This phenomenon is referred to as the **bystander effect.** For example, in the first stage, if there are a lot of people present, each person is less likely to notice an event. The bystander effect on noticing an emergency is demonstrated in an experiment by Latané and Darley (1968). When three people were present as smoke was introduced into a room, they each tended to pay attention to the form they were filling out, not to the smoke. These subjects took much longer to notice the smoke than did those who were alone in the room. People alone tended to spot the smoke within 5 seconds, while those in groups of three averaged 20 seconds before noticing.

The bystander effect also applies to defining the situation as an emergency. Looking at the same experiment described in the last paragraph, people alone in the room quickly went to investigate the smoke. They sniffed it and then went to report it to the experimenter. Those who were in the room with two other people

> The media exacerbated the trauma for the victim. Several newspapers reported the name of the victim and NBC television left it in an interview they conducted with an attorney despite requests to remove the name.
>
> Threats were made against the victim and reportedly collections were taken at local taverns to hire someone to kill her. The victim eventually had to leave the area she had called home her whole life.
>
> Although the extent to which the community in New Bedford, Massachusetts, reacted is extreme, it is not unusual for people to blame the victim, particularly in a rape. However, as Linda-Marie Delloff points out, this did not occur in the case of mass murderer John Wayne Gacy's sex crimes. The victims in the Gacy case were young men and boys. "No blame was placed on those victims—many of them young drifters who had left home. Our society assumes that males may move around independently. Thus they are to be pitied—not blamed—if they become crime victims. But this view is not extended to women" (*The Christian Century,* p. 356).
>
> ♦
>
> Social stereotypes concerning the appropriate behavior of males and females influence our perceptions of behavior. How much do these sex-role stereotypes influence society's tendency to blame the victim? Should the media be allowed to use the name of a victim of a rape? Should the past sex life of a victim be brought up at a rape trial?

Sources: "Big Dan's Tavern," *National Review* (April 20, 1984), pp. 20–21; L. M. Delloff, "Society's Shame: Attitudes Toward Rape," *The Christian Century* (April 11, 1984), pp. 355–356.

did not investigate. Only one man of the twenty-four in groups reported the smoke within 4 minutes. This time lapse occurred even though the room was so full of smoke by 6 minutes into the experiment that the subjects could no longer read their forms. In addition, only three men in the eight groups ever reported the smoke, while the majority of the men working alone did so. The subjects working in groups had unique explanations for the smoke, none of which constituted an emergency. These men thought it was steam, a leak in an air-conditioning vent, smog introduced to simulate life in the city, or "truth gas" that the experimenter introduced into the room to guarantee their truthful answers.

In a study more closely related to criminal behavior, Takooshian and Bodinger (1982) staged a series of car burglaries in New York. A confederate unlocked a car with a coat hanger to obtain a valued object (a television or fur coat). Few passersby noticed the event. Those who did notice stopped and joked with the burglar. Some even offered to help, assuming that the owner of the car was locked out. Apparently, these observers did not define the situation as a crime. However, making the event more obviously a crime did not have a tremendous influence on the amount of reaction. Even when the burglar was a 14-year-old or a person different from the one who had just parked the car, very few New Yorkers intervened.

♦ **FIGURE 14.1**
Latane and Darley's Decision Tree. Only one path up the tree leads to helping. At each fork of the path, the presence of other bystanders may divert a person down a branch toward not helping. (illustrated by Reen Foley)

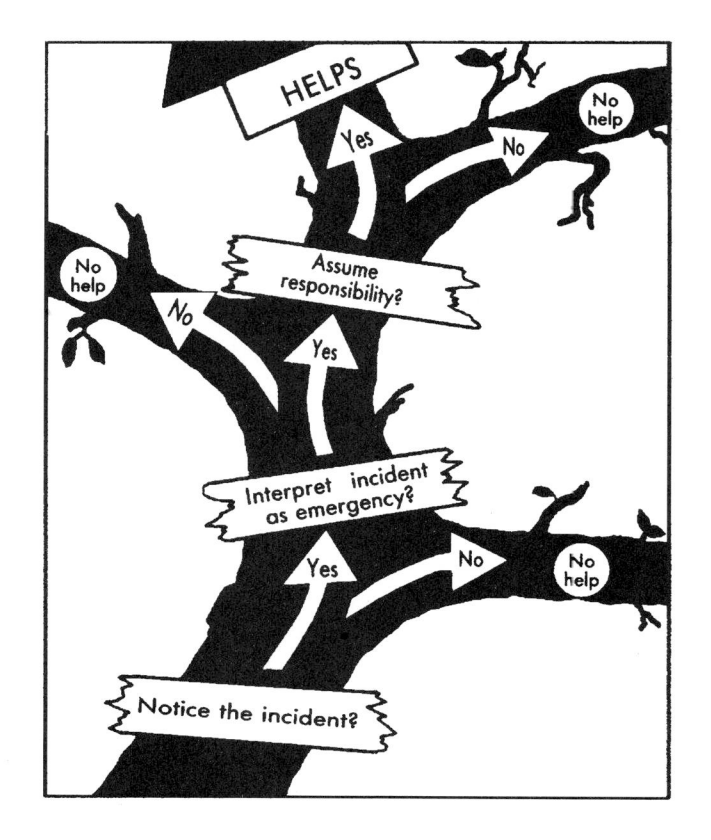

Assuming the observer defines a situation as an emergency, that person will not act unless he or she feels responsible. Again, the bystander effect has occurred; the more people present, the less responsible each person feels. Darley and Latané (1968) explained this reaction in terms of *diffusion of responsibility*. When there are a number of people present, the responsibility for acting is shared among the witnesses. Therefore, each person feels less responsible and is less likely to act than if he or she were the sole witness to the incident. In the Kitty Genovese situation, the witnesses knew that there were many others also viewing the incident. Therefore, each person assumed that someone else had already called the police.

If the bystander has noticed the event, defined it as an emergency, and assumed responsibility, then the bystander must **decide on what assistance to give,** the fourth stage of the model. Finally, the bystander must **actually help.** Although the bystander effect does not affect the last two stages of the model, it does determine whether a witness gets to those decision-making stages.

> **Box 14.2**
>
> **Death on a Bus**
>
> Barney W. Trail was riding the city bus in Jacksonville, Florida, a little after midnight on July 15, 1989. He had been drinking and was asleep when another rider, Terry Lamar Bing, began to torment him verbally. Apparently, Trail was chosen randomly. Bing, who was black, was reported to have said he was "gonna kick this white man's ass." After a few minutes of harassment, Bing, who had also been drinking, began beating Trail. Although there were about twelve other passengers on the bus, none physically intervened until Trail was unconscious on the floor. People were concerned that Bing was armed. The bus driver and at least one passenger did tell Bing to stop.
> When the beating began, the 51-year-old bus driver, Randie Hill, sealed the bus. Bing unsuccessfully attempted to kick open the back door of the bus. One of the passengers guarded the female bus driver from the assailant while she drove to the police station. By the time the bus arrived at the police station, Barney Trail was dead of head trauma. Bing was arrested on the bus.
>
> ♦
>
> Would intervention by the other passengers have prevented the death of Trail? Would Bing have directed his violence toward the other passengers?

Sources: D. Hosansky, "Bus Beating Suspect Out on Early Release," *The Florida Times-Union* (July 17, 1989), pp. A-1, A-2; S. Patterson, "Man Beaten to Death as Bus Riders Look On," *The Florida Times-Union* (July 16, 1989), pp. A-1, A-11.

Cost-Reward Model

One explanation for the presence or absence of helping behavior is found in the cost-reward model developed by Piliavin and her colleagues (Piliavin et al. 1981). This theory hypothesizes that people evaluate the costs and benefits of helping before assisting the victim. The evaluation of the costs and rewards occurs after the witness has observed the incident and defined it as an emergency. At this point, there are a number of factors that determine whether the observer will assist. The decision to help or not help is made very quickly, without the observer being extremely conscious of the decision-making process.

An important factor in the decision to help is the cost of helping to the witness. If there is obvious danger or risk involved, people are more reluctant to assist. If observers think that they will be perceived as incompetent, they are also less likely to help. In addition, observers are more reluctant to assist if they are worried about being embarrassed, since no one else appears to evaluate the situation as an emergency. Finally, people are less likely to assist if they are in a hurry, since the cost of lost time is higher. Read DEATH ON A BUS for a description of an incident in which bystanders did not intervene.

Weighed against the costs of helping are the rewards for helping. These rewards are not as compelling as the costs. They include feeling good about yourself and praise from others around you. These factors hardly appear strong enough to motivate a witness to intervene in an armed robbery.

In addition to the costs and rewards for helping, this model includes costs and rewards for not helping. The costs for not helping include feelings that the observer has about himself such as self-blame and public disapproval. The observer is rewarded for not helping by being able to continue with his own activities and not exerting effort.

This model suggests that observers are most likely to assist when the costs for helping are low and the costs for not helping are high. Let us look at a hypothetical situation which illustrates these conditions. Suppose an observer sees a child who is about to run into the street in front of a car. If this observer is the only person close enough to stop the child, the observer will blame himself if the child is injured. If there are many people watching the incident from a distance, the observer will receive much public disapproval for not helping (high costs of not helping). If this person is merely waiting for a bus and it takes little effort to stop the child (low costs of helping), he is likely to do so.

People are likely to give indirect help (call the police) when the costs are high for both helping and not helping. An example of this situation is one in which an observer sees an armed criminal abduct a child. The witness is the only person close enough to read the license plate. This person realizes that the child will not be rescued unless she reports the license to the police. She will feel very guilty and receive public condemnation for not doing so (high costs for not helping). Therefore, she is likely to wait for the police even if she is late for her final examination in economics (high costs for helping). Overall, however, help, even indirect help, in situations in which the costs are high is unlikely.

When the costs for helping are high and the costs for not helping are low, the observer is likely to leave the scene or deny the situation. For example, suppose someone sees a robber snatch an elderly woman's purse. The robber is carrying a gun and threatens the witness. If no one realizes that this person saw the incident, he is unlikely to report the robbery. This person can reason that the woman is unharmed and he is late for an important business meeting. He is particularly unlikely to assist if no one else knows he observed the crime (low costs for not helping). Someone who also disparages the victim will feel less guilt. Thus, this witness might decide that the woman was flaunting her wealth and deserved to have her purse stolen. Someone in this situation is likely to leave without helping.

Piliavin and her associates (1981) recognize that there are times when the observer acts on impulse. Some situations cause "impulsive helping" in which all bystanders quickly help the victim. However, it is extremely rare that a bystander will risk great bodily harm to assist someone else.

♦ FIGURE 14.2
Costs of helping (illustrated by Reen Foley)

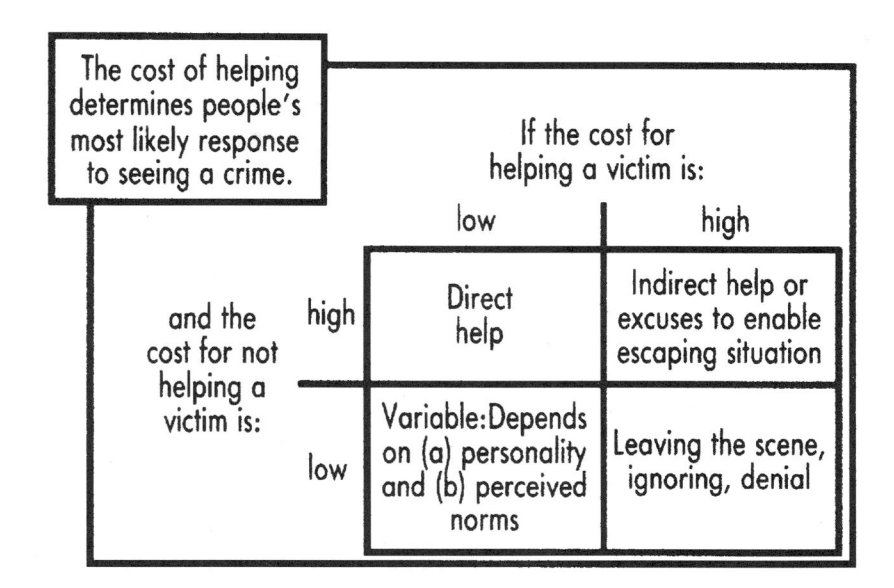

		If the cost for helping a victim is: low	If the cost for helping a victim is: high
and the cost for not helping a victim is:	high	Direct help	Indirect help or excuses to enable escaping situation
and the cost for not helping a victim is:	low	Variable: Depends on (a) personality and (b) perceived norms	Leaving the scene, ignoring, denial

The cost of helping determines people's most likely response to seeing a crime.

Pornography

The previous section discussed bystander intervention, which is one way in which some types of crime might be decreased. The limitation or elimination of exposure to pornography and/or sexually violent material is another method that some people propose to diminish other types of crime and sexual violence. However, there is much debate about the effect of pornography on an individual's behavior.

Pornography, its definition, usage, and potential harm, has been the center of controversy in both the courts and U.S. society for the past two decades. In that time, two national commissions have been appointed to study pornography and the issues related to it. Although their conclusions and recommendations were almost diametrically opposite to each other, each of the commissions was widely criticized for its findings.

Presidential Commissions on Pornography

President Johnson's Commission on Obscenity and Pornography was appointed in 1968 to study the distribution of pornography and its effect on society. The commission was to analyze laws on pornography and recommend measures to regulate traffic in obscenity and pornography without violating constitutional rights. However, the findings of the commission's report were not as expected. The commission concluded, "In sum empirical research designed to clarify the question has found no evidence to date that exposure to explicit sexual materials plays a significant role in the causation of delinquent or criminal behavior among youth or adults. The commission cannot conclude that exposure to erotic materials is a factor in the causation of sex crimes or sex delinquency" (U.S. Commission, 1970, p. 27).

When this commission reported its results in 1970, its findings were greeted with a public outcry. People thought the report supported and even encouraged pornography. Within a short period of time, President Nixon repudiated it.

Following the Johnson Commission report, censorship decreased and the availability of sexually explicit material increased. Material that was formerly considered pornographic or obscene is now found in easily available films, books, and periodicals. Not only has the availability of pornographic materials changed, but also the distribution of this type of explicit material has changed. While pornographic books and magazines could be found in the 1960s, they were expensive and typically bought and viewed at "sex shops." In contrast, sexually explicit magazines and books can now be purchased at many kinds of local stores or by mail. This change has brought sexually explicit material into the home where it can more easily be viewed by children. "The availability of rental videocassettes has made the American middle-class living room into a theatre of the sexually explicit" (Hawkins & Zimring 1988, p. 71).

One aspect of pornography of particular concern is the violence found in some material. There is little doubt that violence in the media has a negative impact on viewers. The 1972 Commission on Television and Violence concluded that nonsexual violent portrayals had a harmful impact on audiences. There is a general assumption that the amount of violence and aggression in pornography has increased since the 1970s. While there may have been an increase in availability of sexually explicit material, the increase in violence is not documented (Donnerstein, Linz & Penrod 1987). An area where violence has increased dramatically is in graphic violence directed toward women portrayed in the media.

In 1985, President Reagan requested that Attorney General Meese form another commission on pornography. He asked the commission to review the content of pornography and its impact on society. He further mandated that the commission propose ways in which to restrict the distribution of pornography without violating constitutional rights. The Meese Commission's findings were readily acceptable to the President. The report states: "We have reached the conclusion, unanimously and confidently, that the available evidence strongly supports the hypothesis that substantial exposure to sexually violent materials as described here bear a causal relationship to antisocial acts of sexual violence, and for some subgroups possibly to unlawful acts of sexual violence" (U.S. Department of Justice, 1986, p. 326).

The negative reactions to the Meese Commission came not from the public, but from the social scientists who conducted research on pornography. The commission claimed its findings were based on the available social science research. However, the commission was accused of biased selection of studies and misrepresentation in its evaluation of the research (Donnerstein, Linz & Penrod 1987; Hawkins & Zimring 1988).

Research on Violent Pornography

Most of the laboratory research on violent pornography has used the same paradigm. In this research paradigm, the subjects are exposed to the pornography.

Later they are given the opportunity to be aggressive to a confederate of the experimenter. This aggressiveness is generally the imposition of an electric shock or a blast of noise. Most of the laboratory research has been conducted with the same subject population, college males. Criticism of the research, which will be discussed later, centers on this paradigm and the limited segment of society studied.

Laboratory research has found that viewing aggressive pornography influenced male aggression toward females. Men were aggressive toward women whether the men were angered or not (Donnerstein 1980). Furthermore, male aggressiveness toward women increased when aggression was condoned (Malamuth 1978). Later research differentiated between violent pornography in which the female victim appeared to enjoy the victimization and find rape pleasurable and pornography in which the female victim obviously found the experience to be noxious. Donnerstein and Berkowitz (1981) found both types of film increased aggressiveness toward women when the male subjects were angered. However, when the subjects were not angered, only the films ending with the women enjoying the experience increased aggression toward females.

The research described above was conducted in laboratories and some experts question whether laboratory research can be generalized to the real world. These critics question the similarity between the imposition of a shock or blast of noise to assault and/or rape. Donnerstein, Linz, and Penrod (1987) enumerate the criticisms of, and limitations to, research on pornography and aggression in the laboratory. First, the aggression measured in laboratory studies is artificial and the subjects do not perceive that they are causing harm. In addition, there is no acceptable definition of aggressive behavior or of violence portrayed in the media. The subjects' acts of aggression are not only condoned, they are also encouraged by the experiment. This contrasts with natural environments where aggression is punished and illegal. Furthermore, the subjects tend to be limited to college populations between the ages of 18 and 22. This is hardly a representative sample of society. Another criticism focuses on the evidence that subjects in an experiment attempt to figure out the experimenter's hypothesis and confirm that prediction. Therefore, subjects do not behave in the manner they ordinarily might. A different type of criticism is that only experiments with positive results are published. Thus, results that fail to verify the relationship between violent pornography and aggression are not disseminated.

Despite the criticisms of the laboratory research, it does provide the only source of information on causality. The controlled experiment is the only method of determining, unambiguously, a cause and effect. Research from the real world is correlational. While this latter type of data can support the conclusions of causality found in laboratory studies, it cannot prove causality.

Violent Pornography and Rape

Abel, Blanchard, and Becker (1978; Abel et al. 1976) conducted research with rapists. Arousal increased in rapists whether they were viewing rape or consenting sex. Nonrapists, in contrast, showed no arousal when viewing rape in

> **Box 14.3**
>
> **Olivia**
>
> In 1978, a 9-year-old girl filed a civil suit against the National Broadcasting Company. This young girl had been "artificially raped" by a group of assailants who had previously viewed a similar scene in a televised movie, *Born Innocent*. In the television drama, an institutionalized adolescent girl was attacked in the communal bath of the home. The television victim was artificially raped with the handle of a plumber's helper by four girls. The actual victim was attacked on the beach with a bottle by a group of juveniles. The suit alleged that the scene in the movie "caused" the assailants "to decide to do a similar act to a minor girl." The plaintiffs attempted to demonstrate that the television broadcasting company should be held responsible for the injuries inflicted on the victim. Attorneys for NBC argued that the drama did not constitute "incitement" of the action. The court agreed with the defendant and dismissed the case. The California court ruled that the television drama was protected by the First Amendment since it did not advocate or encourage violence and, therefore, was not "incitement."

Source: *Olivia v. National Broadcasting Company*, 1978.

which the victim had a negative reaction. Malamuth and his colleagues (1983a & b, 1985, 1986) also found a difference in arousal between subjects viewing rape and consenting sex. This difference in arousal was predictive of the subjects' behavior and their desire to hurt women. The researchers found self-reported sexual aggression in real life was related to dominance as a sexual motive, hostility toward women, attitudes facilitating violence, and sexual arousal to rape. This is not to say that other men do not become aroused by violent pornography. But other men are especially likely to become aroused if the victim is depicted as enjoying the episode. See OLIVIA.

Nonviolent Pornography

Researchers question whether the increase in aggressiveness after viewing violent pornography is due to the violence or to the explicit sexual portrayal. Although research has found nonaggressive pornography may sometimes increase aggressiveness against members of the same sex, Donnerstein, Linz, and Penrod (1987) contend that the aggressiveness is due to the arousal quality of the media rather than to its being sexually explicit. They argue that any arousing or exciting portrayal, such as a humorous one, would have a similar impact on aggressiveness.

Studies have not been consistent in their findings related to the impact of nonaggressive pornography on aggressiveness toward women. Malamuth and Ceniti (1986) found no changes in males' likelihood of raping after 4 weeks of viewing nonviolent pornography. Even in studies in which the subject was angered and witnessed an aggressive model, aggressiveness toward women was not always found. One or two studies did find a relationship between nonaggressive pornography and aggression toward women. However, the support for that conclusion is not very strong.

Zillman and Bryant (1982, 1984) conducted a series of studies to evaluate the impact on subjects of viewing large amounts of nonaggressive pornography. While the films viewed were nonaggressive, they did portray the females in a negative manner, as permissive, promiscuous, and somewhat debased. And while the male subjects did not display increased aggressiveness toward women, they did demonstrate an increased insensitivity toward them. For example, these subjects became more tolerant of violent pornography. They also were more lenient toward rapists and had less positive attitudes toward female equality.

In general, the data do not indicate that viewing nonviolent pornography leads to aggression. There appears to be little negative impact from viewing nudity. However, the impact of nonaggressive pornography which is dehumanizing is more problematic. Data on the effect of "degrading" pornography that is nonviolent are inconsistent but appear to be negative. Further research is being conducted to determine the precise effect.

Violence

Donnerstein, Berkowitz, and Linz (cited in Donnerstein, Linz & Penrod 1987) conducted a study to differentiate the impact of violence and explicit sex. They showed male subjects one of four films: an aggressive pornographic film, a sexually explicit film, a film depicting aggression against women without sex, and a neutral film. Very little aggressiveness was displayed after viewing the sexually explicit or neutral films. The aggressive pornographic film led to the most aggression against women, followed by the film depicting aggression against women without sex. It appears, therefore, that violence is more detrimental to viewers than explicit sex.

Because of the negative impact of violence on viewers, Donnerstein, Linz, and Penrod express concern over the emergence in the past 10 years of a genre of movies called "slasher" or "splatter" films. While sex is not explicit in these films, they do contain graphic violence which is usually directed toward women. These films vividly depict mutilation and brutality, leading to a desensitization toward violence in the viewers. "Desensitization is defined as decreased responsiveness to a stimulus after extensive exposure to it" (1987, p. 115). The desensitization decreases anxiety about violence to women. While it does not lead to violence in everyone, it does make people less sensitive to the victimization of women. This desensitization is demonstrated in research by a decrease in concern for victims by subjects making judgments impacting rape victims. For example, one study found that subjects desensitized by viewing violence against women evaluated injuries to women who were raped as less severe and evaluated the victim as less worthy than those viewers who were not desensitized. Those subjects who enjoyed the films more and thought them less violent judged the female as more responsible for the rape and the defendant less responsible (Linz, Donnerstein & Penrod 1984).

Donnerstein, Linz, and Penrod (1987) believe the violence depicted in the media toward women is more problematic than explicit sex. They maintain that the combination of sex and violence in the media is ignored. "We contend that the violence against women in some types of R-rated films shown in neighborhood theatres and on cable television far exceeds that portrayed in even the most graphic pornography" (p. ix). They conclude that it is not the sexually explicit material, but rather the violent images fused with the explicit sex or violence alone, which create the antisocial and aggressive behavior toward women. In their book on pornography, they conclude "that some forms of pornography, under some conditions, promote certain antisocial attitudes and behavior. Specifically, we should be most concerned about the detrimental effects of exposure to violent images in pornography and elsewhere, particularly material that portrays the myth that women enjoy or in some way benefit from rape, torture, or other forms of sexual violence. It is important to remember, however, that a portrayal of this theme is not limited to pornography. Many mass media depictions that contain little explicit sex or are only mildly sexually explicit portray the same myth" (p. 171).

Alleviating the Effects of Sexual Violence

Donnerstein, Linz, and Penrod (1987) disagree with both the conclusions and recommendations of the Meese Commission. These authors do not support the imposition of harsher penalties for trafficking in violent pornography recommended by the commission. Instead, they suggest the institution of educational programs to teach viewers, particularly young people, to be more critical in their choices in media viewing.

Graphic violence against women is pervasive in the media. It is found in books, television, and movies that are not sexually explicit. Rape is a topic in many forms of media and women's positive response to the violence is frequently portrayed. The Meese Commission's recommendation to strengthen obscenity laws would be useless in controlling this type of violence. Legal remedies would have to extend to every mass media form and still would be unlikely to cover every media presentation. Therefore, these authors maintain that education is the only possible way of decreasing the viewing of this type of violence.

Documentation of the effectiveness of education is found in follow-up studies of debriefings in research on the impact of violent pornography. In the debriefing sessions, myths about rape are contradicted. For example, subjects are told that women's enjoyment of rape is fictitious. The debriefing is quite effective. Subjects who are debriefed are less willing to accept the myths about rape than those in the control group who do not receive this form of debriefing. This difference is maintained for up to 6 months following the debriefing, after which time it levels off (Donnerstein & Berkowitz 1981).

Malamuth and Check (1984) also compared subjects debriefed on myths related to rape to nondebriefed subjects. The debriefed subjects were less likely to see rape as normal or to think the victim caused the rape or wanted to be raped. These subjects were also more likely to impose a severe sentence on the rapist.

Deterrence

The previous two sections explored ways in which crime could be decreased by changes in the public's behavior. This section will discuss how the criminal justice system can decrease crime.

The criminal justice system in general, and corrections in particular, are based on the assumption that punishment of criminals will deter future criminal activity. This deterrent effect of punishment or sanctions is generally divided into two categories: **general** deterrence and **specific** deterrence. "All theories of general deterrence are based on the premise that sanctions are negative inducements and that their imposition on detected offenders serves to discourage at least some others from engaging in similar pursuits" (Blumstein, Cohen & Nagin 1978, p. 19). Specific or primary deterrence, in contrast, merely assumes that a sanction will discourage the punished offender from future criminal activity.

Both aspects of deterrence are based on the assumption that attaching negative sanctions to a particular behavior will decrease people's inclination toward that behavior (Zimring & Hawkins 1973). However, there is considerable debate among social scientists about the actual effect of punishment on an individual's behavior and serious questions concerning the evidence used to support the existence of a deterrent effect of legal sanctions (Klepper & Nagin 1989a, 1989b, Tittle & Rowe 1973, Waldo & Chiricos 1972, Zimring & Hawkins 1973).

Limitations of Early Research on Deterrence

Early research on deterrence was evaluated by the Panel on Research on Deterrent and Incapacitative Effects (Blumstein, Cohen & Nagin 1978) which concluded that "taken as a whole, the reported evidence consistently finds a negative association between crime rates and the risks of apprehension, conviction, or imprisonment" (p. 4). However, the evidence for deterrence was not quite as decisive as it might appear. There were many limitations in the data that had been used to determine the reported consistent effect. This same panel lists three primary sources of bias in those data. The first source of bias is **error in measuring crimes.**

Most early research on deterrence employed official crime statistics to measure both the amount of crime and the level of sanction. Usually a sanction was defined in terms of a ratio. The numerator of the ratio was the number of times the sanction was imposed (apprehension, correction, or sentence), and the denominator of the ratio was the number of offenses committed. The primary source of these statistics was the FBI Uniform Crime Reports. The unreliability of this data is widely recognized (see Chapter 2 for a complete discussion of crime statistics).

Individual police departments are the source of both the number of offenses and the number of arrests, leading to recognized distortion. In addition, the number of offenses is the numerator in the rate of offenses (offenses/population) and is the denominator in the sanction variable (arrests/offenses). As the panel indicates, "because of the way the sanction risk and the crime rate are defined, any variation in the reporting or recording rates in different jurisdictions could cause a negative association, even in the absence of a deterrent effect" (Blumstein et al. 1978, p. 5).

The second bias listed by the panel is **confounding of deterrence and incapacitation.** When offenders are in prison, they cannot commit offenses. A decrease in the number of crimes is not necessarily related to the deterrent effect of the sanction but rather could be attributed to the incapacitation of some offenders. Thus, "a negative association between crimes and sanctions reflects the combined effects of deterrence and incapacitation, rather than a deterrent effect alone" (Blumstein, Cohen & Nagin 1978, p. 5).

The third source of bias which the panel indicates is **simultaneous effect.** This bias focuses on the possibility that the causal direction of the negative association between crime and sanctions could occur in either direction. In other words, the crime rate might decrease as a result of increased sanctions or, alternatively, jurisdictions might lower their sanctions (decrease the amount of time criminals are sentenced to incarceration) as a result of higher crime rate. These authors cite several possible reasons for this latter relationship. If the criminal justice system becomes overburdened with a large number of offenses, the sanctions might be decreased in order to ease the load. There is also the possibility of an increase in tolerance for particular crimes in jurisdictions when those crimes become frequent.

In addition to the biases enumerated by the panel, there are other difficulties with the research on deterrence. One of the concerns expressed by a number of authors is the use of aggregate data (Klepper & Nagin 1989a, Tittle & Logan 1973, Waldo & Chiricos 1972). Aggregate data do not provide information on how sanctions are perceived by individual potential criminals and cannot be used to evaluate the impact of a particular sanction on a particular offender. In addition, the use of aggregate data makes it very difficult to isolate the factor responsible for a decrease in criminal activity. For example, the individual might have been deterred by the threat of social embarrassment associated with an arrest or by the risk of the legal punishment associated with the crime. Increasing the sanction for a particular offense could cause the individual offender to commit a different crime instead of the one having the increased sanction. Or, the increased sanction could lead the individual offender to increase his resistance to apprehension. This information cannot be obtained from aggregate data.

Survey Research

In an attempt to alleviate the problems associated with aggregate data, researchers turned to the use of self-report or survey data. This research method asks people to report on their own criminal behavior and their perceptions of detection risk and sanction severity for criminal behavior.

Cross-Sectional Studies
Initial survey research used cross-sectional data. This method involves the measurement of two variables at the same point in time. One of these variables may allude to an event or behavior which occurred earlier or which might occur in

the future. In deterrence research, the variables were generally an individual's current perception of severity and/or certainty of sanction and involvement in criminal or deviant behavior which occurred in the preceding 6 months to a year. Typically, these studies have found that certainty of punishment is a deterrent, but that severity of punishment is not.

There are two primary criticisms of cross-sectional survey research. The first of these criticisms has centered on the possibility that the relationship between the perceptions of risk of detection and prior criminal behavior is due to an **experiential effect** rather than a deterrent effect. The research measures current perceptions of certainty and previous behavior. The causal direction of this relationship could occur in the direction opposite to that assumed by the researchers, indicating that prior criminal behavior affects perceptions of risk, not the reverse. In other words, the individual who has had no experience with criminal activity might perceive the risks involved as much higher than the person who has been actively engaged in criminal behavior (Bishop 1984, Greenberg 1981, Saltzman et al. 1982).

The experiential effect is a logical outcome of involvement in the criminal justice system. Most people are not punished for their criminal behavior. Someone who has committed a crime without being caught might easily lower his expectations of the risks of receiving a sanction. Therefore, when research finds a negative correlation between criminal activity and perceptions of risks, it could conceivably be due to experience with crime rather than deterrence. See AN INNOVATIVE DETERRENT.

After reviewing cross-sectional studies used to support the deterrent effect of sanctions, Paternoster (1987) concluded that all the studies are examples of the experiential effect. Research using a **lagged relationship,** in which perceptions were measured at one point in time and behavior was measured 6 months later, supported the experiential effect. These studies showed that people involved in crime later have decreased perceptions of risks of sanctions. Later research which differentiated the experiential and deterrent effects found the deterrent effect to be considerably weaker than previously reported.

A second criticism of cross-sectional research on deterrence is that the results might be **spurious.** Prior to assuming that an inverse relationship between certainty of sanction and criminal behavior indicates a deterrent effect, other possible interpretations of the relationship must be explored. It is possible that some other variable, such as social pressure, is responsible for both certainty and criminal involvement. And in fact, when Paternoster reviewed studies which included more variables, he found that the "deterrent effect for perceived certainty becomes highly questionable" (1987, p. 184).

Panel Studies
In response to the criticisms of cross-sectional data, a new approach to research on deterrence surfaced. This method involves the use of panel studies to collect self-report data from the same individuals through surveys repeated over time. These studies measure individuals' current perceptions of risks of sanctions and their subsequent criminal involvement. Panel studies were designed to control the

> **Box 14.4**
>
> **An Innovative Deterrent**
>
> Passengers riding the Manhattan subway are used to panhandlers. However, the saxophone player had a new approach. He began playing his instrument at an ear-piercing pitch. He then demanded that the riders give him some money or he would continue their torture. Not everyone was bullied. One large woman calmly put away her crossword puzzle and took out some sheet music. Standing in front of the threatening saxophone player, she proceeded to belt out a loud, clear operatic tune. Having met his match, the saxophone player moved to another car. The operatic singer received a round of applause when she left at the next subway station.

Source: "Woman Picks a Song Over Sax and Violence," *The Florida Times-Union,* (November 29, 1988), p. A-2.

impact of experience on perceptions of risk and, thus, evaluate the "true" deterrent effect. These studies separate the deterrent effect from the experiential effect.

Generally, panel studies found little or no relationship between deterrence and certainty or severity of sentence, bringing into question the deterrent effect of criminal sanctions. Instead, these studies found deterrence to be related to informal sanctions, socialization, and morals (Bishop 1984, Klepper & Nagin 1989b, Paternoster et al. 1983, Saltzman et al. 1982). However, panel studies have also been criticized for methodological problems and some newer work is returning to the cross-sectional survey method with improvements in design. And, in fact, research by Lundman (1986) found the effects of experience with crime on perceptions of risk to be small. However, Paternoster disagrees with the return to cross-sectional methods. He maintains that even improved cross-sectional methods will have limited usefulness because people's perceptions are changeable.

One recent study has reaffirmed the deterrent effect of criminal sanctions. Using an improved cross-sectional survey design, Klepper and Nagin (1989b) found a relationship between perceptions of detection risk and deterrence of tax noncompliance. These authors contend that severity of punishment and fear of criminal prosecution have a strong deterrent impact on criminal behavior.

Severity and Deterrence

Although theories of deterrence discuss both certainty and severity of sanctions, in actuality very little research has focused on severity. Paternoster enumerates three reasons for this inattention to severity in the research. First, theorists have contended that certainty is more important than severity. In addition, aggregate data not only have not found an inverse relationship between severity and crime, but many studies actually found a positive relationship. In essence, these data indicate that the more severe the punishment, the more likely someone was to commit a crime. And finally, the early research using individual perceptions found little support for severity having a deterrent effect on criminal or deviant behavior.

An experiential effect in severity research is not a concern. The commission of a crime does not logically influence an individual's perceptions of sanctions. However, spuriousness is a viable concern. When studies include other explanatory variables, severity appears to have virtually no effect on criminal behavior (Paternoster 1987).

Generalizability

Despite the improvements in methodology, there are still some limitations to acceptance of deterrence research. For one thing, almost exclusively, the research has been conducted on college students. The behavior of this population does not necessarily reflect that of the general population. The people who are most apt to be involved in serious criminal behavior are not likely to be those surveyed. In addition, the forms of deviance surveyed tend to be quite minor. These limitations bring into question the generalizability of results to serious criminals and serious forms of lawbreaking.

Guns and Their Control

Most of the proposals for crime intervention and prevention explored in this chapter are controversial and the final one is probably the most contentious. Gun ownership and restriction of gun ownership are hotly debated topics. One position maintains that control of guns will decrease violence in society. The opposition contends that if gun ownership is restricted, "only the criminals will have guns." The latter group argues that with the amount of violence in society, honest citizens need firearms in order to protect themselves. Surveys indicate that the vast majority of the population is in favor of gun control (Young, McDowall & Loftin 1987). However, when determining policies, citizens tend to vote against restrictions to gun ownership. These results are generally assumed to be due to the efforts of the National Rifle Association and a strong gun lobby. While there is some truth to that assumption, it is not the only explanation.

Collective Security Model

Young, McDowall, and Loftin (1987) use the collective security model to explain why people vote against gun control when surveys indicate most people favor it. These authors explain that the "expected benefits of gun control are collective in nature, while the expected benefits of gun ownership are individual" (p. 56). If the ownership of guns is restricted, society benefits since the risk of violence and injury are decreased. But this benefit occurs only if everyone complies with the restricted ownership of guns. People would be happy to vote for a society in which no one owned a gun. But they are not willing to give up their right if others (specifically, criminals) still have guns. If there is a great deal of violence in the community, individuals do not want restrictions on their right to have a gun for protection. They are particularly reluctant to forego this right if there is a perception that the institutions that control crime are ineffective. Therefore, gun control is most widely supported when and where it is least needed—in areas where the crime rate is low and self-protection is unnecessary. "Crime and disorder play a double-barreled role: they create both a perceived need for controls on gun possession and, at the same time, they are a major source of resistance to controls" (McDowall & Loftin 1985, p. 411).

Civilized societies maintain control and order through collective mechanisms, such as police, courts, and corrections. Violence decreases when security is provided by the community instead of having individuals or families protecting themselves. Therefore, if the criminal justice institutions are effective and citizens can depend on them for protection, individuals have no need to keep private weapons for self-protection. However, the security of the individual is threatened if the community efforts are ineffective. In these situations, the individual is more vulnerable to victimization since that individual is unprepared for self-protection. If confidence in the collective security weakens, the individual has a desire to own defense weapons. By arming themselves, individuals feel more secure, but the amount of violence in the community increases. See THE SUBWAY VIGILANTE.

The collective security model is supported by research (Young, McDowall & Loftin 1987). Both confidence in police and confidence in the courts are negatively related to gun ownership for protection. Gun sales and ownership increase with the increase in violent crime and riots. At the same time, gun sales and ownership decrease with the increase in allocations to the criminal justice system. However, this same research found no relationship between the perception of crime rate or fear of crime with the likelihood of gun ownership.

Firearm Accidents

The dangers associated with firearms extend beyond actual criminal incidents. Injuries from firearms are not confined to victims of crimes or to perpetrators who encounter armed victims; there are many accidental injuries from firearms. Private ownership of guns for protection increases the risk of injury and death by accident. McDowall and Loftin (1985) reviewed the literature and found that "three major variables determine the risk of firearm accidents: (1) the prevalence of guns (gun density), (2) gun accessibility, and (3) conduct" (p. 403). In other words, the number of firearm accidents is dependent on the number of guns in a community; the more guns there are, the more accidents are likely to occur. In contrast, accidents are less likely when there is greater difficulty involved in obtaining an operable gun. Finally, accidents are related to the behavior of the gun user. Untrained gun users are more likely to cause accidents than those who are trained.

McDowall and Loftin support a collective security model. They contend that all three factors influencing firearm accidents are related to people's perceptions of the effectiveness of the social institutions used to control crime and society's confidence in these institutions. If people in a community perceive the police and

Box 14.5

The Subway Vigilante

Bernhard Hugo Goetz led a quiet, unassuming life until December 22, 1984. On that evening, the 36-year-old electronics technician rode the subway home from work in New York City as he did every weekday. But this ride was different. Four young black males approached Goetz and asked for $5.00. Goetz, a slightly-built man, felt that the black youths were threatening him. Goetz had been seriously injured in a mugging 3 years earlier by three black youths. After that first incident, Goetz carried a gun. This night, he pulled out his gun and shot all four alleged muggers. After reporting the incident to the conductor, Goetz left the subway and fled to New Hampshire.

News of his escapade rapidly spread, and Bernie Goetz became a folk hero. All four of the youths involved in the Goetz incident had police records. People who rode the subway and were terrorized by young thugs cheered Goetz's actions. In the wake of this publicity, Bernhard Goetz turned himself in to the police 9 days after the incident. He confessed to the police in Concord, New Hampshire, and was returned to New York for trial.

The district attorney in New York brought the case to a grand jury who declined to indict Goetz for attempted murder but merely indicted him on a weapons possession charge. However, as more information about the case became available, it was not as clear that Bernie Goetz was a hero. Some people began to view him as a racist. Two of the boys were shot in the back and one was paralyzed with a second shot. Witnesses said that Goetz came up to the boy lying on the ground and said, "Here's another one for you."

As more evidence was revealed, public sentiment took another turn. Some people were upset that Goetz was carrying an unlicensed gun. There was public pressure to try Goetz for attempted murder. Two months later, another grand jury decided to indict Goetz and he went to trial.

The jury selected for the trial was composed of ten whites and two blacks. Six jury members had been victims of crime; four were mugged on the New York subway. In June, 1987, Goetz was adjudicated not guilty of seventeen charges, including four charges of attempted murder and assault. He was found guilty of illegal possession of a gun.

♦

Should citizens have the right to defend themselves with weapons? Would this be so even if the attackers do not have weapons? Do you think people should have the right to protect themselves with guns in high-crime areas such as the New York subway? Would the jury's decision have been the same if Goetz had been black and the attackers white? Would the jury's decision have been the same if an innocent bystander had been killed or seriously injured by a bullet?

Sources: O. Friedrich, "Not Guilty," *Time* (June 29, 1987), pp. 10–11; "The Goetz Trial 'Sideshow' Can Be Startling to Visitors," *The Florida Times-Union* (May 3, 1987), p. A–19.

courts as being unable to control crime, citizens are more likely to buy guns, guns are likely to be more accessible, and people who are not trained in their use will own guns. Therefore, the incidence of firearm accidents will tend to increase.

These authors propose three determinants of confidence in institutional control of crime: the amount of violent crime, police strength, and civil disorder. These three factors are related to the use of guns for protection in a given community. Therefore, confidence in institutional control of crime predicts the three variables which determine the risk of firearm accidents: density, accessibility, and conduct. Using time-series data from Detroit over a 26-year period from 1951 to 1977, McDowall and Loftin found that the data fit their model "quite well." In general, a decrease in collective security led to an increase in the risk of fatal firearm accidents. The number of accidental gunshot deaths increased with the increase in violent crime and civil disturbances. At the same time, accidental gunshot deaths increased with the decrease in allocation of resources to police. They suggest that a policy that increases confidence in the institutions designated to protect society will decrease gun accidents more than restricted access to guns. See WHAT WOULD HAPPEN TO A BLACK BERNHARD GOETZ?

Guns and Deterrence Theory

An important aspect of the argument for gun control lies in whether or not gun control laws will deter crime. Grasmick and Green (1980) propose three inhibitors to deviance: fear of social sanctions (e.g., incarceration), fear of informal sanctions (e.g., violence by victim), and morality. Beginning with the last inhibitor, Green (1987) contends that there are people whose moral values prevent them from committing crimes. No matter what the laws are in reference to gun control, these people will not change their behavior. There is another group of people whose motivation to commit crime is so strong that none of these factors will deter them. Therefore, the group of interest is the remaining population, those who do not have internal constraints against crime, but who will be deterred by external factors.

Gary Kleck reanalyzed the National Crime Survey data in order to determine the incidence and impact of armed resistance to crime. He found that citizen use of guns against violent criminals and burglars occurred approximately as frequently as arrests. He concluded that victim gun use "is a more prompt negative consequence of crime than legal punishment, and is more severe, at its most serious, than legal system punishments" (1988, p. 16). In addition, victims who resist criminals with guns are less likely to lose their property and less likely to be injured than if they resisted in any other manner or offered no resistance.

Green maintains that "deterrence refers to the prevention of crimes from occurring altogether rather than to the altering of crimes already in progress" (1987, p. 64). Deterrence is once again divided into general deterrence and specific deterrence. If gun ownership is a general deterrent, then a victim shooting a perpetrator or holding him at bay with a gun would discourage other criminals from attempting the same crime. If gun ownership is a specific deterrent, then a

> **Box 14.6**
>
> **What Would Happen to a Black Bernhard Goetz?**
>
> No one knows for sure what would have happened if Bernhard Goetz had been black and his antagonists had been white. However, a similar incident did occur in which the races of the actors were reversed. Austin Weeks, a 29-year-old black man was riding the subway in New York City in April, 1980, when two white youths accosted him. Terry Zilimbinaks, 17, leaned over the black adult and recited a series of racial insults. Weeks, like Goetz, was carrying an unlicensed gun. He used this gun to kill Zilimbinaks. Like Goetz, Weeks fled the scene. However, he did not come forth and confess. It took the police 6 years to find Weeks and arrest him. But the grand jury refused to indict Weeks. Weeks was a free man. In addition, there was little publicity surrounding this case.
>
> ♦
>
> Why was there so much publicity surrounding the Goetz case and so little surrounding the Weeks case? Why did the grand jury refuse to indict Weeks? Should the grand jury indict someone for carrying an unlicensed gun on the subway?

Source: O. Friedrich, "Not Guilty," *Time* (June 29, 1987), pp. 10–11.

criminal who is shot without being mortally wounded, shot at, or held at bay by a potential victim would decide never to commit a crime again.

Researchers have attempted to examine the deterrent effect of gun ownership by interviewing convicted criminals. One survey found that inmates were more afraid of being caught and sent to prison than of being shot by police or victims (Wright & Rossi 1985). However, inmates indicated that they were more afraid of an armed victim than of the police. Gary Kleck (1988) reanalyzed Wright and Rossi's data and found that 43 percent of inmates interviewed had decided at some time against committing a crime because of their knowledge or belief that the potential victim had a gun.

Research with inmates who have actually encountered an armed victim have supported the deterrent effect of guns. These inmates are more likely to consider the danger of guns in future attacks than those inmates who have never been confronted by a victim with a weapon. However, the research did not obtain evidence that these inmates have curtailed their criminal activity as a result of being confronted with a weapon (Green 1987).

Summary

A number of methods for crime intervention and prevention were explored. Bibb Latané and John Darley developed a five-stage model to explain helping in an emergency. A witness must **notice the incident,** then **define the situation as an**

emergency. Next the bystander must determine whether he should **assume responsibility for acting** and **decide on what assistance to give.** Finally, the bystander must **actually help.** At each of the first three stages, there is an inverse relationship between the number of observers and the likelihood that any one of them will intervene. This phenomenon is referred to as the **bystander effect.** The cost-reward model hypothesizes that people evaluate the costs and benefits of helping and not helping before assisting the victim.

Two national commissions have studied pornography and came to conflicting conclusions. President Johnson's commission concluded that viewing erotic materials did not cause sex crimes, while the Meese Commission concluded that sexually violent material caused sexual violence.

Research differentiates between violent pornography in which the female victim appears to enjoy the victimization and pornography in which the female victim obviously finds the experience to be noxious. Men rated with a high likelihood of raping and convicted rapists were more likely to be aroused by rape than were other men.

Violence is more detrimental to viewers than explicit sex. Films that vividly depict mutilation and brutality toward women lead to a desensitization toward violence in the viewers. Educational programs to teach viewers to be more critical in their choices of media viewing are suggested as a means of decreasing the impact of violent pornography.

Deterrence is based on the assumption that attaching negative sanctions to a particular behavior will decrease people's inclination toward that behavior. However, there is much debate among social scientists about the actual effect of punishment on an individual's behavior. Early research findings on deterrence have been limited by biases within the data. Survey research attempted to overcome the biases but used cross-sectional data which has been criticized on the basis of an **experiential effect** and **spurious results.** A new approach to research, panel studies, found little or no relationship between deterrence and certainty or severity of sentence. This method has also been criticized for methodological problems. In addition, the generalizability of results to serious criminals and serious forms of lawbreaking is questioned.

The collective security model maintains that restricted ownership of guns reduces the risk of violence and injury in society only if everyone complies with the restriction. If confidence in the collective security weakens, the individual has a desire to own defense weapons and the amount of violence in the community increases, as does the risk of firearm accidents.

An important aspect of the argument for gun control lies in whether or not gun control laws will deter crime. Research with convicted criminals found that those who had encountered an armed victim were more likely to consider the danger of guns in future attacks than those inmates who have never been confronted by a victim with a weapon.

References

Abel, G. G., Blanchard, E. B., Barlow, D. H., & Mavissakalian, M. 1976. Psychological treatment of rapists. In *Sexual Assault: The Victim and the Rapist,* M. Walker & S. Brody, eds. Lexington, Mass.: Lexington.

Abel, G. G., Blanchard, E. B., & Becker, J. V. 1978. An integrated treatment program for rapists. In *Clinical Aspects of the Rapist,* R. Rada, ed. New York: Grune & Straton.

Adams, T. F. 1972. Philosophy of police discretion. In *Criminal Justice Readings,* T. J. Adams, ed. Pacific Palisades, Calif.: Palisades.

Adler, F. 1975. *Sisters in Crime.* New York: McGraw-Hill.

Adorno, T. W., Frenkel-Brunswik, E., Levinson, D. J., & Sanford, R. N. 1950. *The Authoritarian Personality.* New York: Harper & Row.

Aichhorn, A. 1935. *Wayward Youth.* New York: Viking.

Akers, R. L., LaGreca, A. J., Sellers, C., & Cochran, J. 1987. Fear of crime and victimization among the elderly in different types of communities. *Criminology* 25(3): 487–505.

Albonetti, C. A. 1987. Prosecutorial discretion: The effects of uncertainty. *Law & Society Review* 21(2): 291–314.

Alexander, M., & Licker, J. 1975. Selecting a rigid or flexible juror. *Social Action and the Law* 2: 4.

Allport, F. H. 1933. *Institutional Behavior: Essays Toward a Reinterpreting of Contemporary Social Organization.* Chapel Hill, N.C.: University of North Carolina Press.

Allport, G. W., & Postman, L. 1947. *The Psychology of Rumor.* New York: Henry Holt.

Allsopp, J. F. 1976. Criminality and delinquency. In *A Textbook of Human Psychology,* H. J. Eysenck & G. D. Wilson, eds. Baltimore: University Park Press.

Alschuler, A. W. 1968. The prosecutor's role in plea bargaining. *University of Chicago Law Review* 36: 50–112.

Alschuler, A. W. 1979. Sentencing reform and prosecutorial power: A critique of recent proposals for "fixed" and "presumptive" sentencing. In *Criminology Review Yearbook,* vol. 1, S. L. Messinger & E. Bittner, eds. Beverly Hills, Calif.: Sage.

American Correctional Association. 1983. *The American Prison: From the Beginning.* Washington, D.C.: American Correctional Assoc.

Amir, M. 1971. *Patterns in Forcible Rape.* Chicago: University of Chicago Press.

Anderson, E. A. 1976. The chivalrous treatment of the female offender in the arms of the criminal justice system: A review of the literature. *Social Problems* 23: 350–357.

Aronfreed, J. 1961. The nature, variety, and social patterning of moral responses to transgression. *Journal of Abnormal and Social Psychology* 63: 223–240.

Asch, S. E. 1952. *Social Psychology.* New York: Prentice-Hall.

Asch, S. E. 1956. Studies of independence and submission to group pressure. *Psychological Monographs* 70.

Austin, W. 1979. The concept of desert and its influence on simulated decision makers' sentencing decisions. *Law and Human Behavior* 3: 163–187.

Baker, L. 1983. *Miranda: Crime, Law and Politics.* New York: Atheneum.

Baker, M. 1985. *Cops: Their Lives in Their Own Words.* New York: Simon & Schuster.

Balkin, J. 1988. Why policemen don't like policewomen. *Journal of Police Science and Administration* 16(1): 29–38.

Band, S. R., & Manuele, C. A. 1987. Stress and police officer performance: An examination of effective coping behavior. *Police Studies* 10(3): 122–131.

Bandura, A. 1973. Social learning theory of aggression. In *The Control of Aggression,* J. F. Knutson, ed. Chicago: Aldine.

Bandura, A. 1977. *Social Learning Theory.* Englewood Cliffs, N.J.: Prentice-Hall.

Bandura, A., & Mischel, W. 1965. Modification of self-imposed delay of reward through exposure to live and symbolic models. *Journal of Personality and Social Psychology* 2: 698–705.

Bandura, A., & Walters, R. H. 1959. *Adolescent Aggression.* New York: Ronald.

Bard, M., & Sangrey, D. 1979. *The Crime Victim's Book.* New York: Basic.

Barkowitz, P., & Brigham, J. C. 1982. Recognition of faces: Own-race bias, incentive, and time delay. *Journal of Applied Social Psychology* 12: 255–268.

Baron, R. A. 1977. *Human Aggression.* New York: Plenum.

Bartol, C. R. 1980. *Criminal Behavior: A Psychosocial Approach.* Englewood Cliffs, N.J.: Prentice-Hall.

Bayley, D. H. 1979. Police function, structure, and control in Western Europe and North America: Comparative and historical studies. In *Crime and Justice: An Annual Review of Research,* N. Morris & M. Tonry, eds. Chicago: University of Chicago Press.

Beckham, J. C., Annis, L. V., & Gustafson, D. L. 1989. Decision making and examiner bias in forensic expert recommendations for not guilty by reason of insanity. *Law and Human Behavior* 13(1): 79–88.

Bell, D. J. 1982. Policewomen: Myths and reality. *Journal of Police Science and Administration* 10(1): 112–120.

Bem, D. J. 1972. Self-perception theory. In *Advances in Experimental Social Psychology,* vol. 6, L. Berkowitz, ed. New York: Academic Press.

Benjamin, G. A. H., Kaszniak, A., Sales, B., & Shanfield, S. B. 1986. The role of legal education in producing psychological distress among law students and lawyers. *American Bar Foundation Research Journal,* Vol. 11 pp. 225–252.

Bennis, W., & Cleveland, C. 1980. Ripping off the cops. *Chronicle of Higher Education* 20(6): 64.

Berg, K., & Vidmar, N. 1975. Authoritarianism and recall of evidence about criminal behavior. *Journal of Research in Personality* 9: 147–157.

Berkowitz, L. 1969. Control of aggression. In *Review of Child Development Research,* B. M. Caldwell & H. Ricciuti, eds. 3, Chicago: University of Chicago Press.

Berkowitz, L. 1982. Simple views of aggression: An essay review. In *Contemporary Issues in Social Psychology,* 4th ed., J. C. Brigham & L. S. Wrightsman, eds. Monterey: Brooks/Cole, pp. 39–47.

Berliner, L., & Barbieri, M. K. 1984. The testimony of the child victim of sexual assault. *Journal of Social Issues* 40(2): 125–138.

Bermant, G. 1985. Issues in trial management: Conducting the voir dire examination. In *The Psychology of Evidence and Trial Procedure,* S. M. Kassin & L. S. Wrightsman, eds. Beverly Hills, Calif.: Sage.

Bermant, G., Nemeth, C., & Vidmar, N., eds. 1976. *Psychology and the Law.* Lexington, Mass.: Lexington.

Bernstein, I. N., Kelly, W. R., & Doyle, P. A. 1977. Societal reaction to deviants. *American Sociological Review* 42: 743–755.

References

Bersoff, D. N., & Ogden, D. W. 1987. In the Supreme Court of the United States: *Lockhart v. McCree*, Amicus Curiae Brief for the American Psychological Association. *American Psychologist* 42(1): 59–68.

Bierei, J. 1955. Cognitive complexity-simplicity and predictive behavior. *Journal of Abnormal and Social Psychology* 51: 163–268.

Bishop, D. 1984. Legal and extralegal barriers to delinquency: A panel analysis. *Criminology* 22: 403–419.

Bittner, E. 1974. Florence Nightingale in pursuit of Willie Sutton: A theory of the police. In *The Potential for Reform in Criminal Justice*, H. Jacob, ed. Beverly Hills, Calif.: Sage.

Black, D. 1971. The social organization of arrest. *Stanford Law Review* 23: 1087–1111.

Blades, J. 1985. *Family Mediation: Cooperative Divorce Settlement*. Englewood Cliffs, N.J.: Prentice Hall.

Blanck, P. D., Rosenthal, R., & Cordell, L. H. 1985. The appearance of justice: Judges' verbal and nonverbal behavior in criminal jury trials. *Stanford Law Review* 38: 89–164.

Block, C. R., & Block, R. L. 1984. Crime definition, crime measurement, and victim surveys. *Journal of Social Issues* 40(1): 137–160.

Block, R. 1977. *Violent Crime*. Lexington, Mass.: Lexington.

Blumberg, A. S. 1979. *Criminal Justice: Issues and Ironies,* 2nd ed. New York: New Viewpoints.

Blumstein, A., Cohen, J., & Nagin, D., eds. 1978. *Deterrence and Incapacitation: Estimating the Effects of Criminal Sanctions on Crime Rates*. Washington, D.C.: National Academy of Sciences.

Blunk, R. A., & Sales, B. D. 1977. Persuasion during the voir dire. In *Psychology in the Legal Process,* B. D. Sales, ed. New York: Spectrum.

Boehm, V. R. 1968. Mr. Prejudice, Miss Sympathy, and the authoritarian personality. *Wisconsin Law Review* (1968), pp. 734–750.

Boehnert, C. E. 1989. Characteristics of successful and unsuccessful insanity pleas. *Law and Human Behavior* 13(1): 31–40.

Bonn, R. L. 1984. *Criminology.* New York: McGraw-Hill.

Bonsignore, J. J., Katsh, E., d'Errico, P., Pipkin, R. M., & Arons, S. 1974. *Before the Law: An Introduction to the Legal Process*. Boston: Houghton Mifflin.

Bothwell, R. K., Brigham, J. C., & Malpass, R. S. 1989. Cross-racial identification. *Personality and Social Psychology Bulletin* 15(1): 19–25.

Bothwell, R. K., Deffenbacher, K. A., & Brigham, J. C. 1987. Correlation of eyewitness accuracy and confidence: Optimality hypothesis revised. *Journal of Applied Psychology* 72: 691–695.

Bozza, C. M. 1973. Motivation guiding police in arrest process. *Journal of Police Science & Administration* 1: 468–476.

Bray, R. M., & Kerr, N. L. 1982. Methodological issues in the study of the psychology of the courtroom. In *The Psychology of the Courtroom,* Kerr, N. L. & Bray, R. M., eds. New York: Academic Press.

Bray, R. M., & Noble, A. M. 1978. Authoritarianism and decisions of mock juries: Evidence of jury bias and group polarization. *Journal of Personality and Social Psychology* 36: 1424–1430.

Brewer, D., Beckett, G. E., & Holt, N. 1981. Determinate sentencing in California. *Journal of Research in Crime and Delinquency* 18: 200–231.

Brickman, P., Rabinowitz, V. C., Karuza, J., Coates, D., Cohn, E., & Kidder, L. 1982. Models of helping and coping. *American Psychologist* 37: 368–384.

Brigham, J. C., & Bothwell, R. K. 1983. The ability of prospective jurors to estimate the accuracy of eyewitness identifications. *Law and Human Behavior* 1: 19–30.

Brigham, J. C., & WolfsKeil, M. P. 1983. Opinions of attorneys and law enforcement personnel on the accuracy of eyewitness identifications. *Law and Human Behavior* 7: 337–349.

Broeder, D. W. 1965. Voir dire examinations: An empirical study. *Southern California Law Review* 38:503–528.

Bronson, E. J. 1970. On the conviction proneness and representativeness of the death qualified jury: An empirical study of Colorado veniremen. *University of Colorado Law Review* 42: 1–3.

Brown, R. M. 1979. Historical patterns of American violence. In *Violence in America: Historical and Comparative Perspectives,* H. D. Graham & T. R. Gurr, eds. Beverly Hills, Calif.: Sage, pp. 19–48.

Brown, E. L., Deffenbacher, K. A., & Sturgill, W. 1977. Memory for faces and the circumstances of encounter. *Journal of Applied Psychology* 62: 311–318.

Bruner, J. S., & Postman, L. J. 1949. On the perception of incongruity: A paradigm. *Journal of Personality* 18: 206–223.

Bruner, J. S., Postman, L. J., & Rodrigues, J. 1951. Expectations and the perceptions of color. *American Journal of Psychology* 64: 216–227.

Buckhout, R. 1975. Nearly 2,000 witnesses can be wrong. *Social Action and the Law* 2: 7.

Buckhout, R. 1986. Personal values and expert testimony. *Law and Human Behavior* 10(1/2): 127–144.

Buckhout, R., Rabinowitz, M., Alfonso, V., Kanellis, D., & Anderson, J. 1988. Empirical assessment of lineups: Getting down to cases. *Law and Human Behavior* 12(3): 323–332.

Bunch, B. J., Foley, L. A., & Urbina, S. P. 1983. The psychology of violent female offenders. *The Prison Journal* 58(2): 66–79.

Burbeck, E. 1988. Predictive validity of the recruit selection interview. *Police Journal* 61(4): 304–311.

Burgess, A. W., ed. 1984. *Research Handbook on Rape and Sexual Assault.* New York: Garland.

Burgess, A. W., & Holmstrom, L. L. 1974a. Rape trauma syndrome. *American Journal of Psychiatry* 131: 980–986.

Burgess, A. W., & Holmstrom, L. L. 1974b. Coping behavior of the rape victim. *American Journal of Psychiatry* 136: 1278–1282.

Burgess, A. W., & Holmstrom, L. L. 1978. Recovery from rape and prior life stress. *Research in Nursing and Health* 1: 165–174.

Burtt, H. 1931. *Legal Psychology.* New York: Prentice-Hall.

Cadoret, R. J. 1978. Psychopathology in adopted-away offspring of biological parents with antisocial behavior. *Archives of General Psychiatry* 35(2): 176–184.

Calhoun, L. G., Selby, J. W., & Warring, L. J. 1976. Social perception of the victim's causal role in rape. *Human Relations* 29: 517–526.

Caplan, L. 1984. *The Insanity Defense and the Trial of John W. Hinckley, Jr.* Boston: David R. Godine.

Carroll, J. S. 1982. Committing a crime: The offender's decision. In *The Criminal Justice System: A Social-Psychological Analysis,* V. J. Konečni & E. B. Ebbesen, eds. San Francisco: Freeman, pp. 49–67.

Carter, R. M., Glaser, D., & Wilkins, L. T., eds. 1972. *Correctional Institutions.* Philadelphia: Lippincott.

Carter, R. M., & Wilkins, L. T. 1967. Some factors in sentencing policy. *Journal of Criminal Law, Criminology, and Police Science* 58: 503–514.

Casper, J. D. 1972. *American Criminal Justice: The Defendant's Perspective.* Englewood Cliffs, N.J.: Prentice-Hall.

Catania, A. C. 1984. *Learning,* 2nd ed. Englewood Cliffs, N.J.: Prentice-Hall.

Ceci, S. J., Ross, D. F., & Toglia, M. P. 1987. Age differences in suggestibility: Narrowing the uncertainties. In *Children's Eyewitness Memory,* S. J. Ceci, M. P. Toglia, & D. F. Ross, eds. New York: Springer Verlag, pp. 79–91.

Chambliss, W. J., & Seidman, R. B. 1971. *Law, Order and Power.* Reading, Mass.: Addison-Wesley.

Chance, J. E., & Goldstein, A. G. 1984. Face-recognition memory: Implications for children's eyewitness testimony. *Journal of Social Issues* 40(2): 69–86.

Chi, M. T. H. 1978. Knowledge structures and memory development. In *Children's Thinking: What Develops?* R. S. Sieglee, ed. Hillsdale, N.J.: Erlbaum, pp. 73–96.

Chiricos, T. G., & Waldo, G. P. 1975. Socioeconomic status and criminal sentencing. *American Sociological Review* 40: 753–772.

Christiansen, K. O. 1977. A preliminary study of crime among twins. In *Biosocial Bases of Criminal Behavior,* S. A. Mednick & K. O. Christiansen, eds. New York: Gardner Press.

Clare, P. K., & Kramer, J. H. 1976. *Introduction to American Corrections.* Boston: Holbrook Press.

Claridge, G. 1973. Final remarks. In *Personality Differences and Biological Variations,* G. Claridge, S. Canter, & W. I. Hume, eds. New York: Pergamon Press.

Clark, L. D. 1975. *The Grand Jury: The Use and Abuse of Political Power.* New York: Quadrangle Books.

Clark, S. H., Freeman, J. L., & Koch, G. G. 1976. Bail risk: A multivariate analysis. *Journal of Legal Studies* 5: 341–386.

Clarke, S. H. 1976. Influences of income and other factors on whether criminal defendants go to prison. *Law and Society Review* 11: 57–92.

Cloward, R. A., & Ohlin, L. E. 1960. *Delinquency and Opportunity: A Theory of Delinquent Gangs.* Glencoe, Ill.: Free Press.

Coates, D., & Winston, T. 1983. Countering the deviance of depression: Peer support groups for victims. *Journal of Social Issues* 39(2): 169–194.

Coates, D., Wortman, C. B., & Abbey, A. 1979. Reactions to victims. In *New Approaches to Social Problems: Applications of Attribution Theory,* I. H. Frieze, D. Bar-Tal, & J. S. Carroll, eds. San Francisco, Calif.: Jossey-Bass.

Cohen, A. K. 1955. *Delinquent Boys: The Culture of the Gang.* Glencoe, Ill.: Free Press.

Cohen, R. L. 1991. Prisoners in 1990. Washington, D.C.: Bureau of Justice Statistics.

Cohen, R. L., & Harnick, M. A. 1980. The susceptibility of child witnesses to suggestion. *Law and Human Behavior* 4: 201–210.

Cohn, Y. 1974. Crisis intervention and the victim of robbery. In *Victomology: A New Focus,* vol. 2, I. Drapkin & E. Viano, eds. Lexington, Mass.: Heath.

Cohn, A., & Udolf, R. 1979. *The Criminal Justice System and Its Psychology.* New York: Van Nostrand Reinhold.

Cole, G. F. 1986. *The American System of Criminal Justice,* 4th ed. Monterey, Calif.: Brooks/Cole.

Colman, A. M., & Gorman, L. P. 1982. Conservatism, dogmatism, and authoritarianism in British police officers. *Sociology* 16: 1–11.

Cortes, J. B., & Gatti, F. M. 1972. *Delinquency and Crime: A Biopsychological Approach.* New York: Seminar Press.

Cowan, C. C., Thompson, W. C., & Ellsworth P. C. 1984. The effects of death qualification on jurors' predisposition to convict and on the quality of deliberation. *Law and Human Behavior* 8: 53–80.

Crites, L., ed. 1976. *The Female Offender.* Lexington, Mass.: Lexington.

Crowe, R. 1972. The adopted offspring of women criminal offenders. *Archives of General Psychiatry* 27: 600–603.

Cumming, E., Cumming, I. M., & Edell, L. 1965. Policemen as philosopher, guide and friend. *Social Problems* 12: 276–286.

Cutler, B. L., Penrod, S. D., & Dexter, H. R. 1989. The eyewitness, the expert psychologist, and the jury. *Law and Human Behavior* 13(3): 311–332.

Darley, J. M., & Latané, B. 1968. Bystander intervention in emergencies: Diffusion of responsibility. *Journal of Personality and Social Psychology* 8: 377–383.

Darrow, C. 1936. Attorney for the defense. *Esquire Magazine.* Reprinted in *California Trial Lawyers Journal,* 1974–1975.

Das, D. K. 1988. Should we include criminology in police recruitment training? *Police Journal* 61(2): 137–151.

Davies, G., Stevenson-Robb, Y., & Flin, R. 1988. Tales out of school: Children's memory for an unexpected event. In *Practical Aspects of Memory,* vol 1, *Memory in Everyday Life,* M. M. Gruneberg, R. N. Sykes, & P. Morris, eds. London: Wiley, pp. 122–127.

Davis, J. H., Kerr, N. L., Stasser, G., Meek, D., & Holt, R. W. 1977. Victim consequences, sentence severity, and decision processes in mock jurors. *Organizational Behavior and Human Performance* 18: 346–365.

Davis, K. 1947. Final note on a case of extreme isolation. *American Journal of Sociology* 57: 432–457.

Davis, K. E. 1975. *Police Discretion.* St. Paul, Minn.: West.

Davis, P. C. 1978. Death penalty and the current state of the law. *Criminal Law Bulletin* 14: 7–17.

DeFleur, L. 1975. Biasing influences on drug arrest records: Implications for deviance research. *American Sociological Review* 40: 88–103.

Dershowitz, A. 1982. *The Best Defense.* New York: Random House.

Diamond, B. L. 1980. Inherent problems in the use of pretrial hypnosis on a prospective witness. *California Law Review* 68: 313–349.

Diamond, S. S., & Zeisel, H. 1974. A courtroom experiment on juror selection and decision-making. *Personality and Social Psychology Bulletin* 1: 276–277.

Dodge, L. 1990. *Death Penalty Sentencing* (Report No. B–236876). Washington, D.C.: U.S. General Accounting Office.

Donnerstein, E. 1980. Aggressive erotica and violence against women. *Journal of Personality and Social Psychology* 39: 269–277.

Donnerstein, E., & Berkowitz, L. 1981. Victim reactions in aggressive erotic films as a factor in violence against women. *Journal of Personality and Social Psychology* 41: 710–724.

Donnerstein, E., Linz, D., & Penrod, S. 1987. *The Question of Pornography.* New York: The Free Press.

Doob, A. N., & Kirschenbaum, H. M. 1973. Bias in police lineups—partial remembering. *Journal of Police Science and Administration* 1(3): 287–293.

Duncan, E. M., Whitney, P., & Kunen, S. 1982. Integration of visual and verbal information in children's memories. *Child Development* 53: 1215–1223.

Dvorkin, E., Himmelstein, J., & Lesnick, H. 1981. *Becoming a Lawyer: A Humanistic Perspective on Legal Education and Professionalism.* St. Paul, Minn.: West.

Ebbesen, E. B., & Konečni, V. J. 1982a. An analysis of the bail system. In *The Criminal Justice System: A Social-Psychological Analysis,* V. J. Konečni & E. B. Ebbesen, eds. San Francisco: Freeman, pp. 191–230.

Ebbesen, E. B., & Konečni, V. J. 1982b. Social psychology and the law: A decision-making approach to the criminal justice system. In *The Criminal Justice System: A Social-Psychological Analysis,* V. J. Konečni & E. B. Ebbesen, eds. San Francisco: Freeman, pp. 3–23.

Edwards, H. T. 1988. The role of legal education in shaping the profession. *Journal of Legal Education* 38: 285–293.

Efran, M. G. 1974. The effect of physical appearance on the judgment of guilt, interpersonal attraction, and severity of recommended punishment in a simulated jury task. *Journal of Research in Personality* 8: 45–54.

Eisler, R. T. 1977. *Dissolution: No-Fault Divorce, Marriage and the Future of Women.* New York: McGraw-Hill.

Elkins, J. R. 1988. The quest for meaning: Narrative accounts of legal education. *Journal of Legal Education* 38: 577–598.

Elliott, E. S., Wills, E. J., & Goldstein, A. G. 1973. The effects of discrimination training on the recognition of white and oriental faces. *Bulletin of the Psychonomic Society* 2: 71–73.

Elliott, R., & Robinson, R. J. 1991. Death penalty attitudes and the tendency to convict or acquit: Some data. *Law and Human Behavior* 15(4): 389–404.

Ellis, H. D. 1975. Recognizing faces. *British Journal of Psychology* 6: 409–426.

Ellison, K. W., & Genz, J. L. 1983. *Stress and the Police Officer.* Springfield, Ill.: Charles C. Thomas.

Elwork, A., & Sales, B. D. 1985. Jury instructions. In *The Psychology of Evidence and Trial Procedure,* S. M. Kassin & L. S. Wrightsman, eds. Beverly Hills, Calif.: Sage.

Emler, N. P., Winton, M., & Heather, N. 1977. Moral reasoning and delinquency: Some limitations of Kohlberg's theory. *Bulletin of the British Psychological Society* 30: 161.

Erickson, M. L., & Empey, L. T. 1963. Court records, undetected delinquency and decision-making. *Journal of Criminal Law, Criminology, and Police Science* 54: 456–469.

Eron, L. D., Huesmann, L. R., Dubow, E., Romanoff, R., & Yarmel, P. 1987. Aggression and its correlates over 22 years. In *Childhood Aggression and Violence: Sources of Influence, Prevention and Control,* D. Crowell, I. Evans, & C. O'Donnell, eds. New York: Plenum.

Espenshade, T. 1979. The economic consequences of divorce. *Journal of Marriage and the Family* 41: 615–625.

Eysenck, H. J. 1977. *Crime and Personality.* London: Routledge and Kegan Paul.

Eysenck, H. J. 1981. The nature of intelligence. In *Intelligence and Learning,* M. Friedman, J. Das, & N. O'Connor, eds. New York: Plenum.

Eysenck, H. J. 1983. Personality, conditioning, and antisocial behavior. In *Personality Theory, Moral Development and Criminal Behavior,* W. S. Laufer & J. M. Day, eds. Lexington, Mass.: Lexington Books.

Eysenck, H. J. 1984. Crime and conditioning. In *Psychological Approaches to Crime and Its Correction: Theory, Research, and Practice,* I. Jacks & S. G. Cox, eds. Chicago: Nelson-Hall, pp. 46–64.

Eysenck, H. J., & Gudjonsson, G. H. 1989. *The Causes and Cures of Criminality.* New York: Plenum.

Eysenck, H. J., & Rachman, S. 1965. *The Causes and Cures of Neurosis.* San Diego: Robert R. Knapp.

Fahringer, H. P. 1977. Even victors by victory are undone. *Criminal Law Bulletin* 13(3): 212–213.

Feather, N. T. 1967. An expectancy-value model of information-seeking behavior. *Psychological Review* 74: 342–360.

Feldman, M. P. 1977. *Criminal Behavior: A Psychological Analysis.* London: John Wiley.

Feldman-Summers, S. 1976. Conceptual and empirical issues associated with rape. In *Victims and Society,* E. C. Viano, ed. Washington, D.C.: Visage.

Feldman-Summers, S., & Lindner, K. 1976. Perceptions of victims and defendants in criminal assault cases. *Criminal Justice and Behavior* 3: 135–149.

Felkenes, G. T. 1973. *The Criminal Justice System.* Englewood Cliffs, N.J.: Prentice-Hall.

Fine, R. A. 1986. *Escape of the Guilty.* New York: Dodd, Mead.

Finkel, N. J. 1982. Insanity defenses: Jurors' assessment of mental disease, responsibility, and culpability. Paper presented at the Annual Convention of the American Psychological Association, August 1982, Washington, D.C.

Finkel, N. J., & Handel, S. F. 1989. How jurors construe "insanity." *Law and Human Behavior* 13(1): 41–60.

Finkel, N. J., Shaw, R., Bercaw, S., & Koch, J. 1985. Insanity defenses: From the jurors' perspective. *Law and Psychology Review* 9: 77–92.

Fisher, R. P., Geiselman, R. E., & Amador, M. 1989. Field test of the cognitive interview: Enhancing the recollection of actual victims and witnesses of crime. *Journal of Applied Psychology* 74(5): 722–727.

Fisk, J. G. 1974. Some dimensions in police discretion. In *The Police Community,* J. Goldsmith & S. S. Goldsmith, eds. Pacific Palisades, Calif.: Palisades Publishers.

Fitzgerald, R., & Ellsworth, P. C. 1984. Due process vs. crime control: Death qualification and jury attitudes. *Law and Human Behavior* 8: 31–52.

Flango, V. E. 1980. Would jurors do a better job if they could take notes? *Judicature* 63(9): 436–443.

Foley, L. A. 1976. Personality and situational influences on changes in prejudice: Replication of Cook's railroad game in a prison setting. *Journal of Personality and Social Psychology* 34: 846–856.

Foley, L. A. 1977. Personality characteristics and interracial contact as determinants of black prejudice toward whites. *Human Relations* 30: 709–720.

Foley, L. A. 1981. The grand jury selection process. Paper presented at the annual convention of Society of Southeastern Social Psychologists. October 24, Tampa, Florida.

Foley, L. A. 1987. Florida after the Furman decision: The effect of extralegal factors on the processing of capital offense cases. *Behavioral Sciences & the Law* 5(4): 457–465.

Foley, L. A., & Chamblin, M. H. 1982. The effect of race and personality on mock jurors' decisions. *The Journal of Psychology* 112: 47–51.

Foley, L. A., & Powell, R. S. 1982. The discretion of prosecutors, judges, and juries in capital cases. *Criminal Justice Review* 7(2): 16–22.

Foley, L. A., & Rasche, C. E. 1979. The effect of race on sentence, actual time served and final disposition of female offenders. In *Theory and Research in Criminal Justice: Current Perspectives,* J. A. Conley, ed. Cincinnati: Anderson.

Fontaine, G., & Kiger, R. 1978. The effects of defendant dress and supervision on judgments of simulated jurors: An exploratory study. *Law and Human Behavior* 2: 63–71.

Fox, S. G., & Walters, H. A. 1986. The impact of general versus specific expert testimony and eyewitness confidence upon mock juror judgment. *Law and Human Behavior* 10: 215–228.

Frank, J., & Frank, B. 1957. *Not Guilty.* Garden City, N.Y.: Doubleday.

Frankel, M. E., & Naftalis, G. P. 1977. *The Grand Jury: An Institution on Trial.* New York: Hill & Wang.

Freed, D. J., & Foster, H. H., Jr. 1984. Family law in the fifty states: An overview. *Family Law Quarterly* 18 (47): 321–333.

Freedman, C. D. 1988. Structuring investigative discretion in Canada: Recommendations and guideline for police questioning. *Police Studies* 11(3): 139–152.

Friedlander, K. 1947. *The Psychoanalytic Approach to Juvenile Delinquency.* New York: International Universities Press.

Friedman, K., Bischoff, H., Davis, R., & Person, A. 1982. Samaritan blues. *Psychology Today* (July), pp. 26–28.

Furstenberg, F. F., Nord, C. W., Peterson, J. L., & Zill, N. 1983. The life course of children of divorce: Marital disruption and parental contact. *American Sociological Review* 48: 656–668.

Gallup, G. 1976. Death penalty OK rises. *Jacksonville Journal,* April 29, p. 3.

Geiselman, R. E., & Fisher, R. P. 1985. *Interviewing Victims and Witnesses of Crime.* Washington, D.C.: National Institute of Justice.

Geiselman, R. E., Fisher, R. P., MacKinnon, D. P., & Holland, H. L. 1986. Enhancement of eyewitness memory with the cognitive interview. *American Journal of Psychology* 99: 385–401.

Gelman, A. M. 1982. Prosecutorial decision-making: The screening process. In *The Criminal Justice System: A Social-Psychological Analysis,* V. J. Konečni & E. B. Ebbesen, eds. San Francisco: Freeman, pp. 235–256.

Gerber, R. J. 1984. *The Insanity Defense.* Port Washington, N.Y.: Associated Faculty.

Gibson, J. L. 1978. Race as a determinant of criminal sentences: A methodological critique and a case study. *Law & Society Review* 12: 455–478.

Glueck, S., & Glueck, E. 1956. *Physique and Delinquency.* New York: Harper & Row.

Golden, K. 1981. Women as patrol officers: A study of attitudes. *Police Studies* 4: 29–33.

Goldfarb, W. 1943. Infant rearing and problem behavior. *American Journal of Orthopsychiatry* 13: 249–256.

Goldman, A. H. 1986. Cognitive psychologists as expert witnesses: A problem in professional ethics. *Law and Human Behavior* 10(1/2): 29–46.

Goldsmith, A. J. 1988. New directions in police complaints procedures: Some conceptual and comparative departures. *Police Studies* 11(2): 60–71.

Goldstein, J. H. 1986. *Aggression and Crimes of Violence.* 2nd ed. New York: Oxford University Press.

Goodman, G. S. 1984. The child witness: An introduction; and Children's testimony in historical perspective. *Journal of Social Issues* 40(2): 1–32.

Goodman, G. S., Golding, J. M., & Haith, M. M. 1984. Jurors' reactions to child witnesses. *Journal of Social Issues* 40(2): 139–156.

Goodman, G. S., Golding, J. M., Helgeson, V. S., Haith, M. M., & Michelli, J. 1987. When a child takes the stand: Jurors' perceptions of children's eyewitness testimony. *Law and Human Behavior* 11(1): 27–40.

Goodman, G. S., & Hahn, A. 1987. Evaluating eyewitness testimony. In *Handbook of Forensic Psychology,* I. B. Weiner & A. K. Hess, eds. New York: Wiley.

Goodman, G. S., & Reed, R. S. 1986. Age differences in eyewitness testimony. *Law and Human Behavior* 10(4): 317–332.

Gordon, D. 1976. Capitalism, class, and crime in America. In *Classes, Conflict, and Control,* J. Munroe, ed. Cincinnati: Anderson.

Gordon, M. T., Riger, S., LeBailly, R. K., & Heath, L. 1980. Crime, women and the quality of urban life. *Signs* 5(3): 144–160.

Gottfredson, M. R., & Gottfredson, D. M. 1988. *Decision Making in Criminal Justice: Toward the Rational Exercise of Discretion,* 2nd ed. New York: Plenum.

Graham, H. D., & Gurr, T. R. 1969. *The History of Violence in America: Historical and Comparative Perspective.* New York: Praeger.

Graham, H. D., & Gurr, T. R. 1979. *Violence in America: Historical and Comparative Perspectives.* Beverly Hills, Calif.: Sage.

Grant, J. D., & Grant, M. Q. 1959. A group dynamics approach to the treatment of nonconformists in the Navy. *Annals of the American Academy of Political and Social Science,* pp. 126–135.

Grant, J. D., Grant, J., & Toch, H. H. 1982. Police-citizen conflict and decisions to arrest. In *The Criminal Justice System: A Social-Psychological Analysis,* V. J. Konečni & E. B. Ebbesen, eds. San Francisco: Freeman, pp. 133–158.

Grasmick, H., & Green, D. E. 1980. Legal punishment, social disapproval, and internalization as inhibitors of illegal behavior. *Journal of Criminal Law and Criminology* 71: 325–335.

Gray, T. C. 1975. Selecting for a police subculture. In *Police in America,* J. H. Skolnick & T. C. Gray, eds. Boston: Educational Associates.

Green, E. 1964. Inter- and intra-racial crime relative to sentencing. *Journal of Criminal Law, Criminology, and Police Science* 55: 348–358.

Green, G. S. 1987. Citizen gun ownership and criminal deterrence: Theory, research, and policy. *Criminology* 25(1): 63–82.

Greenberg, D. F. 1981. Methodological issues in survey research on the inhibition of crime. *The Journal of Criminal Law and Criminology* 72(3): 1094–1101.

Greenberg, M. S., & Ruback, R. B. 1982. *Social Psychology of the Criminal Justice System.* Monterey, Calif.: Brooks/Cole.

Greenberg, M. S., Wilson, C. E., & Mills, M. K. 1982. Victim decision-making: An experimental approach. In *The Criminal Justice System: A Social-Psychological Analysis,* V. J. Konečni & E. B. Ebbesen, eds. San Francisco: Freeman, pp. 73–94.

Greene, E., Schooler, J. W., & Loftus, E. F. 1985. Expert psychological testimony. In *The Psychology of Evidence and Trial Procedure,* S. M. Kassin & L. S. Wrightsman, eds. Beverly Hills, Calif.: Sage.

Greenfield, L. A. 1990. *Capital Punishment 1989.* Washington, D.C.: Bureau of Justice Statistics.

Grisso, T. 1991. A developmental history of the American Psychology-Law Society. *Law and Human Behavior* 15:213–232.

Guinther, J. 1988. *The Jury in America.* New York: Facts on File.

Gurr, T. R. 1979. On the history of violent crime in Europe and America. In *Violence in America: Historical and Comparative Perspectives,* H. D. Graham & T. R. Gurr, eds. Beverly Hills, Calif.: Sage.

Gurr, T. R. 1989. Historical trends in violent crime: Europe and the United States. In *Violence in America: The History of Crime,* T. R. Gurr, ed. Newbury Park, Calif.: Sage, pp. 21–54.

Hagan, J. 1985. *Modern Criminology: Crime, Criminal Behavior, and Its Control.* New York: McGraw-Hill.

Haney, C. 1980. Psychology and legal change: On the limits of a factual jurisprudence. *Law and Human Behavior* 4: 147–200.

Hare, R. D. 1970. *Psychopathy: Theory and Research.* New York: John Wiley.

Harlow, C. W. 1985. *Reporting Crimes to the Police.* Special report. Washington, D.C.: U.S. Printing Office, U.S. Department of Justice.

Harries, K. D., & Lura, R. P. 1974. The geography of justice: Sentencing variations in U.S. judicial districts. *Judicature* 57: 392–401.

Harvey, O. J. 1966. System structure, flexibility, and creativity. In *Experience, Structure, and Adaptability,* O. J. Harvey, ed. New York: Springer.

Harvey, O. J., Hunt, D. E., & Schroder, H. M. 1961. *Conceptual Systems Personality Organization.* New York: Wiley.

Hastie, R. 1986. Notes on the psychologist expert witness. *Law and Human Behavior* 10(1/2): 79–82.

Hastie, R., Penrod, S. D., & Pennington, N. 1983. *Inside the Jury.* Cambridge, Mass.: Harvard University Press.

Hawkins, G., & Zimring, F. E. 1988. *Pornography in a Free Society.* New York: Cambridge University Press.

Heilbrun, K., Heilbrun, P. G., & Griffin, N. 1988. Comparing females acquitted by reasons of insanity, convicted, and civilly committed in Florida: 1977–1984. *Law and Human Behavior* 12(3): 295–312.

Hendrick, C., & Shaffer, D. R. 1975. Effect of pleading the Fifth Amendment on perceptions of guilt and morality. *Bulletin of the Psychonomic Society* 6: 449–452.

Hepburn, J., & Voss, H. L. 1970. Patterns of criminal homicide: A comparison of Chicago and Philadelphia. *Criminology* 8: 19–45.

Hetherington, E. M., & Parke, R. D. 1975. *Child Psychology: A Contemporary Viewpoint.* New York: McGraw-Hill.

Heuer, L., & Penrod, S. 1988. Increasing juror participation in trials: A field experiment with jury notetaking and question asking. *Law and Human Behavior* 12(3): 231–262.

Hiatt, D., & Hargrave, G. E. 1988. Predicting job performance problems with psychological screening. *Journal of Police Science and Administration* 16(2): 122–125.

Hilberman, E. 1976. Rape: The ultimate violation of the self. *American Journal of Psychiatry* 133: 436–437.

Hindelang, M. J. 1978. Race and involvement in common law personal crimes. *American Sociological Review* 43: 93–109.

Hindman, R. E. 1975. A survey related to use of female law enforcement officers. *Police Chief* 42(4): 58–59.

Hirsch, A. V. 1976. *Doing Justice: The Choice of Punishments—Report of the Committee for the Study of Incarceration.* New York: Hill and Wang.

Hirschi, T. 1969. *Causes of Delinquency.* Berkeley, Calif.: University of California Press.

Hoffman, M. L. 1970. Moral development. In *Carmichael's Manual of Child Psychology,* vol. 2, P. Mussen, ed. New York: Wiley.

Hoffman, P. B., & Beck, J. L. 1984. Burnout—age at release from prison and recidivism. *Journal of Criminal Justice* 12(6): 617–623.

Hogan, R., & Jones, W. H. 1983. A role-theoretical model of criminal conduct. In *Personality Theory, Moral Development and Criminal Behavior,* W. S. Laufer & J. M. Day, eds. Lexington, Mass.: Lexington Books, pp. 3–22.

Hogarth, J. 1971. *Sentencing as a Human Process.* Toronto: University of Toronto.

Holmes, T., & Rahe, R. 1967. The social readjustment rating scale. *Journal of Psychosomatic Research* 11: 213–218.

Horowitz, I. A. 1980. Juror selection: A comparison of two methods in several criminal cases. *Journal of Applied Social Psychology* 10: 86–99.

Horowitz, I. A. 1985. The effect of jury nullification instruction on verdicts and jury functioning in criminal trials. *Law and Human Behavior* 9: 25–36.

Horowitz, I. A. 1988. Jury nullification: The impact of judicial instructions, arguments, and challenges on jury decision making. *Law and Human Behavior* 12(4): 439–454.

Horowitz, I. A., & Willging, T. E. 1984. *The Psychology of Law: Integrations and Applications.* Boston: Little, Brown.

Horowitz, I. A., & Willging, T. E. 1991. Changing views of jury power: The nullification debate, 1787–1988. *Law and Human Behavior* 15(2): 165–182.

Humphrey, J. A., & Milakovick, M. E. 1981. *The Administration of Justice.* New York: Human Sciences Press.

Hunt, Y. C., Jr. 1971. *Minority Recruiting in the New York City Police Department: Part I. The Attraction of Candidates.* New York: Rand Institute.

Inglis, B. 1986. *The Hidden Power.* London: Cape.

Irwin, J. 1980. *Prisons in Turmoil.* Boston: Little, Brown.

Izzett, R., & Leginski, W. 1974. Group discussion and the influence of defendant characteristics in a simulated jury setting. *Journal of Social Psychology* 93: 271–279.

Janoff-Bulman, R. 1979. Characterological versus behavioral self-blame. *Journal of Personality and Social Psychology* 37: 1798–1809.

Janoff-Bulman, R., & Frieze, I. H. 1983. A theoretical perspective for understanding reactions to victimization. *Journal of Social Issues* 39(2): 1–18.

Janus, S. S., Janus, C., Lord, L. K., & Power, T. 1988. Women in police work—Annie Oakley or Little Orphan Annie? *Police Studies* 11(3): 124–127.

Jarvik, L. F., Klodin, V., & Matsuyama, S. S. 1973. Human aggression and the extra Y chromosome. *American Psychologist* 28: 574–682.

Jennings, W. S., Kilkenny, R., & Kohlberg, L. 1983. Moral development theory and practice for youthful and adult offenders. In *Personality Theory, Moral Development and Criminal Behavior,* W. S. Laufer & J. M. Day, eds. Lexington, Mass.: Lexington Books.

Johnson, G. B. 1970. The negro and crime. In *The Sociology of Crime and Delinquency,* 2nd ed., M. E. Wolfgang, L. Savitz, & N. Johnston, eds. New York: John Wiley, pp. 419–429.

Johnson, E. H. 1974. *Crime, Correction, and Society.* Homewood, Ill.: Dorsey.

Johnson, J. M., & DeBerry, M. M. 1990. Criminal victimization 1989. Washington, D.C.: Bureau of Justice Statistics.

Johnson, M. K., & Foley, M. A. 1984. Differentiating fact from fantasy: The reliability of children's memory. *Journal of Social Issues* 40: 33–50.

Johnson, R. 1987. *Hard Time: Understanding and Reforming the Prison.* Monterey, Calif.: Brooks/Cole.

Jones, C., & Aronson, E. 1973. Attribution of fault to a rape victim as a function of respectability of the victim. *Journal of Personality and Social Psychology* 26: 415–419.

Jurow, G. 1971. New data on the effect of a "death qualified" jury on the guilt determination process. *Harvard Law Review* 84: 567–611.

Kalish, C. B. 1974. *Crimes and Victims: A Report on the Dayton-San Jose Pilot Survey of Victimization.* Washington, D.C.: National Criminal Justice Information and Statistics Service, Law Enforcement Assistance Administration, U.S. Department of Justice.

Kalven, H., Jr. 1957. A report on the jury project of the University of Chicago Law School. *Insurance Counsel Journal* 24: 368–381.

Kalven, H., Jr., & Zeisel, H. 1966. *The American Jury.* Boston: Little, Brown.

Kamin, L. J. 1986. Is crime in the genes? The answer may depend on who chooses what evidence. *Scientific American* 247: 22–25.

Kaplan, M. F. 1977. Discussion polarization effects in a modified jury decision paradigm: Information influences. *Sociometry* 40(3): 262–271.

Kaplan, M. F., ed. 1986. *The Impact of Social Psychology on Procedural Justice.* Springfield, Ill.: Charles C. Thomas.

Kaplan, M. F., & Kemmerick, G. D. 1974. Juror judgment as information integration: Combining evidential and nonevidential information. *Journal of Personality and Social Psychology* 30: 493–499.

Kaplan, M. F., & Miller, L. E. 1978. Reducing the effects of juror bias. *Journal of Personality and Social Psychology* 36: 1443–1455.

Kargon, R. 1986. Expert testimony in historical perspective. *Law and Human Behavior* 10(1/2): 15–28.

Karmen, A. 1984. *Crime Victims: An Introduction to Victimology.* Monterey, Calif.: Brooks/Cole.

Kassin, S. M., & McNall, K. 1991. Police interrogations and confessions: Communicating promises and threats by pragmatic implication. *Law and Human Behavior* 15(3): 233–252.

Kassin, S. M., & Wrightsman, L. S. 1983. The construction and validation of a juror bias scale. *Journal of Research in Personality* 17: 423–441.

Kassin, S. M., & Wrightsman, L. S. 1985. Confession evidence. In *The Psychology of Evidence and Trial Procedure,* S. M. Kassin & L. S. Wrightsman, eds. Beverly Hills, Calif.: Sage.

Kassin, S. M., & Wrightsman, L. S. 1988. *The American Jury on Trial.* New York: Hemisphere.

Katz, S., & Masur, M. A. 1979. *Understanding the Rape Victim: A Synthesis of Research Findings.* New York: Wiley.

Kelling, G. L. 1988. *Police and Communities: The Quiet Revolution.* Washington, D.C.: National Institute of Justice.

Kelling, G. L., & Moore, M. K. 1988. *The Evolving Strategy of Policing.* Washington, D.C.: National Institute of Justice.

Kelling, G. L., Wasserman, R., & Williams, H. 1988. *Police Accountability and Community Policing.* Washington, D.C.: National Institute of Justice.

Kenrick, D. T., Dantchik, A., & MacFarlane, S. 1983. Personality, environment, and criminal behavior: An evolutionary perspective. In *Personality Theory, Moral Development and Criminal Behavior,* W. S. Laufer & J. M. Day, eds. Lexington, Mass.: Lexington Books.

Kerr, N. L. 1978. Severity of prescribed penalty and mock jurors' verdicts. *Journal of Personality and Social Psychology* 36: 1431–1442.

Kerr, N. L. 1982. Trial participants' behaviors and jury verdicts: An exploratory field study. In *The Criminal Justice System: A Social-Psychological Analysis,* V. J. Konečni & E. B. Ebbesen, eds. San Francisco: Freeman, pp. 261–290.

Kerr, N. L. 1986. Social science and the U.S. Supreme Court. In *The Impact of Social Psychology on Procedural Justice,* M. F. Kaplan, ed. Springfield, Ill.: Charles C. Thomas, pp. 56–82.

Kerr, N. L., Nerenz, D., & Herrick, D. 1979. Role playing and the study of jury behavior. *Sociological Methods and Research* 7: 337–355.

Kidd, R. F. 1979. Crime reporting: Toward a social psychological model. *Criminology* 17: 380–394.

Kidd, R. F., & Chayet, E. F. 1984. Why do victims fail to report? The psychology of criminal victimization. *Journal of Social Issues* 40(1): 39–50.

Kidder, L. H., Boell, J. L., & Moyer, M. M. 1983. Rights consciousness and victimization prevention: Personal defense and assertiveness training. *Journal of Social Issues* 39(2): 153–168.

King, M. A., & Yuille, J. C. 1987. Suggestibility and the child witness. In *Children's Eyewitness Memory*, S. J. Ceci, M. P. Toglia, & D. F. Ross, eds. New York: Springer Verlag, pp. 24–35.

Kinnane, A. 1979. *Policing.* Chicago: Nelson-Hall.

Kittrie, N. N. 1984. Will the XYY syndrome abolish guilt? In *Psychological Approaches to Crime and Its Correction: Theory, Research, Practice*, I. Jacks & S. G. Cox, eds. Chicago: Nelson-Hall, pp. 36–45.

Kleck, G. 1981. Racial discrimination in criminal sentencing: A critical evaluation of the evidence with additional evidence on the death penalty. *American Sociological Review* 46: 783–805.

Kleck, G. 1988. Crime control through the private use of armed force. *Social Problems* 35(1): 1–21.

Kleck, R. E., & Wheaton, J. 1967. Dogmatism and responses to opinion-consistent and opinion-inconsistent information. *Journal of Personality and Social Psychology* 5: 249–252.

Klein, D., & Kress, J. 1976. Any woman's blues: A critical overview of women, crime, and the criminal justice system. *Crime and Social Justice* 34: 34–49.

Klepper, S., & Nagin, D. 1989a. The deterrent effect of perceived certainty and severity of punishment revisited. *Criminology* 27(4): 721–746.

Klepper, S., & Nagin, D. 1989b. Tax compliance and perceptions of the risks of detection and criminal prosecution. *Law & Society Review* 23(2): 209–240.

Knudten, R. D., Meade, A. C., Knudten, M. S., & Doerner, W. G. 1976. The victim in the administration of justice. In *Criminal Justice and the Victim*, W. F. McDonald, ed. Beverly Hills, Calif.: Sage.

Kohlberg, L. 1964. Development of moral character and moral ideology. In *Review of Child Development Research*, vol. 1, M. L. Hoffmann & L. W. Hoffmann, eds. New York: Russell Sage.

Konečni, V. J., & Ebbesen, E. B. 1982. Analysis of the sentencing system. In *The Criminal Justice System: A Social-Psychological Analysis*, V. J. Konečni & E. B. Ebbesen, eds. San Francisco: Freeman, pp. 293–332.

Konečni, V. J., & Ebbesen, E. B. 1986. Courtroom testimony by psychologists on eyewitness identification issues: Critical notes and reflections. *Law and Human Behavior* 10(1/2): 117–126.

Kramer, G. P., & Kerr, N. L. 1989. Laboratory simulation and bias in the study of juror behavior: A methodological note. *Law and Human Behavior* 13(1): 89–100.

Kramer, G. P., Kerr, N. L., & Carroll, J. S. 1990. Pretrial publicity, judicial remedies, and jury bias. *Law and Human Behavior* 14(5): 409–438.

Kressel, K., Jaffee, N., Tuchman, B., Watson, C., & Deutsch, M. 1980. A typology of divorcing couples: Implications for mediation and the divorce process. *Family Process* 19: 101–116.

Kroes, W. H. 1988. *Broken Cops.* Springfield, Ill.: Charles C. Thomas.

Krupnick, J. 1980. Brief psychotherapy with victims of violent crimes. *Victomology* 5(2–4): 347–354.

LaFave, W. R. 1965. *Arrest: The Decision to Take a Suspect into Custody.* Boston: Little, Brown.

LaFree, G. D. 1980. The effect of sexual stratification by race on official reactions to rape. *American Sociological Review* 45: 842–854.

Landers, S. 1989. AIDS test repealed for marriage license. *APA Monitor* 20(8): 26.

Landes, W. M. 1974. Legality and reality: Some evidence on criminal procedure. *Journal of Legal Studies* 3: 287–338.

Landy, F. J. 1976. The validity of the interview in police officer selection. *Journal of Applied Psychology* 25: 95–106.

L'Armand, K., & Pepitone, A. 1977. *On Attribution of Responsibility and Punishment for Rape.* Paper presented at the meeting of the American Psychological Association, August, San Francisco.

Latané, B., & Darley, J. 1968. Group inhibition of bystander intervention in emergencies. *Journal of Personality and Social Psychology* 10(3): 215–221.

Latané, B., & Darley, J. 1970. *The Unresponsive Bystander: Why Doesn't He Help?* New York: Appleton-Century-Crofts.

References

Leippe, M. R., & Romanczyk, A. 1989. Reactions to child (versus adult) eyewitnesses: The influence of jurors' preconceptions and witness behavior. *Law and Human Behavior* 13(2): 103–132.

Leizer, J. I., & Rogers, R. W. 1974. Effects of method of discipline, timing of punishment, and timing of test on resistance to temptation. *Child Development* 45: 790–792.

LeJeune, R., & Alex, N. 1973. On being mugged: The event and its aftermath. *Urban Life and Culture* 2: 259–287.

Lempert, R. O. 1986. Social sciences in court: On "eyewitness experts" and other issues. *Law and Human Behavior* 10(1/2): 167–182.

Lerner, M. J. 1970. The desires for justice and reactions to victims. In *Altruism and Helping Behavior,* J. Macaulay & L. Berkowitz, eds. New York: Academic.

Lerner, M. J. 1980. *The Belief in a Just World: A Fundamental Delusion.* New York: Plenum.

Lester, D., & Brink, W. T. 1985. Police solidarity and tolerance for police misbehavior. *Psychological Reports* 57: 326.

Levine, J. P. 1976. The potential for crime overreporting in criminal victimization surveys. *Criminology* 14: 307–327.

Levine, M. A. 1976. Urban politics and policy outcomes: The criminal courts. In *Criminal Justice: Law and Politics,* 2nd ed., G. F. Cole, ed. North Scituate, Mass.: Duxbury.

Levine, F. J., & Tapp, J. L. 1982. Eyewitness identification: Problems and pitfalls. In *The Criminal Justice System: A Social-Psychological Analysis,* V. J. Konečni & E. B. Ebbesen, eds. San Francisco: W. H. Freeman.

Lewin, K. 1947. Group decisions and social change. In *Readings in Social Psychology,* T. M. Newcomb & E. L. Hartley, eds. New York: Holt, Rinehart & Winston.

Lewin, K. 1948. *Resolving Social Conflicts: Selected Papers on Group Dynamics.* New York: Harper & Row.

Lind, E. A., & Ke, G. Y. 1985. Opening and closing statements. In *The Psychology of Evidence and Trial Procedure,* S. M. Kassin & L. S. Wrightsman, eds. Beverly Hills, Calif.: Sage.

Lind, E. A., & O'Barr, W. M. 1978. The social significance of speech in the courtroom. In *Language and Social Psychology,* H. Giles & R. St. Clair, eds. Oxford, Eng.: Blackwell.

Linden, E. 1988. The preppie killer cops a plea. *Time,* April 4, p. 22.

Linz, D., Donnerstein, E., & Penrod, S. 1984. The effects of multiple exposures to filmed violence against women. *Journal of Communication* 34: 130–147.

Linz, D., & Penrod, S. 1982. A meta-analysis of the influence of research methodology on the outcomes of jury simulation studies. Paper presented at the Academy of Criminal Justice Sciences, Louisville, Kentucky.

Linz, D., Penrod, S., & McDonald, E. 1986. Attorney communication and impression making in the courtroom: Views from off the bench. *Law and Human Behavior* 10(4): 281–302.

List, J. A. 1986. Age and schematic differences in the reliability of eyewitness testimony. *Developmental Psychology* 22: 50–57.

Loftus, E. F. 1979. *Eyewitness Testimony.* Cambridge, Mass.: Harvard University Press.

Loftus, E. F. 1986. Experimental psychologist as advocate or impartial educator. *Law and Human Behavior* 10(1/2): 63–78.

Loftus, E. F., Altman, D., & Geballe, R. 1975. Effects of questioning upon a witness's later recollections. *Journal of Police Science and Administration* 3: 165.

Loftus, E. F., Loftus, G. R., & Messo, J. 1987. Some facts about "weapon focus." *Law and Human Behavior* 11(1): 55–62.

Loftus, E. F., Miller, D. G., & Burns, H. G. 1978. Semantic integration of verbal information into a visual memory. *Journal of Experimental Psychology: Human Learning and Memory* 4: 19–31.

Loftus, E. F., & Palmer, J. C. 1974. Reconstruction of automobile destruction: An example of the interaction between language and memory. *Journal of Verbal Learning and Verbal Behavior* 13: 585–589.

Loh, W. D. 1985. The evidence and trial procedure. In *The Psychology of Evidence and Trial Procedure,* S. M. Kassin & L. S. Wrightsman, eds. Beverly Hills, Calif.: Sage.

Love, K., & Singer, M. 1988. Self-efficacy, psychological well-being, job satisfaction and job involvement: A comparison of male and female police officers. *Police Studies* 11(2): 98–102.

Low, P. W., Jeffries, J. C., Jr., & Bonnie, R. J. 1986. *The Trial of John W. Hinckley, Jr.* Mineola, N.Y.: Foundation.

Luce, T. S. 1974. Blacks, whites, and yellows: They all look alike to me. *Psychology Today* (November), pp. 105–108.

Luginbuhl, J., & Middendorf, K. 1988. Death penalty beliefs and jurors' responses to aggravating and mitigating circumstances in capital trials. *Law and Human Behavior* 12(3): 263–282.

Lundman, R. J. 1986. One-wave perceptual deterrence research: Some grounds for the renewed examination of cross-sectional methods. *Journal of Research in Crime and Delinquency* 23: 370–388.

Lundman, R., Sykes, R., & Clark, J. 1978. Police control of juveniles: A replication. *Journal of Research in Crime and Delinquency* 15: 74–91.

McCahill, T. W., Meyer, L. C., & Fischman, A. M. 1979. *The Aftermath of Rape.* Lexington, Mass.: Heath.

McClearn, G. E., & DeFries, J. C. 1973. *Introduction to Behavioral Genetics.* San Francisco: W. H. Freeman.

McCloskey, M., & Egeth, H. 1983. Eyewitness identification: What can a psychologist tell a jury? *The American Psychologist* 38: 550–563.

McCloskey, M., Egeth, H., & McKenna, J. 1986. The experimental psychologist in court: The ethics of expert testimony. *Law and Human Behavior* 10(1/2): 1–14.

McCormick, C. T. 1972. *Handbook of the Law of Evidence,* 2nd ed. St. Paul, Minn.: West.

McDowall, D., & Loftin, C. 1985. Collective security and fatal firearm accidents. *Criminology* 23(3): 401–416.

McEvoy, D. W. 1975a. Training for the new centurions. In *The Police and the Behavioral Sciences,* J. L. Steinberg & D. W. McEvoy, eds. Springfield, Ill.: Charles C. Thomas.

McEvoy, D. W. 1975b. Games policemen play. In *The Police and the Behavioral Sciences,* J. L. Steinberg & D. W. McEvoy, eds. Springfield, Ill.: Charles C. Thomas.

McGlynn, R. P., Megas, J. C., & Benson, D. H. 1976. Sex and race as factors affecting the attribution of insanity in a murder trial. *The Journal of Psychology* 93: 93–99.

Maass, A., Brigham, J. C., & West, S. G. 1985. Testifying on eyewitness reliability: Expert advice is not always persuasive. *Journal of Applied Psychology* 66: 482–489.

Maccoby, E. E. 1980. *Social Development: Psychological Growth and the Parent-Child Relationship.* New York: Harcourt Brace Jovanovich.

Maeder, T. 1985. *Crime and Madness.* New York: Harper & Row.

Malamuth, N. 1978. Erotica, aggression and perceived appropriateness. Paper presented at the annual meeting of the American Psychological Association, September, Toronto.

Malamuth, N. 1983a. Factors associated with rape as predictors of laboratory aggression against women. *Journal of Personality and Social Psychology* 45: 432–442.

Malamuth, N. 1983b. Predictors of naturalistic sexual aggression. *Journal of Personality and Social Psychology* 50: 953–962.

Malamuth, N., & Ceniti, J. 1986. Repeated exposure to violent and nonviolent pornography: Likelihood of raping ratings and laboratory aggression against women. *Aggressive Behavior* 12: 129–137.

Malamuth, N., & Check, J. V. P. 1984. Debriefing effectiveness following exposure to pornographic rape depictions. *Journal of Sex Research* 20: 1–13.

Malamuth, N., & Check, J. V. P. 1985. The effects of aggressive pornography on beliefs of rape myths: Individual differences. *Journal of Research in Personality* 19: 299–320.

Maltz, M. D. 1975. Crime statistics: A mathematical perspective. *Journal of Criminal Justice* 3: 177–194.

Margolick, D. 1991. White dies for killing black, for the first time in decades. *New York Times* (September 7), p. 1.

Marin, B. V., Holmes, D. L., Guth, M., & Kovac, P. 1979. The potential of children as eyewitnesses. *Law and Human Behavior* 3: 295–306.

Mark, V. H., & Erwin, F. R. 1970. *Violence and the Brain.* Hagerstown, Md.: Harper & Row.

References

Marshall, J. 1969. *Law and Psychology in Conflict*. Garden City, N.Y.: Doubleday.

Martinson, R. 1974. What works? Questions and answers about prison reform. *The Public Interest* 35: 22–54.

Maynard, D. W. 1988. Narratives and narrative structure in plea bargaining. *Law & Society Review* 22(3): 449–482.

Meehl, P. E. 1977. Law and the fireside inductions. In *Law, Justice, and the Individual in Society*, J. L. Tapp & F. J. Levine, eds. New York: Holt, Rinehart and Winston, pp. 10–28.

Melton, G. B. 1984. Child witnesses and the First Amendment: A psycholegal dilemma. *Journal of Social Issues* 40(2): 109–124.

Melton, G. B., & Thompson, R. A. 1987. Getting out of a rut: Detours to less traveled paths in child witness research. In *Children's Eyewitness Memory*, S. J. Ceci, M. P. Toglia, & D. F. Ross, eds. New York: Springer Verlag, pp. 209–229.

Menninger, K. 1966. *The Crime of Punishment*. New York: Viking.

Merton, R. K. 1957. *Social Theory and Social Structure*. Glencoe, Ill.: Free Press.

Miller, D. T., & Porter, C. A. 1983. Self-blame in victims of violence. *Journal of Social Issues* 39(2): 139–152.

Miller, G. R. 1975. Jurors' responses to videotaped trial materials: Some recent findings. *Personality and Social Psychology Bulletin* 1: 561–569.

Miller, G. R., & Boster, F. J. 1977. Three images of the trial: Their implications for psychological research. In *Psychology in the Legal Process*, B. D. Sales, ed. New York: Spectrum, pp. 19–38.

Miller, G. R., & Burgoon, J. K. 1982. Factors affecting assessments of witness credibility. In *The Psychology of the Courtroom*, N. L. Kerr & R. M. Bray, eds. New York: Academic Press.

Miller, W. B. 1958. Lower class culture as a generating milieu of gang delinquency. *Journal of Social Issues* 14: 5–19.

Mitchell, H. E., & Byrne, D. 1973. The defendant's dilemma: Effects of jurors' attitudes and authoritarianism. *Journal of Personality and Social Psychology* 25: 123–129.

Monahan, J., & Loftus, E. 1982. The psychology of law. *Annual Review of Psychology* 33: 441–475.

Moore, M. H., Trojanowicz, R. C., & Kelling, G. L. 1988. *Crime and Policing*. Washington, D.C.: National Institute of Justice.

Moran, G., & Comfort, J. C. 1986. Neither "tentative" nor "fragmentary": Verdict preference of impaneled felony jurors as a function of attitude toward capital punishment. *Journal of Applied Psychology* 71: 146–155.

Morash, M. 1981. Cognitive development theory: A basis for juvenile correctional reform? *Criminology* 19: 360–371.

Morgan, R. F. 1989. New custody trends in divorce and their implications on the lives of parents and children. Paper presented at the meeting of the Southeastern Psychological Association, Washington, D.C.

Moulds, E. F. 1980. Chivalry and paternalism: Disparities of treatment in the criminal justice system. In *Women, Crime and Justice*, S. Datesman & R. Scarpitti, eds. New York: Oxford.

Myers, D. G., & Kaplan, M. F. 1976. Group-induced polarization in simulated juries. *Personality and Social Psychology Bulletin* 2: 63–66.

Myers, D. G., & Lamm, H. 1976. The group polarization phenomenon. *Psychological Bulletin* 83: 602–627.

Myers, M. A. 1980. Social contexts and attributions of criminal responsibility. *Social Psychology Quarterly* 43: 405–419.

Myers, M. A. 1988. Social background and the sentencing behavior of judges. *Criminology* 26(4): 649–676.

Myers, M. A., & Hagan, J. 1979. Private and public trouble: Prosecutors and the allocation of court resources. *Social Problems* 26: 439–451.

Nagel, S. S. 1969. *The Legal Process from a Behavioral Perspective*. Homewood, Ill.: Dorsey.

Nagel, S. S., & Weitzman, L. J. 1971. Women as litigants. *The Hastings Law Journal* 23: 171–198.

National Council of Crime and Delinquency. 1978. Federal sentencing and prisons. *American Journal of Corrections* 40: 29, 32.

Neises, M. L., & Dillehay, R. C. 1987. Death qualification and conviction proneness: *Witt* and *Witherspoon* compared. *Behavioral Sciences & the Law* 5(4): 479–494.

Nemeth, C., & Sosis, R. 1973. A simulated jury: Characteristics of the defendant and the jurors. *Journal of Social Psychology* 90: 221–229.

Nicholson, R. A., Robertson, H. C., Johnson, W. G., & Jensen, G. 1988. A comparison of instruments for assessing competency to stand trial. *Law and Human Behavior* 12(3): 313–322.

Niederhoffer, A., & Niederhoffer, E. 1978. *The Police Family: From Station House to Ranch House.* Lexington, Mass.: Heath.

Nietzel, M. T. 1979. *Crime and Its Modification.* New York: Pergamon.

Nietzel, M. T., & Dillehay, R. C. 1979. *Psychologists and Voir Dire: A Strategy and Its Applications.* Paper presented at annual meeting of the American Psychological Association, New York.

Noblit, G. W., & Burcart, J. M. 1976. Ethics, powerless peoples, and methodologies for the study of trouble. *Humboldt Journal of Social Relations* 2: 20–25.

Noon, E., & Hollin, C. R. 1987. Lay knowledge of eyewitness behaviour: A British survey. *Applied Cognitive Psychology* 1: 143–153.

Norland, S., & Shover, N. 1977. Gender roles and female criminality. *Criminology* 15: 87–104.

Notman, M., & Nadelson, C. 1976. The rape victim: Psychodynamic considerations. *American Journal of Psychiatry* 133: 408–412.

O'Leary, L. R. 1979. *The Selection and Promotion of the Successful Police Officer.* Springfield, Ill.: Charles C. Thomas.

Pachella, R. G. 1986. Personal values and the value of expert testimony. *Law and Human Behavior* 10 (1/2): 145–150.

Parke, R. D. 1970. The role of punishment in the socialization process. In *Early Experiences and the Processes of Socialization,* R. A. Hoppe, G. A. Milton, & E. C. Simmel, eds. New York: Academic Press.

Parker, J. F., & Carranza, L. E. 1989. Eyewitness testimony of children in target-present and target-absent lineups. *Law and Human Behavior* 13(2): 133–150.

Parker, J. F., Haverfield, E., & Baker-Thomas, S. 1986. Eyewitness testimony of children. *Journal of Applied Social Psychology* 16: 287–302.

Pasewark, R., Pantle, M., & Steadman, H. 1982. Detention and rearrest rates of persons found not guilty by reason of insanity and convicted felons. *American Journal of Psychiatry* 139: 892–897.

Passingham, R. E. 1972. Crime and personality: A review of Eysenck's theory. In *Biological Bases of Individual Behavior,* V. D. Nebylkitsyn & J. A. Gray, eds. New York: Academic.

Paternoster, R. 1984. Prosecutorial discretion in requesting the death penalty: A case of victim-based racial discrimination. *Law & Society Review* 18(3): 435–478.

Paternoster, R. 1987. The deterrent effect of the perceived certainty and severity of punishment: A review of the evidence and issues. *Justice Quarterly* 42: 173–217.

Paternoster, R., Saltzman, L. E., Chiricos, T. G., & Waldo, G. P. 1983. Perceived risk and social control: Do sanctions really deter? *Law and Society Review* 17: 457–479.

Pearson, J., & Thoennes, N. 1984. Child custody, child support arrangements and child support payment patterns. Paper presented at the Child Support Enforcement Research Workshop, August, Washington, D.C.

Pedersen, N. L., Plomin, R., McClearn, G. E., & Friberg, L. 1988. Neuroticism, extraversion, and related traits in adult twins reared apart and reared together. *Journal of Personality and Social Psychology* 55(6): 950–957.

Pennington, D. C. 1982. Witnesses and their testimony: Effects of ordering on juror verdicts. *Journal of Applied Social Psychology* 12: 318–333.

Penrod, S. 1980. Evaluating social scientific methods of jury selection. Paper presented at the meeting of the Midwestern Psychological Association, St. Louis, Mo.

Pepinsky, H. E. 1975. Police decision making. In *Decision Making in the Criminal Justice System: Reviews and Essays,* D. M. Gottfredson, ed. Rockville, Md.: NIMH, pp. 21–51.

Perloff, L. S. 1983. Perceptions of vulnerability to victimization. *Journal of Social Issues* 39(2): 41–61.

Perry, W. 1977. The justice system and sentencing: The importance of race in the military. *Criminology* 15: 225–234.

Peters, D. P. 1987. The impact of naturally occurring stress on children's memory. In *Children's Eyewitness Memory,* S. J. Ceci, M. P. Toglia, & D. F. Ross, eds. New York: Springer Verlag, pp. 122–141.

Peterson, C., & Seligman, M. E. P. 1983. Learned helplessness and victimization. *Journal of Social Issues* 39(2): 103–116.

Pettigrew, T. F. 1958. Personality and socio-cultural factors in intergroup attitudes: A cross-national comparison. *Journal of Conflict Resolution* 2: 29–42.

Pettigrew, T. F. 1959. Racial change and social policy. *Annals of the American Academy of Political and Social Sciences* 44: 114–134.

Phares, E. .J., & Wilson, K. G. 1972. Responsibility attribution: Role of outcome severity, situational ambiguity, and internal-external control. *Journal of Personality* 40: 392–406.

Phillips, B., & Pasewark, R. 1980. Insanity plea in Connecticut. *Bulletin of the American Academy of Psychiatry and the Law* 8: 335–344.

Piliavin, I., & Briar, S. 1964. Police encounters with juveniles. *American Journal of Sociology* 70: 206–214.

Piliavin, J. A., Dovidio, J. F., Gaertner, S. L., & Clark, R. D., III. 1981. *Emergency Intervention.* New York: Academic.

Piliavin, J. A., Piliavin, I. M., & Broll, L. 1976. Time of arrival at an emergency and likelihood of helping. *Personality and Social Psychology Bulletin* 2(3): 273–276.

Polikoff, N. D. 1983. Gender and child custody determinations: Exploding the myths. In *Families, Politics and Public Policies: A Feminist Dialogue on Women and the State,* I. Diamond, ed. New York: Longman.

Pollak, O. 1950. *The Criminality of Women.* New York: A. S. Barnes.

President's Commission on Law Enforcement and the Administration of Justice. 1967. *The Challenge of Crime in a Free Society.* Washington, D.C.: U.S. Government Printing Office.

Price, W. H., & Whatmore, P. B. 1967. Behaviour disorders and patterns of crime among XYY males identified at a maximum security hospital. *British Medical Journal* 1: 533–536.

Pynoos, R. S., & Eth, S. 1984. The child as witness to homicide. *Journal of Social Issues* 40(2): 87–108.

Pyszczynski, T., & Wrightsman, L. S. 1981. The effects of opening statements on mock jurors' verdicts in a simulated criminal trial. *Journal of Applied Social Psychology* 11: 301–313.

Quinney, R. 1970. *The Social Reality of Crime.* Boston: Little, Brown.

Rasche, C. E., & Foley, L. A. 1978. *The Effect of Race on Sentencing Patterns of Offenders.* Paper presented at the annual meeting of the Academy of Criminal Justice Sciences, New Orleans.

Rattner, A. 1988. Convicted but innocent: Wrongful conviction and the criminal justice system. *Law and Human Behavior* 12(3): 283–294.

Reaves, B. A. 1991. *Pretrial Release of Felony Defendants, 1988.* Washington, D.C.: Bureau of Justice Statistics.

Reiss, A. J., Jr. 1971. *The Police and the Public.* New Haven, Conn.: Yale University Press.

Riedel, M. 1976. Discrimination in the imposition of the death penalty: A comparison of the characteristics of offenders sentenced pre-Furman and post-Furman. *Temple Law Quarterly* 42(2): 261–287.

Robinson, E. 1935. *Law and the Lawyers.* New York: Macmillan.

Roesch, R., & Golding, S. L. 1980. *Competency to Stand Trial.* Urbana, Ill.: University of Illinois.

Rogers, J. L., Bloom, J. D., & Manson, S. M. 1984. Insanity defenses: Contested or conceded? *American Journal of Psychiatry* 141: 885–888.

Rokeach, M. 1960. *The Open and Closed Mind.* New York: Basic Books.

Rokeach, M., & Vidmar, N. 1973. Testimony concerning possible jury bias in a Black Panther murder trial. *Journal of Applied Social Psychology* 3(1): 19–29.

Rose, R. J., Koskenvuo, M., Kaprio, J., Sarna, S., & Langinvainia, H. 1988. Shared genes, shared experiences, and similarity of personality: Data from 14,288 adult Finnish Co-Twins. *Journal of Personality and Social Psychology* 54(1): 161–171.

Rosenthal, D. 1970. *Genetic Theory and Abnormal Behavior.* New York: McGraw-Hill.

Rosenthal, D. 1971. *Genetics of Psychopathology.* New York: McGraw-Hill.

Rosett, A., & Cressy, D. R. 1976. *Justice by Consent: Plea Bargains in the American Courthouse.* Philadelphia: Lippincott.

Ross, D. F., Miller, B. S., & Moran, P. B. 1987. The child in the eyes of the jury. In *Children's Eyewitness Memory,* S. J. Ceci, M. P. Toglia, & D. F. Ross, eds. New York: Springer-Verlag, pp. 142–154.

Rotter, J. B. 1954. *Social Learning and Clinical Psychology.* Englewood Cliffs, N.J.: Prentice-Hall.

Rotter, J. B. 1972. Beliefs, social attitudes and behavior: A social learning analysis. In *Applications of a Social Learning Theory of Personality,* J. B. Rotter, J. E. Chana, & E. J. Phares, eds. New York: Holt, Rinehart & Winston.

Rowe, D. C. 1986. Genetic and environmental components of antisocial behavior: A study of 265 twin pairs. *Criminology* 24(3): 513–532.

Ruback, R. B., Greenberg, M. S., & Westcott, D. R. 1984. Social influence and crime-victim decision making. *Journal of Social Issues* 40(1): 51–76.

Rubin, Z., & Peplau, L. A. 1975. Who believes in a just world? *Journal of Social Issues* 31: 65–90.

Rumbaut, R. G., & Bittner, E. 1979. Changing conceptions of the police role: A sociological review. In *Crime and Justice: An Annual Review of Research,* N. Morris & M. Tonry, eds. Chicago: University of Chicago Press.

Ryan, W. 1971. *Blaming the Victim.* New York: Vintage Books.

Ryckman, R. M., Burns, M. J., & Robbins, M. A. 1986. Authoritarianism and sentencing strategies for low and high severity crimes. *Personality and Social Psychology Bulletin* 12(2): 227–235.

Sack, S. M. 1987. *The Complete Legal Guide to Marriage, Divorce, Custody and Living Together.* New York: McGraw-Hill.

Saks, M. J. 1977. *Jury Verdicts: The Role of Group Size and Social Decision Rule.* Lexington, Mass.: Lexington Books.

Saks, M. J., & Hastie, R. 1978. *Social Psychology in Court.* New York: Van Nostrand Reinhold.

Salpukas, A. 1976. Detroit gangs become "more bold, violent." *Jacksonville Journal,* August 21, p. 9.

Salzman, L. E., Paternoster, R., Waldo, G. P., & Chiricos, T. G. 1982. Deterrent and experiential effects: The problem of causal order in perceptual deterrence research. *Journal of Research in Crime and Delinquency* 19: 172–189.

Sampson, R. J., & Cohen, J. 1988. Deterrent effects of the police on crime: A replication and theoretical extension. *Law & Society Review* 22(1): 163–189.

Sand, L. B., & Reiss, S. A. 1985. A report on seven experiments conducted by district court judges in the second circuit. *New York University Law Review* 60: 423–497.

Savitsky, J. C., & Sim, M. E. 1974. Trading emotions: Equity theory of reward and punishment. *Journal of Communication* 24(3): 140–147.

Saywitz, K. J. 1987. Children's testimony: Age-related patterns of memory errors. In *Children's Eyewitness Memory,* S. J. Ceci, M. P. Toglia, & D. F. Ross, eds. New York: Springer Verlag, pp. 36–52.

Scheflin, A., & Van Dyke, J. 1980. Jury nullification: The contours of a controversy. *Law and Contemporary Problems* 4: 52–115.

Scheppele, K. L., & Bart, P. B. 1983. Through women's eyes: Defining danger in the wake of sexual assault. *Journal of Social Issues* 39(2): 63–81.

Schulman, J. 1973. A systematic approach to successful jury selection. *Guild Notes* 2: 13–20.

Schulman, J., & Pitt, V. 1982. Second thoughts on joint custody: Analysis of legislation and its impact for women and children. *Golden Gate University Law Review* 12(3): 539–577.

Schulsinger, F. 1972. Psychopathy: Heredity and environment. *International Journal of Mental Health* 1: 190–206.

Schwartz, J. A., Liebman, D. A., & Phelps, L. G. 1975. The development of an in-service child and juvenile training program for patrol officers. In *The Police and the Behavioral Sciences,* J. L. Steinberg & D. W. McEvoy, eds. Springfield, Ill.: Charles C. Thomas, pp. 47–60.

Scott, W. A. 1962. Cognitive complexity and cognitive flexibility. *Sociometry* 25: 405–414.

Sealy, A., & Cornish, W. 1973. Jurors and their verdicts. *Modern Law Review* 36: 496–508.

Seidman, D., & Couzens, M. 1974. Getting the crime rate down: Political pressure and crime reporting. *Law and Society Review* 8: 457–493.

Selby, J. W., Calhoun, L. G., & Brock, T. A. 1977. Sex differences in social perception of rape victims. *Personality and Social Psychology Bulletin* 3: 412–415.

Seligman, M. 1975. *Helplessness: On Depression, Development and Death.* San Francisco: Freeman.

Severance, L. J., & Loftus, E. F. 1982. Improving the ability of jurors to comprehend and apply criminal jury instructions. *Law and Society Review* 17: 153–198.

Shaffer, D. R. 1985. The defendant's testimony. In *The Psychology of Evidence and Trial Procedure,* S. M. Kassin & L. S. Wrightsman, eds. Beverly Hills, Calif.: Sage.

Shaffer, D. R., & Case, T. 1982. On the decision to testify in one's own behalf: Effects of withheld evidence, defendant's sexual preferences, and juror dogmatism on juridic decisions. *Journal of Personality and Social Psychology* 42: 335–346.

Shaffer, D. R., Plummer, D., & Hammock, G. 1986. Hath he suffered enough? Effects of jury dogmatism, defendant similarity, and defendant's pretrial suffering on juridic decisions. *Journal of Personality and Social Psychology* 50(5): 1059–1067.

Shaffer, T., & Redmount, R. 1977. *Lawyers, Law Students, and People.* Colorado Springs, Colo.: Shepard's.

Shapland, J. 1986. Victim assistance and the criminal justice system: The victim's perspective. In *From Crime Policy to Victim Policy,* E. A. Fattah, ed. New York: St. Martin's, pp. 218–233.

Sheehan, P. W., & Tilden, J. 1983. Effects of suggestibility and hypnosis on accurate and distorted retrieval from memory. *Journal of Experimental Psychology: Learning Memory and Cognition* 9: 283–293.

Sheldon, W. H. 1949. *Varieties of Delinquent Youth: An Introduction to Constitutional Psychiatry.* New York: Harper & Row.

Sherman, L. J. 1975. An evaluation of policewomen on patrol in a suburban police department. *Journal of Police Science and Administration* 3(4): 434–438.

Sherman, L. W., Gartin, P. R., & Buerger, M. E. 1989. Hot spots of predatory crime: Routine activities and the criminology of place. *Criminology* 27(1): 27–55.

Sigall, H., & Ostrove, N. 1975. Beautiful but dangerous: Effects of offender attractiveness and nature of the crime on juridic judgment. *Journal of Personality and Social Psychology* 31: 410–414.

Silver, R. L., & Wortman, C. B. 1980. Coping with undesirable life events. In *Human Helplessness: Theories and Application,* J. Garber & M. E. P. Seligman, eds. New York: Academic Press.

Silverstein, L. 1965. *Defense of the Poor in Criminal Cases in American State Courts.* Chicago: American Bar Association Foundation.

Simon, R. 1967. *The Jury and the Defense of Insanity.* Boston: Little, Brown.

Simon, R. 1975. *Women and Crime.* Lexington, Mass.: Lexington Books.

Simon, R., & Mahan, L. 1971. Quantifying burdens of proof: A view from the bench, the jury, and the classroom. *Law & Society Review* 5: 319–330.

Skinner, B. F. 1953. *Science and Human Behavior.* New York: Free Press.

Skinner, B. F. 1969. *Contingencies of Reinforcement.* New York: Appleton-Century-Crofts.

Skogan, W. G. 1975. Measurement problems in official and survey crime rates. *Journal of Criminal Justice* 3: 17–32.

Skogan, W. G. 1976. Citizens reporting of crime: Some national panel data. *Criminology* 13: 535–549.

Skogan, W. G. 1977. Dimensions of the dark figure of unreported crime. *Crime and Delinquency* 23: 41–50.

Skogan, W. G. 1979. Crime in contemporary America. In *Violence in America: Historical and Comparative Perspectives,* H. D. Graham & T. R. Gurr, eds. Beverly Hills, Calif.: Sage, pp. 375–392.

Skogan, W. G. 1989. Social change and the future of violent crime. In *Violence in America,* T. R. Gurr, ed. Newbury Park, Calif.: Sage, pp. 235–250.

Skogan, W. G., & Maxfield, M. G. 1981. *Coping with Crime: Individual and Neighborhood Reactions.* Beverly Hills, Calif.: Sage.

Skolnick, J. H. 1975. *Justice Without Trial: Law Enforcement in Democratic Society,* 2nd ed. New York: Wiley.

Skolnick, J. H., & Bayley, D. H. 1986. *The NEW Blue Line.* New York: The Free Press.

Smith, D., & Swanson, R. M. 1979a. Architectural reform and corrections: An attributional analysis. *Criminal Justice and Behavior* 6(3): 275–295.

Smith, D., & Swanson, R. M. 1979b. Privacy and corrections: A social learning approach. *Criminal Justice and Behavior* 6(4): 339–357.

Smith, D. A., & Visher, C. 1981. Street level justice: Situational determinants of police arrest decisions. *Social Problems* 29: 167–177.

Smith, D. E., & Smith, D. D. 1977. Eysenck's psychoticism scale and reconviction. *British Journal of Criminology* 17: 387–388.

Smith, S. R., & Freinkel, S. 1988. *Adjusting the Balance*. New York: Greenwood.

Snodgrass, S. E., Higgins, J. G., & Todisco, L. 1986. The Effects of Walking Behavior on Mood. Paper presented at the meeting of the American Psychological Association, August, Washington, D.C.

Solomon, R. L. 1964. Punishment. *American Psychologist* 19: 239–253.

Spanos, N. P., Gwynn, S. L., Baltruweit, W. J., & deGroh, M. 1989. Are hypnotically induced pseudomemories resistant to cross-examination? *Law and Human Behavior* 13(3): 271–290.

Sparrow, M. K. 1988. Perspectives on policing: Implementing community policing. Washington, D.C.: U.S. Department of Justice, National Institute of Justice.

Stanovich, K. E. 1986. *How to Think Straight about Psychology*. Glenview, Ill.: Scott, Foresman.

Steadman, H. J., & Cocozza, J. J. 1974. *Careers of the Criminally Insane*. Lexington, Mass.: Lexington Books.

Steffensmeier, D. J. 1980. Sex differences in patterns of adult crime, 1965–1977: A review and assessment. *Social Forces* 58: 1080–1108.

Steffensmeier, D. J. 1983. Flawed arrest "rates" and overlooked reliability problems in UCR arrest statistics: A comment on Wilson's "The masculinity of violent crime—Some second thoughts." *Journal of Criminal Justice* 11(2): 167–172.

Steinman, S. 1981. The experience of children in a joint-custody arrangement: A report of a study. *American Journal of Orthopsychiatry* 51: 403–414.

Stephens, C. 1975. Selective characteristics of jurors and litigants: Their influence on juries' verdicts. In *The Jury System in America,* R. J. Simon, ed. Beverly Hills, Calif.: Sage.

Stevens R. 1983. *Law School*. Chapel Hill, N.C.: University of North Carolina Press.

Stinchcombe, A. L., Adams. R., Heimer, C. A., Scheppele, K. L., Smith, T. W., & Taylor, D. G. 1980. *Crime and Punishment: Changing Attitudes in America*. San Francisco: Jossey-Bass.

Stotland, E. 1982. The police feedback cycle. In *The Criminal Justice System: A Social-Psychological Analysis,* V. J. Konečni & E. B. Ebbesen, eds. San Francisco: Freeman, pp. 159–188.

Stotland, E., & Berberich, J. 1979. The psychology of the police. In *Psychology of Crime and Criminal Justice,* H. Toch, ed. New York: Holt, Rinehart & Winston, pp. 24–67.

Strickland, B. R. 1988. Clinical psychology comes of age. *American Psychologist* 43(2): 104–107.

Strommen, E. A., McKinney, J. P., & Fitzgerald, H. E. 1983. *Developmental Psychology: The School-Aged Child*. Homewood, Ill.: Dorsey.

Sudnow, D. 1965. Normal crimes: Sociological features of the penal code in a public defender's office. *Social Problems* 12(3): 255–276.

Sue, S., Smith, R. E., & Caldwell, C. 1973. Effects of inadmissible evidence on the decision of simulated jurors: A moral dilemma. *Journal of Applied Social Psychology* 3: 344–353.

Suggs, D., & Sales, B. D. 1979. Using communication process to evaluate prospective jurors during the voir dire. *Arizona Law Review* 20: 629–642.

Sullivan, C. E., Grant, M. Q., & Grant, J. D. 1957. The development of interpersonal maturity: Applications to delinquency. *Psychiatry* 20: 272–283.

Sutherland, E. H., & Cressey, D. R. 1974. *Criminology,* 9th ed. Philadelphia: L. J. B. Lippincott.

Swigert, V. L., & Farrell, R. A. 1976. *Murder, Inequality, and the Law: Differential Treatment in the Legal Process*. Lexington, Mass.: Lexington.

Symonds, M. 1976. The rape victim: Psychological patterns of response. *American Journal of Psychoanalysis* 36: 27–34.

References

Takooshian, H., & Bodinger, H. 1982. Bystander indifference to street crime. In *Contemporary Criminology,* L. Savitz & N. Johnston, eds. New York: Wiley.

Tapp, J. L. 1977. Psychology and law: A look at the interface. In *Psychology in the Legal Process,* B. D. Sales, ed. New York: Spectrum, pp. 1–15.

Tapp, J. L. 1980. Psychology and policy perspectives on the law: Reflections on a decade. *Journal of Social Issues* 36(2): 1980.

Tapp, J. L., & Levine, F. J. 1977. *Law, Justice, and the Individual in Society.* New York: Holt, Rinehart and Winston.

Taylor, S. E., Wood, J. V., & Lichtman, R. R. 1983. It could be worse: Selective evaluation as a response to victimization. *Journal of Social Issues* 39(2): 19–40.

Teich, P. F. 1986. Research on American law teaching. *Journal of Legal Education* 36: 167–188.

Tellegen, A., Lykken, D. T., Bouchard, T. J., Jr., Wilcox, K. J., Segal, N. L., & Rich, S. 1988. Personality similarity in twins reared apart and together. *Journal of Personality and Social Psychology* 54(6): 1031–1039.

Territo, L., Swanson, C. R., Jr., & Chamelin, N. C. 1977. *The Police Personnel Selection Process.* Indianapolis: Bobbs-Merrill.

Territo, L., & Vetter, H. J. 1981. Stress and police personnel. *Journal of Police Science and Administration* 9(2): 195–208.

Thibaut, J., & Walker, L. 1975. *Procedural Justice: A Psychological Analysis.* Hillside, N.J.: Lawrence Earlbaum Associates.

Thomas, E. 1986. America's crusade: What is behind the latest war on drugs. *Time,* September 15, pp. 60–68.

Thrasher, F. 1927. *The Gang.* Chicago: University of Chicago Press.

Tittle, C. R., & Logan, C. H. 1973. Sanctions and deviance: Evidence and remaining questions. *Law and Society Review* 7: 372–392.

Tittle, C. R., & Rowe, A. R. 1973. Moral appeal, sanction threat, and deviance: An experimental test. *Social Problems,* 20: 488–498.

Tittle, C. R., & Villemez, W. J. 1977. Social class and criminality. *Social Forces* 56: 474–502.

Toch, H. 1977. *Living in Prison: The Ecology of Survival.* New York: Free Press.

Toch, H., ed. 1979. *Psychology of Crime and Criminal Justice.* New York: Holt, Rinehart & Winston.

Trautman, N. E. 1988. *Law Enforcement—The Making of a Profession.* Springfield, Ill.: Charles C. Thomas.

Turk, A. T. 1969. *Criminality and Legal Order.* Chicago: Rand-McNally.

Turow, S. 1977. *One L.* New York: G. P. Putnam's Sons.

Ugwuegbu, D. C. E. 1979. Racial and evidential factors in juror attribution of legal responsibility. *Journal of Experimental Social Psychology* 15: 133–146.

Uhlig, M. F. 1988. The making of a lawyer. *Journal of Legal Education* 38: 611–617.

Valenstein, E. S. 1973. *Brain Control.* New York: John Wiley.

Valenti, A., & Downing, L. 1975. Differential effects of jury size on verdicts following deliberation as a function of the apparent guilt of a defendant. *Journal of Personality and Social Psychology* 32: 655–663.

van Dijk, J. 1986. Responding to crime: Reflections on the reactions of victims and non-victims to the increase in petty crime. In *From Crime Policy to Victim Policy,* E. A. Fattah, ed. New York: St. Martin's, pp. 156–166.

Vega, M., & Silverman, I. J. 1982. Female police officers as viewed by their male counterparts. *Police Studies* 5: 31–39.

Vidmar, N. 1972. Effects of decision alternatives on the verdicts and social perceptions of simulated jurors. *Journal of Personality and Social Psychology* 22: 211–218.

Villasenor, V. 1977. *Jury: The People vs. Juan Corona.* Boston: Little, Brown.

Visher, C. A. 1983. Gender, police arrest decisions, and notions of chivalry. *Criminology* 21(1): 5–28.

Visher, C. A. 1987. Juror decision making: The importance of evidence. *Law and Human Behavior* 11(1): 1–18.

von Munsterberg, H. 1908. *On the Witness Stand.* New York: Doubleday, Page.

Wagenaar, W. A. 1988. The proper seat: A Bayesian discussion of the position of expert witness. *Law and Human Behavior* 12(4): 499–510.

Wagstaff, G. F. 1984. The enhancement of witness testimony by "hypnosis": A review and methodological critique of the experimental literature. *British Journal of Experimental and Clinical Hypnosis* 22: 3–12.

Waldo, G. P., & Chiricos, T. G. 1972. Perceived penal sanction and self-reported criminality: A neglected approach to deterrence research. *Social Problems* 19: 522–540.

Walker, L., Thibaut, J., & Andreoli, V. 1972. Order of presentation at trial. *Yale Law Journal* 82: 216–226.

Wallerstein, J. S. 1985. Effect of divorce on children. *The Harvard Medical School Mental Health Letter* 2(3): 8.

Wallerstein, J. S., & Blakeslee, S. 1989. *Second Chances: Men, Women and Children a Decade after Divorce.* New York: Ticknor and Fields.

Wallerstein, J. S., & Kelly, J. B. 1980. *Surviving the Breakup.* New York: Basic Books.

Walters, G. D., & White, T. W. 1989. Heredity and crime: Bad genes or bad research. *Criminology* 27(3): 455–486.

Warren, M. Q. 1976. Intervention with juvenile delinquents. In *Pursuing Justice for the Child,* M. Rosenhein, ed. Chicago: University of Chicago Press.

Warren, M. Q. 1983. Applications of interpersonal maturity theory to offender populations. In *Personality Theory, Moral Development and Criminal Behavior,* W. S. Laufer & J. M. Day, eds. Lexington, Mass.: Lexington Books, pp. 23–50.

Warren, M. Q., & Hindelang, M. J. 1979. Current explanations of offender behavior. In *Psychology of Crime and Criminal Justice,* H. Toch, ed. New York: Holt, Rinehart & Winston, pp. 166–182.

Webster, J. A. 1973. *The Realities of Police Work.* Dubuque, Iowa: Kendall/Hunt.

Weinstein, N. D., & Lachendro, E. 1982. Egocentrism as a source of unrealistic optimism. *Personality and Social Psychology Bulletin* 8: 195–200.

Weiss, R. S. 1984. The impact of marital dissolution on income and consumption in single-parent households. *Journal of Marriage and the Family* 46: 115–127.

Weitzman, L. J. 1985. *The Divorce Revolution.* New York: The Free Press, Collier Macmillan.

Wells, G. L. 1986. Expert psychological testimony: Empirical and conceptual analyses of effects. *Law and Human Behavior* 10(1/2): 83–96.

Wells, G. L., & Murray, D. M. 1984. Eyewitness confidence. In *Eyewitness Testimony: Psychological Perspectives.* G. L. Wells & E. F. Loftus, eds. New York: Cambridge University Press.

Westley, W. 1970. *Violence and the Police: A Sociological Study.* Cambridge, Mass.: MIT Press.

Wheeler, M. 1980. *Divided Children: A Legal Guide for Divorcing Parents.* New York: Norton.

Widgery, R. M. 1974. Sex of receiver and physical attractiveness of source as determinants of initial credibility perception. *Western Speech Communicator* 38: 13–17.

Wigmore, J. H. 1970. *Evidence,* vol. 3, rev. by J. H. Chadbourn. Boston: Little, Brown.

Wilson, E. O. 1975. *Sociobiology: The New Synthesis.* Cambridge, Mass.: Belknap Press of Harvard University Press.

Wilson, J. Q. 1968. *Varieties of Police Behavior.* Cambridge, Mass.: Harvard University Press.

Wilson, J. Q. 1975. *Thinking About Crime.* New York: Basic Books.

Wilson, J. Q., & Boland, B. 1978. The effects of the police on crime. *Law & Society Review* 12: 367–390.

Wilson, J. Q., & Boland, B. 1982. The effects of the police on crime: A response to Jacob and Rich. *Law & Society Review* 16(1): 163–169.

Wilson, J. Q., & Herrnstein, R. J. 1985. *Crime and Human Nature.* New York: Simon & Schuster.

Winick, C. 1979. The psychology of the courtroom. In *Psychology of Crime and Criminal Justice,* H. Toch, ed. New York: Holt, Rinehart & Winston.

Wolf, S., & Montgomery, D. A. 1977. Effects of inadmissible evidence and level of judicial admonishment to disregard on the judgments of mock jurors. *Journal of Applied Social Psychology* 7: 205–219.

References

Wolfgang, M. E. 1963. Uniform Crime Reports: A critical appraisal. *University of Pennsylvania Law Review* 111: 708–738.

Wolfgang, M. E. 1978. Real and perceived changes of crime and punishment. *Daedalus* 107(1): 143–158.

Wolfgang, M. E., & Reidel, M. 1973. Race, judicial discretion, and the death penalty. *The Annals of the American Academy of Political and Social Science* 407: 119–133.

Wolfgang, M. E., Savitz, L., & Johnston, N., eds. 1970. *The Sociology of Crime and Delinquency.* New York: Wiley.

Wong, M., & Singer, K. 1973. Abnormal homicide in Hong Kong. *British Journal of Psychiatry* 123: 37–46.

Woocher, F. D. 1986. Legal principles governing expert testimony by experimental psychologists. *Law and Human Behavior* 10(1/2): 47–62.

Woods, L., Been, V., & Schulman, J. 1983. Sex and economic discrimination in child custody awards. *Clearinghouse Review* 16(11): 1133–1134.

Wortman, C. B. 1976. Causal attributions and personal control. In *New Directions in Attribution Research,* vol. 1, J. H. Harvey, W. J. Ickes, & R. F. Kidd, eds. Hillsdale, N.J.: Erlbaum Associates.

Wortman, C. B. 1983. Coping with victimization: Conclusions and implications for future research. *Journal of Social Issues* 39(2): 195–221.

Wright, J. D., & Rossi, P. H. 1981. Weapons, crime, and violence in America: Executive summary. Washington, D.C.: National Institute of Justice.

Wright, J. D., & Rossi, P. H. 1985. *The Armed Criminal in America.* Washington, D.C.: U.S. Government Printing Office.

Wrightsman, L. S. 1987. *Psychology and the Legal System.* Pacific Grove, Calif.: Brooks/Cole.

Yarmey, A. D. 1986. Ethical responsibilities governing the statements experimental psychologists make in expert testimony. *Law and Human Behavior* 10(1/2): 101–116.

Yarmey, A. D. 1990. *Understanding Police and Police Work.* New York: New York University.

Yarmey, A. D., & Jones, H. P. T. 1983. Is the psychology of eyewitness identification a matter of common sense? In *Evaluating Witness Evidence,* S. M. Lloyd & B. R. Clifford, eds. New York: Wiley, pp. 13–40.

Yochelson, S., & Samenow, S. E. 1976. *The Criminal Personality,* vol. 1, *A Profile for Change.* New York: Jason Aronson.

Young, R. L., McDowall, D., & Loftin, C. 1987. Collective security and the ownership of firearms for protection. *Criminology* 25(1): 47–62.

Yuille, J. C., & McEwan, N. H. 1985. Use of hypnosis as an aid to eyewitness memory. *Journal of Applied Psychology* 70(2): 389–400.

Zeisel, H., & Diamond, S. S. 1976. The jury selection in the Mitchell-Stans conspiracy trial. *American Bar Foundation Research Journal* 87: 151–174.

Zillman, D., & Bryant, J. 1982. Pornography, sexual callousness, and the trivialization of rape. *Journal of Communication* 32: 10–21.

Zillman, D., & Bryant, J. 1984. Effects of massive exposure to pornography. In *Pornography and Sexual Aggression,* N. Malamuth & E. Donnerstein, eds. New York: Academic.

Zimring, F., & Hawkins, G. 1973. *Deterrence: The Legal Threat in Crime Control.* Chicago: University of Chicago Press.

Zimring, F. E., & Hawkins, G. 1986. *Capital Punishment and the American Agenda.* Cambridge, N.Y.: Cambridge University Press.

Index

INDEX OF CASES

Brown v. Board of Education (1954), 5, 7
Durham v. U.S. (1954), 267
Dusky v. United States (1960), 276, 278
Frye v. United States (1923), 220
Furman v. Georgia (1972), 298, 299, 301
Globe v. Superior Court (Globe III) (1982), 226
Gregg v. Georgia (1972), 299, 301
Jackson v. Indiana (1972), 276
Jurek v. Texas (1972), 299, 301
Manson v. Braithwaite (1977), 217
McCleskey v. Kemp (1987), 300, 301
Muller v. Oregon (1908), 5
Neil v. Biggers (1972), 217
Olivia v. National Broadcasting Co. (1978), 338
People v. McDonald (1984), 225
Profitt v. Florida (1972), 299, 301
State v. Chappele (1983), 225
United States v. Amaral (1973), 224
United States v. Downing (1985), 224, 225
United States v. Jackson (1975), 225
United States v. Smith (1984), 224, 225
United States v. Watson (1978), 225
Wainwright v. Witt (1985), 247
Webster v. Reproductive Health Services (1988), 68, 305
Witherspoon v. Illinois (1968), 247

INDEX OF AUTHORS

Abbey, A., 98
Abel, G. G., 337
Adams, R., 103
Adams, T. F., 141
Adler, F., 93, 219
Adorno, T. W., 205
Aichhorn, A., 89
Akers, R. L., 102, 103
Albonetti, C. A., 160, 162
Alex, N., 107
Alexander, M., 205
Alfonso, V., 217
Allport, G. W., 3, 210, 211, 227
Allsopp, J. F., 88
Alschuler, A. W., 161, 165, 176, 177, 180, 257
Altman, D., 215
Amador, M., 216
Amir, M., 123
Anderson, E. A., 143
Anderson, J., 217
Andrioli, V., 193
Annis, L. V., 266
Arieti, S., 270, 271
Aronfreed, J., 60
Arons, S., 7
Aronson, E., 246, 255
Asch, S. E., 212, 213, 238, 244
Austin, W., 255, 349

Index

Baker, L., 6
Baker, M., 132–34
Baker-Thomas, S., 228
Balkin, J., 137
Baltruweit, W. J., 215
Band, S. R., 137, 138
Bandura, A., 55–57, 85
Barbieri, M. K., 225, 226, 228, 229, 231
Bard, M., 105, 107
Barkowitz, P., 210
Barlow, D. H., 337
Baron, R. A., 81, 133
Bart, P. B., 105, 107, 112, 117, 121, 122
Bartol, C. R., 62, 65, 74, 76–78, 80, 85, 88, 104
Bayley, D. H., 138, 139, 146
Beck, J. L., 65, 292
Becker, J. V., 337
Beckett, G. E., 257
Beckham, J. C., 266
Been, V., 318
Bell, D. J., 53, 136, 154
Bem, D. J., 131
Benjamin, G. A. H., 16
Bennis, W., 129, 138
Benson, D. H., 244
Berberich, J., 126, 129, 130, 138
Berg, K., 205, 252
Berkowitz, L., 91, 133, 158, 337, 339, 340
Berliner, L., 225, 226, 229, 231
Bermant, G., 3, 5, 197
Bernstein, I. N., 256
Bersoff, D. N., 248
Bierei, J., 205
Bischoff, H., 105
Bishop, D., 67, 343, 344
Bittner, E., 139
Black, D., 142
Blades, J., 317
Blakeslee, S., 325
Blanchard, E. B., 337
Blanck, P. D., 185
Block, C. R., 32, 37, 38,
Block, R., 104
Block, R. L., 32, 37, 38
Bloom, J. D., 272
Blumberg, A. S., 132, 133, 151
Blumstein, A., 341
Blunk, R. A., 199, 200
Bodinger, H., 331
Boehm, V. R., 205, 252

Boehnert, C. E., 272
Boell, J. L., 123
Boland, B., 144
Bonn, R. L., 35, 172, 194, 207, 251, 280
Bonnie, R. J., 260, 261, 263, 264, 266, 267, 275
Boster, F. J., 246
Bothwell, R. W., 11, 210, 218, 223, 228
Bouchard, T. J., Jr., 79
Bozza, C. M., 143
Bray, R. M., 203, 205, 239, 252
Brewer, D., 257
Briar, S., 142, 143
Brickman, P., 118
Brigham, J. C., 11, 210, 218, 223, 228
Brink, W. T., 133
Brock, T. A., 206
Broll, L., 329
Bronson, E. J., 166, 236
Brown, E. L., 214
Brown, R. M., 45, 75
Bruner, J. S., 211–13
Bryant, J., 339
Buckhout, R., 216, 217, 221, 222
Bunch, B. J., 93
Burbeck, E., 127
Burcart, J. M., 93
Burgess, A. W., 107, 109, 111–13, 121, 123
Burgoon, J. K., 246
Burns, H. S., 215
Burns, M. J., 252, 255
Burtt, H., 3
Byrne, D., 205, 252

♦

Cadoret, R. J., 78
Caldwell, C., 238
Calhoun, L. G., 206, 246
Caplan, L., 262
Carranza, L. E., 228
Carroll, J. S., 68, 173
Carter, R. M., 251, 298
Case, T., 191
Casper, J. D., 159
Catania, A. C., 58
Ceci, S. J., 228
Ceniti, J., 338
Chamblin, M. H., 205, 238
Chambliss, W. J., 245
Chamelin, N. C., 126
Chance, J. E., 210, 228
Chayet, E. F., 36, 40, 107
Check, J. V. P., 340

Chi, M. T. H., 227
Chiricos, T. G., 34, 256, 341–43
Christiansen, K. O., 78
Clare, P. K., 285
Claridge, G., 78
Clark, J., 142
Clark, K., 5
Clark, L. D., 167
Clark, R. D., 333
Clark, S. H., 158
Cleveland, C., 129, 138
Cloward, R. A., 82
Coates, D., 98, 118, 119
Cochran, J., 102
Cocozza, J. J., 276
Cohen, A. K., 81–83
Cohen, J., 144, 341
Cohen, R. L., 228, 283
Cohn, A., 126, 138
Cohn, E., 118
Cohn, Y., 121
Cole, G. F., 2, 154, 157, 159, 163, 165, 167, 169, 171, 172, 185, 188, 191, 249, 251, 252, 254, 255, 258, 282
Colman, A. M., 131
Comer, S. L., 215
Comfort, J. C., 159, 166, 229, 248, 289
Cordell, L. H., 185
Cornish, W., 204
Cortes, J. B., 74
Couzens, M., 30, 31
Cowan, C. C., 166, 248
Cressey, D. R., 86, 177
Crites, L., 143
Crowe, R., 80
Cumming, E., 138
Cumming, I. M., 138
Cutler, B. L., 223, 224, 233

♦

D'Errico, P., 7
Dantchik, A., 77
Darley, J., 329, 330, 332, 349
Darrow, C., 205, 245
Das, D. K., 129
Davies, G., 228
Davis, J. H., 206
Davis, K., 63
Davis, K. E., 142
Davis, R., 105
DeBerry, M. M., 280
Deffenbacher, K. A., 214, 218
DeFleur, L., 143
DeFries, J. C., 78
Dershowitz, A., 187, 189, 192, 198

Deutsch, M., 319
Dexter, H. R., 223, 224, 233
Diamond, B. L., 216
Diamond, S. S., 201, 202, 204
Dillehay, R. C., 198, 199, 201, 247
Doerner, W. G., 40
Dodge, L., 236, 245, 256
Donnerstein, E., 336–40
Doob, A. N., 216
Dovidio, J. F., 333
Downing, L., 224, 225, 242
Doyle, P. A., 256
Dubow, E., 57
Duncan, E. M., 227
Dvorkin, E., 12, 13

♦

Ebbesen, E. B., 37, 139, 158–61, 220, 251, 256, 280, 282
Edwards, H. T., 15, 255
Efran, M. G., 245
Egeth, H., 220, 223
Eisler, R. T., 304, 307
Elkins, J. R., 9, 13, 15
Elliott, E. S., 210
Elliott, R., 248
Ellis, H. D., 210
Ellison, K. W., 25, 76, 138
Ellsworth, P. C., 166, 248
Elwork, A., 236
Emler, N. P., 92
Empey, L. T., 35
Erickson, M. L., 35
Eron, L. D., 57
Espenshade, T., 313
Eth, S., 229, 230
Eysenck, H. J., 59, 62, 72, 78, 86–88

♦

Fahringer, H. P., 238
Farrell, R. A., 171
Feather, N. T., 205
Feldman, M. P., 88, 112, 246
Feldman-Summers, S., 112, 246
Felkenes, G. T., 167
Fine, R. A., 175
Finkel, N. J., 268, 269
Fischman, A. M., 112
Fisher, R. P., 216, 217, 243
Fisk, J. G., 139
Fitzgerald, H. E., 62
Fitzgerald, R., 248
Flango, V. E., 237
Flin, R., 228
Foley, L. A., 93, 166, 168, 205, 214, 238, 257, 299

Foley, M. A., 227, 245, 256
Fontaine, G., 246
Foster, H. H., Jr., 81, 263, 314, 317
Fox, S. G., 223, 298
Frank, B., 6, 148
Frank, J., 6, 148
Frankel, M. E., 167, 168
Freed, D. J., 314, 317
Freedman, C. D., 150
Freeman, J. L., 158
Freinkel, S., 100
Frenkel-Brunswik, E., 205
Friberg, L., 79, 88
Friedlander, K., 89
Friedman, K., 105
Frieze, I. H., 105, 107, 117, 118, 121, 123
Furstenberg, F. F., 321, 322

♦

Gaertner, S. L., 333
Gallup, G., 206
Gartin, P. R., 104
Gatti, F. M., 74
Geballe, R., 215
Geiselman, R. E., 216, 217
Gelman, A. M., 160
Genz, J. L., 25, 76, 138
Gerber, R. J., 260
Gibson, J. L., 253
Glaser, D., 298
Glueck, E., 74
Glueck, S., 74
Golden, K., 137
Goldfarb, W., 63
Golding, J. M., 230, 232
Golding, S. L., 277
Goldman, A. H., 221–23, 309
Goldsmith, A. J., 130
Goldstein, A. G., 210, 228
Goldstein, J. H., 44, 45
Goodman, G. S., 210, 225–30, 232
Gordon, D., 245, 257
Gordon, M. T., 103
Gorman, L. P., 131
Gottfredson, D. M., 100, 139, 284
Gottfredson, M. R., 100, 139, 284
Graham, H. D., 31, 41
Grant, J. D., 90, 143
Grant, M. Q., 90
Gray, T. C., 131
Green, E., 256
Green, G. S., 348, 349
Greenberg, D. F., 343

Greenberg, M. S., 34, 36–38, 40, 118, 157, 158, 165, 174, 176, 186, 188, 193, 199, 204, 206, 239, 245, 252, 253, 255, 256
Greene, E., 111
Greenfield, L. A., 247, 250
Griffin, N., 269
Grisso, T., 3
Gudjonsson, G. H., 78, 86, 88
Guinther, J., 196, 197, 244
Gurr, T. R., 31, 41, 43, 45–48
Gustafson, D. L., 266
Guth, M., 227
Gwynn, S. L., 215

♦

Hagan, J., 30, 31, 35, 41, 44, 48, 162
Hahn, A., 210
Haith, M. M., 230
Hammock, G., 239
Handel, S. F., 268, 269
Haney, C., 21, 22, 24, 26
Hare, R. D., 77
Hargrave, G. E., 126
Harlow, C. W., 32, 34, 36, 38, 40
Harnick, M. A., 228
Harries, K. D., 251
Harvey, O. J., 205, 206, 316
Hastie, R., 201, 223, 236
Haverfield, E., 228
Hawkins, G., 336, 341
Heath, L., 103
Heather, N., 92
Heilbrun, K., 269
Heilbrun, P. G., 269
Heimer, C. A., 103
Helgeson, V. S., 232
Hendrick, C., 191
Hepburn, J., 104
Herrick, D., 204
Herrnstein, R. J., 76, 92
Hetherington, E. M., 78
Heuer, L., 237
Heusmann, L. R., 57
Hiatt, D., 126
Higgins, J. G., 131
Hilberman, E., 111
Himmelstein, J., 12
Hindelang, M. J., 53, 81, 83, 85, 89, 100, 256
Hindman, R. E., 135
Hirsch, A. V., 257
Hirschi, T., 35, 83, 84
Hoffman, M. L., 6
Hoffman, P. B., 64, 292

Hogan, R., 57, 85, 89
Hogarth, J., 251, 253
Holland, H. L., 217
Hollin, C. R., 223
Holmes, D. L., 227
Holmes, T., 324
Holmstrom, L. L., 107, 109, 112, 113, 121, 123
Holt, N., 257
Holt, R. W., 206
Horowitz, I. A., 20, 131, 141, 147, 173, 174, 177, 189, 203, 242, 251
Huesmann, L. R., 57
Humphrey, J. A., 283, 284, 292
Hunt, D. E., 205
Hunt, Y. C., 126

◆

Inglis, B., 57, 62, 63, 212
Irwin, J., 287
Izzett, R., 245

◆

Jaffee, N., 319
Janoff-Bulman, R., 105, 107, 109, 117, 118, 121, 123
Janus, C., 136, 137
Janus, S. S., 136, 137
Jarvik, L. F., 76
Jeffries, J. C., Jr., 260, 261, 263, 264, 266, 267, 275
Jennings, W. S., 90, 92
Jensen, G., 277
Johnson, J. M., 280
Johnson, M. K., 227, 245, 256
Johnson, R., 5, 283, 291–93, 295–97
Johnson, W. G., 277
Johnston, N., 31, 35, 41, 280, 282
Jones, C., 246, 255
Jones, H. P. T., 230
Jones, W. H., 57, 85, 89
Jurow, G., 205, 248

◆

Kalish, C. B., 30
Kalven, H., Jr., 3, 238, 246
Kamin, L. J., 74
Kanellis, D., 217
Kaplan, M. F., 20, 21, 191, 206, 239, 242, 244, 245
Kaprio, J., 79
Kargon, R., 221
Karmen, A., 68, 98, 100–105, 114, 115, 119

Karuza, J., 118
Kassin, S. M., 147, 148, 150, 151, 190, 192, 196, 204, 246
Kaszniak, A., 16
Katsh, E., 7
Katz, S., 112
Ke, G. Y., 189, 193
Kelling, G. L., 129, 138, 139, 144–46
Kelly, J. B., 320, 324, 325
Kelly, W. R., 256
Kemmerick, G. D., 191, 245
Kenrick, D. T., 77
Kerr, N. L., 5, 7, 173, 185, 188, 203, 204, 206, 242, 244, 245
Kidd, R. F., 36, 40, 107
Kidder, L. H., 123
Kiger, R., 246
Kilkenny, R., 90, 92
King, M. A., 228
Kinnane, A., 127, 128, 137, 146
Kirshenbaum, H. M., 216
Kittrie, N. N., 75, 76
Kleck, G., 256, 257, 348, 349
Kleck, R. E., 205
Klein, D., 93
Klepper, S., 341, 342, 344
Klodin, V., 76
Knudten, M. S., 40
Knudten, R. D., 40
Koch, G. G., 158
Kohlberg, L., 73, 90, 92
Konečni, V. J., 37, 139, 158–61, 220, 251, 256, 280, 282
Koskenvuo, M., 79
Kovac, P., 227
Kramer, G. P., 173, 204
Kramer, J. H., 285
Kress, J., 93
Kressel, K., 319
Kroes, W. H., 131, 132, 137, 138
Krupnick, J., 105, 107
Kunen, S., 227

◆

L'Armand, K., 246
Lachendro, E., 106
LaFave, W. R., 205
LaFree, G. D., 256
La Greca, A. J., 102, 103
Lamm, H., 239
Landers, S., 305
Landes, W. M., 158
Landy, F. J., 127
Langinvainia, H., 79
Latane, B., 329, 330, 332, 349
LeBailly, R. K., 103

Leginski, W., 245
Leippe, M. R., 232
Leizer, J. I., 60
LeJeune, R., 107
Lempert, R. O., 222, 223
Lerner, M. J., 98, 107, 255
Lesnick, H., 12
Lester, D., 133
Levine, F. J., 8, 26, 213, 215, 216
Levine, J. P., 34
Levinson, D. J., 205
Lewin, K., 3
Lichtman, R. R., 98, 106, 116, 117
Licker, J., 205
Liebman, D. A., 129
Lind, E. A., 21, 189, 193, 246
Linden, E., 175
Lindner, K., 246
Linz, D., 189, 203, 336–40
List, J. A., 7, 15, 165, 173, 196, 228, 289
Loftin, C., 345, 346, 348
Loftus, E., 7, 111, 214, 215, 221–23, 233, 236
Loftus, G. R., 214
Logan, C. H., 342
Loh, W. D., 189, 193, 242
Lord, L. K., 136, 247, 261
Love, K., 136
Low, P. W., 260, 261
Luce, T. S., 210
Luginbuhl, J., 166, 247, 248
Lundman, R. J., 142, 143, 344
Lura, R. P., 251
Lykken, D. T., 79

◆

Maass, A., 223
Maccoby, E. E., 63
MacFarlane, S., 77
MacKinnon, D. P., 217
Maeder, T., 260, 261, 263–66, 269, 272, 276
Mahan, L., 204
Malamuth, N., 337, 338, 340
Malpass, R. S., 210
Maltz, M. D., 30
Manson, S. M., 217, 272
Manuele, C. A., 137
Margolick, D., 300
Marin, B. V., 227
Mark, V. H., 77, 133, 170, 243
Marshall, J., 237
Martinson, R., 4, 257
Masur, M. A., 112

Index

Matsuyama, S. S., 76
Mavissakalian, M., 337
Maxfield, M. G., 101
Maynard, D. W., 176, 178, 179
McCahill, T. W., 112
McClearn, G. E., 78, 79, 88
McCloskey, M., 220, 223
McCormick, C. T., 246
McDonald, E., 189, 225
McDowall, D., 345, 346, 348
McEvoy, D. W., 129, 130, 143
McEwan, N. H., 216
McGlynn, R. P., 244
McKenna, J., 220, 223
McKinney, J. P., 62
McNall, K., 147, 150, 151
Meade, A. C., 40
Meehl, P. E., 21, 22
Meek, D., 206
Megas, J. C., 244
Melton, G. B., 226, 228
Menninger, K., 4
Merton, R. K., 73, 81, 82
Messo, J., 214
Meyer, L. C., 112
Middendorf, K., 166, 247, 248
Milakovick, M. E., 283
Miller, B. S., 232
Miller, D. G., 215
Miller, D. T., 109
Miller, G. R., 204, 246
Miller, L. E., 206, 239, 245
Miller, W. B., 83
Mills, M. K., 34, 36, 40, 100, 289
Mischel, W., 57
Mitchell, H. E., 205, 252
Monahan, J., 7
Montgomery, D. A., 238
Moore, M. H., 139, 144
Moore, M. K., 145
Moran, G., 166, 248
Moran, P. B., 232
Morash, M., 92
Morgan, R. F., 314, 317, 319, 322
Moulds, E. F., 143
Moyer, M. M., 123
Murray, D. M., 198, 218
Myers, D. G., 239
Myers, M. A., 162, 246, 252, 253

♦

Nadelson, C., 105
Naftalis, G. P., 167, 168
Nagel, S. S., 143, 257
Nagin, D., 341, 342, 344

Neises, M. L., 247
Nemeth, C., 3, 204
Nerenz, D., 204
Nicholson, R. A., 277
Niederhoffer, A., 137
Niederhoffer, E., 137
Nietzel, M. T., 28, 30, 31, 34, 35, 38, 40, 92, 198, 199, 201, 280
Noble, A. M., 9, 239, 252
Noblit, G. W., 93
Noon, E., 223
Nord, C. W., 321, 322
Norland, S., 93
Notman, M., 105

♦

O'Barr, W. M., 246
O'Leary, L. R., 127
Ohlin, L. E., 82
Ostrove, D. W., 248

♦

Pachella, R. G., 220
Palmer, J. C., 215
Pantle, M., 269
Parke, R. D., 60, 78, 108
Parker, J. F., 228, 262
Pasewark, R., 269
Passingham, R. E., 88
Paternoster, R., 299, 301, 343–45
Pearson, J., 319
Pedersen, N. L., 79, 88
Pennington, D. C., 193
Penrod, S. D., 189, 203, 223, 224, 233, 237, 336–40
Pepinsky, H. E., 139, 142–44
Pepitone, A., 246
Peplau, L. A., 248
Perloff, L. S., 106, 107, 121
Perry, W., 245
Person, A., 105
Peters, D. P., 228
Petersen, J. L., 321, 322
Peterson, C., 109, 110, 117, 118
Pettigrew, T. F., 205, 206
Phares, E. J., 252
Phelps, L. G., 129
Phillips, B., 269
Pigott, M., 11
Piliavin, I., 142, 143, 329
Piliavin, J. A., 329, 333, 334
Pipkin, R. M., 7
Pitt, V., 319
Plomin, R., 79, 88

Plummer, D., 239
Polikoff, N. D., 317, 318
Pollak, O., 93, 143
Porter, C. A., 109
Postman, L., 210–12, 227
Powell, R. S., 256, 257, 299
Power, T., 136
Price, W. H., 76, 88
Pynoos, R. S., 229, 230
Pyszczynski, T., 189

♦

Quinney, R., 245

♦

Rabinowitz, M., 118, 217
Rachman, S., 87
Rahe, R., 324
Rasche, C. E., 93, 245
Rattner, A., 148, 218
Reaves, B. A., 156, 158, 160
Redmount, R., 17
Reed, R. S., 226–28
Reiss, A. J., Jr., 139
Reiss, S. A., 237
Rich, S., 79, 317
Riedel, M., 298
Riger, S., 103
Robbins, M. A., 252, 255
Robertson, H. C., 277
Robinson, E., 3
Robinson, R. J., 248
Roesch, R., 277
Rogers, J. L., 272
Rogers, R. W., 60
Rokeach, M., 205, 244
Romanczyk, A., 232
Romanoff, R., 57
Rose, R. J., 79
Rosenthal, D., 78
Rosenthal, R., 185
Rosett, A., 177
Ross, D. F., 228, 232
Rossi, P. H., 104, 349
Rotter, J. B., 85
Rowe, A. R., 341
Rowe, D. C., 78, 79
Ruback, R. B., 36–38, 118, 157, 158, 165, 169, 174, 176, 186, 188, 193, 199, 204, 206, 239, 245, 252, 253, 255, 256
Rubin, Z., 248
Rumbaut, R. G., 139
Ryan, W., 100
Ryckman, R. M., 252, 255

♦

Sack, S. M., 305–7, 313
Saks, M. J., 201, 236, 244
Sales, B., 16
Sales, B. D., 198, 199, 236
Salpukas, A., 57
Saltzman, L. E., 343, 344
Samenow, S. E., 92
Sampson, R. J., 144
Sand, L. R., 237
Sanford, R. N., 205
Sangrey, D., 105, 107
Sarna, S., 79
Savitsky, J. D., 245
Savitz, L., 31, 35, 41, 280, 282
Saywitz, K. J., 228
Scheflin, A., 242
Scheppele, K. L., 103, 105, 107, 112, 117, 121, 122
Schooler, J. W., 111
Schreiber, F. R., 270, 271
Schroder, H. M., 205
Schulman, J., 201, 318, 319
Schulsinger, F., 78
Schwartz, J. A., 129, 219
Scott, W. A., 13, 205
Sealy, A., 204
Segal, N. L., 79
Seidman, D., 31
Seidman, R. B., 245
Selby, J. W., 206, 246
Seligman, M., 109, 110, 117, 118
Sellers, C., 102
Severance, L. J., 236, 292
Shaffer, D. R., 17, 191, 239, 246
Shaffer, T., 17
Shanfield, S. B., 16
Shapland, J., 100, 115
Sheehan, P. W., 216
Sheldon, W. H., 73, 74
Sherman, L. J., 137
Sherman, L. W., 104
Shover, N., 93
Sigall, H., 5
Silver, R. L., 113
Silverman, I. J., 135
Silverstein, L., 5, 257
Sim, M. E., 245
Simon, R., 93, 143, 204, 239, 242
Singer, K., 104, 344
Singer, M., 136
Skinner, B. F., 53, 58–60, 85
Skogan, W. G., 33, 34, 41, 43, 46–49, 101, 104, 105
Skolnick, J. H., 131, 132, 138, 146

Smith, D., 5
Smith, D. A., 141–43
Smith, D. D., 88
Smith, D. E., 88
Smith, R. E., 238
Smith, T. W., 103
Snodgrass, S. E., 131
Solomon, R. L., 59, 238, 317
Sosis, R., 204
Spanos, N. P., 215, 216
Sparrow, M. K., 136, 146
Stanovich, K. E., 11, 79
Stasser, G., 206
Steadman, H., 269
Steadman, H. J., 276
Steffensmeier, D. J., 47, 93
Steinman, S., 320
Stephens, C., 245, 257
Stevens, R., 12
Stevenson-Robb, Y., 228
Stinchcombe, A. L., 103
Stotland, E., 126, 129, 130, 138, 143
Strickland, B. R., 3, 9
Strommen, E. A., 62
Sturgill, W., 214
Sudnow, D., 171
Sue, S., 140, 164, 238, 311
Suggs, D., 198
Sullivan, C. E., 90
Sutherland, E. H., 86
Swanson, C. R., Jr., 126
Swanson, R. M., 5
Swigert, V. L., 171
Sykes, R., 142, 143
Symonds, M., 111

♦

Takooshian, H., 331
Tapp, J. L., 3, 8, 21, 22, 25, 26, 213, 215, 216
Taylor, D. G., 103
Taylor, S. E., 98, 105, 106, 116, 117
Teich, P. F., 17, 18
Tellegen, A., 79
Territo, L., 126, 127, 133, 137
Thibaut, J., 193
Thoennes, N., 319
Thomas, E., 66, 67, 79, 157, 206, 228, 261, 313
Thompson, W. C., 166, 228, 248, 308
Thrasher, F., 83
Tilden, J., 216
Tittle, C. R., 34, 341, 342
Toch, H., 72, 294, 301
Toch, H. H., 144

Todisco, L., 131
Toglia, M. P., 228
Trautman, N. E., 126, 129, 132
Trojanowicz, R. C., 144
Tuchman, B., 319
Turk, A. T., 82, 83
Turow, S., 13, 15, 17

♦

Udolf, R., 126, 138
Ugwuegbu, D. C. E., 244
Uhlig, M. F., 13, 14, 17
Urbina, S. P., 93

♦

Valenstein, E. S., 77
Valenti, A., 242
Van Dijk, J., 328
Van Dyke, J., 242
Van Verst, M., 228
Vega, M., 135
Vetter, H. J., 133, 137
Vidmar, N., 3, 205, 242, 244, 252
Villasenor, V., 239, 240
Villemez, W. J., 34
Visher, C., 141–43, 206, 244
Von Munsterberg, H., 3
Voss, H. L., 104

♦

Wagenaar, W. A., 221, 222
Wagstaff, G. F., 216
Waldo, G. P., 34, 256, 341–43
Walker, L., 193, 211, 236
Wallerstein, J. S., 320, 324, 325
Walters, G. D., 79, 80
Walters, H. A., 223
Walters, R. H., 57
Warren, M. Q., 53, 81, 83, 85, 89, 90
Warring, L. J., 246
Wasserman, R., 129
Watson, C., 225, 319
Webster, J. A., 68, 138, 305
Weinstein, N. D., 106
Weiss, R. S., 111, 313
Weitzman, L. J., 143, 304, 310, 312–14, 318
Wells, G. L., 214, 218, 223
West, S. G., 44, 172, 223, 309, 318
Westcott, D. R., 36–38, 118
Westley, W., 131, 132, 151
Whatmore, P. B., 76
Wheaton, J., 205
Wheeler, M., 310–12, 314, 315, 317, 321, 323, 325

White, T. W., 79, 80
Whitney, P., 227
Widgery, R. M., 191
Wigmore, J. H., 246
Wilcox, K. J., 79
Wilkins, L. T., 251, 298
Willging, T. E., 20, 131, 141, 147, 173, 174, 177, 189, 242, 251
Williams, H., 129, 242, 244
Wills, E. J., 210
Wilson, C. E., 34, 36, 38, 40
Wilson, E. O., 76
Wilson, J. Q., 76, 92, 93, 138, 145
Wilson, K. G., 252
Winick, C., 184, 186, 187, 196, 197, 201, 236, 238

Winston, T., 118, 119
Winton, M., 92
Wolf, S., 238
Wolfgang, M. E., 31, 35, 41, 61, 104, 245, 256, 280, 282
WolfSkeil, M. P., 223
Wong, M., 104
Woocher, F. D., 221, 224, 225
Wood, J. V., 98, 106, 116, 117, 164
Woods, L., 318
Wortman, C. B., 98, 109, 113, 115, 121
Wright, J. D., 104, 349
Wrightsman, L. S., 148, 150, 159, 169, 174, 189, 190, 192, 196, 199, 204, 246

Yarmel, P., 57
Yarmey, A. D., 25, 126, 129–32, 216, 221, 230
Yochelson, S., 92
Young, R. L., 345, 346
Yuille, J. C., 216, 228

♦

Zeisel, H., 4, 201, 202, 204, 238, 246
Zill, N., 321, 322
Zillman, D., 339
Zimring, F. E., 298, 336, 341

SUBJECT INDEX

♦

Abortion, 5, 66–69, 305
Abused spouse syndrome, 7
Adam Walsh Society, 119
Adultery, 9, 298, 305, 307, 310, 315
Adverse witness, 191
Affirmative action, 126
Aggravating circumstances, 247, 248, 250
Aggression, 62, 77, 89, 90, 133, 336–39
AIDS, 305
Alcoholism, 78, 138, 297
Alimony, 310–12, 323
American Correctional Association, 287
American Law Institute's Model Penal Code Test, 267
American Psychiatric Association, 221, 260, 266
American Psychological Association, 3, 248
Anaclitic depression, 63
Annulment, 307
Anomie, 81
Anticipatory socialization 130, 151
Appeals, 164, 193, 207, 265, 267
Appellate courts, 193
Arbitration, 166
Arraignment, 169, 172, 181
Assertiveness, 123, 135, 297
Attractiveness, 77, 203, 244–46
Attributions, 109, 117, 239, 245

Attribution theory, 10, 245
Authoritarian, 23, 26, 131, 190, 205, 247, 252, 255, 290

♦

Baccaria, 280
Banishment, 283, 284, 298, 301
Battered wife, 319
Battered woman syndrome, 220
Bazelon, Judge David, 267, 278
Bedlam, 261
Bench trial, 187, 272
Bentham, 280
Bethlehem Hospital, 261
Bias, 23, 173, 197, 199, 206, 244, 317, 341, 342
Bifurcated trial, 248, 265
Big Houses, 287
Bill of Rights, 120, 167
Biosocial, 72, 77, 95
Birth control, 220, 305
Bondsmen, 154, 156
Brandeis briefs, 5
Burglar, 121, 331
Burn out syndrome, 138
Bystander Effect, 21, 330, 332, 350
Bystander intervention, 328, 329, 332, 335

♦

Capital offenses, 158, 244
Capital punishment, 5, 247, 298
Case load, 163, 172, 177, 248
Case method, 12–15, 17, 26
Cause and effect, 12, 76, 78, 145, 337

Challenge, 9, 136, 141, 197
Change of venue, 173
Child abuse, 144, 166, 225, 271, 297, 322
Child custody, 7, 310, 314, 315, 317, 322
Child-rearing, 63, 64
Child support, 311–14, 317, 319–21, 323, 326
Child victimization, 226
Chivalry, 143, 310
Civil cases, 173, 191, 193, 201, 244
Civil rights, 145, 243
Classical conditioning, 53, 69
Clinical psychologist, 3, 275
Clinical psychology, 20
Closing arguments, 193, 200, 236
Closing statement, 192
Cocaine, 49, 66, 67, 159, 174
Cognition, 18, 107
Cohabitation, 305
Collective Security Model, 345, 346, 350
Commission on Television and Violence, 336
Commitment, 84, 252, 268, 269, 273, 277, 278
Common-law, 305, 313
Community policing, 146
Community problem-solving era, 145, 151
Community property, 304, 305, 313
Competency, 218, 226
Complainant, 142, 151, 186
Compliance, 238, 314, 326
Concordance rate, 78

Conditioning, 53, 54, 62, 69, 86, 331
Confession, 6, 147–51, 173, 194, 195, 246
Conformity, 94, 201, 206, 212, 238, 239
Conscience, 62–64, 69, 86, 88, 89, 242
Constitution, 8, 154, 169, 172, 190, 192, 316
Contingencies, 85
Continuance, 173, 189
Conviction rate, 161, 175, 180
Convicts, 74, 289, 291, 292, 295
Coping mechanisms, 115, 116, 123, 325
Correctional Institutions, 283, 288, 290, 301
Corruption, 133, 145, 168, 169
Cost-Reward Model, 333, 350
Counterfeiting, 93
Court appointed attorneys, 171, 172, 176
Crime control, 129, 132, 136, 268, 278
Crime reporting, 38
Criminally insane, 269, 272, 276
Criminal type, 72–74, 143
Cross-examination, 190, 216, 226, 231
Cross-race identification, 210
Custody, 7, 156, 163, 170, 261, 292, 307, 309–11, 314–24, 326
Cynicism, 132, 266

♦

Dangerousness, 112, 113, 218, 221
Death penalty, 8, 122, 166, 175, 221, 247, 248, 250, 256, 258, 298, 299, 300, 301
Death qualified, 166, 247, 258
Debriefings, 340
Deductive reasoning, 12
Dehumanizing, 339
Delayed gratification, 83
Deliberations, 167, 193, 196, 202, 203, 232, 236–40, 244
Demeanor, 136, 141–44, 151, 239, 244, 245
Depression, 45, 63, 64, 105, 110, 112, 117, 118, 138, 292, 325, 326
Deprivation, 63, 80, 82, 83
Desensitization, 339, 350
Desocialization, 154
Detention, 170, 241, 250, 283, 291
Determinate sentences, 250
Deterrence, 61, 144, 253–55, 257, 258, 280, 284, 301, 341–45, 348, 350
Deterrent effect, 254, 341–44, 349
Deviant behavior, 52, 65, 73, 82, 86, 343, 345

De-victimizing, 115, 123
Diagnostic and Statistical Manual, 260
Directed verdict, 190
Discovery, 173, 195, 220
Discrimination, 5, 136, 256, 257, 299–301
Displaced aggression, 89
Dissolution, 304, 306, 310
District Attorneys, 253
Divorced child syndrome, 325, 326
Dizygotic, 78
Dogmatism, 205, 206
Driving under the influence, 166, 172, 250
Drugs, 49, 66–69, 86, 87, 108, 111, 128, 177, 179, 212, 250, 272, 285, 297
Due process, 194, 207, 277
Durham decision, 267

♦

Ecclesiastical courts, 307
Ectomorph, 74
Efficacy, 126, 151, 297
Ego, 88, 89
Eighth Amendment, 249, 298
Embezzlement, 28, 47
Endomorph, 74
Environmental, 77–80, 86, 121, 294, 295
Equal Credit Opportunity Act, 305
Erotic materials, 335, 350
Ethics, 24, 180, 181, 203, 207, 220, 221, 223, 232
Execution, 261, 283–85, 298–301
Ex parte, 310
Experiment, 11, 12, 25, 59, 66, 223, 230, 266, 267, 278, 328, 330, 331, 337
Experimental method, 12, 23, 26
Extralegal factors, 244, 257, 258, 300
Extraversion, 87, 88

♦

Facial recognition, 228
False confessions, 6, 148, 152
Fear of crime, 103, 329, 346
Federal Jury Selection and Service Act, 167
Federal Rules of Evidence, 223
Federal Speedy Trial Act, 189
Felony, 61, 160, 165–67, 192, 196
Fifth Amendment, 191
Fingerprinting, 154

First Amendment, 226, 338
First appearance, 157, 169–72, 181
Folkways, 65–69
Foot patrol, 146
Foreperson, 24, 168, 193, 236, 243, 247
Forgery, 93, 252, 294
Fourth Amendment, 172
Fraud, 93
Frustration, 83, 133
Furloughs, 290

♦

Gangs, 57, 73, 82, 83, 291, 292
Gender, 304, 310, 315, 317, 326
General deterrence, 253, 284, 301, 341, 348
Generalizability, 222, 345, 350
Genetic, 72, 77–80, 86, 95, 194, 195
Genovese, Kitty, 328, 329, 332
Goetz, 168, 347–49
Goring, 74
Grand jury, 24, 122, 166–69, 172, 180, 241, 243, 347, 349
Grand Stand Play, 199, 207
Group polarization effect, 239
Guided discretion, 299, 301
Guilty but insane, 264, 277
Guilty but mentally ill, 264, 273, 278
Gun accidents, 348

♦

Hearsay, 192, 226, 251
Helplessness, 40, 50, 105, 109, 110, 123
Hereditary, 72, 78–80, 95, 265
Hinckley, John W. Jr., 260, 262, 263, 273
Homicide, 41–45, 50, 68, 100, 102, 229, 230, 250, 299, 301
Homicide rates, 41, 44
Hostage, 56, 114
Hypnosis, 148, 216

♦

Immunity, 165, 198, 243
Inadmissible evidence, 189, 192, 238
In camera, 318
Incapacitation, 253, 254, 258, 284, 301, 342
Incest, 113, 166
Incompetent to stand trial, 272, 273, 276–78
Index Crimes, 28, 31, 32, 280
Indictment, 149, 163, 167, 169, 172, 181, 189, 300

Index

Indoctrination, 199
Inductive, 12, 17, 64, 69
Informants, 144
Inmate code, 287, 288, 292
Inmate culture, 287, 292
Insanity Defense Reform Act, 273
Institutionalization, 287
Instrumental conditioning, 53, 69
Intangible assets, 313, 326
Intervention, 90, 327–29, 332, 333, 335, 345, 349
Intestate, 14, 305
Introvert, 87
Intrusive thoughts, 105, 121
Involuntary commitment, 269, 277, 278
Irresistible impulse, 264, 268, 275, 277
Isolation, 63, 119, 132, 137, 287, 294, 295
Italian School, 72

♦

Joint custody, 315, 319, 320, 326
Juan Corona, 239, 240
Juror confusion, 223, 233
Juror sensitivity, 224, 233
Juror skepticism, 224, 233
Just world theory, 107

♦

Kidnappers, 114

♦

Larceny, 28, 36, 46, 280
Law Enforcement Assistance Administration, 282
Leading questions, 190, 216, 226–28
Learned helplessness, 109, 110
Legal custody, 315
Legal responsibility, 265
Lie-detector, 150
Lineup, 164, 173, 214, 216, 217
Locker room culture, 130
Locus of control, 252, 297
Lombroso, 72–74
LSD, 66

♦

M'Naghten rule, 261–65, 276, 277
MADD, 119, 120, 308
Mandatory sentences, 250
Marijuana, 66, 67, 87
Mass media, 340
Matrimonial Causes Act, 307

Mediation, 146, 166, 319
Meese Commission, 336, 340, 350
Memory, 18, 34, 89, 105, 108, 210, 211, 214–16, 218, 220, 226–28, 232
Mens rea, 186, 273, 278
Mental disorders, 218, 260, 265, 267, 271, 272
Mesomorph, 74
Minority groups, 126
Miranda, 6, 7, 150
Misdemeanors, 140, 157, 165, 249
Mitchell-Stans Trial, 201, 202
Mitigating circumstances, 148, 248, 250, 257
Mock jurors, 150, 151, 203, 204, 206, 236, 239, 244, 252, 268, 269
Monozygotic, 78
Moral Development Theory, 90
Mores, 62, 65, 66, 68, 69, 298, 301
Motivation, 63, 77, 80, 93, 142, 144, 165, 175, 186, 242, 265, 298, 329, 348
Motive, 62, 338

♦

National Council of Crime and Delinquency, 299
National Crime Survey, 32, 33, 35, 38, 40, 42, 49, 348
National Rifle Association, 345
Negative reinforcement, 53, 54
Neurosis, 89, 262
Neuroticism, 87, 88
New-Gate Prison, 285, 286
New Hampshire Rule, 267
Nolo contendere, 120, 172
Nomothetic, 22–24, 26
Nonverbal behavior, 148, 185, 201, 245
Normlessness, 81
Norms, 8, 36, 52, 62, 69, 73, 82–84, 90, 130, 205, 314, 317
Nudity, 339
Nurturing, 318

♦

Obscenity, 335, 340
Oedipus complex, 89
Old Bailey, 286, 287
Opening statement, 189, 240
Operant conditioning, 54
Overcharging, 165, 166, 175, 180
Overcrowding, 248, 283, 290
Own recognizance, 157, 159

♦

Pardon, 260
Parens patriae, 226
Pathologist, 179, 218
Peer support group, 119
Penitentiaries, 287, 290, 301
Perceptions, 38, 85, 106, 107, 113, 116, 119, 131, 136, 210–13, 215, 232, 331, 342–46
Peremptory challenge, 197
Phobias, 87, 105, 112
Photospread, 217, 219
Pleading guilty, 161, 282
Police brutality, 133
Political Era, 145, 151
Polygraph, 126
Posttraumatic stress disorder, 105, 229
Precedence, 8, 188, 207
Prejudice, 58, 199, 205, 224
President's Commission on Law Enforcement and the Administration, 31
Pretrial diversion, 166
Pretrial motions, 173, 174
Pretrial release, 159
Primacy effect, 193, 212
Prison crowding, 5
Private attorneys, 159
Proactive policing, 144
Probable cause, 169, 172, 181
Probation, 59, 61, 159, 175, 178, 248–51, 256, 258, 282
Property crime, 28, 68, 122
Prostitution, 8, 32, 66, 68
Protective custody, 292
Pseudomemories, 216
Psychoactive, 269, 272
Psychoanalytic, 73, 82, 88–90
Psychological stress indicator, 126
Psychometrics, 18
Psychopathology, 78
Psychotic, 88, 262, 271
Psychoticism, 87, 88
Public defenders, 159, 171, 176, 177
Punks, 291

♦

Race, 47, 101, 102, 123, 127, 142, 149, 162, 168, 196, 199, 202, 205, 210, 244, 245, 256–58, 298–300
Racial discrimination, 256, 299
Rape, 6, 28, 30, 31, 34, 38, 100, 103, 107, 109–13, 116, 117, 119, 121, 122, 123, 170, 194, 204, 206, 207, 246, 247, 252, 255, 256, 299, 305, 330, 331, 337–40, 350

Rape crisis syndrome, 111
Rapists, 112, 113, 194, 254, 328, 330, 337, 339, 350
Rea gestae, 226
Reasonable doubt, 23, 25, 186, 187, 190, 239, 262, 267, 278
Rebuttal, 192
Recall, 34, 205, 210, 216, 217, 227, 228, 237
Recency effect, 193, 212
Recidivism, 283, 292
Reform era, 145, 146, 151
Rehabilitation, 4, 251, 253–55, 258, 283, 284, 288, 290, 292, 296, 297, 301, 309
Reinforcement, 53, 54, 57, 73, 77, 84, 85
Release programs, 290
Restitution, 249, 250, 255, 258
Retention, 210, 214, 215, 218, 232
Retribution, 219, 253, 255, 258, 284, 301
Retrieval, 210, 215, 216, 232
Risk of victimization, 100–102, 104
Rorschach, 126

◆

SADD, 119
Sanctions, 8, 67, 113, 254, 255, 257, 258, 341–45, 348, 350
Schemas, 252
Schizophrenia, 78
Scientific Jury Selection, 200, 201, 203
Scientific method, 10, 201
Segregation, 5, 291, 295, 296
Self-blame, 109, 111, 117, 123, 334
Self-defense, 119, 123, 148, 296
Self-esteem, 117–19, 121, 138
Self-fulfilling prophecy, 143
Self-perception, 131
Self-report, 28, 34, 35, 49, 92, 342, 343
Sex discrimination, 136
Sex-role, 89, 93
Sexual abuse, 228, 231
Sexual assault, 38, 170, 206, 225, 226, 228, 229

Sexual battery, 30, 165, 180, 192
Sexually explicit material, 336, 340
Shaping, 92
Show up, 157, 170
Simulated jury studies, 204
Situational testing, 129
Sixth Amendment, 226
Social control, 84, 284, 329
Social disorder, 144
Socialization, 26, 51–53, 62, 69, 84, 130, 131, 151, 154, 344
Social Learning theory, 84–86
Social psychology, 2, 9, 24, 193
Sociobiology, 73, 76, 77
Socratic method, 13, 16
Somatotype, 74
Specific deterrence, 284, 301, 341, 348
Speed of closure, 190, 205
Speedy trial, 189
Split sentences, 250
Spouse abuse, 315
Stare decisis, 22, 23, 26
Statutory law, 8
Stereotypes, 143, 171, 199, 205, 232, 233, 331
Sting operations, 144
Streetwise, 142, 143
Study release programs, 290
Styles of policing, 144–46, 151
Subculture, 65, 66, 73, 82, 83, 86, 147, 205
Suicide, 55, 58, 100, 112, 138, 149, 163, 241, 261, 299
Superego, 62, 88, 89
Suppression, 59, 173, 174
Supreme Court, 5–7, 68, 150, 151, 154, 166, 167, 173, 175, 187, 188, 193, 196, 217, 218, 226, 232, 242, 244, 246, 247, 264, 268, 271, 276–78, 298–301, 305, 316
Symbolic assailants, 132

◆

Tax noncompliance, 344
Television and Violence, 336
Terrorists, 114

Torture, 271, 298, 301, 340, 344
Trade-out agreement, 180
Traffic violations, 134, 139, 144, 169
Transference, 214
Trial of Lunatics Act, 264, 277
Twins, 77–79

◆

U.S. Supreme Court, 5, 6, 154, 173, 175, 188, 196, 217, 226, 232, 242, 271, 276, 278, 298, 301
Unconscious, 89, 111, 214, 333
Uncontested divorce, 307, 310
Undercover agents, 144
Uniform Marriage and Divorce Act, 315
Unmarried couples, 306
Unsecured appearance bond, 157

◆

Victimless crimes, 32, 49, 68, 100
Videotaped depositions, 226
Violent crime, 28, 38, 41, 44–47, 50, 93, 105, 221, 346, 348
Visitation, 166, 288, 309, 315–17, 319–23, 326
Voir dire, 25, 196–203, 207
Vulnerability, 104, 107, 121, 122, 124, 229

◆

Watchman, 145, 151
Watergate, 201, 202
Weapon, 38, 114, 150, 168, 175, 213, 256, 349, 350
Weapon focus, 213
Witchcraft, 298
Working personality, 131, 133, 135, 137, 151

◆

XYY chromosome, 73, 75, 76